Street by Stre

BRIST

AVONMOUTH, BRADFORD-O N,
CHIPPING SODBURY, CLEVEDON,
TROWBRIDGE, WESTON-SUPER-MARE

Bradley Stoke, Congresbury, Keynsham, Kingswood, Mangotsfield, Midsomer Norton, Nailsea, Portishead, Radstock, Severn Beach, Thornbury, Winscombe, Yatton

Ist edition May 2001

Published by AA Publishing (a trading name of Automobile Association Developments Limited, whose registered office is Norfolk House, Priestley Road, Basingstoke, Hampshire, RG24 9NY. Registered number 1878835).

Mapping produced by the Cartographic Department of The Automobile Association.

A CIP Catalogue record for this book is available from the British Library.

Printed by G. Canale & C. S.P.A., Torino, Italy

Ref: MD060

Key to map pages ii-iii

Key to map symbols iv-1

Enlarged scale pages 2-7

Street by Street 8-163

Index – towns & villages 164

Index – streets 166-204

Index – featured places 204-212

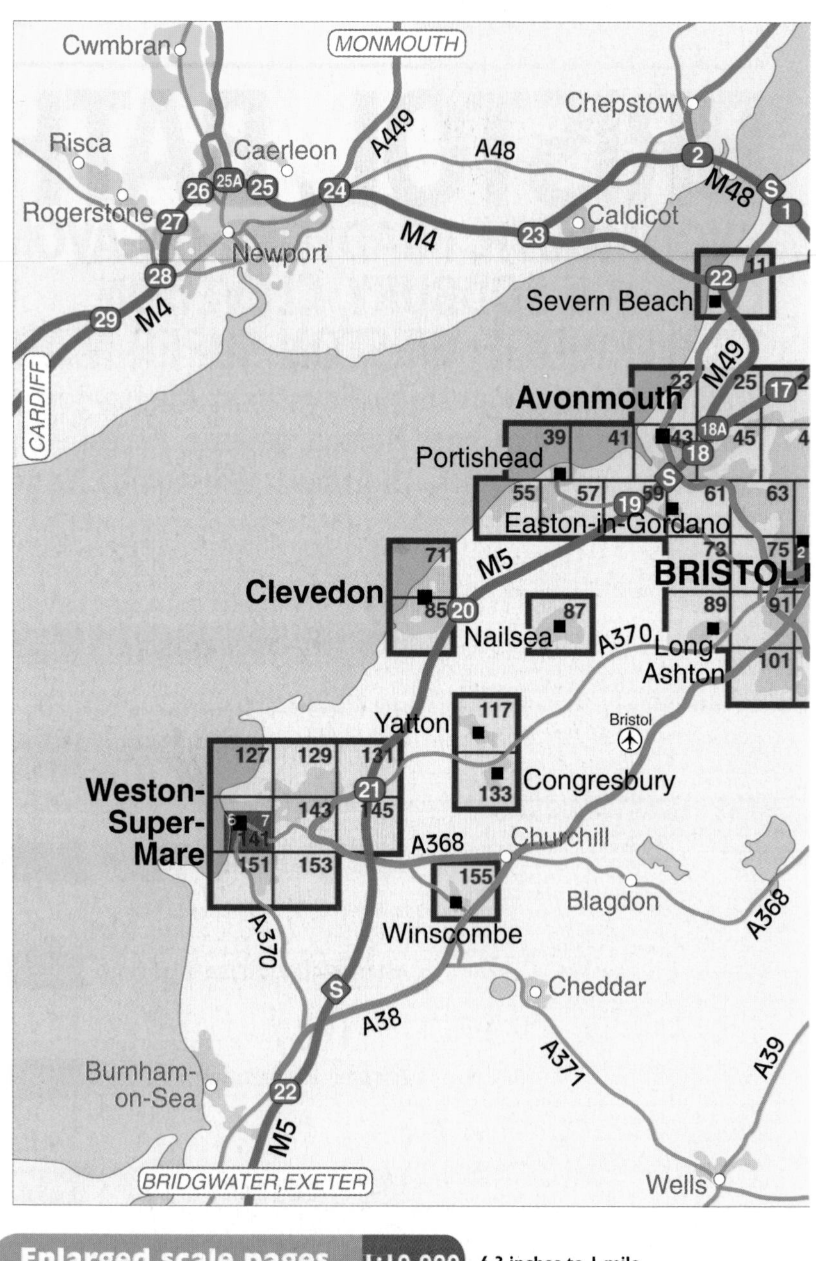

Enlarged scale pages 1:10,000

6.3 inches to 1 mile

0 1/4 miles 1/2

0 1/4 1/2 kilometres 3/4 1

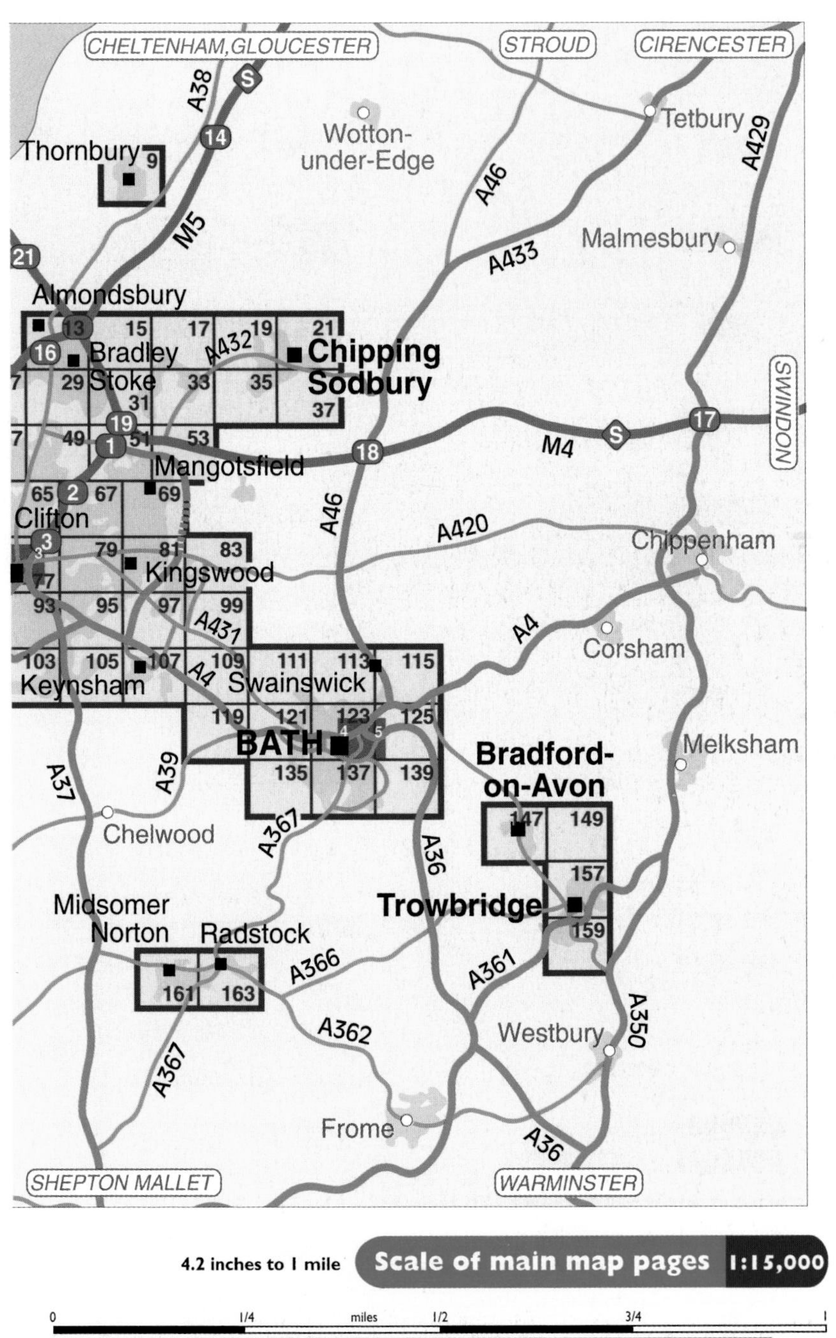

4.2 inches to 1 mile

Scale of main map pages 1:15,000

0 1/4 miles 1/2 3/4 1

0 1/4 1/2 kilometres 3/4 1 1 1/4 1 1/2

Junction 9	Motorway & junction	P+	Park & Ride
Services	Motorway service area		Bus/coach station
	Primary road single/dual carriageway		Railway & main railway station
Services	Primary road service area		Railway & minor railway station
	A road single/dual carriageway		Underground station
	B road single/dual carriageway		Light railway & station
	Other road single/dual carriageway		Preserved private railway
	Restricted road	LC	Level crossing
	Private road		Tramway
	One way street		Ferry route
	Pedestrian street		Airport runway
	Track/ footpath		Boundaries- borough/ district
	Road under construction		Mounds
	Road tunnel	93	Page continuation 1:15,000
P	Parking	7	Page continuation to enlarged scale 1:10,000

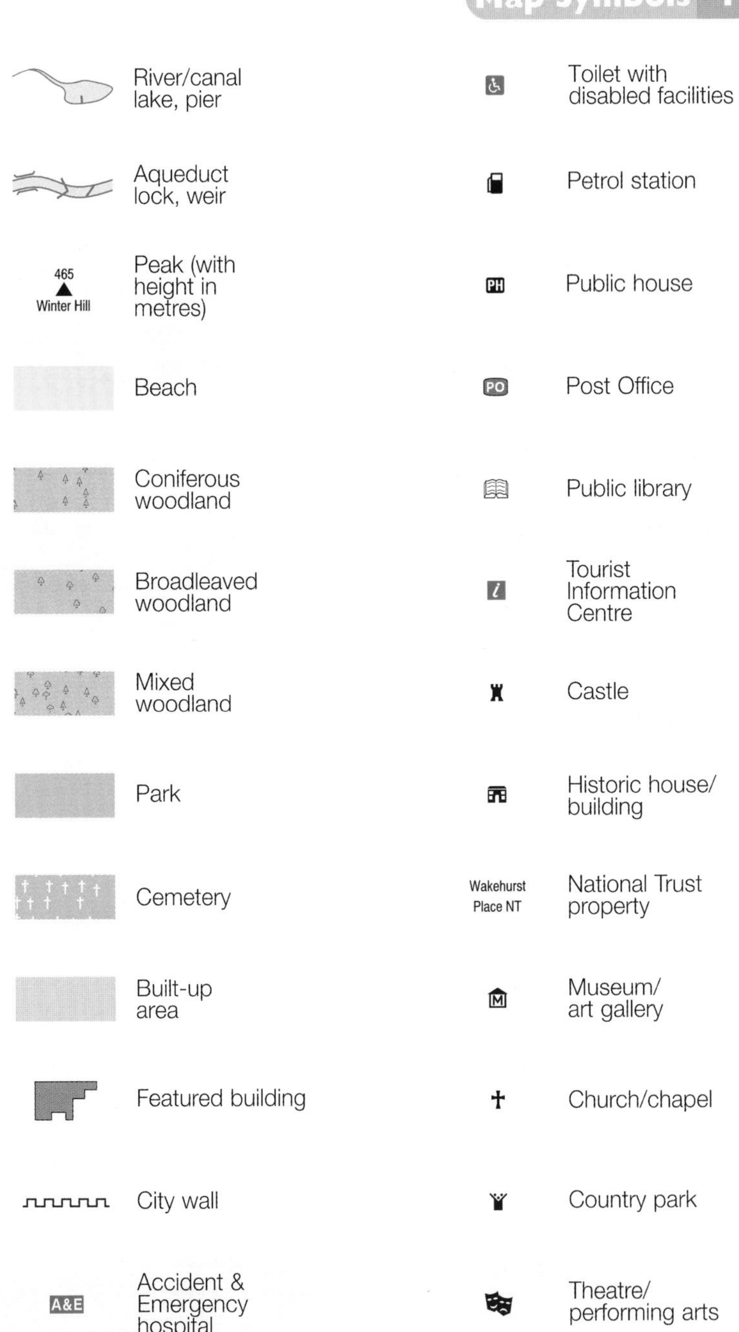
River/canal lake, pier
Aqueduct lock, weir
465
Winter Hill
Peak (with height in metres)
Beach
Coniferous woodland
Broadleaved woodland
Mixed woodland
Park
Cemetery
Built-up area
Featured building
City wall
A&E
Accident & Emergency hospital
Toilet
Toilet with disabled facilities
Petrol station
PH
Public house
PO
Post Office
Public library
i
Tourist Information Centre
Castle
Historic house/ building
Wakehurst Place NT
National Trust property
M
Museum/ art gallery
Church/chapel
Country park
Theatre/ performing arts
Cinema

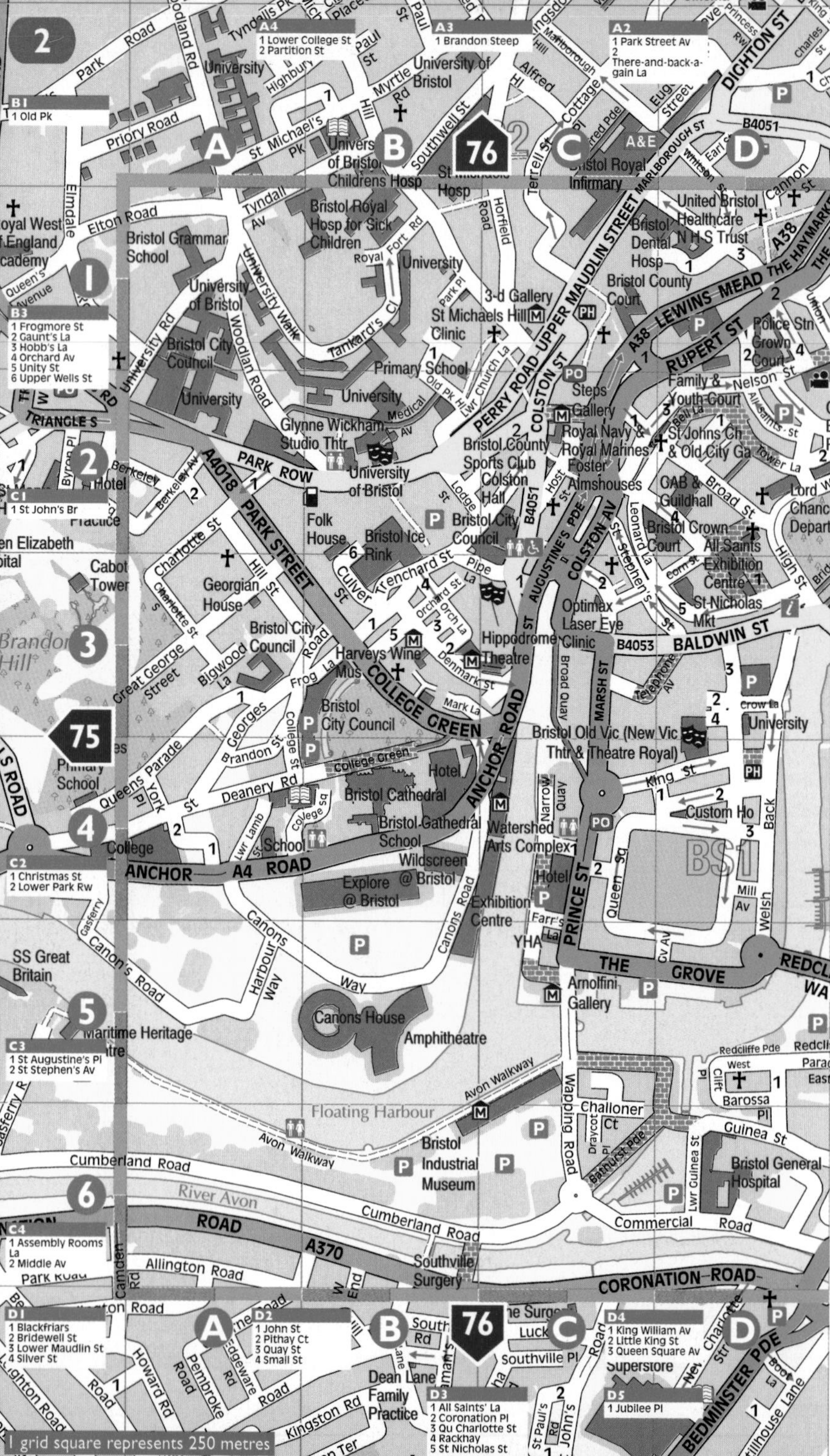

2
A4
1 Lower College St
2 Partition St
A3
1 Brandon Steep
A2
1 Park Street Av
2 There-and-back-again La
B1
1 Old Pk
B3
1 Frogmore St
2 Gaunt's La
3 Hobb's La
4 Orchard Av
5 Unity St
6 Upper Wells St
C1
1 St John's Br
C2
1 Christmas St
2 Lower Park Rw
C3
1 St Augustine's Pl
2 St Stephen's Av
C4
1 Assembly Rooms La
2 Middle Av
D1
1 Blackfriars
2 Bridewell St
3 Lower Maudlin St
4 Silver St
D2
1 John St
2 Pithay Ct
3 Quay St
4 Small St
D3
1 All Saints' La
2 Coronation Pl
3 Qu Charlotte St
4 Rackhay
5 St Nicholas St
D4
1 King William Av
2 Little King St
3 Queen Square Av
D5
1 Jubilee Pl
A
B
C
D
76
75
1
2
3
4
5
6
Park Road
Priory Road
Tyndalls Pk
University
Highbury
Myrtle Rd
Hill
University of Bristol
St Michael's Pk
Univers of Bristol Childrens Hosp
Southwell St
St Michaels Hosp
Alfred Hl
Marlborough Hill
Cottage Pl
Terrell St
Bristol Royal Infirmary
A&E
DIGHTON ST
MARLBOROUGH ST
B4051
Whitson St
Earl St
Cannon St
Elmdale
Royal West of England Academy
Elton Road
Queen's Avenue
Bristol Grammar School
Tyndall Av
University Walk
Bristol Royal Hosp for Sick Children
Royal Fort Rd
University
Horfield Road
UPPER MAUDLIN STREET
United Bristol Healthcare N H S Trust
Bristol Dental Hosp
Bristol County Court
A38 LEWINS MEAD
THE HAYMARKET
University Rd
University of Bristol
Woodland Road
Bristol City Council
Tankard's Cl
Park Pl
3-d Gallery
St Michaels Hill Clinic
PERRY ROAD
COLSTON ST
PH
PO
RUPERT ST
Police Stn
Crown Court
Nelson St
Family & Youth Court
Primary School
Old Pk Hl
Lwr Church La
Steps Gallery
University
TRIANGLE S
Medical Av
Glynne Wickham Studio Thtr
Royal Navy & Royal Marines
Bell La
St Johns Ch & Old City Ga
All Saints' St
Tower La
Byron Pl
Berkeley Hotel
Berkeley Av
A4018
PARK ROW
University of Bristol
Bristol County Sports Club
Colston Hall
Foster Almshouses
Host St
CAB & Guildhall
Broad St
Lord W
Chance Depart
Practice
Queen Elizabeth Hospital
Cabot Tower
Brandon Hill
Charlotte St
PARK STREET
Folk House
Lodge St
Bristol City Council
B4051
ST AUGUSTINE'S PDE
COLSTON AV
Leonard La
St Stephen's St
Bristol Crown Court
All Saints Exhibition Centre
High St
Georgian House
Hill St
Bristol Ice Rink
Culver St
Trenchard St
Pipe La
Corn St
St Nicholas Mkt
Optimax Laser Eye Clinic
Bristol City Council
Great George Street
Bigwood La
Frog La
Harveys Wine Mus
Orchard St
Orch La
Denmark St
Hippodrome Theatre
B4053
BALDWIN ST
Broad Quay
MARSH ST
Telephone Av
COLLEGE GREEN
Mark La
Bristol City Council
Georges Rd
College St
Brandon St
ANCHOR ROAD
Bristol Old Vic (New Vic Thtr & Theatre Royal)
Crow La
University
WELLS ROAD
Primary School
Queens Parade
York Pl
Deanery Rd
College Green
Hotel
Bristol Cathedral
Narrow Quay
King St
Custom Ho
Back
College Sq
Bristol Cathedral School
Watershed Arts Complex
BS1
College
Lwr Lamb St
School
ANCHOR A4 ROAD
Wildscreen @ Bristol
Explore @ Bristol
Canons Road
Hotel
PRINCE ST
Queen Sq
Mill Av
Welsh
Gasferry
Canon's Road
Canons Harbour Way
Exhibition Centre
Farr's La
YHA
Gv Av
THE GROVE
REDCL
SS Great Britain
Canons Way
Arnolfini Gallery
Canons House
Amphitheatre
Maritime Heritage Centre
Redcliffe Pde West
Redclif Parad East
Clift Pl
Barossa Pl
Avon Walkway
Floating Harbour
Wapping Road
Challoner Ct
Draycot Pl
Bathurst Pde
Guinea St
Lwr Guinea St
Bristol General Hospital
Bristol Industrial Museum
Cumberland Road
River Avon
Commercial Road
Gasferry Rd
Cumberland Road
ROAD
A370
Camden Rd
Allington Road
Park Road
Southville Surgery
CORONATION ROAD
W End
Howard Rd
Pembroke Road
Edgeware Road
South Rd
Lane
Dean Lane Family Practice
Kingston Rd
Southville Pl
St Paul's Rd
St John's Road
Superstore
BEDMINSTER PDE
Stillhouse Lane
1 grid square represents 250 metres

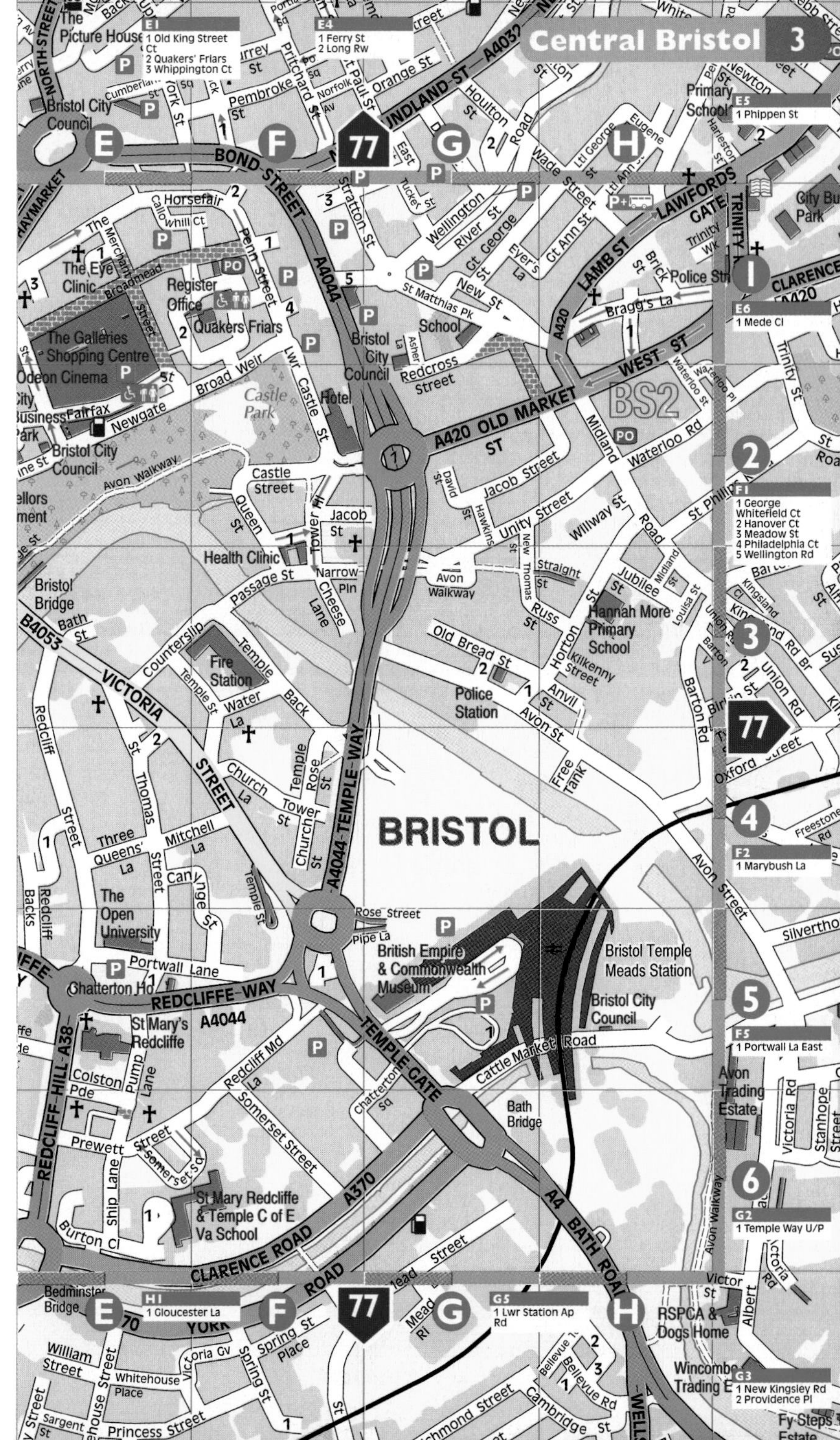

Central Bristol 3
E1
1 Old King Street Ct
2 Quakers' Friars
3 Whippington Ct
E4
1 Ferry St
2 Long Rw
E5
1 Phippen St
E6
1 Mede Cl
F1
1 George Whitefield Ct
2 Hanover Ct
3 Meadow St
4 Philadelphia Ct
5 Wellington Rd
F2
1 Marybush La
F5
1 Portwall La East
G2
1 Temple Way U/P
G3
1 New Kingsley Rd
2 Providence Pl
G5
1 Lwr Station Ap Rd
H1
1 Gloucester La
The Picture House
Bristol City Council
Primary School
BOND STREET
HAYMARKET
NORTH STREET
Pembroke St
Orange St
Houlton Road
Wade Street
LAWFORDS GATE
TRINITY RD
City Business Park
Horsefair
Penn Street
The Eye Clinic
Broadmead
Register Office
Quakers Friars
The Galleries Shopping Centre
Odeon Cinema
Fairfax
Newgate
Broad Weir
Castle Park
Lwr Castle St
Hotel
Redcross Street
School
St Matthias Pk
New St
LAMB ST
Police Station
Bragg's La
WEST ST
CLARENCE RD
A420 OLD MARKET ST
BS2
Midland Rd
Waterloo Rd
Jacob Street
Unity Street
Willway St
St Philips
Avon Walkway
Castle Street
Queen St
Tower Hl
Jacob St
Health Clinic
Narrow Pln
Cheese Lane
Passage St
Straight St
Russ St
Jubilee St
Hannah More Primary School
Old Bread St
Horton St
Kilkenny Street
Anvil St
Avon St
Police Station
Barton Rd
Union Rd
Oxford Street
Bristol Bridge
Bath St
B4053 VICTORIA STREET
Counterslip
Temple Back
Fire Station
Temple St
Water La
Church La
Tower St
Temple Rose St
Church St
A4044 TEMPLE WAY
BRISTOL
Free Tank
Avon Street
Freestone Rd
Silverthorn
Redcliff Street
Thomas St
Three Queens' La
Mitchell La
Canynge St
The Open University
Redcliff Backs
Rose Street
Pipe La
British Empire & Commonwealth Museum
Bristol Temple Meads Station
Bristol City Council
Portwall Lane
Chatterton Ho
REDCLIFFE WAY
A4044
St Mary's Redcliffe
Colston Pde
Pump Lane
Redcliff Md La
Somerset Street
Chatterton Sq
TEMPLE GATE
Cattle Market Road
Bath Bridge
Avon Trading Estate
Victoria Rd
Stanhope Street
REDCLIFF HILL A38
Prewett Street
Somerset Sq
Ship Lane
St Mary Redcliffe & Temple C of E Va School
Burton Cl
CLARENCE ROAD
A370
A4 BATH ROAD
Avon Walkway
Bedminster Bridge
YORK
ROAD
Spring St Place
Victoria Gv
William Street
Whitehouse Place
Sargent St
Princess Street
Mead Rl
Bellevue Rd
Richmond Street
Cambridge St
RSPCA & Dogs Home
Wincombe Trading Estate
Albert Rd
Victor St
WELLS

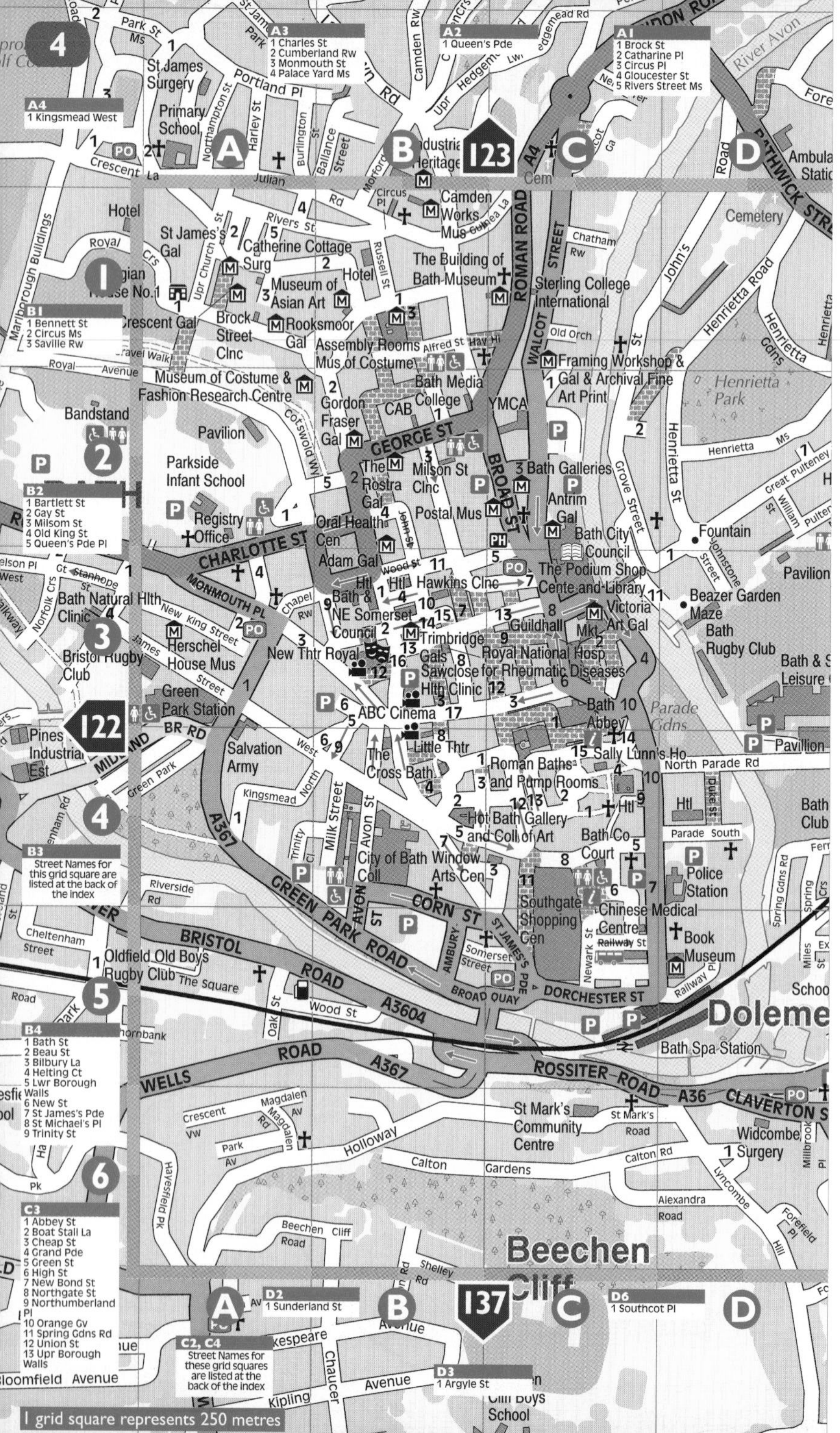
4
A4
1 Kingsmead West
A3
1 Charles St
2 Cumberland Rw
3 Monmouth St
4 Palace Yard Ms
A2
1 Queen's Pde
A1
1 Brock St
2 Catharine Pl
3 Circus Pl
4 Gloucester St
5 Rivers Street Ms
B1
1 Bennett St
2 Circus Ms
3 Saville Rw
B2
1 Bartlett St
2 Gay St
3 Milsom St
4 Old King St
5 Queen's Pde Pl
B3
Street Names for this grid square are listed at the back of the index
B4
1 Bath St
2 Beau St
3 Bilbury La
4 Helting Ct
5 Lwr Borough Walls
6 New St
7 St James's Pde
8 St Michael's Pl
9 Trinity St
C3
1 Abbey St
2 Boat Stall La
3 Cheap St
4 Grand Pde
5 Green St
6 High St
7 New Bond St
8 Northgate St
9 Northumberland Pl
10 Orange Gv
11 Spring Gdns Rd
12 Union St
13 Upr Borough Walls
C2, C4
Street Names for these grid squares are listed at the back of the index
D2
1 Sunderland St
D3
1 Argyle St
D6
1 Southcot Pl
A
B
C
D
1
2
3
4
5
6
123
122
137
St James Surgery
Primary School
Portland Pl
Park St
Northampton St
Harley St
Burlington St
Ballance Street
Camden Rd
Industrial Heritage
Julian Rd
Crescent La
Hotel
Marlborough Buildings
Royal Crs
Georgian House No.1
Crescent Gal
Gravel Walk
Royal Avenue
St James's Gal
Upr Church St
Catherine Cottage Surg
Rivers St
Museum of Asian Art
Brock Street Clnc
Rooksmoor Gal
Russell St
Hotel
Circus Pl
Camden Works Mus
Guinea La
The Building of Bath Museum
Assembly Rooms Mus of Costume
Alfred St
Hay Hl
Museum of Costume & Fashion Research Centre
Gordon Fraser Gal
CAB
Bath Media College
YMCA
George St
Bandstand
Pavilion
Parkside Infant School
Registry Office
Cotswold Way
The Rostra Gal
Milson St Clnc
Postal Mus
Oral Health Cen
Adam Gal
John St
Charlotte St
Monmouth Pl
Chapel Rw
Bath Natural Hlth Clinic
Bristol Rugby Club
Herschel House Mus
New King Street
James Street
Green Park Station
Midland Br Rd
Pines Industrial Est
Salvation Army
New Thtr Royal
Bath & NE Somerset Council
Trimbridge Gals
Sawclose
Hlth Clinic
ABC Cinema
Little Thtr
The Cross Bath
Wood St
Hawkins Clnc
Htl
Guildhall
Royal National Hosp for Rheumatic Diseases
Roman Baths and Pump Rooms
Hot Bath Gallery and Coll of Art
Bath Abbey
Sally Lunn's Ho
Bath Co Court
Kingsmead North
Westgate
Milk Street
Avon St
Trinity Cl
City of Bath Coll
Window Arts Cen
Southgate Shopping Cen
Chinese Medical Centre
Railway St
Newark St
Corn St
Green Park Road
Avon St
Ambury
Somerset Street
St James's Pde
Broad Quay
Dorchester St
Riverside Rd
Cheltenham Street
Oldfield Old Boys Rugby Club
The Square
Bristol Road
A3604
Wood St
Oak St
A367
Wells Road
Rossiter Road
A36
Claverton St
Bath Spa Station
Dolemeads
St Mark's Community Centre
St Mark's Road
Widcombe Surgery
Calton Rd
Calton Gardens
Holloway
Magdalen Av
Magdalen Rd
Crescent Vw
Park Av
Hayesfield Pk
Alexandra Road
Lyncombe Hill
Forefield Pl
Beechen Cliff Road
Shelley Rd
Beechen Cliff
Millbrook Pl
Spring Gdns Rd
Police Station
Book Museum
Parade South
Duke St
North Parade Rd
Parade Gdns
Pavilion
Bath & Somerset Leisure Centre
Bath Rugby Club
Beazer Garden Maze
Victoria Art Gal
Mkt
The Podium Shop Centre and Library
Bath City Council
Antrim Gal
Bath Galleries
Broad St
Roman Road
Walcot Street
Chatham Rw
Sterling College International
Old Orch
Framing Workshop & Gal & Archival Fine Art Print
Grove Street
Henrietta St
Henrietta Ms
Henrietta Park
Henrietta Road
Henrietta Gdns
Great Pulteney St
William St
Johnstone Street
Fountain
Pavilion
St John's Rd
Cemetery
Bathwick Street
River Avon
Ambulance Station
Cem
A4
Kipling Avenue
Chaucer
Shakespeare Avenue
Bloomfield Avenue
Beechen Cliff Boys School
1 grid square represents 250 metres

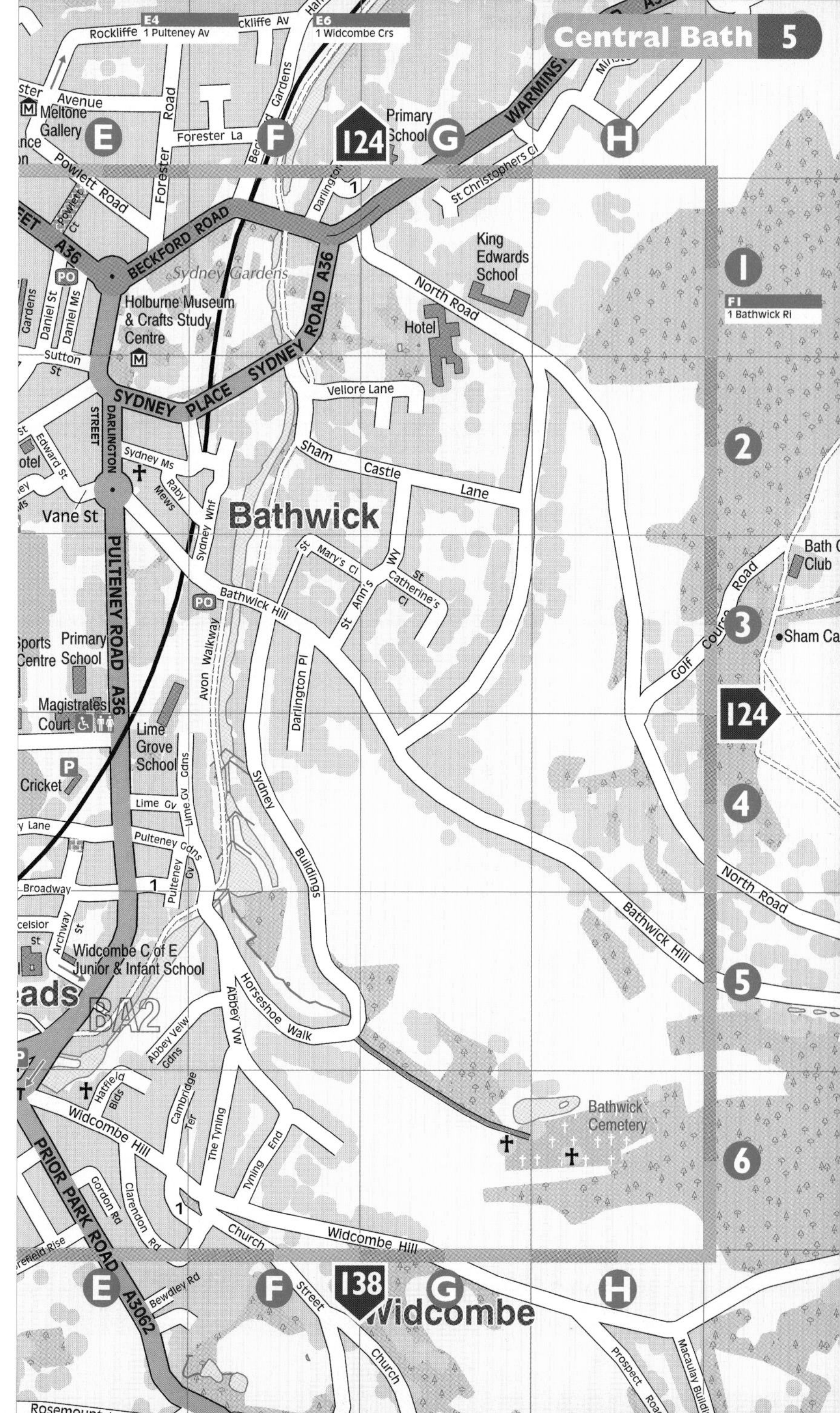

E4 1 Pulteney Av
E6 1 Widcombe Crs
F1 1 Bathwick Ri
Rockliffe
Rockliffe Av
Avenue
Meltone Gallery
Forester Road
Forester La
Beckford Gardens
Primary School
124
Warminster Road
St Christophers Cl
Powlett Road
Powlett Ct
Darlington
A36
BECKFORD ROAD
Sydney Gardens
SYDNEY ROAD A36
King Edwards School
North Road
Hotel
Holburne Museum & Crafts Study Centre
Daniel St
Daniel Ms
Sutton St
SYDNEY PLACE
Vellore Lane
DARLINGTON STREET
Edward St
Sydney Ms
Raby Mews
Sham Castle Lane
Vane St
Bathwick
Sydney Whf
St Mary's Cl
St Catherine's Cl
St Ann's Wy
Bathwick Hill
PULTENEY ROAD A36
Avon Walkway
Darlington Pl
Sports Centre
Primary School
Magistrates Court
Lime Grove School
Lime Gv Gdns
Lime Gv
Cricket
Sydney Buildings
Pulteney Gdns
Pulteney Gv
Broadway
Golf Course Road
Bath Golf Club
Sham Castle
North Road
Bathwick Hill
Archway St
Widcombe C of E Junior & Infant School
BA2
Horseshoe Walk
Abbey Veiw Gdns
Abbey Vw
Hatfield Blds
Cambridge Ter
The Tyning
Tyning End
Widcombe Hill
Bathwick Cemetery
PRIOR PARK ROAD A3062
Gordon Rd
Clarendon Rd
Church Street
Widcombe Hill
138
Widcombe
Bewdley Rd
Prospect Road
Macaulay Buildings
Rosemount Lane
E F G H
1 2 3 4 5 6

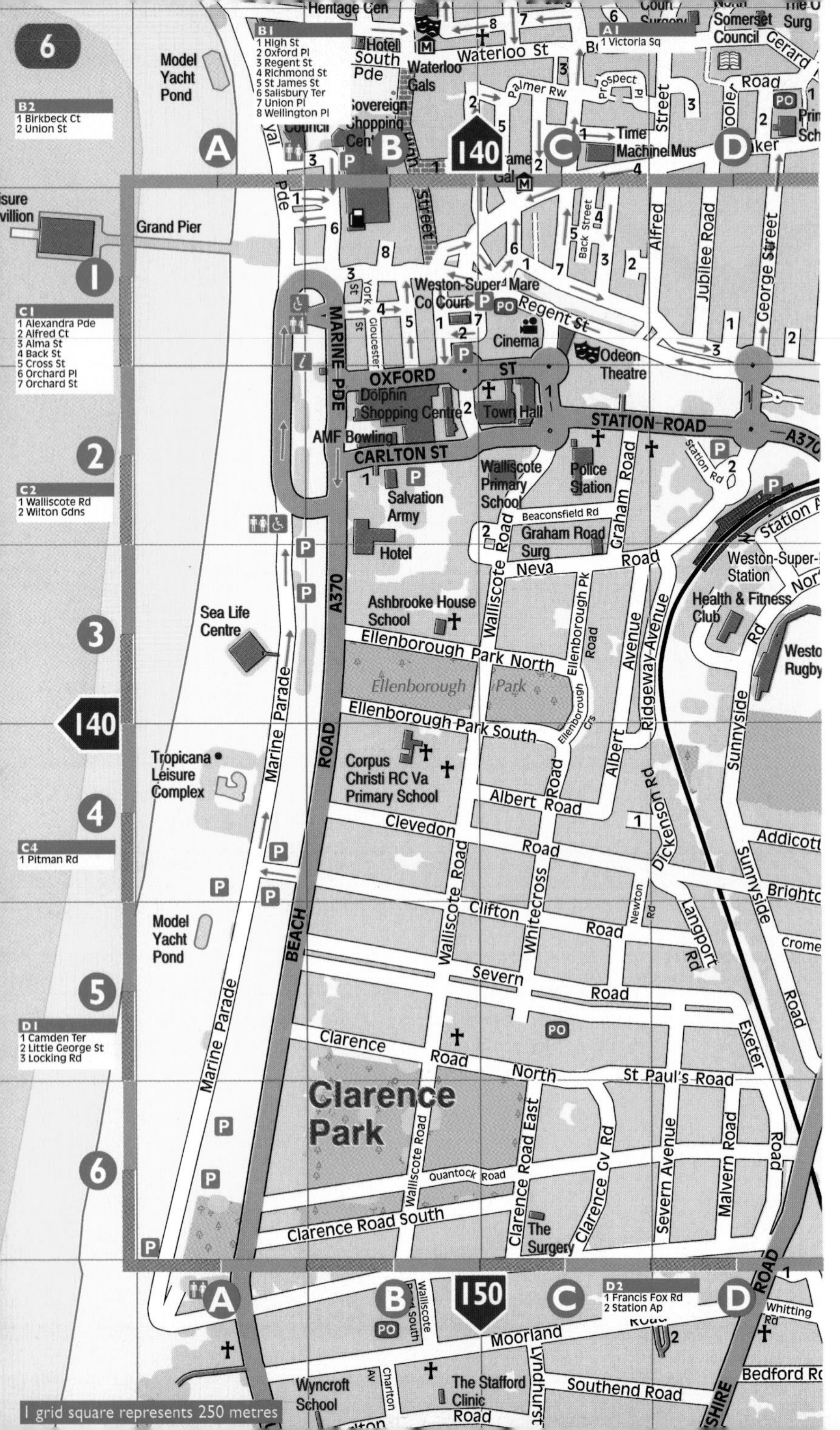
6
B1
1 High St
2 Oxford Pl
3 Regent St
4 Richmond St
5 St James St
6 Salisbury Ter
7 Union Pl
8 Wellington Pl
A1
1 Victoria Sq
B2
1 Birkbeck Ct
2 Union St
C1
1 Alexandra Pde
2 Alfred Ct
3 Alma St
4 Back St
5 Cross St
6 Orchard Pl
7 Orchard St
C2
1 Walliscote Rd
2 Wilton Gdns
C4
1 Pitman Rd
D1
1 Camden Ter
2 Little George St
3 Locking Rd
D2
1 Francis Fox Rd
2 Station Ap
Model Yacht Pond
Grand Pier
Waterloo St
Waterloo Gals
Sovereign Shopping Centre
Somerset Council
Time Machine Mus
Weston-Super-Mare Co Court
Cinema
Odeon Theatre
OXFORD ST
Dolphin Shopping Centre
Town Hall
STATION ROAD
A370
AMF Bowling
CARLTON ST
Salvation Army
Walliscote Primary School
Police Station
Beaconsfield Rd
Graham Road Surg
Neva Road
Hotel
Weston-Super-Mare Station
Health & Fitness Club
Sea Life Centre
Ashbrooke House School
Ellenborough Park North
Ellenborough Park
Ellenborough Park South
Ellenborough Crs
Tropicana Leisure Complex
Corpus Christi RC Va Primary School
Albert Road
Clevedon Road
Clifton Road
Severn Road
Clarence Road North
St Paul's Road
Clarence Park
Quantock Road
Clarence Road South
The Surgery
Marine Parade
BEACH ROAD
MARINE PDE
Walliscote Road
Whitecross Road
Graham Road
Albert Avenue
Ridgeway Avenue
Dickenson Rd
Langport Rd
Newton Rd
Sunnyside Road
Exeter Road
Addicott
Brighton
Clarence Gv Rd
Severn Avenue
Malvern Road
Clarence Road East
Jubilee Road
George Street
Alfred Street
Back Street
Palmer Rw
Prospect Pl
Gloucester St
York St
140
150
Moorland Road
Southend Road
Bedford Rd
Lyndhurst Road
Wyncroft School
The Stafford Clinic
Whitting Rd
1 grid square represents 250 metres

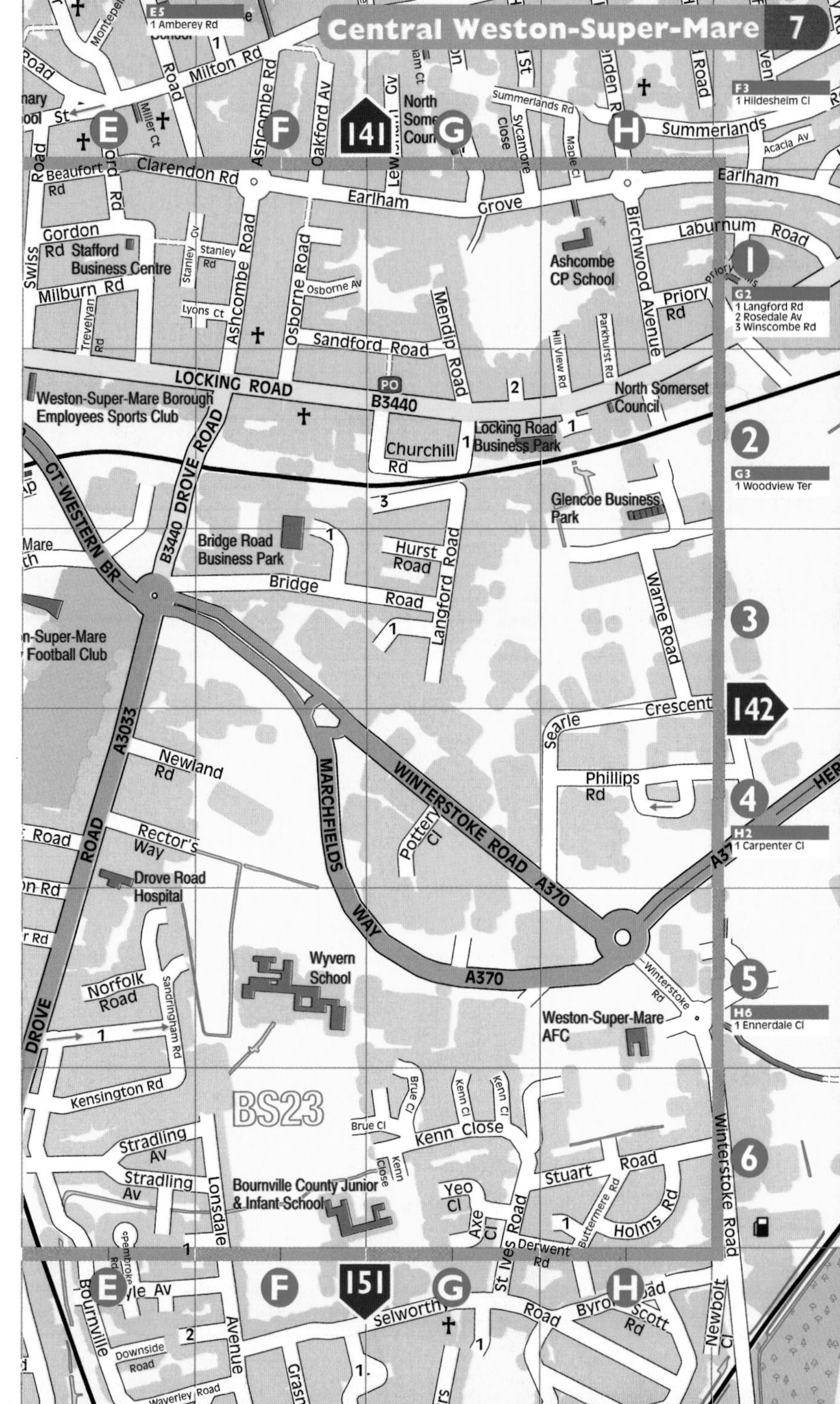
E5
1 Amberey Rd
F3
1 Hildesheim Cl
G2
1 Langford Rd
2 Rosedale Av
3 Winscombe Rd
G3
1 Woodview Ter
H2
1 Carpenter Cl
H6
1 Ennerdale Cl
141
142
151
Milton Rd
Clarendon Rd
Earlham Grove
Summerlands Rd
Summerlands
Acacia Av
Laburnum Road
Beaufort Rd
Gordon Rd
Stafford Business Centre
Milburn Rd
Swiss Road
Trevelyan Rd
Stanley Gv
Stanley Rd
Lyons Ct
Ashcombe Road
Osborne Road
Osborne Av
Oakford Av
Sandford Road
Mendip Road
Ashcombe CP School
Birchwood Avenue
Priory Rd
Hill View Rd
Parkhurst Rd
Sycamore Close
Maple Cl
Miller Ct
North Somerset Council
LOCKING ROAD
B3440
PO
Weston-Super-Mare Borough Employees Sports Club
Locking Road Business Park
Churchill Rd
Glencoe Business Park
B3440 DROVE ROAD
GT-WESTERN BR
Bridge Road Business Park
Hurst Road
Bridge Road
Langford Road
Warne Road
Searle Crescent
Phillips Rd
WINTERSTOKE ROAD A370
MARCHFIELDS WAY
A370
A3033
DROVE ROAD
Newland Rd
Rector's Way
Pottery Cl
Drove Road Hospital
Wyvern School
Norfolk Road
Sandringham Rd
Weston-Super-Mare AFC
Winterstoke Rd
Winterstoke Road
Kensington Rd
BS23
Brue Cl
Kenn Cl
Kenn Close
Stradling Av
Lonsdale Avenue
Bournville County Junior & Infant School
Yeo Cl
Axe Cl
St Ives Road
Derwent Rd
Stuart Road
Buttermere Rd
Holms Rd
Pembroke Rd
Bournville
Downside Road
Waverley Road
Selworthy
Byron Road
Scott Rd
Newbolt Cl
Grasmere

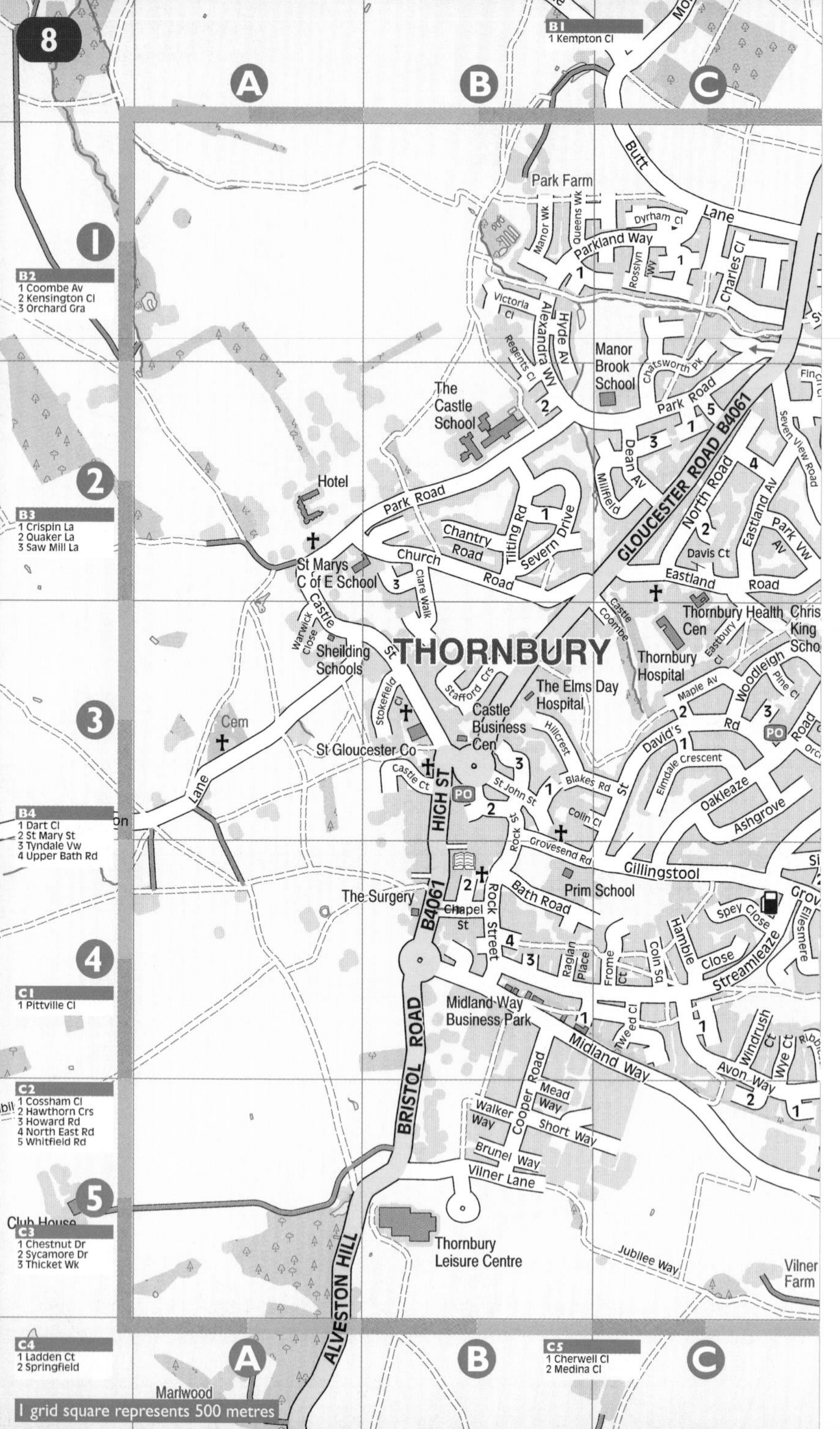
A
B
C
1
2
3
4
5
B1
1 Kempton Cl
B2
1 Coombe Av
2 Kensington Cl
3 Orchard Gra
B3
1 Crispin La
2 Quaker La
3 Saw Mill La
B4
1 Dart Cl
2 St Mary St
3 Tyndale Vw
4 Upper Bath Rd
C1
1 Pittville Cl
C2
1 Cossham Cl
2 Hawthorn Crs
3 Howard Rd
4 North East Rd
5 Whitfield Rd
C3
1 Chestnut Dr
2 Sycamore Dr
3 Thicket Wk
C4
1 Ladden Ct
2 Springfield
C5
1 Cherwell Cl
2 Medina Cl
THORNBURY
Butt Lane
Park Farm
Manor Wk
Queens Wk
Dyrham Cl
Parkland Way
Rosslyn Wy
Charles Cl
Victoria Cl
Alexandra Wy
Hyde Av
Regents Cl
Manor Brook School
Chatsworth Pk
Park Road
The Castle School
Dean Av
Millfield
GLOUCESTER ROAD B4061
North Road
Seven View Road
Eastland Av
Park Vw Av
Hotel
Park Road
Chantry Road
Tilting Rd
Severn Drive
Church Road
Davis Ct
Eastland Road
St Marys C of E School
Clare Walk
Castle St
Castle Coombe
Thornbury Health Cen
Warwick Close
Sheilding Schools
Thornbury Hospital
Eastbury Cl
Maple Av
Woodleigh Rd
Pine Cl
Stafford Crs
The Elms Day Hospital
Stokefield Cl
Castle Business Cen
Hillcrest
David's Rd
Elmdale Crescent
Cem
St Gloucester Co
Lane
Castle Ct
HIGH ST
PO
St John St
Blakes Rd
Colin Cl
Oakleaze
Ashgrove
Rock St
Grovesend Rd
Gillingstool
Prim School
The Surgery
Chapel St
Rock Street
Bath Road
Spey Close
Ellesmere
B4061
Raglan Place
Frome Ct
Colin Sq
Hamble Close
Streamleaze
Midland Way Business Park
Tweed Cl
BRISTOL ROAD
Midland Way
Windrush Ct
Wye Ct
Avon Way
Cooper Road
Mead Way
Walker Way
Short Way
Brunel Way
Vilner Lane
Thornbury Leisure Centre
Jubilee Way
Vilner Farm
Club House
ALVESTON HILL
Marlwood

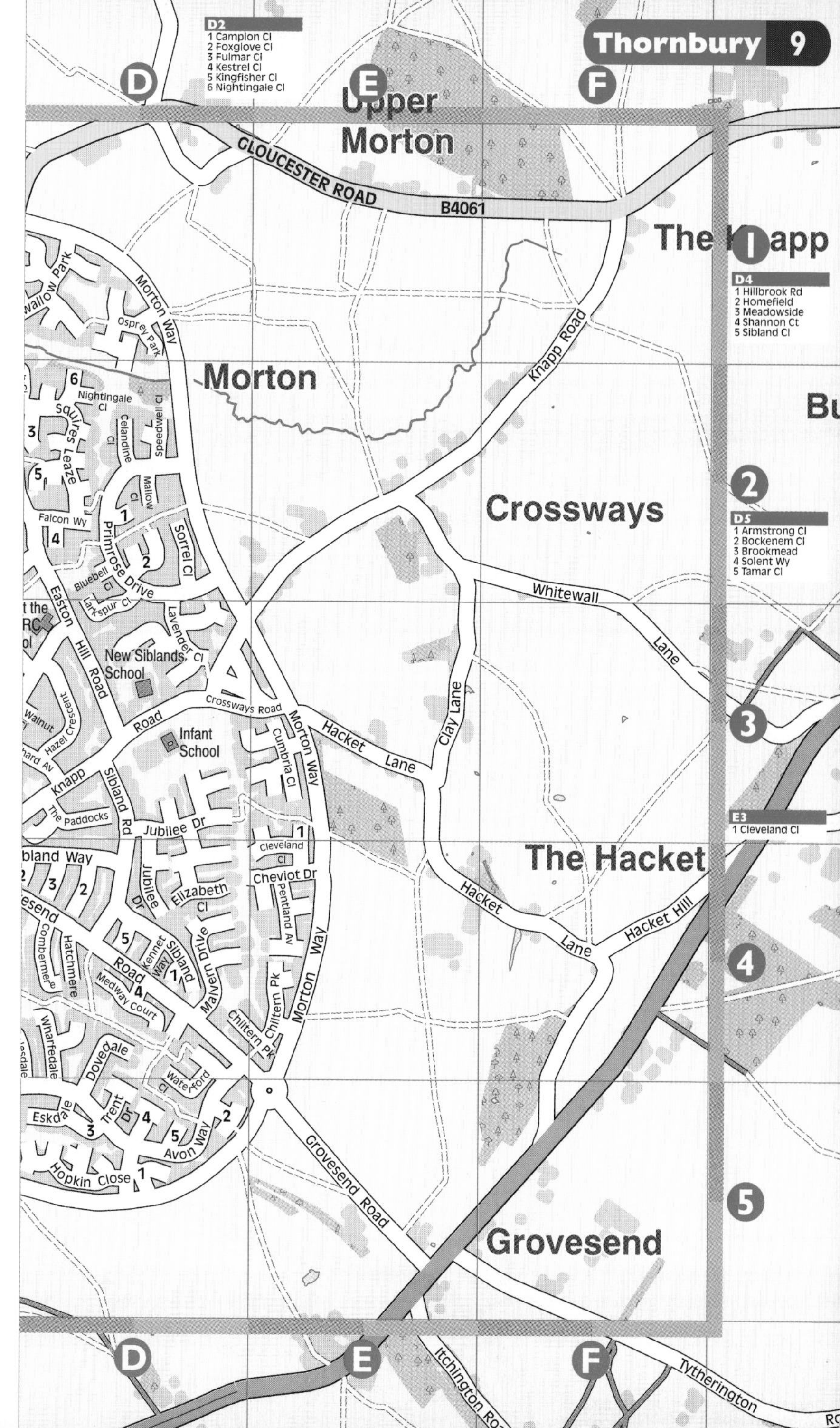
D2
1 Campion Cl
2 Foxglove Cl
3 Fulmar Cl
4 Kestrel Cl
5 Kingfisher Cl
6 Nightingale Cl
D
E
F
Upper Morton
GLOUCESTER ROAD
B4061
The Knapp
D4
1 Hillbrook Rd
2 Homefield
3 Meadowside
4 Shannon Ct
5 Sibland Cl
Knapp Road
Morton Way
Osprey Park
Swallow Park
Morton
Nightingale Cl
Squires Leaze
Celandine Cl
Speedwell Cl
Mallow Cl
Falcon Wy
Primrose Drive
Sorrel Cl
Bluebell Cl
Larkspur Cl
Easton Hill Road
Lavender Cl
Crossways
D5
1 Armstrong Cl
2 Bockenem Cl
3 Brookmead
4 Solent Wy
5 Tamar Cl
Whitewall Lane
New Siblands School
Crossways Road
Clay Lane
Infant School
Hacket Lane
Cumbria Cl
Walnut
Hazel Crescent
Knapp Road
Sibland Rd
The Paddocks
Jubilee Dr
Cleveland Cl
Cheviot Dr
E3
1 Cleveland Cl
The Hacket
Sibland Way
Jubilee Dr
Elizabeth Cl
Pentland Av
Hacket Hill
Kennet Way
Sibland
Malvern Drive
Combermere
Hatchmere
Road
Medway Court
Chiltern Pk
Wharfedale
Dovedale
Waterford Cl
Eskdale
Trent Dr
Avon Way
Hopkin Close
Grovesend Road
Grovesend
Itchington Road
Tytherington

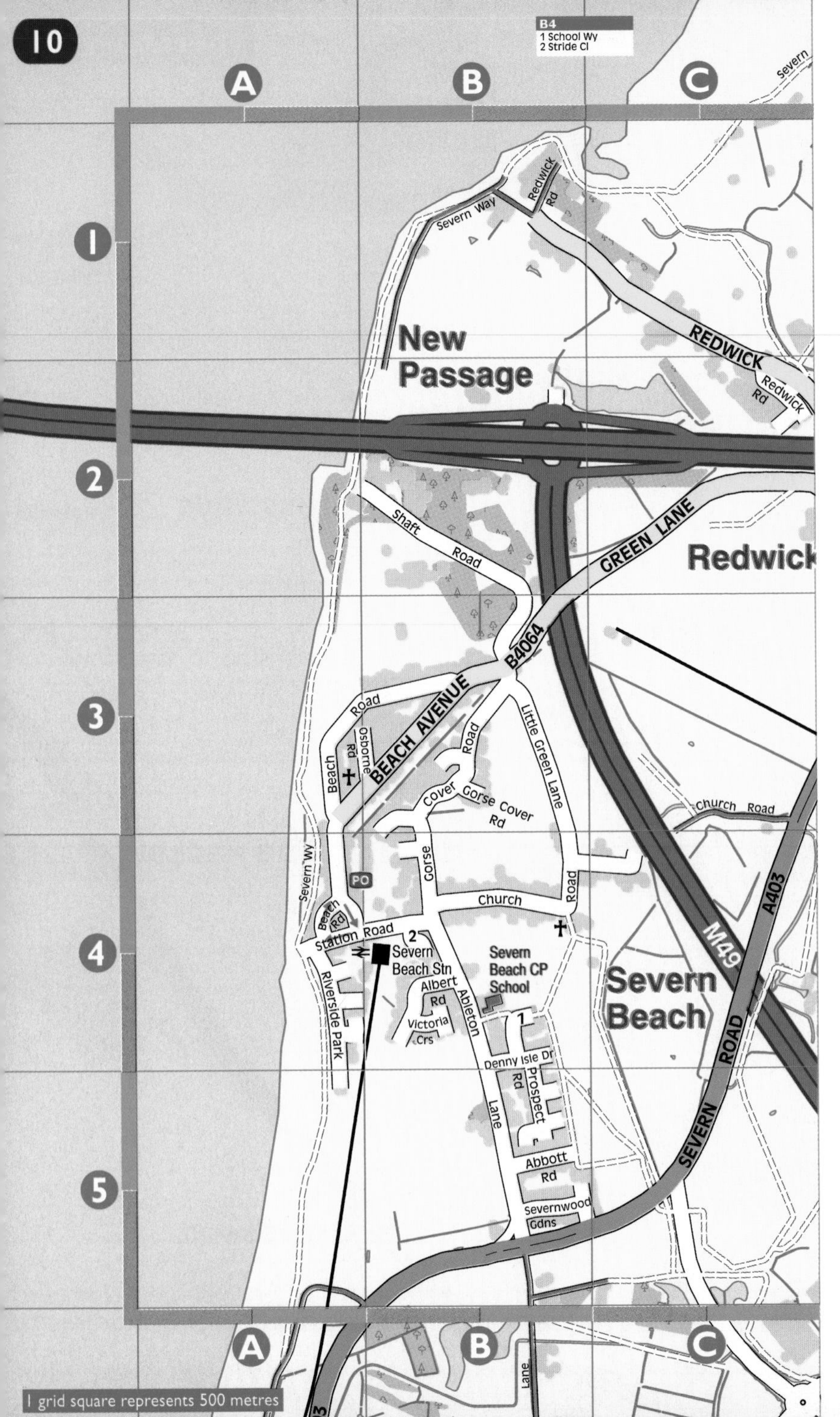

B4
1 School Wy
2 Stride Cl
A
B
C
Severn
Severn Way
Redwick Rd
New Passage
REDWICK
Redwick Rd
1
2
Shaft Road
GREEN LANE
Redwick
B4064
BEACH AVENUE
Road
Osborne Rd
Beach
Road
Little Green Lane
Cover
Gorse Cover Rd
Church Road
3
Severn Wy
PO
Gorse
Church
Road
Beach Rd
Station Road
Severn Beach Stn
Albert Rd
Ableton
Severn Beach CP School
Severn Beach
M49
A403
4
Riverside Park
Victoria Crs
Denny Isle Dr
Rd
Prospect
Lane
ROAD
SEVERN
Abbott Rd
Severnwood Gdns
5
A
B
C
Lane

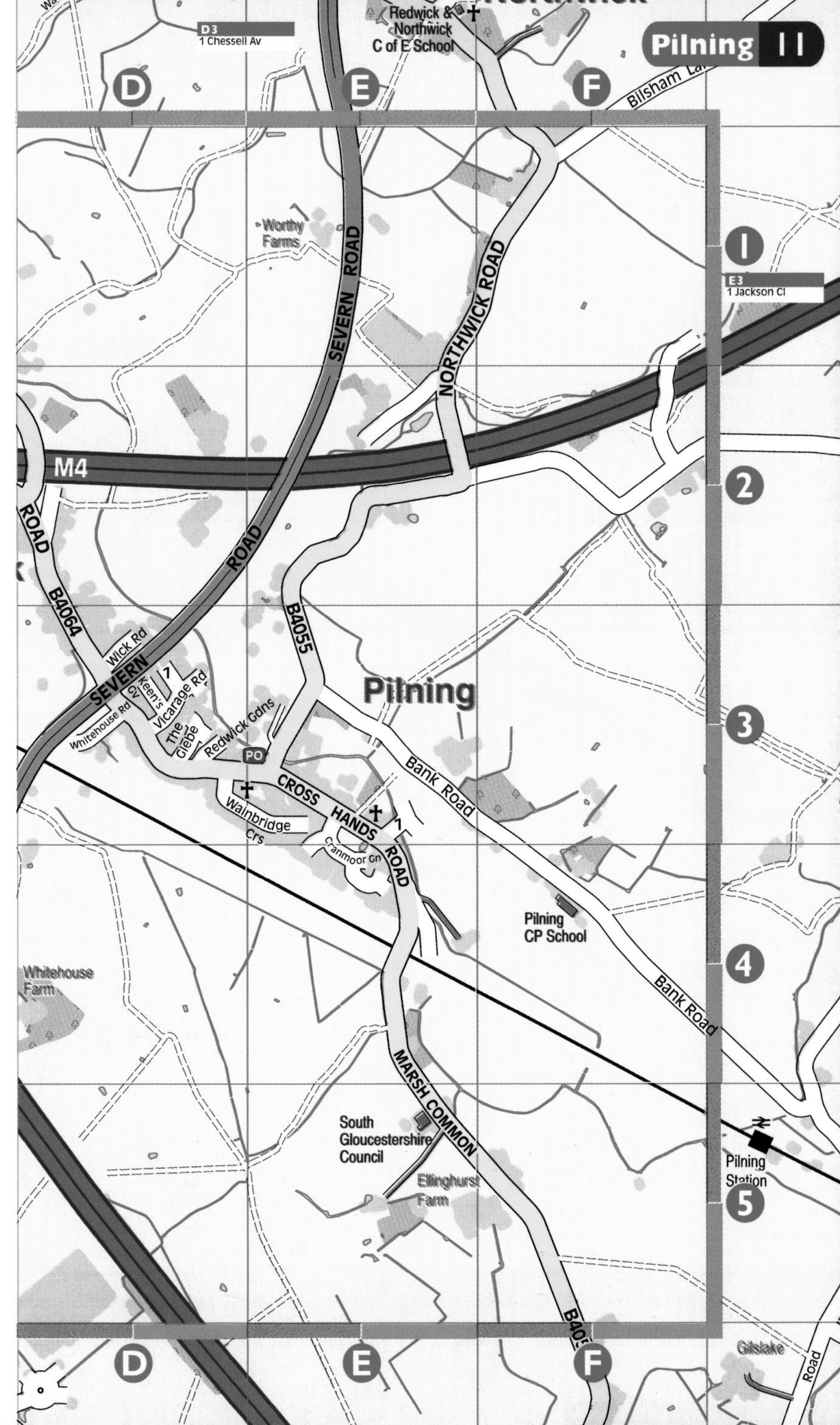
D3
1 Chessell Av
Redwick & Northwick C of E School
Bilsham La
E3
1 Jackson Cl
Worthy Farms
SEVERN ROAD
NORTHWICK ROAD
M4
ROAD
B4064
B4055
Wick Rd
SEVERN
Keen's Gv
Vicarage Rd
Whitehouse Rd
The Glebe
Redwick Gdns
PO
Pilning
Bank Road
CROSS HANDS ROAD
Wainbridge Crs
Cranmoor Gn
Pilning CP School
Whitehouse Farm
MARSH COMMON
South Gloucestershire Council
Ellinghurst Farm
Pilning Station
Gilslake
Road
D
E
F
1
2
3
4
5

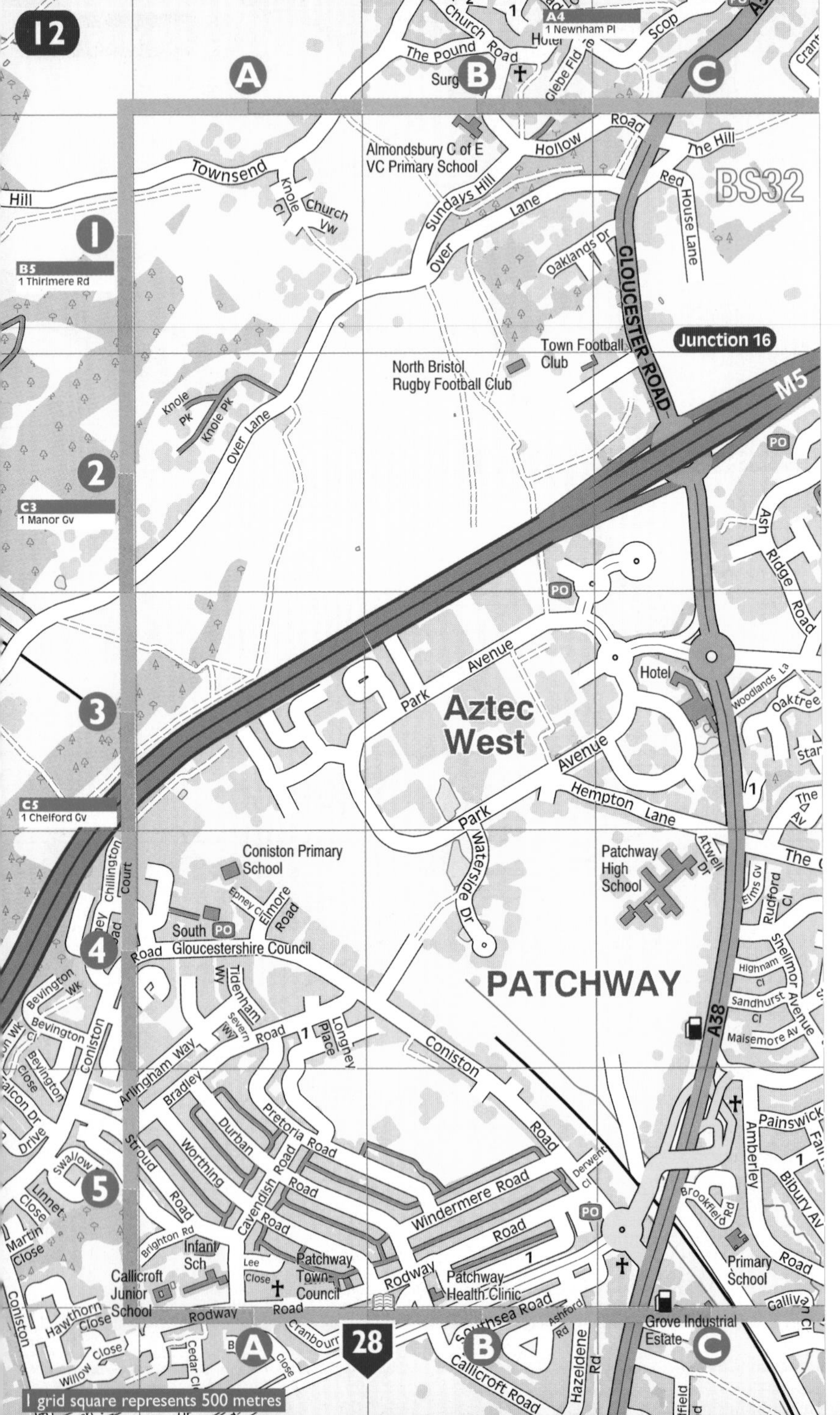

28

1 grid square represents 500 metres

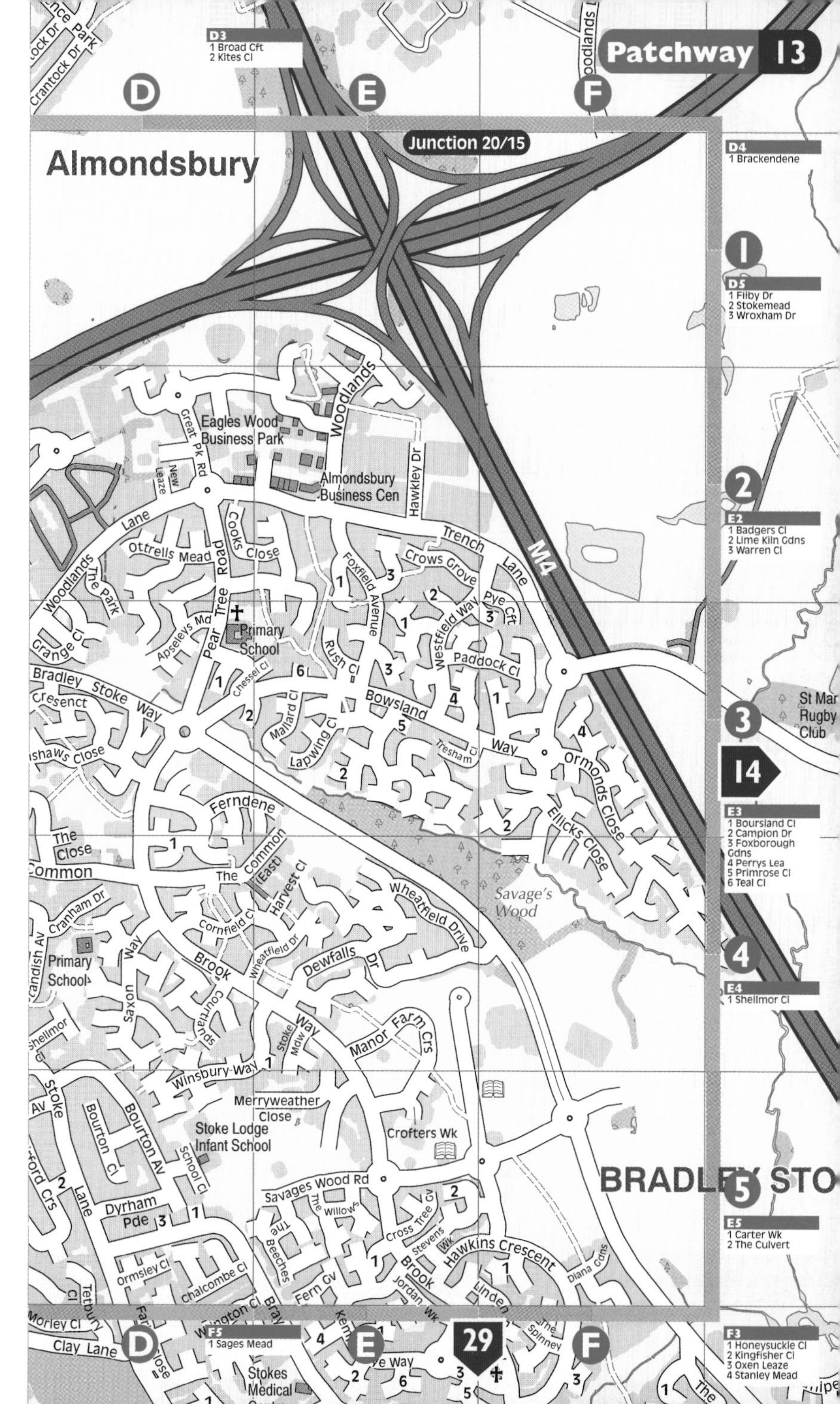
D3
1 Broad Cft
2 Kites Cl
D
E
F
Junction 20/15
Almondsbury
D4
1 Brackendene
1
D5
1 Filby Dr
2 Stokemead
3 Wroxham Dr
Woodlands
Eagles Wood
Business Park
Great Pk Rd
New Leaze
Almondsbury
Business Cen
Hawkley Dr
2
E2
1 Badgers Cl
2 Lime Kiln Gdns
3 Warren Cl
Trench Lane
M4
Crows Grove
Foxfield Avenue
Cooks Close
Ottrells Mead
Pear Tree Road
Woodlands Lane
The Park
Grange Cl
Apseleys Md
Primary School
Chessel Cl
Rush Cl
Westfield Way
Pye Cft
Paddock Cl
Bradley Stoke Way
Cresenct
Bowsland Way
Mallard Cl
Lapwing Cl
Tresham Cl
Ormonds Close
St Mar
Rugby
Club
3
14
Ferndene
E3
1 Boursland Cl
2 Campion Dr
3 Foxborough Gdns
4 Perrys Lea
5 Primrose Cl
6 Teal Cl
Ellicks Close
The Close
Common
The Common (East)
Harvest Cl
Wheatfield Drive
Savage's Wood
Cranham Dr
Cornfield Cl
Wheatfield Dr
Primary School
Brook Way
Dewfalls Dr
4
E4
1 Shellmor Cl
Saxon Way
Courtlands
Stoke Mdw
Manor Farm Crs
Shellmor Cl
Winsbury Way
Merryweather Close
Stoke Lodge
Infant School
Crofters Wk
Bourton Cl
Bourton Av
School Cl
BRADLEY STO
5
Savages Wood Rd
Dyrham Pde
The Willows
Cross Tree Gv
The Beeches
E5
1 Carter Wk
2 The Culvert
Stevens Wk
Hawkins Crescent
Ormsley Cl
Chalcombe Cl
Fern Gv
Brook
Jordan Wk
Linden
Diana Gdns
Tetbury Cl
Morley Cl
Clay Lane
F5
1 Sages Mead
29
The Spinney
F3
1 Honeysuckle Cl
2 Kingfisher Cl
3 Oxen Leaze
4 Stanley Mead
Stokes
Medical
Centre

14
Woodlands
Gaunt's
Earthcott
A
B
C
1
2
3
4
5
13
St Marys
Rugby
Club
Water
Park
North
Woods
Trench Lane
Hotel
Ormonds Close
Close
BRADLEY STOKE
Bradley Brook
B4427
Diana Gdns
30
Lavender Wy
Juniper
Fennel
STER ROAD
1 grid square represents 500 metres

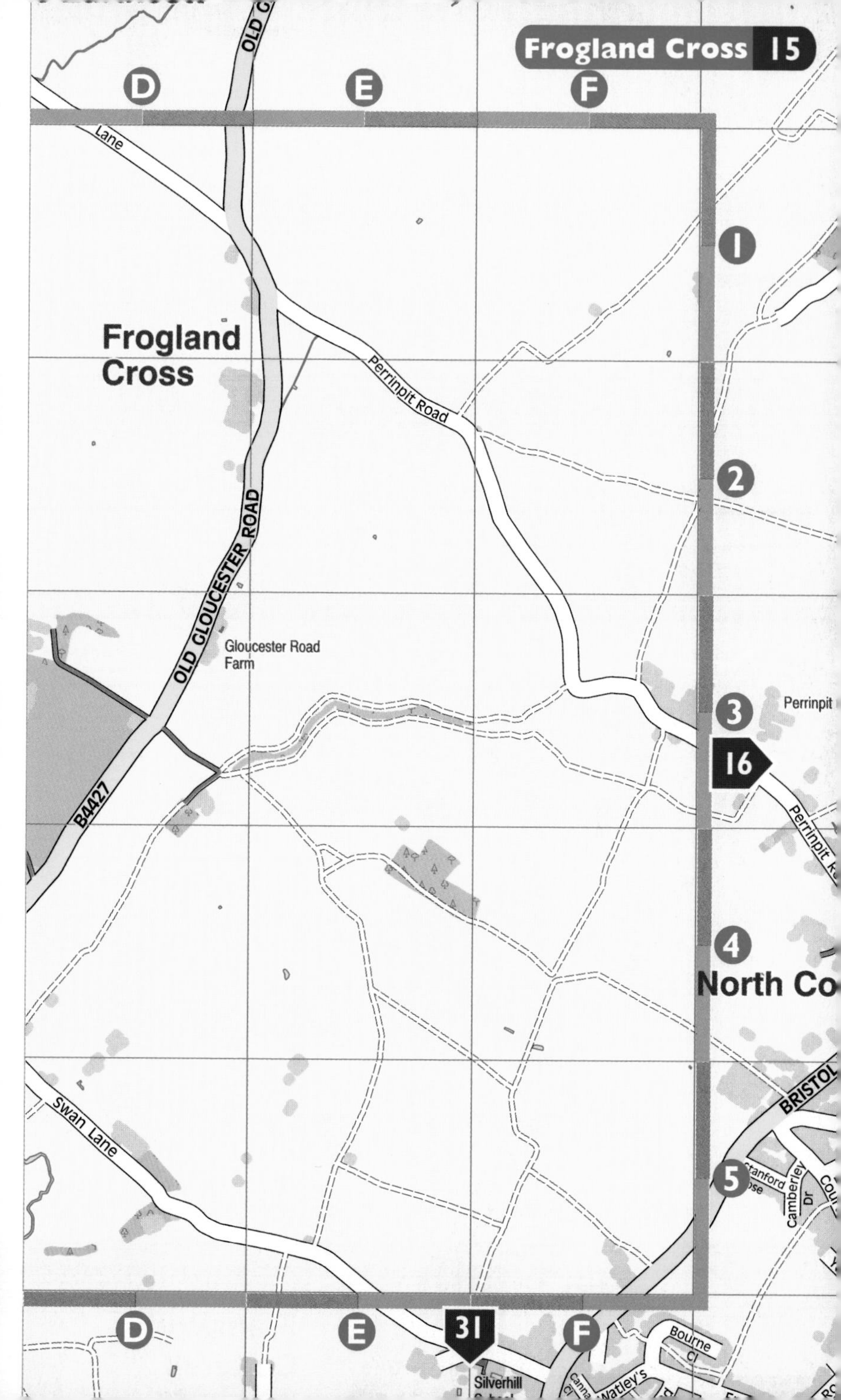
D
E
F
Lane
OLD G
Frogland Cross
Perrinpit Road
OLD GLOUCESTER ROAD
Gloucester Road Farm
B4427
Perrinpit
16
Perrinpit R
North Co
BRISTOL
Swan Lane
Stanford Close
Camberley Dr
31
Bourne Cl
Silverhill
Watley's
1
2
3
4
5

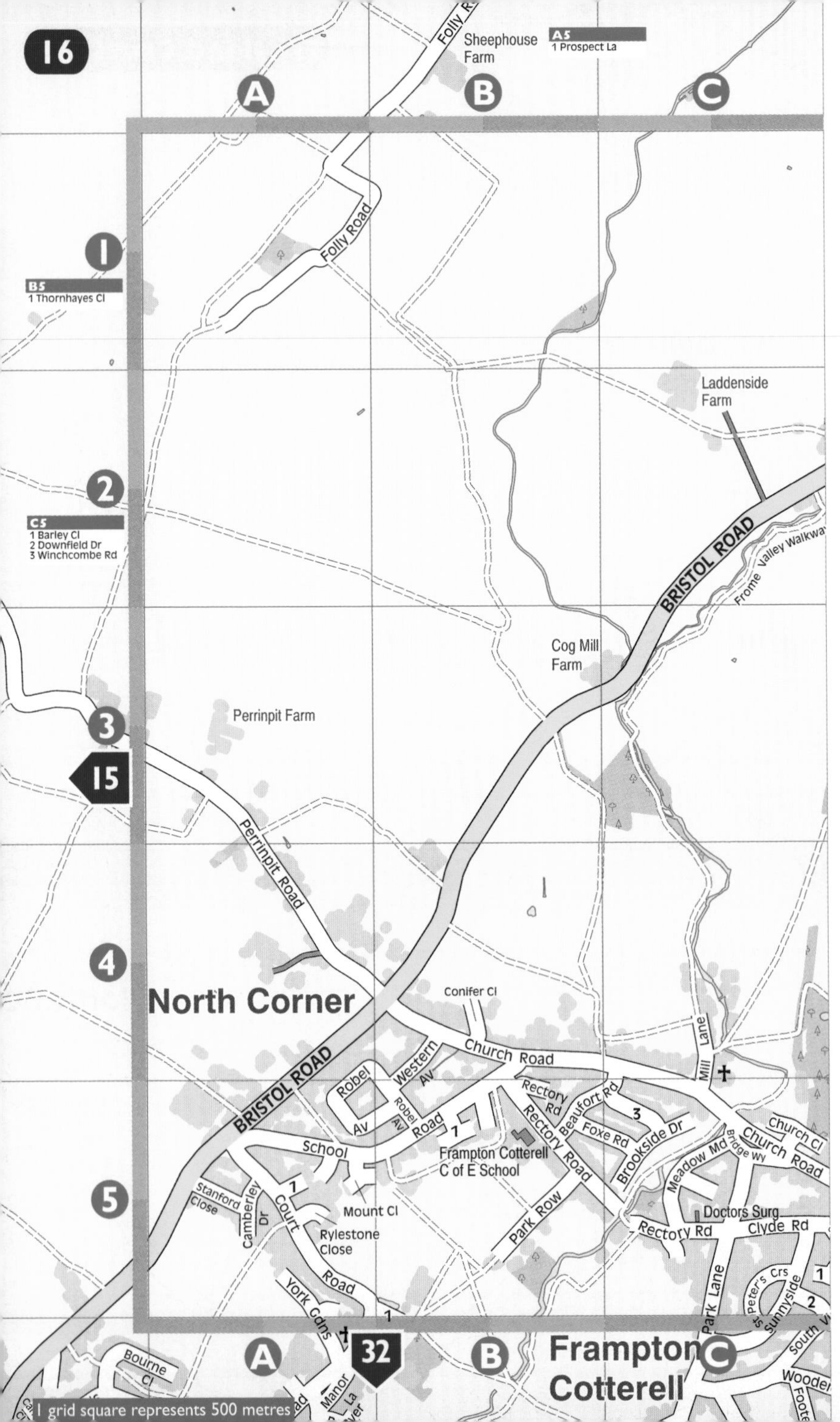

Folly Road
Sheephouse Farm
A5
1 Prospect La
A
B
C
1
B5
1 Thornhayes Cl
2
C5
1 Barley Cl
2 Downfield Dr
3 Winchcombe Rd
3
15
4
5
Laddenside Farm
BRISTOL ROAD
Frome Valley Walkway
Cog Mill Farm
Perrinpit Farm
Perrinpit Road
North Corner
Conifer Cl
Church Road
Mill Lane
Western Av
Robel Av
Robel Av
Road
School
Rectory Rd
Beaufort Rd
Foxe Rd
Brookside Dr
Rectory Road
Church Cl
Church Road
Bridge Wy
Meadow Md
Frampton Cotterell C of E School
Stanford Close
Camberley Dr
Court
Road
Mount Cl
Rylestone Close
Park Row
Rectory Rd
Doctors Surg
Clyde Rd
Park Lane
St Peter's Crs
Sunnyside
South Vi
York Gdns
32
Bourne Cl
Manor La
Frampton Cotterell
Wooden
Foote

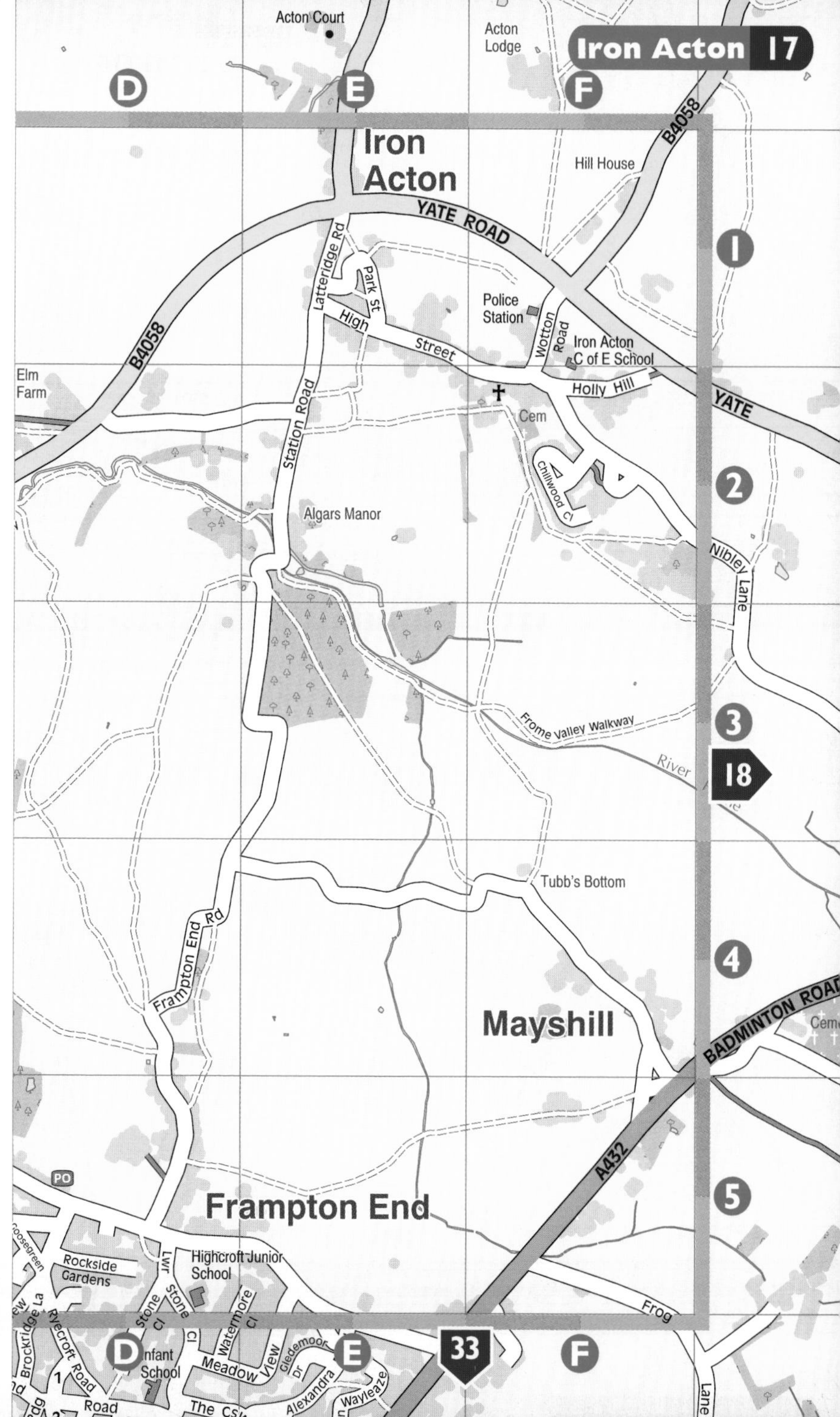
Acton Court
Acton Lodge
D
E
F
Iron Acton
YATE ROAD
B4058
Hill House
Latteridge Rd
Park St
High Street
Police Station
Wotton Road
Iron Acton C of E School
Holly Hill
YATE
Elm Farm
Station Road
Cem
Chillwood Cl
Algars Manor
Nibley Lane
Frome Valley Walkway
River
18
1
2
3
4
5
Tubb's Bottom
Frampton End Rd
Mayshill
BADMINTON ROAD
Cem
A432
PO
Frampton End
Goosegreen
Rockside Gardens
Lwr Stone Cl
Highcroft Junior School
Watermore Cl
Frog
Brockridge La
Ryecroft Road
Stone Cl
Infant School
Meadow View
Gledemoor Dr
Alexandra
Wayleaze
Road
33
Lane

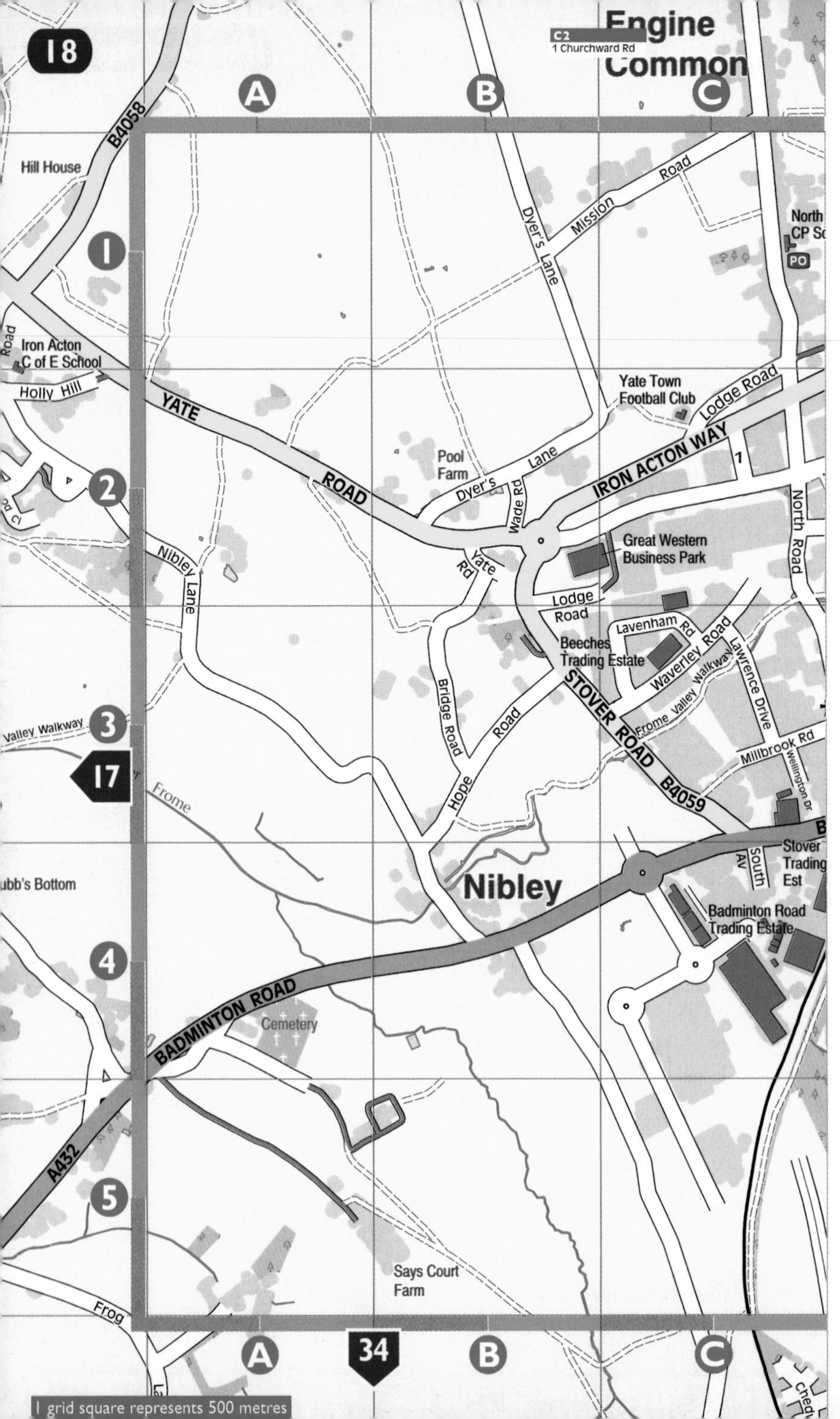
Engine Common
C2
1 Churchward Rd
A
B
C
1
2
3
4
5
B4058
Hill House
Road
Iron Acton C of E School
Holly Hill
YATE ROAD
Mission Road
Dyer's Lane
North CP Sc
PO
Yate Town Football Club
Lodge Road
IRON ACTON WAY
Pool Farm
Dyer's Lane
Wade Rd
North Road
Great Western Business Park
Yate Rd
Nibley Lane
Lodge Road
Lavenham Rd
Beeches Trading Estate
Waverley Road
Lawrence Drive
Bridge Road
Hope Road
STOVER ROAD
B4059
Frome Valley Walkway
Millbrook Rd
Wellington Dr
Valley Walkway
17
Frome
Nibley
South Av
Stover Trading Est
Badminton Road Trading Estate
BADMINTON ROAD
Cemetery
A432
Says Court Farm
Frog
34
1 grid square represents 500 metres

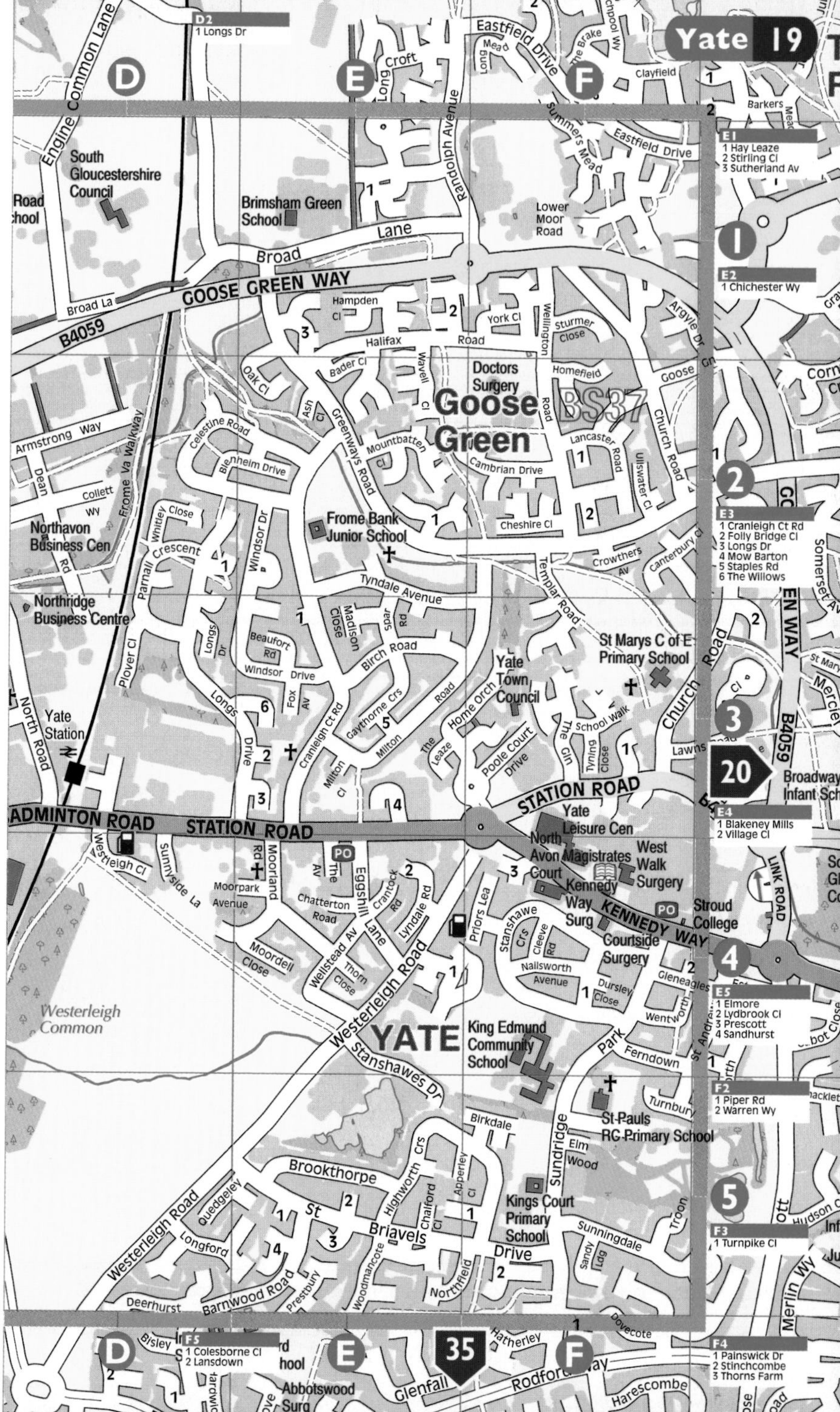
D2
1 Longs Dr
E1
1 Hay Leaze
2 Stirling Cl
3 Sutherland Av
E2
1 Chichester Wy
E3
1 Cranleigh Ct Rd
2 Folly Bridge Cl
3 Longs Dr
4 Mow Barton
5 Staples Rd
6 The Willows
E4
1 Blakeney Mills
2 Village Cl
E5
1 Elmore
2 Lydbrook Cl
3 Prescott
4 Sandhurst
F2
1 Piper Rd
2 Warren Wy
F3
1 Turnpike Cl
F4
1 Painswick Dr
2 Stinchcombe
3 Thorns Farm
F5
1 Colesborne Cl
2 Lansdown
Goose Green
BS37
YATE
South Gloucestershire Council
Brimsham Green School
GOOSE GREEN WAY
B4059
Broad Lane
Doctors Surgery
Frome Bank Junior School
Northavon Business Cen
Northridge Business Centre
Yate Station
St Marys C of E Primary School
Yate Town Council
STATION ROAD
BADMINTON ROAD
Yate Leisure Cen
North Avon Magistrates Court
West Walk Surgery
Kennedy Way Surg
KENNEDY WAY
Stroud College
Courtside Surgery
King Edmund Community School
St Pauls RC Primary School
Kings Court Primary School
Westerleigh Common
Westerleigh Road
Abbotswood Surg
Broadway Infant Sch
20
35

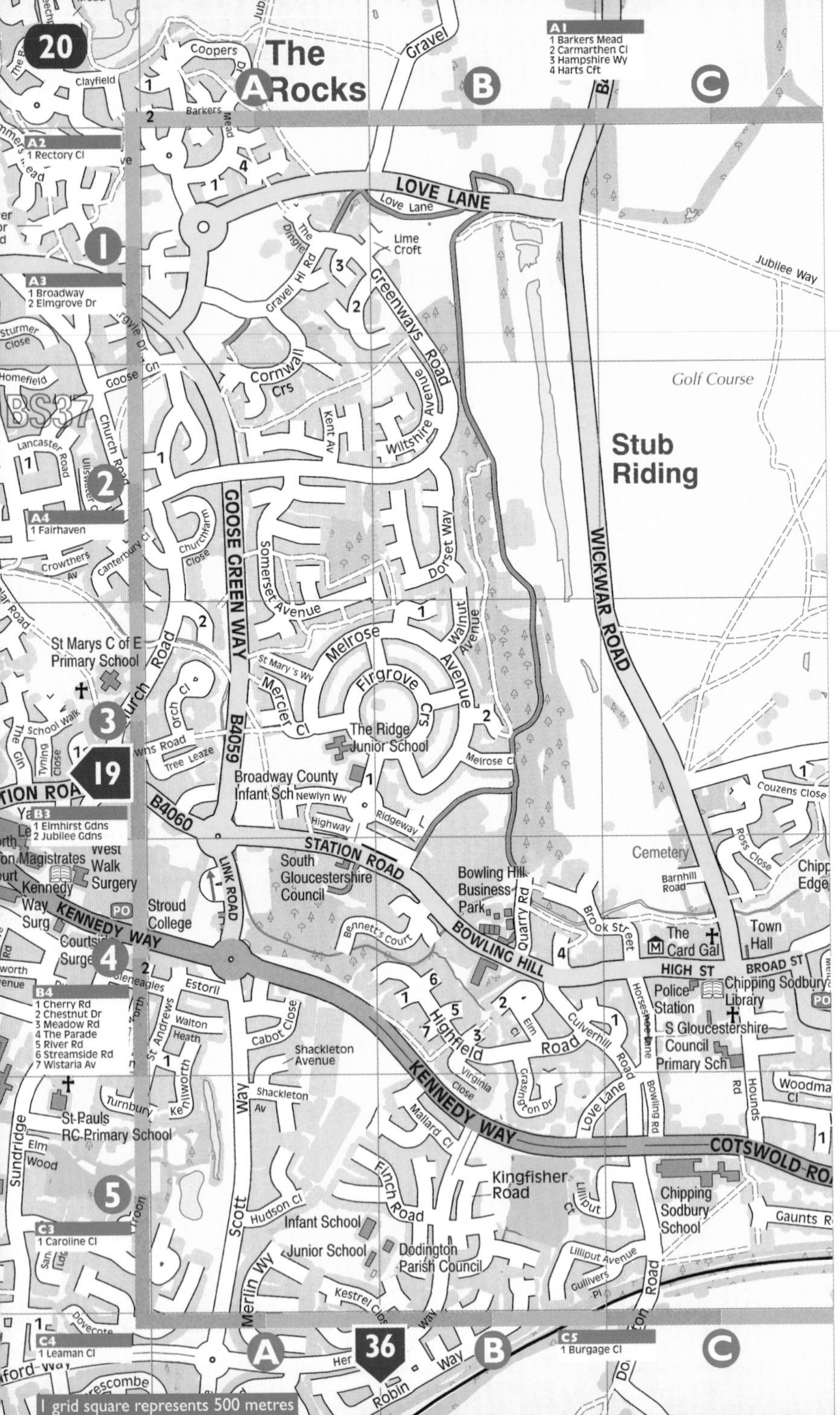
20
The Rocks
A1
1 Barkers Mead
2 Carmarthen Cl
3 Hampshire Wy
4 Harts Cft
A2
1 Rectory Cl
A3
1 Broadway
2 Elmgrove Dr
A4
1 Fairhaven
B3
1 Elmhirst Gdns
2 Jubilee Gdns
B4
1 Cherry Rd
2 Chestnut Dr
3 Meadow Rd
4 The Parade
5 River Rd
6 Streamside Rd
7 Wistaria Av
C3
1 Caroline Cl
C4
1 Leaman Cl
C5
1 Burgage Cl
Love Lane
Jubilee Way
Golf Course
Stub Riding
Wickwar Road
Goose Green Way
B4059
B4060
Station Road
Link Road
Kennedy Way
Bowling Hill
High St
Broad St
Cotswold Road
St Marys C of E Primary School
The Ridge Junior School
Broadway County Infant Sch
South Gloucestershire Council
Bowling Hill Business Park
Cemetery
Town Hall
Chipping Sodbury Library
Police Station
S Gloucestershire Council Primary Sch
Chipping Sodbury School
Stroud College
Kingfisher Road
Infant School
Junior School
Dodington Parish Council
St Pauls RC Primary School
Shackleton Avenue
Scott Way
Merlin Wy
Finch Road
Robin Way
19
36
1 grid square represents 500 metres

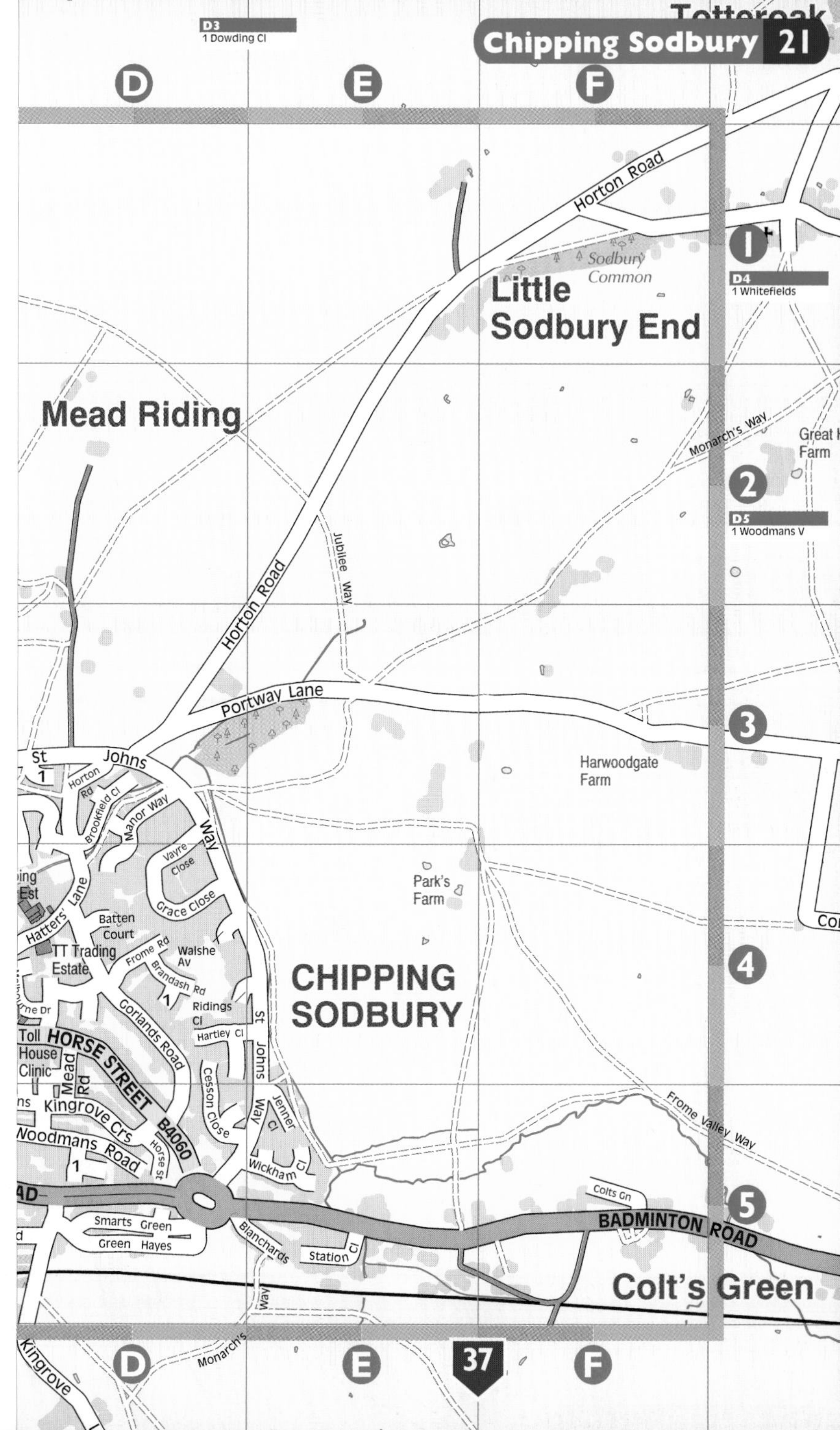

D3
1 Dowding Cl
D
E
F
Horton Road
Sodbury Common
Little Sodbury End
D4
1 Whitefields
Mead Riding
Monarch's Way
Great H
Farm
D5
1 Woodmans V
Jubilee Way
Horton Road
Portway Lane
Harwoodgate Farm
St Johns Way
Horton Rd
Brookfield Cl
Manor Way
Vayre Close
Grace Close
Park's Farm
Hatters' Lane
Batten Court
TT Trading Estate
Frome Rd
Walshe Av
Brandash Rd
CHIPPING SODBURY
Gorlands Road
Ridings Cl
Hartley Cl
St Johns Way
Toll House Clinic
HORSE STREET
Mead Rd
B4060
Kingrove Crs
Cesson Close
Jenner Cl
Frome Valley Way
Woodmans Road
Horse St
Wickham Cl
Colts Gn
BADMINTON ROAD
Smarts Green
Green Hayes
Blanchards
Station Cl
Colt's Green
Way
Monarch's
Kingrove

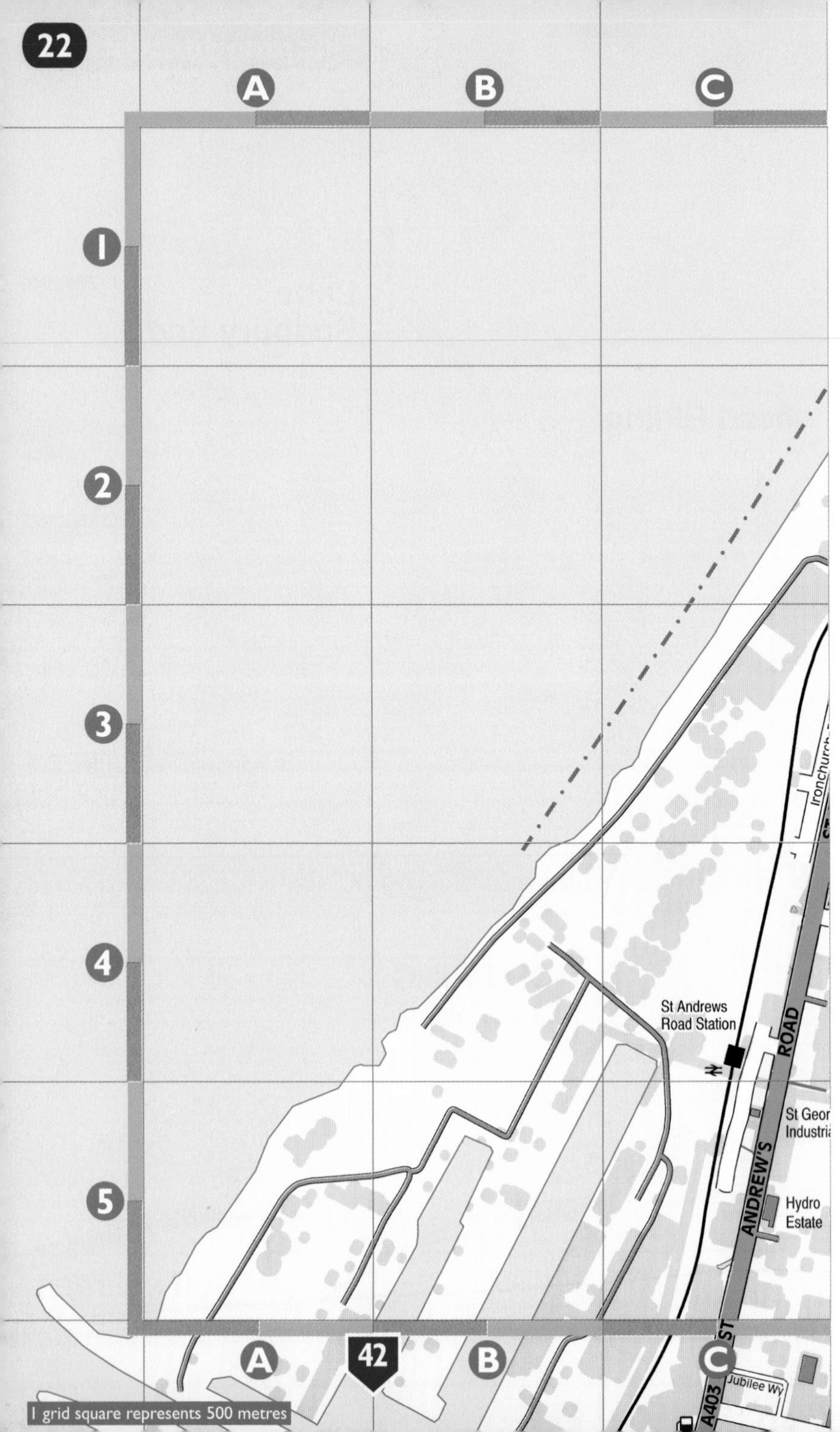
A
B
C
1
2
3
4
5
Ironchurch
St Andrews
Road Station
ROAD
ANDREW'S
ST
A403
St Geor
Industri
Hydro
Estate
Jubilee Wy
42
1 grid square represents 500 metres

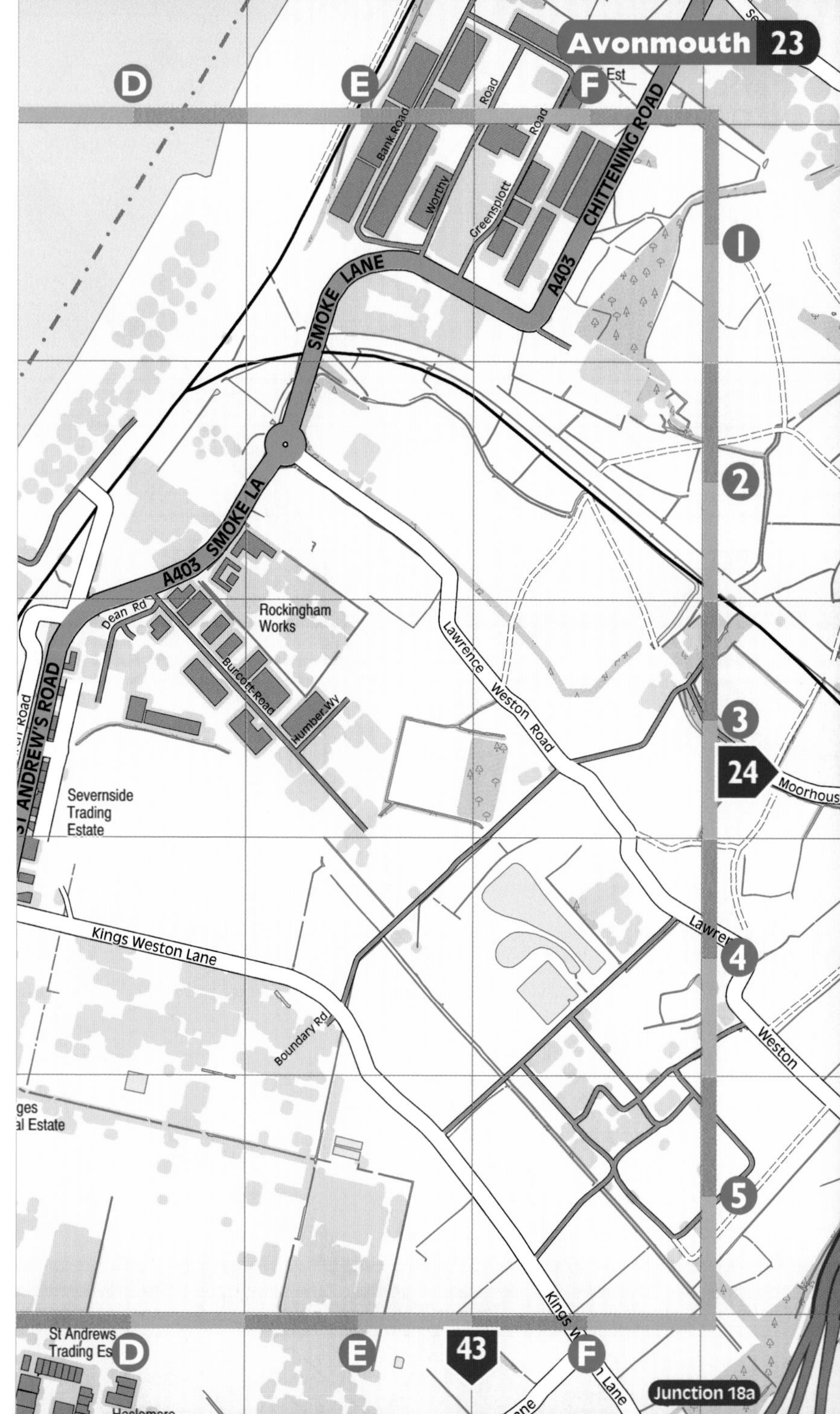
D
E
F
Est
Bank Road
Road
Road
Worthy
Greensplott
CHITTENING ROAD
A403
SMOKE LANE
A403 SMOKE LA
Dean Rd
Rockingham
Works
Burcott Road
Humber Wy
Lawrence Weston Road
ST ANDREW'S ROAD
Severnside
Trading
Estate
Kings Weston Lane
Boundary Rd
Lawren
Weston
Moorhouse
24
1
2
3
4
5
St Andrews
Trading Es
Haslemere
43
Kings Weston Lane
Junction 18a

24
Ind Est
CHITTENING ROAD
Severn Road
Lane
Gas
Works
A
B
C
1
2
3
23
4
5
M49
Hallen
Marsh
Severn Road
Moorhouse
Lane
Moorhouse
Lane
Moor
House
Lawrence
Weston
Road
Poplar
Farm
M49
M5
Lawrence
Weston
Road
Bank Leaze
Primary
School
Atwood Drive
44
Junction 18a
1 grid square represents 500 metres

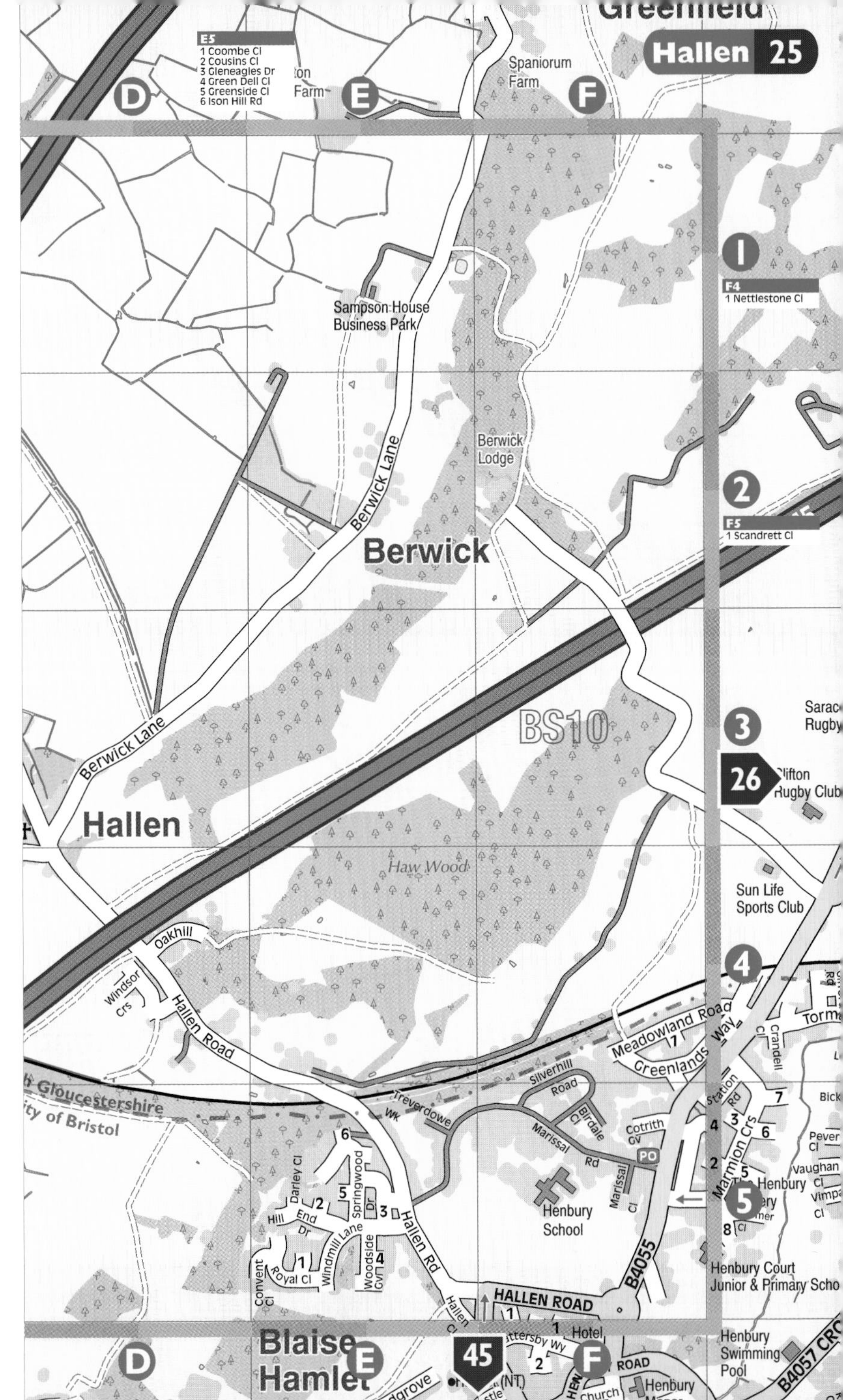
E5
1 Coombe Cl
2 Cousins Cl
3 Gleneagles Dr
4 Green Dell Cl
5 Greenside Cl
6 Ison Hill Rd
Spaniorum Farm
F4
1 Nettlestone Cl
F5
1 Scandrett Cl
Sampson House Business Park
Berwick Lodge
Berwick Lane
Berwick
BS10
Hallen
Haw Wood
Clifton Rugby Club
Sun Life Sports Club
Oakhill
Windsor Crs
Hallen Road
Meadowland Road
Greenlands Way
Crandell Cl
Silverhill Road
Birdale Cl
Treverdowe Wk
Marissal Rd
Marissal Cl
Cotrith Gv
PO
Station Rd
Marmion Crs
Henbury School
Darley Cl
Springwood Dr
Hill End Dr
Windmill Lane
Woodside Gv
Royal Cl
Convent Cl
Hallen Rd
Hallen Cl
HALLEN ROAD
B4055
Henbury Court Junior & Primary Scho
Henbury Swimming Pool
Hotel
Blaise Hamlet
Woodgrove Rd
Castle Cl
Church La
Henbury Manor School
B4057
Gloucestershire
City of Bristol
Pever Cl
Vaughan Cl
Torm
Bick
Sarac Rugby
26
45

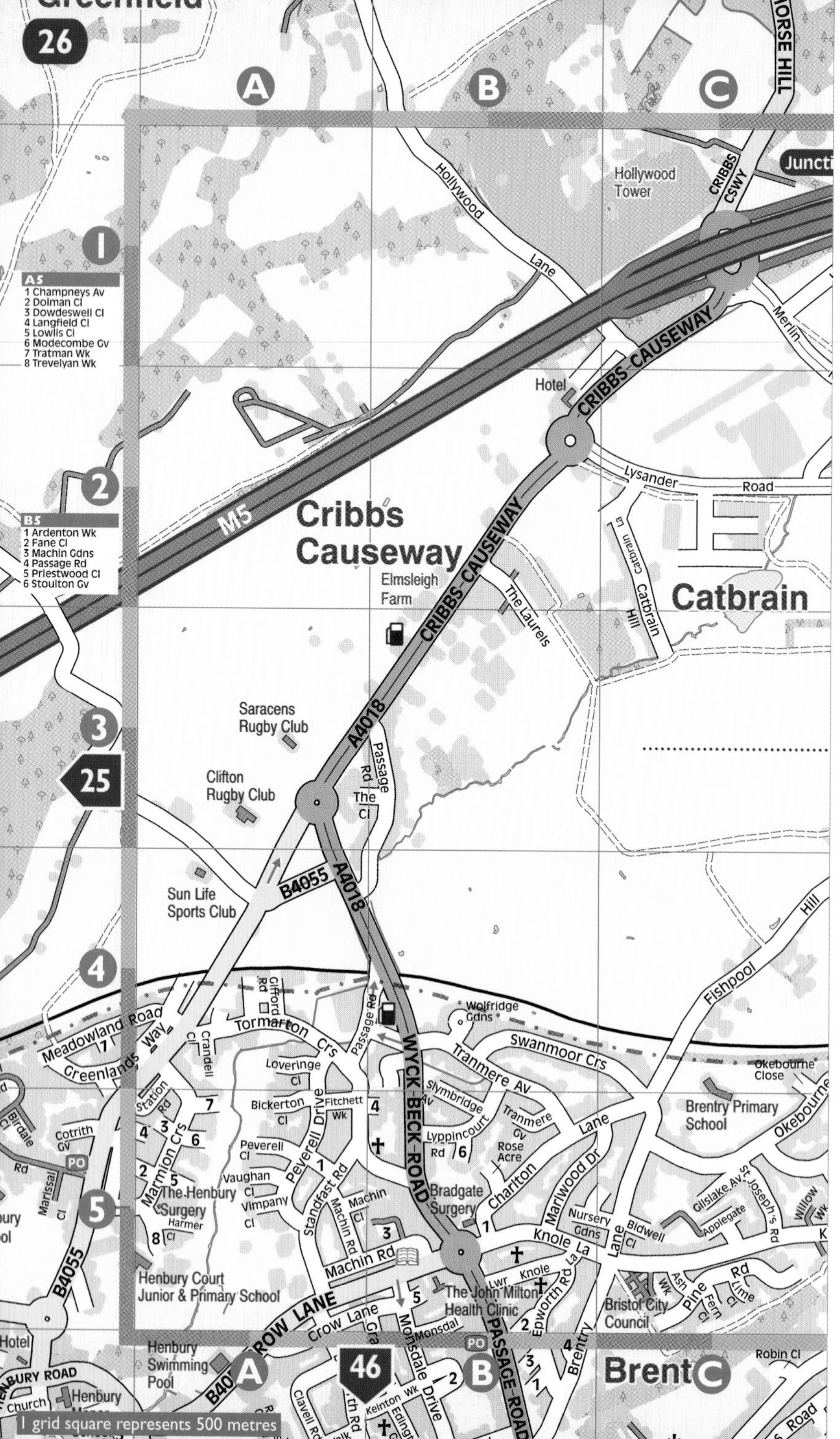
26
A
B
C
A5
1 Champneys Av
2 Dolman Cl
3 Dowdeswell Cl
4 Langfield Cl
5 Lowlis Cl
6 Modecombe Gv
7 Tratman Wk
8 Trevelyan Wk
B5
1 Ardenton Wk
2 Fane Cl
3 Machin Gdns
4 Passage Rd
5 Priestwood Cl
6 Stoulton Gv
Hollywood Lane
Hollywood Tower
CRIBBS CSWY
CRIBBS CAUSEWAY
Hotel
M5
Cribbs Causeway
Elmsleigh Farm
Lysander Road
Catbrain La
Catbrain Hill
Catbrain
The Laurels
Saracens Rugby Club
Clifton Rugby Club
A4018
B4055
Passage Rd
The Cl
Sun Life Sports Club
25
Fishpool Hill
Meadowland Road
Greenlands Way
Crandell Cl
Gifford Rd
Tormarton Crs
Passage Rd
Wolfridge Gdns
WYCK BECK ROAD
Swanmoor Crs
Tranmere Av
Okebourne Close
Brentry Primary School
Loveringe Cl
Bickerton Cl
Fitchett Wk
Peverell Drive
Slymbridge Av
Tranmere Gv
Lyppincourt Rd
Rose Acre
Charlton Lane
Marlwood Dr
Station Rd
Cotrith Gv
Birdale Cl
Marissal Cl
Marmion Crs
The Henbury Surgery
Harmer Cl
Peverell Cl
Vaughan Cl
Vimpany Cl
Standfast Rd
Machin Rd
Machin Cl
Bradgate Surgery
Nursery Gdns
Knole La
Lane
Bidwell Cl
Gilslake Av
St Joseph's Rd
Applegate
Okebourne
Willow Wk
Machin Rd
Henbury Court Junior & Primary School
CROW LANE
Crow Lane
Monsdale Drive
The John Milton Health Clinic
Lwr Knole
Epworth Rd
Brentry
Bristol City Council
Ash Wk
Pine Rd
Fern Cl
Lime Cl
PASSAGE ROAD
Henbury Swimming Pool
46
Hotel
HENBURY ROAD
Church
Henbury
Brent
Robin Cl
B4055
PO
1 grid square represents 500 metres

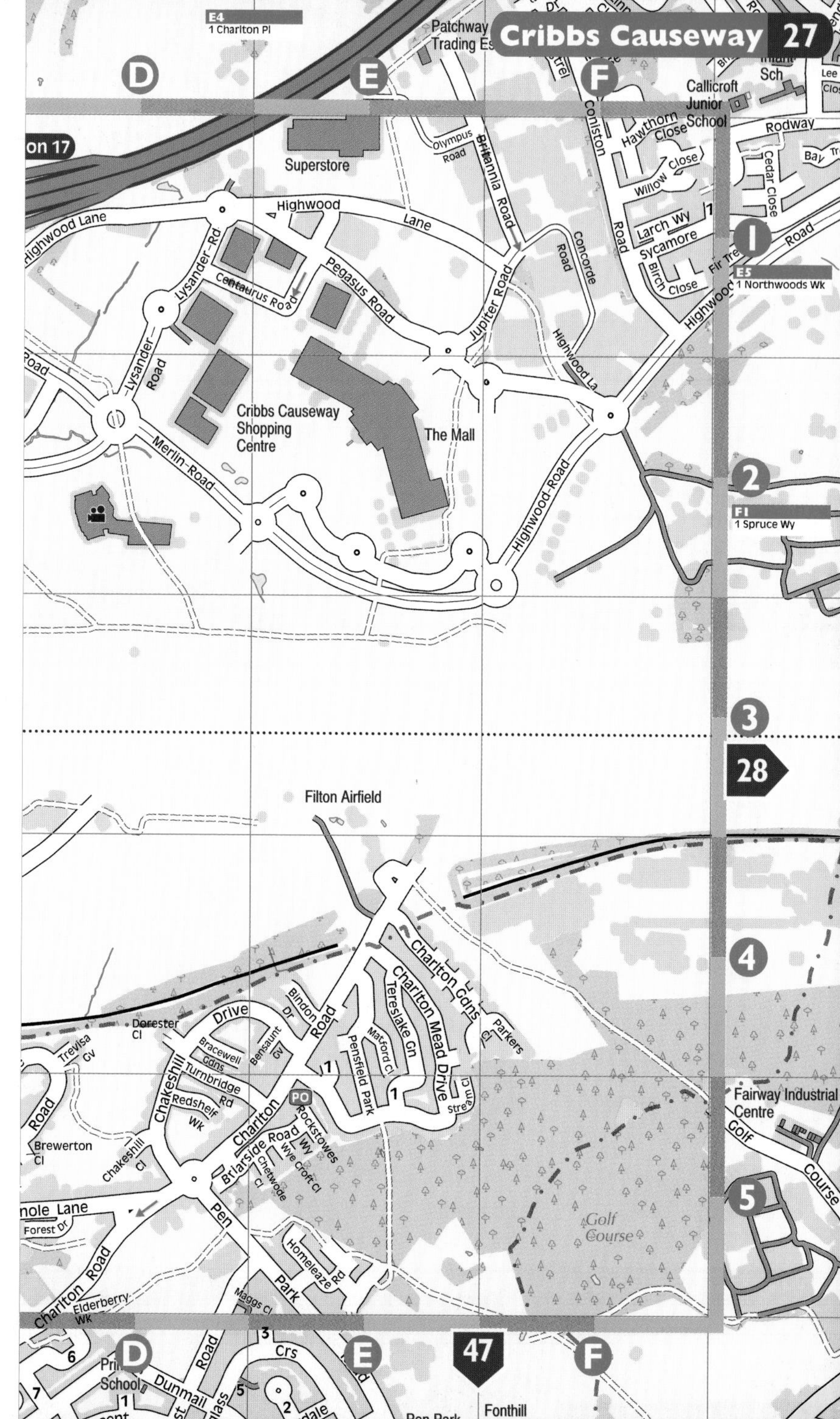
E4
1 Charlton Pl
Patchway
Trading Es
D
E
F
Callicroft
Junior
School
Lee
Close
Rodway
Bay
Cedar Close
Superstore
Olympus
Road
Britannia Road
Coniston
Road
Hawthorn
Close
Willow
Close
Larch Wy
Sycamore
Birch
Close
Fir Tree
Highwood
Road
1
E5
1 Northwoods Wk
Highwood Lane
Highwood
Lane
Lysander Rd
Centaurus Road
Pegasus Road
Jupiter Road
Concorde
Road
Highwood La
Lysander
Road
Road
Cribbs Causeway
Shopping
Centre
The Mall
Merlin Road
Highwood Road
2
F1
1 Spruce Wy
3
28
Filton Airfield
4
Charlton Gdns
Charlton Mead Drive
Tereslake Gn
Matford Cl
Pensfield Park
Parkers
Cl
Stream Cl
Bindon
Dr
Road
Bensaunt
Gv
Drive
Dorester
Cl
Trevisa
Gv
Bracewell
Gdns
Turnbridge
Rd
Redshelf
Wk
Chakeshill
Chakeshill
Cl
Road
Brewerton
Cl
Charlton
PO
Rockstowes
Wy
Briarside Road
Wye Croft Cl
Chetwode
Cl
Pen
Park
Homeleaze
Rd
Maggs Cl
Golf
Course
Fairway Industrial
Centre
Golf
Course
5
Lane
Forest Dr
Charlton Road
Elderberry
Wk
47
3
Crs
6
7
School
Dunmail
Road
5
2
Pen Park
Fonthill

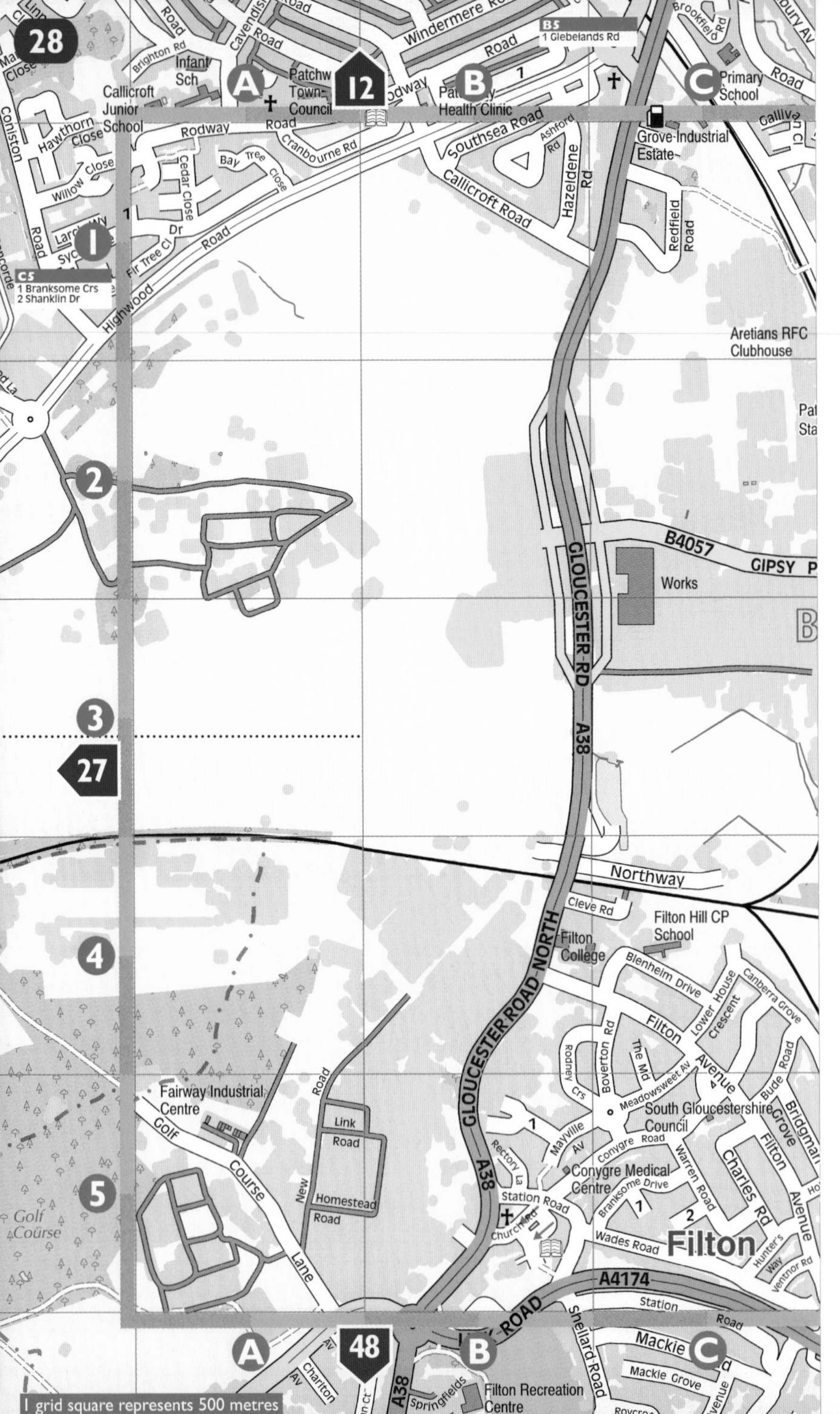

12
27
48
A
B
C
1
2
3
4
5
B5
1 Glebelands Rd
C5
1 Branksome Crs
2 Shanklin Dr
Windermere Road
Cavendish Road
Brighton Rd
Infant Sch
Callicroft Junior School
Patchway Town Council
Patchway Health Clinic
Primary School
Coniston Road
Hawthorn Close
Willow Close
Rodway Road
Cedar Close
Bay Tree Close
Cranbourne Rd
Southsea Road
Ashford Rd
Hazeldene Rd
Callicroft Road
Grove Industrial Estate
Redfield Road
Fir Tree Cl
Highwood Road
Gallivan Cl
Brookfield Rd
Aretians RFC Clubhouse
B4057
GIPSY
Works
GLOUCESTER RD
A38
Northway
Cleve Rd
Filton Hill CP School
Filton College
GLOUCESTER ROAD NORTH
Blenheim Drive
Lower House Crescent
Canberra Grove
Filton Avenue
Rodney Crs
Boverton Rd
The Md
Meadowsweet Av
South Gloucestershire Council
Bude Road
Bridgman Grove
Filton Grove
Charles Rd
Mayville Av
Conygre Road
Conygre Medical Centre
Branksome Drive
Warren Road
Rectory La
Station Road
Church Rd
Wades Road
Filton
Hunter's Way
Ventnor Rd
Filton Avenue
A4174
Station Road
Shellard Road
Mackie Grove
Fairway Industrial Centre
Golf Course Lane
New Road
Link Road
Homestead Road
Golf Course
Charlton Av
Springfields
Filton Recreation Centre
Roycroft

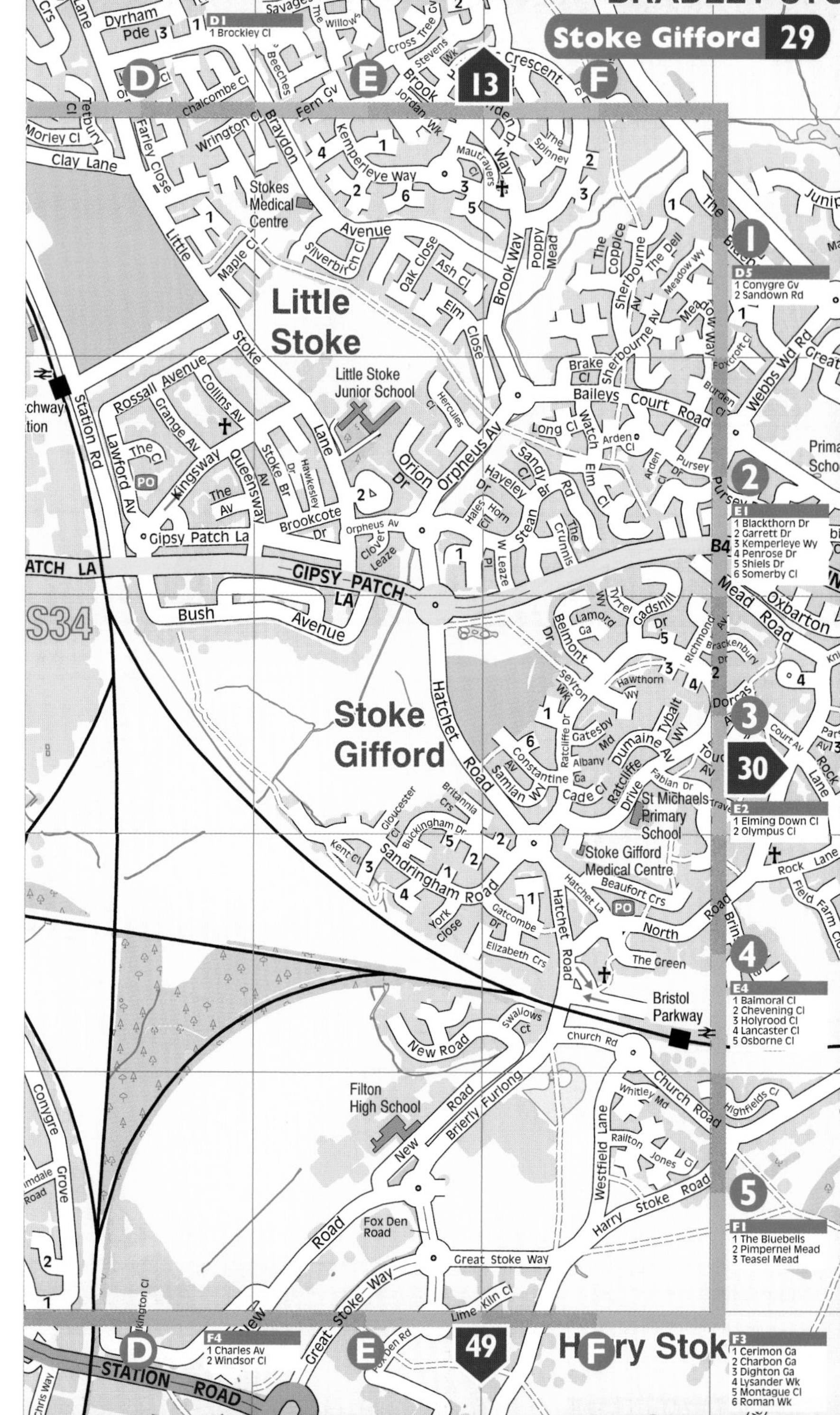

Little Stoke
Stoke Gifford
Stokes Medical Centre
Little Stoke Junior School
St Michaels Primary School
Stoke Gifford Medical Centre
Filton High School
Bristol Parkway
Gipsy Patch La
GIPSY PATCH LA
Station Rd
Bush Avenue
Hatchet Road
Sandringham Road
Great Stoke Way
Harry Stoke Road
Church Road
Church Rd
New Road
Brierly Furlong
Fox Den Road
Westfield Lane
Baileys Court Road
Rossall Avenue
Kingsway
Queensway
Lawford Av
Stoke Lane
Brook Way
Orpheus Av
Orion Dr
Brookcote Dr
Clay Lane
Little Stoke Lane
Braydon Avenue
Kemperleye Way
Silverbirch Cl
Oak Close
Ash Cl
Elm Close
Poppy Mead
The Coppice
Sherbourne Av
The Dell
Meadow Way
Webbs Wd Rd
Mead Road
Oxbarton
Gadshill Dr
Belmont Dr
Ratcliffe Drive
Dumaine Av
Tybalt Wy
Constantine Av
Samian Wy
Cade Cl
Court Av
Rock Lane
North Road
The Green
Beaufort Crs
Hatchet La
Elizabeth Crs
Gatcombe Dr
York Close
Buckingham Dr
Britannia Crs
Gloucester Cl
Kent Cl
Swallows Ct
Whitley Md
Railton Jones Cl
Highfields Cl
Lime Kiln Cl
Field Farm Close
Conygre Grove
STATION ROAD
S34
13
30
49
D1 1 Brockley Cl
D5 1 Conygre Gv 2 Sandown Rd
E1 1 Blackthorn Dr 2 Garrett Dr 3 Kemperleye Wy 4 Penrose Dr 5 Shiels Dr 6 Somerby Cl
E2 1 Elming Down Cl 2 Olympus Cl
E4 1 Balmoral Cl 2 Chevening Cl 3 Holyrood Cl 4 Lancaster Cl 5 Osborne Cl
F1 1 The Bluebells 2 Pimpernel Mead 3 Teasel Mead
F4 1 Charles Av 2 Windsor Cl
F3 1 Cerimon Ga 2 Charbon Ga 3 Dighton Ga 4 Lysander Wk 5 Montague Cl 6 Roman Wk

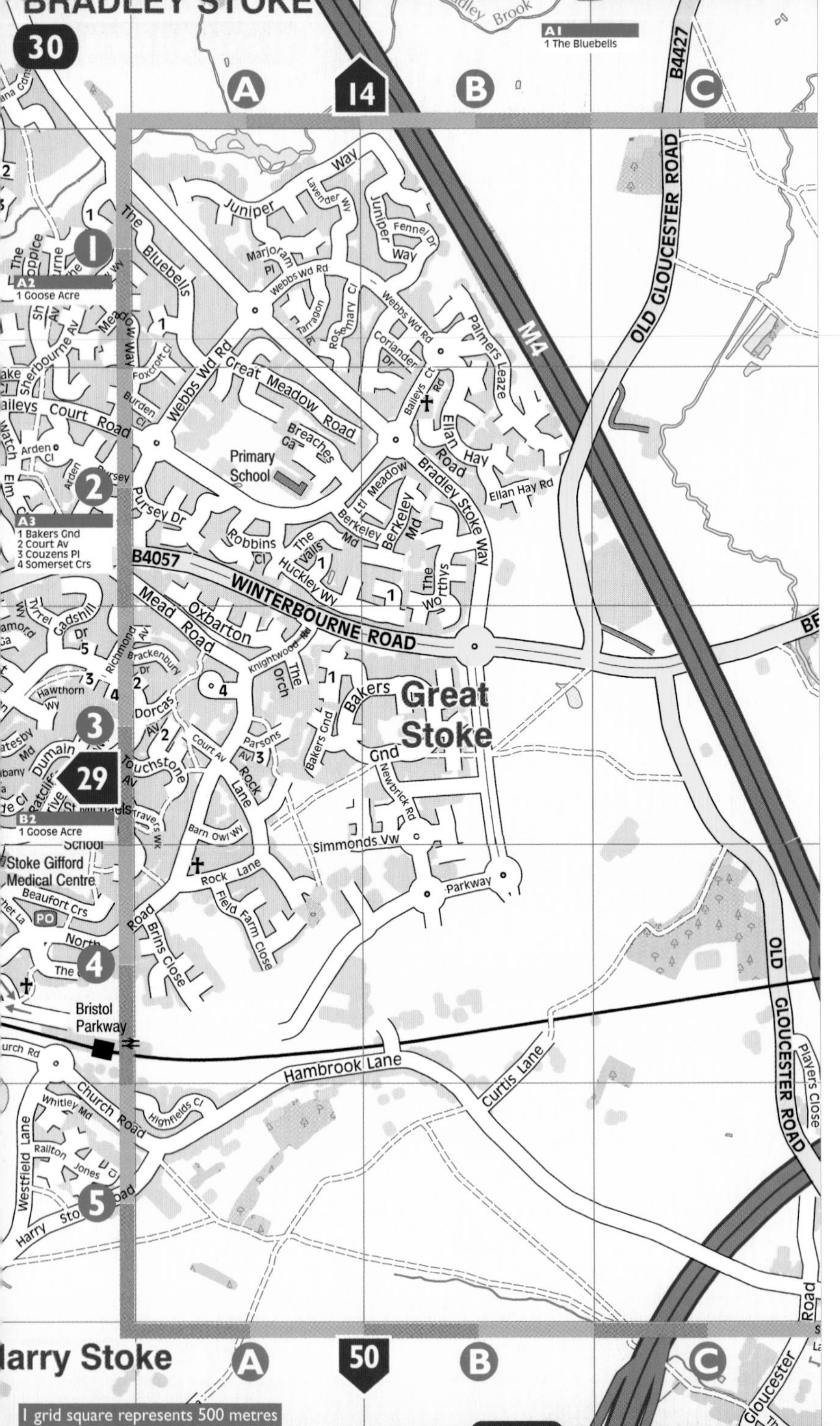

BRADLEY STOKE
30
14
A
B
C
A1
1 The Bluebells
A2
1 Goose Acre
A3
1 Bakers Gnd
2 Court Av
3 Couzens Pl
4 Somerset Crs
B2
1 Goose Acre
29
50
Juniper Way
Lavender Wy
Fennel Dr
Marjoram Pl
Webbs Wd Rd
Tarragon Pl
Rosemary Cl
Coriander Dr
Palmers Leaze
M4
OLD GLOUCESTER ROAD
B4427
The Bluebells
Foxcroft Cl
Burden Cl
Great Meadow Road
Baileys Court Road
Breaches Ga
Primary School
Ellan Hay Road
Ellan Hay Rd
Bradley Stoke Way
Ltl Meadow
Berkeley Md
Pursey Dr
Robbins Cl
The Valls
Huckley Wy
The Worthys
B4057
WINTERBOURNE ROAD
Mead Road
Oxbarton
Knightwood Rd
The Orch
Gadshill Dr
Richmond Av
Brackenbury Dr
Hawthorn Wy
Dorcas Av
Touchstone Av
Court Av
Parsons Av
Rock Lane
Bakers Gnd
Great Stoke
Newbrick Rd
Simmonds Vw
Parkway
Barn Owl Wy
Travers Wk
Field Farm Close
Brins Close
Stoke Gifford Medical Centre
Beaufort Crs
PO
Bristol Parkway
Church Rd
Church Road
Whitley Md
Highfields Cl
Hambrook Lane
Curtis Lane
Player's Close
Westfield Lane
Railton Jones Cl
Harry Stoke
Gloucester Road
1 grid square represents 500 metres

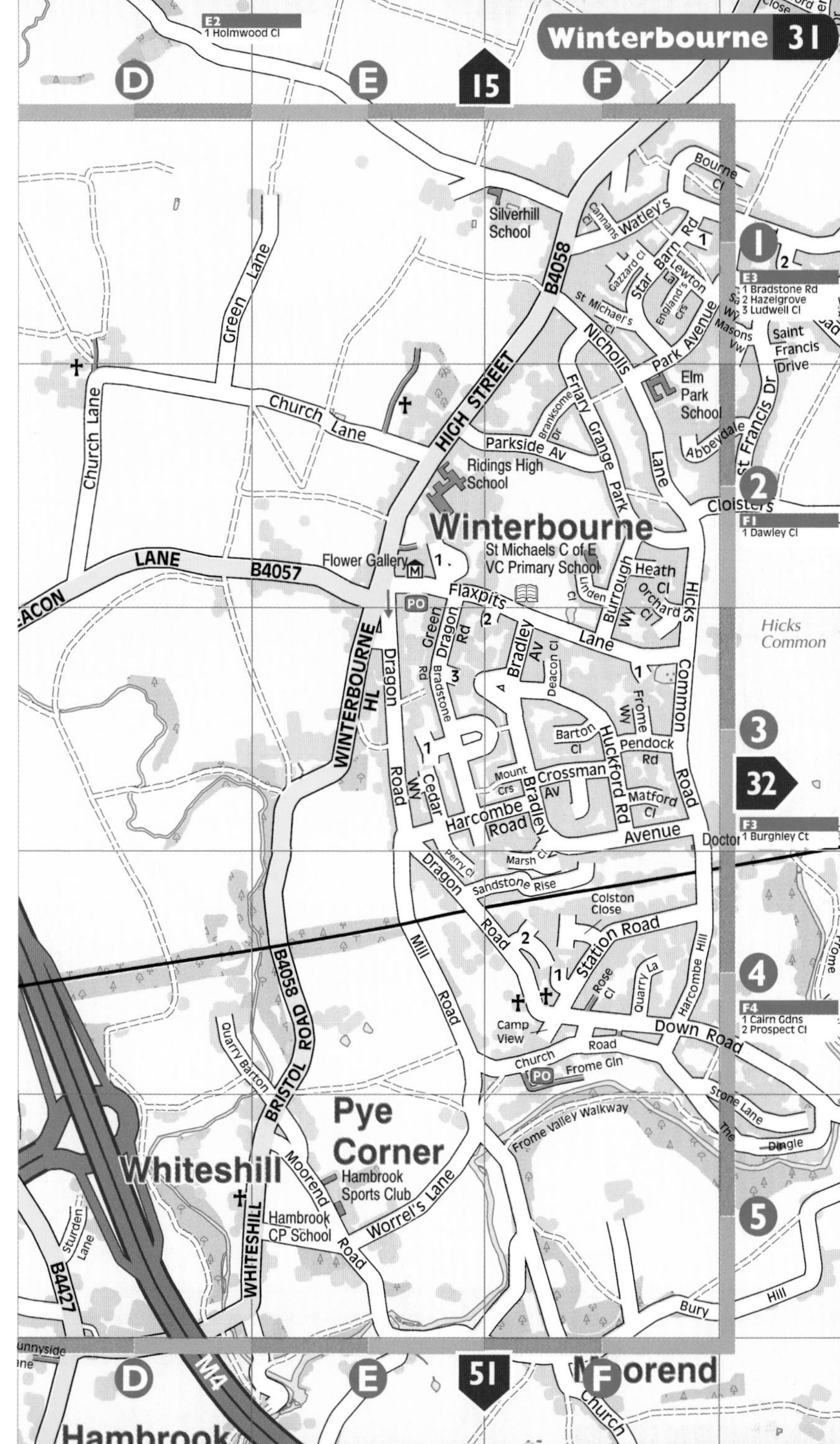

E2
1 Holmwood Cl
D
E
15
F
Silverhill School
Green Lane
Church Lane
Church Lane
HIGH STREET
B4058
Watley's
Cannans Cl
Bourne Cl
Gazzard Cl
Star Barn Rd
Lewton La
England's Crs
St Michael's Cl
Nicholls Lane
Park Avenue
Friary Grange Park
Branksome Dr
Parkside Av
Ridings High School
Elm Park School
Abbeydale
St Francis Dr
Saint Francis Drive
Masons Vw
E3
1 Bradstone Rd
2 Hazelgrove
3 Ludwell Cl
Cloisters
F1
1 Dawley Cl
Winterbourne
Flower Gallery
St Michaels C of E VC Primary School
LANE
B4057
DEACON
PO
Flaxpits Lane
Linden Cl
Burrough Wy
Heath Cl
Orchard Cl
Hicks Common Road
Hicks Common
WINTERBOURNE HL
Dragon Road
Green Dragon Rd
Bradstone Rd
Bradley Av
Deacon Cl
Frome Wy
Barton Cl
Pendock Rd
Huckford Rd
Crossman Av
Mount Crs
Bradley Road
Cedar Wy
Harcombe Road
Matford Cl
Avenue
Doctor
F3
1 Burghley Ct
32
Perry Cl
Marsh Cl
Dragon Road
Sandstone Rise
Colston Close
Station Road
Rose Cl
Quarry La
Harcombe Hill
Mill Road
Camp View
Church Road
Down Road
Frome Gln
PO
F4
1 Cairn Gdns
2 Prospect Cl
B4058
BRISTOL ROAD
Quarry Barton
Pye Corner
Frome Valley Walkway
Stone Lane
The Dingle
Frome
Whiteshill
Moorend Road
Hambrook Sports Club
Worrel's Lane
Hambrook CP School
WHITESHILL
Sturden Lane
B4427
Bury Hill
M4
Sunnyside Lane
D
E
51
F
Moorend
Church
Hambrook
1
2
3
4
5

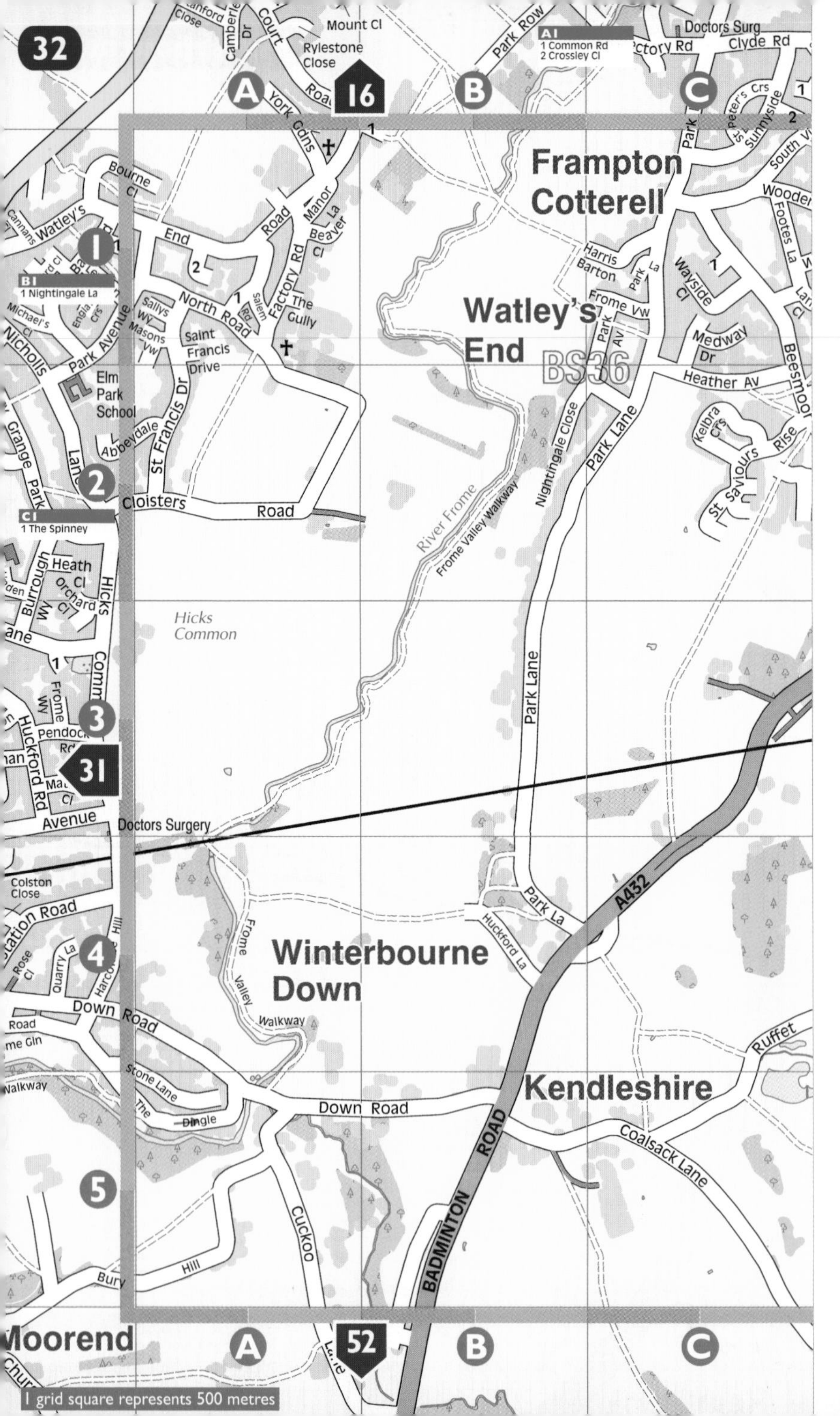

16
A1
1 Common Rd
2 Crossley Cl
B1
1 Nightingale La
C1
1 The Spinney
31
52
Frampton Cotterell
Watley's End
BS36
Winterbourne Down
Kendleshire
Moorend
Hicks Common
River Frome
Frome Valley Walkway
Park Lane
Park La
Badminton Road
A432
Down Road
Coalsack Lane
Cloisters Road
North Road
St Francis Dr
Saint Francis Drive
Nightingale Close
Heather Av
Medway Dr
Wayside Cl
Frome Vw
Harris Barton
Factory Rd
The Gully
Manor La
Beaver Cl
Bourne Cl
Watley's End
Park Avenue
Elm Park School
Abbeydale
Cuckoo La
Bury Hill
Stone Lane
The Dingle
Huckford La
Huckford Rd
Doctors Surgery
Doctors Surg
Station Road
Colston Close
Quarry La
Rose Cl
Ruffet
St Saviours Rise
Kelbra Crs
Mount Cl
Rylestone Close
York Gdns
Park Row
Clyde Rd
Sunnyside
Footes La
Heath Cl
Orchard Cl
Burrough Wy
Frome Wy
Pendock Rd
Grange Park
Nicholls
Sallys Wy
Masons Vw
Salem Rd

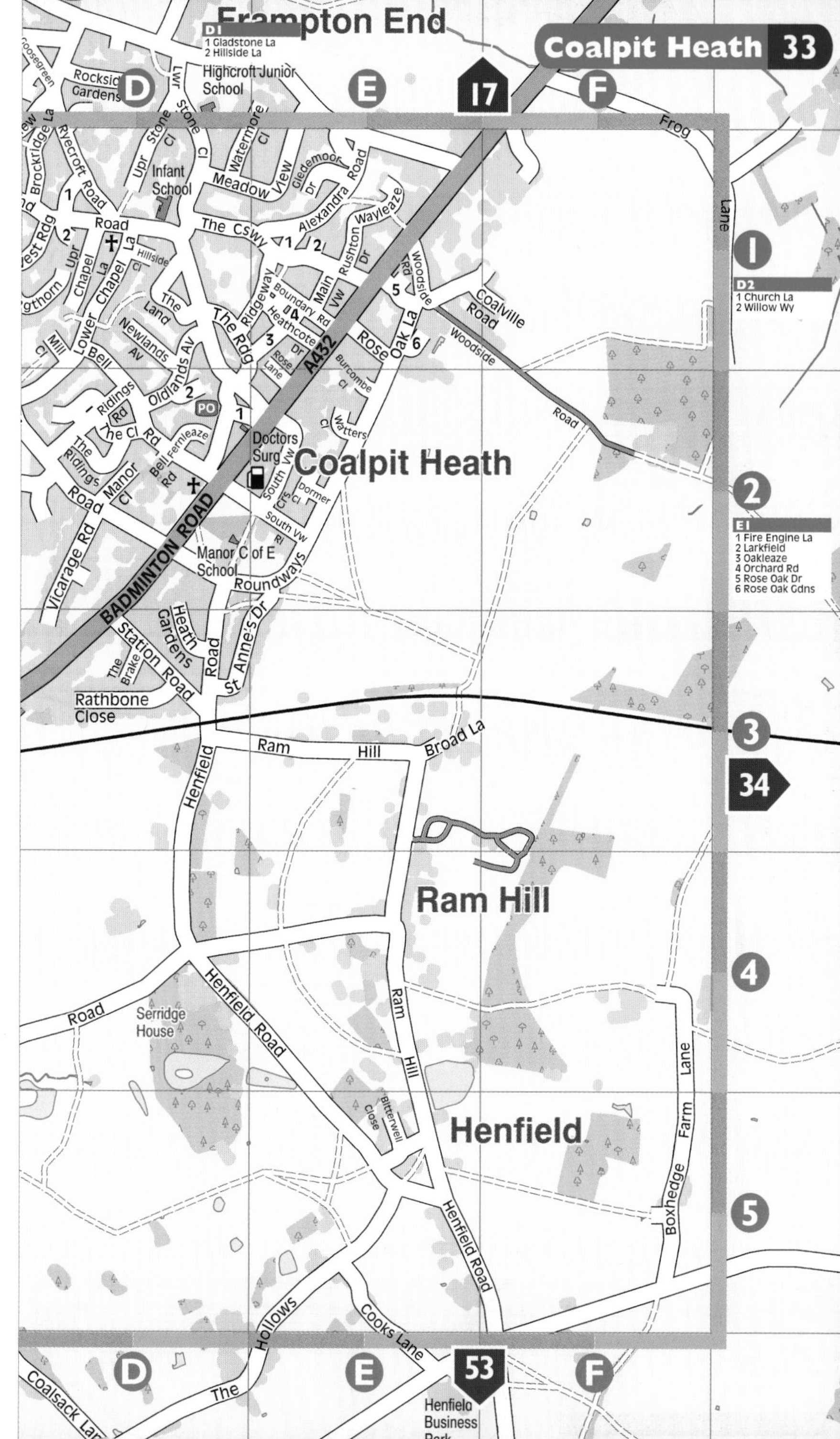
Frampton End
D1
1 Gladstone La
2 Hillside La
Highcroft Junior School
Rockside Gardens
D
E
17
F
Frog Lane
Goosegreen
Brockridge La
Ryecroft Road
Upr Stone Cl
Lwr Stone Cl
Watermore Cl
Infant School
Meadow View
Gledemoor Dr
Alexandra Road
Wayleaze
Rushton Dr
Road
The Cswy
Upr Chapel La
Chapel La
Hillside
Lower Chapel La
The Land
Ridgeway
Boundary Rd
Heathcote Dr
Main Vw
The Rdg
Newlands Av
Oldlands Av
Mill Cl
Bell
Rose Lane
Rose Oak La
Woodside Rd
Woodside
Coalville Road
Woodside Road
A432
Burcombe Cl
Watters Cl
Ridings Rd
The Cl
Fernleaze
PO
Doctors Surg
Coalpit Heath
The Ridings
Manor Cl
Bell Rd
South Vw
South Vw Crs
Dormer Cl
South Vw Ri
Road
Vicarage Rd
BADMINTON ROAD
Manor C of E School
Roundways
Heath Gardens
Station Road
The Brake
Road
St Anne's Dr
Rathbone Close
Ram Hill
Broad La
Henfield
Ram Hill
Henfield
Road
Serridge House
Henfield Road
Ram Hill
Bitterwell Close
Henfield Road
Boxhedge Farm Lane
The Hollows
Cooks Lane
Coalsack La
The
Henfield Business Park
53
D
E
F
1
D2
1 Church La
2 Willow Wy
2
E1
1 Fire Engine La
2 Larkfield
3 Oakleaze
4 Orchard Rd
5 Rose Oak Dr
6 Rose Oak Gdns
3
34
4
5

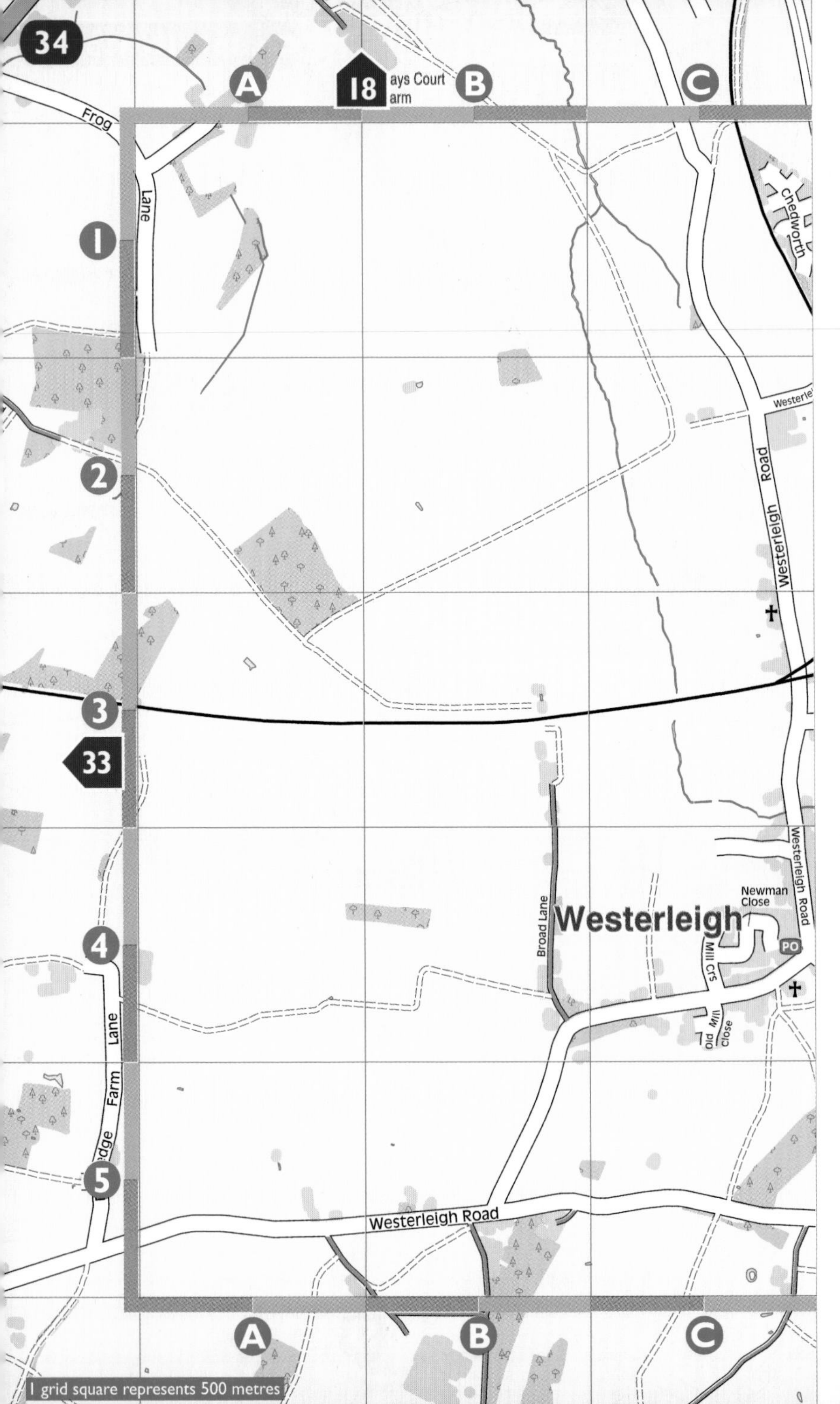
34
A
18
ays Court
arm
B
C
Frog
Lane
Chedworth
1
2
Westerleigh Road
Westerle
3
33
Broad Lane
Westerleigh
Newman
Close
Westerleigh Road
PO
Mill Crs
Old Mill Close
4
Lane
Farm
5
Westerleigh Road
A
B
C
1 grid square represents 500 metres

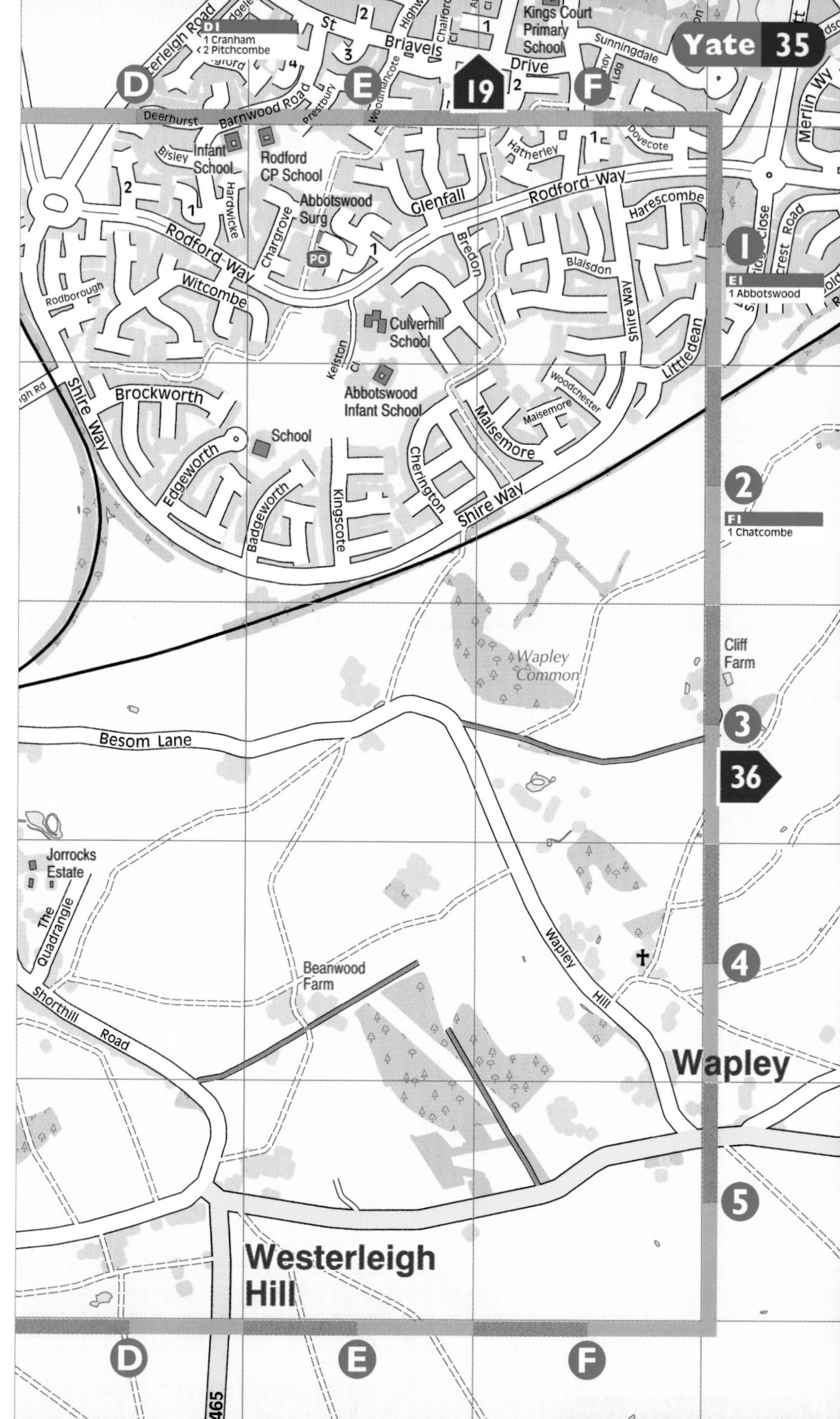
D1
1 Cranham
2 Pitchcombe
E1
1 Abbotswood
F1
1 Chatcombe
Kings Court
Primary
School
St Briavels
Drive
Sunningdale
Merlin Wy
Deerhurst
Barnwood Road
Prestbury
Woodmancote
Chalford
Infant
School
Rodford
CP School
Bisley
Hardwicke
Chargrove
Abbotswood
Surg
PO
Glenfall
Rodford Way
Hatherley
Dovecote
Harescombe
Bredon
Blaisdon
Witcombe
Rodborough
Culverhill
School
Shire Way
Littledean
Kelston
Cl
Abbotswood
Infant School
Brockworth
Woodchester
Maisemore
School
Edgeworth
Badgeworth
Kingscote
Cherington
Cliff
Farm
Wapley
Common
Besom Lane
Jorrocks
Estate
The
Quadrangle
Beanwood
Farm
Wapley
Hill
Shorthill
Road
Wapley
Westerleigh
Hill
19
36
1
2
3
4
5
D
E
F

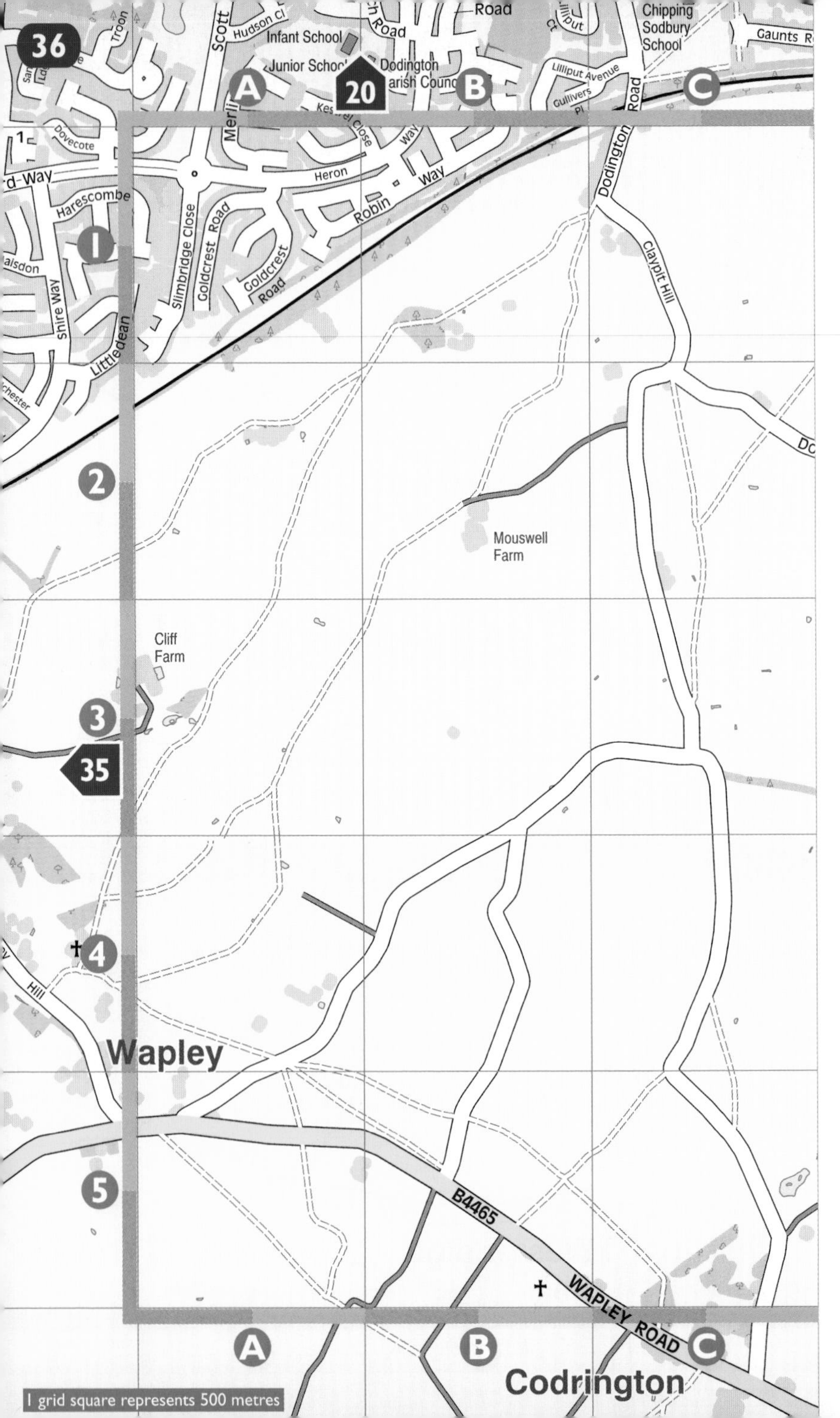
36
20
35
Road
Chipping
Sodbury
School
Gaunts R
Hudson Cl
Infant School
Junior School
Dodington
Parish Council
Scott
Troon
Lilliput Avenue
Gullivers Pl
Dodington Road
Kestrel Close
Dovecote
Merlin
Heron
Robin Way
Harescombe
Slimbridge Close
Goldcrest Road
Shire Way
Littledean
Claypit Hill
Mouswell Farm
Cliff Farm
Hill
Wapley
B4465
WAPLEY ROAD
Codrington
A
B
C
1
2
3
4
5
1 grid square represents 500 metres

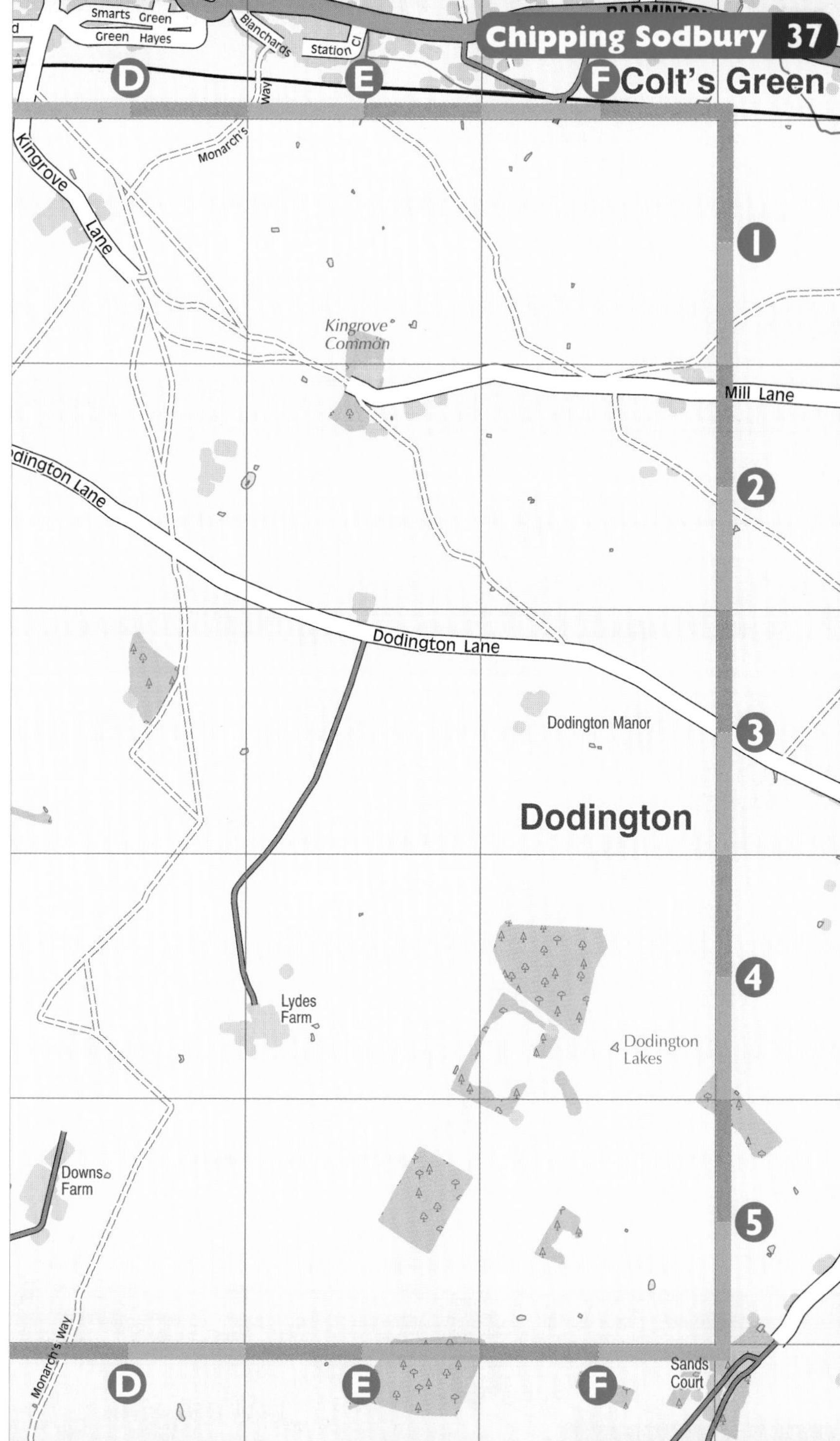
Smarts Green
Green Hayes
Blanchards
Station Cl
Monarch's Way
D
E
F
Colt's Green
Kingrove Lane
Monarch's
I
Kingrove Common
Mill Lane
Dodington Lane
2
Dodington Lane
Dodington Manor
3
Dodington
4
Lydes Farm
Dodington Lakes
Downs Farm
5
Monarch's Way
Sands Court
D
E
F

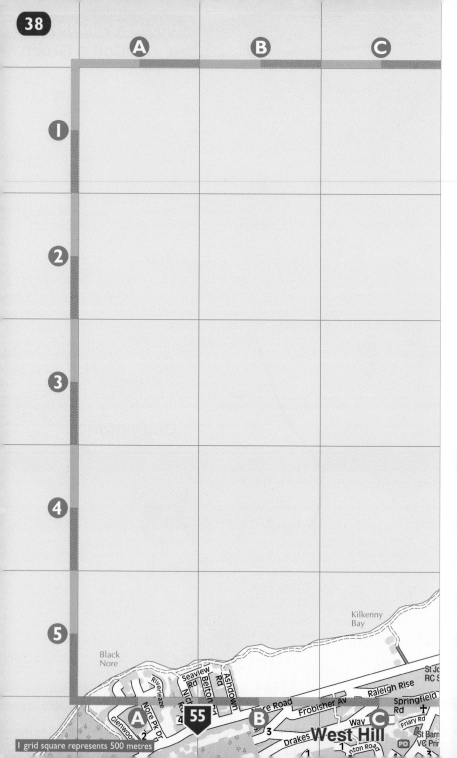

A
B
C
1
2
3
4
5
Kilkenny Bay
Black Nore
Seaview Rd
Belton Rd
Ashdown Rd
Riverleaze
Raleigh Rise
St Jo
RC S
Springfield Rd
Frobisher Av
Nore Road
Nore Pk Dr
Glenwoo
55
Way
Drakes
West Hill
Friary Rd
St Barn
VC Pri
PO
1 grid square represents 500 metres

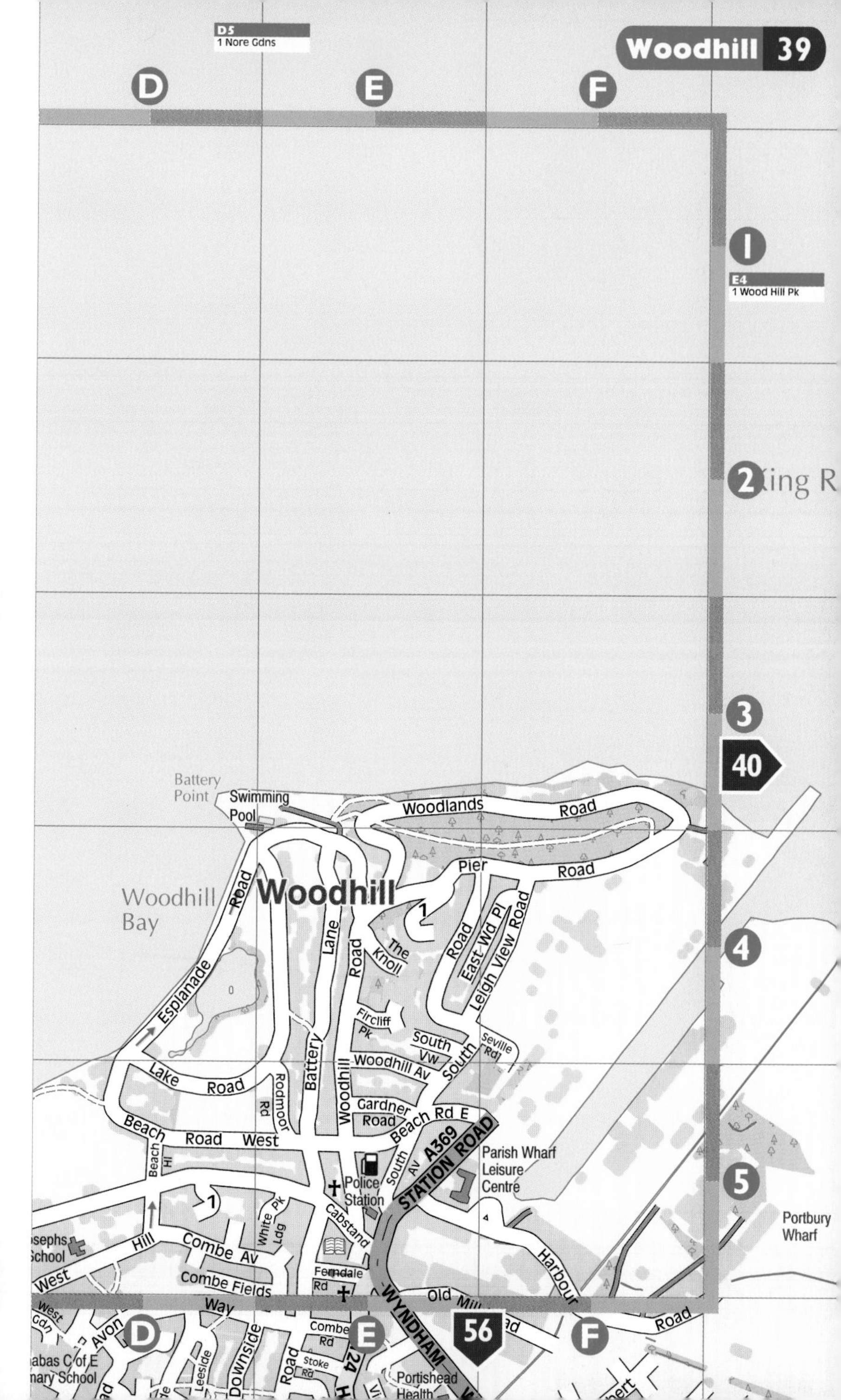

D5
1 Nore Gdns
E4
1 Wood Hill Pk
D
E
F
1
2
3
4
5
40
56
King R
Battery Point
Swimming Pool
Woodlands Road
Pier Road
Woodhill
Woodhill Bay
Esplanade Road
Lane
Woodhill Road
The Knoll
Road
East Wd Pl
Leigh View Road
Fircliff Pk
South Vw
Seville Rd
South
Woodhill Av
Lake Road
Rodmoor Rd
Battery
Woodhill
Gardner Road
Beach Rd E
Beach Road West
Beach Hl
South Av
A369 STATION ROAD
Parish Wharf Leisure Centre
Police Station
Cabstand
White Pk Ldg
Combe Av
Combe Fields
Hill
West
Way
Ferndale Rd
Old Mill Road
Harbour Road
WYNDHAM
Portbury Wharf
Combe Rd
Stoke Rd
Downside
Leeside
Avon
Portishead Health

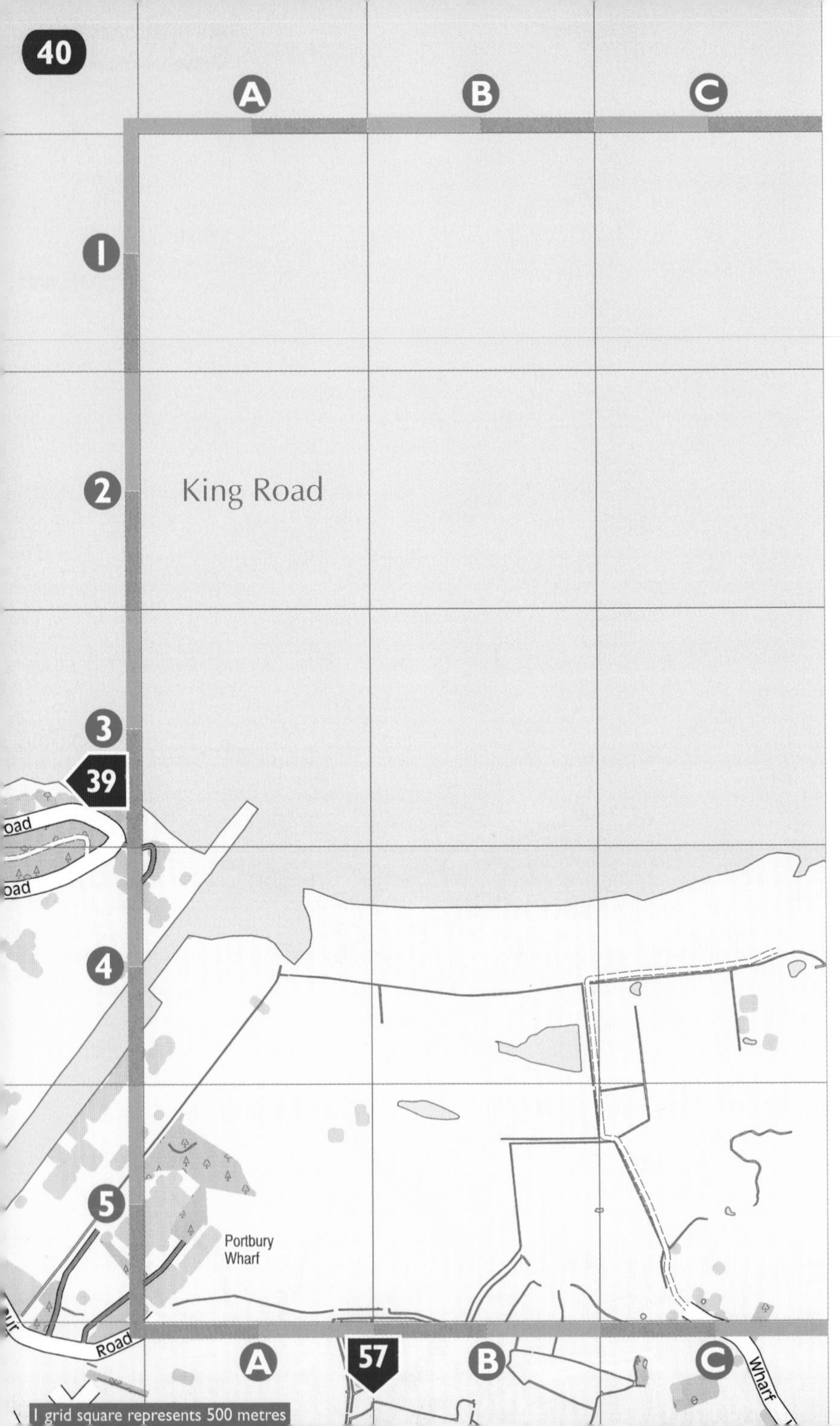
A
B
C
1
2
3
4
5
King Road
39
Road
Road
Portbury
Wharf
Road
57
Wharf
1 grid square represents 500 metres

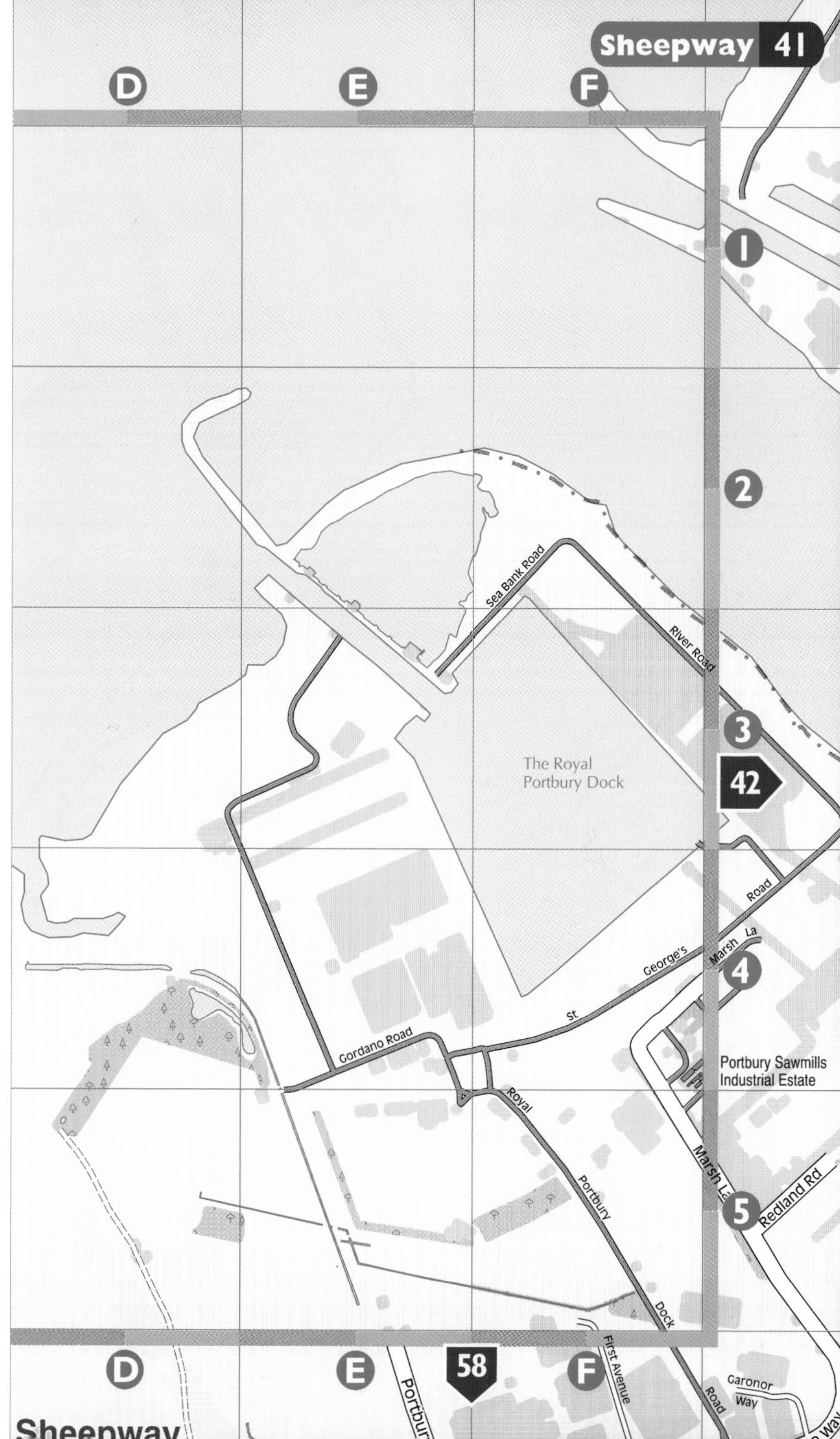

D
E
F
1
2
3
4
5
Sea Bank Road
River Road
The Royal
Portbury Dock
42
Road
Marsh La
George's
St
Gordano Road
Royal
Portbury
Dock
Road
Portbury Sawmills
Industrial Estate
Marsh La
Redland Rd
First Avenue
Portbury
58
Caronor
Way
Way
Sheepway

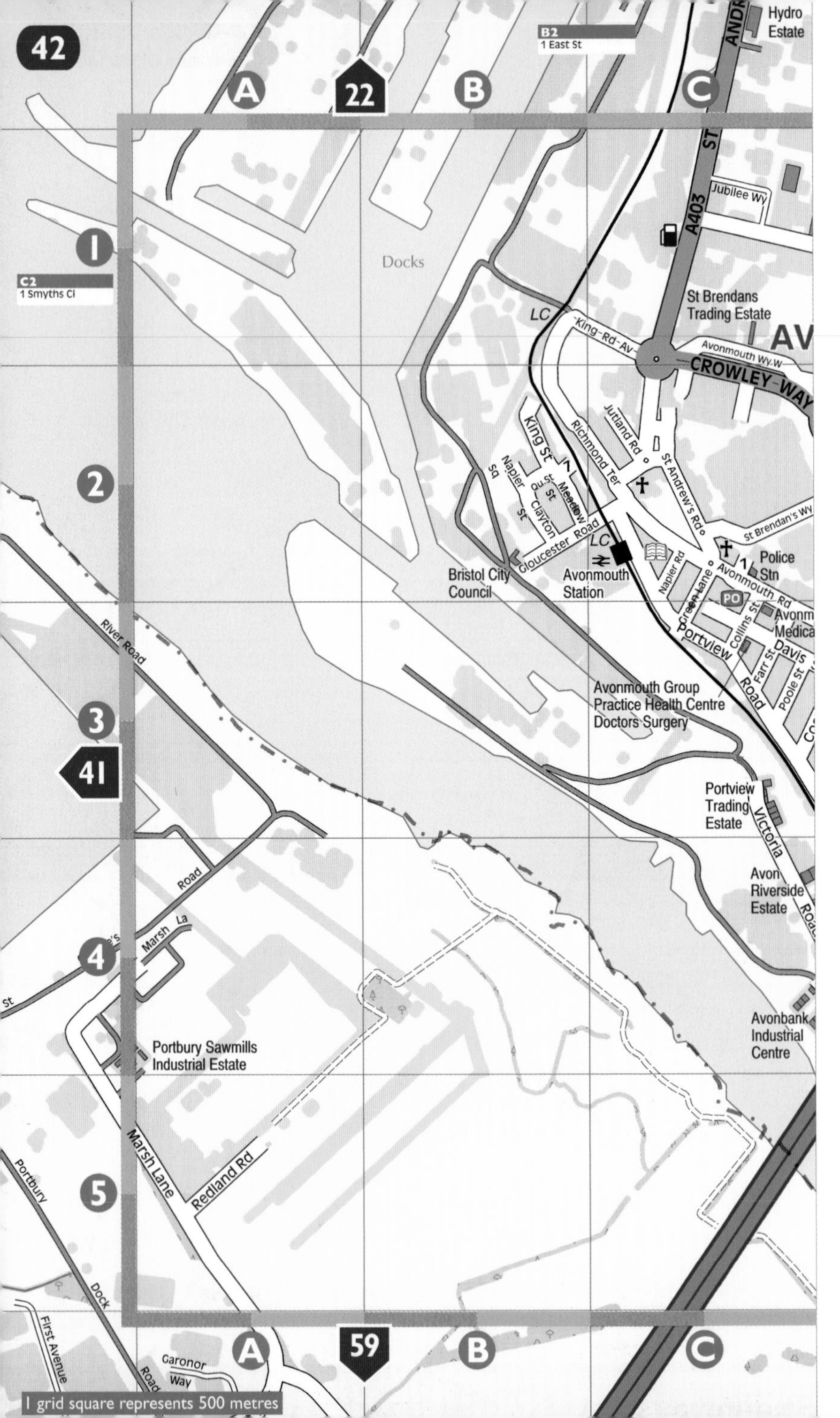
B2
1 East St
C2
1 Smyths Cl
22
41
59
Hydro Estate
Docks
St Brendans Trading Estate
King Rd Av
Avonmouth Wy W
CROWLEY WAY
A403
ST
Jubilee Wy
Jutland Rd
Richmond Ter
St Andrew's Rd
St Brendan's Wy
King St
Napier Sq
Napier St
Clayton St
Meadow St
Gloucester Road
LC
Avonmouth Station
Bristol City Council
Police Stn
Avonmouth Rd
Napier Rd
Green Lane
Collins St
PO
Portview Road
Farr St
Davis
Poole St
Avonmouth Group Practice Health Centre Doctors Surgery
Portview Trading Estate
Victoria Road
Avon Riverside Estate
Avonbank Industrial Centre
River Road
Road
Marsh La
St
Portbury Sawmills Industrial Estate
Marsh Lane
Redland Rd
Portbury Dock Road
First Avenue
Garonor Way
1 grid square represents 500 metres

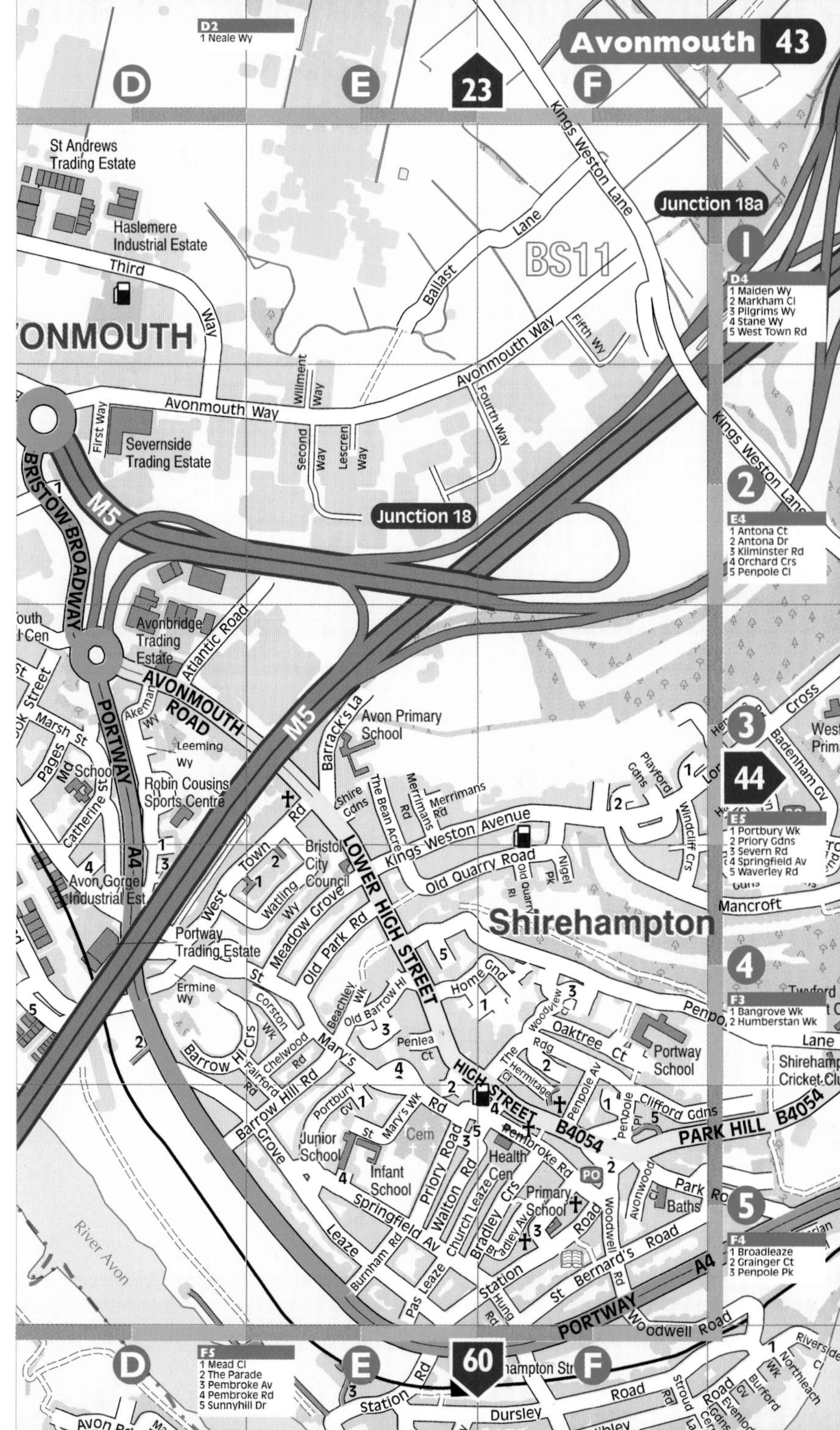
D2
1 Neale Wy
D
E
23
F
St Andrews Trading Estate
Haslemere Industrial Estate
Third Way
AVONMOUTH
Kings Weston Lane
Junction 18a
Ballast Lane
BS11
D4
1 Maiden Wy
2 Markham Cl
3 Pilgrims Wy
4 Stane Wy
5 West Town Rd
Avonmouth Way
Fifth Wy
Willment Way
Fourth Way
First Way
Severnside Trading Estate
Second Way
Lescren Way
Junction 18
BRISTOW BROADWAY
M5
E4
1 Antona Ct
2 Antona Dr
3 Kilminster Rd
4 Orchard Crs
5 Penpole Cl
Avonbridge Trading Estate
Atlantic Road
AVONMOUTH ROAD
PORTWAY
Akeman Wy
Leeming Wy
Marsh St
Pages Md
School
Catherine St
Robin Cousins Sports Centre
Avon Primary School
Barrack's La
Shire Gdns
The Bean Acre
Merrimans Rd
Cross
Badenham Gv
Playford Gdns
Windcliff Crs
44
E5
1 Portbury Wk
2 Priory Gdns
3 Severn Rd
4 Springfield Av
5 Waverley Rd
Kings Weston Avenue
Old Quarry Road
Old Quarry Rl
Nigel Pk
Town Rd
Bristol City Council
Watling Wy
LOWER HIGH STREET
A4
Avon Gorge Industrial Est
West
Meadow Grove
Old Park Rd
Mancroft
Shirehampton
Portway Trading Estate
St
Ermine Wy
Corston Wk
Beachley Wk
Old Barrow Hl
Home Gnd
Woodview Cl
Oaktree Ct
Penpole Lane
Portway School
F3
1 Bangrove Wk
2 Humberstan Wk
Twyford H
Shirehampton Cricket Club
Barrow Hl Crs
Chelwood Rd
Fairford Rd
Mary's
Penlea Ct
The Rdg
The Hermitage Cl
Penpole Av
Penpole Pl
Clifford Gdns
PARK HILL B4054
Barrow Hill Rd
Portbury Gv
Mary's Wk
Rd
HIGH STREET B4054
Pembroke Rd
Barrow Grove
St
Junior School
Cem
Infant School
Priory Road
Walton Rd
Church Leaze
Health Cen
PO
Avonwood Cl
Park Road
Baths
F4
1 Broadleaze
2 Grainger Ct
3 Penpole Pk
Springfield Av
Bradley Crs
Bradley Av
Primary School
Woodwell Rd
River Avon
Leaze
Burnham Rd
Pas Leaze
Station Road
Hung Rd
St Bernard's Road
A4
PORTWAY
Woodwell Road
Riverside Cl
Northleach Wk
Burford Gv
F5
1 Mead Cl
2 The Parade
3 Pembroke Av
4 Pembroke Rd
5 Sunnyhill Dr
60
Station Rd
Dursley Road
Stroud Rd
Avon Rd

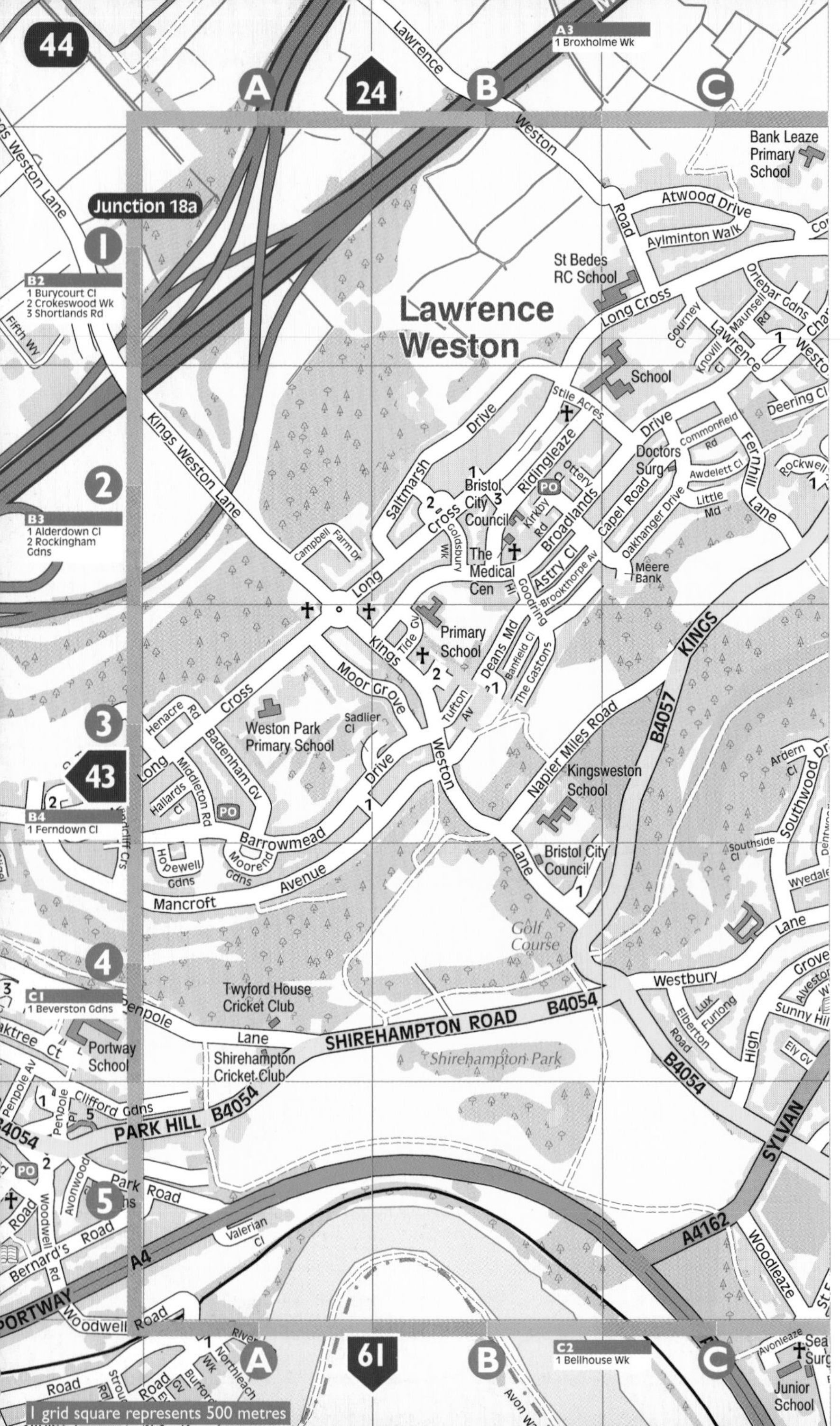
24
A
B
C
A3
1 Broxholme Wk
Junction 18a
B2
1 Burycourt Cl
2 Crokeswood Wk
3 Shortlands Rd
B3
1 Alderdown Cl
2 Rockingham Gdns
43
B4
1 Ferndown Cl
C1
1 Beverston Gdns
C2
1 Bellhouse Wk
61
Lawrence Weston
Bank Leaze Primary School
Atwood Drive
Aylminton Walk
St Bedes RC School
Long Cross
Lawrence Weston Road
School
Kings Weston Lane
Saltmarsh Drive
Ridingleaze
Bristol City Council
Doctors Surg
The Medical Cen
Broadlands
Capel Road
Oakhanger Drive
Fernhill Lane
Deering Cl
Primary School
Moor Grove
Weston Park Primary School
Barrowmead Drive
Mancroft Avenue
Napier Miles Road
Kingsweston School
B4057
KINGS
Golf Course
Twyford House Cricket Club
Penpole Lane
SHIREHAMPTON ROAD
B4054
Shirehampton Park
Shirehampton Cricket Club
Portway School
PARK HILL
Park Road
Valerian Cl
A4
PORTWAY
Woodwell Road
Bernard's Road
Westbury Lane
Elberton Road
High Grove
SYLVAN
A4162
Woodleaze
Junior School
Avon Way
1 grid square represents 500 metres

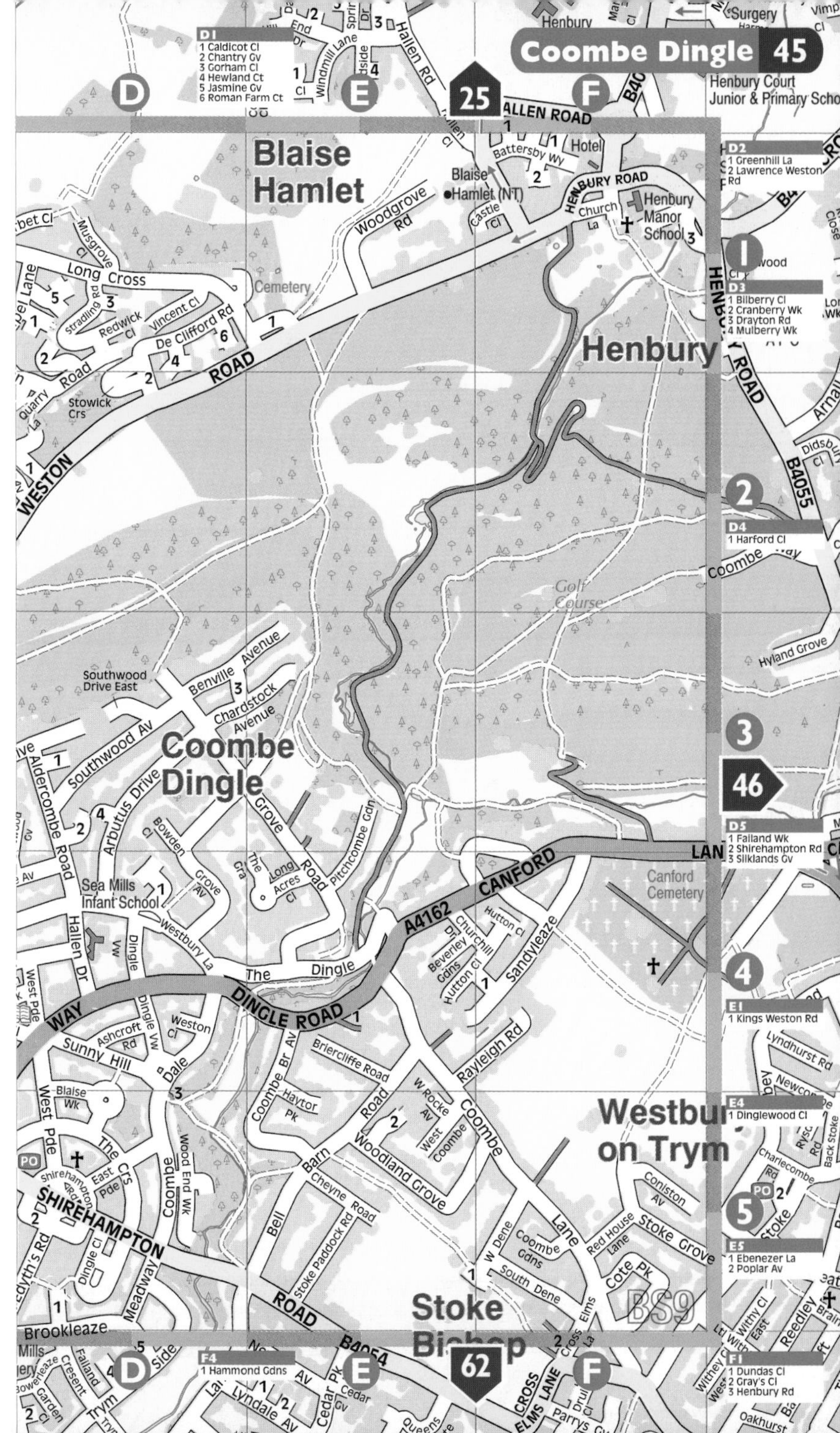
D1
1 Caldicot Cl
2 Chantry Gv
3 Gorham Cl
4 Hewland Ct
5 Jasmine Gv
6 Roman Farm Ct
D2
1 Greenhill La
2 Lawrence Weston Rd
D3
1 Bilberry Cl
2 Cranberry Wk
3 Drayton Rd
4 Mulberry Wk
D4
1 Harford Cl
D5
1 Falland Wk
2 Shirehampton Rd
3 Silklands Gv
E1
1 Kings Weston Rd
E4
1 Dinglewood Cl
E5
1 Ebenezer La
2 Poplar Av
F1
1 Dundas Cl
2 Gray's Cl
3 Henbury Rd
F4
1 Hammond Gdns
Blaise Hamlet
Blaise Hamlet (NT)
Henbury
Henbury Manor School
Henbury Court Junior & Primary School
Coombe Dingle
Westbury on Trym
Stoke Bishop
Cemetery
Golf Course
Canford Cemetery
Sea Mills Infant School
Southwood Drive East
Hallen Road
Henbury Road
Weston Road
Dingle Road
Canford Lane
A4162
B4055
B4054
Shirehampton Road
Woodgrove Rd
Long Cross
Redwick Cl
Vincent Cl
De Clifford Rd
Stradling Rd
Musgrove Cl
Stowick Crs
Quarry Road
Battersby Wy
Castle Cl
Church La
Hotel
Surgery
Benville Avenue
Chardstock Avenue
Southwood Av
Aldercombe Road
Arbutus Drive
Bowden Cl
Grove Av
Grove Road
The Long Acres Cl
Pitchcombe Gdn
Westbury La
The Dingle
Churchill Dr
Beverley Gdns
Hutton Cl
Sandyleaze
Rayleigh Rd
Briercliffe Road
Coombe Br Av
Haytor Pk
Barn Road
W Rocke Av
West Coombe
Coombe Lane
Woodland Grove
Cheyne Road
Bell
Stoke Paddock Rd
W Dene
Coombe Gdns
South Dene
Red House Lane
Stoke Grove
Coniston Av
Cote Pk
Cross Elms La
Cross Elms Lane
Parrys Gv
Druid Cl
Hallen Dr
Dingle Vw
West Pde
Ashcroft Rd
Sunny Hill
Dale
Weston Cl
Blaise Wk
The Crs
East Pde
Coombe
Wood End Wk
Dingle Cl
Meadway
Brookleaze
Falland
Boweleaze
Cresent
Garden
Trym
Side
Lyndale Av
Cedar Pk
Cedar Gv
Queens
Coombe Way
Hyland Grove
Didsbury Cl
Arnall
Lyndhurst Rd
Newcombe
Charlecombe Rd
Back Stoke
Withey Cl
Withy Cl East
Reedley
Oakhurst
BS9
25
46
62

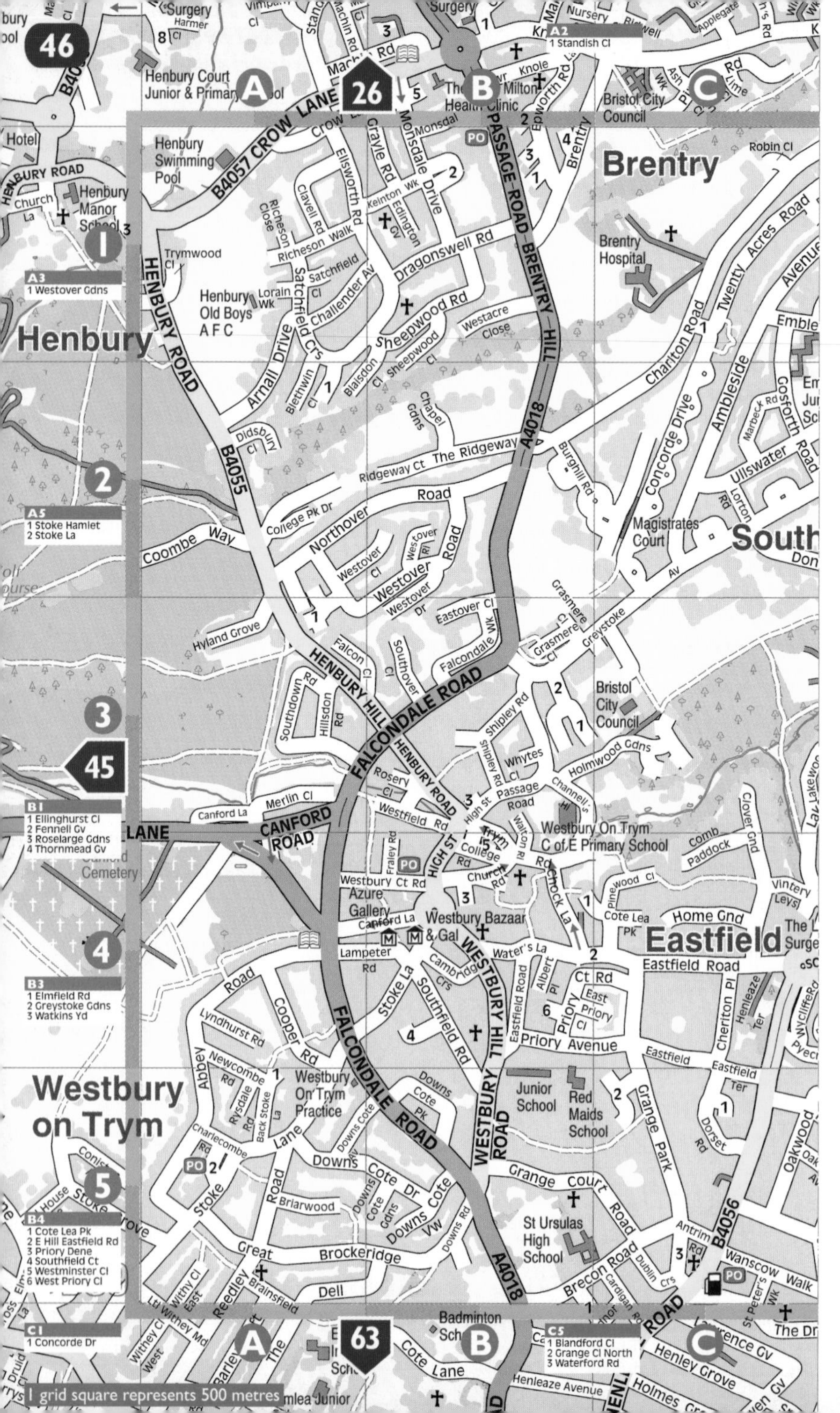

46
26
45
63
A
B
C
1
2
3
4
5
Brentry
Henbury
Westbury on Trym
Eastfield
B4057 CROW LANE
PASSAGE ROAD
BRENTRY HILL
A4018
HENBURY ROAD
B4055
HENBURY HILL
FALCONDALE ROAD
CANFORD ROAD
WESTBURY HILL
WESTBURY ROAD
B4056
Henbury Court Junior & Primary School
Henbury Swimming Pool
Henbury Manor School
Henbury Old Boys A F C
Brentry Hospital
Bristol City Council
Magistrates Court
Westbury On Trym C of E Primary School
Westbury Azure Gallery
Westbury Bazaar & Gal
Westbury On Trym Practice
Junior School
Red Maids School
St Ursulas High School
Canford Cemetery
The Ridgeway
Charlton Road
Twenty Acres Road
Concorde Drive
Greystoke Av
Northover Road
Westover Road
Coombe Way
Canford La
Eastfield Road
Priory Avenue
Grange Court Road
Grange Park
Brecon Road
Wanscow Walk
Henley Grove
Cote Lane
Henleaze Avenue
Great Brockeridge
Stoke Lane
Dragonswell Rd
Sheepwood Rd
Arnall Drive
A3
1 Westover Gdns
A5
1 Stoke Hamlet
2 Stoke La
B1
1 Ellinghurst Cl
2 Fennell Gv
3 Roselarge Gdns
4 Thornmead Gv
B3
1 Elmfield Rd
2 Greystoke Gdns
3 Watkins Yd
B4
1 Cote Lea Pk
2 E Hill Eastfield Rd
3 Priory Dene
4 Southfield Ct
5 Westminster Cl
6 West Priory Cl
C1
1 Concorde Dr
A2
1 Standish Cl
C5
1 Blandford Cl
2 Grange Cl North
3 Waterford Rd
1 grid square represents 500 metres

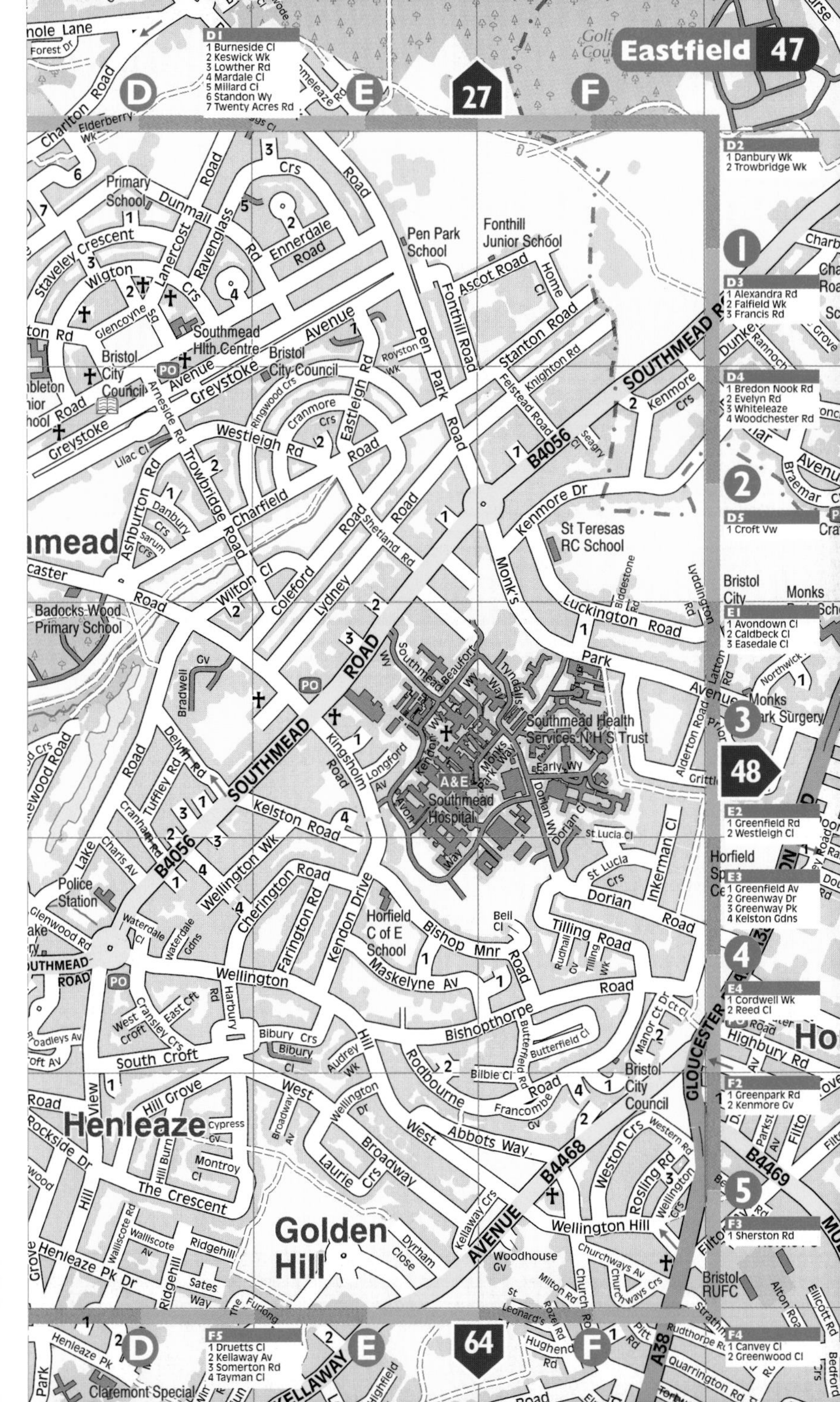
D1
1 Burneside Cl
2 Keswick Wk
3 Lowther Rd
4 Mardale Cl
5 Millard Cl
6 Standon Wy
7 Twenty Acres Rd
D2
1 Danbury Wk
2 Trowbridge Wk
D3
1 Alexandra Rd
2 Falfield Wk
3 Francis Rd
D4
1 Bredon Nook Rd
2 Evelyn Rd
3 Whiteleaze
4 Woodchester Rd
D5
1 Croft Vw
E1
1 Avondown Cl
2 Caldbeck Cl
3 Easedale Cl
E2
1 Greenfield Rd
2 Westleigh Cl
E3
1 Greenfield Av
2 Greenway Dr
3 Greenway Pk
4 Kelston Gdns
E4
1 Cordwell Wk
2 Reed Cl
F2
1 Greenpark Rd
2 Kenmore Gv
F3
1 Sherston Rd
F4
1 Canvey Cl
2 Greenwood Cl
F5
1 Druetts Cl
2 Kellaway Av
3 Somerton Rd
4 Tayman Cl
27
48
64
D
E
F
1
2
3
4
5
Southmead
Henleaze
Golden Hill
Southmead Road
Southmead Hospital
Southmead Health Services N H S Trust
A&E
Pen Park School
Fonthill Junior School
St Teresas RC School
Badocks Wood Primary School
Horfield C of E School
Police Station
Bristol City Council
Southmead Hlth Centre
Bristol RUFC
Monks Park Surgery
Claremont Special School
Woodhouse Gv
Wellington Road
Wellington Hill
Gloucester Road
Kellaway Avenue
Greystoke Avenue
Charlton Road
Dunmail Road
Ennerdale Road
Ravenglass Rd
Staveley Crescent
Lanercost Crs
Wigton Crs
Glencoyne Sq
Westleigh Rd
Eastleigh Rd
Cranmore Crs
Ringwood Crs
Royston Wk
Pen Park Road
Fonthill Road
Ascot Road
Home Cl
Stanton Road
Knighton Rd
Felstead Road
Kenmore Crs
Kenmore Dr
Seagry Cl
Monk's Park Avenue
Luckington Road
Biddestone Rd
Lyddington Rd
Latton Rd
Alderton Road
Trowbridge Road
Ashburton Rd
Arnesside Rd
Lilac Cl
Danbury Crs
Sarum Crs
Charfield Road
Shetland Rd
Coleford Road
Lydney Road
Wilton Cl
Bradwell Gv
Delvin Rd
Tuffley Rd
Cranham Rd
Kelston Road
Kingsholm Road
Longford Av
Wellington Wk
Cherington Road
Farington Rd
Kendon Drive
Bishop Mnr Road
Maskelyne Av
Bishopthorpe Road
Butterfield Rd
Butterfield Cl
Dorian Road
Tilling Road
Rudhall Gv
Tilling Wk
Inkerman Cl
St Lucia Cl
St Lucia Crs
Manor Ct Dr
Waterdale Cl
Waterdale Gdns
Glenwood Rd
Charis Av
Lake Road
Cransley Crs
East Cft
West Croft
South Croft
Harbury Rd
Bibury Crs
Bibury Cl
Audrey Wk
Rodbourne Road
Bilbie Cl
Francombe Gv
Abbots Way
West Broadway
Broadway Av
Wellington Dr
Laurie Crs
Dyrham Close
Kellaway Crs
Weston Crs
Western Rd
Rosling Rd
Wellington Crs
Churchways Av
Churchways Crs
Church Rd
Milton Rd
St Leonard's Rd
Rozel Rd
Hughenden Rd
Strathmore Rd
Rudthorpe Rd
Quarrington Rd
Pitt Rd
Alton Rd
Ellicott Rd
Highbury Rd
Hill Grove
Henleaze Rd
View Road
Cypress Gv
Hill Burn
Montroy Cl
The Crescent
Rockside Dr
Walliscote Rd
Walliscote Av
Ridgehill
Sates Way
Henleaze Pk Dr
The Furlong
Broadleys Av
Elderberry Wk
Forest Dr
B4056
B4468
B4469
A38
Golf Course

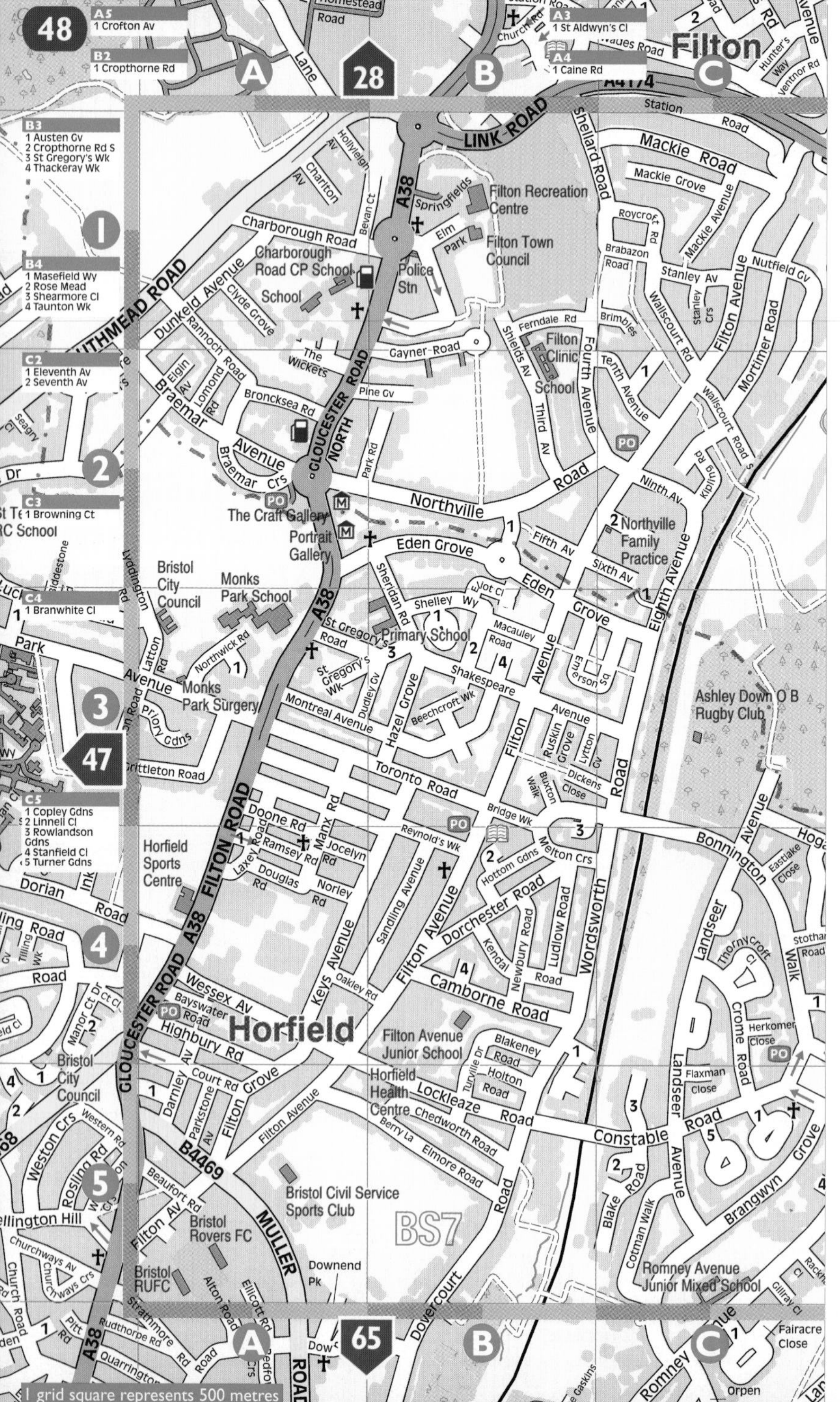
A5
1 Crofton Av
B2
1 Cropthorne Rd
B3
1 Austen Gv
2 Cropthorne Rd S
3 St Gregory's Wk
4 Thackeray Wk
B4
1 Masefield Wy
2 Rose Mead
3 Shearmore Cl
4 Taunton Wk
C2
1 Eleventh Av
2 Seventh Av
C3
1 Browning Ct
C4
1 Branwhite Cl
C5
1 Copley Gdns
2 Linnell Cl
3 Rowlandson Gdns
4 Stanfield Cl
5 Turner Gdns
A3
1 St Aldwyn's Cl
A4
1 Caine Rd
28
47
65
A
B
C
1
2
3
4
5
Filton
Homestead Road
Station Road
Church Rd
Wades Road
A4174
Station Road
LINK ROAD
Shellard Road
Mackie Road
Mackie Grove
Mackie Avenue
Roycroft Rd
Brabazon Road
Stanley Av
Stanley Crs
Nutfield Gv
Filton Avenue
Mortimer Road
Wallscourt Rd
Brimbles
Tenth Avenue
Ninth Av
Kipling Rd
Hollyleigh Av
Charlton Av
Bevan Ct
Springfields
Filton Recreation Centre
Filton Town Council
Elm Park
Police Stn
Charborough Road
Charborough Road CP School
School
SOUTHMEAD ROAD
Dunkeld Avenue
Clyde Grove
Rannoch Road
Elgin Av
Lomond Rd
Braemar Avenue
Braemar Crs
Broncksea Rd
The Wickets
Gayner Road
Pine Gv
Park Rd
GLOUCESTER ROAD NORTH
A38
Ferndale Rd
Shields Av
Filton Clinic
School
Third Av
Fourth Avenue
Northville Road
The Craft Gallery
Portrait Gallery
Eden Grove
Fifth Av
Sixth Av
Northville Family Practice
Eighth Avenue
Sheridan Rd
Shelley Wy
Macauley Road
Primary School
St Gregory's Road
St Gregory's Wk
Dudley Gv
Hazel Grove
Shakespeare Avenue
Beechcroft Wk
Emerson Sq
Bristol City Council
Monks Park School
Lyddington Rd
Latton Rd
Northwick Rd
Park Avenue
Monks Park Surgery
Priory Gdns
Crittleton Road
Montreal Avenue
Toronto Road
Filton Road
Ruskin Grove
Lytton Gv
Dickens Close
Buxton Walk
Bridge Wk
Ashley Down O B Rugby Club
Bonnington Avenue
Eastlake Close
Doone Rd
Manx Rd
Ramsey Rd
Laxey Road
Jocelyn Rd
Douglas Rd
Norley Rd
Reynold's Wk
Hottom Gdns
Melton Crs
Horfield Sports Centre
FILTON ROAD
A38
Dorian Road
Sandling Avenue
Keys Avenue
Filton Avenue
Dorchester Road
Kendal Road
Newbury Road
Ludlow Road
Wordsworth Road
Landseer Avenue
Thornycroft Cl
Crome Road
Stothard Road
Walk
Herkomer Close
Camborne Road
Oakley Rd
Wessex Av
Bayswater Road
Highbury Rd
Horfield
Filton Avenue Junior School
Blakeney Road
Turville Dr
Holton Road
Lockleaze Road
Flaxman Close
Constable Road
Horfield Health Centre
Chedworth Road
Berry La
Elmore Road
Darnley Av
Court Rd
Parkstone Av
Filton Grove
GLOUCESTER ROAD
Bristol City Council
Weston Crs
Western Rd
Rosling Rd
Wellington Hill
Churchways Av
Churchways Crs
Church Road
B4469
Beaufort Rd
Filton Av Rd
Bristol Rovers FC
Bristol RUFC
MULLER ROAD
Bristol Civil Service Sports Club
BS7
Downend Pk
Dovercourt Road
Blake Road
Cotman Walk
Brangwyn Grove
Romney Avenue Junior Mixed School
Gilliray Cl
Fairacre Close
Romney Avenue
Orpen Gardens
Alton Road
Ellicott Rd
Strathmore Rd
Rudthorpe Rd
Pitt Rd
Quarrington Rd
The Gaskins
A38
1 grid square represents 500 metres

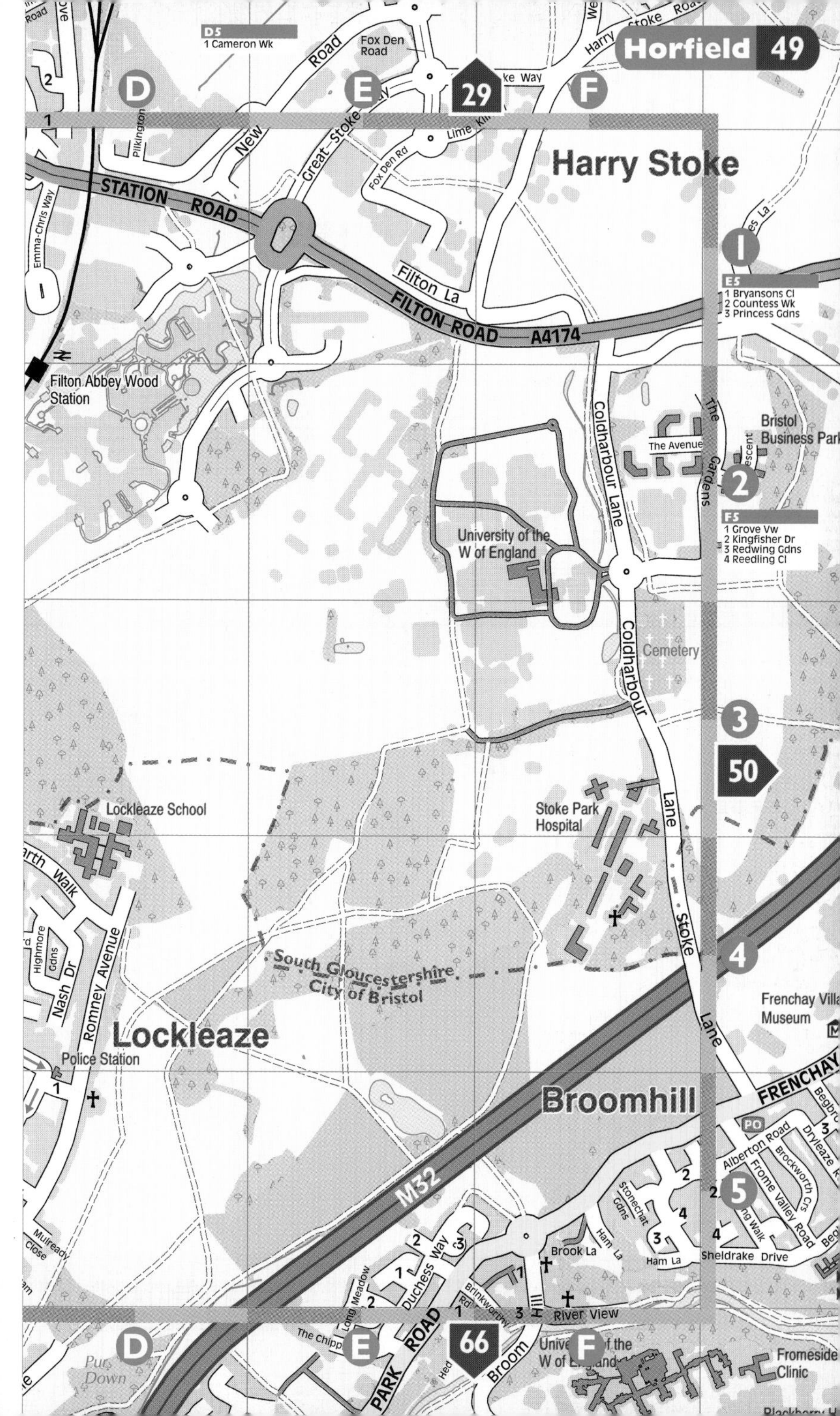
D5
1 Cameron Wk
Fox Den Road
New Road
Great Stoke
29
Harry Stoke
Fox Den Rd
Pilkington
STATION ROAD
Emma-Chris Way
Filton La
FILTON ROAD
A4174
E5
1 Bryansons Cl
2 Countess Wk
3 Princess Gdns
Filton Abbey Wood Station
Coldharbour Lane
The Gardens
The Avenue
Bristol
F5
1 Grove Vw
2 Kingfisher Dr
3 Redwing Gdns
4 Reedling Cl
University of the W of England
Cemetery
Coldharbour Lane
50
Lockleaze School
Stoke Park Hospital
Stoke Lane
South Gloucestershire
City of Bristol
Highmore Gdns
Nash Dr
Romney Avenue
Lockleaze
Police Station
Museum
Broomhill
M32
FRENCHAY
Alberton Road
Brockworth Crs
Frome Valley Road
Stonechat Gdns
Ham La
Brook La
Sheldrake Drive
Duchess Way
Long Meadow
Broom Hill
River View
PARK ROAD
66
Pur Down
Fromeside Clinic
Mulready Close

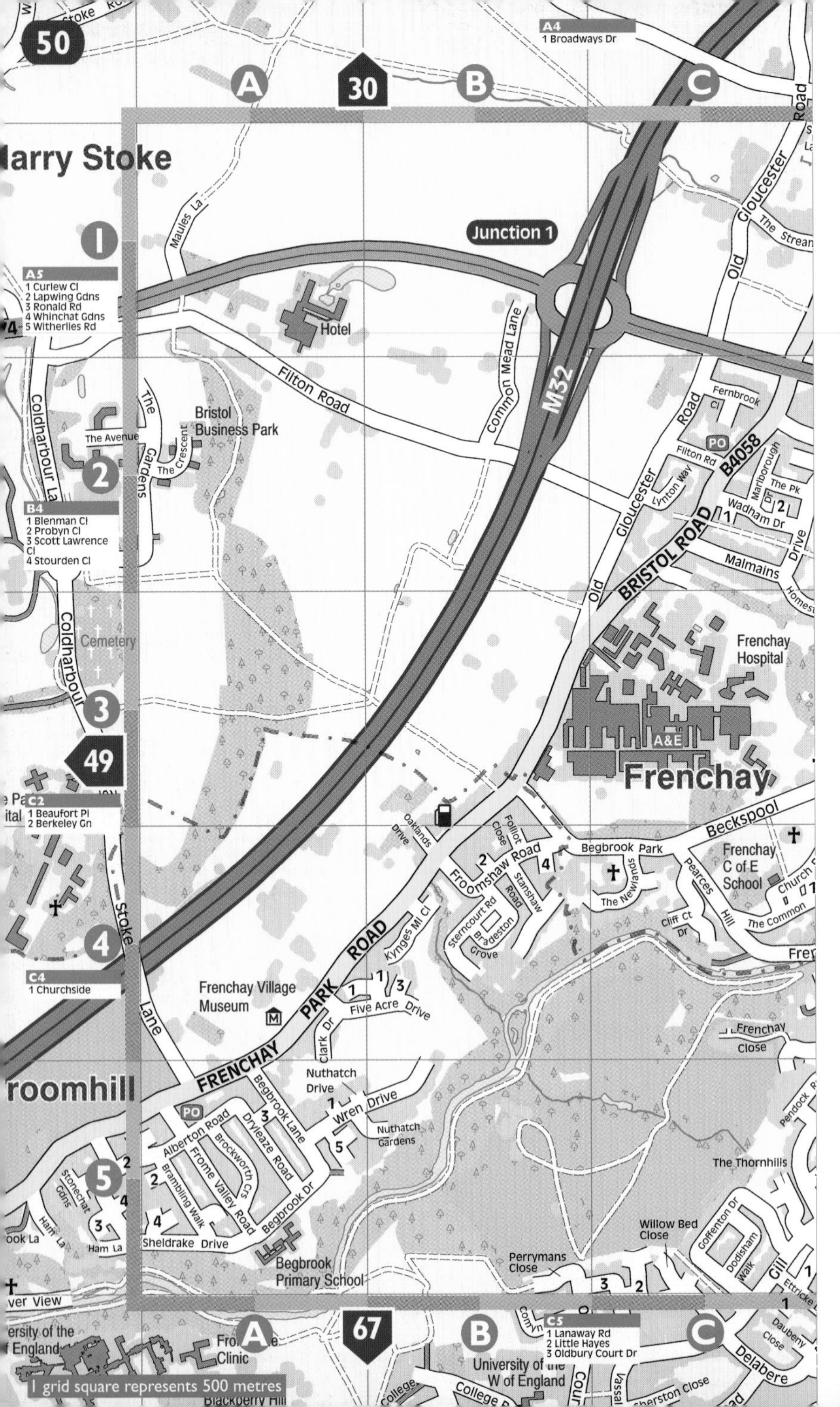

50
30
A
B
C
A4
1 Broadways Dr
Harry Stoke
1
A5
1 Curlew Cl
2 Lapwing Gdns
3 Ronald Rd
4 Whinchat Gdns
5 Witherlies Rd
Maules La
Junction 1
Hotel
Filton Road
Common Mead Lane
M32
Old Gloucester Road
The Stream
Coldharbour La
The Avenue
The Gardens
The Crescent
Bristol Business Park
2
B4
1 Blenman Cl
2 Probyn Cl
3 Scott Lawrence Cl
4 Stourden Cl
Fernbrook Cl
PO
Filton Rd
B4058
Lynton Way
Marlborough Dr
The Pk
Wadham Dr
Drive
BRISTOL ROAD
Malmains
Homestead
Coldharbour
Cemetery
3
49
Frenchay Hospital
A&E
Frenchay
C2
1 Beaufort Pl
2 Berkeley Gn
Oaklands Drive
Folliot Close
Froomshaw Road
Begbrook Park
Beckspool
Frenchay C of E School
Church
The Newlands
Pearces Hill
Stanshaw Road
Sterncourt Rd
Bradeston Grove
Kynges Ml Cl
Cliff Ct Dr
The Common
4
Stoke Lane
C4
1 Churchside
Frenchay Village Museum
FRENCHAY PARK ROAD
Five Acre Drive
Clark Dr
Frenchay Close
roomhill
Nuthatch Drive
Wren Drive
Nuthatch Gardens
Begbrook Lane
Dryleaze Road
Alberton Road
Brockworth Crs
Frome Valley Road
Brambling Walk
Begbrook Dr
Stonechat Gdns
Ham La
Sheldrake Drive
Begbrook Primary School
The Thornhills
Pendock
Willow Bed Close
Goffenton Dr
Dodisham Walk
Gill
Ettricke
Perrymans Close
5
ver View
University of the W of England
Frome Clinic
67
C5
1 Lanaway Rd
2 Little Hayes
3 Oldbury Court Dr
University of the W of England
Daubeny Close
Delabere
College
Vassal
Blackberry Hill
1 grid square represents 500 metres

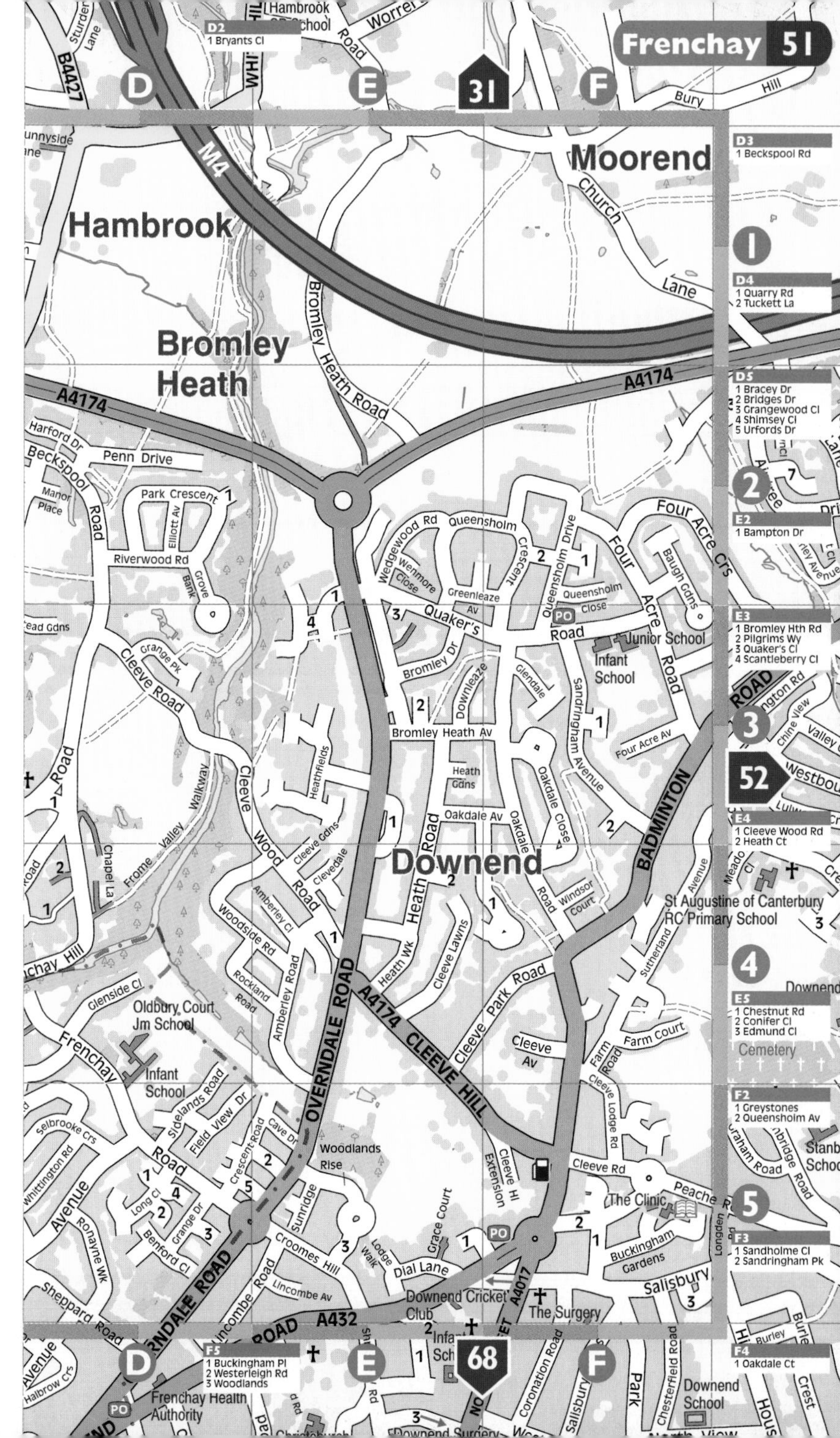
D2
1 Bryants Cl
D
E
F
31
Hambrook
Bury
Hill
Worrel
Sturden Lane
B4427
M4
Moorend
Church
Lane
Hambrook
Bromley Heath
Bromley Heath Road
A4174
A4174
D3
1 Beckspool Rd
1
D4
1 Quarry Rd
2 Tuckett La
D5
1 Bracey Dr
2 Bridges Dr
3 Grangewood Cl
4 Shimsey Cl
5 Urfords Dr
2
E2
1 Bampton Dr
Harford Dr
Penn Drive
Beckspool Road
Manor Place
Park Crescent
Elliott Av
Riverwood Rd
Grove Bank
Wedgewood Rd
Queensholm Crescent
Wenmore Close
Greenleaze Av
Queensholm Drive
Queensholm Close
Four Acre Crs
Four Acre Road
Baugh Gdns
Quaker's Road
PO
Junior School
Infant School
E3
1 Bromley Hth Rd
2 Pilgrims Wy
3 Quaker's Cl
4 Scantleberry Cl
Grange Pk
Cleeve Road
Bromley Dr
Downleaze
Glendale
Sandringham Avenue
Bromley Heath Av
Heath Gdns
Four Acre Av
Heathfields
Oakdale Av
Oakdale Close
Oakdale Road
3
52
Westbour
Valley
Chine View
BADMINTON ROAD
Cleeve Wood Road
Frome Valley Walkway
Cleeve Gdns
Clevedale
Heath Road
Downend
Windsor Court
E4
1 Cleeve Wood Rd
2 Heath Ct
Chapel La
Amberley Cl
Woodside Rd
St Augustine of Canterbury RC Primary School
Meadow Cl
Sutherland Avenue
4
Frenchay Hill
Rockland Road
Amberley Road
Heath Wk
Cleeve Lawns
Cleeve Park Road
Downend
E5
1 Chestnut Rd
2 Conifer Cl
3 Edmund Cl
Glenside Cl
Oldbury Court Jm School
OVERNDALE ROAD
A4174 CLEEVE HILL
Cleeve Av
Farm Court
Farm Road
Cemetery
Frenchay Road
Infant School
Sidelands Road
Field View Dr
Crescent Road
Cave Dr
Cleeve Lodge Rd
F2
1 Greystones
2 Queensholm Av
Selbrooke Crs
Whittington Rd
Avenue
Woodlands Rise
Cleeve Hl Extension
Cleeve Rd
Graham Road
Stanbridge Road
Stanbri School
Long Cl
Grange Dr
Sunridge
Grace Court
The Clinic
Peache Rd
5
Ronayne Wk
Benford Cl
Croomes Hill
Lodge Walk
Dial Lane
PO
Buckingham Gardens
Longden
F3
1 Sandholme Cl
2 Sandringham Pk
Sheppard Road
OVERNDALE ROAD
Lincombe Road
Lincombe Av
Downend Cricket Club
A4017
The Surgery
Salisbury
ROAD
A432
Infant School
68
F4
1 Oakdale Ct
F5
1 Buckingham Pl
2 Westerleigh Rd
3 Woodlands
Avenue
Halbrow Crs
PO
Frenchay Health Authority
Coronation Road
Salisbury
Park
Chesterfield Road
Downend School
Burley
Crest
Downend Surgery

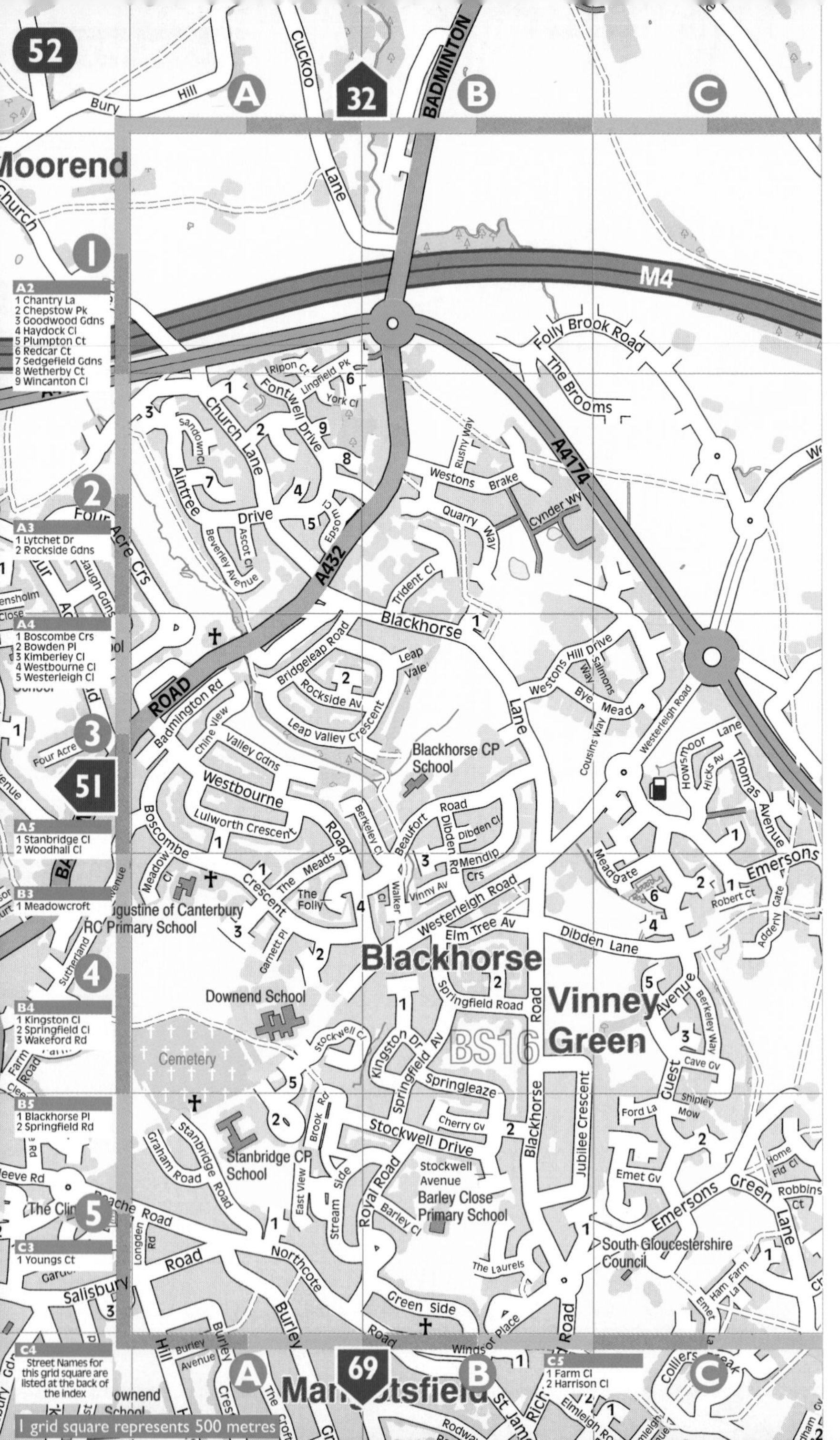
Moorend
Blackhorse
Vinney Green
BS16
M4
A432
A4174
Blackhorse CP School
Downend School
Stanbridge CP School
Barley Close Primary School
South Gloucestershire Council
Cemetery
A2
1 Chantry La
2 Chepstow Pk
3 Goodwood Gdns
4 Haydock Cl
5 Plumpton Ct
6 Redcar Ct
7 Sedgefield Gdns
8 Wetherby Ct
9 Wincanton Cl
A3
1 Lytchet Dr
2 Rockside Gdns
A4
1 Boscombe Crs
2 Bowden Pl
3 Kimberley Cl
4 Westbourne Cl
5 Westerleigh Cl
A5
1 Stanbridge Cl
2 Woodhall Cl
B3
1 Meadowcroft
B4
1 Kingston Cl
2 Springfield Cl
3 Wakeford Rd
B5
1 Blackhorse Pl
2 Springfield Rd
C3
1 Youngs Ct
C4
Street Names for this grid square are listed at the back of the index
C5
1 Farm Cl
2 Harrison Cl
1 grid square represents 500 metres

32
51
69

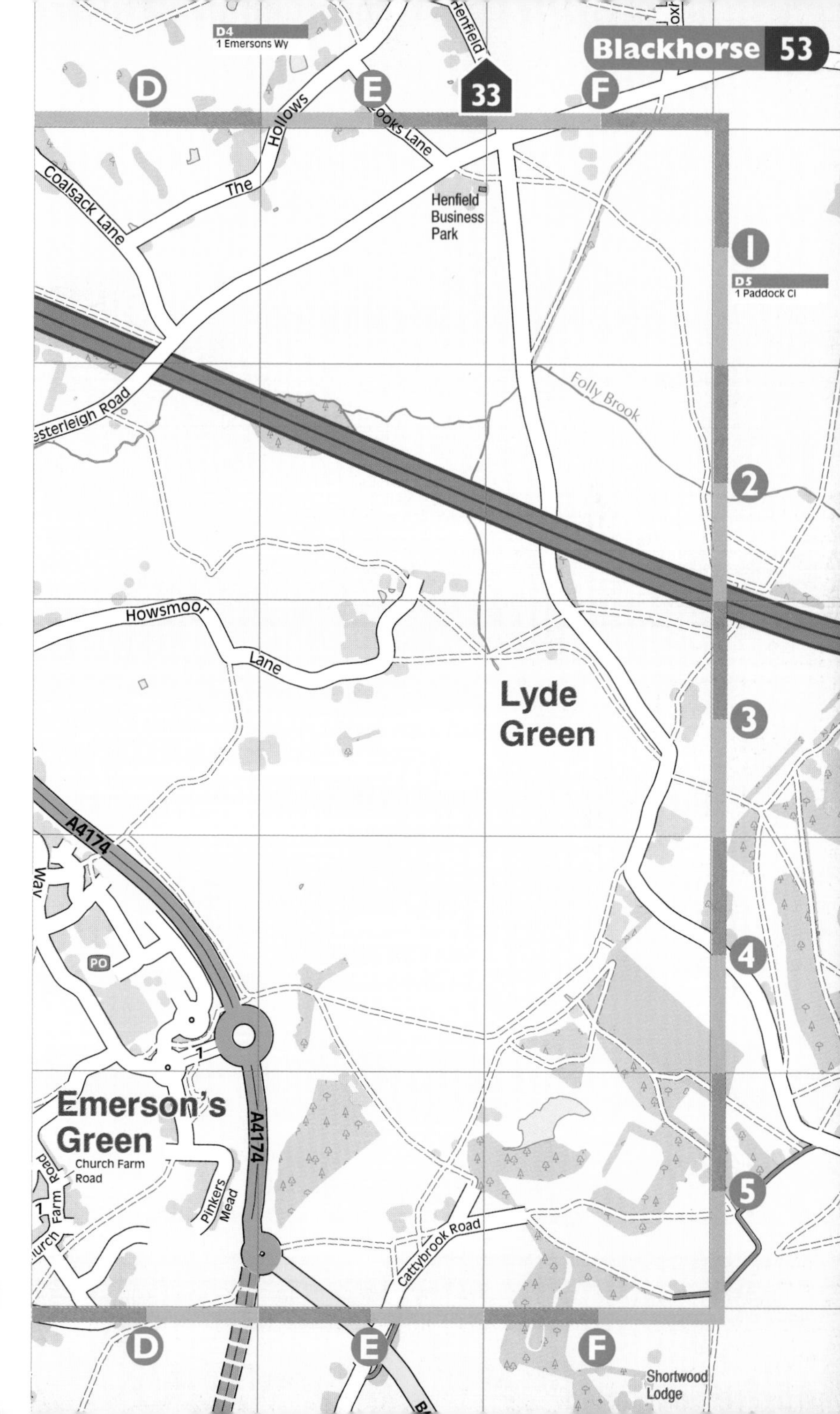
D4
1 Emersons Wy
Henfield
33
D
E
F
Cooks Lane
The Hollows
Coalsack Lane
Henfield
Business
Park
1
D5
1 Paddock Cl
Westerleigh Road
Folly Brook
2
Howsmoor
Lane
Lyde
Green
3
A4174
Way
4
PO
1
Emerson's
Green
A4174
Church Farm
Road
Pinkers
Mead
Church Farm Road
1
Cattybrook Road
5
D
E
F
Shortwood
Lodge

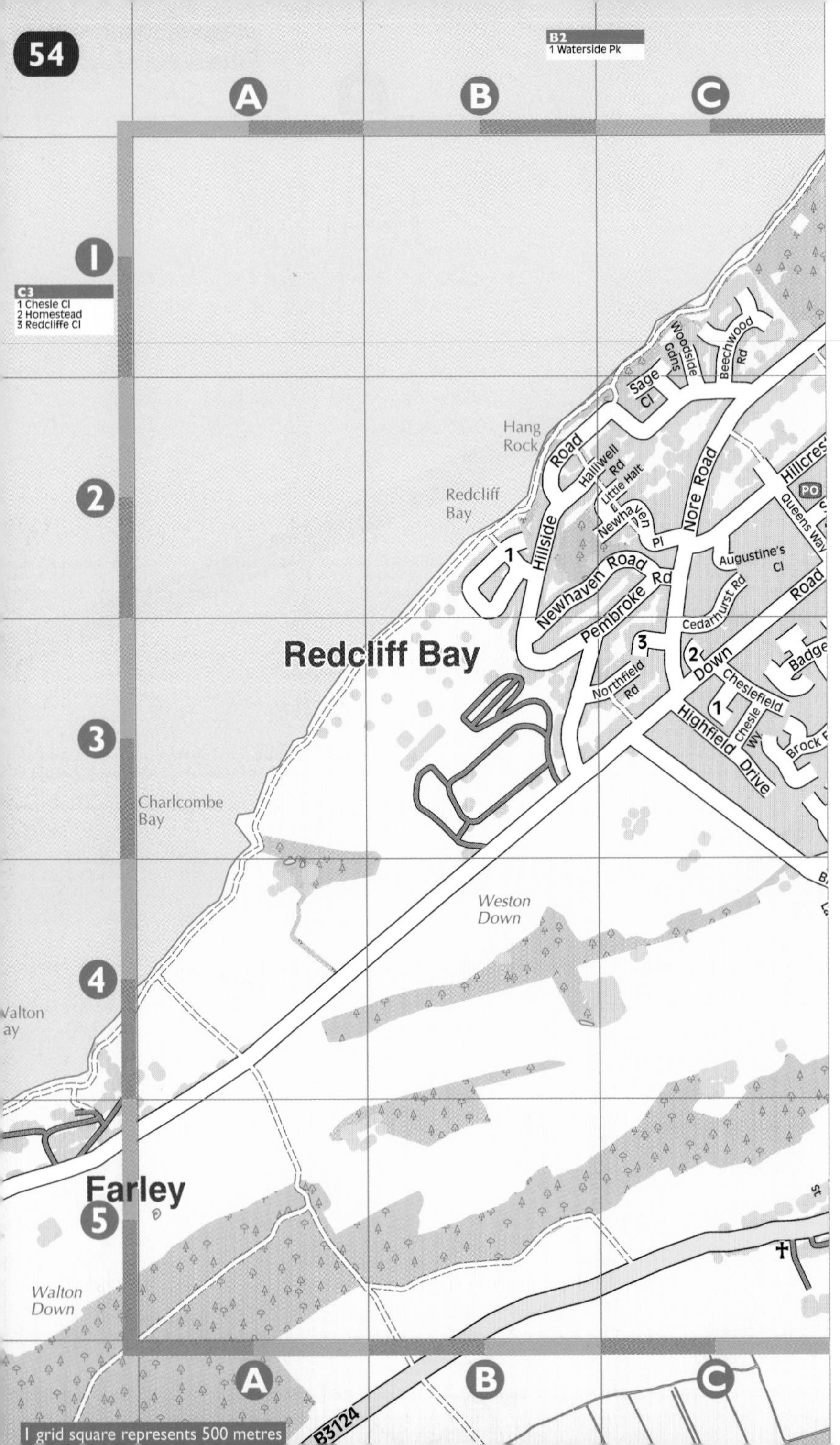
B2
1 Waterside Pk
C3
1 Chesle Cl
2 Homestead
3 Redcliffe Cl
A
B
C
1
2
3
4
5
Redcliff Bay
Hang Rock
Redcliff Bay
Charlcombe Bay
Weston Down
Walton Down
Farley
Woodside Gdns
Beechwood Rd
Sage Cl
Road
Halliwell Rd
Little Halt
Newhaven Pl
Nore Road
Hillcrest
PO
Queens Way
Hillside
Newhaven Road
Pembroke Rd
Augustine's Cl
Cedarhurst Rd
Road
Down
Northfield Rd
Cheslefield
Highfield Drive
Chesle Wy
Badger
Brock
B3124
1 grid square represents 500 metres

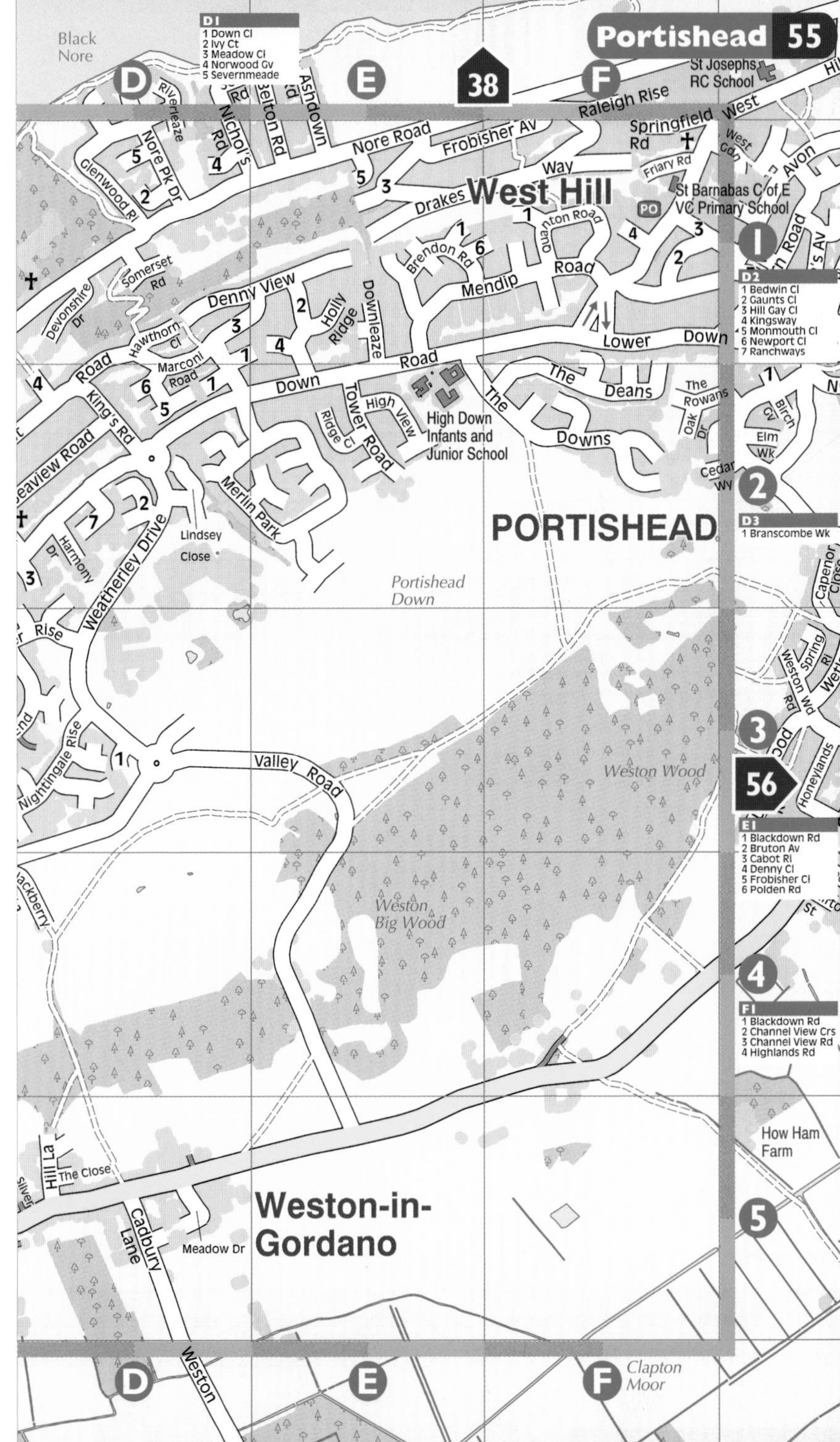
D1
1 Down Cl
2 Ivy Ct
3 Meadow Cl
4 Norwood Gv
5 Severnmeade
D2
1 Bedwin Cl
2 Gaunts Cl
3 Hill Gay Cl
4 Kingsway
5 Monmouth Cl
6 Newport Cl
7 Ranchways
D3
1 Branscombe Wk
E1
1 Blackdown Rd
2 Bruton Av
3 Cabot Ri
4 Denny Cl
5 Frobisher Cl
6 Polden Rd
F1
1 Blackdown Rd
2 Channel View Crs
3 Channel View Rd
4 Highlands Rd
Black Nore
West Hill
PORTISHEAD
Portishead Down
Weston Wood
Weston Big Wood
Weston-in-Gordano
Clapton Moor
How Ham Farm
St Josephs RC School
St Barnabas C of E VC Primary School
High Down Infants and Junior School
Raleigh Rise
Nore Road
Frobisher Av
Springfield Rd
Drakes Way
Mendip Road
Lower Down Road
Denny View
Valley Road
Weatherley Drive
Seaview Road
King's Rd
Tower Road
Merlin Park
Lindsey Close
Nightingale Rise
Cadbury Lane
Meadow Dr
The Close
Hill La
Weston
38
56

St Josephs RC School
Raleigh Rise
Springfield Rd
West
Combe Fields
Way
Friary Rd
West Gdn
Avon
St Barnabas C of E VC Primary School
PO
Severn Road
Queen's Av
Rippleside
Briary Road
Leeside
Downside
Slade Road
Combe Rd
Stoke Rd
Ferndale Rd
Police Station
Cabstan
STATION
Leisure Centre
Harbour Road
Old Mill Road
WYNDHAM WAY A369
B3124 HIGH STREET
Victoria Sq
Portishead Health Centre
Albert Rd
Serbert Rd
Quays Av
Conference Av
Roath Road
Portishead CP School
Church Cl
Portishead & North Weston Town Council
Brampton Way
Lower Down Road
Deans
Newlands Hill
North Church Rd
South Church Rd
Primary School
Mendip Leisure Cen
Forester Rd
Norfolk Road
Burford Cl
Exeter Rd
Winford Cl
Denston Dr
The Rowans
Oak Dr
Birch Gv
Elm Wk
Cedar Wy
The Garstons
St Peters Road
Greystoke Business Cen
The Paddock
Court Cl
Falcon Cl
Cadbury Rd
Glebe Av
Glebe Rd
Portland Dr
Heron
B3124 PORTB
COMM
BRISTOL ROAD
St Mary's Road
Capenor Close
Lane
Gordano School
Spring Rl
Weston Rd
Weston Wd
Wetlands
Greenfield Park
Maysfield Cl
Clapton Lane
Underwood Road
Honeylands
CLEVEDON ROAD
Cemetery
Hollis Av
Mead Rd
George St
Clifton St
North Weston
How Ham Farm
Drove
Moor La
Clapton
Clapton in Gordano
Clapton Moor
39
55
A1
1 Charlton Vw
2 Dano View Gdns
3 Link Rd
A2
1 Willow Cl
A3
1 Hollis Crs
B1
1 Halletts Wy
2 Orchard Cl
3 Victoria Cl
B2
1 Thatcher Cl
C1
1 Blenheim Wy
2 Mulberry Av
3 Richmond Cl
C2
1 Bladen Cl
2 Clayton Cl
3 Cotswold Cl
4 Dandy's Meadow
5 Lynton Cl
6 Stafford Rd
7 Tudor Rd
1 grid square represents 500 metres

Portbury
Wharf
D
E
40
F
Wharf
Lane
Sheepw
Galingale
Wy
Queenscote
Tydeman
Rd
Lambourne Way
Sheepway
Gdns
URY
MON
2
THE
PORTBURY
Middle
Bridge
3
58
Gordano
Football C
BS20
Upper
Caswell
Farm
4
Caswell
Cross
Caswell Lane
5
Naish
Hill
Hill
D
E
F

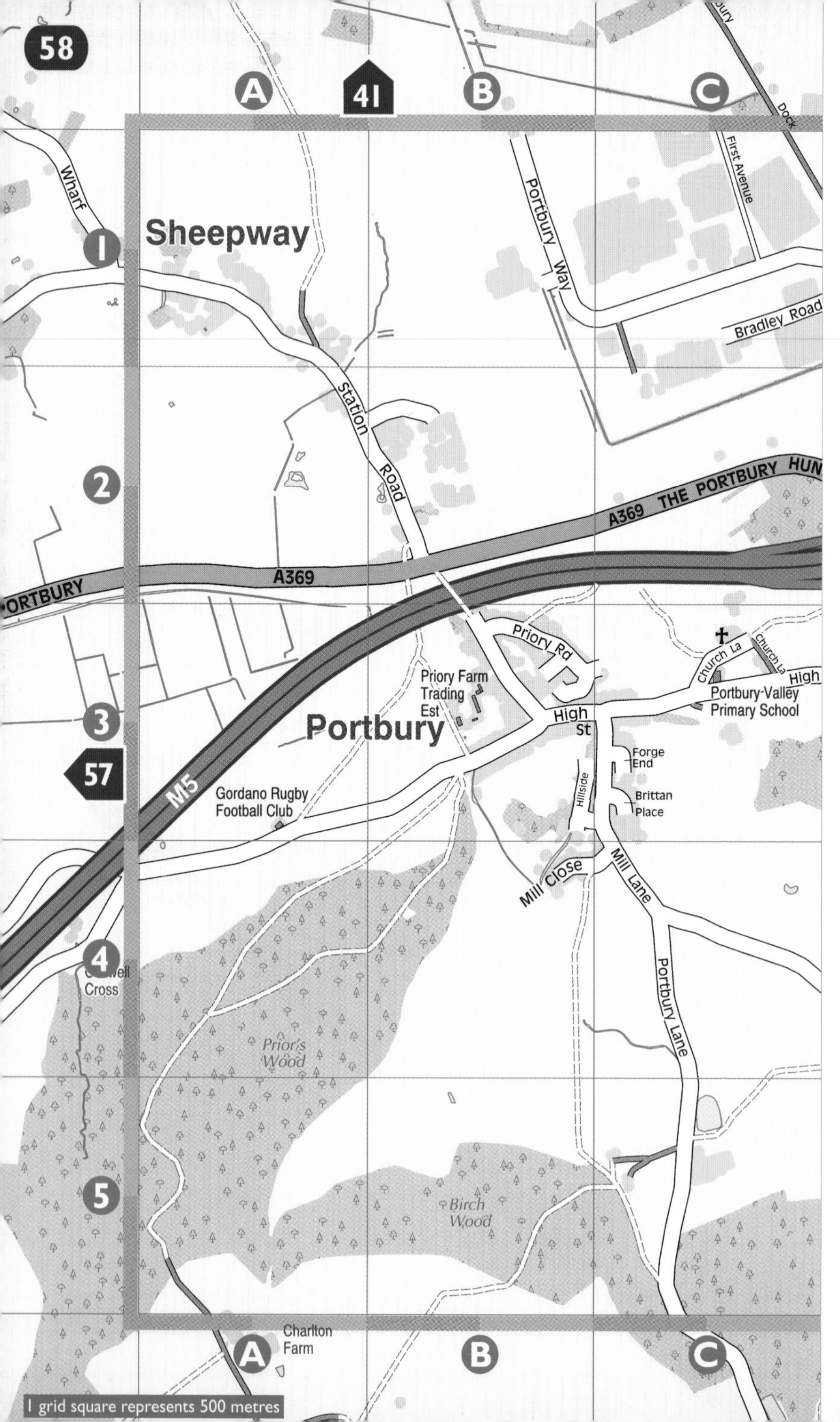

41
57
A
B
C
1
2
3
4
5
Sheepway
Portbury
Wharf
Portbury Way
First Avenue
Dock
Bradley Road
Station Road
A369 THE PORTBURY HUN
A369
PORTBURY
M5
Priory Rd
Priory Farm Trading Est
High St
Church La
High
Portbury-Valley Primary School
Forge End
Brittan Place
Hillside
Mill Close
Mill Lane
Portbury Lane
Gordano Rugby Football Club
Cross
Prior's Wood
Birch Wood
Charlton Farm
1 grid square represents 500 metres

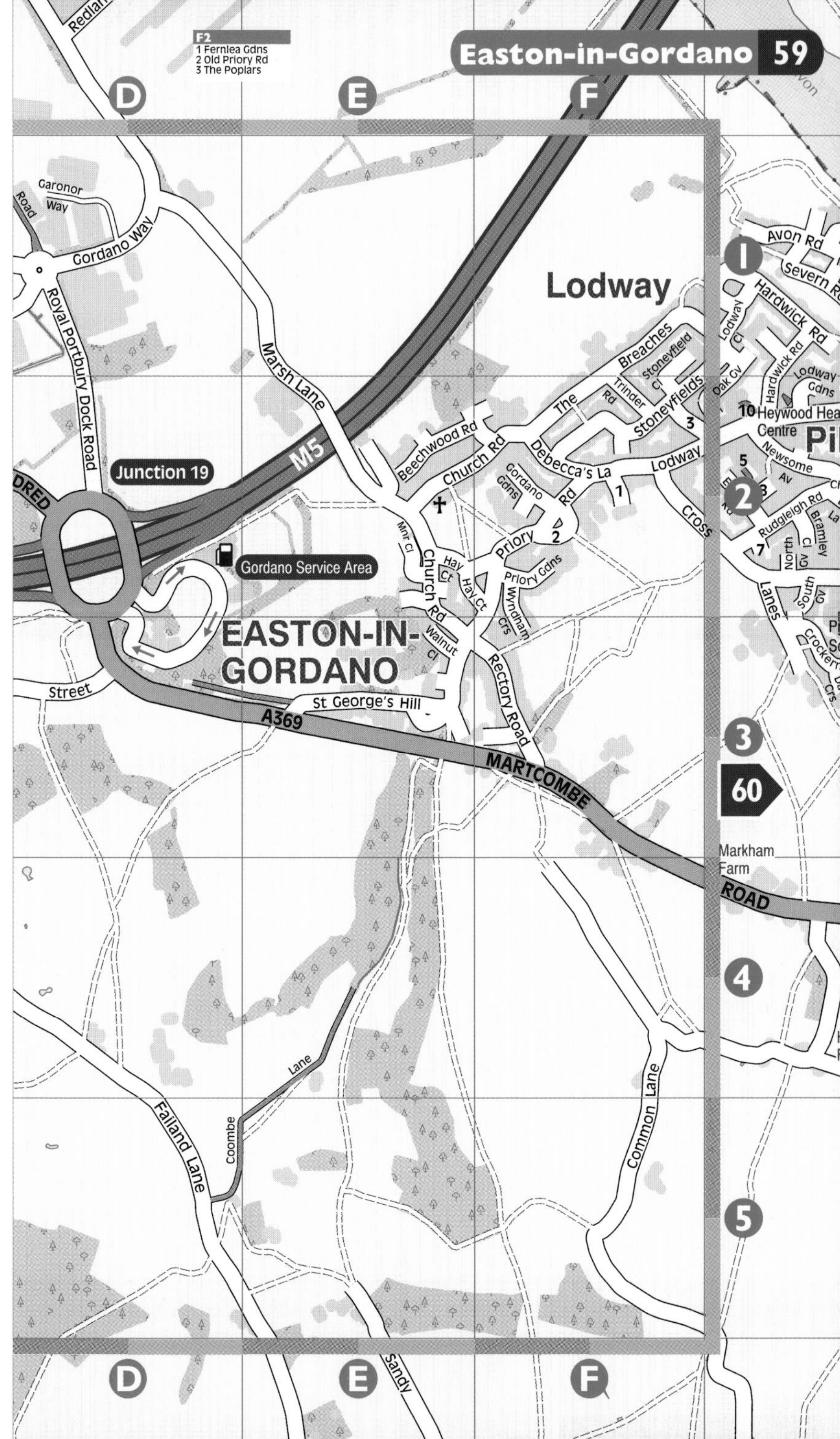
F2
1 Fernlea Gdns
2 Old Priory Rd
3 The Poplars
D
E
F
Lodway
Garonor Way
Gordano Way
Royal Portbury Dock Road
Marsh Lane
M5
Junction 19
Gordano Service Area
EASTON-IN-GORDANO
Beechwood Rd
Church Rd
The Breaches
Stoneyfield Cl
Trinder Rd
Stoneyfields
Debecca's La
Gordano Gdns
Lodway
Cross
Priory Rd
Priory Gdns
Wyndham Crs
Hay Ct
Mnr Cl
Walnut Cl
Rectory Road
St George's Hill
Street
A369
MARTCOMBE ROAD
Avon Rd
Severn Rd
Hardwick Rd
Lodway Cl
Oak Gv
Lodway Gdns
10 Heywood Health Centre
Newsome Av
Rudgleigh Rd
Bramley
North Gv
South Gv
Lanes
Crockerne
Markham Farm
60
Lane
Coombe
Failand Lane
Common Lane
Sandy
1
2
3
4
5

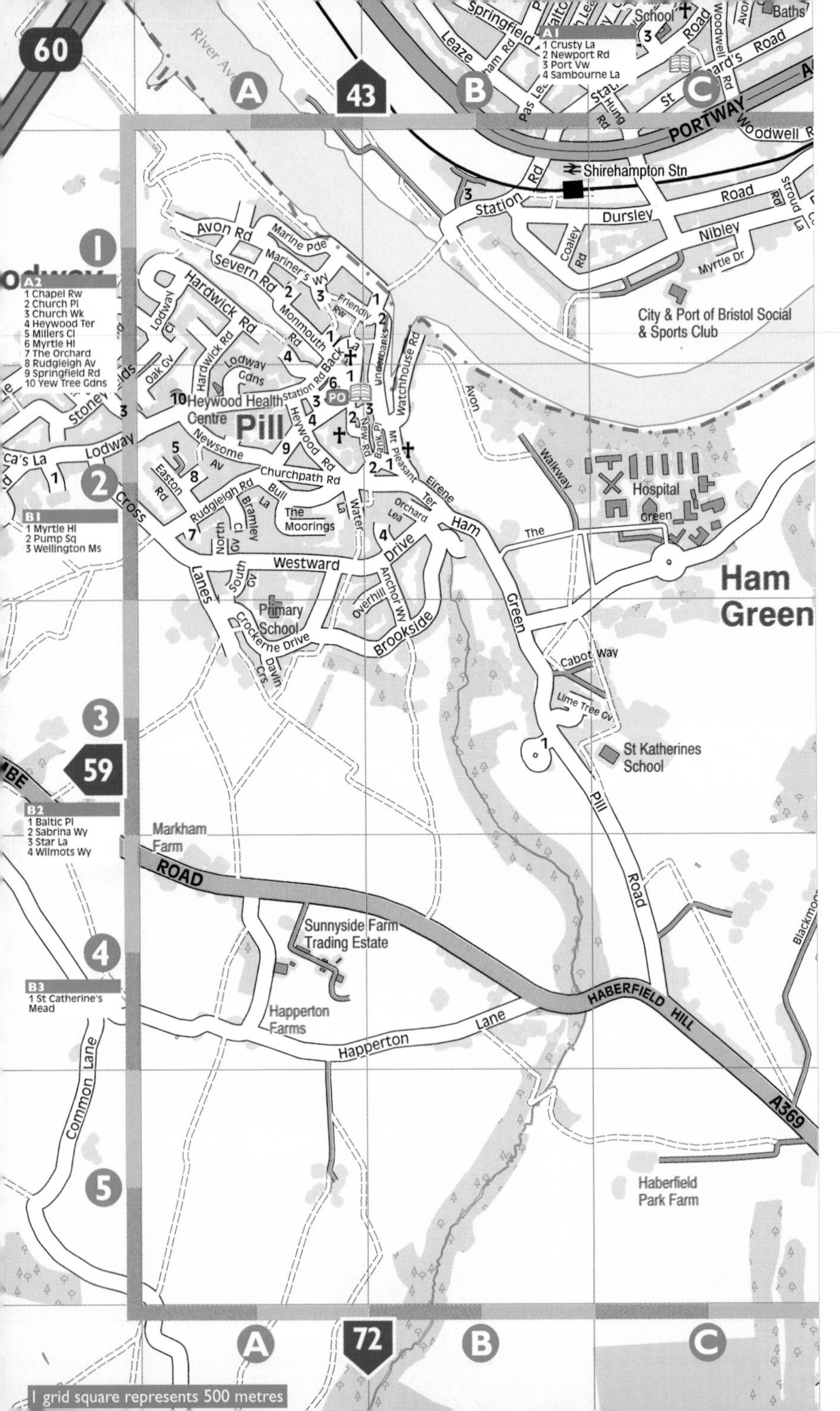

60
43
59
72
A
B
C
1
2
3
4
5
A1
1 Crusty La
2 Newport Rd
3 Port Vw
4 Sambourne La
A2
1 Chapel Rw
2 Church Pl
3 Church Wk
4 Heywood Ter
5 Millers Cl
6 Myrtle Hl
7 The Orchard
8 Rudgleigh Av
9 Springfield Rd
10 Yew Tree Gdns
B1
1 Myrtle Hl
2 Pump Sq
3 Wellington Ms
B2
1 Baltic Pl
2 Sabrina Wy
3 Star La
4 Wilmots Wy
B3
1 St Catherine's Mead
River Avon
PORTWAY
Shirehampton Stn
Station Rd
Dursley Road
Nibley
Coaley Rd
Myrtle Dr
Stroud Rd
City & Port of Bristol Social & Sports Club
Pill
Heywood Health Centre
Avon Rd
Marine Pde
Mariner's Wy
Severn Rd
Hardwick Rd
Monmouth Rd
Friendly Rw
Back La
Underbanks
Watchhouse Rd
Lodway Cl
Lodway Gdns
Oak Gv
Station Rd
Heywood Rd
New Rd
Bank Pl
Mt Pleasant
Newsome Av
Churchpath Rd
Easton Rd
Rudgleigh Rd
Bull La
Bramley Cl
North Gv
The Moorings
Water La
Orchard Lea
Eirene Ter
Westward Drive
South Gv
Primary School
Overhill
Anchor Wy
Brookside
Crockerne Drive
Davin Crs
Lodway
Cross Lanes
Avon Walkway
Hospital
The Green
Ham Green
Cabot Way
Lime Tree Gv
St Katherines School
Pill Road
Markham Farm
ROAD
Sunnyside Farm Trading Estate
Happerton Farms
Happerton Lane
HABERFIELD HILL
A369
Common Lane
Haberfield Park Farm
Blackmoor
1 grid square represents 500 metres

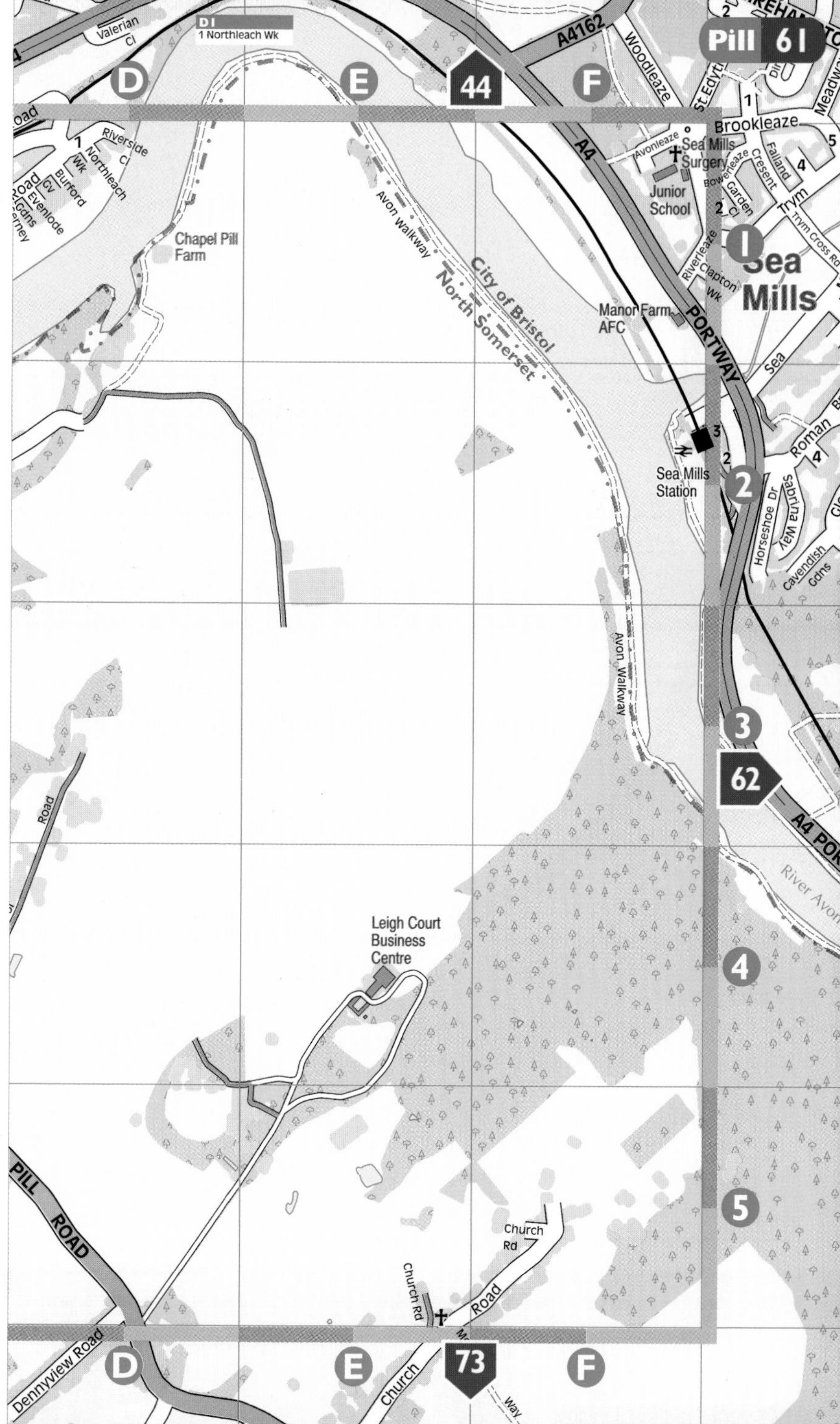
Valerian Cl
D1
1 Northleach Wk
A4162
Woodleaze
D
E
F
44
Brookleaze
Avonleaze
Sea Mills Surgery
Boweleaze
Cresent
Falland
Junior School
Garden Cl
Trym
Trym Cross Rd
Riverleaze
Clapton Wk
Sea Mills
Riverside Cl
Northleach Wk
Burford Cv
Evenlode
Chapel Pill Farm
Avon Walkway
City of Bristol
North Somerset
A4
Manor Farm AFC
PORTWAY
Sea
Roman
Sea Mills Station
Horseshoe Dr
Sabrina Way
Cavendish Gdns
1
2
3
4
5
62
A4 POR
River Avon
Road
Leigh Court Business Centre
Church Rd
Church Rd
Road
PILL ROAD
Dennyview Road
Church
73
Way

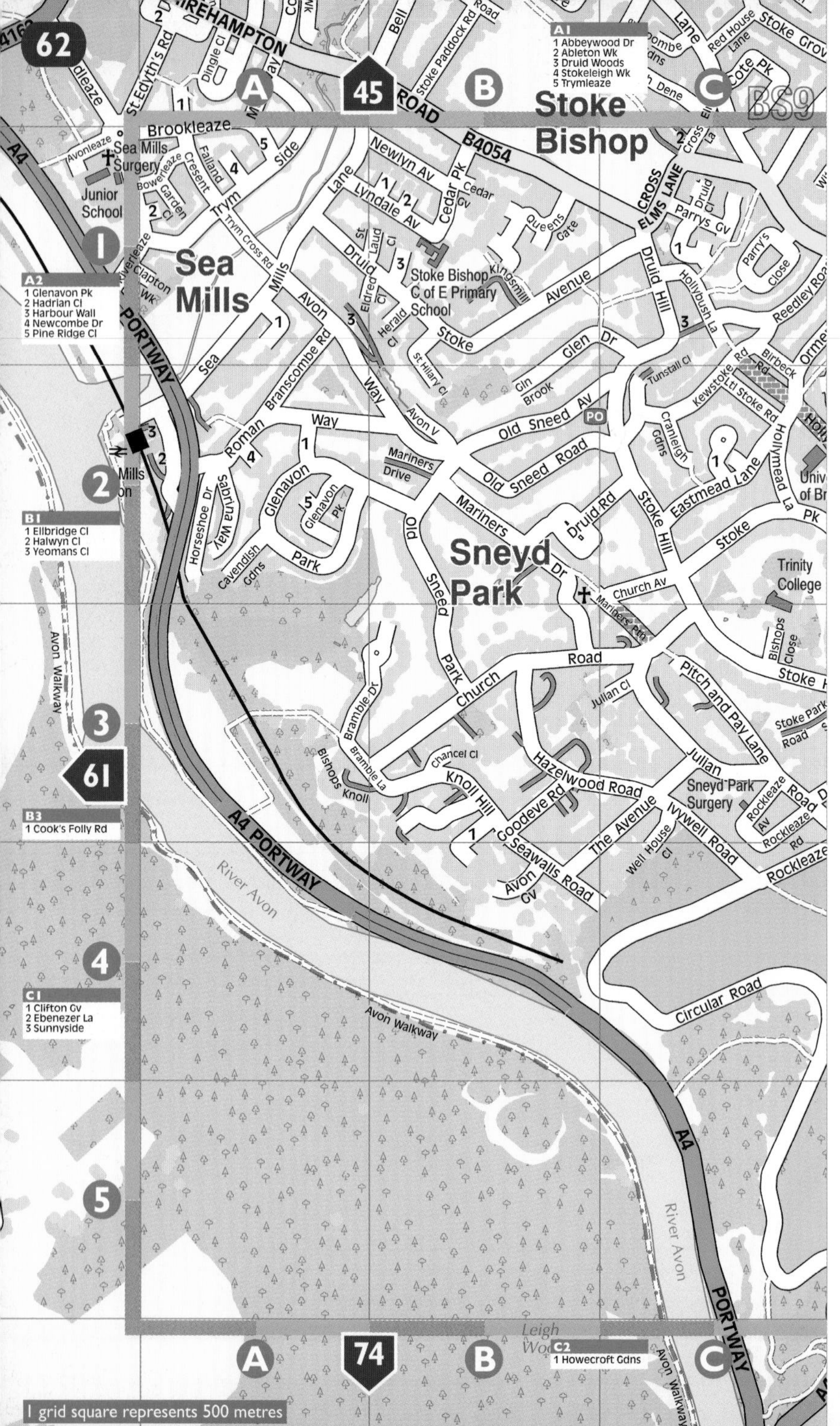

45
74
61
A
B
C
1
2
3
4
5
BS9
Stoke Bishop
Sea Mills
Sneyd Park
A1
1 Abbeywood Dr
2 Ableton Wk
3 Druid Woods
4 Stokeleigh Wk
5 Trymleaze
A2
1 Glenavon Pk
2 Hadrian Cl
3 Harbour Wall
4 Newcombe Dr
5 Pine Ridge Cl
B1
1 Ellbridge Cl
2 Halwyn Cl
3 Yeomans Cl
B3
1 Cook's Folly Rd
C1
1 Clifton Gv
2 Ebenezer La
3 Sunnyside
C2
1 Howecroft Gdns
SHIREHAMPTON ROAD
B4054
Stoke Paddock Rd
Bell
Red House Lane
Stoke Grove
Cote Pk
Brookleaze
Avonleaze
Sea Mills Surgery
Junior School
Bowerleaze
Crescent
Falland
Garden Cl
Trym Side
Trym Cross Rd
Newlyn Av
Lyndale Av
Cedar Pk
Cedar Gv
Queens Gate
CROSS ELMS LANE
Druid Cl
Parrys Gv
Parry's Close
Reedley Road
Stoke Bishop C of E Primary School
Kingsmill
Avenue
Druid Hill
Hollybush La
Sea Mills
Avon Way
Branscombe Rd
Druid Stoke Avenue
St Laud Cl
Eldred Cl
Herald Cl
St Hilary Cl
Glen Dr
Gln Brook
Tunstall Cl
Kewstoke Rd
Birbeck Rd
Ltl Stoke Rd
Roman Way
Old Sneed Av
PO
Old Sneed Road
Avon V
Mariners Drive
Cranleigh Gdns
Eastmead Lane
Hollymead La
Stoke Pk
University of Br
Trinity College
Sabrina Way
Horseshoe Dr
Glenavon Park
Glenavon Pk
Cavendish Gdns
Mariners Dr
Druid Rd
Stoke Hill
Church Av
Mariners Path
Old Sneed Park
Church Road
Bishops Close
Stoke Hill
Julian Cl
Pitch and Pay Lane
Stoke Park Road
Bramble Dr
Bramble La
Bishops Knoll
Chancel Cl
Knoll Hill
Hazelwood Road
Julian Road
Sneyd Park Surgery
Rockleaze Av
Rockleaze Rd
Rockleaze
Goodeve Rd
The Avenue
Well House Cl
Ivywell Road
Seawalls Road
Avon Gv
A4 PORTWAY
A4
PORTWAY
River Avon
Avon Walkway
Circular Road
Leigh Woods
1 grid square represents 500 metres

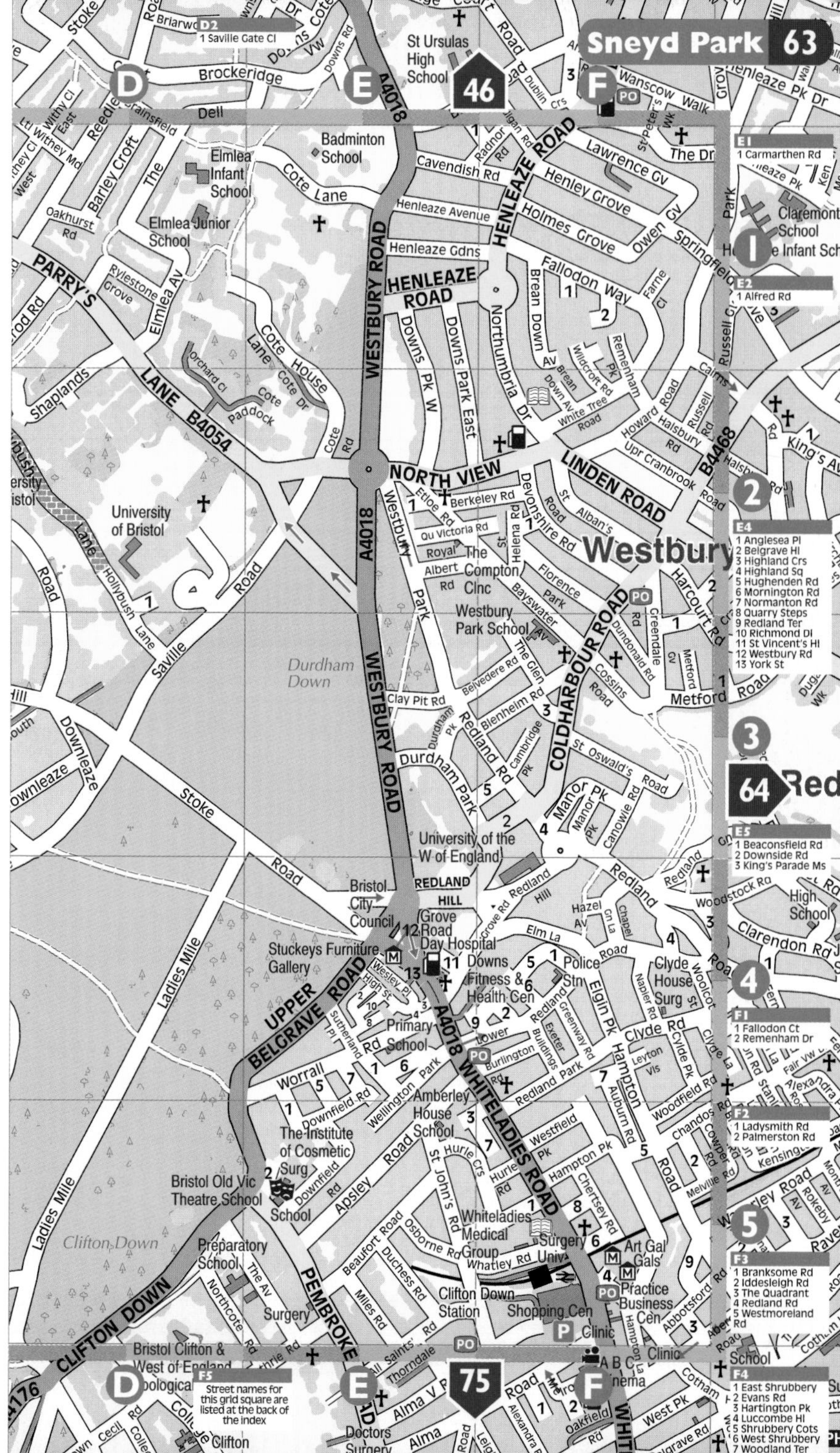
D2
1 Saville Gate Cl
46
E1
1 Carmarthen Rd
E2
1 Alfred Rd
E4
1 Anglesea Pl
2 Belgrave Hl
3 Highland Crs
4 Highland Sq
5 Hughenden Rd
6 Mornington Rd
7 Normanton Rd
8 Quarry Steps
9 Redland Ter
10 Richmond Dl
11 St Vincent's Hl
12 Westbury Rd
13 York St
64
Redl
E5
1 Beaconsfield Rd
2 Downside Rd
3 King's Parade Ms
F1
1 Fallodon Ct
2 Remenham Dr
F2
1 Ladysmith Rd
2 Palmerston Rd
F3
1 Branksome Rd
2 Iddesleigh Rd
3 The Quadrant
4 Redland Rd
5 Westmoreland Rd
F4
1 East Shrubbery
2 Evans Rd
3 Hartington Pk
4 Luccombe Hl
5 Shrubbery Cots
6 West Shrubbery
7 Woodland Ter
F5
Street names for this grid square are listed at the back of the index
75
Westbury
St Ursulas High School
Badminton School
Elmlea Infant School
Elmlea Junior School
Claremont School
University of Bristol
Durdham Down
The Compton Clnc
Westbury Park School
University of the W of England
Bristol City Council
Grove Road Day Hospital
Stuckeys Furniture Gallery
Downs Fitness & Health Cen
Primary School
Police Stn
Clyde House Surg
Amberley House School
The Institute of Cosmetic Surg
Bristol Old Vic Theatre School
School
Clifton Down
Preparatory School
Surgery
Whiteladies Medical Group
Surgery
Univ
Art Gal
Gals
Practice Business Cen
Clifton Down Station
Shopping Cen
Clinic
Bristol Clifton & West of England Zoological
A B C Cinema
Doctors Surgery
High School
WESTBURY ROAD
A4018
HENLEAZE ROAD
NORTH VIEW
LINDEN ROAD
B4468
PARRY'S LANE B4054
COLDHARBOUR ROAD
UPPER BELGRAVE ROAD
A4018 WHITELADIES ROAD
PEMBROKE
CLIFTON DOWN
A4176
REDLAND HILL
Cote Lane
Henleaze Avenue
Henleaze Gdns
Cavendish Rd
Henley Grove
Holmes Grove
Lawrence Gv
Springfield
Fallodon Way
Downs Pk W
Downs Park East
Northumbria Dr
Bream Down Av
Remenham
Howard Road
Halsbury Rd
Upr Cranbrook Road
Berkeley Rd
Devonshire Rd
St Alban's Road
Qu Victoria Rd
Royal
Albert Rd
Westbury Park
Florence Park
Bayswater Av
Harcourt Rd
Greendale Rd
Dundonald Rd
Cossins Road
Metford Road
Belvedere Rd
The Glen
Blenheim Rd
Clay Pit Rd
Redland Rd
Durdham Park
St Oswald's Road
Manor Pk
Canowie Rd
Stoke Road
Ladies Mile
Downleaze
Saville Road
Hollybush Lane
Shaplands
Cote House Lane
Cote Paddock
Orchard Cl
Oakhurst Rd
Barley Croft
Rylestone Grove
Elmlea Av
Brockeridge
Dell
Redland
Woodstock Rd
Clarendon Rd
Elm La
Hazel Av
Chapel
Elgin Pk
Clyde Rd
Hampton Road
Redland Park
Worrall Rd
Downfield Rd
Wellington Park
Apsley Road
Hurle Crs
Westfield Pk
Hampton Pk
Chertsey Rd
Woodfield Rd
Chandos Rd
Cowper Rd
Melville Rd
Waverley Road
Rokeby Av
Beaufort Road
Osborne Rd
Duchess Rd
Miles Rd
Whatley Rd
St John's Rd
Northcote Rd
Abbotsford Rd
Cotham
Thorndale
Alma Vale
Alma
Oakfield Rd
West Pk
Belgrave Rd
Alexandra Rd
King's Ave
Wanscow Walk
The Dr

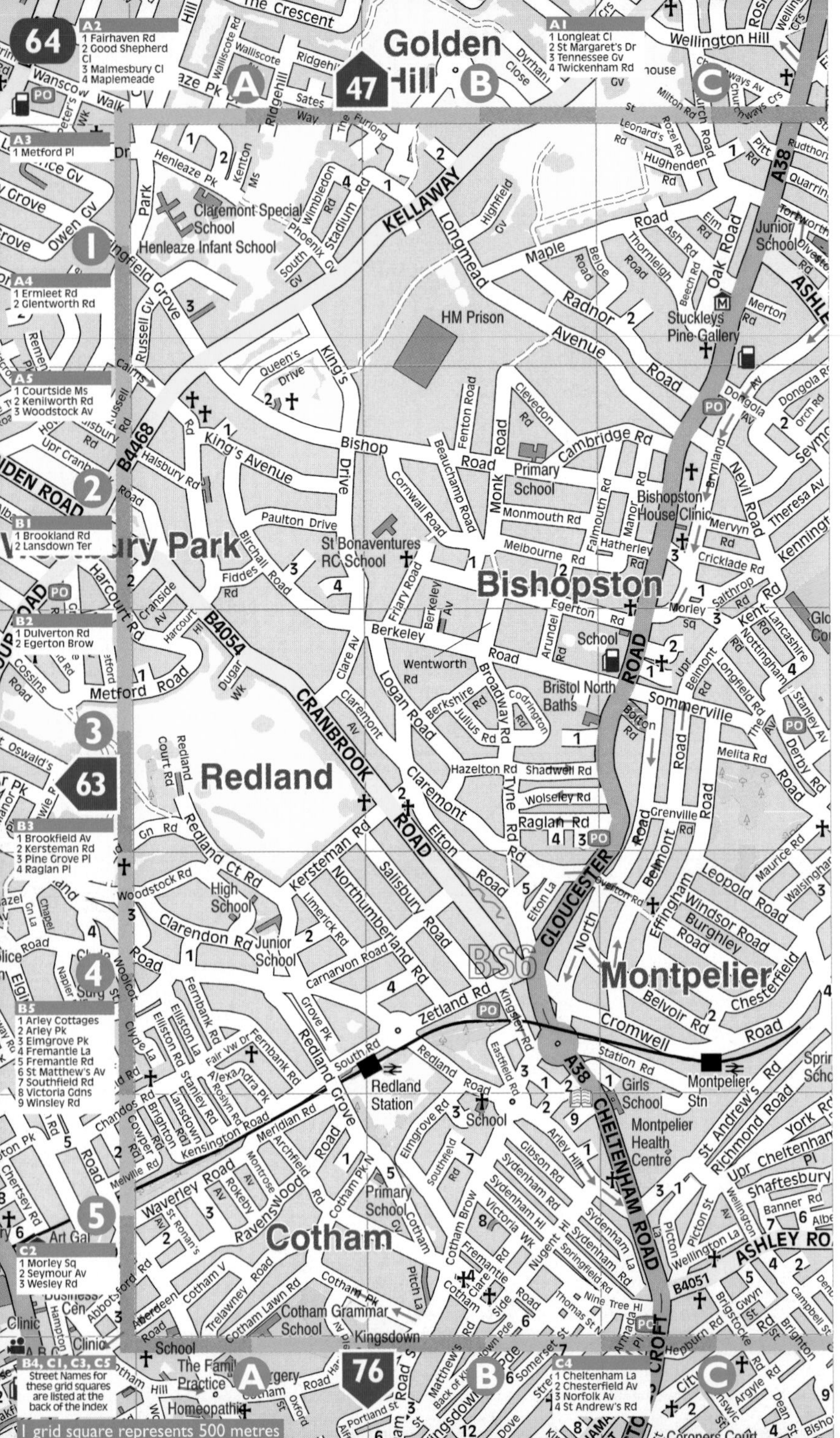
64
A2
1 Fairhaven Rd
2 Good Shepherd Cl
3 Malmesbury Cl
4 Maplemeade
A1
1 Longleat Cl
2 St Margaret's Dr
3 Tennessee Gv
4 Twickenham Rd
A3
1 Metford Pl
A4
1 Ermleet Rd
2 Glentworth Rd
A5
1 Courtside Ms
2 Kenilworth Rd
3 Woodstock Av
B1
1 Brookland Rd
2 Lansdown Ter
B2
1 Dulverton Rd
2 Egerton Brow
B3
1 Brookfield Av
2 Kersteman Rd
3 Pine Grove Pl
4 Raglan Pl
B5
1 Arley Cottages
2 Arley Pk
3 Elmgrove Pk
4 Fremantle La
5 Fremantle Rd
6 St Matthew's Av
7 Southfield Rd
8 Victoria Gdns
9 Winsley Rd
C2
1 Morley Sq
2 Seymour Av
3 Wesley Rd
C4
1 Cheltenham La
2 Chesterfield Av
3 Norfolk Av
4 St Andrew's Rd
B4, C1, C3, C5
Street Names for these grid squares are listed at the back of the index
1 grid square represents 500 metres
47
63
76
Golden Hill
Bishopston
Redland
Montpelier
Cotham
BS6
The Crescent
Wellington Hill
KELLAWAY
Longmead
Maple Road
Radnor Avenue Road
HM Prison
Claremont Special School
Henleaze Infant School
Stuckleys Pine Gallery
Junior School
Primary School
Bishopston House Clinic
St Bonaventures RC School
Bristol North Baths
High School
Junior School
Redland Station
Montpelier Stn
Girls School
Montpelier Health Centre
Primary School
Cotham Grammar School
Kingsdown
The Family Practice Surgery
Homeopathic
Clinic
School
Art Gal
B4468
B4054
A38
B4051
CRANBROOK ROAD
GLOUCESTER ROAD
CHELTENHAM ROAD
ASHLEY ROAD
STOKES CROFT
King's Avenue
Bishop Road
Berkeley Road
Zetland Rd
Cromwell Road
Station Rd
Coroners Court

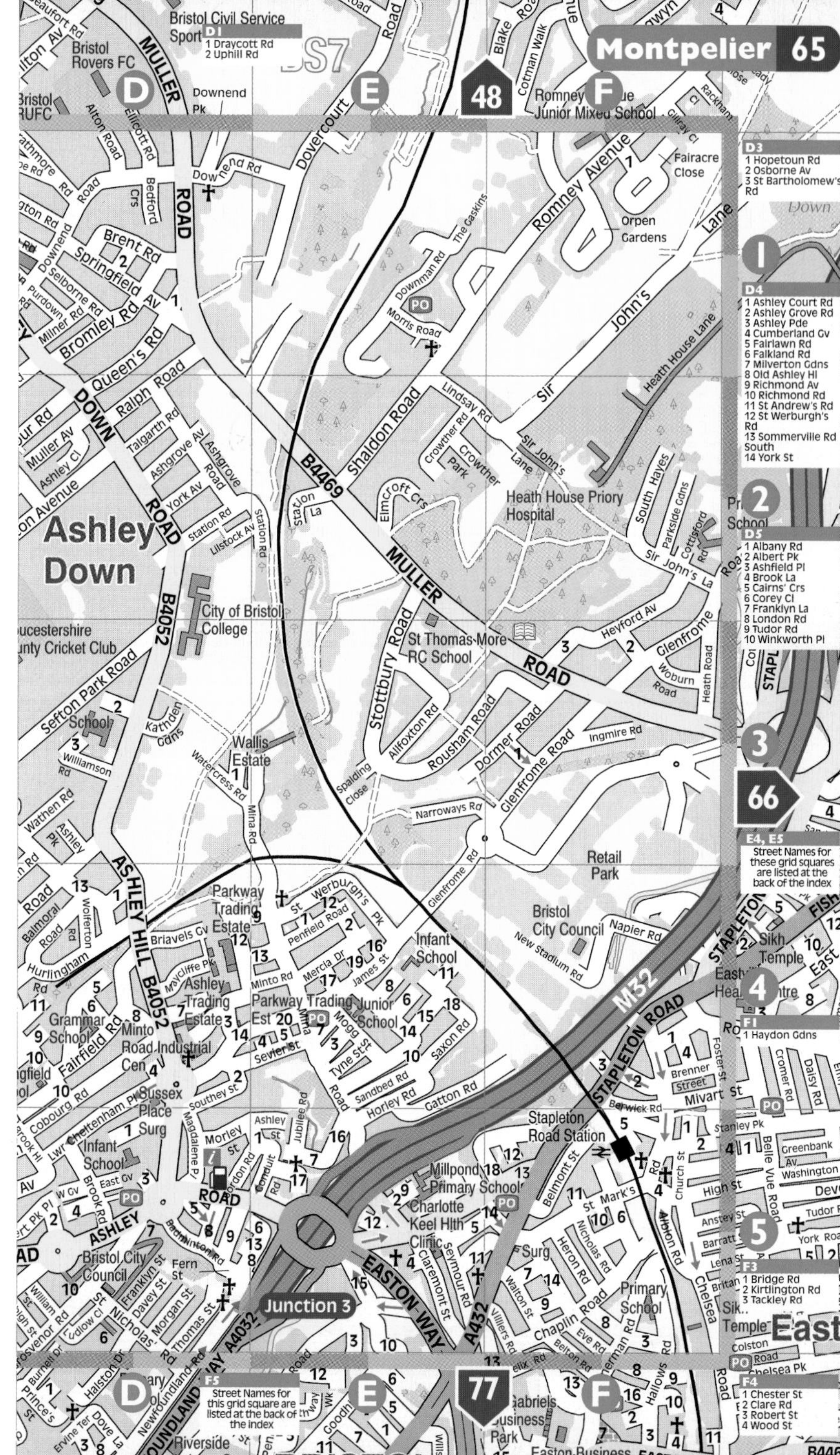

Montpelier 65
48
66
77
D1
1 Draycott Rd
2 Uphill Rd
D3
1 Hopetoun Rd
2 Osborne Av
3 St Bartholomew's Rd
D4
1 Ashley Court Rd
2 Ashley Grove Rd
3 Ashley Pde
4 Cumberland Gv
5 Fairlawn Rd
6 Falkland Rd
7 Milverton Gdns
8 Old Ashley Hl
9 Richmond Av
10 Richmond Rd
11 St Andrew's Rd
12 St Werburgh's Rd
13 Sommerville Rd South
14 York St
D5
1 Albany Rd
2 Albert Pk
3 Ashfield Pl
4 Brook La
5 Cairns' Crs
6 Corey Cl
7 Franklyn La
8 London Rd
9 Tudor Rd
10 Winkworth Pl
E4, E5
Street Names for these grid squares are listed at the back of the index
F1
1 Haydon Gdns
F3
1 Bridge Rd
2 Kirtlington Rd
3 Tackley Rd
F4
1 Chester St
2 Clare Rd
3 Robert St
4 Wood St
F5
Street Names for this grid square are listed at the back of the index
BS7
Bristol Civil Service Sport
Bristol Rovers FC
Bristol RUFC
Downend Pk
Romney Avenue Junior Mixed School
Fairacre Close
Orpen Gardens
Ashley Down
Muller Road
Ashley Down Road
B4469
B4052
Ashley Hill B4052
Sir John's Lane
Heath House Lane
Heath House Priory Hospital
City of Bristol College
Gloucestershire County Cricket Club
St Thomas More RC School
Wallis Estate
Parkway Trading Estate
Ashley Trading Estate
Parkway Trading Est
Infant School
Junior School
Retail Park
Bristol City Council
Minto Road Industrial Cen
Grammar School
Sussex Place Surg
Stapleton Road Station
Stapleton Road
Millpond Primary School
Charlotte Keel Hlth Clinic
Surg
Primary School
Sikh Temple
Eastville Health Centre
M32
A432
A4032
Easton Way
Junction 3
Newfoundland Way
Riverside Leisure Cen
Gabriels Business Park
Easton Business
B4465

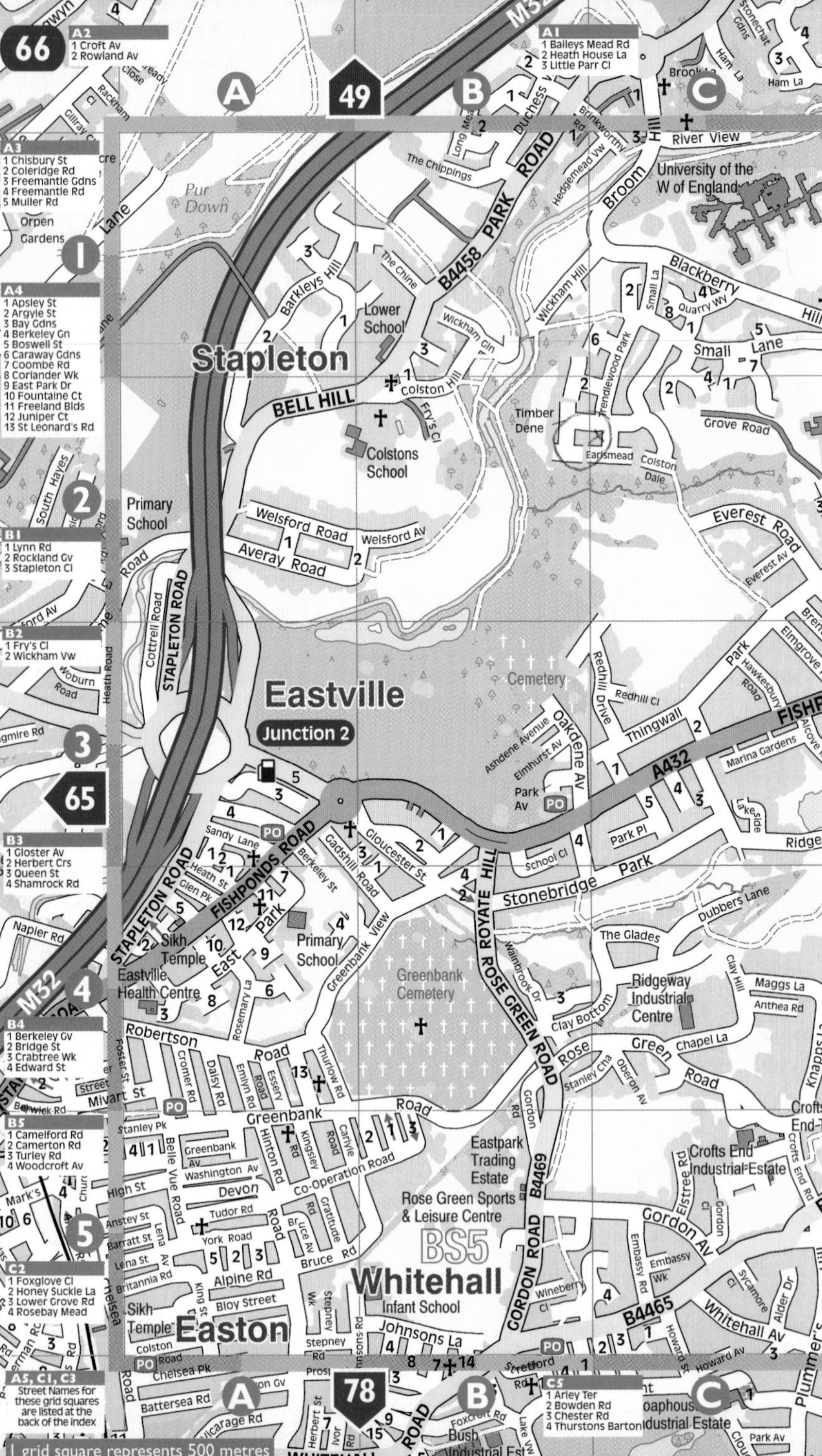
A2
1 Croft Av
2 Rowland Av
A1
1 Baileys Mead Rd
2 Heath House La
3 Little Parr Cl
A3
1 Chisbury St
2 Coleridge Rd
3 Freemantle Gdns
4 Freemantle Rd
5 Muller Rd
A4
1 Apsley St
2 Argyle St
3 Bay Gdns
4 Berkeley Gn
5 Boswell St
6 Caraway Gdns
7 Coombe Rd
8 Coriander Wk
9 East Park Dr
10 Fountaine Ct
11 Freeland Blds
12 Juniper Ct
13 St Leonard's Rd
B1
1 Lynn Rd
2 Rockland Gv
3 Stapleton Cl
B2
1 Fry's Cl
2 Wickham Vw
B3
1 Gloster Av
2 Herbert Crs
3 Queen St
4 Shamrock Rd
B4
1 Berkeley Gv
2 Bridge St
3 Crabtree Wk
4 Edward St
B5
1 Camelford Rd
2 Camerton Rd
3 Turley Rd
4 Woodcroft Av
C2
1 Foxglove Cl
2 Honey Suckle La
3 Lower Grove Rd
4 Rosebay Mead
A5, C1, C3
Street Names for these grid squares are listed at the back of the index
C5
1 Arley Ter
2 Bowden Rd
3 Chester Rd
4 Thurstons Barton
49
65
78
M32
Stapleton
Eastville
Junction 2
Whitehall
Easton
BS5
B4458 PARK ROAD
BELL HILL
STAPLETON ROAD
FISHPONDS ROAD
A432
ROSE GREEN ROAD
ROYATE HILL
GORDON ROAD
B4469
B4465
University of the W of England
Lower School
Colstons School
Primary School
Cemetery
Greenbank Cemetery
Sikh Temple
Eastville Health Centre
Ridgeway Industrial Centre
Crofts End Industrial Estate
Eastpark Trading Estate
Rose Green Sports & Leisure Centre
Infant School
Timber Dene
Pur Down
Orpen Gardens
The Chippings
The Chine
Barkleys Hill
Wickham Hill
Wickham Gln
Colston Hill
Hedgemead Vw
Brinkworthy Rd
Broom Hill
River View
Blackberry Hill
Quarry Wy
Small La
Small Lane
Trendlewood Park
Grove Road
Earlsmead
Colston Dale
Everest Road
Everest Av
Welsford Road
Welsford Av
Averay Road
Cottrell Road
Heath Road
Woburn Road
Ingmire Rd
Napier Rd
Redhill Drive
Redhill Cl
Oakdene Av
Ashdene Avenue
Elmhurst Av
Park Av
Thingwall Park
Hawkesbury Road
Elmgrove
Marina Gardens
Alcove Rd
Lake Side
Park Pl
School Cl
Stonebridge Park
Ridgeway
Dubbers Lane
The Glades
Clay Hill
Maggs La
Anthea Rd
Knapps La
Wainbrook Dr
Clay Bottom
Chapel La
Rose Green Road
Stanley Cha
Oberon Av
Crofts End
Crofts End Rd
Elstree Rd
Gordon Cl
Gordon Av
Embassy Rd
Embassy Wk
Wineberry Cl
Sycamore Cl
Alder Dr
Whitehall Av
Howard Av
Howard St
Plummer's Hill
Sandy Lane
Heath St
Glen Pk
East Park
Berkeley St
Gadshill Road
Gloucester St
Greenbank View
Rosemary La
Robertson Road
Cromer Rd
Daisy Rd
Emlyn Rd
Essery Road
Thurlow Rd
Mivart St
Greenbank Road
Stanley Pk
Greenbank Av
Hinton Rd
Kingsley Rd
Carlyle Road
Co-Operation Road
Belle Vue Road
Washington Av
High St
Devon Road
Gratitude Rd
Bruce Av
Bruce Rd
Tudor Rd
York Road
Anstey St
Barratt St
Lena Av
Lena St
Britannia Rd
Alpine Rd
King St
Bloy Street
Stepney Wk
Stepney Rd
Johnsons La
Johnsons Rd
Colston Road
Chelsea Pk
Chelsea Rd
Foster St
Berwick Rd
St Mark's
Nicholas Rd
Eve Rd
Battersea Rd
Vicarage Rd
Herbert St
Ivor Rd
Foxcroft Rd
Lake Vw
Bush Industrial Est
Soaphouse Industrial Estate
Stretford Rd
Park Av
Stonechat Gdns
Ham La
Brook La
Duchess Way
Long Mead
Rackham Cl
Gillray Cl
South Hayes
1 grid square represents 500 metres

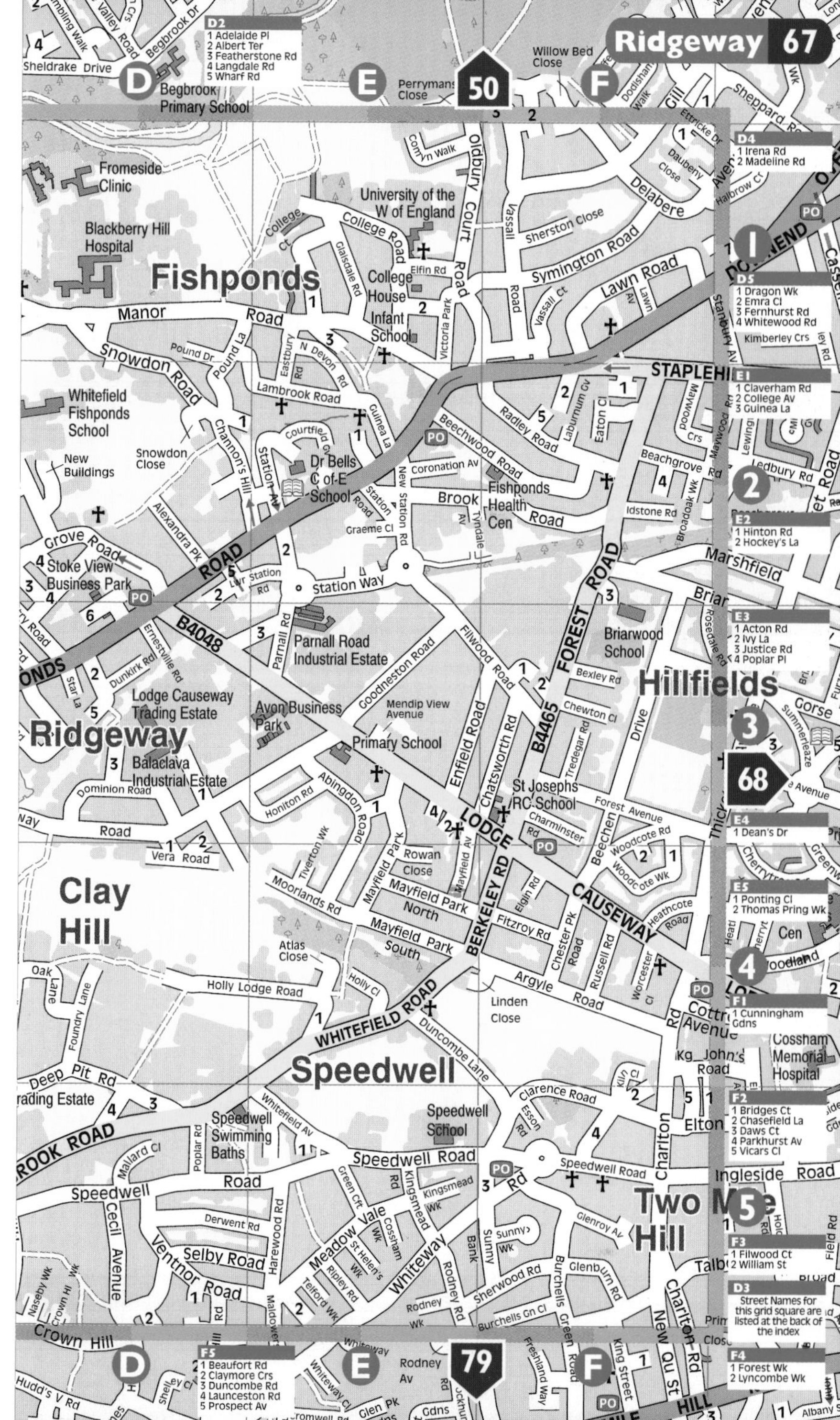

Ridgeway 67
D2
1 Adelaide Pl
2 Albert Ter
3 Featherstone Rd
4 Langdale Rd
5 Wharf Rd
D4
1 Irena Rd
2 Madeline Rd
D5
1 Dragon Wk
2 Emra Cl
3 Fernhurst Rd
4 Whitewood Rd
E1
1 Claverham Rd
2 College Av
3 Guinea La
E2
1 Hinton Rd
2 Hockey's La
E3
1 Acton Rd
2 Ivy La
3 Justice Rd
4 Poplar Pl
E4
1 Dean's Dr
E5
1 Ponting Cl
2 Thomas Pring Wk
F1
1 Cunningham Gdns
F2
1 Bridges Ct
2 Chasefield La
3 Daws Ct
4 Parkhurst Av
5 Vicars Cl
F3
1 Filwood Ct
2 William St
D3
Street Names for this grid square are listed at the back of the index
F4
1 Forest Wk
2 Lyncombe Wk
F5
1 Beaufort Rd
2 Claymore Crs
3 Duncombe Rd
4 Launceston Rd
5 Prospect Av
50
68
79
Fishponds
Ridgeway
Hillfields
Clay Hill
Speedwell
Two Mile Hill
Fromeside Clinic
Blackberry Hill Hospital
University of the W of England
College House Infant School
Whitefield Fishponds School
Dr Bells C of E School
Fishponds Health Cen
Briarwood School
Parnall Road Industrial Estate
Lodge Causeway Trading Estate
Avon Business Park
Mendip View Avenue Primary School
Balaclava Industrial Estate
St Josephs RC School
Speedwell Swimming Baths
Speedwell School
Cossham Memorial Hospital
Begbrook Primary School
Stoke View Business Park
Sheldrake Drive
Begbrook Dr
Perrymans Close
Willow Bed Close
Oldbury Court Road
Vassall Road
Sherston Close
Symington Road
Lawn Road
Delabere
Daubeny Close
Manor Road
Snowdon Road
Snowdon Close
Pound Dr
Pound La
Channon's Hill
Lambrook Road
College Road
Victoria Park
Beechwood Road
Radley Road
Coronation Av
Brook Road
New Station Rd
Station Road
Graeme Cl
Station Way
Grove Road
Alexandra Pk
Fishponds Road
B4048
Lodge Causeway
Forest Road
B4465
Filwood Road
Goodneston Road
Enfield Road
Chatsworth Rd
Beachgrove Rd
Idstone Rd
Marshfield
Bexley Rd
Chewton Cl
Tredegar Rd
Forest Avenue
Charminster Rd
Woodcote Rd
Woodcote Wk
Dominion Road
Vera Road
Honiton Rd
Abingdon Road
Rowan Close
Mayfield Park North
Mayfield Park South
Moorlands Rd
Berkeley Rd
Fitzroy Rd
Argyle Road
Heathcote Road
Atlas Close
Holly Lodge Road
Holly Cl
Whitefield Road
Duncombe Lane
Linden Close
Oak Lane
Foundry Lane
Deep Pit Rd
Begbrook Road
Clarence Road
Esson Rd
Kiln Cl
Charlton
Elton
Ingleside Road
Speedwell Road
Whitefield Av
Poplar Rd
Mallard Cl
Cecil Avenue
Derwent Rd
Selby Road
Ventnor Road
Harewood Rd
Meadow Vale
Kingsmead Wk
Whiteway
Rodney Rd
Sunny Wk
Glenroy Av
Sherwood Rd
Glenburn Rd
Burchells Green Road
Burchells Gn Cl
Charlton Rd
New Qu St
King Street
Crown Hill
Rodney Av
Freshland Way
Two Mile Hill

68
51
67
80
A3, B4
Street Names for these grid squares are listed at the back of the index
C1, C3, C5
Street Names for these grid squares are listed at the back of the index
A1
1 Pemberton Ct
A2
1 Edgeware Rd
A4
1 Coulson Wk
2 Henshaw Cl
3 Welton Wk
4 Wentforth Dr
5 Willow Gv
6 Woodland Cl
A5
1 Dalkeith Av
2 Lodgeside Av
3 Seymour Rd
4 Soundwell Rd
B1
1 Christchurch Av
2 Christchurch La
3 Downend Pk Rd
4 Nelson Rd
5 Tyler's La
B2
1 Alexandra Cl
2 Kensington Rd
3 Nelson Rd
4 North Vw
5 Pendennis Av
B3
1 Beazer Cl
2 Colston Cl
3 Leicester Sq
4 Portland Pl
5 Wesley Cl
B5
1 Brighton Pl
2 Chesham Wy
3 Gladstone Rd
4 Hampton St
5 Kennington Av
6 Kimberley Rd
7 Morley Ter
8 Wesley Hl
9 Worcester Rd
C2
1 Byron Pl
2 Eastleigh Cl
3 Fiennes Cl
4 Irving Cl
5 James Cl
6 Saunders Rd
7 Shipnran Ct
8 Teewell Cl
C4
1 Blackthorn Wk
2 Deerhurst
3 Frys Hl
4 Pembroke Rd
5 Tyndale Rd
Staple Hill
Soundwell
Hillfields
Downend Road
Overndale Road
A432
North Street
Victoria Street
High Street
Staplehill Road
Broad Street A4175
Teewell Hill
Soundwell Road
Lodge Hill
Lodge Road
Downend Road
A4017
A420
Frenchay Health Authority
Christchurch Junior School
Downend Surgery
Doctors Surgery
Downend Cricket Club
Infant School
The Surgery
The Clinic
Kingswood Borough Council
Primary School
Hayward Road Industrial Estate
Kingswood Leisure Centre
Soundwell Coll
St Stephens C of E VC Junior School
Avondale Business Cen
Lonsdale Business Cen
Cossham Memorial Hospital
Oatley Trading Estate
Kings Chase Shop Cen
Kingswood Health Cen
Civic Centre
The Orchard Medical Cen
Beachgrove Gardens
Marshfield Road
Briar Way
Corse Hill
Maple Avenue
The Greenway
Cherrytree Crs
Woodland Way
Cotswold View
Syston Way
New Cheltenham Road
Ingleside Road
Elton Road
Talbot Av
Broad Rd
Portland Street
Midland Road
Gladstone Street
Pool Road
Church Road
Hilltop Road
Crown Road
Teewell Avenue
West Park Road
Pleasant Road
Upper Station Road
Acacia Road
Uplands Road
Colston St
Morley Road
Narrow Lane
Seymour Road
1 grid square represents 500 metres

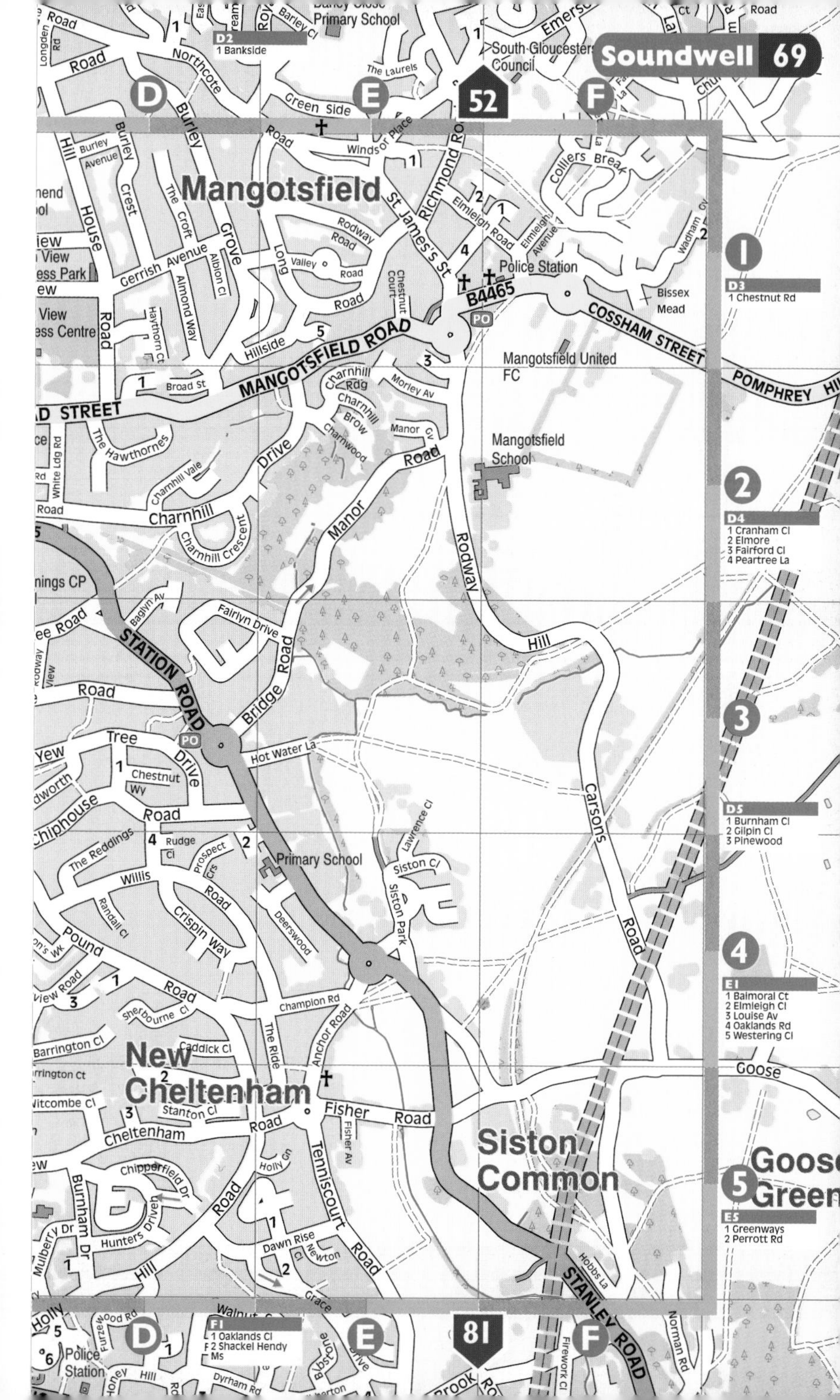

Mangotsfield
New Cheltenham
Siston Common
Goose Green
D2
1 Bankside
D3
1 Chestnut Rd
D4
1 Cranham Cl
2 Elmore
3 Fairford Cl
4 Peartree La
D5
1 Burnham Cl
2 Gilpin Cl
3 Pinewood
E1
1 Balmoral Ct
2 Elmleigh Cl
3 Louise Av
4 Oaklands Rd
5 Westering Cl
E5
1 Greenways
2 Perrott Rd
F1
1 Oaklands Cl
2 Shackel Hendy Ms
52
81
MANGOTSFIELD ROAD
COSSHAM STREET
POMPHREY HILL
STATION ROAD
STANLEY ROAD
B4465
Police Station
Mangotsfield United FC
Mangotsfield School
Primary School
South Gloucestershire Council
Rodway Hill
Carsons Road
Manor Road
Bridge Road
Fisher Road
Tenniscourt Road
Siston Park
Hot Water La
Charnhill Drive
Charnhill Crescent
Richmond Road
St James's St
Northcote Road
Burley Grove
Gerrish Avenue
Chiphouse Road
Pound Road
Willis Road
Crispin Way
Deerswood
Champion Rd
Anchor Road
The Ride
Cheltenham Road
Burnham Dr
Hunters Drive
Dawn Rise
Goose

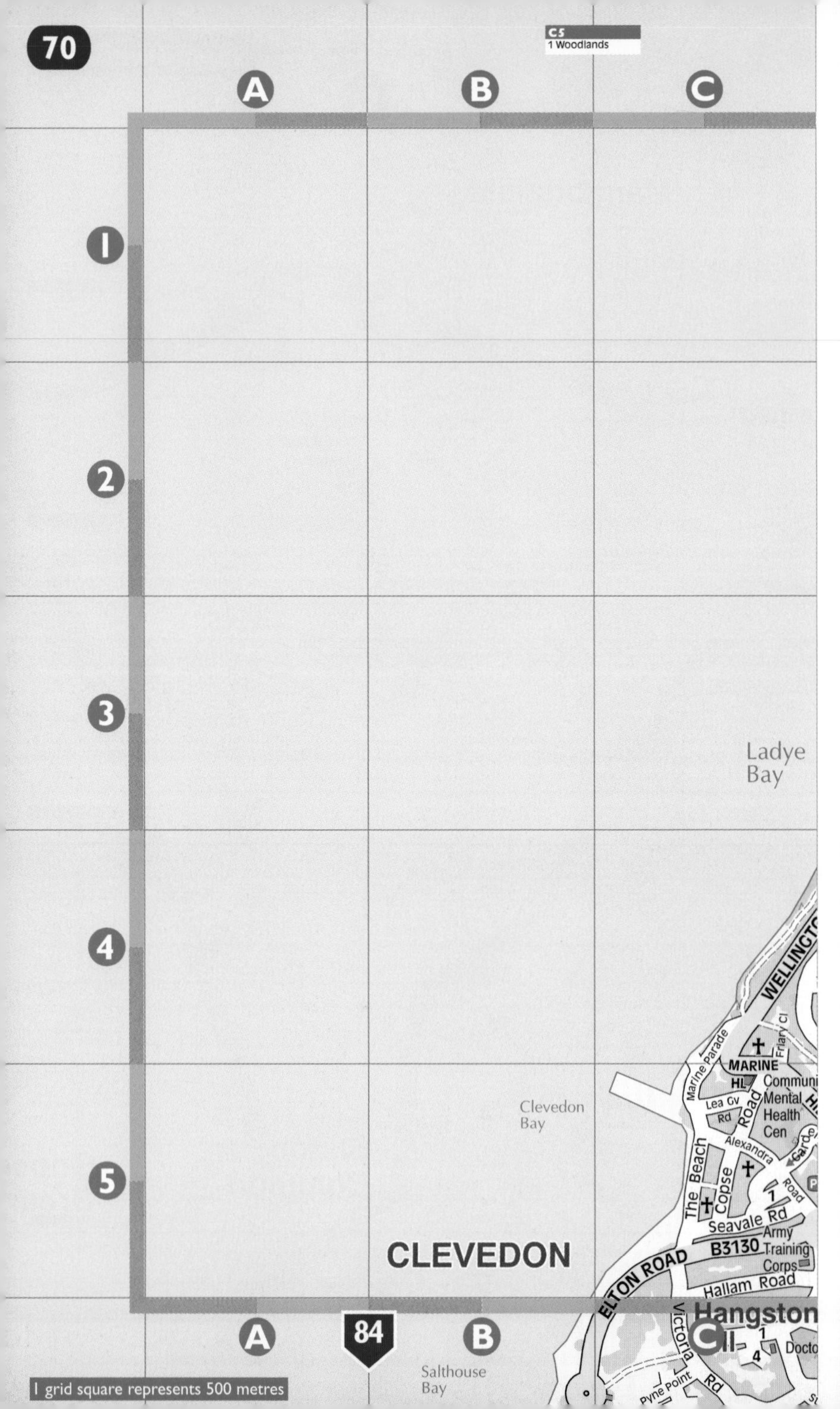
C5
1 Woodlands
A
B
C
1
2
3
4
5
Ladye
Bay
WELLINGTON
Marine Parade
Friary Cl
MARINE
HL
Communi
Mental
Health
Cen
Lea Gv
Rd
Road
Alexandra
Road
The Beach
Copse
1
Seavale Rd
Army
Training
Corps
B3130
ELTON ROAD
Hallam Road
Clevedon
Bay
CLEVEDON
Hangston
Hill
Victoria
Rd
Pyne Point
1
4
Docto
84
Salthouse
Bay
1 grid square represents 500 metres

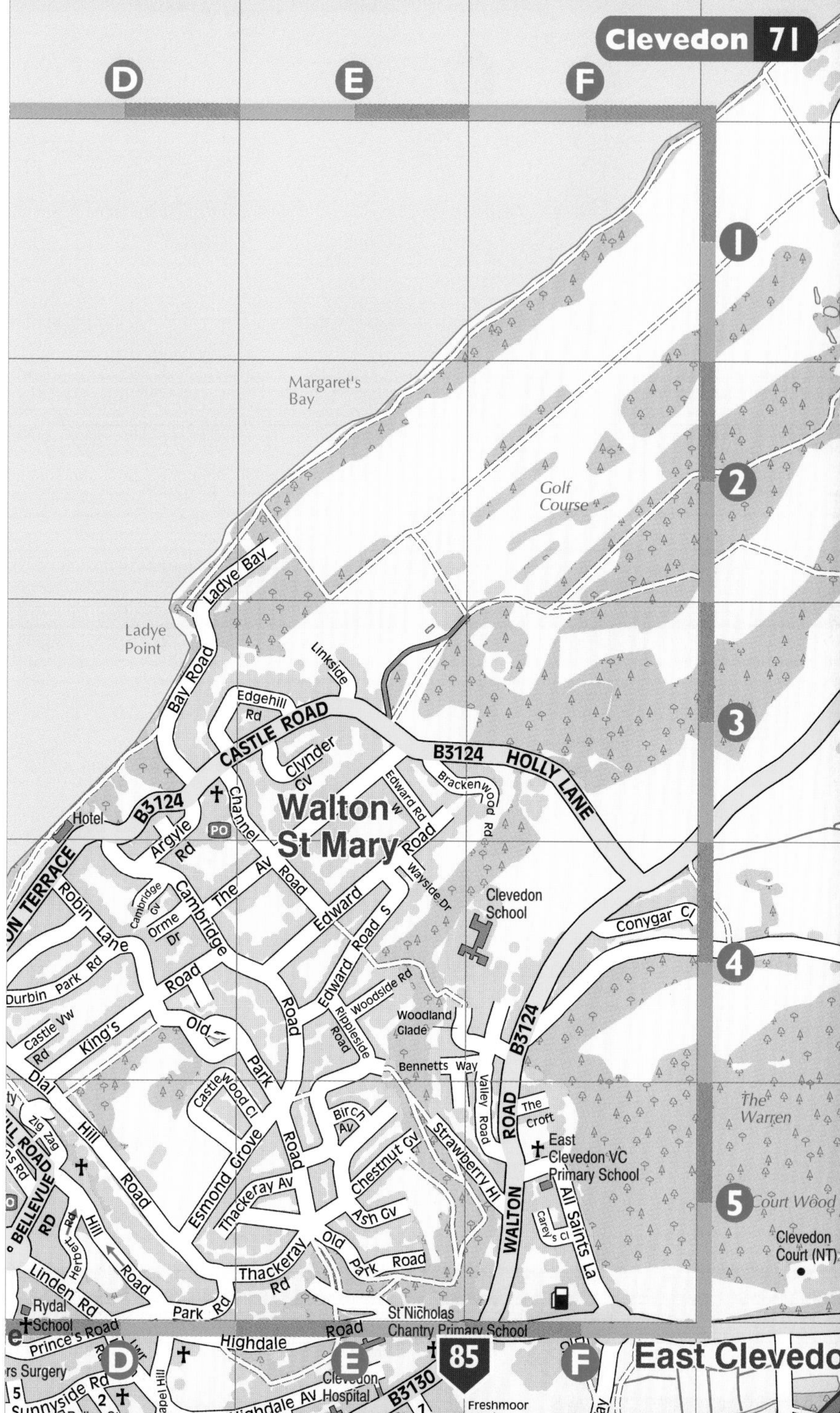
D
E
F
1
2
3
4
5
Margaret's Bay
Golf Course
Ladye Point
Ladye Bay
Bay Road
Linkside
Edgehill Rd
CASTLE ROAD
Clynder Gv
B3124
HOLLY LANE
Hotel
Argyle Rd
Channel Road
Walton St Mary
Edward Rd W
Edward Road
Brackenwood Rd
Wayside Dr
Clevedon School
Conygar Cl
Robin Lane
Cambridge Gv
Orme Dr
Cambridge Road
The Av
Edward Road S
Durbin Park Rd
King's Road
Old Park Road
Woodside Rd
Woodland Glade
Ripple Road
Bennetts Way
Valley Road
WALTON ROAD
Castle Vw Rd
Dial Hill Road
Castlewood Cl
Esmond Grove
Birch Av
Chestnut Gv
Strawberry Hl
The Croft
East Clevedon VC Primary School
All Saints La
Carey's Cl
The Warren
Court Wood
Clevedon Court (NT)
BELLEVUE RD
HILL ROAD
Zig Zag
Herbert Rd
Hill Road
Linden Rd
Thackeray Av
Ash Gv
Thackeray Rd
Old Park Road
Park Rd
Rydal School
Prince's Road
Highdale Road
St Nicholas Chantry Primary School
85
East Clevedon
Surgery
Sunnyside Rd
Police Stn
Chapel Hill
Highdale Av
Clevedon Hospital
B3130
Freshmoor
Clevedon Health

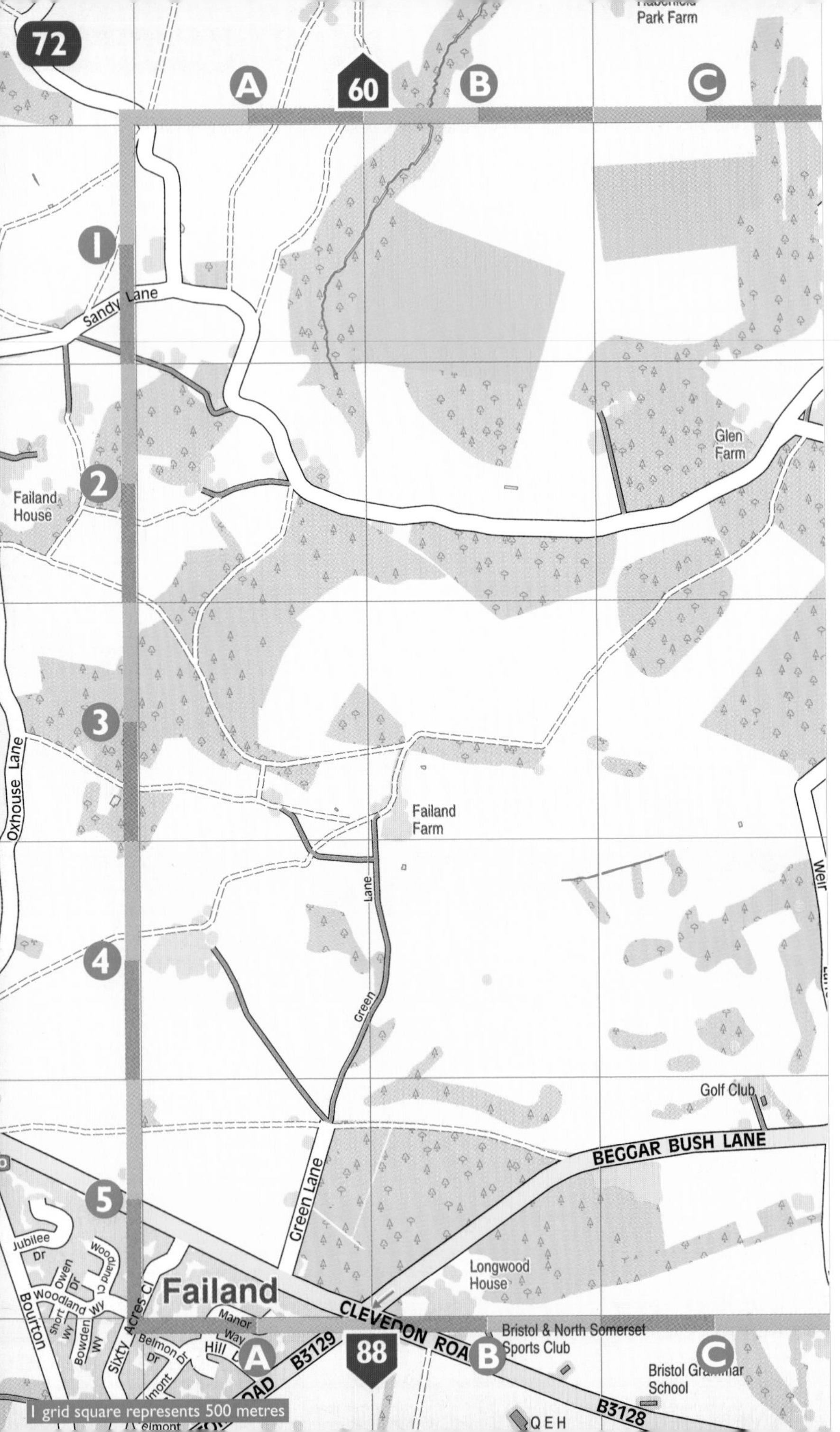
Park Farm
A
60
B
C
1
Sandy Lane
2
Failand House
Glen Farm
3
Oxhouse Lane
Failand Farm
Lane
4
Green
Weir
Golf Club
BEGGAR BUSH LANE
5
Green Lane
Jubilee Dr
Woodland Cl
Owen Dr
Woodland Wy
Bourton
Short Wy
Bowden Wy
Sixty Acres Cl
Failand
Longwood House
Manor Way
Hill
Belmont Dr
CLEVEDON ROAD
B3129
A
88
B
Bristol & North Somerset Sports Club
C
Bristol Grammar School
B3128
QEH
1 grid square represents 500 metres

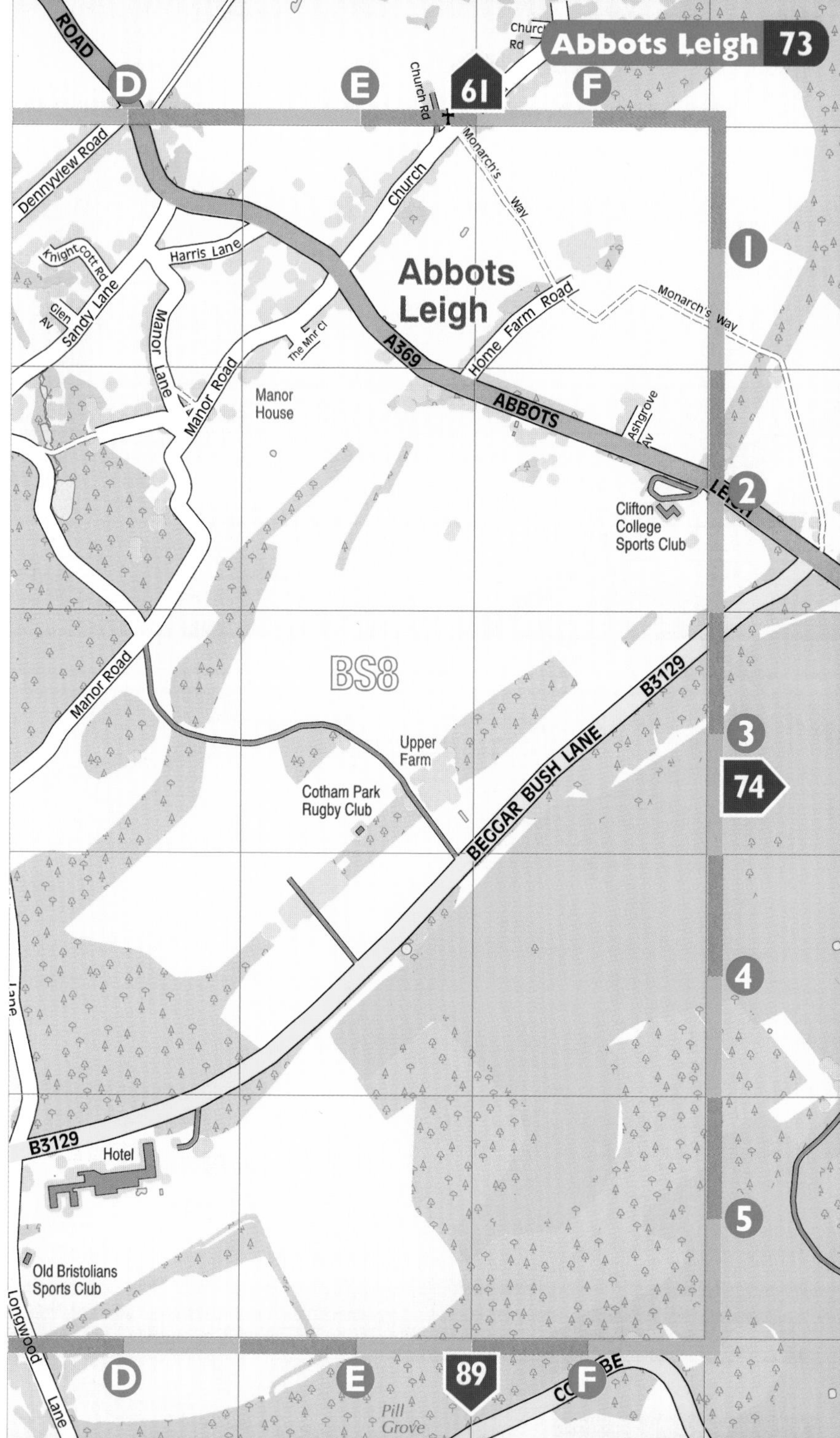
ROAD
D
E
F
Church Rd
61
Church Rd
Dennyview Road
Church
Monarch's Way
Knight Cott Rd
Harris Lane
Abbots Leigh
Glen Av
Sandy Lane
Manor Lane
The Mnr Cl
Home Farm Road
Monarch's Way
A369
Manor Road
Manor House
ABBOTS
Ashgrove Av
LEIGH
Clifton College Sports Club
1
2
3
4
5
BS8
Manor Road
B3129
BEGGAR BUSH LANE
Upper Farm
Cotham Park Rugby Club
74
Lane
B3129
Hotel
Old Bristolians Sports Club
Longwood Lane
89
Pill Grove
COMBE

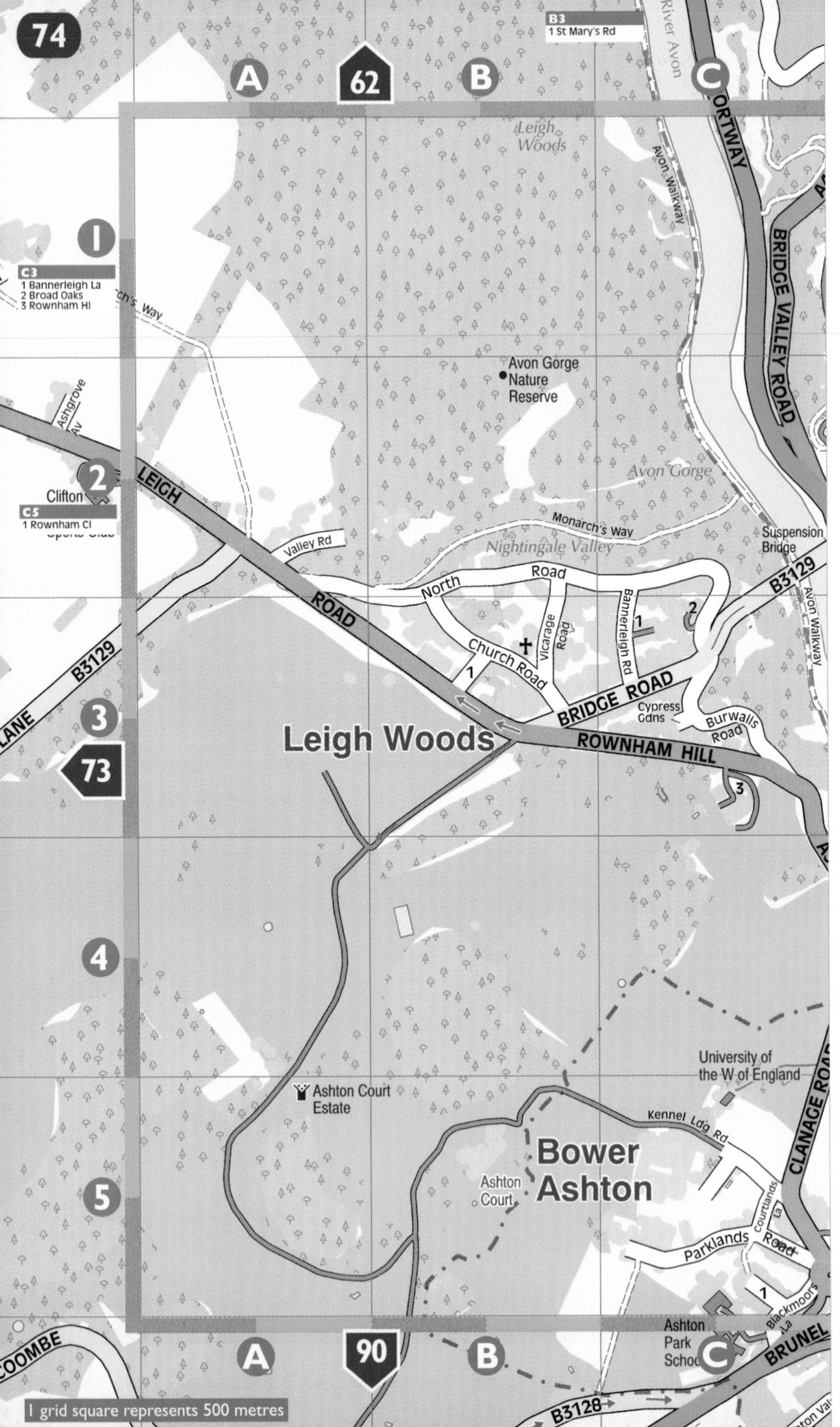
62
A
B
C
B3
1 St Mary's Rd
River Avon
PORTWAY
Leigh Woods
Avon Walkway
BRIDGE VALLEY ROAD
C3
1 Bannerleigh La
2 Broad Oaks
3 Rownham Hl
Monarch's Way
Avon Gorge Nature Reserve
Ashgrove Av
Avon Gorge
Clifton
C5
1 Rownham Cl
LEIGH ROAD
Valley Rd
Monarch's Way
Nightingale Valley
Suspension Bridge
North Road
B3129
Vicarage Road
Bannerleigh Rd
Church Road
BRIDGE ROAD
Cypress Gdns
Burwalls Road
Leigh Woods
ROWNHAM HILL
LANE
B3129
73
Ashton Court Estate
University of the W of England
Kennel Ldg Rd
Bower Ashton
Ashton Court
CLANAGE ROAD
Courtlands La
Parklands Road
Blackmoors La
Ashton Park Schoo
COOMBE
90
BRUNEL
B3128
1 grid square represents 500 metres

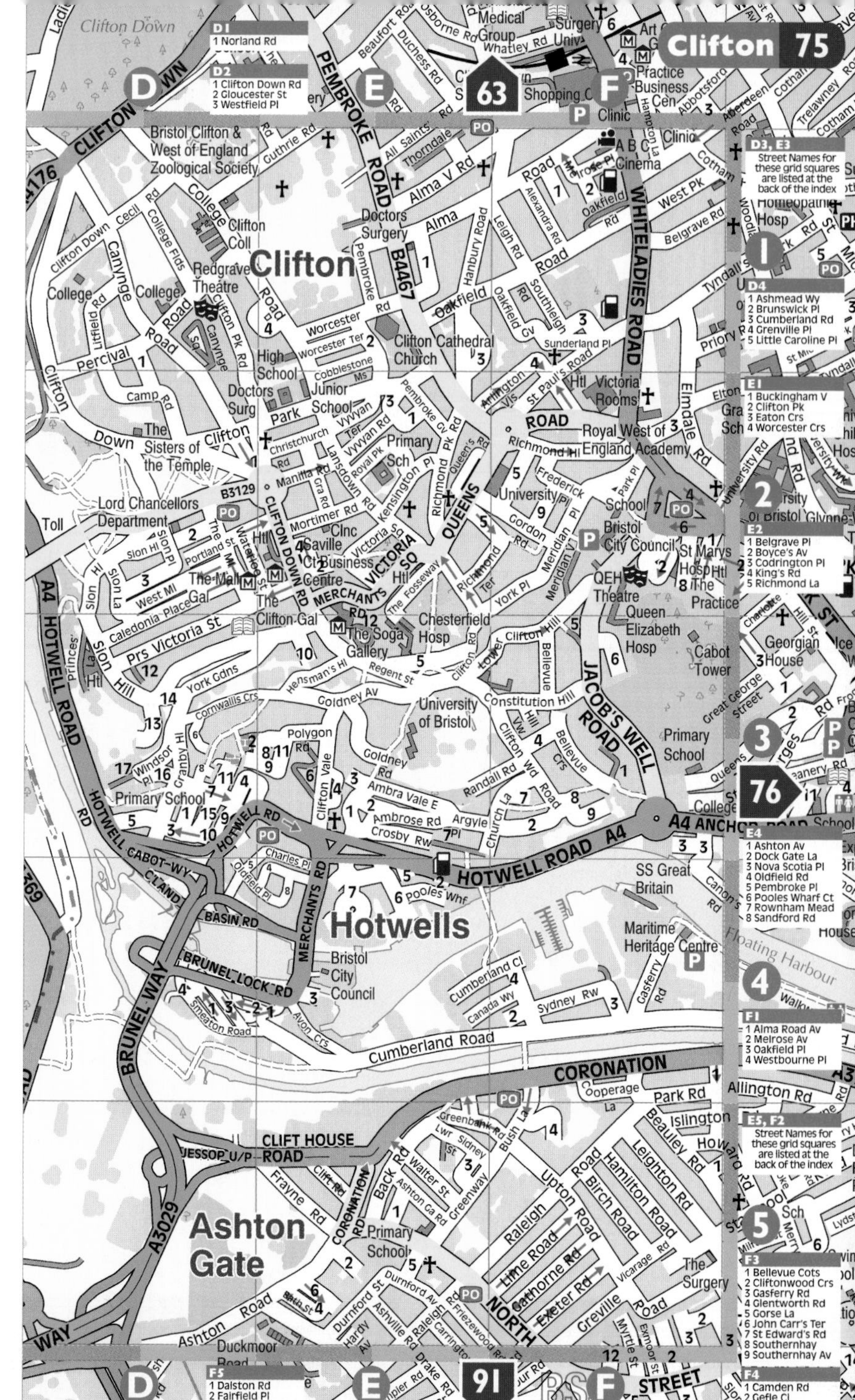
D1
1 Norland Rd
D2
1 Clifton Down Rd
2 Gloucester St
3 Westfield Pl
D3, E3
Street Names for these grid squares are listed at the back of the index
D4
1 Ashmead Wy
2 Brunswick Pl
3 Cumberland Rd
4 Grenville Pl
5 Little Caroline Pl
E1
1 Buckingham V
2 Clifton Pk
3 Eaton Crs
4 Worcester Crs
E2
1 Belgrave Pl
2 Boyce's Av
3 Codrington Pl
4 King's Rd
5 Richmond La
E4
1 Ashton Av
2 Dock Gate La
3 Nova Scotia Pl
4 Oldfield Rd
5 Pembroke Pl
6 Pooles Wharf Ct
7 Rownham Mead
8 Sandford Rd
F1
1 Alma Road Av
2 Melrose Av
3 Oakfield Pl
4 Westbourne Pl
E5, F2
Street Names for these grid squares are listed at the back of the index
F3
1 Bellevue Cots
2 Cliftonwood Crs
3 Gasferry Rd
4 Glentworth Rd
5 Gorse La
6 John Carr's Ter
7 St Edward's Rd
8 Southernhay
9 Southernhay Av
F4
1 Camden Rd
2 Gefle Cl
3 Hanover Pl
4 Mardyke Ferry Rd
F5
1 Dalston Rd
2 Fairfield Pl
3 King William St
4 Phipps St
Clifton Down
Bristol Clifton & West of England Zoological Society
Clifton
Clifton Coll
Redgrave Theatre
Clifton Cathedral Church
High School
Junior School
Royal West of England Academy
Victoria Rooms
University of Bristol
Bristol City Council
QEH Theatre
Queen Elizabeth Hosp
Cabot Tower
Georgian House
Chesterfield Hosp
The Soga Gallery
The Clifton Gal
Lord Chancellors Department
Hotwells
SS Great Britain
Maritime Heritage Centre
Floating Harbour
Ashton Gate
Bristol City FC
WHITELADIES ROAD
QUEENS ROAD
JACOB'S WELL ROAD
HOTWELL ROAD A4
A4 HOTWELL ROAD
A4 ANCHOR ROAD
CLIFTON DOWN RD
MERCHANTS RD
BRUNEL WAY
CORONATION
CLIFT HOUSE ROAD
Cumberland Road
PEMBROKE ROAD
B4467
B3129
A3029
A4176
63
76
91
D
E
F
1
2
3
4
5

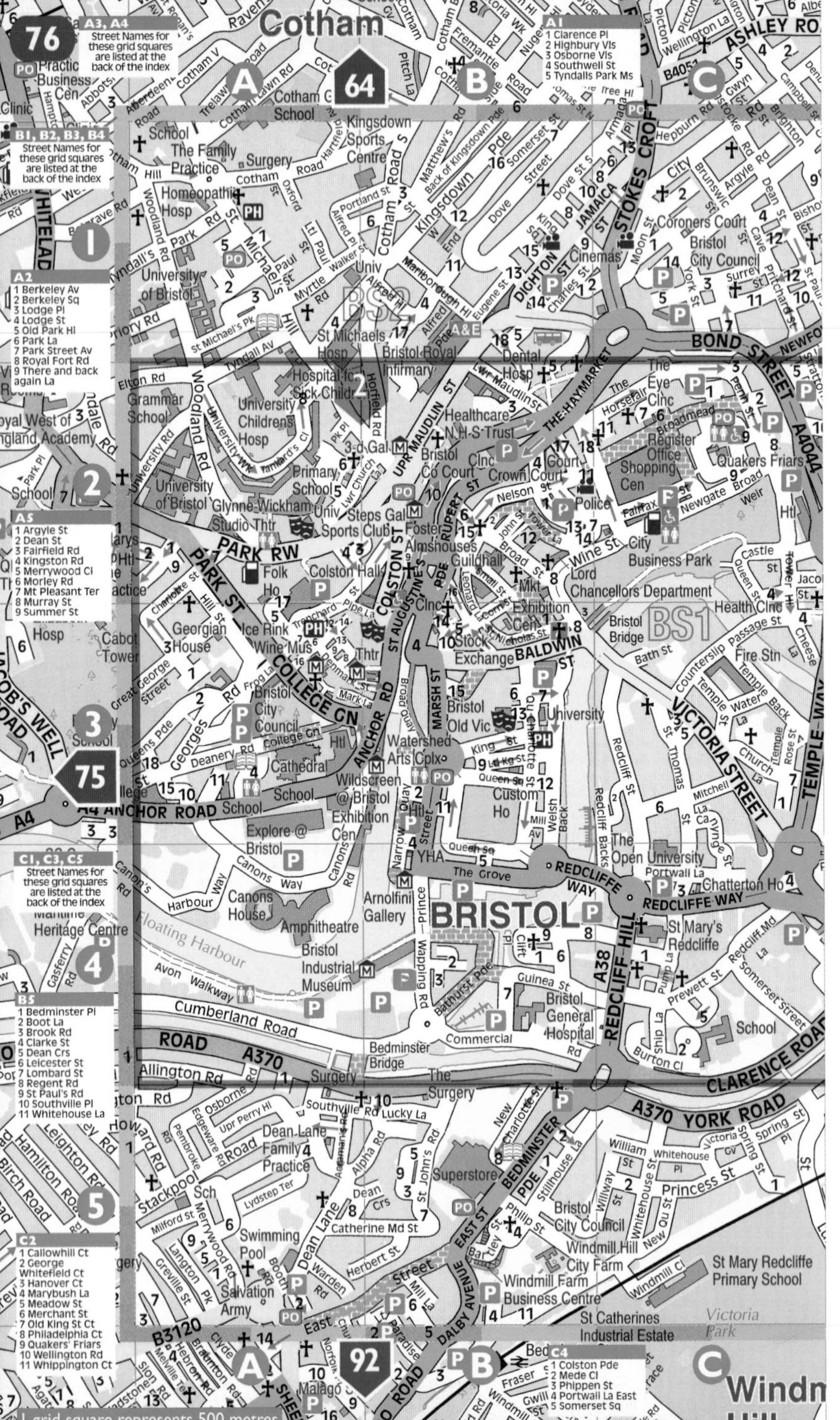
76
A3, A4
Street Names for these grid squares are listed at the back of the index
Cotham
64
A1
1 Clarence Pl
2 Highbury Vls
3 Osborne Vls
4 Southwell St
5 Tyndalls Park Ms
B1, B2, B3, B4
Street Names for these grid squares are listed at the back of the index
A2
1 Berkeley Av
2 Berkeley Sq
3 Lodge Pl
4 Lodge St
5 Old Park Hl
6 Park La
7 Park Street Av
8 Royal Fort Rd
9 There and back again La
A5
1 Argyle St
2 Dean St
3 Fairfield Rd
4 Kingston Rd
5 Merrywood Cl
6 Morley Rd
7 Mt Pleasant Ter
8 Murray St
9 Summer St
75
C1, C3, C5
Street Names for these grid squares are listed at the back of the index
B5
1 Bedminster Pl
2 Boot La
3 Brook Rd
4 Clarke St
5 Dean Crs
6 Leicester St
7 Lombard St
8 Regent Rd
9 St Paul's Rd
10 Southville Pl
11 Whitehouse La
C2
1 Callowhill Ct
2 George Whitefield Ct
3 Hanover Ct
4 Marybush La
5 Meadow St
6 Merchant St
7 Old King St Ct
8 Philadelphia Ct
9 Quakers' Friars
10 Wellington Rd
11 Whippington Ct
C4
1 Colston Pde
2 Mede Cl
3 Phippen St
4 Portwall La East
5 Somerset Sq
92
BS2
BS1
BRISTOL
STOKES CROFT
BOND STREET
THE HAYMARKET
PARK RW
PARK ST
COLLEGE GN
ANCHOR RD
COLSTON ST
ST AUGUSTINE'S PDE
MARSH ST
BALDWIN ST
VICTORIA STREET
TEMPLE WAY
REDCLIFFE WAY
REDCLIFF HILL
A4 ANCHOR ROAD
CUMBERLAND ROAD
A370
CLARENCE ROAD
A370 YORK ROAD
BEDMINSTER PDE
EAST ST
DALBY AVENUE
Floating Harbour
Bristol Royal Infirmary
Bristol Cathedral
Bristol Old Vic
Bristol Industrial Museum
Bristol General Hospital
St Mary's Redcliffe
Shopping Cen
Lord Chancellors Department
City Business Park
Windmill Hill City Farm
St Mary Redcliffe Primary School
St Catherines Industrial Estate
Victoria Park
Windmill Hill
1 grid square represents 500 metres

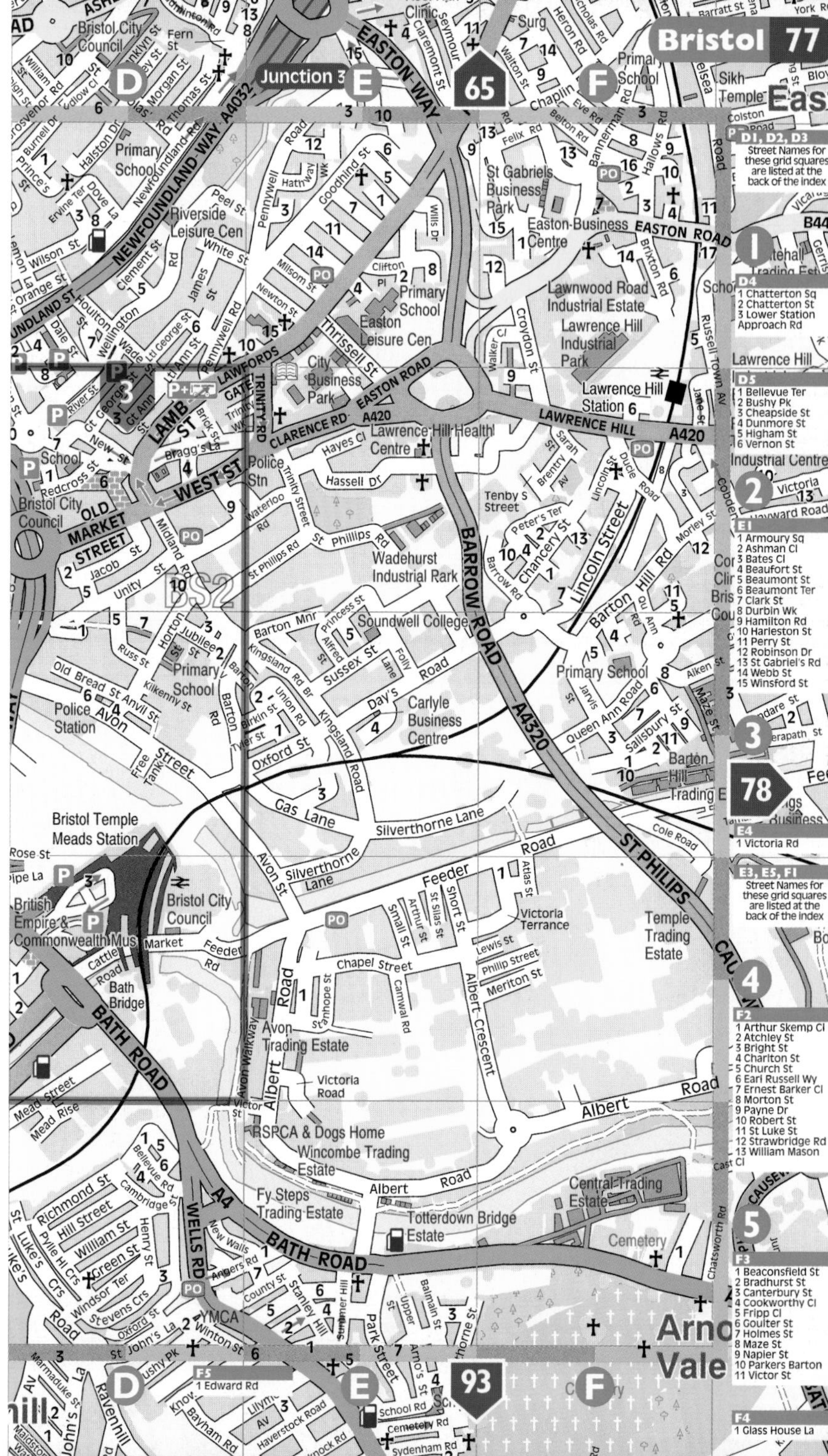

D1, D2, D3
Street Names for these grid squares are listed at the back of the index

D4
1 Chatterton Sq
2 Chatterton St
3 Lower Station Approach Rd

D5
1 Bellevue Ter
2 Bushy Pk
3 Cheapside St
4 Dunmore St
5 Higham St
6 Vernon St

E1
1 Armoury Sq
2 Ashman Cl
3 Bates Cl
4 Beaufort St
5 Beaumont St
6 Beaumont Ter
7 Clark St
8 Durbin Wk
9 Hamilton Rd
10 Harleston St
11 Perry St
12 Robinson Dr
13 St Gabriel's Rd
14 Webb St
15 Winsford St

E4
1 Victoria Rd

E3, E5, F1
Street Names for these grid squares are listed at the back of the index

F2
1 Arthur Skemp Cl
2 Atchley St
3 Bright St
4 Charlton St
5 Church St
6 Earl Russell Wy
7 Ernest Barker Cl
8 Morton St
9 Payne Dr
10 Robert St
11 St Luke St
12 Strawbridge Rd
13 William Mason Cl

F3
1 Beaconsfield St
2 Bradhurst St
3 Canterbury St
4 Cookworthy Cl
5 Fripp Cl
6 Goulter St
7 Holmes St
8 Maze St
9 Napier St
10 Parkers Barton
11 Victor St

F4
1 Glass House La

F5
1 Edward Rd

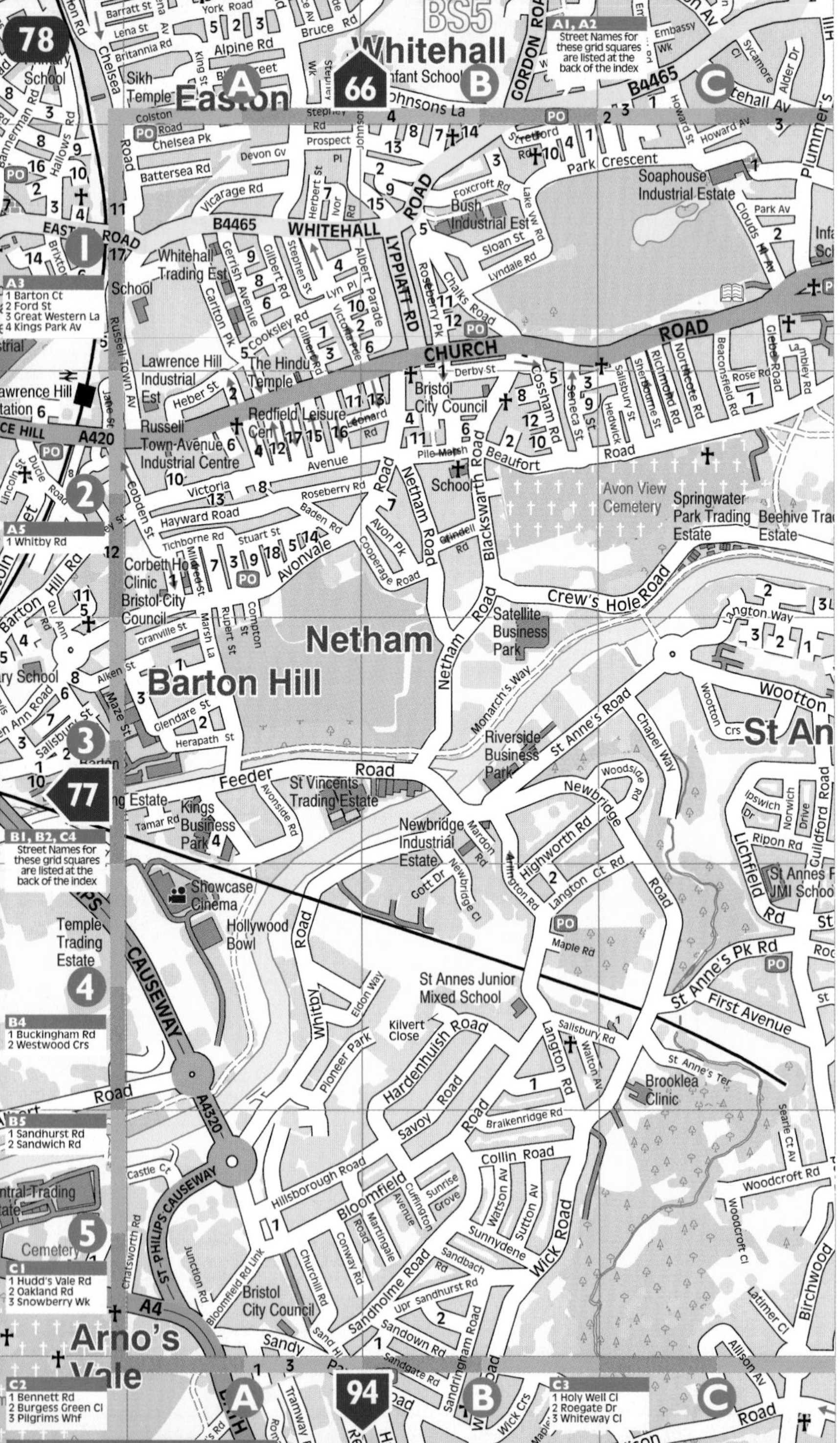

78
66
77
94
BS5
Whitehall
Easton
A1, A2
Street Names for these grid squares are listed at the back of the index
A3
1 Barton Ct
2 Ford St
3 Great Western La
4 Kings Park Av
A5
1 Whitby Rd
B1, B2, C4
Street Names for these grid squares are listed at the back of the index
B4
1 Buckingham Rd
2 Westwood Crs
B5
1 Sandhurst Rd
2 Sandwich Rd
C1
1 Hudd's Vale Rd
2 Oakland Rd
3 Snowberry Wk
C2
1 Bennett Rd
2 Burgess Green Cl
3 Pilgrims Whf
C3
1 Holy Well Cl
2 Roegate Dr
3 Whiteway Cl
York Road
Alpine Rd
Bruce Rd
Barratt St
Lena St
Britannia Rd
Chelsea Rd
Sikh Temple
Primary School
Bannerman Rd
Hallows Rd
Colston Road
Chelsea Pk
Devon Gv
Battersea Rd
Vicarage Rd
Prospect Pl
Johnsons La
Infant School
GORDON ROAD
Embassy Wk
B4465
Sycamore Cl
Alder Dr
Whitehall Av
Howard St
Howard Av
Plummer's Hill
Stretford Rd
Park Crescent
Soaphouse Industrial Estate
Park Av
Clouds Hill Av
Foxcroft Rd
Bush Industrial Est
Lake Vw Rd
Sloan St
Lyndale Rd
Chalks Road
Rosebery Pk
Herbert St
Ivor Rd
WHITEHALL ROAD
LYPPIATT RD
EASTON ROAD
Whitehall Trading Est
Gerrish Avenue
Gilbert Rd
Stephen St
Albert Parade
Lyn Pl
Victoria Pde
Carlton Pk
Cooksley Rd
School
Russell Town Av
Lawrence Hill Industrial Est
The Hindu Temple
CHURCH ROAD
Derby St
Bristol City Council
Cossham Rd
Seneca St
Salisbury St
Sherbourne St
Richmond Rd
Northcote Rd
Beaconsfield Rd
Rose Rd
Glebe Road
Lambley Rd
Lawrence Hill Station
LAWRENCE HILL
A420
Heber St
Redfield Leisure Cen
Leonard Rd
Russell Town Avenue Industrial Centre
Pile Marsh
Beaufort Road
Avon View Cemetery
Springwater Park Trading Estate
Beehive Trading Estate
Lincoln St
Ducie Road
Cobden St
Victoria Avenue
Roseberry Rd
Hayward Road
Baden Rd
Netham Road
Blackswarth Road
Tichborne Rd
Stuart St
Avonvale
Avon Pk
Cooperage Road
Grindell Rd
Mildred St
Corbett House Clinic
Bristol City Council
Barton Hill Rd
Crew's Hole Road
Langton Way
Satellite Business Park
Netham
Granville St
Marsh La
Rupert St
Compton St
Alken St
Barton Hill
Maze St
Monarch's Way
Wootton Crs
Wootton
St Anne's Road
Chapel Way
St Annes
Glendare St
Herapath St
Salisbury St
Jarvis
Queen Ann Road
Riverside Business Park
Woodside Rd
Newbridge Road
Feeder Road
St Vincents Trading Estate
Avonside Rd
Kings Business Park
Tamar Rd
Trading Estate
Newbridge Industrial Estate
Mardon Rd
Highworth Rd
Ipswich Dr
Norwich Drive
Guildford Road
Ripon Rd
Lichfield Rd
St Annes Park JMI School
Showcase Cinema
Hollywood Bowl
Gott Dr
Newbridge Cl
Arlington Rd
Langton Ct Rd
Maple Rd
Temple Trading Estate
ST PHILIPS CAUSEWAY
Whitby Road
Eldon Way
St Annes Junior Mixed School
St Anne's Pk Rd
First Avenue
Kilvert Close
Pioneer Park
Hardenhuish Road
Langton Rd
Salisbury Rd
Walton Av
St Anne's Ter
Brooklea Clinic
Searle Ct Av
A4320
Albert Road
Savoy Road
Braikenridge Rd
Castle Ct
Collin Road
Woodcroft Rd
Woodcroft Cl
Central Trading Estate
Hillsborough Road
Bloomfield Road
Cuffington Avenue
Sunrise Grove
Watson Av
Sutton Av
Wick Road
Cemetery
Chatsworth Rd
Junction Rd
Bloomfield Rd Link
Conway Rd
Martingale Road
Sunnydene
Sandbach Rd
Churchill Rd
Sandholme Road
Upr Sandhurst Rd
Latimer Cl
Birchwood Road
A4
Bristol City Council
Arno's Vale
Sandown Rd
Sandringham Road
Sandgate Rd
Allison Av
Sandy Park Road
Tramway Road
Wick Crs
Allison Road
Rugby
1 grid square represents 500 metres

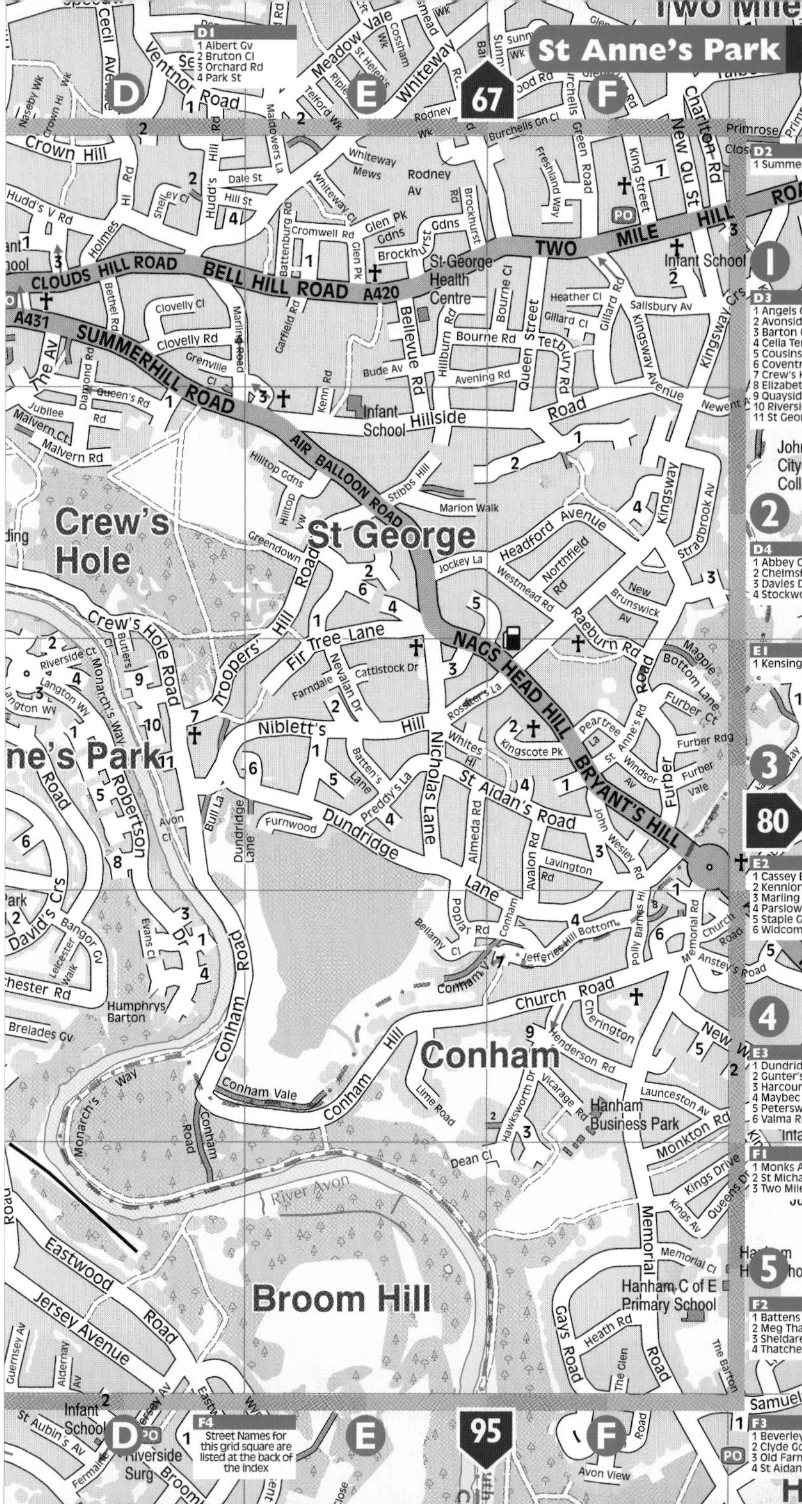
D1
1 Albert Gv
2 Bruton Cl
3 Orchard Rd
4 Park St
D2
1 Summerhill Ter
D3
1 Angels Gnd
2 Avonside Wy
3 Barton Cl
4 Celia Ter
5 Cousins Ms
6 Coventry Wk
7 Crew's Hole Rd
8 Elizabeths Ms
9 Quayside La
10 Riverside Wk
11 St Georges Av
D4
1 Abbey Ct
2 Chelmsford Wk
3 Davies Dr
4 Stockwood Ms
E1
1 Kensington Rd
E2
1 Cassey Bottom La
2 Kennion Rd
3 Marling Rd
4 Parslow Barton
5 Staple Grove Crs
6 Widcombe Cl
E3
1 Dundridge Gdns
2 Gunter's Hl
3 Harcourt Av
4 Maybec Gdns
5 Petersway Gdns
6 Valma Rocks
F1
1 Monks Av
2 St Michaels Ct
3 Two Mile Ct
F2
1 Battens Rd
2 Meg Thatchers Cl
3 Sheldare Barton
4 Thatchers Cl
F3
1 Beverley Cl
2 Clyde Gdns
3 Old Farm La
4 St Aidan's Cl
F4
Street Names for this grid square are listed at the back of the index
67
80
95
St George
Crew's Hole
Conham
Broom Hill
Two Mile Hill Road
Clouds Hill Road
Bell Hill Road A420
Summerhill Road A431
Air Balloon Road
Nags Head Hill
Bryant's Hill
Crew's Hole Road
Conham Road
Conham Hill
Church Road
Hillside Road
Dundridge Lane
Nicholas Lane
St Aidan's Road
Niblett's Hill
Fir Tree Lane
Troopers' Hill Road
Headford Avenue
Kingsway
Kingsway Avenue
Memorial Road
Eastwood Road
Jersey Avenue
River Avon
St George Health Centre
Infant School
John Cabot City Technology College
Hanham Business Park
Hanham C of E Primary School
Riverside Surg

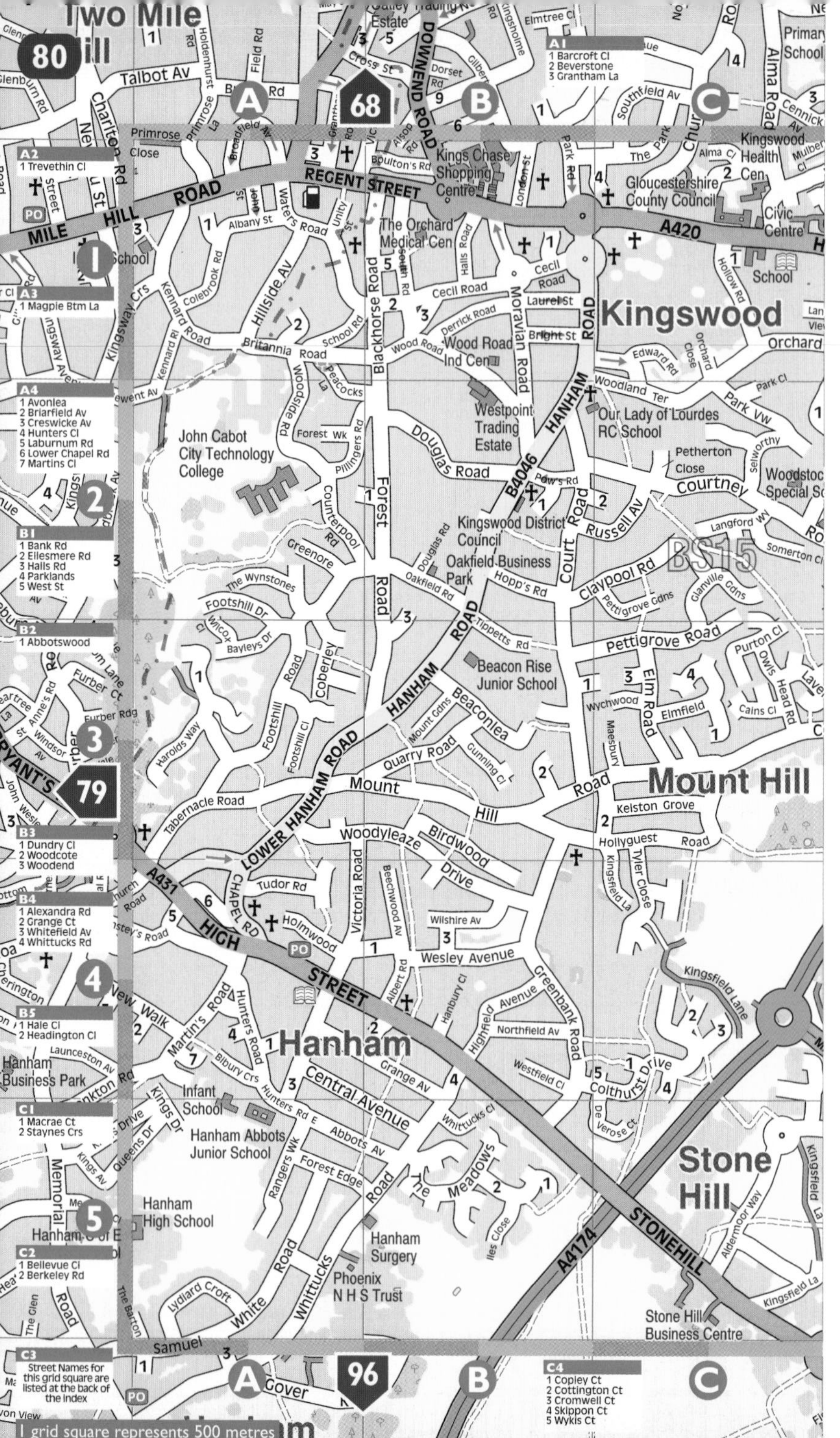
Two Mile Hill
Talbot Av
Charlton Rd
Primrose Close
Broadfield Av
Cross St
68
DOWNEND ROAD
Kings Chase Shopping Centre
REGENT STREET
MILE HILL ROAD
A420
Gloucestershire County Council
Kingswood Health Cen
Civic Centre
School
The Orchard Medical Cen
Albany St
Waters Road
Colebrook Rd
Hillside Av
Kennard Road
Kingsway Crs
Britannia Road
School Rd
Blackhorse Road
Cecil Road
Derrick Road
Wood Road
Wood Road Ind Cen
Moravian Road
Laurel St
Bright St
Kingswood
Orchard
Edward Rd
Orchard Close
Woodland Ter
Park Vw
Park Cl
Our Lady of Lourdes RC School
Westpoint Trading Estate
HANHAM ROAD
B4046
Woodside Rd
Peacocks La
Forest Wk
Pillingers Rd
Douglas Road
Forest Road
John Cabot City Technology College
Counterpool Rd
Greenore
Pow's Rd
Court Road
Russell Av
Courtney
Petherton Close
Selworthy
Woodstock Special Sc
Langford Wy
Somerton Cl
BS15
Kingswood District Council
Oakfield Business Park
Oakfield Rd
Douglas Rd
Hopp's Rd
Claypool Rd
Pettigrove Gdns
Glanville Gdns
The Wynstones
Footshill Dr
Wilcox Cl
Bayleys Dr
Tippetts Rd
Pettigrove Road
Purton Cl
Owls Head Rd
Beacon Rise Junior School
Elm Road
Wychwood
Elmfield
Cains Cl
Coberley
Footshill Road
Footshill Cl
Harolds Way
Beaconlea
Mount Gdns
Quarry Road
Gunning Cl
Maesbury
LOWER HANHAM ROAD
Mount Hill Road
Mount Hill
Kelston Grove
Hollyguest Road
Tabernacle Road
Woodyleaze
Birdwood Drive
Kingsfield La
Tyler Close
A431
HIGH STREET
CHAPEL RD
Tudor Rd
Holmwood
Victoria Road
Beechwood Av
Wilshire Av
Wesley Avenue
Albert Rd
Hanbury Cl
Greenbank Road
Highfield Avenue
Northfield Av
Kingsfield Lane
New Walk
Martin's Road
Hunters Road
Hanham
Bibury Crs
Central Avenue
Grange Av
Westfield Cl
Colthurst Drive
De Verose Ct
Infant School
Hunters Rd E
Abbots Av
Whittucks Cl
Hanham Abbots Junior School
Rangers Wk
Forest Edge
Road
The Meadows
Stone Hill
Kingsfield La
Hanham High School
Hanham Surgery
Phoenix N H S Trust
Iles Close
Aldermoor Way
STONEHILL
A4174
Lydiard Croft
White Road
Whittucks Road
Stone Hill Business Centre
Samuel
Gover
79
96
Hanham Business Park
Launceston Av
Memorial Road
Kings Dr
Queens Dr
Kings Av
The Glen
The Barton
BRYANT'S
A1
1 Barcroft Cl
2 Beverstone
3 Grantham La
A2
1 Trevethin Cl
A3
1 Magpie Btm La
A4
1 Avonlea
2 Briarfield Av
3 Creswicke Av
4 Hunters Cl
5 Laburnum Rd
6 Lower Chapel Rd
7 Martins Cl
B1
1 Bank Rd
2 Ellesmere Rd
3 Halls Rd
4 Parklands
5 West St
B2
1 Abbotswood
B3
1 Dundry Cl
2 Woodcote
3 Woodend
B4
1 Alexandra Rd
2 Grange Ct
3 Whitefield Av
4 Whittucks Rd
B5
1 Hale Cl
2 Headington Cl
C1
1 Macrae Ct
2 Staynes Crs
C2
1 Bellevue Cl
2 Berkeley Rd
C3
Street Names for this grid square are listed at the back of the index
C4
1 Copley Ct
2 Cottington Ct
3 Cromwell Ct
4 Skippon Ct
5 Wykis Ct
1 grid square represents 500 metres

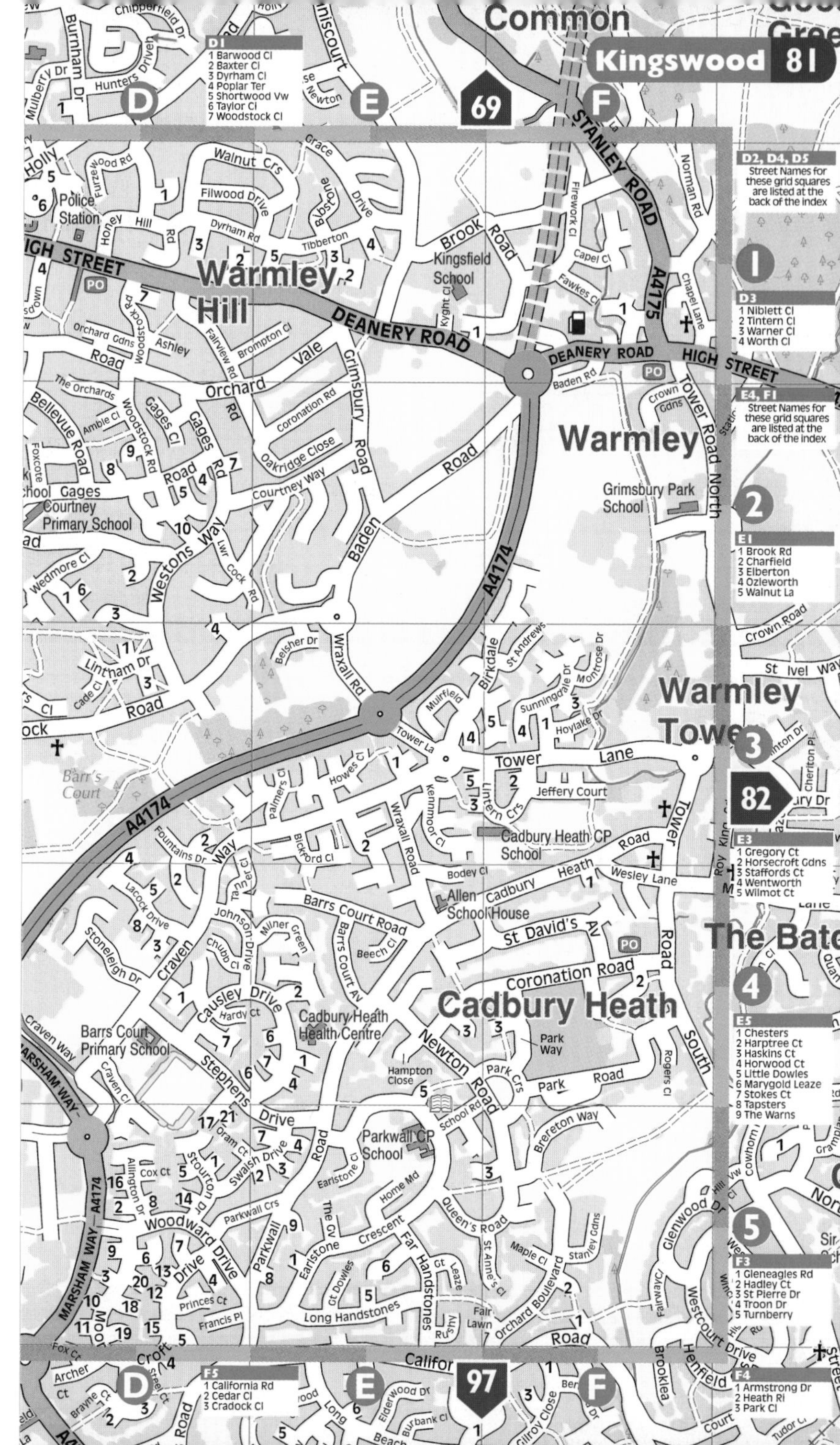
Common
69
D
E
F
D1
1 Barwood Cl
2 Baxter Cl
3 Dyrham Cl
4 Poplar Ter
5 Shortwood Vw
6 Taylor Cl
7 Woodstock Cl
D2, D4, D5
Street Names for these grid squares are listed at the back of the index
D3
1 Niblett Cl
2 Tintern Cl
3 Warner Cl
4 Worth Cl
E4, F1
Street Names for these grid squares are listed at the back of the index
E1
1 Brook Rd
2 Charfield
3 Elberton
4 Ozleworth
5 Walnut La
E3
1 Gregory Ct
2 Horsecroft Gdns
3 Staffords Ct
4 Wentworth
5 Wilmot Ct
E5
1 Chesters
2 Harptree Ct
3 Haskins Ct
4 Horwood Ct
5 Little Dowles
6 Marygold Leaze
7 Stokes Ct
8 Tapsters
9 The Warns
F3
1 Gleneagles Rd
2 Hadley Ct
3 St Pierre Dr
4 Troon Dr
5 Turnberry
F5
1 California Rd
2 Cedar Cl
3 Cradock Cl
F4
1 Armstrong Dr
2 Heath Ri
3 Park Cl
1
2
3
4
5
82
97
Warmley Hill
Warmley
Warmley Tower
Cadbury Heath
The Batch
HIGH STREET
DEANERY ROAD
STANLEY ROAD
A4175
A4174
MARSHAM WAY
Police Station
Kingsfield School
Grimsbury Park School
Gages Courtney Primary School
Cadbury Heath CP School
Allen School House
Cadbury Heath Health Centre
Barrs Court Primary School
Parkwall CP School
Barr's Court
Walnut Crs
Filwood Drive
Dyrham Rd
Tibberton
Bibstone
Grace Drive
Brook Road
Firework Cl
Capel Cl
Fawkes Cl
Norman Rd
Chapel Lane
Honey Hill Rd
Furzewood Rd
Orchard Gdns
Ashley Road
Orchard Rd
Vale
Brompton Cl
Fairview Rd
Woodstock Rd
Grimsbury Road
Coronation Rd
Oakridge Close
Courtney Way
Baden Road
Baden Rd
Crown Gdns
Tower Road North
Bellevue Road
The Orchards
Amble Cl
Gages Cl
Gages Rd
Foxcote
Westons Way
Lwr Cock Rd
Wedmore Cl
Lintham Dr
Cade Cl
Belsher Dr
Wraxall Rd
Muirfield
Birkdale
St Andrews
Montrose Dr
Sunningdale Dr
Hoylake Dr
Tower La
Tower Lane
Crown Road
St Ivel Way
Jeffery Court
Lintern Crs
Kenmoor Cl
Howes Cl
Palmers Cl
Bickford Cl
Wraxall Road
Fountains Dr
Tanner Cl
Lacock Drive
Stoneleigh Dr
Craven Way
Johnson Drive
Chubb Cl
Milner Green
Barrs Court Road
Barrs Court Av
Beech Cl
Bodey Cl
Cadbury Heath Road
Wesley Lane
Tower Road
St David's Av
Coronation Road
Causley Drive
Hardy Ct
Stephens Drive
Newton Road
Hampton Close
Park Crs
Park Way
Park Road
Rogers Cl
South Road
School Rd
Brereton Way
Oram Ct
Stourton Dr
Swaish Drive
Earlstone Cl
Home Md
Cox Ct
Allington Dr
Woodward Drive
Parkwall Crs
Parkwall Road
The Gv
Earlstone Crescent
Queen's Road
St Anne's Cl
Stanley Gdns
Maple Cl
Orchard Boulevard
Glenwood Dr
Westcourt Drive
Gt Dowles
Far Handstones
Gt Leaze
Long Handstones
Rushy
Fair Lawn
Princes Ct
Francis Pl
Moor Croft
Fox Ct
Archer Ct
Brayne Ct
Croft Street
California
Elderwood Dr
Burbank Cl
Gilroy Close
Brooklea
Henfield
Cheriton Pl
Grampian Cl
Cowhorn Hill
PO

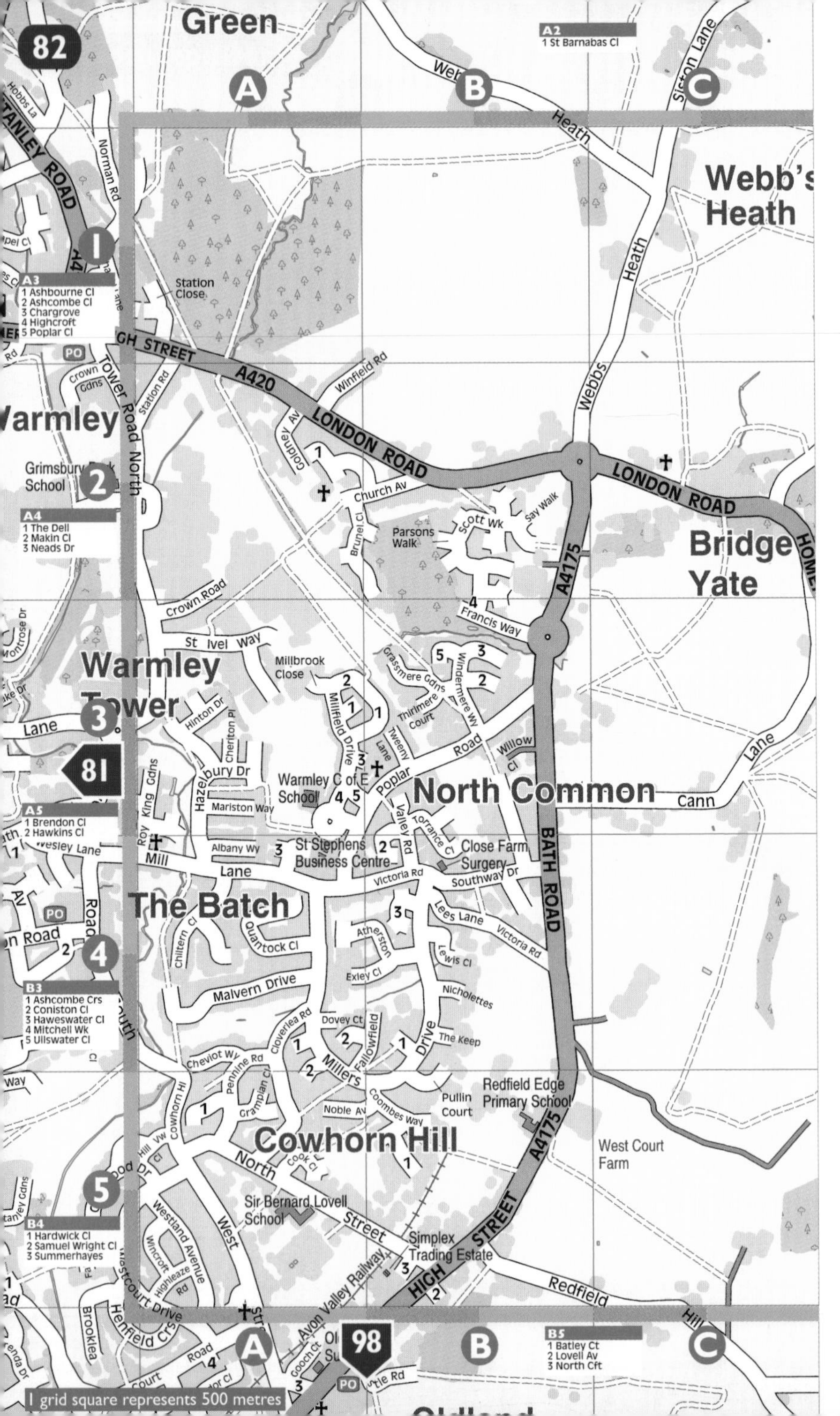
Green
A2
1 St Barnabas Cl
Webbs Heath
Siston Lane
Webb's Heath
A3
1 Ashbourne Cl
2 Ashcombe Cl
3 Chargrove
4 Highcroft
5 Poplar Cl
Station Close
HIGH STREET
A420
LONDON ROAD
Winfield Rd
Warmley
Grimsbury Park School
A4
1 The Dell
2 Makin Cl
3 Neads Dr
Church Av
Brunel Cl
Parsons Walk
Scott Wk
Say Walk
A4175
Bridge Yate
Crown Road
Francis Way
St Ivel Way
Millbrook Close
Grassmere Gdns
Windermere Wy
Thirlmere Court
Warmley Tower
Hinton Dr
Cheriton Pl
Millfield Drive
Tweeny Lane
Poplar Road
Willow Cl
Lane
Hazelbury Dr
Warmley C of E School
North Common
Cann Lane
Mariston Way
A5
1 Brendon Cl
2 Hawkins Cl
Wesley Lane
Albany Wy
St Stephens Business Centre
Valley Rd
Torrance Cl
Close Farm Surgery
BATH ROAD
Mill Lane
Victoria Rd
Southway Dr
The Batch
Lees Lane
Quantock Cl
Atherston
Chiltern Cl
Lewis Cl
Exley Cl
Malvern Drive
Nicholettes
B3
1 Ashcombe Crs
2 Coniston Cl
3 Haweswater Cl
4 Mitchell Wk
5 Ullswater Cl
Cloverlea Rd
Dovey Ct
Fallowfield
Drive
The Keep
Cheviot Wy
Pennine Rd
Millers
Grampian Cl
Cowhorn Hl
Redfield Edge Primary School
Pullin Court
Noble Av
Coombes Way
Cowhorn Hill
West Court Farm
Hill Vw
Cook Cl
North Street
B4
1 Hardwick Cl
2 Samuel Wright Cl
3 Summerhayes
Sir Bernard Lovell School
Westland Avenue
Wincroft
Highleaze Rd
Simplex Trading Estate
HIGH STREET
Avon Valley Railway
Redfield Hill
Westcourt Drive
Henfield Crs
Brooklea
B5
1 Batley Ct
2 Lovell Av
3 North Cft
81
98
1 grid square represents 500 metres

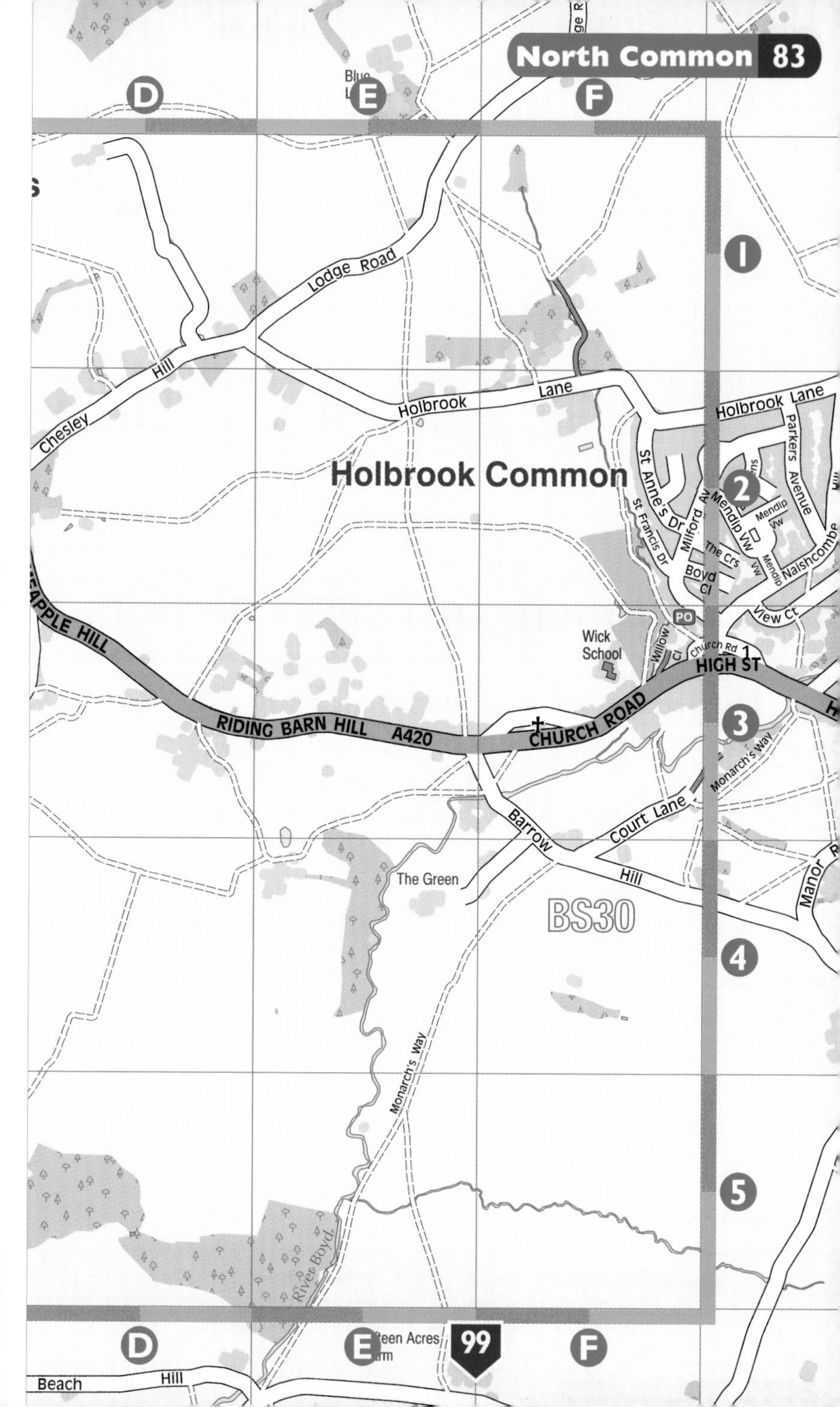
D
E
F
Blue
Lodge Road
Chesley
Hill
Holbrook
Lane
Holbrook Lane
Holbrook Common
St Anne's Dr
St Francis Dr
Milford Av
Mendip Vw
Mendip Vw
Parkers Avenue
The Crs
Boyd Cl
Naishcombe
View Ct
PO
Wick School
Willow Cl
Church Rd
HIGH ST
RIDING BARN HILL
A420
CHURCH ROAD
Monarch's Way
Court Lane
Barrow
Hill
The Green
BS30
Manor
Monarch's Way
River Boyd
Beach
Hill
1
2
3
4
5
99

70
CLEVEDON
A
B
C
A2
1 Macleod Cl
A3
1 The Tynings
B2
1 Saltings Cl
B3
1 Concorde Dr
2 Crawford Cl
3 Hedges Cl
4 Ladycroft
5 Riverside Cl
6 Sandford Cl
B4
1 Baker Cl
C1
1 Albert Rd
2 Coleridge Rd
3 Jesmond Rd
4 Russell Rd
C2
1 Coleridge V Rd W
2 Fearnville Est
3 Hanson's Wy
4 Lwr Knowles Rd
5 Newport Cl
6 Wains Cl
7 Westbourne Av
8 Westbourne Crs
9 Wordsworth Rd
C3
Street Names for this grid square are listed at the back of the index
C4
1 Parsons Gn
1
2
3
4
5
Salthouse Bay
Hangstone Hill
West End
Cemetery
ELTON ROAD
B3130
Hallam Road
Seavale Rd
Army Training Corps
Victoria Rd
Pyne Point
St Brandons School
West Way
The Homestead
OLD CHURCH
Beach Av
Knowles Rd
Glebe Rd
Speedwell Industrial Est
Coleridge Vale Rd
Salthouse Rd
Old Church Road
Long Av
West Croft
Pizey Close
Pizey Avenue
Westbourne Avenue
Church Cl
Pill Way
Yeo Way
Westbourne Crs
Keene's Way
Churchill
Kimberley Rd
Tennyson Avenue
Saint Andrew's Drive
Southern Way
Westerleigh Road
Ashton Cl
Strode Road
Tweed Rd
St John the Evangelist Primary School
Hayward Cl
Butterfield Pk
Farleigh Road
Sunnyvale
Ashley Rd
Wedmore Road
Lavington Close
The Leys
Saxby Cl
Five C Business Centre
Strode Wy
Blackmoor
Southern
Holland Rd
Turner Way
Netherways
Ransford
Primary School
Strode Rd
Millcross
Rushmoor
Yeolands Drive
Eastlea
Deer Mead
Tuckmill
Chipping Cross
Cavell Ct
Ltl Ham
Cobley Cft
Cannons
Longacre
Oakley
Garstons
Catemead
The Hyde
Patch Cft
Freelands
Byfields
Strode Road
Colehouse Lane
Dowlais Farm
Lower Strode Road
1 grid square represents 500 metres

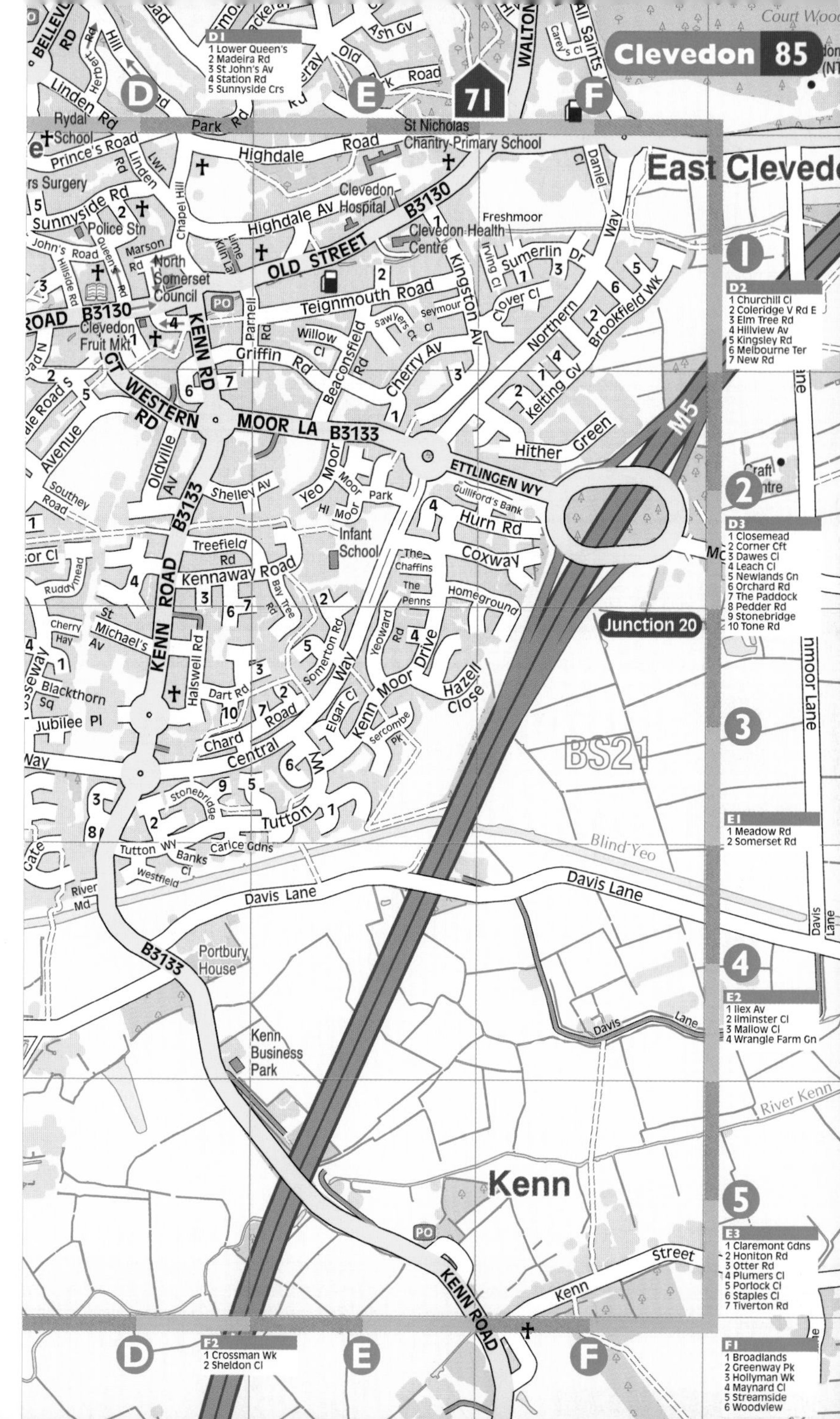

D1
1 Lower Queen's
2 Madeira Rd
3 St John's Av
4 Station Rd
5 Sunnyside Crs
71
East Clevedon
D2
1 Churchill Cl
2 Coleridge V Rd E
3 Elm Tree Rd
4 Hillview Av
5 Kingsley Rd
6 Melbourne Ter
7 New Rd
D3
1 Closemead
2 Corner Cft
3 Dawes Cl
4 Leach Cl
5 Newlands Gn
6 Orchard Rd
7 The Paddock
8 Pedder Rd
9 Stonebridge
10 Tone Rd
E1
1 Meadow Rd
2 Somerset Rd
E2
1 Ilex Av
2 Ilminster Cl
3 Mallow Cl
4 Wrangle Farm Gn
E3
1 Claremont Gdns
2 Honiton Rd
3 Otter Rd
4 Plumers Cl
5 Porlock Cl
6 Staples Cl
7 Tiverton Rd
F1
1 Broadlands
2 Greenway Pk
3 Hollyman Wk
4 Maynard Cl
5 Streamside
6 Woodview
F2
1 Crossman Wk
2 Sheldon Cl
Junction 20
BS21
Kenn
Kenn Business Park
Portbury House
Blind Yeo
River Kenn
Davis Lane
M5
B3133
B3130
OLD STREET
MOOR LA
KENN ROAD
ETTLINGEN WY
Clevedon Hospital
Clevedon Health Centre
St Nicholas Chantry Primary School
North Somerset Council
Police Stn
Clevedon Fruit Mkt
Infant School
Court Wood

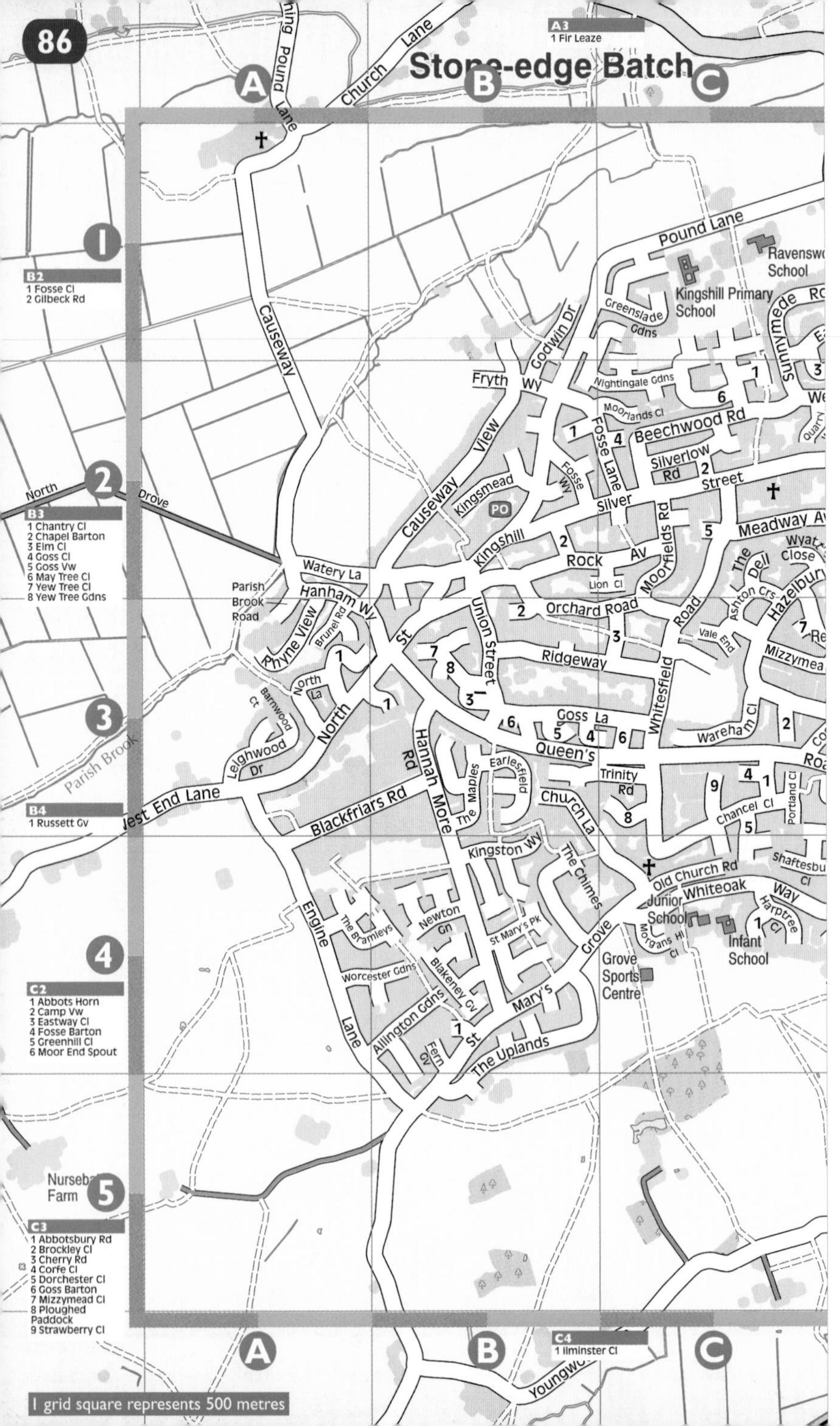
Stone-edge Batch
A3
1 Fir Leaze
B2
1 Fosse Cl
2 Gilbeck Rd
B3
1 Chantry Cl
2 Chapel Barton
3 Elm Cl
4 Goss Cl
5 Goss Vw
6 May Tree Cl
7 Yew Tree Cl
8 Yew Tree Gdns
B4
1 Russett Gv
C2
1 Abbots Horn
2 Camp Vw
3 Eastway Cl
4 Fosse Barton
5 Greenhill Cl
6 Moor End Spout
C3
1 Abbotsbury Rd
2 Brockley Cl
3 Cherry Rd
4 Corfe Cl
5 Dorchester Cl
6 Goss Barton
7 Mizzymead Cl
8 Ploughed Paddock
9 Strawberry Cl
C4
1 Ilminster Cl
Church Lane
Pound Lane
Causeway
North Drove
Parish Brook Road
Parish Brook
Watery La
Hanham Wy
Rhyne View
Brunel Rd
North La
Barnwood Ct
Leighwood Dr
North St
Blackfriars Rd
Hannah More Rd
Engine Lane
The Bramleys
Newton Gn
Worcester Gdns
Blakeney Gv
Allington Gdns
Fern Gv
St Mary's
St Mary's Pk
The Uplands
Kingston Wy
The Maples
Earlesfield
Church La
The Chimes
Grove
Grove Sports Centre
Morgans Hl Cl
Junior School
Infant School
Old Church Rd
Whiteoak Way
Harptree Cl
Shaftesbu Cl
Chancel Cl
Portland Cl
Trinity Rd
Queen's
Goss La
Whitesfield Road
Wareham Cl
Ridgeway
Union Street
Orchard Road
Lion Cl
Rock Av
Kingshill
Kingsmead
PO
Causeway View
Fryth Wy
Godwin Dr
Fosse Wy
Fosse Lane
Silver Street
Silverlow Rd
Beechwood Rd
Moorlands Cl
Nightingale Gdns
Greenslade Gdns
Kingshill Primary School
Sunnymede
Moorfields Rd
Meadway Av
The Dell
Ashton Crs
Vale End
Wyat Close
Mizzymea
Pound Lane
School
Quarry
Youngwo
1 grid square represents 500 metres

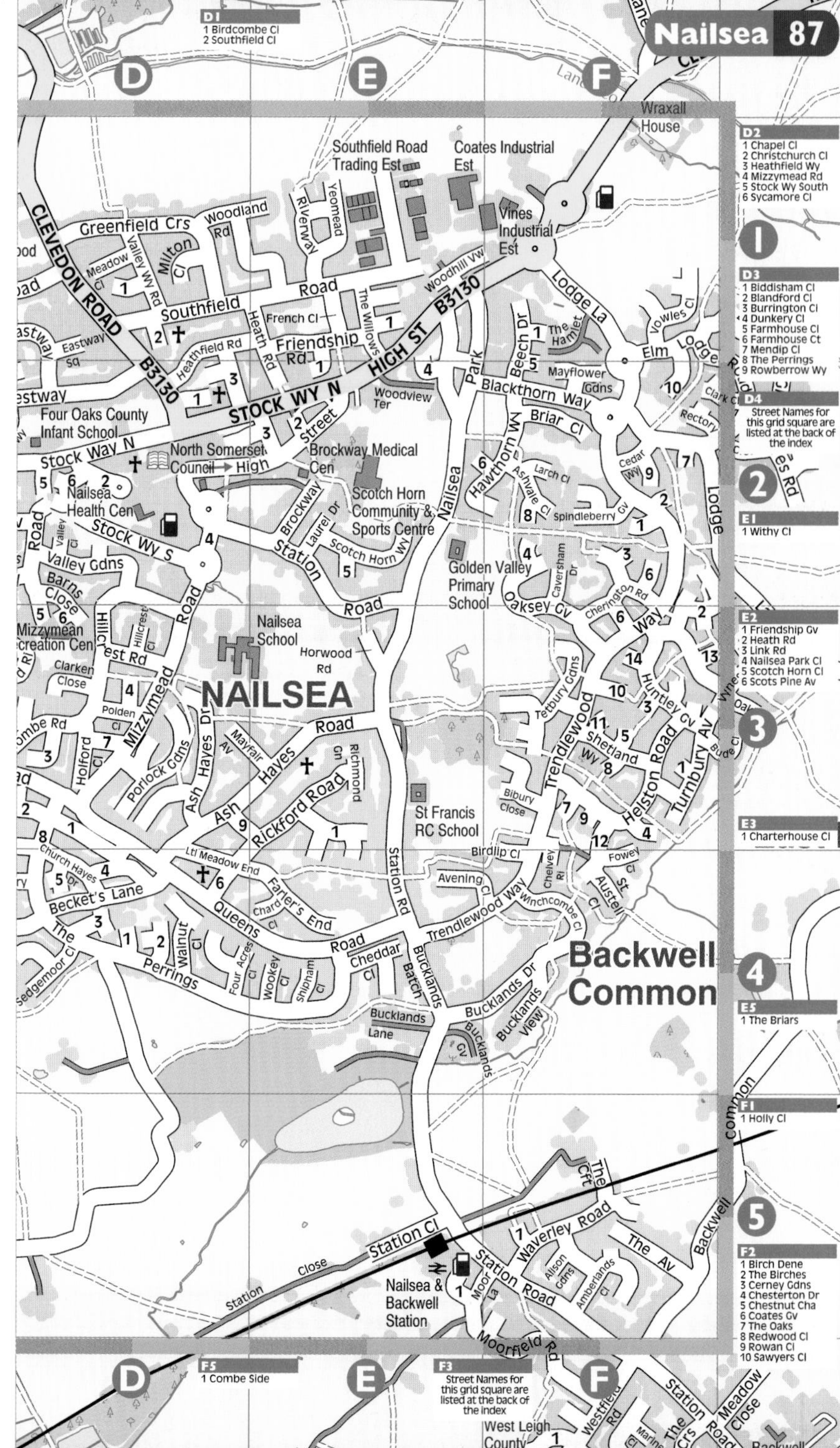
D1
1 Birdcombe Cl
2 Southfield Cl
D2
1 Chapel Cl
2 Christchurch Cl
3 Heathfield Wy
4 Mizzymead Rd
5 Stock Wy South
6 Sycamore Cl
D3
1 Biddisham Cl
2 Blandford Cl
3 Burrington Cl
4 Dunkery Cl
5 Farmhouse Cl
6 Farmhouse Ct
7 Mendip Cl
8 The Perrings
9 Rowberrow Wy
D4
Street Names for this grid square are listed at the back of the index
E1
1 Withy Cl
E2
1 Friendship Gv
2 Heath Rd
3 Link Rd
4 Nailsea Park Cl
5 Scotch Horn Cl
6 Scots Pine Av
E3
1 Charterhouse Cl
E5
1 The Briars
F1
1 Holly Cl
F2
1 Birch Dene
2 The Birches
3 Cerney Gdns
4 Chesterton Dr
5 Chestnut Cha
6 Coates Gv
7 The Oaks
8 Redwood Cl
9 Rowan Cl
10 Sawyers Cl
F5
1 Combe Side
F3
Street Names for this grid square are listed at the back of the index
NAILSEA
Backwell Common
Wraxall House
Southfield Road Trading Est
Coates Industrial Est
Vines Industrial Est
Four Oaks County Infant School
North Somerset Council
Brockway Medical Cen
Nailsea Health Cen
Scotch Horn Community & Sports Centre
Golden Valley Primary School
Nailsea School
Mizzymead Recreation Cen
St Francis RC School
Nailsea & Backwell Station
West Leigh County
CLEVEDON ROAD
B3130
HIGH ST
STOCK WY N
Stock Way N
Stock Wy S
Southfield Road
Greenfield Crs
Woodland Rd
Friendship Rd
Heathfield Rd
Station Road
Nailsea Park
Blackthorn Way
Lodge La
Trendlewood Way
Queens Road
Ash Hayes Road
Rickford Road
Station Rd
Becket's Lane
The Perrings
Bucklands Lane
Bucklands Dr
Bucklands View
Station Cl
Station Close
Waverley Road
Moorfield Rd
Backwell Common
Helston Road
Turnbury Av
Mizzymead Road
Hillcrest Rd
Valley Gdns
Barns Close
Clarken Close
Oaksey Gv
Caversham Dr
Cherington Rd
Shetland Wy
Bibury Close
Birdlip Cl
Avening Cl
Winchcombe Cl
Farler's End
Cheddar Cl
Walnut Cl
Four Acres Cl
Wookey Cl
Shipham Cl
Sedgemoor Cl
Church Hayes Dr
Porlock Gdns
Mayfair Av
Richmond Gn
Horwood Rd
Laurel Dr
Scotch Horn Wy
Brockway
Hawthorn Wy
Briar Cl
Mayflower Gdns
Beech Dr
The Hamlet
Elm
Vowles Cl
Rectory
Clark Cl
Woodview Ter
The Willows
French Cl
Riverway
Yeomead
Milton Cl
Valley Wy Rd
Meadow Cl
Eastway Sq
Woodhill Vw
Larch Cl
Ashvale Cl
Spindleberry Gv
Cedar Wy
Tetbury Gdns
Trendlewood
Huntley Gv
Chelvey Ri
Fowey Cl
St Austell Cl
Holford Cl
Polden Cl
Ltl Meadow End
Chard Cl
Bucklands Batch
Bucklands Gv
The Cft
The Av
Allison Gdns
Amberlands Cl
Moor La
Westfield Rd
Mariners
The Crs
Meadow Close
Backwell

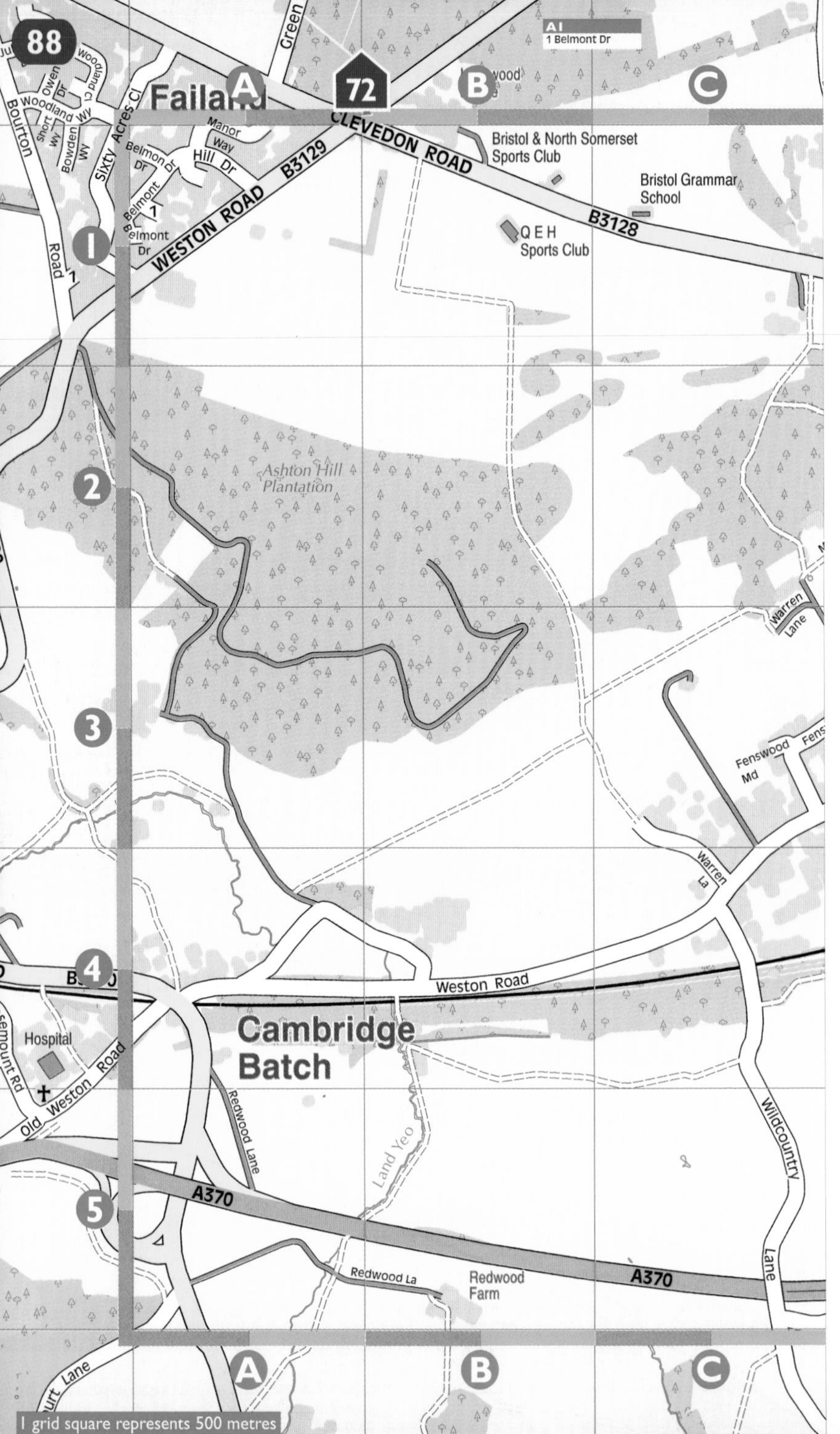

72
A1
1 Belmont Dr
Failand
Woodland Wy
Owen Dr
Woodland Cl
Short Wy
Bowden Wy
Bourton Road
Sixty Acres Cl
Manor Way
Hill Dr
Belmont Dr
Belmont Dr
WESTON ROAD
B3129
CLEVEDON ROAD
Bristol & North Somerset Sports Club
Bristol Grammar School
Q E H Sports Club
B3128
Ashton Hill Plantation
Warren Lane
Fenswood Md
Warren La
Weston Road
Cambridge Batch
Hospital
Old Weston Road
Redwood Lane
Land Yeo
A370
A370
Wildcountry Lane
Redwood La
Redwood Farm
1 grid square represents 500 metres

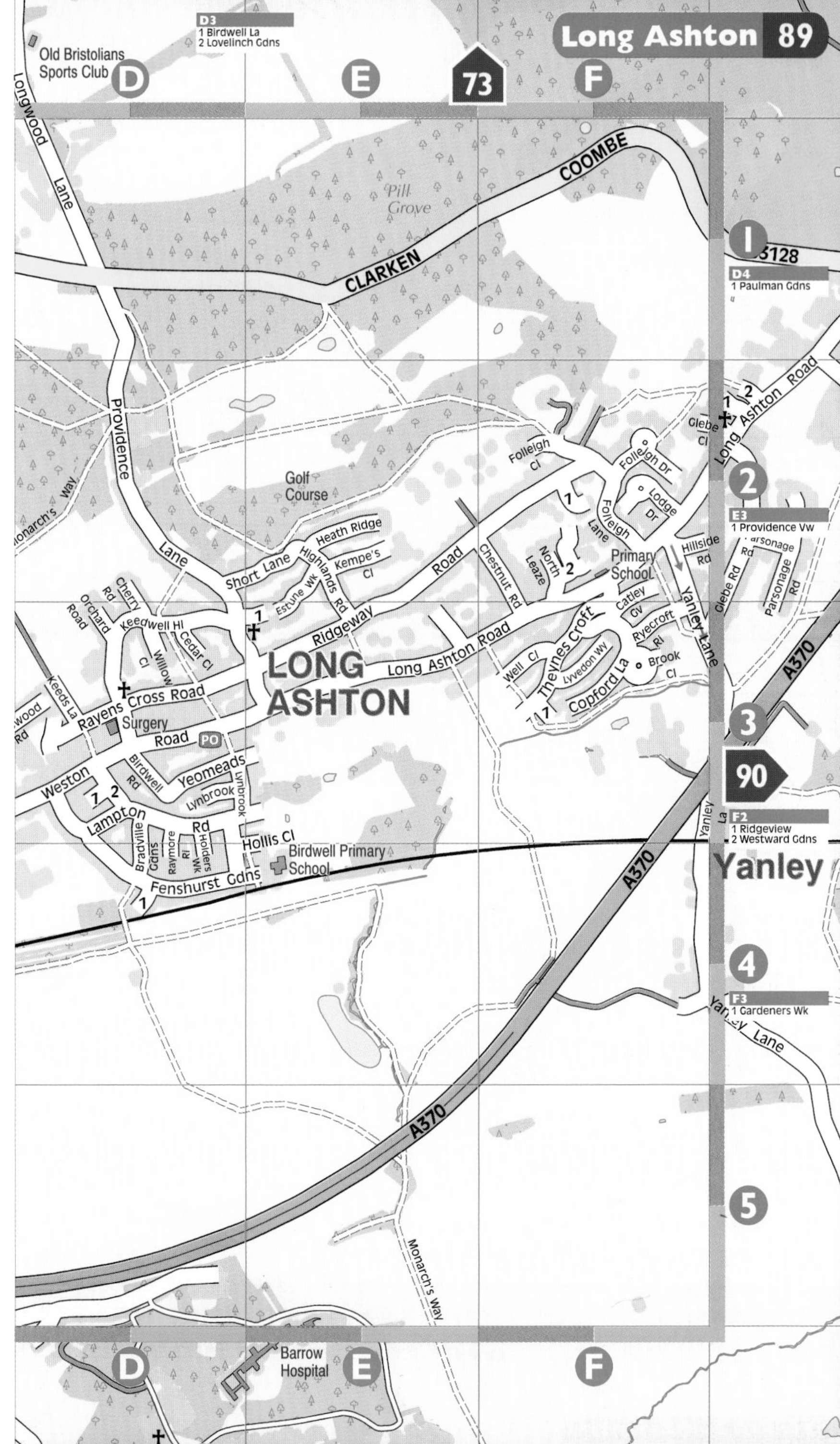
D3
1 Birdwell La
2 Lovelinch Gdns
Old Bristolians Sports Club
D
E
73
F
Longwood Lane
COOMBE
Pill Grove
CLARKEN
B3128
D4
1 Paulman Gdns
Long Ashton Road
Glebe Cl
Providence Lane
Golf Course
Folleigh Cl
Folleigh Dr
Lodge Dr
Folleigh Lane
E3
1 Providence Vw
Monarch's Way
Heath Ridge
Short Lane
Highlands Rd
Kempe's Cl
Estune Wk
Road
Chestnut Rd
North Leaze
Primary School
Hillside Rd
Parsonage Rd
Glebe Rd
Orchard Road
Cherry Rd
Keedwell Hl
Willow Cl
Cedar Cl
Ridgeway
Catley Gv
Yanley Lane
Ryecroft Ri
LONG ASHTON
Long Ashton Road
Well Cl
Theynes Croft
Lyvedon Wy
Brook Cl
A370
Keeds La
Rayens Cross Road
Copford La
Surgery
Road
PO
Weston
Birdwell Rd
Yeomeads
Lynbrook
90
Lampton Rd
Bradville Gdns
Raymore Ri
Holders Wk
Hollis Cl
Birdwell Primary School
F2
1 Ridgeview
2 Westward Gdns
Yanley La
Yanley
Fenshurst Gdns
F3
1 Gardeners Wk
Yanley Lane
A370
Monarch's Way
Barrow Hospital
1
2
3
4
5

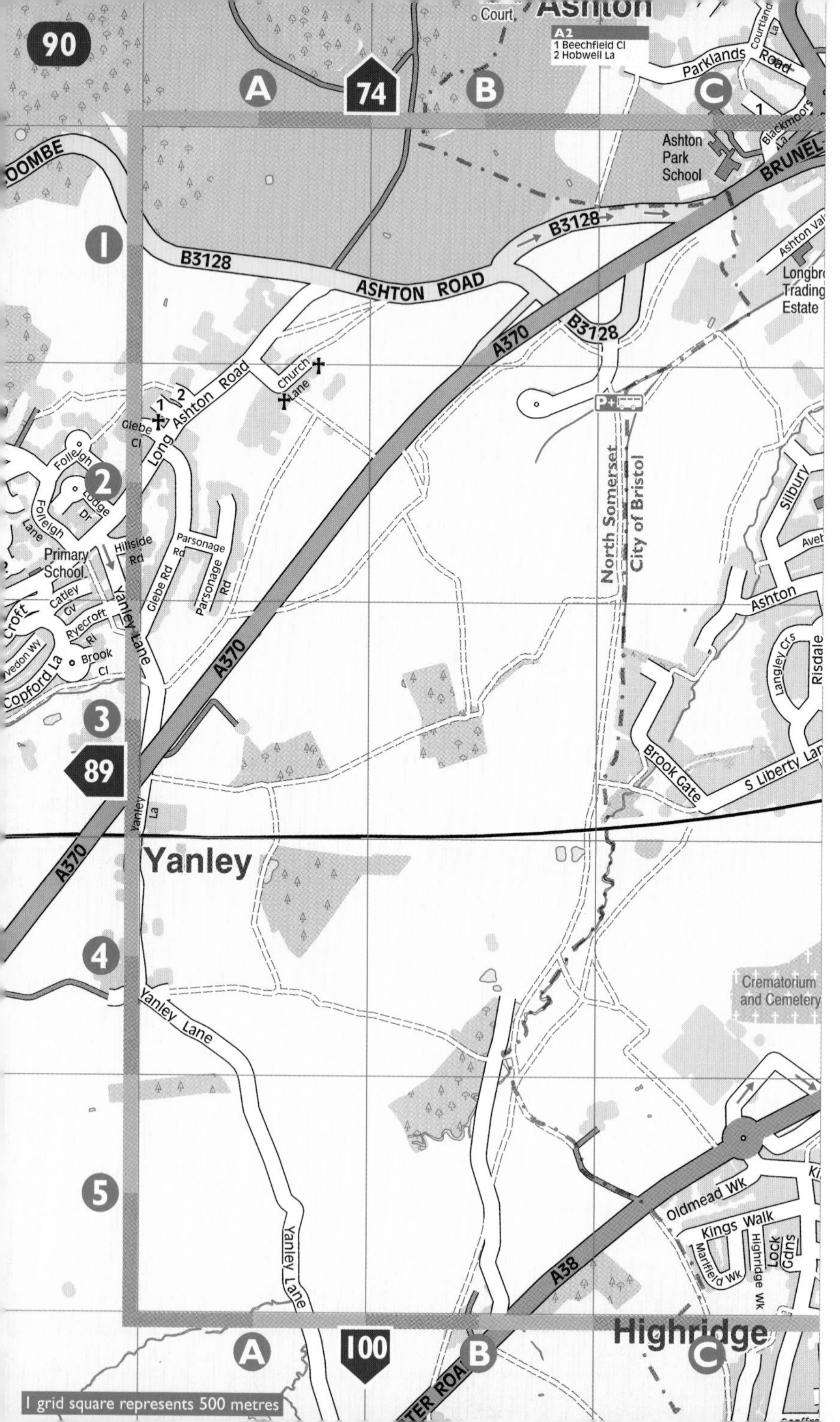
Court
Ashton
A2
1 Beechfield Cl
2 Hobwell La
Courtland La
Parklands Road
74
A
B
C
Ashton Park School
Blackmoors La
BRUNEL
B3128
Ashton Vale
Longbro Trading Estate
1
B3128
ASHTON ROAD
A370
B3128
Church Lane
Long Ashton Road
Glebe Cl
Folleigh
Lodge Dr
Folleigh Lane
2
Primary School
Hillside Rd
Parsonage Rd
Parsonage Rd
Glebe Rd
Catley Gv
Ryecroft Ri
Yanley Lane
Brook Cl
Copford La
Croft
A370
North Somerset
City of Bristol
Silbury
Ashton
Langley Crs
Risdale
Brook Gate
S Liberty Lane
3
89
Yanley La
Yanley
A370
4
Yanley Lane
Crematorium and Cemetery
5
Oldmead Wk
Kings Walk
Marifield Wk
Highridge Wk
Lock Gdns
A38
Yanley Lane
Highridge
100
I grid square represents 500 metres

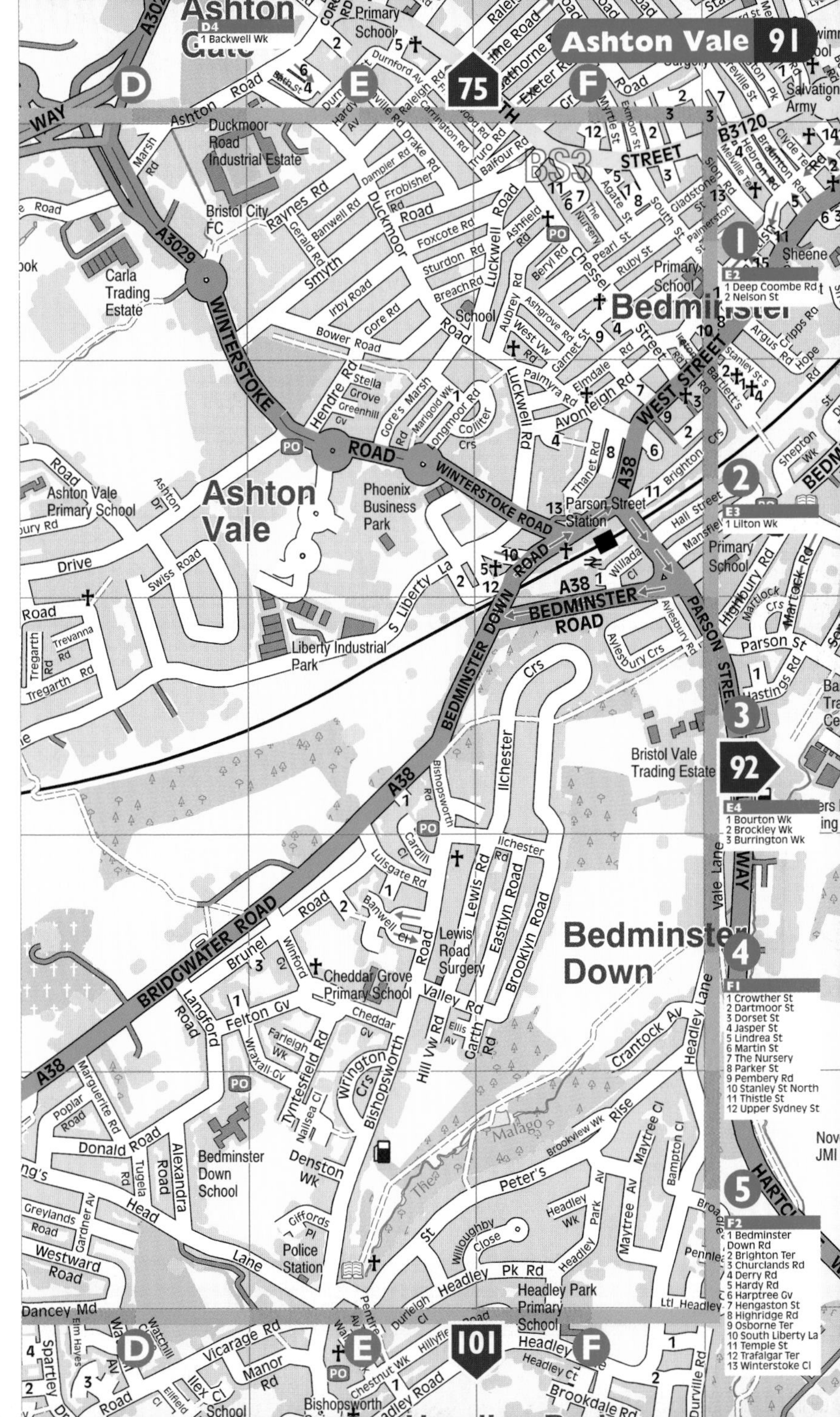

Ashton Gate
D4
1 Backwell Wk
D
E
75
F
A3029
Ashton Road
Duckmoor Road Industrial Estate
Bristol City FC
Carla Trading Estate
Raynes Rd
Gerald Rd
Banwell Rd
Duckmoor Road
Dampier Rd
Frobisher Rd
Foxcote Rd
Sturdon Rd
Breach Rd
Smyth Road
Irby Road
Gore Rd
Bower Road
Luckwell Road
Ashfield Rd
Chessel St
Beryl Rd
Pearl St
Ruby St
Agate St
South St
Gladstone St
Palmerston St
The Nursery
BS3
STREET
B3120
Primary School
Bedminster
E2
1 Deep Coombe Rd
2 Nelson St
Aubrey Rd
Ashgrove Rd
West Vw Rd
Garnet St
Elmdale Rd
Palmyra Rd
Avonleigh Rd
WEST STREET
Stanley St S
Bartlett's Rd
Argus Rd
Cripps Rd
Hope Rd
School
Hendre Rd
Stella Grove
Greenhill Gv
Gore's Marsh Rd
Marigold Wk
Longmoor Rd
Colliter Crs
Luckwell Rd
WINTERSTOKE ROAD
Thanet Rd
A38
Brighton Crs
Shepton Wk
Ashton Vale Primary School
Ashton Dr
Ashton Vale
Phoenix Business Park
Parson Street Station
Hall Street
Mansfield
E3
1 Lilton Wk
Primary School
Drive
Swiss Road
Road
S Liberty La
Willada Cl
A38
BEDMINSTER ROAD
BEDMINSTER DOWN ROAD
Aylesbury Rd
Aylesbury Crs
PARSON STREET
Highbury Rd
Martock Rd
Parson St
Hastings Rd
Trevanna Rd
Tregarth Rd
Liberty Industrial Park
Crs
Ilchester
Bristol Vale Trading Estate
92
E4
1 Bourton Wk
2 Brockley Wk
3 Burrington Wk
Bishopsworth Rd
Cardill Cl
Lulsgate Rd
Ilchester Rd
Lewis Rd
Eastlyn Road
Brooklyn Road
Banwell Cl
Vale Lane
WAY
BRIDGWATER ROAD
Road
Brunel
Winford Gv
Cheddar Grove Primary School
Lewis Road Surgery
Bedminster Down
F1
1 Crowther St
2 Dartmoor St
3 Dorset St
4 Jasper St
5 Lindrea St
6 Martin St
7 The Nursery
8 Parker St
9 Pembery Rd
10 Stanley St North
11 Thistle St
12 Upper Sydney St
Langford Road
Felton Gv
Cheddar Gv
Valley Rd
Hill Vw Rd
Ellis Av
Garth Rd
Crantock Av
Headley Lane
Farleigh Wk
Wraxall Gv
Tyntesfield Rd
Wrington Crs
Bishopsworth
Nailsea Cl
A38
Marguerite Rd
Poplar Road
Donald Road
Tugela Rd
Alexandra Road
Bedminster Down School
Denston Wk
Malago
Brookview Wk
Rise
Maytree Cl
Maytree Av
Bampton Cl
Peter's
St
Headley Wk
Park Av
Willoughby Close
Headley
Pennlea
HARTCLIFFE
5
F2
1 Bedminster Down Rd
2 Brighton Ter
3 Churchlands Rd
4 Derry Rd
5 Hardy Rd
6 Harptree Gv
7 Hengaston St
8 Highridge Rd
9 Osborne Ter
10 South Liberty La
11 Temple St
12 Trafalgar Ter
13 Winterstoke Cl
Greylands Road
Gardner Av
Westward Road
Head
Lane
Giffords Pl
Police Station
Headley Pk Rd
Headley Park Primary School
Ltl Headley
Dancey Md
Elm Hayes
Spartley
Watchill
Vicarage Rd
Manor Rd
Ilex Cl
Elfield Cl
Road
School
Chestnut Wk
Bishopsworth
Durleigh Cl
Pentire Av
Hillyfield
101
Headley
Headley Ct
Brookdale Rd
Ourville Rd

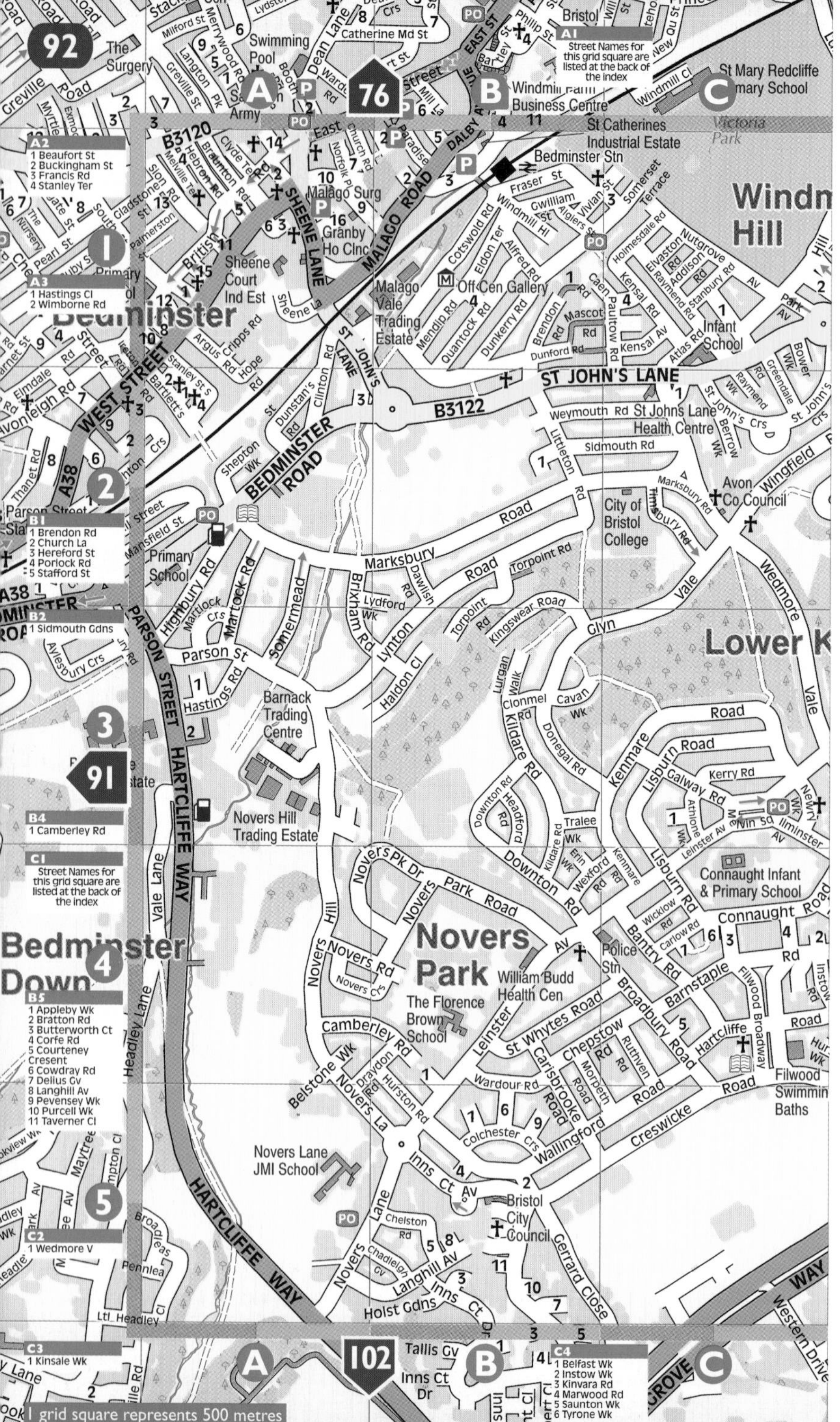
92
76
91
102
A
B
C
1
2
3
4
5
A1
Street Names for this grid square are listed at the back of the index
A2
1 Beaufort St
2 Buckingham St
3 Francis Rd
4 Stanley Ter
A3
1 Hastings Cl
2 Wimborne Rd
B1
1 Brendon Rd
2 Church La
3 Hereford St
4 Porlock Rd
5 Stafford St
B2
1 Sidmouth Gdns
B4
1 Camberley Rd
C1
Street Names for this grid square are listed at the back of the index
B5
1 Appleby Wk
2 Bratton Rd
3 Butterworth Ct
4 Corfe Rd
5 Courteney Cresent
6 Cowdray Rd
7 Delius Gv
8 Langhill Av
9 Pevensey Wk
10 Purcell Wk
11 Taverner Cl
C2
1 Wedmore V
C3
1 Kinsale Wk
C4
1 Belfast Wk
2 Instow Wk
3 Kinvara Rd
4 Marwood Rd
5 Saunton Wk
6 Tyrone Wk
Bedminster
Windmill Hill
Lower K
Novers Park
Bedminster Down
St Mary Redcliffe Primary School
Windmill Farm Business Centre
St Catherines Industrial Estate
Bedminster Stn
Victoria Park
Malago Vale Trading Estate
Sheene Court Ind Est
Off Cen Gallery
City of Bristol College
Avon Co Council
St Johns Lane Health Centre
Barnack Trading Centre
Novers Hill Trading Estate
Connaught Infant & Primary School
William Budd Health Cen
The Florence Brown School
Novers Lane JMI School
Bristol City Council
Filwood Swimming Baths
Police Stn
BEDMINSTER ROAD
ST JOHN'S LANE
MALAGO ROAD
SHEENE LANE
WEST STREET
PARSON STREET
HARTCLIFFE WAY
B3120
B3122
A38
1 grid square represents 500 metres

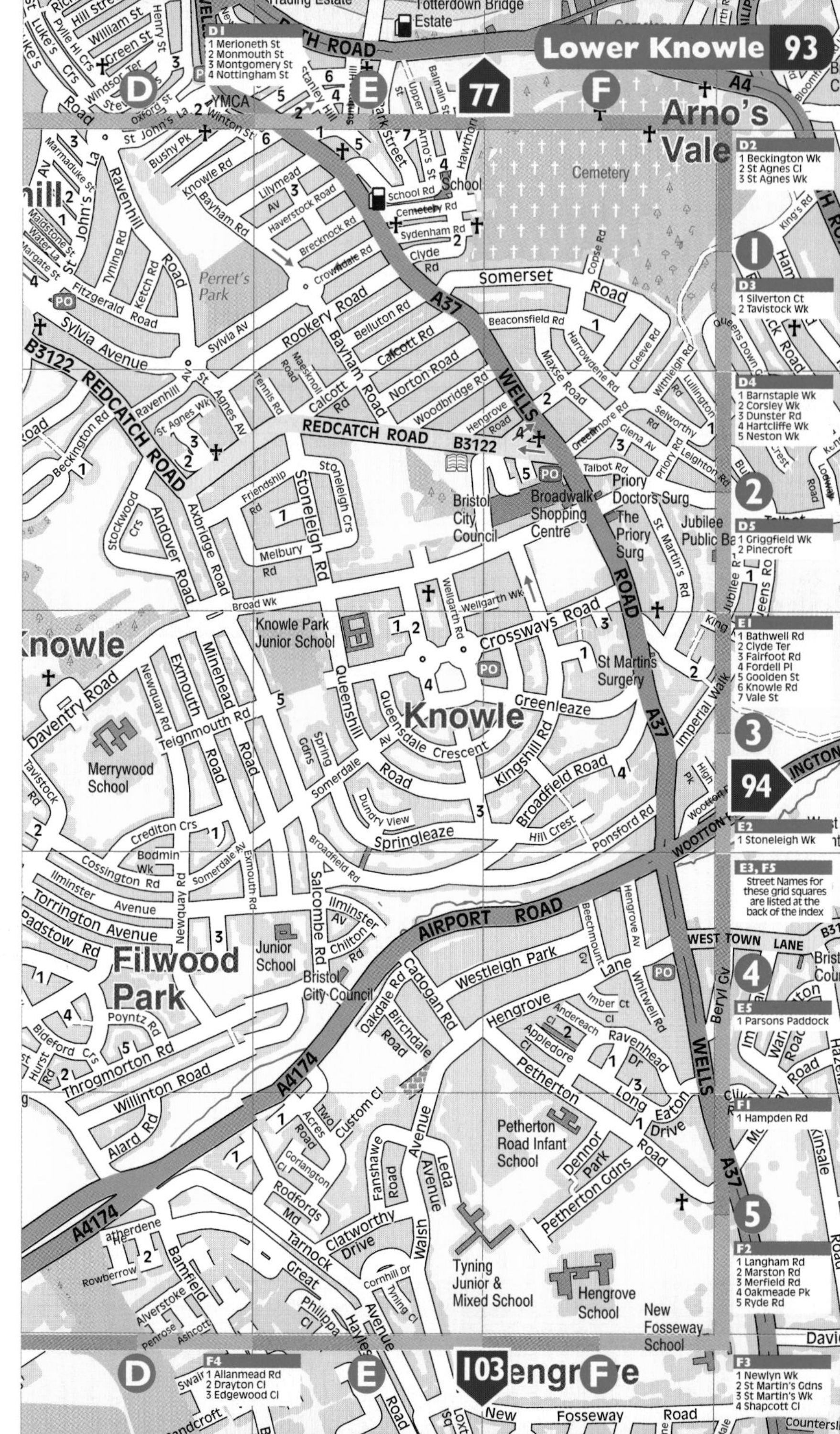
D1
1 Merioneth St
2 Monmouth St
3 Montgomery St
4 Nottingham St
D2
1 Beckington Wk
2 St Agnes Cl
3 St Agnes Wk
D3
1 Silverton Ct
2 Tavistock Wk
D4
1 Barnstaple Wk
2 Corsley Wk
3 Dunster Rd
4 Hartcliffe Wk
5 Neston Wk
D5
1 Griggfield Wk
2 Pinecroft
E1
1 Bathwell Rd
2 Clyde Ter
3 Fairfoot Rd
4 Fordell Pl
5 Goolden St
6 Knowle Rd
7 Vale St
E2
1 Stoneleigh Wk
E3, F5
Street Names for these grid squares are listed at the back of the index
E5
1 Parsons Paddock
F1
1 Hampden Rd
F2
1 Langham Rd
2 Marston Rd
3 Merfield Rd
4 Oakmeade Pk
5 Ryde Rd
F3
1 Newlyn Wk
2 St Martin's Gdns
3 St Martin's Wk
4 Shapcott Cl
F4
1 Allanmead Rd
2 Drayton Cl
3 Edgewood Cl
Arno's Vale
Cemetery
Knowle
Filwood Park
Totterdown Bridge Estate
Perret's Park
Knowle Park Junior School
Merrywood School
Broadwalk Shopping Centre
Bristol City Council
Priory Doctors Surg
The Priory Surg
St Martins Surgery
Jubilee Public Ba
Junior School
Petherton Road Infant School
Tyning Junior & Mixed School
Hengrove School
New Fosseway School
Redcatch Road
Wells Road
Airport Road
Somerset Road
Crossways Road
West Town Lane
Wootton
New Fosseway Road
A37
A4174
B3122
77
94
103

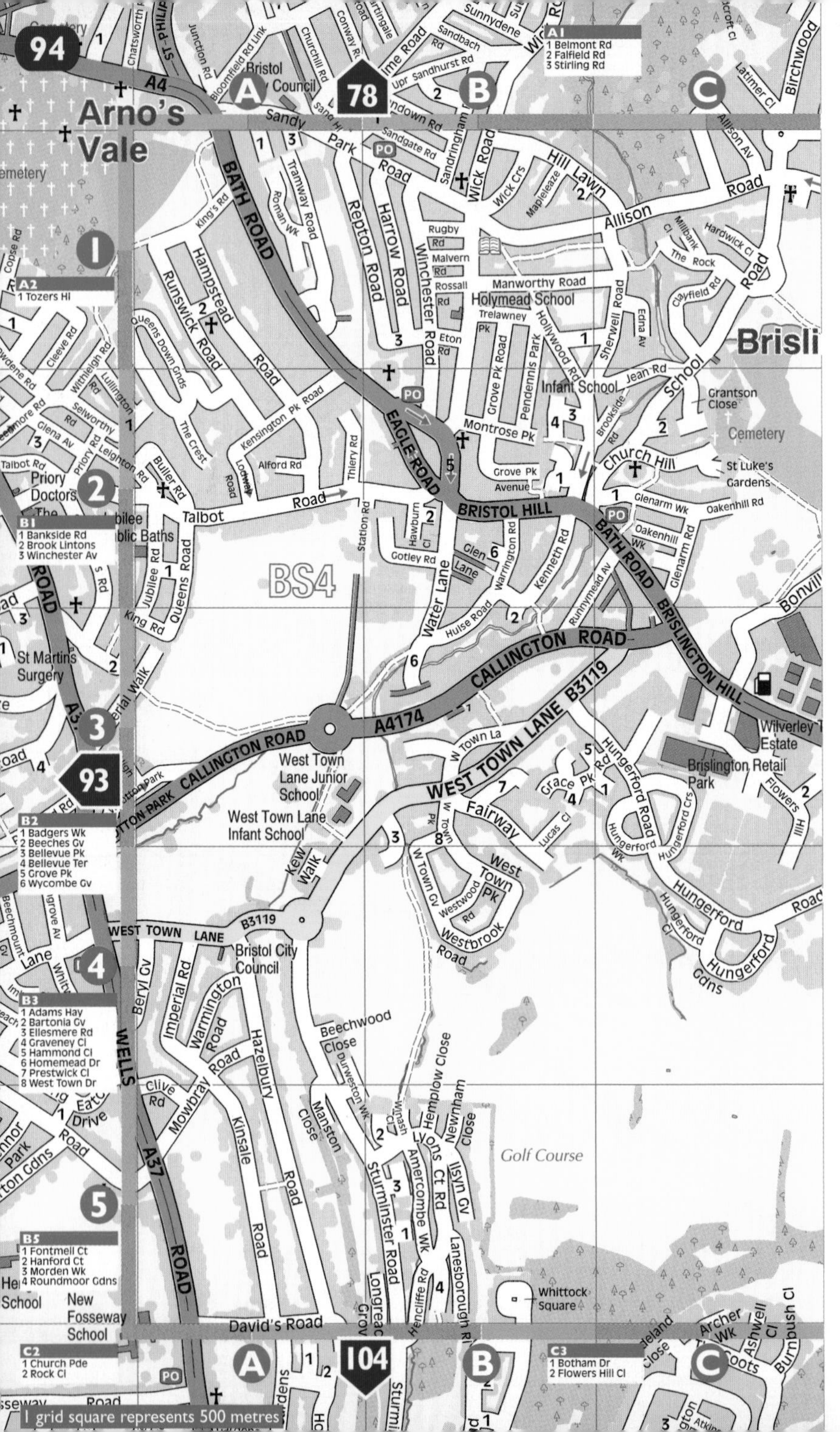
94
78
A
B
C
A1
1 Belmont Rd
2 Falfield Rd
3 Stirling Rd
Arno's Vale
Cemetery
A4
Junction Rd
Bloomfield Rd Link
Bristol City Council
Churchill Rd
Conway Rd
Sunnydene
Sandbach Rd
Upr Sandhurst Rd
Sandown Rd
Sandgate Rd
Sandy Park Road
PO
Sandringham Rd
Wick Road
Wick Crs
Hill Lawn
Mapleleaze
Allison Road
Allison Av
Latimer Cl
Birchwood
Millbank Cl
Hardwick Cl
The Rock
Clayfield Rd
School Road
Brisli
BATH ROAD
Tramway Road
Roman Wk
King's Rd
Repton Road
Harrow Road
Winchester Road
Rugby Rd
Malvern Rd
Rossall Rd
Eton Rd
Manworthy Road
Holymead School
Trelawney Pk
Grove Pk Road
Pendennis Park
Hollywood Rd
Sherwell Road
Edna Av
Infant School
Jean Rd
Grantson Close
Cemetery
St Luke's Gardens
Church Hill
Copse Rd
A2
1 Tozers Hl
Hampstead Road
Runswick Road
Queens Down Gdns
The Crest
Kensington Pk Road
Cleeve Rd
Withleigh Rd
Lullington Rd
Selworthy Rd
Glena Av
Priory Rd
Leighton Rd
Talbot Rd
Priory Doctors
Buller Rd
Lockwell Road
Alford Rd
Thiery Rd
EAGLE ROAD
Montrose Pk
Grove Pk Avenue
Glenarm Wk
Oakenhill Rd
Oakenhill Wk
Glenarm Rd
B1
1 Bankside Rd
2 Brook Lintons
3 Winchester Av
Jubilee Public Baths
Talbot Road
Queens Road
Jubilee Rd
King Rd
Station Rd
Hawburn Cl
Gotley Rd
BRISTOL HILL
Glen Lane
Warrington Rd
Kenneth Rd
Runnymead Av
BATH ROAD
BRISLINGTON HILL
Bonvill
BS4
Water Lane
Hulse Road
CALLINGTON ROAD
A4174
St Martins Surgery
WEST TOWN LANE B3119
W Town La
Hungerford Road
Grace Pk Rd
Wilverley Estate
Brislington Retail Park
Flowers Hill
93
CALLINGTON ROAD
Sutton Park
West Town Lane Junior School
West Town Lane Infant School
Fairway
Lucas Cl
Hungerford Wk
Hungerford Crs
B2
1 Badgers Wk
2 Beeches Gv
3 Bellevue Pk
4 Bellevue Ter
5 Grove Pk
6 Wycombe Gv
Kew Walk
W Town Pk
W Town Gv
Westwood Rd
West Town Pk
Westbrook Road
Hungerford Road
Hungerford Cl
Hungerford Gdns
WEST TOWN LANE B3119
Bristol City Council
Beryl Gv
Imperial Rd
Warmington Road
Hazelbury Road
B3
1 Adams Hay
2 Bartonia Gv
3 Ellesmere Rd
4 Graveney Cl
5 Hammond Cl
6 Homemead Dr
7 Prestwick Cl
8 West Town Dr
WELLS ROAD
A37
Mowbray Road
Clive Rd
Eaton Drive
Kinsale Road
Beechwood Close
Durweston Wk
Manston Close
Wynash Cl
Hemplow Close
Newnham Close
Lyons Ct Rd
Amercombe Wk
Ilsyn Gv
Sturminster Road
Lanesborough Rise
Hencliffe Rd
Golf Course
Whittock Square
B5
1 Fontmell Ct
2 Hanford Ct
3 Morden Wk
4 Roundmoor Gdns
New Fosseway School
David's Road
104
Archer Wk
Ashwell Cl
Burnbush Cl
C2
1 Church Pde
2 Rock Cl
C3
1 Botham Dr
2 Flowers Hill Cl
1 grid square represents 500 metres

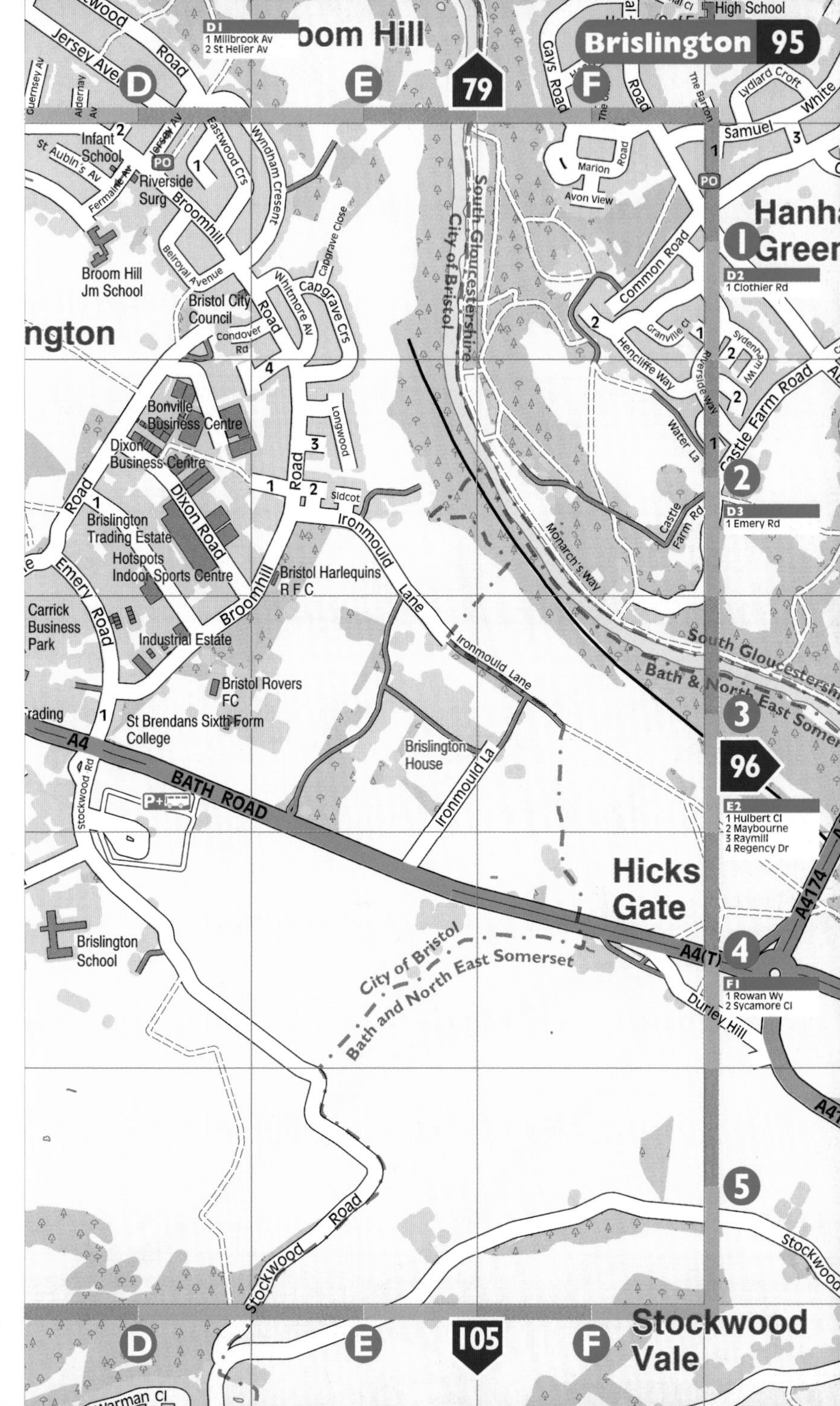
Broom Hill
D1
1 Millbrook Av
2 St Helier Av
79
High School
Jersey Ave
Road
Guernsey Av
Alderney Av
D
E
F
Gays Road
Road
The Barton
Lydiard Croft
White
Samuel
Infant School
St Aubin's Av
Fermaine Av
Jersey Av
Eastwood Crs
Wyndham Cresent
PO
Riverside Surg
Broomhill
Belroyal Avenue
Capgrave Close
Marion
Road
Avon View
South Gloucestershire
City of Bristol
Hanham Green
Broom Hill Jm School
Bristol City Council
Whitmore Av
Capgrave Crs
Road
Common Road
D2
1 Clothier Rd
ngton
Condover Rd
Granville Cl
Hencliffe Way
Riverside Way
Sydenham Wy
Castle Farm Road
Bonville Business Centre
Longwood
Water La
Dixon Business Centre
Road
Sidcot
Ironmould Lane
Castle Farm Rd
D3
1 Emery Rd
Brislington Trading Estate
Dixon Road
Hotspots Indoor Sports Centre
Monarch's Way
Broomhill
Bristol Harlequins R F C
Emery Road
Carrick Business Park
Industrial Estate
Ironmould Lane
South Gloucestershire
Bath & North East Somerset
Bristol Rovers FC
Trading
St Brendans Sixth Form College
A4
Brislington House
Ironmould La
96
Stockwood Rd
BATH ROAD
E2
1 Hulbert Cl
2 Maybourne
3 Raymill
4 Regency Dr
Hicks Gate
A4174
Brislington School
City of Bristol
Bath and North East Somerset
A4(T)
F1
1 Rowan Wy
2 Sycamore Cl
Durley Hill
Stockwood Road
Stockwood
Stockwood Vale
105
Warman Cl

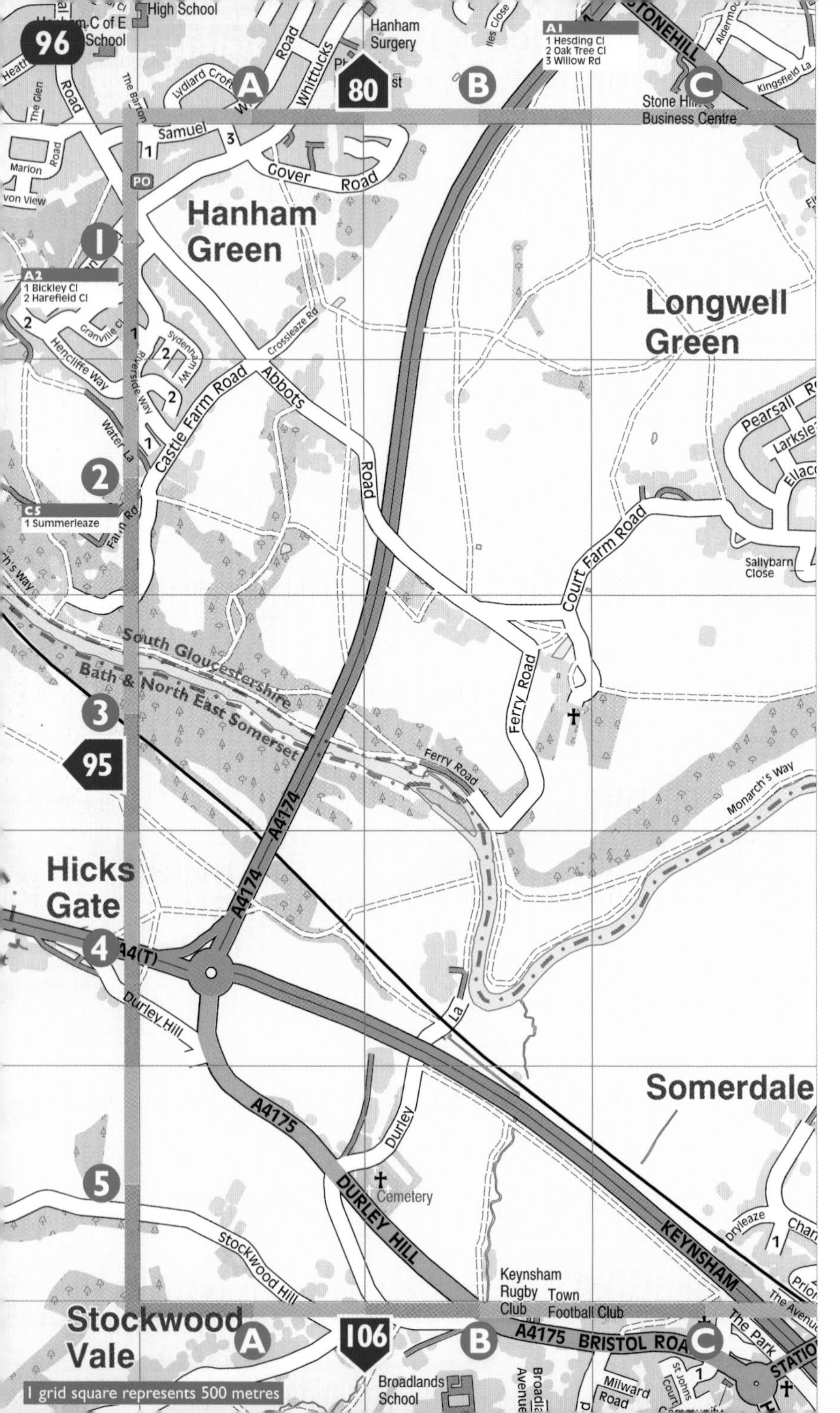
96
80
95
106
A
B
C
1
2
3
4
5
High School
Hanham C of E School
Hanham Surgery
A1
1 Hesding Cl
2 Oak Tree Cl
3 Willow Rd
Stone Hill Business Centre
Kingsfield La
Iles Close
Lydiard Croft
Whittucks Road
The Glen
Road
The Barton
Samuel
Marion
Road
Gover Road
PO
Hanham Green
A2
1 Bickley Cl
2 Harefield Cl
Granville Cl
Hencliffe Way
Sydenham Way
Crossleaze Rd
Riverside Way
Castle Farm Road
Abbots Road
Water La
Longwell Green
Pearsall Rd
Court Farm Road
Sallybarn Close
C5
1 Summerleaze
Farm Rd
South Gloucestershire
Bath & North East Somerset
Ferry Road
Monarch's Way
A4174
Hicks Gate
A4(T)
Durley Hill
La
Durley
A4175
DURLEY HILL
Cemetery
Somerdale
KEYNSHAM
Drylease
Stockwood Hill
Keynsham Rugby Club
Town Football Club
The Avenue
The Park
Stockwood Vale
A4175 BRISTOL ROAD
Broadlands School
Milward Road
St Johns Court
STATION
I grid square represents 500 metres

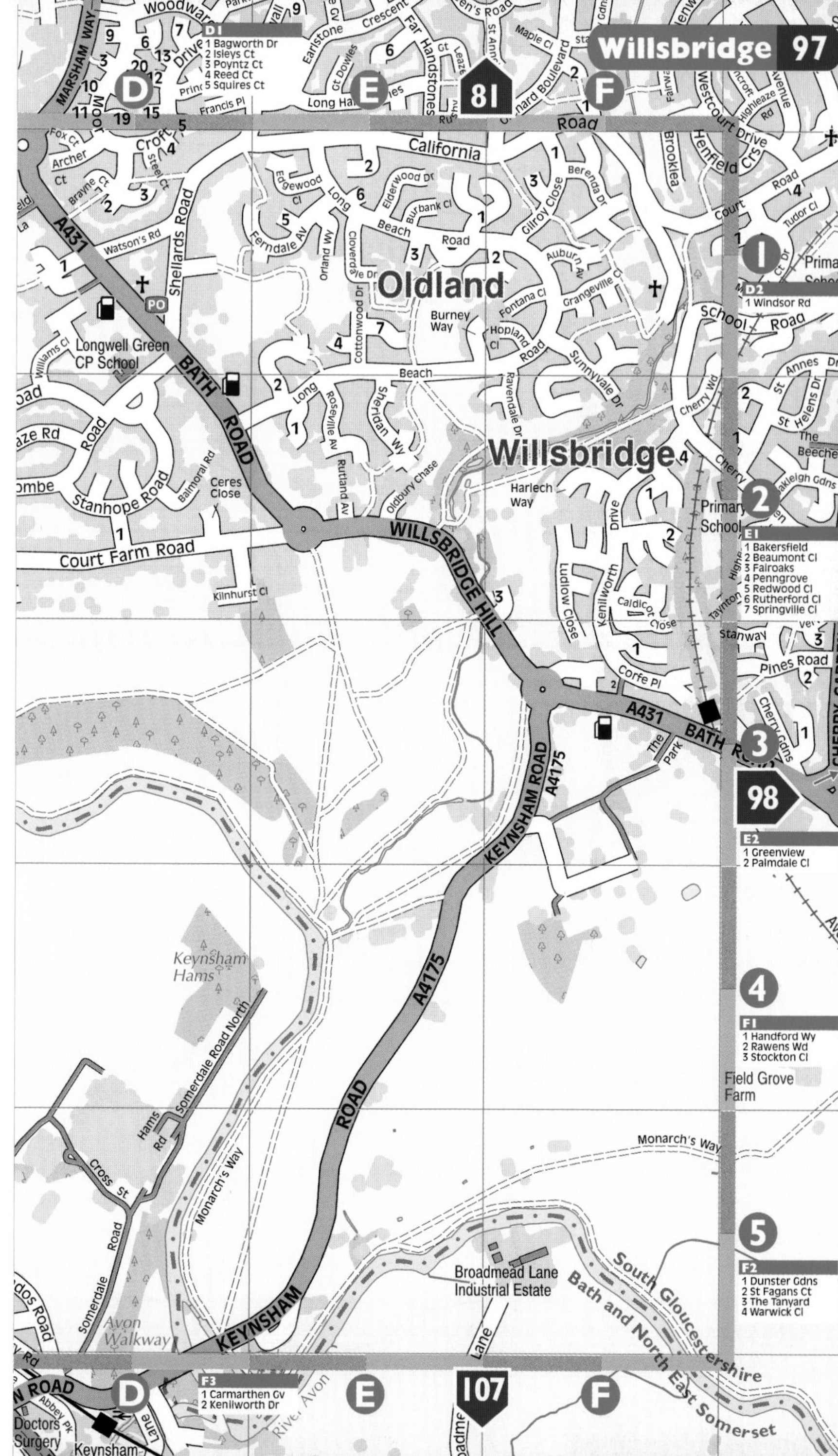
Oldland
Willsbridge
81
98
107
D1
1 Bagworth Dr
2 Isleys Ct
3 Poyntz Ct
4 Reed Ct
5 Squires Ct
D2
1 Windsor Rd
E1
1 Bakersfield
2 Beaumont Cl
3 Fairoaks
4 Penngrove
5 Redwood Cl
6 Rutherford Cl
7 Springville Cl
E2
1 Greenview
2 Palmdale Cl
F1
1 Handford Wy
2 Rawens Wd
3 Stockton Cl
F2
1 Dunster Gdns
2 St Fagans Ct
3 The Tanyard
4 Warwick Cl
F3
1 Carmarthen Gv
2 Kenilworth Dr
California Road
Court Farm Road
Willsbridge Hill
Bath Road
A431
Keynsham Road
A4175
Longwell Green CP School
Keynsham Hams
Somerdale Road North
Monarch's Way
Broadmead Lane Industrial Estate
Field Grove Farm
Avon Walkway
South Gloucestershire
Bath and North East Somerset
Cherry Garden Road
Doctors Surgery
Keynsham
Primary School

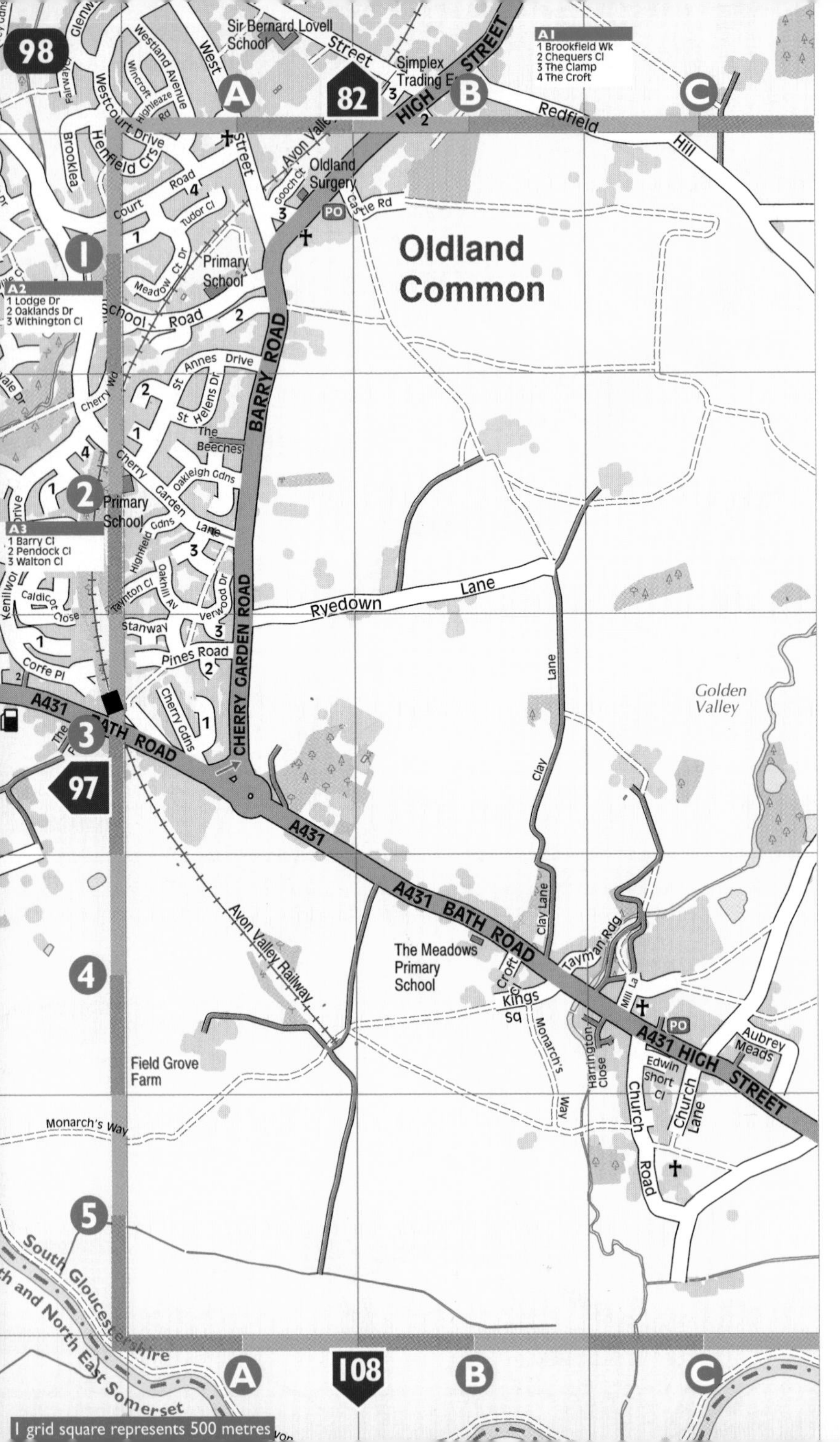
98
82
97
108
A
B
C
1
2
3
4
5
A1
1 Brookfield Wk
2 Chequers Cl
3 The Clamp
4 The Croft
A2
1 Lodge Dr
2 Oaklands Dr
3 Withington Cl
A3
1 Barry Cl
2 Pendock Cl
3 Walton Cl
Oldland
Common
Golden
Valley
Sir Bernard Lovell
School
Simplex
Trading Est
West Street
HIGH STREET
Redfield Hill
Westcourt Drive
Henfield Crs
Brooklea
Court Road
Tudor Cl
Oldland
Surgery
Castle Rd
Gooch Ct
Avon Valley
Primary
School
Meadow Ct Dr
School Road
BARRY ROAD
St Annes Drive
St Helens Dr
The
Beeches
Cherry Wd
Cherry Garden Lane
Oakleigh Gdns
Primary
School
Highfield Gdns
Taynton Cl
Oakhill Av
Verwood Dr
Caldicot Close
Stanway
Pines Road
Corfe Pl
CHERRY GARDEN ROAD
Cherry Gdns
Ryedown Lane
Clay Lane
A431 BATH ROAD
A431
The Meadows
Primary
School
Croft Cl
Kings Sq
Monarch's Way
Tayman Rdg
Mill La
PO
A431 HIGH STREET
Aubrey
Meads
Harrington Close
Edwin Short Cl
Church Road
Church Lane
Avon Valley Railway
Field Grove
Farm
Monarch's Way
South Gloucestershire
Bath and North East Somerset
1 grid square represents 500 metres

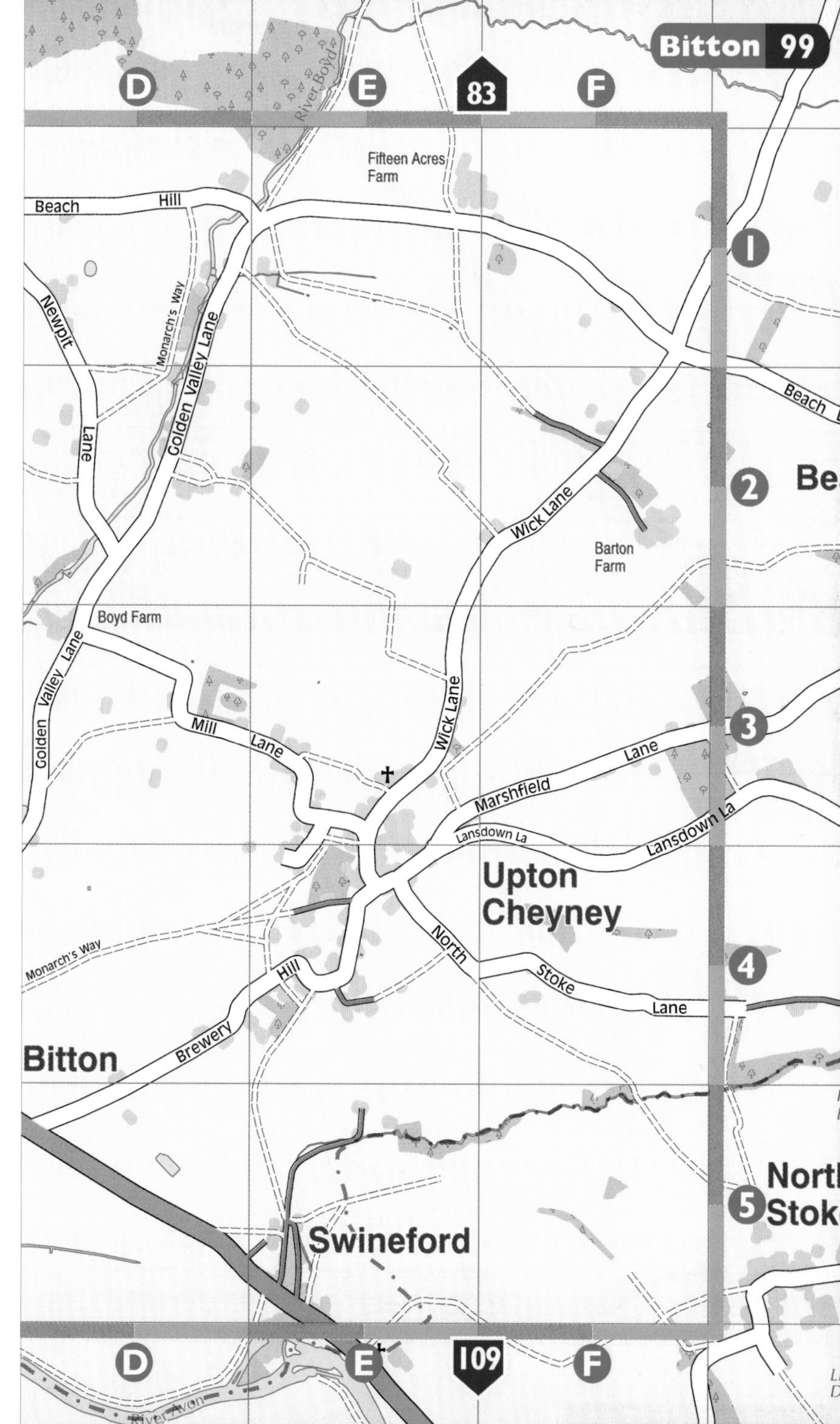
D
E
83
F
River Boyd
Fifteen Acres
Farm
Beach
Hill
Newpit
Lane
Monarch's Way
Golden Valley Lane
1
2
Beach L
Bea
Wick Lane
Barton
Farm
Boyd Farm
Golden Valley Lane
Mill
Lane
Wick Lane
3
Marshfield
Lane
Lansdown La
Lansdown La
Upton
Cheyney
North
Stoke
Lane
4
Monarch's Way
Hill
Brewery
Bitton
North
Stoke
5
Swineford
D
E
109
F
River Avon

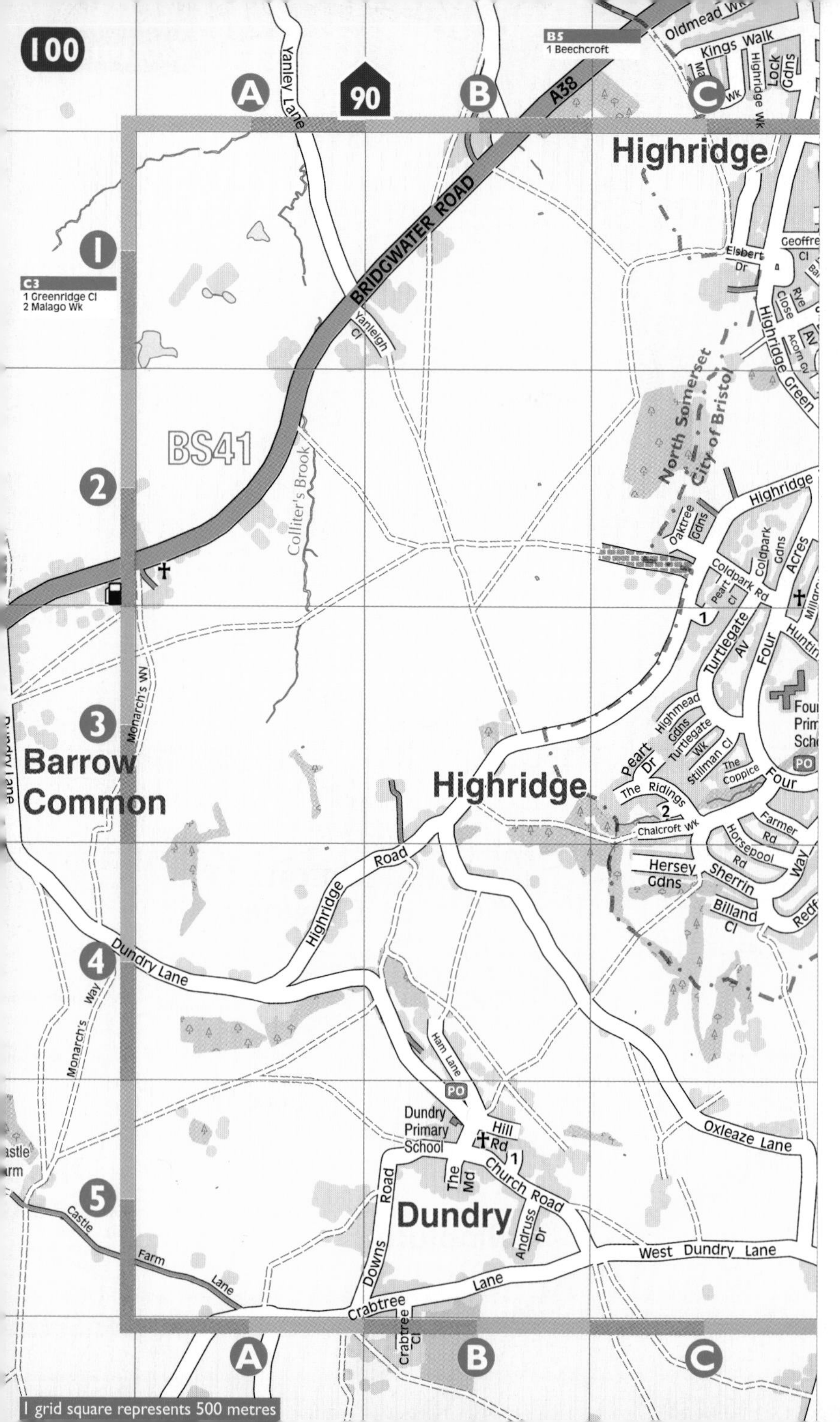
90
A
B
C
1
2
3
4
5
B5
1 Beechcroft
C3
1 Greenridge Cl
2 Malago Wk
Yanley Lane
A38
BRIDGWATER ROAD
Yanleigh Cl
Highridge
Oldmead Wk
Kings Walk
Highridge Wk
Lock Gdns
Elsbert Dr
Geoffrey Cl
Rye Close
Acorn Gv
Highridge Green
North Somerset
City of Bristol
BS41
Colliter's Brook
Highridge
Oaktree Gdns
Coldpark Gdns
Coldpark Rd
Acres
Peart Cl
Turtlegate Av
Four
Monarch's Wy
Barrow Common
Highmead Gdns
Turtlegate Wk
Stillman Cl
The Coppice
Peart Dr
The Ridings
Chalcroft Wk
Highridge
Four
Farmer Rd
Horsepool Rd
Way
Hersey Gdns
Sherrin
Billand Cl
Highridge Road
Dundry Lane
Monarch's Way
Ham Lane
PO
Dundry Primary School
Hill Rd
Oxleaze Lane
The Md
Church Road
Castle Farm
Castle Farm Lane
Downs Road
Dundry
Andruss Dr
West Dundry Lane
Crabtree Lane
Crabtree Cl
1 grid square represents 500 metres

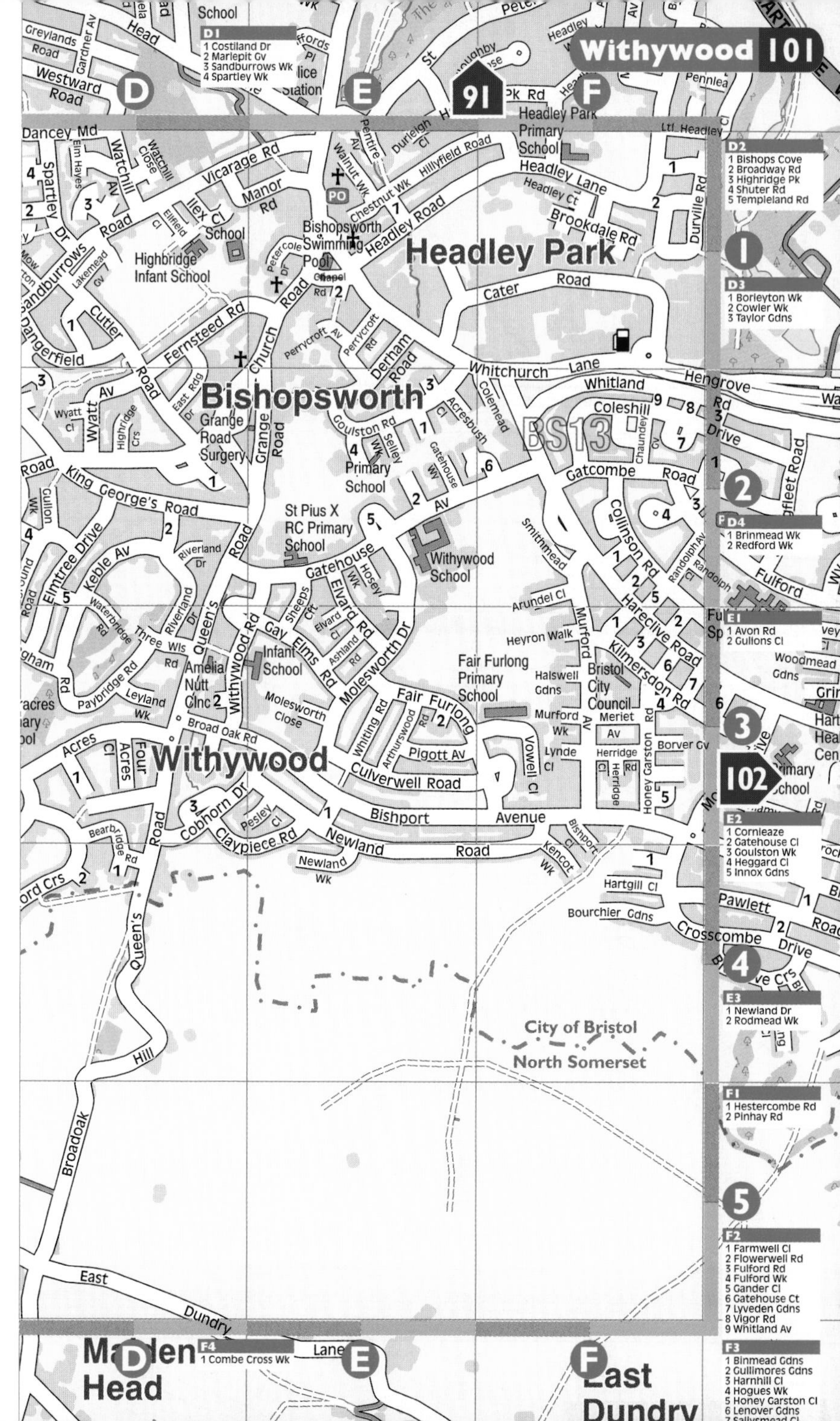
D1
1 Costiland Dr
2 Marlepit Gv
3 Sandburrows Wk
4 Spartley Wk
91
D
E
F
D2
1 Bishops Cove
2 Broadway Rd
3 Highridge Pk
4 Shuter Rd
5 Templeland Rd
D3
1 Borleyton Wk
2 Cowler Wk
3 Taylor Gdns
D4
1 Brinmead Wk
2 Redford Wk
E1
1 Avon Rd
2 Gullons Cl
E2
1 Cornleaze
2 Gatehouse Cl
3 Goulston Wk
4 Heggard Cl
5 Innox Gdns
E3
1 Newland Dr
2 Rodmead Wk
F1
1 Hestercombe Rd
2 Pinhay Rd
F2
1 Farmwell Cl
2 Flowerwell Rd
3 Fulford Rd
4 Fulford Wk
5 Gander Cl
6 Gatehouse Ct
7 Lyveden Gdns
8 Vigor Rd
9 Whitland Av
F3
1 Binmead Gdns
2 Gullimores Gdns
3 Harnhill Cl
4 Hogues Wk
5 Honey Garston Cl
6 Lenover Gdns
7 Sallysmead Cl
F4
1 Combe Cross Wk
102
1
2
3
4
5
Headley Park
Bishopsworth
Withywood
BS13
Maiden Head
East Dundry
City of Bristol
North Somerset
Headley Park Primary School
Highbridge Infant School
Bishopsworth Swimming Pool
Grange Road Surgery
St Pius X RC Primary School
Withywood School
Primary School
Infant School
Amelia Nutt Clnc
Fair Furlong Primary School
Bristol City Council
School
Whitchurch Lane
Hengrove Way
Headley Lane
Headley Road
Cater Road
Vicarage Rd
King George's Road
Queen's Road
Broad Oak Rd
Bishport Avenue
Newland Road
Culverwell Road
Gatehouse Av
Molesworth Dr
Hareclive Road
Collinson Rd
Gatcombe Road
Kilmersdon Rd
Church Road
Grange Road
Withywood Rd
Broadoak Hill
East Dundry Lane
Crosscombe Drive
Pawlett Road
Fulford Rd
Whitland Rd
Coleshill Drive

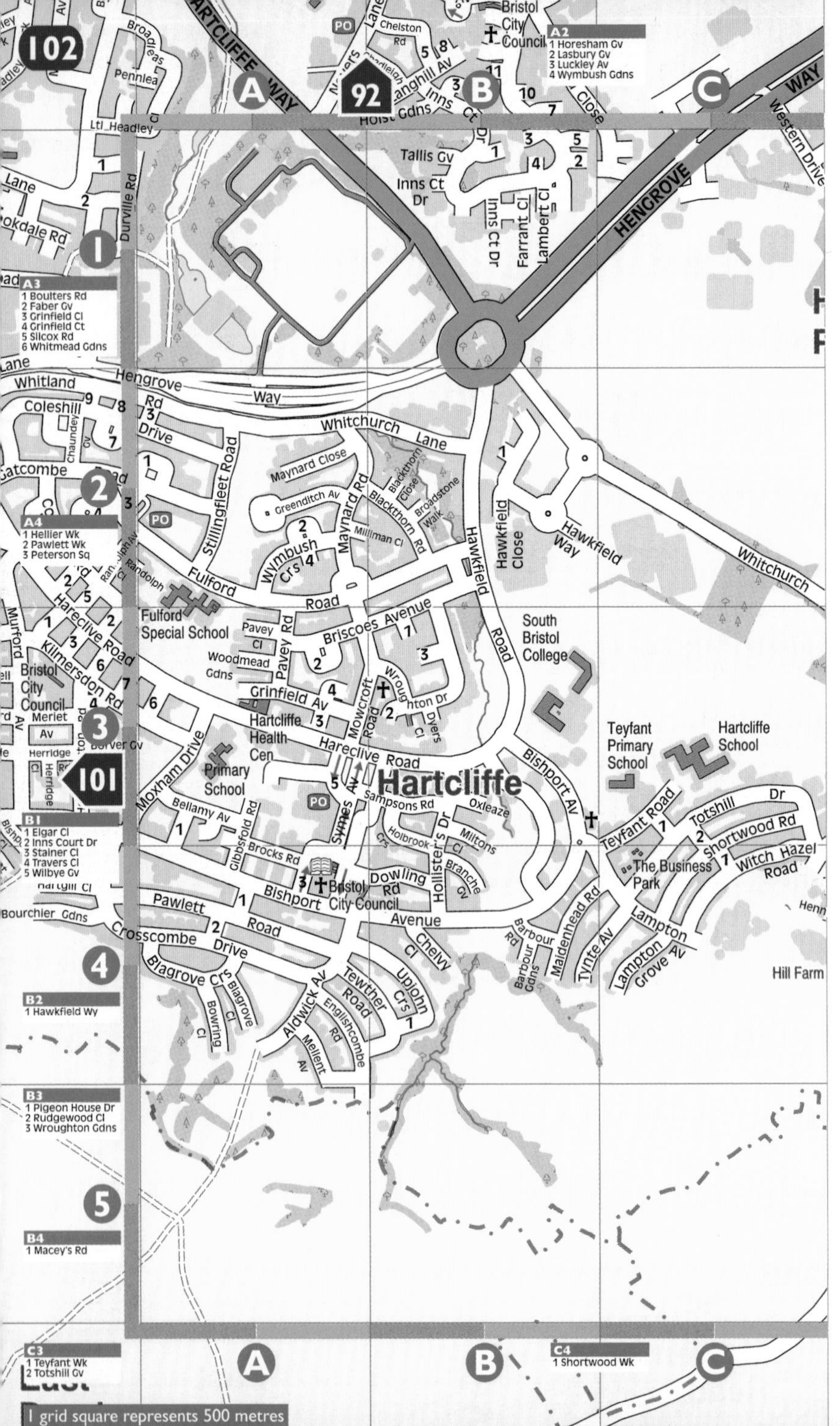

102
92
101
A
B
C
1
2
3
4
5
HARTCLIFFE WAY
HENGROVE WAY
WAY
Bristol City Council
A2
1 Horesham Gv
2 Lasbury Gv
3 Luckley Av
4 Wymbush Gdns
Chelston Rd
Holst Gdns
Inns Ct Dr
Tallis Gv
Farrant Cl
Lambert Cl
Close
Western Drive
Broadleas
Pennlea
Ltl Headley
Durville Rd
Lane
Brookdale Rd
A3
1 Boulters Rd
2 Faber Gv
3 Grinfield Cl
4 Grinfield Ct
5 Silcox Rd
6 Whitmead Gdns
Whitland Rd
Hengrove Way
Coleshill Drive
Chaundey Gv
Gatcombe Road
A4
1 Hellier Wk
2 Pawlett Wk
3 Peterson Sq
Randolph Av
Whitchurch Lane
Stillingfleet Road
Maynard Close
Greenditch Av
Maynard Rd
Blackthorn Close
Blackthorn Rd
Broadstone Walk
Millman Cl
Wymbush Crs
Hawkfield Road
Hawkfield Close
Hawkfield Way
Whitchurch
Fulford Road
Fulford Special School
Briscoes Avenue
Pavey Rd
Pavey Cl
Woodmead Gdns
Murford Av
Hareclive Road
Kilmersdon Rd
Bristol City Council
Grinfield Av
Wroughton Dr
Dyers Cl
Mowcroft Road
South Bristol College
Meriet Av
Herridge Cl
Herridge Rd
Hartcliffe Health Cen
Moxham Drive
Primary School
Hartcliffe
Symes Av
Sampsons Rd
Oxleaze
Bishport Av
Teyfant Primary School
Hartcliffe School
Teyfant Road
Totshill Dr
Shortwood Rd
Witch Hazel Road
The Business Park
B1
1 Elgar Cl
2 Inns Court Dr
3 Stainer Cl
4 Travers Cl
5 Wilbye Gv
Bellamy Av
Gibbsfold Rd
Brocks Rd
Holbrook Crs
Hollister's Dr
Miltons Cl
Branche Gv
Dowling Rd
Bristol City Council
Bishport Avenue
Hartgill Cl
Bourchier Gdns
Pawlett Road
Crosscombe Drive
Chelvy Cl
Barbour Rd
Barbour Gdns
Maidenhead Rd
Tynte Av
Lampton Av
Lampton Grove
Hill Farm
Blagrove Crs
Blagrove Cl
Bowring Cl
Aldwick Av
Englishcombe Rd
Mellent Av
Tewther Road
Uphon Crs
B2
1 Hawkfield Wy
B3
1 Pigeon House Dr
2 Rudgewood Cl
3 Wroughton Gdns
B4
1 Macey's Rd
C3
1 Teyfant Wk
2 Totshill Gv
C4
1 Shortwood Wk
1 grid square represents 500 metres

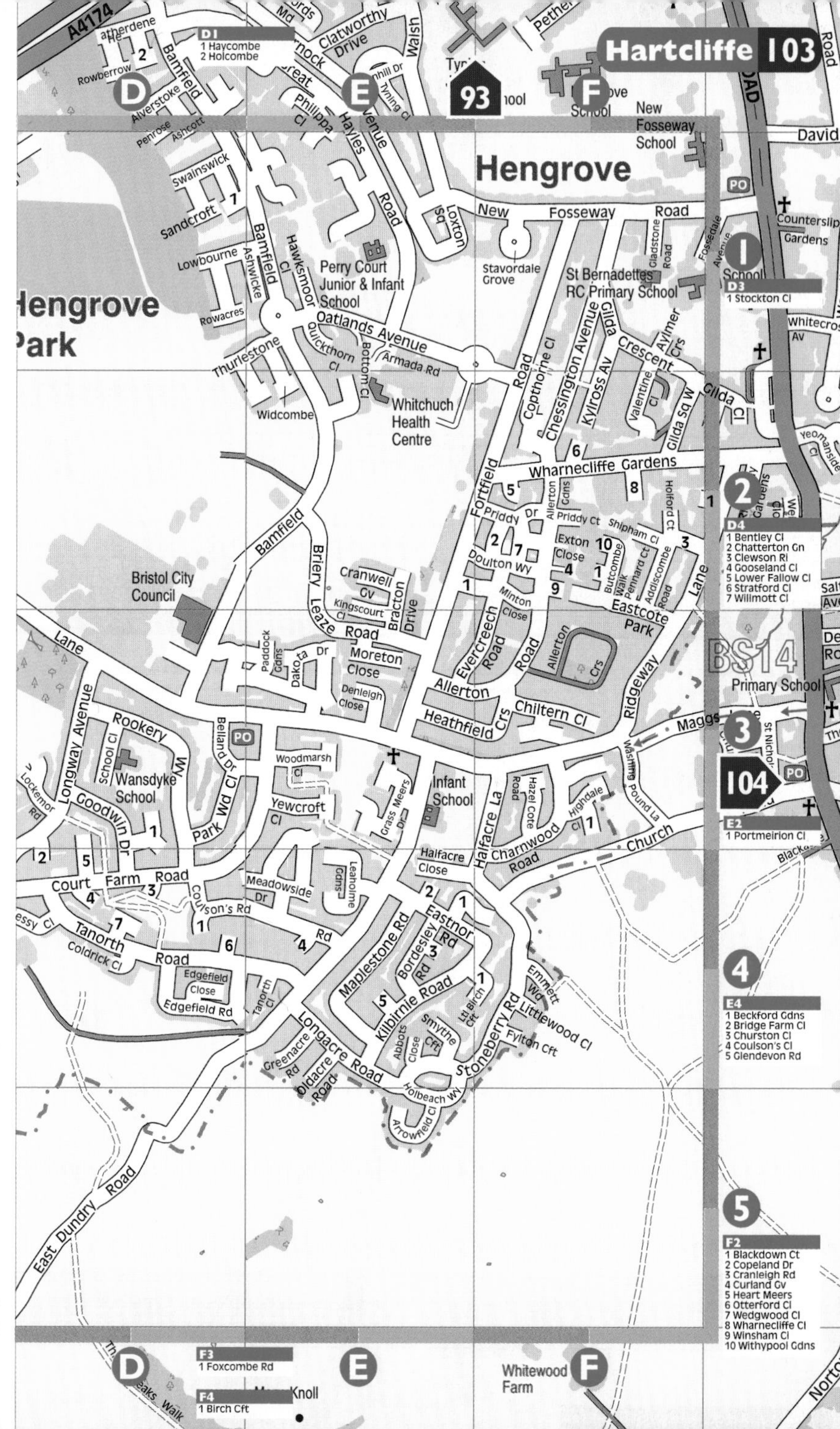
Hengrove
Hengrove Park
D1
1 Haycombe
2 Holcombe
D3
1 Stockton Cl
D4
1 Bentley Cl
2 Chatterton Gn
3 Clewson Ri
4 Gooseland Cl
5 Lower Fallow Cl
6 Stratford Cl
7 Willmott Cl
E2
1 Portmeirion Cl
E4
1 Beckford Gdns
2 Bridge Farm Cl
3 Churston Cl
4 Coulson's Cl
5 Glendevon Rd
F2
1 Blackdown Ct
2 Copeland Dr
3 Cranleigh Rd
4 Curland Gv
5 Heart Meers
6 Otterford Cl
7 Wedgwood Cl
8 Wharnecliffe Cl
9 Winsham Cl
10 Withypool Gdns
F3
1 Foxcombe Rd
F4
1 Birch Cft
93
104
BS14
New Fosseway Road
Oatlands Avenue
Perry Court Junior & Infant School
St Bernadettes RC Primary School
New Fosseway School
Whitchuch Health Centre
Bristol City Council
Wansdyke School
Infant School
Primary School
Wharnecliffe Gardens
Allerton Road
Briery Leaze Road
Fortfield Road
Court Farm Road
Tanorth Road
Longacre Road
Kilbirnie Road
Stoneberry Rd
East Dundry Road
Church Road
Maggs Lane
Whitewood Farm
Moat Knoll

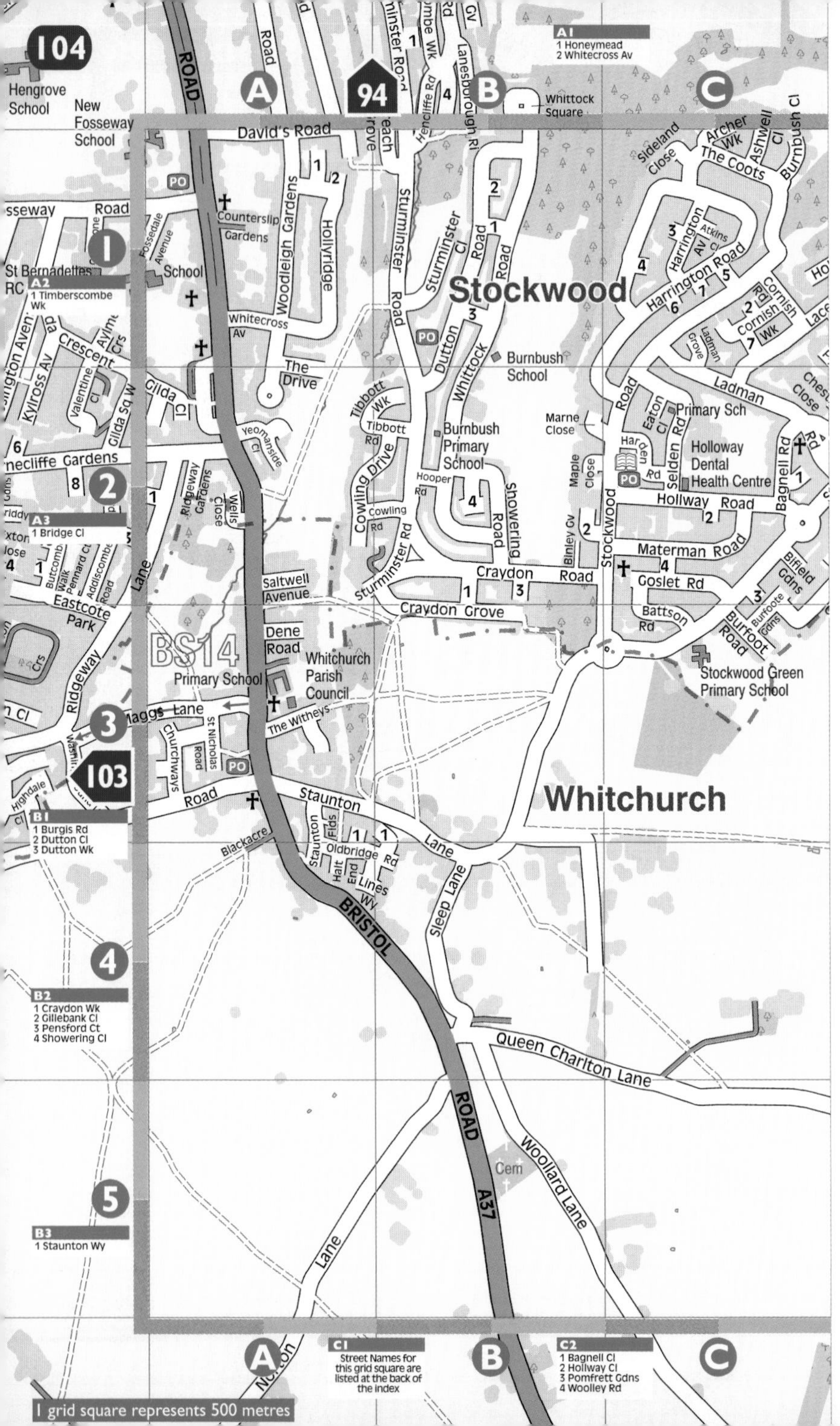
104
Hengrove School
New Fosseway School
94
A1
1 Honeymead
2 Whitecross Av
Whittock Square
David's Road
Woodleigh Gardens
Hollyridge
Sturminster Road
Sturminster Cl
Lanesborough Ri
Hencliffe Rd
Counterslip Gardens
Fossedale Avenue
School
St Bernadettes RC
A2
1 Timberscombe Wk
Whitecross Av
The Drive
Crescent
Kylross Av
Valentine Cl
Gilda Cl
Gilda Sq W
Yeomanside Cl
Ridgeway Gardens
Wells Close
A3
1 Bridge Cl
Butcombe Walk
Pennard Ct
Addiscombe Road
Eastcote Park
Ridgeway
Lane
Saltwell Avenue
Dene Road
BS14
Primary School
Whitchurch Parish Council
Maggs Lane
The Witheys
Churchways
St Nicholas Road
103
Highdale
B1
1 Burgis Rd
2 Dutton Cl
3 Dutton Wk
Road
Staunton Lane
Staunton Flds
Oldbridge Rd
Halt End
Lines Wy
Blackacre
BRISTOL ROAD
Sleep Lane
B2
1 Craydon Wk
2 Gillebank Cl
3 Pensford Ct
4 Showering Cl
Queen Charlton Lane
ROAD A37
Woollard Lane
Cem
Lane
B3
1 Staunton Wy
Norton
C1
Street Names for this grid square are listed at the back of the index
C2
1 Bagnell Cl
2 Hollway Cl
3 Pomfrett Gdns
4 Woolley Rd
1 grid square represents 500 metres
Stockwood
Tibbott Wk
Tibbott Rd
Cowling Drive
Cowling Rd
Dutton Road
Whittock Road
Burnbush School
Burnbush Primary School
Hooper Rd
Showering Road
Craydon Road
Craydon Grove
Sturminster Rd
Sideland Close
Archer Wk
The Coots
Ashwell Cl
Burnbush Cl
Harrington Av
Atkins Cl
Harrington Road
Cornish Rd
Cornish Wk
Ladman Grove
Ladman Road
Primary Sch
Eaton Cl
Selden Rd
Harden Rd
Holloway Dental Health Centre
Marne Close
Maple Close
Binley Gv
Stockwood Road
Hollway Road
Bagnell Rd
Materman Road
Goslet Rd
Battson Rd
Burfoot Road
Burfoote Gdns
Bifield Gdns
Stockwood Green Primary School
Whitchurch
PO

D1
1 Cogsall Rd
2 Holsom Rd
3 Swane Rd
Stockwood Road
95
D
E
F
Stockwood
Vale
1
D2
1 Cantell Gv
2 Warren Gdns
Warman Cl
Warman Rd
Road
Cottle Gdns
Derricke Road
Cottle Road
Matthews Close
Lane
Pynne Cl
Pynne Rd
Townsend Road
Townsend Close
Stockwood Road
Coape Rd
Bifield Road
Bifield Close
2
Lays Farm
Caroline Cl
3
106
Walnut Close
4
Queen
Charlton
Queen Charlton Lane
Lane
Dapwell Lane
Charlton Road
Parkhouse
5
High
D
E
F

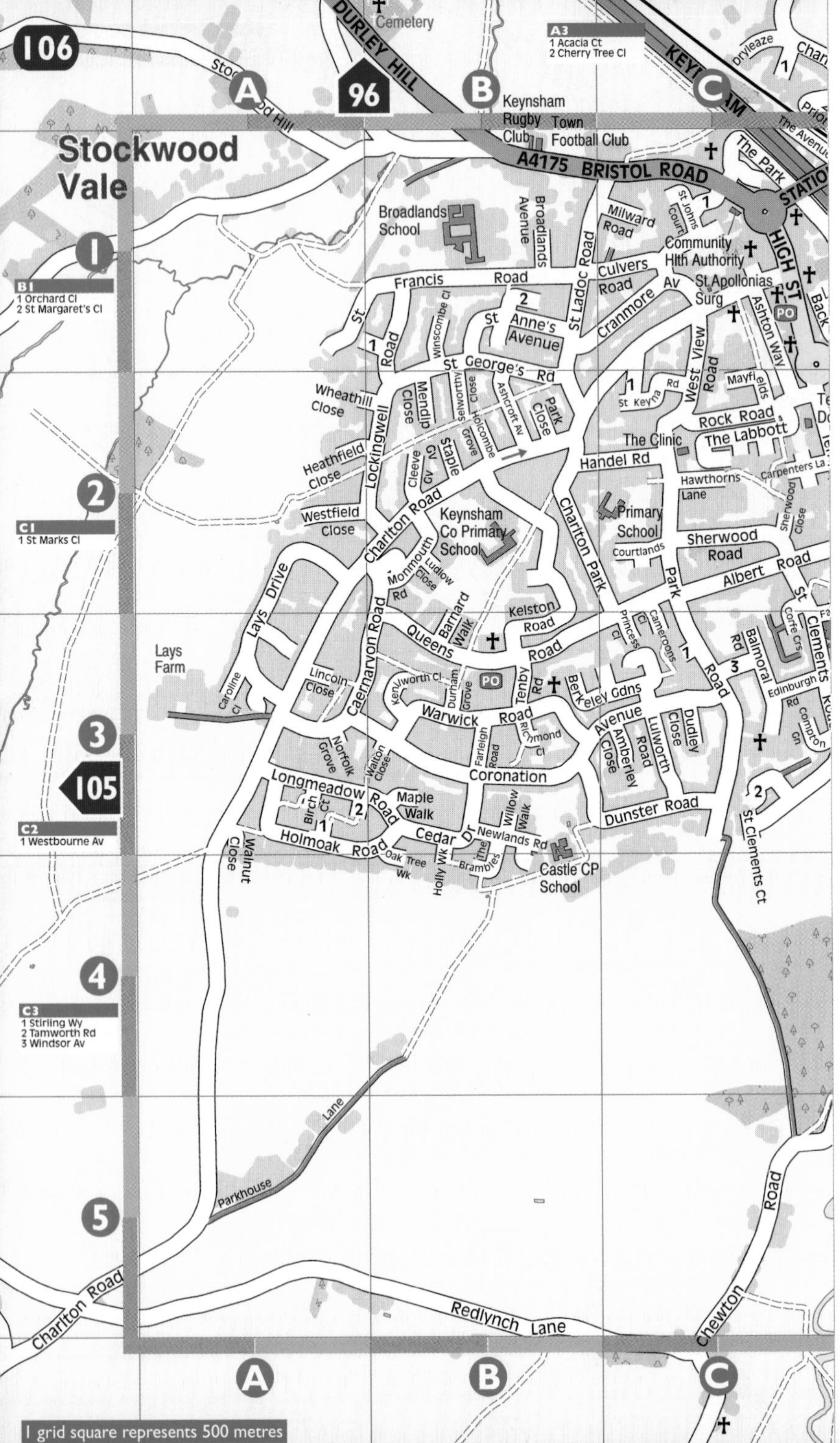
106
96
105
A
B
C
1
2
3
4
5
Stockwood Vale
Stockwood Hill
Durley Hill
Cemetery
Keynsham Rugby Club
Town Football Club
A4175 Bristol Road
Keynsham
Station
High St
A3
1 Acacia Ct
2 Cherry Tree Cl
B1
1 Orchard Cl
2 St Margaret's Cl
C1
1 St Marks Cl
C2
1 Westbourne Av
C3
1 Stirling Wy
2 Tamworth Rd
3 Windsor Av
Broadlands School
Broadlands Avenue
Milward Road
St Johns Court
Community Hlth Authority
St Apollonias Surg
Francis Road
St Ladoc Road
Culvers Road
Cranmore Av
St Anne's Avenue
Winscombe Cl
St Francis Road
St George's Rd
Wheathill Close
Lockingwell Road
Mendip Close
Selworthy Close
Holcombe Grove
Ashcroft Av
Park Close
St Keyna Rd
West View Road
Ashton Way
Mayfields
Rock Road
The Labbott
The Clinic
Handel Rd
Hawthorns Lane
Carpenters La
Sherwood Close
Heathfield Close
Cleeve Gv
Staple Gv
Westfield Close
Charlton Road
Keynsham Co Primary School
Charlton Park
Primary School
Courtlands
Sherwood Road
Albert Road
Park Road
St Clements Road
Monmouth Rd
Ludlow Close
Barrard Walk
Kelston Road
Princess Cl
Camerons Cl
Coffe Crs
Balmoral Rd
Edinburgh Rd
Compton Gn
Lays Drive
Lays Farm
Caernarvon Road
Queens Road
Lincoln Close
Kenilworth Cl
Durham Grove
PO
Tenby Rd
Berkeley Gdns
Caroline Cl
Warwick Road
Richmond Cl
Avenue
Amberley Close
Lulworth Road
Dudley Close
Norfolk Grove
Walton Close
Farleigh Road
Coronation
Longmeadow Road
Birch Ct
Maple Walk
Willow Walk
Dunster Road
Holmoak Road
Cedar Dr
Newlands Rd
Oak Tree Wk
Holly Wk
The Brambles
Castle CP School
Walnut Close
St Clements Ct
Parkhouse Lane
Chewton Road
Charlton Road
Redlynch Lane
Dryleaze
The Park
The Avenue
1 grid square represents 500 metres

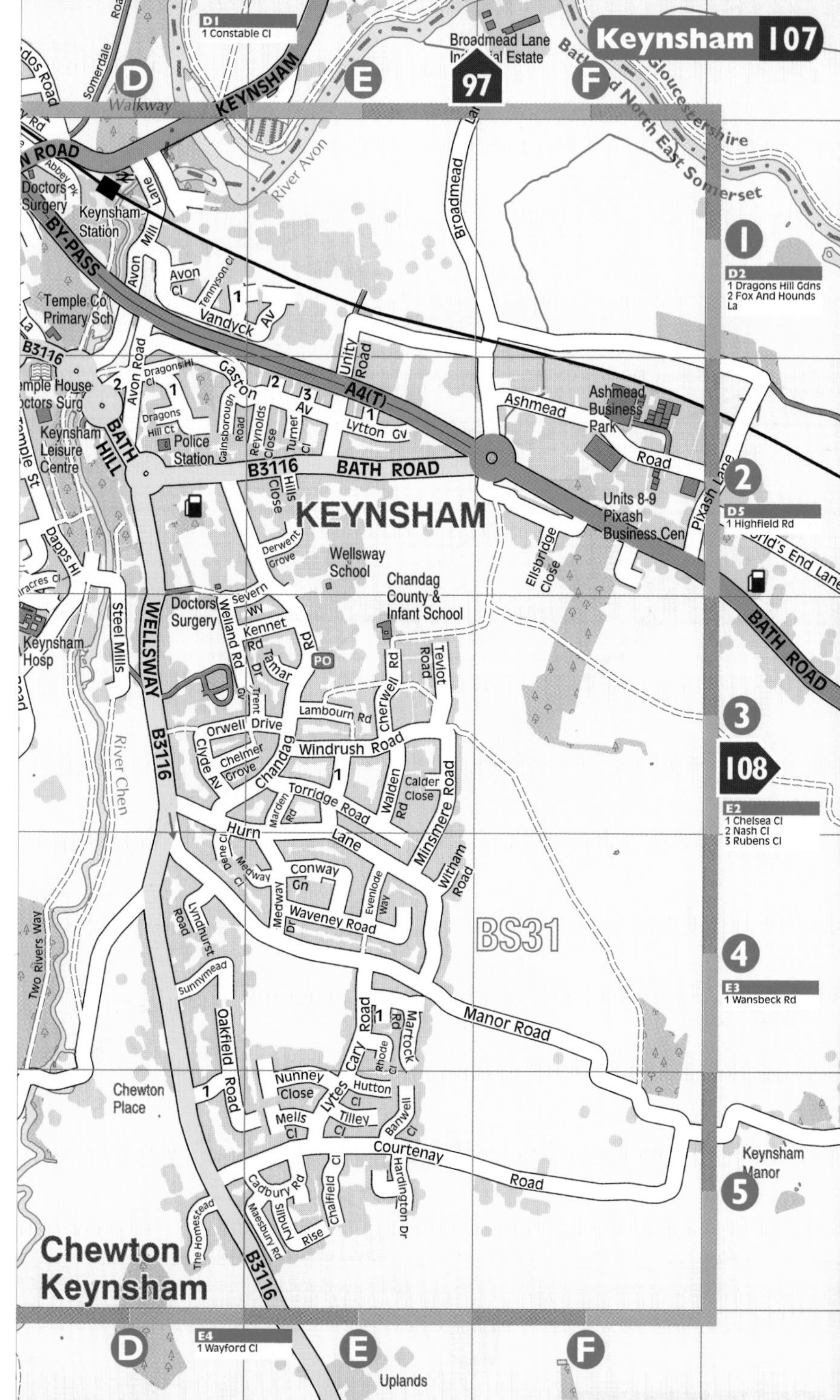
D1
1 Constable Cl
Broadmead Lane Industrial Estate
97
D
E
F
KEYNSHAM
Walkway
Somerdale
Keynsham Station
Doctors Surgery
Abbey Pk
BY-PASS
Temple Co Primary Sch
Temple House Doctors Surg
Keynsham Leisure Centre
Police Station
B3116
BATH ROAD
A4(T)
BATH HILL
Avon Mill Lane
Avon Cl
Tennyson Cl
Vandyck Av
Dragons Hl Cl
Dragons Hill Ct
Avon Road
Gaston Av
Gainsborough Road
Reynolds Close
Turner Cl
Lytton Gv
Unity Road
Hills Close
Broadmead Lane
River Avon
Ashmead Business Park
Ashmead Road
Units 8-9 Pixash Business Cen
Pixash Lane
Ellsbridge Close
Bath and North East Somerset
Gloucestershire
D2
1 Dragons Hill Gdns
2 Fox And Hounds La
D5
1 Highfield Rd
World's End Lane
KEYNSHAM
Derwent Grove
Wellsway School
Chandag County & Infant School
Doctors Surgery
Severn Wy
Welland Rd
Kennet Rd
Tamar Dr
Trent Gv
PO
Chandag Rd
Cherwell Rd
Teviot Road
Lambourn Rd
Orwell Drive
Clyde Av
Chelmer Grove
Windrush Road
Torridge Road
Marden Rd
Walden Rd
Calder Close
Minsmere Road
Hurn Lane
Dene Cl
Medway Cl
Conway Gn
Medway Dr
Evenlode Way
Waveney Road
Witham Road
WELLSWAY
B3116
Steel Mills
Dapps Hl
Keynsham Hosp
Temple St
River Chen
Two Rivers Way
Lyndhurst Road
Sunnymead
Oakfield Road
BS31
Manor Road
Cary Road
Martock Rd
Rhode Cl
Nunney Close
Lytes Cary
Hutton Cl
Mells Cl
Tilley Cl
Banwell Cl
Courtenay Road
Cadbury Rd
Chalfield Cl
Hardington Dr
Silbury Rise
Maesbury Rd
The Homestead
Chewton Place
Chewton Keynsham
B3116
Keynsham Manor
1
2
3
4
5
108
E2
1 Chelsea Cl
2 Nash Cl
3 Rubens Cl
E3
1 Wansbeck Rd
E4
1 Wayford Cl
Uplands

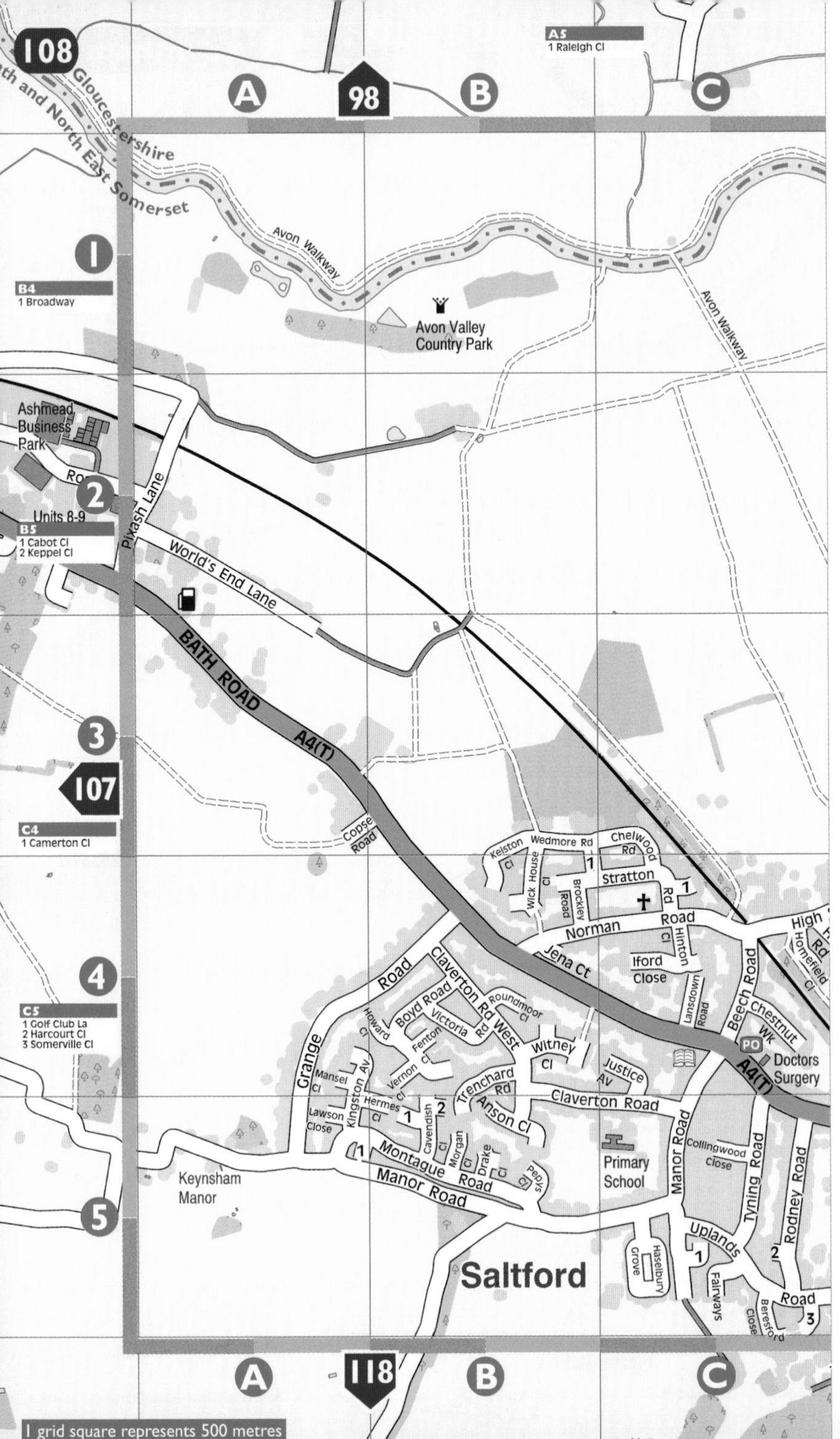
108
98
A5
1 Raleigh Cl
A
B
C
Gloucestershire
Bath and North East Somerset
Avon Walkway
Avon Valley
Country Park
1
B4
1 Broadway
Ashmead
Business
Park
2
Units 8-9
B5
1 Cabot Cl
2 Keppel Cl
Pixash Lane
World's End Lane
BATH ROAD
A4(T)
3
107
C4
1 Camerton Cl
Copse Road
Kelston Cl
Wedmore Rd
Chelwood Rd
Wick House Cl
Brockley Road
Stratton Rd
Norman Road
Hinton Cl
Jena Ct
Iford Close
High St
Homefield Cl
Beech Road
Chestnut Wk
Lansdown Road
4
C5
1 Golf Club La
2 Harcourt Cl
3 Somerville Cl
Grange Road
Claverton Rd West
Boyd Road
Victoria Rd
Roundmoor Cl
Howard Cl
Fenton Cl
Witney Cl
Justice Av
Doctors Surgery
Mansel Cl
Kingston Av
Vernon Cl
Trenchard Rd
Claverton Road
Hermes Cl
Cavendish Cl
Anson Cl
Lawson Close
Morgan Cl
Drake Cl
Sayes Cl
Montague Road
Manor Road
Primary School
Collingwood Close
Tyning Road
Rodney Road
Keynsham Manor
5
Saltford
Uplands
Grove
Haselbury
Fairways
Beresford Close
Road
118
1 grid square represents 500 metres

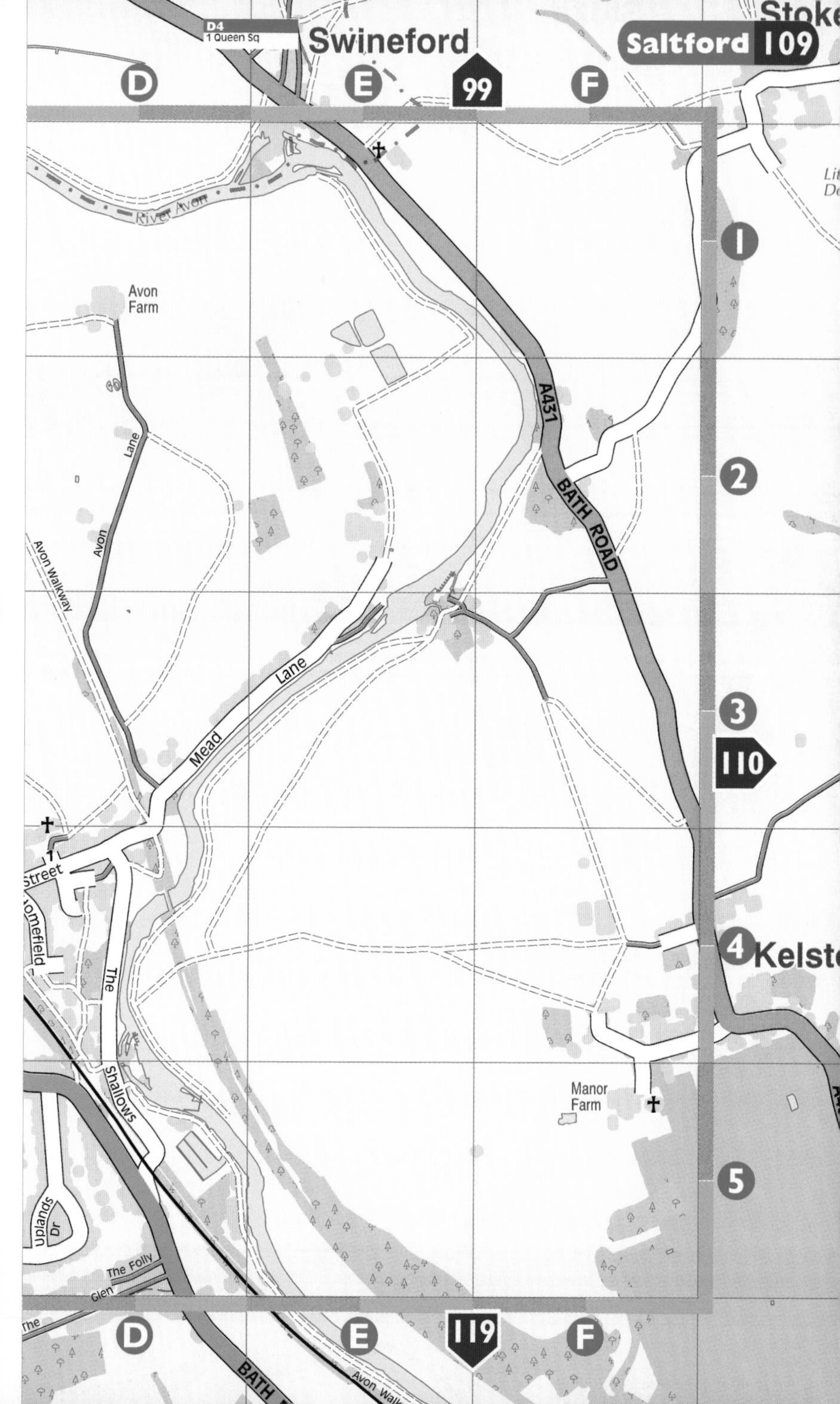
D4
1 Queen Sq
Swineford
Saltford 109
Stoke
D
E
F
99
River Avon
Avon Farm
Avon Lane
Avon Walkway
A431
BATH ROAD
Mead Lane
110
Street
The Shallows
Kelst
Manor Farm
Uplands Dr
The Folly
Glen
The
119
BATH
Avon Walk
1
2
3
4
5

Stoke
110
A
B
C
Little Down
1
2
BATH ROAD
Prospect Stile
3
109
4
Kelston
Cotswold Way
Manor Farm
A431
5
Kelston Park
Dean Hill House
A
120
B
C
1 grid square represents 500 metres
KELSTON

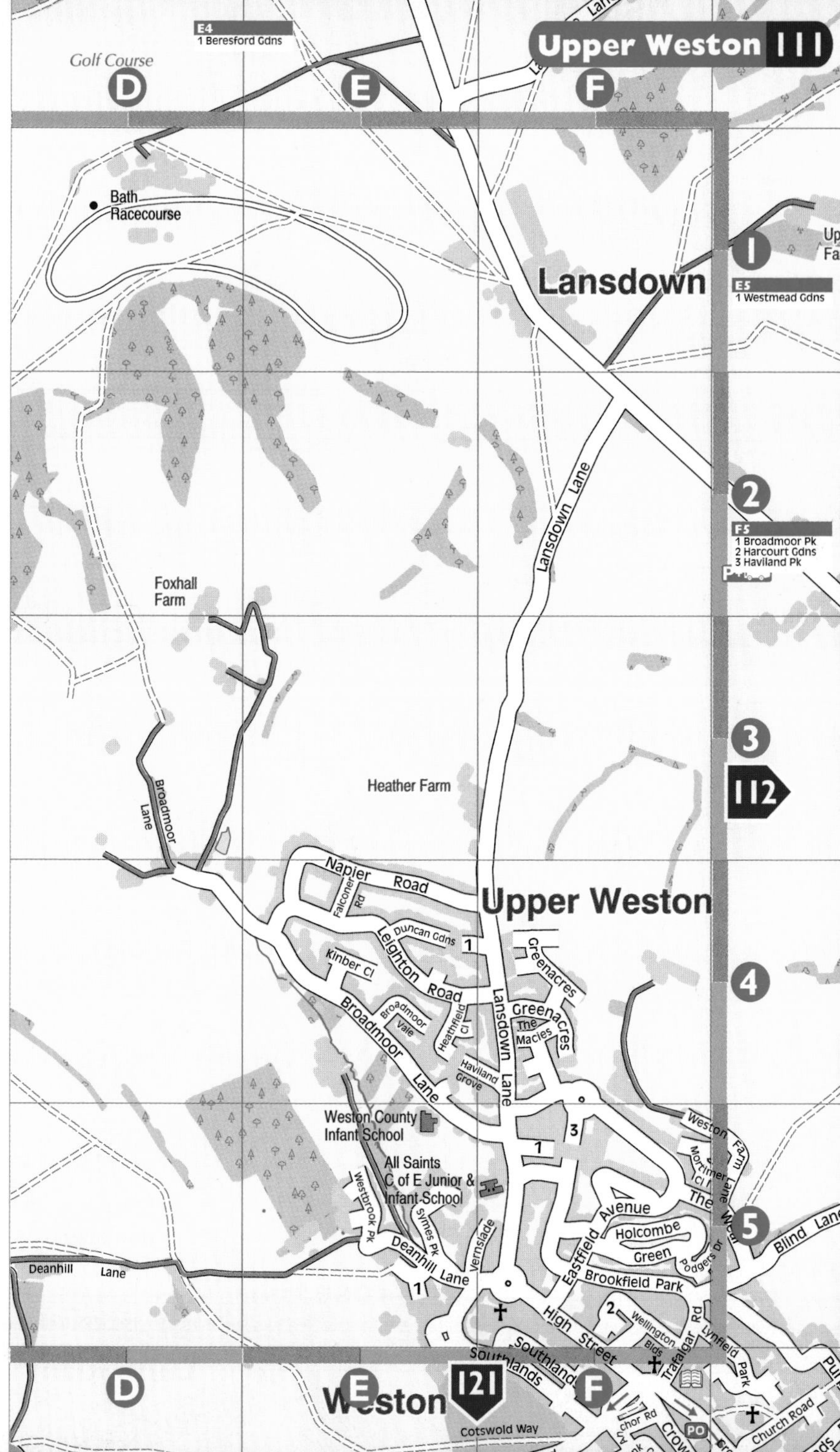
E4
1 Beresford Gdns
Golf Course
D
E
F
Bath Racecourse
Lansdown
E5
1 Westmead Gdns
Lansdown Lane
F5
1 Broadmoor Pk
2 Harcourt Gdns
3 Haviland Pk
Foxhall Farm
Broadmoor Lane
Heather Farm
112
Napier Road
Falconer Rd
Upper Weston
Duncan Gdns
Leighton Road
Kinber Cl
Greenacres
The Macies
Broadmoor Vale
Heathfield Cl
Broadmoor Lane
Haviland Grove
Weston County Infant School
All Saints C of E Junior & Infant School
Weston Farm Lane
Mortimer Cl
The Weal
Westbrook Pk
Symes Pk
Vernslade
Eastfield Avenue
Holcombe Green
Podgers Dr
Blind Lane
Deanhill Lane
Brookfield Park
High Street
Wellington Bldgs
Trafalgar Rd
Lynfield Park
Southlands
Weston
121
Cotswold Way
Anchor Rd
PO
Church Road
1
2
3
4
5

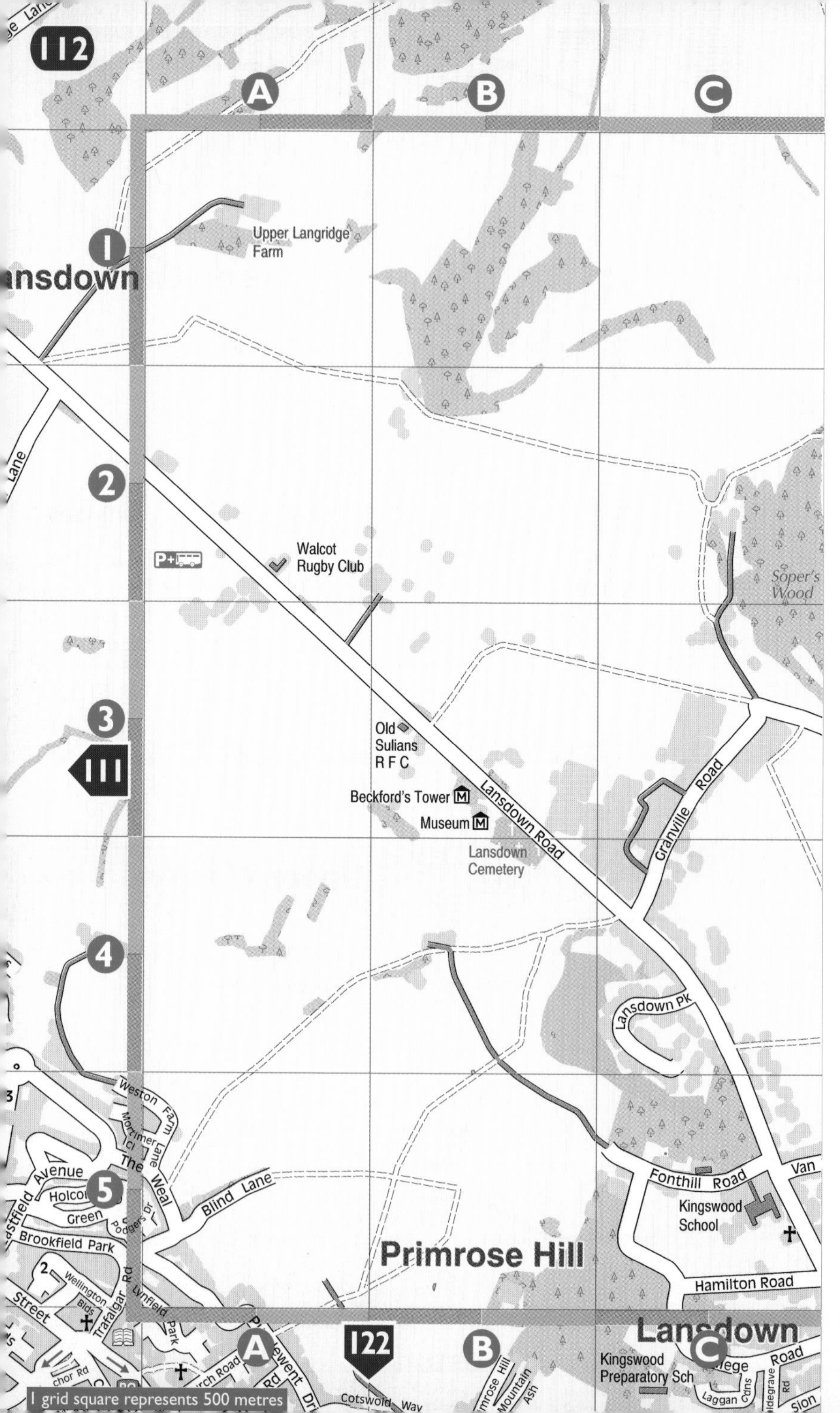
112
A
B
C
1
Lansdown
Upper Langridge Farm
2
Lane
Walcot Rugby Club
Soper's Wood
3
111
Old Sulians R F C
Beckford's Tower
Museum
Lansdown Road
Granville Road
Lansdown Cemetery
4
Lansdown Pk
Weston Farm Lane
Mortimer Cl
The Weal
Avenue
Holcombe
5
Green
Brookfield Park
Podgers Dr
Blind Lane
Fonthill Road
Van
Kingswood School
Primrose Hill
Hamilton Road
Wellington Blds
Street
Trafalgar Rd
Lynfield
Park
Lansdown
A
122
B
C
Kingswood Preparatory Sch
College
Road
Laggan Gdns
Primrose Hill
Mountain Ash
Sion
Cotswold Way
1 grid square represents 500 metres

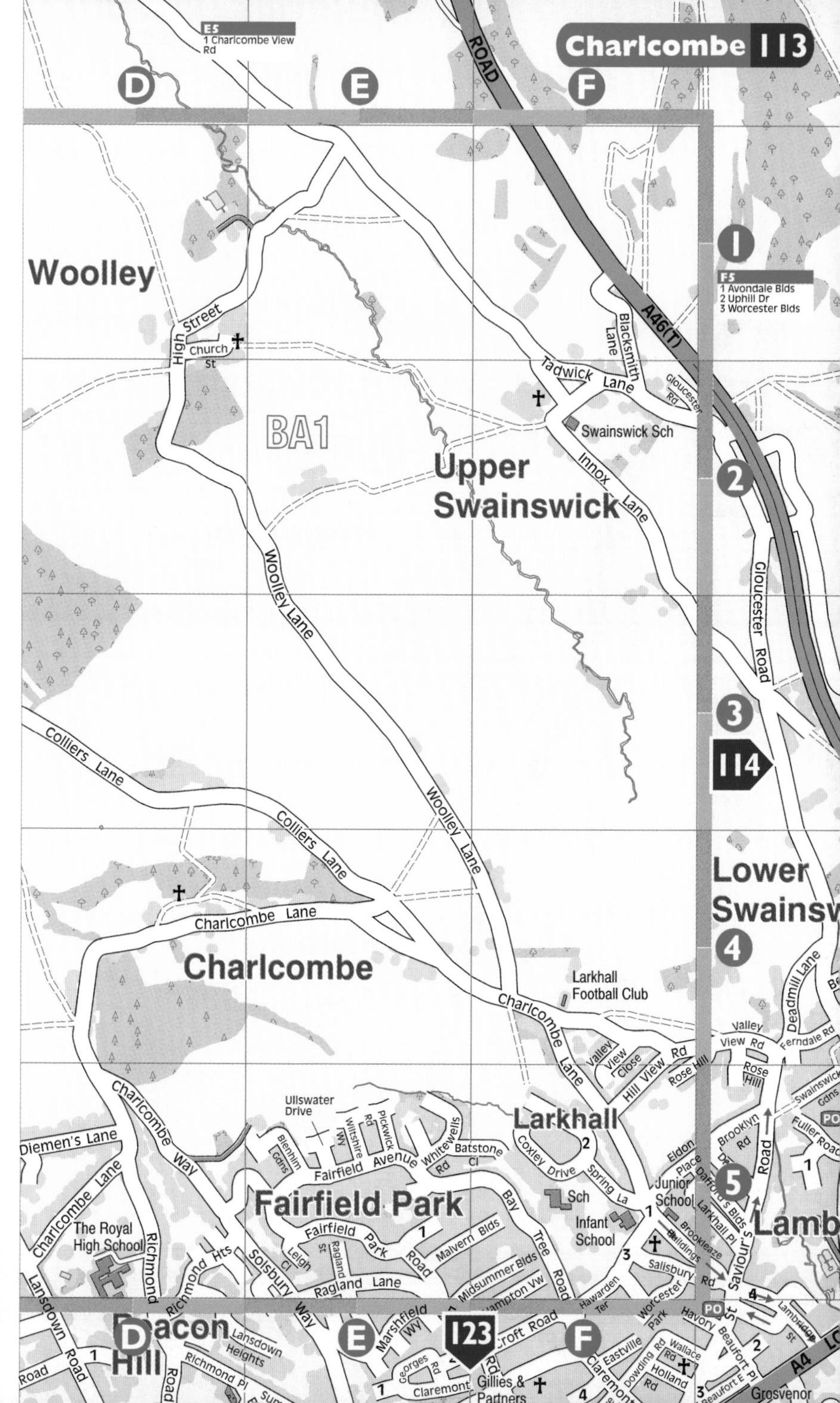
E5
1 Charlcombe View Rd
D
E
F
ROAD
Woolley
High Street
Church St
BA1
Upper Swainswick
Tadwick Lane
Blacksmith Lane
A46(T)
Gloucester Rd
Swainswick Sch
Innox Lane
F5
1 Avondale Blds
2 Uphill Dr
3 Worcester Blds
1
2
3
4
5
114
Gloucester Road
Woolley Lane
Colliers Lane
Charlcombe Lane
Charlcombe
Lower Swainsw
Larkhall Football Club
Deadmill Lane
Valley View Rd
Ferndale Rd
Valley View Close
Hill View Rd
Rose Hill
Charlcombe Way
Ullswater Drive
Blenheim Gdns
Wiltshire Wy
Pickwick Rd
Whitewells Rd
Batstone Cl
Fairfield Avenue
Larkhall
Coxley Drive
Spring La
Eldon Place
Daffords Blds
Junior School
Brooklyn Rd
Swainswick Gdns
Fuller Road
Diemen's Lane
Charlcombe Lane
The Royal High School
Richmond
Fairfield Park
Fairfield Park Road
Leigh Cl
Ragland St
Malvern Blds
Bay Tree Road
Sch
Infant School
Larkhall Pl
Brookleaze Buildings
Saviour's Road
Lamb
Lansdown Road
Richmond Hts
Solsbury Way
Ragland Lane
Midsummer Blds
Hampton Vw
Salisbury Rd
Hawarden Ter
Worcester Park
Havory
St
Lambridge St
Beaufort Pl
PO
Beacon Hill
Lansdown Heights
Richmond Pl
Marshfield Wy
123
Croft Road
Georges Rd
Claremont
Gillies & Partners
Eastville
Dowding Rd
Wallace Rd
Holland Rd
Beaufort E
Grosvenor
A4

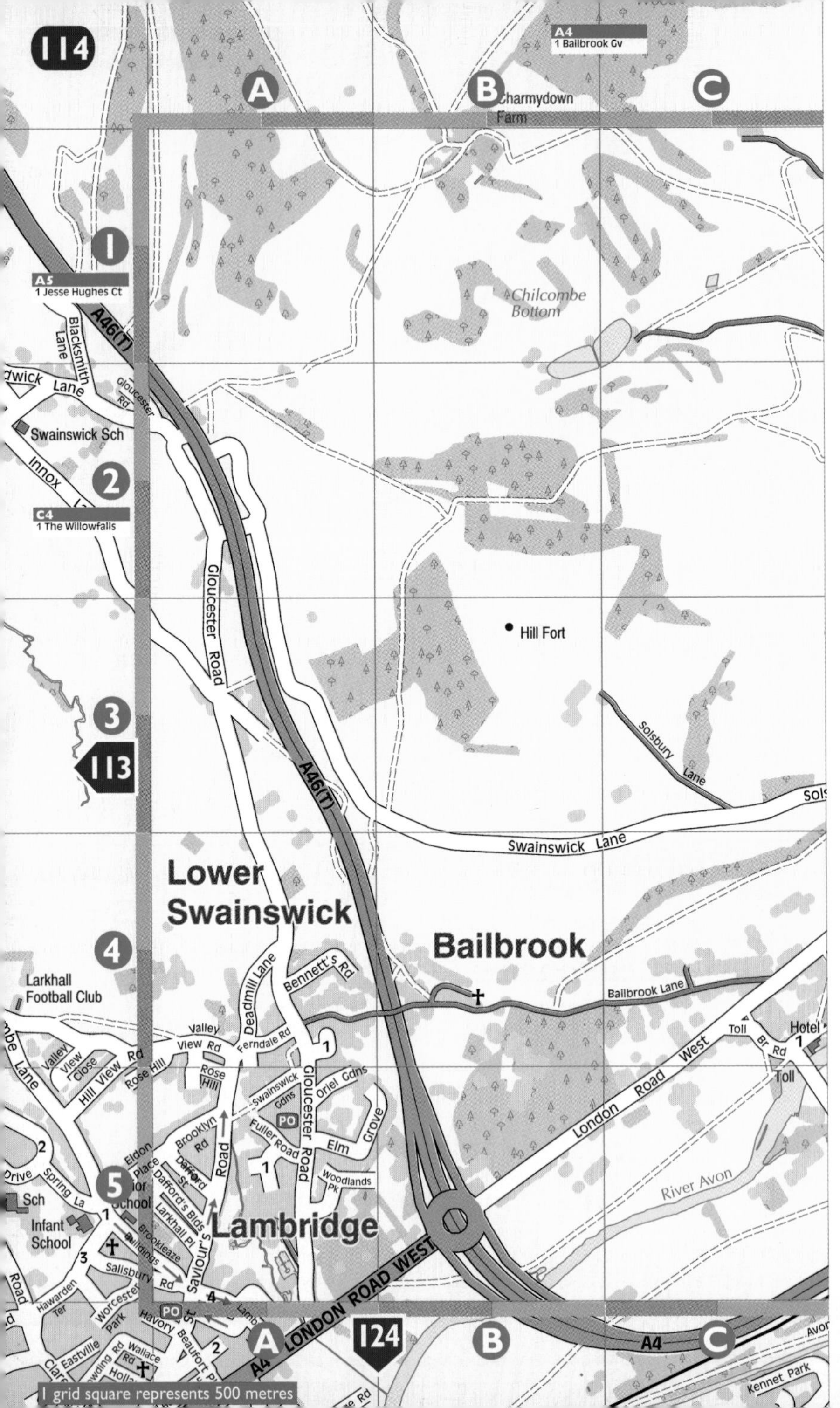
A4
1 Bailbrook Gv
A
B
C
Charmydown
Farm
1
A5
1 Jesse Hughes Ct
A46(T)
Blacksmith Lane
Lane
Gloucester Rd
Swainswick Sch
Innox
2
C4
1 The Willowfalls
Chilcombe
Bottom
Gloucester Road
Hill Fort
3
113
A46(T)
Solsbury Lane
Sols
Swainswick Lane
Lower
Swainswick
Bailbrook
4
Larkhall
Football Club
Deadmill Lane
Bennett's Rd
Bailbrook Lane
Valley
View Rd
Ferndale Rd
1
Toll
Br
Rd
Hotel
1
Toll
London Road West
Valley View Close
Hill View Rd
Rose Hill
Rose Hill
Swainswick Gdns
Oriel Gdns
Gloucester Road
PO
Brooklyn Rd
Fuller Road
Elm
Grove
Eldon Place
Dafford St
Road
1
Woodlands Pk
River Avon
Drive
Spring La
2
5
Sch
Dafford's Blds
Larkhall Pl
School
1
Infant
School
Brookleaze Buildings
Saviour's
Lambridge
3
Salisbury Rd
Road
Hawarden Ter
Worcester Park
PO
Havory
St
4
Lamb
A4 LONDON ROAD WEST
124
A
B
C
A4
Avon
Eastville
Wallace Rd
Beaufort Pl
2
Kennet Park
1 grid square represents 500 metres

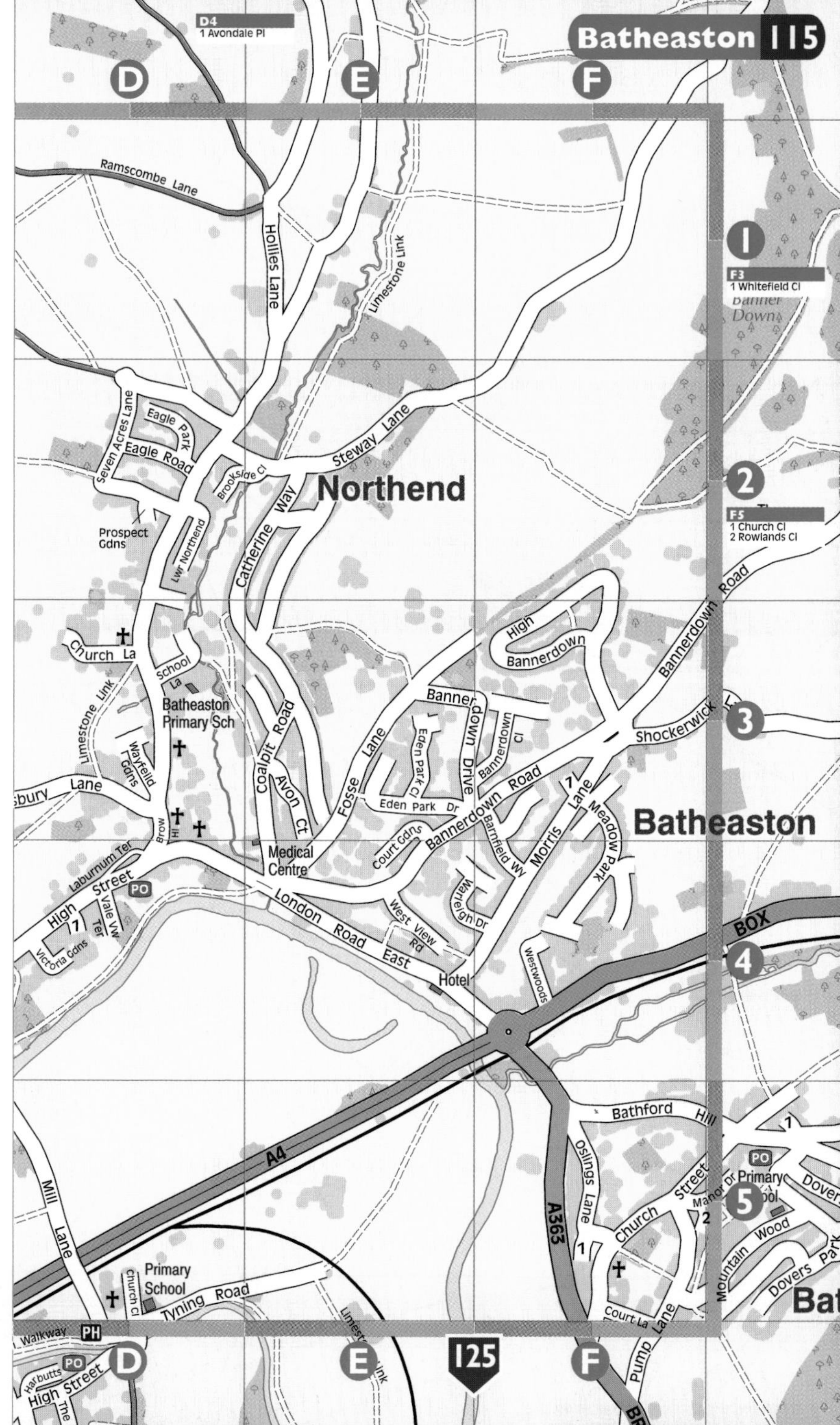
D4
1 Avondale Pl
D
E
F
F3
1 Whitefield Cl
F5
1 Church Cl
2 Rowlands Cl
Ramscombe Lane
Hollies Lane
Limestone Link
Banner Down
Seven Acres Lane
Eagle Park
Eagle Road
Steway Lane
Brookside Cl
Northend
Catherine Way
Prospect Gdns
Lwr Northend
Church La
School La
Batheaston Primary Sch
High Bannerdown
Bannerdown Road
Shockerwick La
Banner-down Drive
Bannerdown Cl
Eden Park Cl
Eden Park Dr
Fosse Lane
Coalpit Road
Avon Ct
Wayfield Gdns
Lane
Brow
Hi
Bannerdown Road
Barnfield Wy
Morris Lane
Meadow Park
Batheaston
Court Gdns
Medical Centre
Laburnum Ter
High Street
PO
Vale Vw
Ter
Victoria Gdns
London Road East
West View Rd
Warleigh Dr
Westwoods
Hotel
BOX
A4
Bathford Hill
Oslings Lane
Church Street
Manor Dr
Primary School
Dovers
Mountain Wood
Dovers Park
A363
Mill Lane
Primary School
Church Cl
Tyning Road
Court La
Pump Lane
Bat
Walkway
PH
Harbutts
High Street
125
1
2
3
4
5

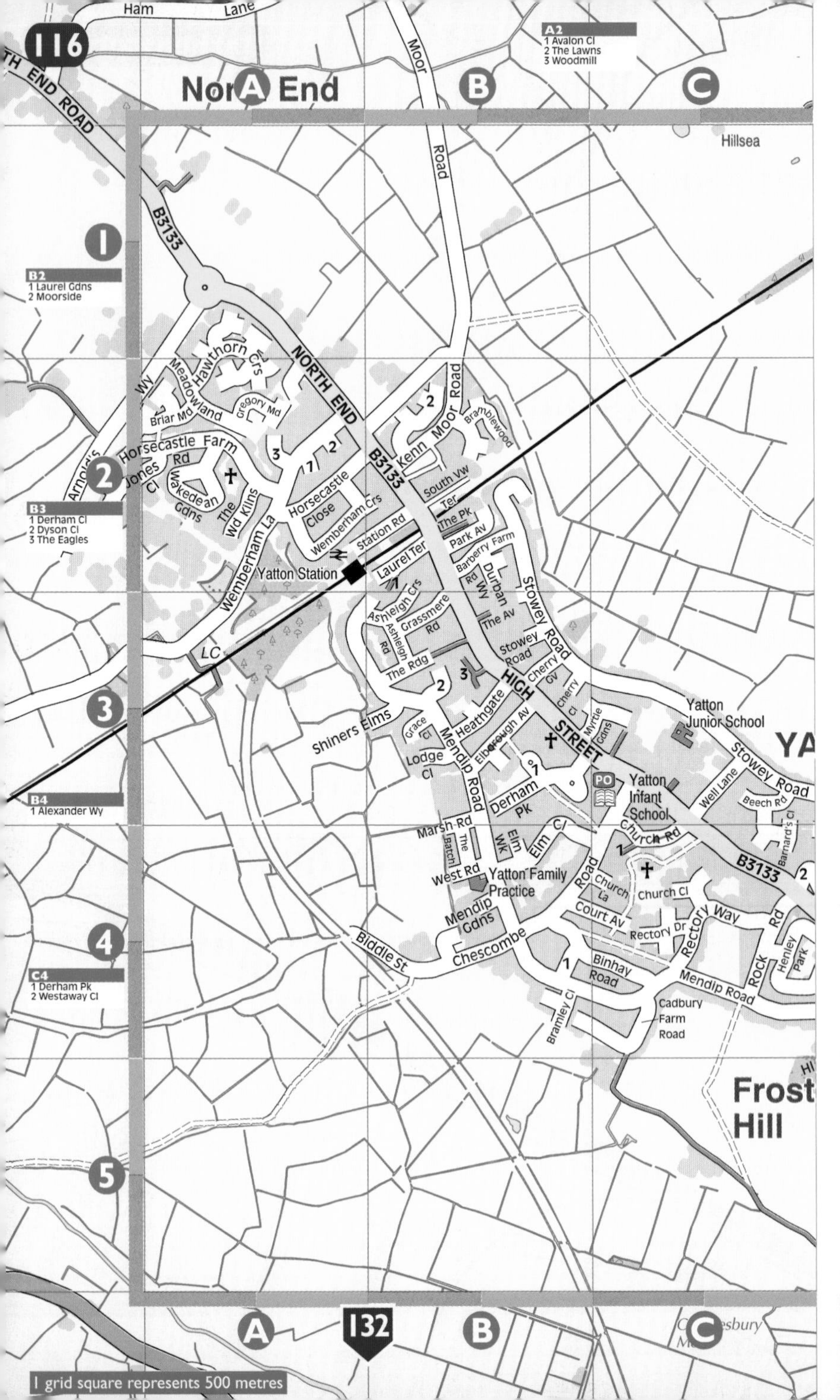
116
North End
A
B
C
A2
1 Avalon Cl
2 The Lawns
3 Woodmill
Ham
Lane
Moor Road
NORTH END ROAD
Hillsea
B3133
1
B2
1 Laurel Gdns
2 Moorside
NORTH END
Hawthorn Crs
Meadowland
Wy
Briar Md
Gregory Md
Kenn Moor Road
Bramblewood
Horsecastle Farm Rd
Arnold's
Jones Cl
Wakedean Gdns
The Wd Kilns
Horsecastle Close
Wemberham Crs
Wemberham La
South Vw
Ter
The Pk
Park Av
Station Rd
2
B3
1 Derham Cl
2 Dyson Cl
3 The Eagles
Yatton Station
Laurel Ter
Barberry Farm Rd
Durban Wy
Stowey Road
Ashleigh Crs
Ashleigh Rd
Grassmere Rd
The Av
The Rdg
Stowey Road
LC
Cherry Gv
Cherry Cl
HIGH STREET
Myrtle Gdns
Heathgate
Yatton Junior School
3
Shiners Elms
Grace Cl
Lodge Cl
Mendip Road
Elborough Av
Derham Pk
PO
Yatton Infant School
Well Lane
Stowey Road
Beech Rd
Barnard's Cl
YA
B4
1 Alexander Wy
Marsh Rd
The Batch
Elm Wk
Elm Cl
Church Rd
West Rd
Yatton Family Practice
Church La
Church Cl
B3133
Mendip Gdns
Court Av
Rectory Dr
Rectory Way
Rock Rd
Henley Park
4
C4
1 Derham Pk
2 Westaway Cl
Biddle St
Chescombe Road
Binhay Road
Mendip Road
Bramley Cl
Cadbury Farm Road
Frost Hill
5
A
132
B
C
1 grid square represents 500 metres

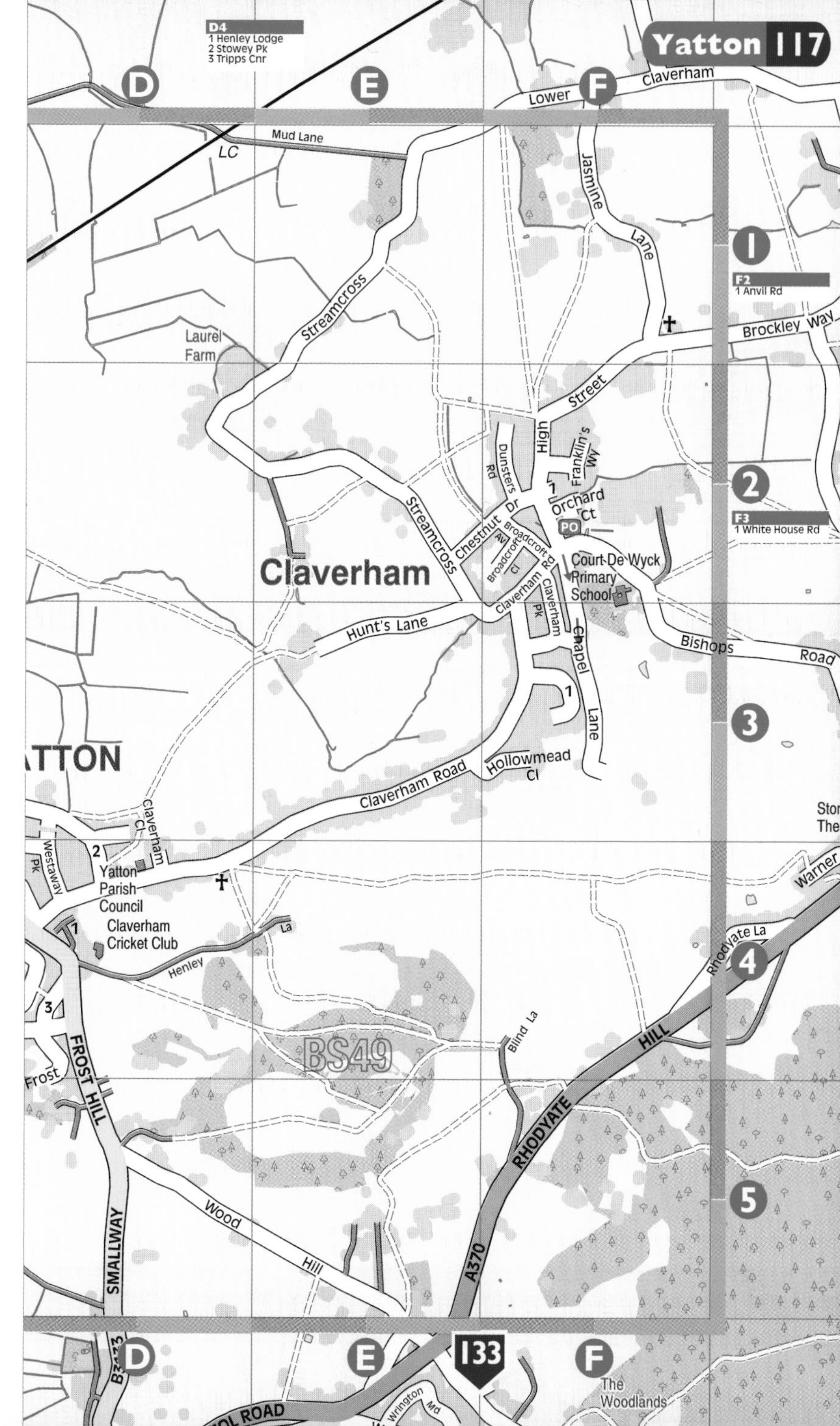
D4
1 Henley Lodge
2 Stowey Pk
3 Tripps Cnr
Lower Claverham
Mud Lane
LC
Jasmine Lane
F2
1 Anvil Rd
Brockley Way
Streamcross
Laurel Farm
High Street
Dunsters Rd
Franklin's Wy
Orchard Ct
F3
1 White House Rd
PO
Chestnut Dr
Broadcroft Av
Broadcroft Cl
Claverham Rd
Court De Wyck Primary School
Claverham
Claverham Pk
Hunt's Lane
Chapel Lane
Bishops Road
Hollowmead Cl
Claverham Road
YATTON
Claverham Cl
Westaway Pk
Yatton Parish Council
Claverham Cricket Club
Henley La
Warner
Rhodyate La
Blind La
BS49
HILL
RHODYATE
FROST HILL
Frost
Wood Hill
A370
SMALLWAY
B3133
133
The Woodlands
Wrington Md
D
E
F
1
2
3
4
5

118
108
Saltford
Uplands
Haselbury Grove
Road
Beresford Close
Golf Course
North Breach
Ashton Hill
Depot
Gypsy Lane
Middlepiece Lane
Corston Field
A39
Stantonbury House
A
B
C
1
2
3
4
5
1 grid square represents 500 metres

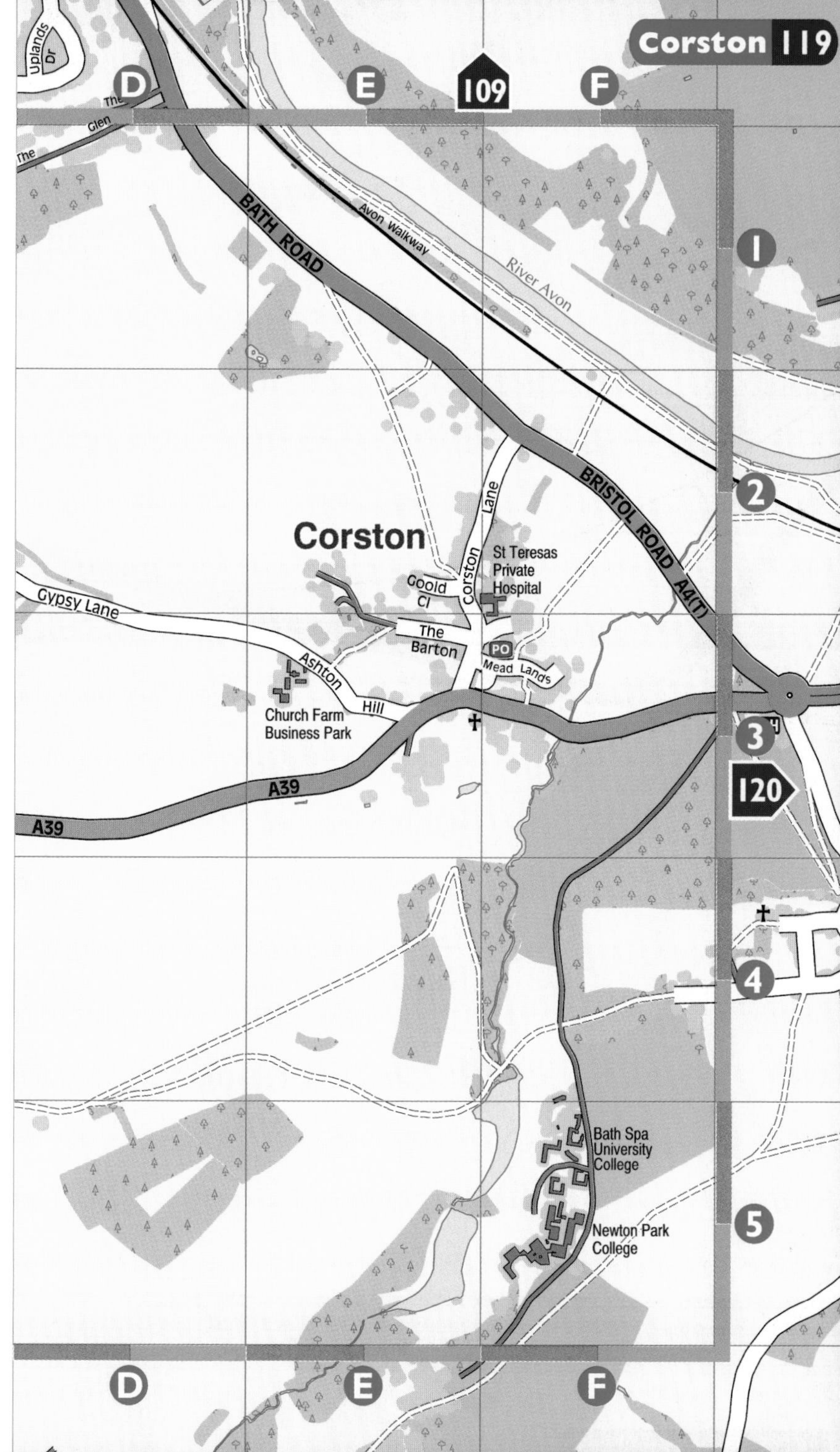
Uplands Dr
The Glen
The
D
E
109
F
BATH ROAD
Avon Walkway
River Avon
1
2
BRISTOL ROAD A4(T)
Corston
Corston Lane
St Teresas
Private
Hospital
Goold Cl
Gypsy Lane
The Barton
PO
Mead Lands
Ashton Hill
Church Farm
Business Park
A39
A39
3
120
4
Bath Spa
University
College
5
Newton Park
College
D
E
F

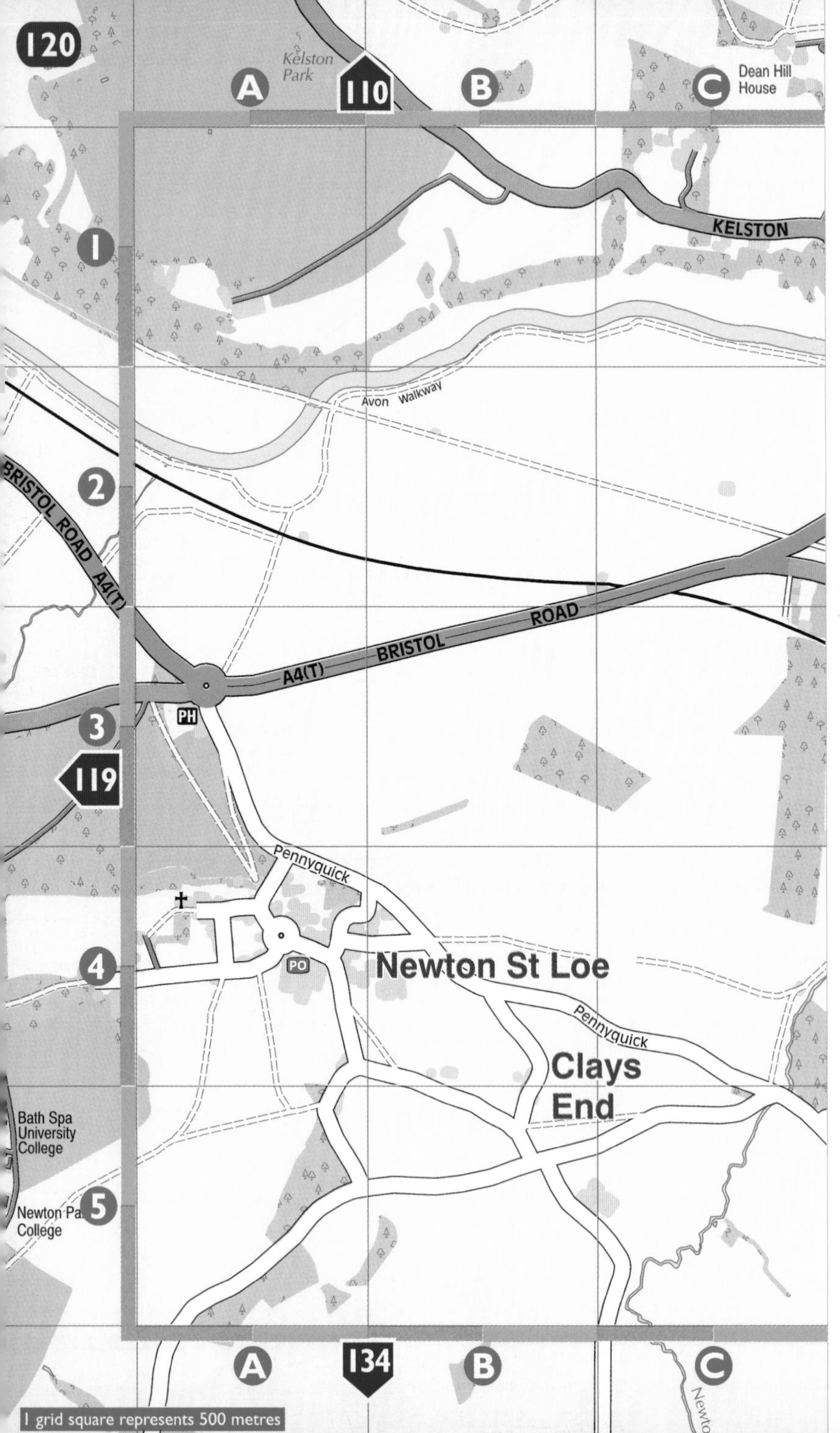
120
Kelston Park
A
110
B
C
Dean Hill House
KELSTON
1
Avon Walkway
2
BRISTOL ROAD A4(T)
ROAD
BRISTOL
A4(T)
PH
3
119
Pennyquick
4
PO
Newton St Loe
Pennyquick
Clays End
Bath Spa University College
5
Newton Park College
A
134
B
C
I grid square represents 500 metres

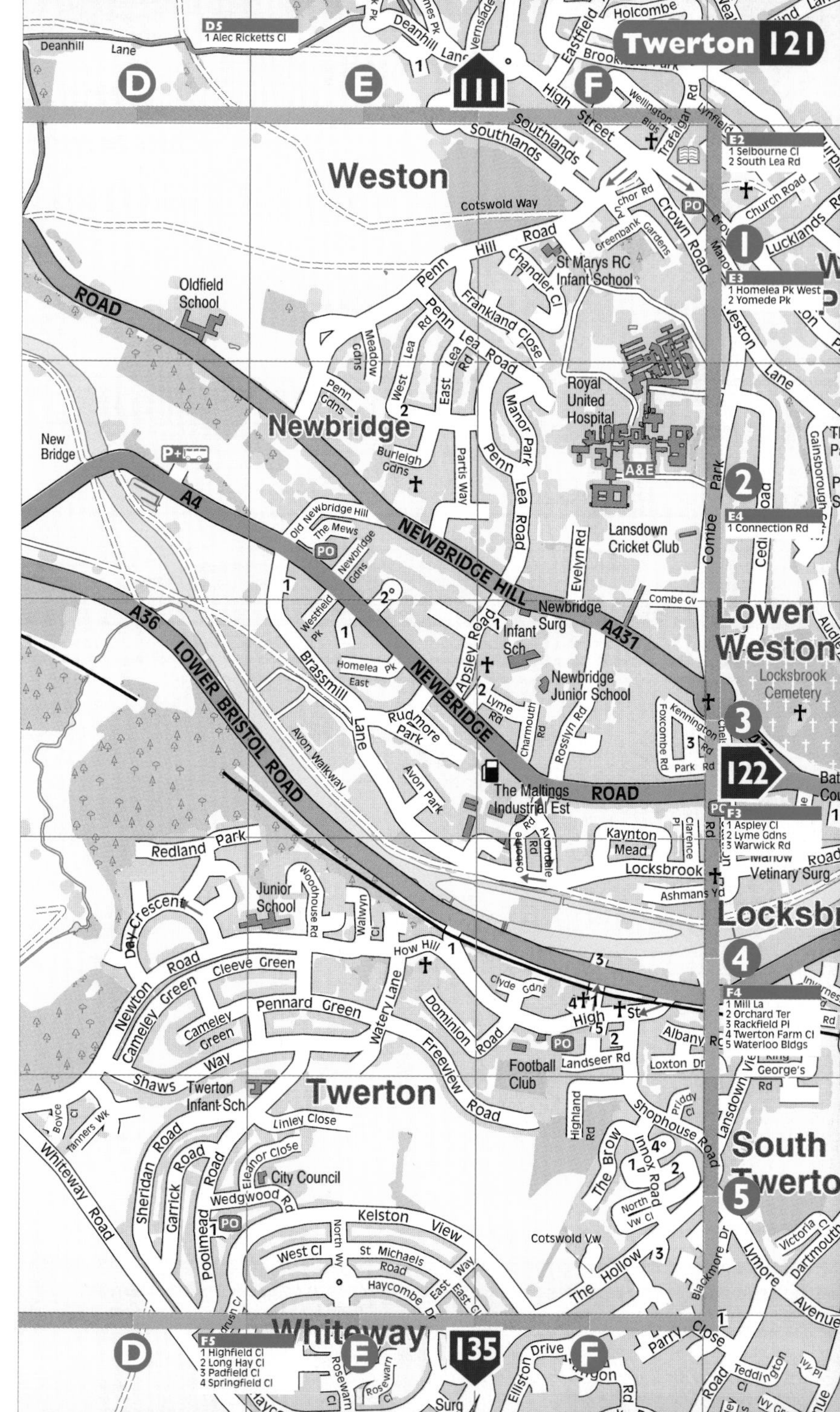

D5
1 Alec Ricketts Cl
Deanhill Lane
D
E
F
111
Weston
Cotswold Way
Southlands
High Street
Penn Hill Road
Chandler Cl
St Marys RC Infant School
Frankland Close
Penn Lea Road
Royal United Hospital
A&E
Oldfield School
ROAD
Newbridge
New Bridge
A4
Meadow Gdns
West Lea Rd
East Lea Rd
Penn Gdns
Burleigh Gdns
Partis Way
Manor Park
Penn Lea Road
Evelyn Rd
Lansdown Cricket Club
Combe Park
Combe Gv
NEWBRIDGE HILL
A431
Newbridge Surg
Old Newbridge Hill
The Mews
Newbridge Gdns
PO
Westfield Pk
Homelea Pk East
Brassmill Lane
Apsley Road
Infant Sch
Newbridge Junior School
Lyme Rd
Charmouth Rd
Rosslyn Rd
Kennington Rd
Foxcombe Rd
Park Rd
NEWBRIDGE ROAD
Rudmore Park
Avon Walkway
Avon Park
The Maltings Industrial Est
A36
LOWER BRISTOL ROAD
Lower Weston
Locksbrook Cemetery
122
E2
1 Selbourne Cl
2 South Lea Rd
E3
1 Homelea Pk West
2 Yomede Pk
E4
1 Connection Rd
F3
1 Aspley Cl
2 Lyme Gdns
3 Warwick Rd
Church Road
Lucklands Rd
Weston Lane
Crown Road
Greenbank Gardens
Anchor Rd
Trafalgar Rd
Lynfield
Wellington Bldgs
Holcombe
Eastfield
Brookleaze
Deanhill Lane
Vernslade
Gainsborough
Cedric Rd
Redland Park
Day Crescent
Junior School
Woodhouse Rd
Walwyn Cl
Kaynton Mead
Locksbrook Road
Ashmans Yd
Osborne Rd
Avondale Rd
Clarence Pl
Manor Vetinary Surg
Locksbrook
How Hill
Newton Road
Cleeve Green
Cameley Green
Pennard Green
Watery Lane
Dominion Road
Clyde Gdns
High St
Albany Rd
Freeview Road
Football Club
Landseer Rd
Loxton Dr
Shaws Way
Twerton Infant Sch
Twerton
Linley Close
Boyce Cl
Tanners Wk
Whiteway Road
Sheridan Road
Garrick Road
Eleanor Close
City Council
Wedgwood Rd
Poolmead Road
Kelston View
North Wy
West Cl
St Michaels Road
Haycombe Dr
East Way
East Cl
Highland Rd
The Brow
Innox Road
Shophouse Road
Priddy Cl
North Vw Cl
Cotswold Vw
The Hollow
Blackmore Dr
F4
1 Mill La
2 Orchard Ter
3 Rackfield Pl
4 Twerton Farm Cl
5 Waterloo Bldgs
King George's Rd
Lansdown View
South Twerton
Victoria Cl
Dartmouth Avenue
Lymore Avenue
Whiteway
135
F5
1 Highfield Cl
2 Long Hay Cl
3 Padfield Cl
4 Springfield Cl
Rosewarn Cl
Elliston Drive
Parry Close
Teddington Cl
Ivy Pl
Surg

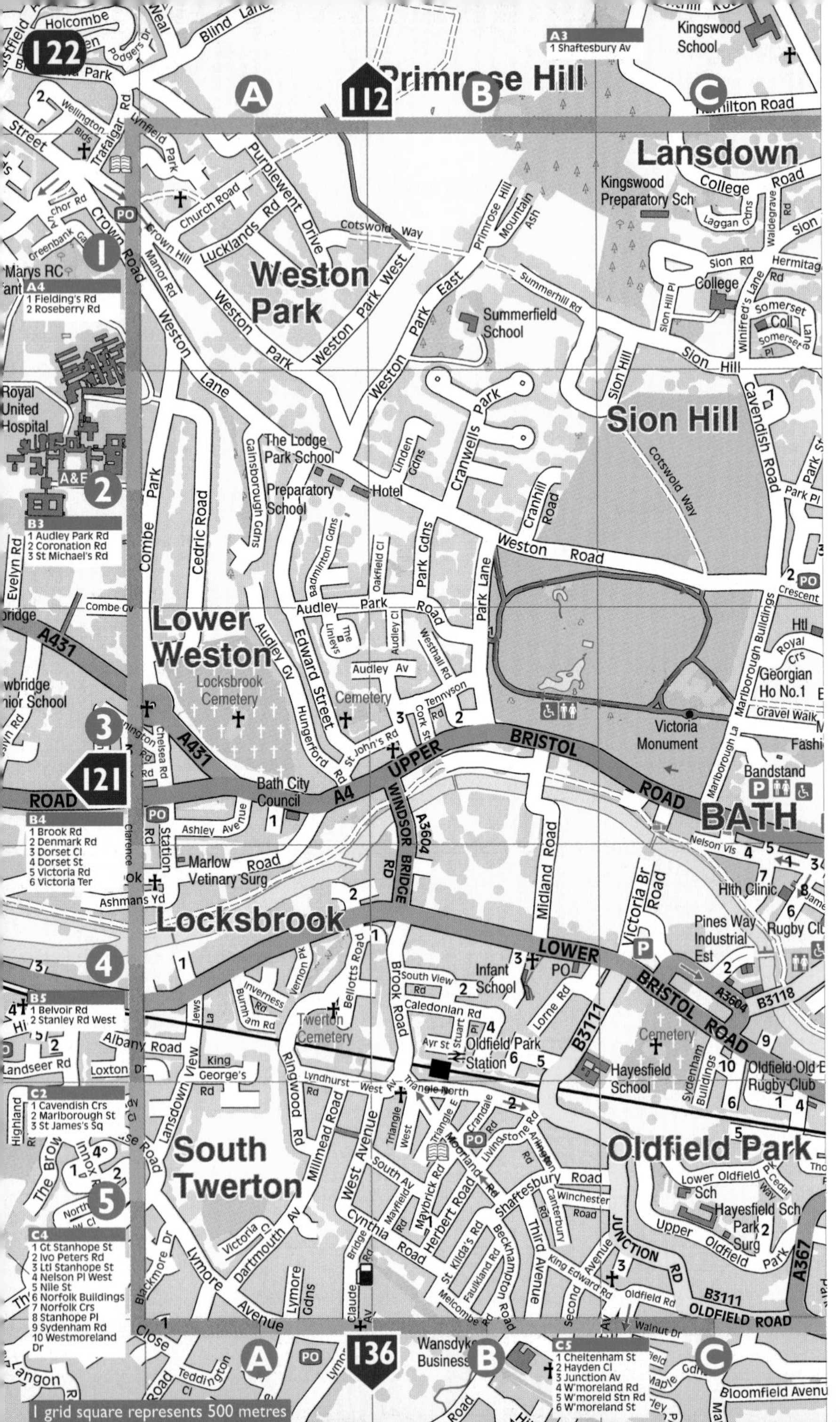

122
112
121
136
A
B
C
1
2
3
4
5
Primrose Hill
Lansdown
Weston Park
Sion Hill
Lower Weston
Locksbrook
South Twerton
Oldfield Park
BATH
A3
1 Shaftesbury Av
A4
1 Fielding's Rd
2 Roseberry Rd
B3
1 Audley Park Rd
2 Coronation Rd
3 St Michael's Rd
B4
1 Brook Rd
2 Denmark Rd
3 Dorset Cl
4 Dorset St
5 Victoria Rd
6 Victoria Ter
B5
1 Belvoir Rd
2 Stanley Rd West
C2
1 Cavendish Crs
2 Marlborough St
3 St James's Sq
C4
1 Gt Stanhope St
2 Ivo Peters Rd
3 Ltl Stanhope St
4 Nelson Pl West
5 Nile St
6 Norfolk Buildings
7 Norfolk Crs
8 Stanhope Pl
9 Sydenham Rd
10 Westmoreland Dr
C5
1 Cheltenham St
2 Hayden Cl
3 Junction Av
4 W'moreland Rd
5 W'moreld Stn Rd
6 W'moreland St
Kingswood School
Hamilton Road
Kingswood Preparatory Sch
College Road
Laggan Gdns
Waldegrave Rd
Sion Rd
Hermitage Rd
College
Somerset Coll
Somerset Pl
Somerset Lane
Winifred's Lane
Sion Hill Pl
Sion Hill
Cavendish Road
Summerhill Rd
Summerfield School
Cotswold Way
Primrose Hill
Mountain Ash
Weston Park East
Weston Park West
Weston Park
Purplewent Drive
Lucklands Rd
Church Road
Crown Hill
Manor Rd
Lynfield Park
Trafalgar Rd
Wellington Bldgs
Holcombe
Blind Lane
Podgers Dr
Neal
Crown Road
Anchor Rd
Greenbank Gdns
Marys RC
Royal United Hospital
A&E
Weston Lane
Cranwells Park
Linden Gdns
The Lodge Park School
Hotel
Preparatory School
Gainsborough Gdns
Cranhill Road
Weston Road
Park Pl
Park St
Crescent
PO
Marlborough Buildings
Royal Crs
Htl
Georgian Ho No.1
Gravel Walk
Victoria Monument
Marlborough La
Bandstand
Combe Park
Cedric Road
Evelyn Rd
Combe Gv
A431
Badminton Gdns
Oakfield Cl
Park Gdns
Park Lane
Audley Park Road
The Linleys
Audley Cl
Westhall Rd
Audley Av
Audley Gv
Edward Street
Hungerford Rd
Cemetery
Locksbrook Cemetery
Tennyson Rd
Cork St
St John's Rd
Chelsea Rd
UPPER BRISTOL ROAD
A4
ROAD
Bath City Council
Ashley Avenue
Station Rd
Marlow Road
Marlow Vetinary Surg
Ashmans Yd
Clarence St
WINDSOR BRIDGE RD
A3604
Midland Road
Victoria Br Road
Nelson Vls
Hlth Clinic
Pines Way Industrial Est
Rugby Club
LOWER BRISTOL ROAD
A3604
B3118
Infant School
Lorne Rd
B3111
Cemetery
Hayesfield School
Sydenham Buildings
Oldfield Old Bristolians Rugby Club
Vernon Pk
Bellotts Road
Brook Road
South View Rd
Caledonian Rd
Stuart Pl
Ayr St
Oldfield Park Station
Inverness Rd
Burnham Rd
Twerton Cemetery
Jews La
Albany Road
Loxton Dr
Landseer Rd
King George's Rd
Lansdown View
Ringwood Rd
Lyndhurst Rd
West Av
Triangle North
Triangle West
Triangle E
Crandale Rd
Livingstone Rd
Arlington Rd
Millmead Road
West Avenue
South Av
Mayfield Rd
Moorland Rd
Maybrick Rd
Herbert Road
Cynthia Road
Shaftesbury Road
Winchester Road
Canterbury Rd
Third Avenue
Beckhampton Road
St Kilda's Rd
Faulkland Rd
Melcombe Rd
Bridge Rd
Claude Av
Lymore Gdns
Lymore Avenue
Dartmouth Av
Victoria Cl
Blackmore Dr
Lymore Close
Highland Rd
The Brow
Innox Rd
North Cl
Second Avenue
King Edward Rd
JUNCTION RD
Oldfield Rd
B3111
OLDFIELD ROAD
Walnut Dr
Lower Oldfield Pk
Cedar Way
Sch
Hayesfield Sch
Park Surg
Upper Oldfield Park
A367
Wansdyke Business
Teddington Cl
Langon
Maple Gdns
Bloomfield Avenue
Lowbridge
Newbridge Junior School
1 grid square represents 500 metres

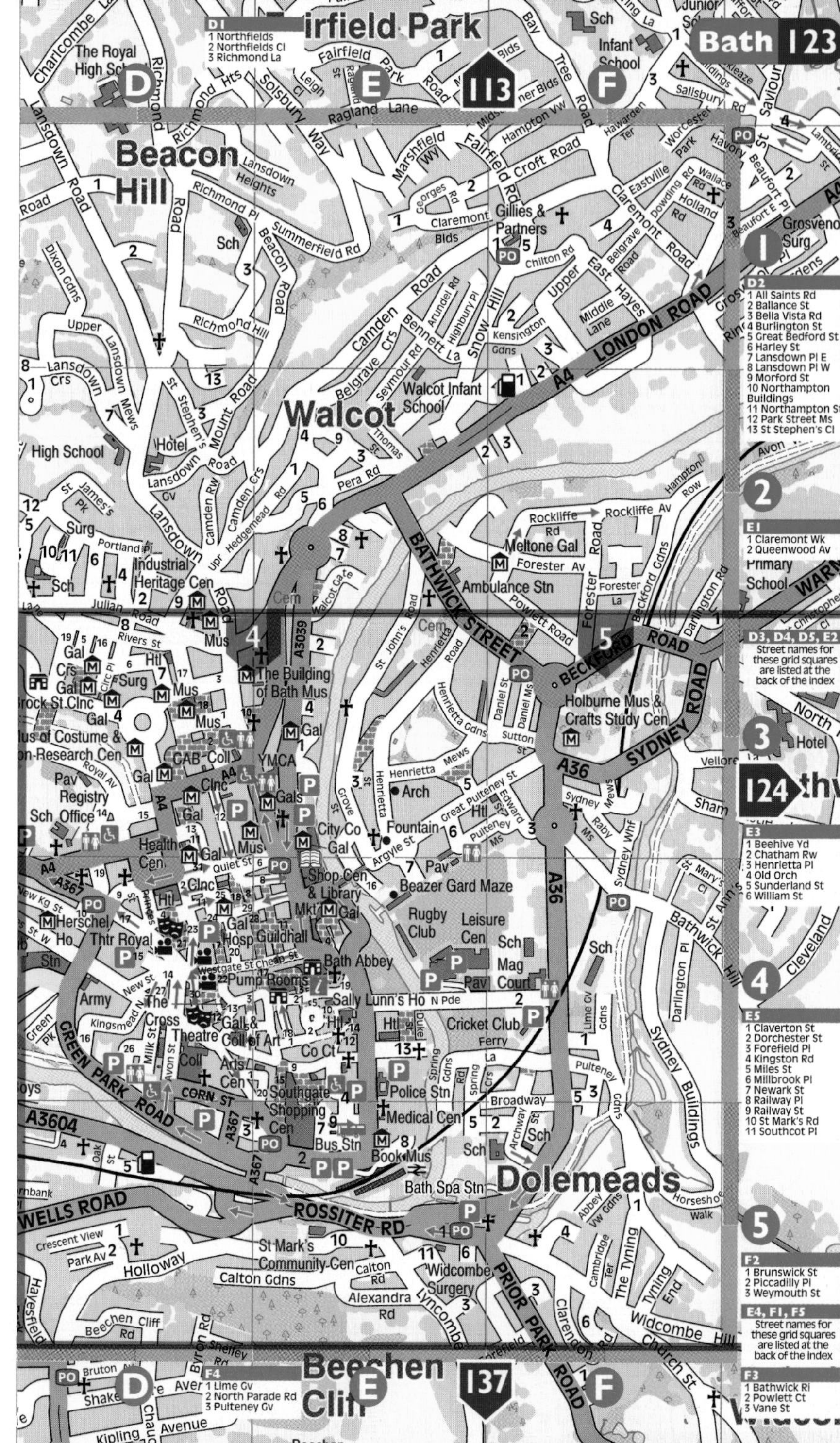

D1
1 Northfields
2 Northfields Cl
3 Richmond La
D2
1 All Saints Rd
2 Ballance St
3 Bella Vista Rd
4 Burlington St
5 Great Bedford St
6 Harley St
7 Lansdown Pl E
8 Lansdown Pl W
9 Morford St
10 Northampton Buildings
11 Northampton St
12 Park Street Ms
13 St Stephen's Cl
E1
1 Claremont Wk
2 Queenwood Av
D3, D4, D5, E2
Street names for these grid squares are listed at the back of the index
E3
1 Beehive Yd
2 Chatham Rw
3 Henrietta Pl
4 Old Orch
5 Sunderland St
6 William St
E5
1 Claverton St
2 Dorchester St
3 Forefield Pl
4 Kingston Rd
5 Miles St
6 Millbrook Pl
7 Newark St
8 Railway Pl
9 Railway St
10 St Mark's Rd
11 Southcot Pl
F2
1 Brunswick St
2 Piccadilly Pl
3 Weymouth St
E4, F1, F5
Street names for these grid squares are listed at the back of the index
F3
1 Bathwick Ri
2 Powlett Ct
3 Vane St
F4
1 Lime Gv
2 North Parade Rd
3 Pulteney Gv
113
124
137
Beacon Hill
Walcot
Dolemeads
Beechen Cliff
The Royal High Sch
Lansdown Road
Richmond Road
Solsbury Way
Ragland Lane
Fairfield Park Road
Fairfield Rd
Croft Road
Hampton Vw
Claremont Road
Summerfield Rd
Camden Road
Snow Hill
LONDON ROAD
A4
Walcot Infant School
Gillies & Partners
Upr Hedgemead Rd
Lansdown Crs
Mount Road
St Stephen's Rd
Industrial Heritage Cen
The Building of Bath Mus
BATHWICK STREET
BECKFORD ROAD
SYDNEY ROAD
Holburne Mus & Crafts Study Cen
Meltone Gal
Forester Av
Ambulance Stn
Rockliffe Av
Henrietta Gdns
Great Pulteney St
Argyle St
Beazer Gard Maze
Rugby Club
Leisure Cen
Cricket Club
Mus of Costume & Fashion-Research Cen
Registry Office
Thtr Royal
Pump Rooms
Bath Abbey
Sally Lunn's Ho
Guildhall
Shop Cen & Library
Southgate Shopping Cen
Bus Stn
Bath Spa Stn
Police Stn
Medical Cen
Book Mus
GREEN PARK ROAD
CORN ST
A3604
A367
A36
A3039
WELLS ROAD
ROSSITER RD
PRIOR PARK ROAD
Holloway
Widcombe Surgery
St Mark's Community Cen
Calton Gdns
Alexandra Rd
Lyncombe
Widcombe Hill
Sydney Buildings
Bathwick Hill
Cleveland
Darlington Pl
Horseshoe Walk
The Tyning
Tyning End
Church St
Clarendon Rd

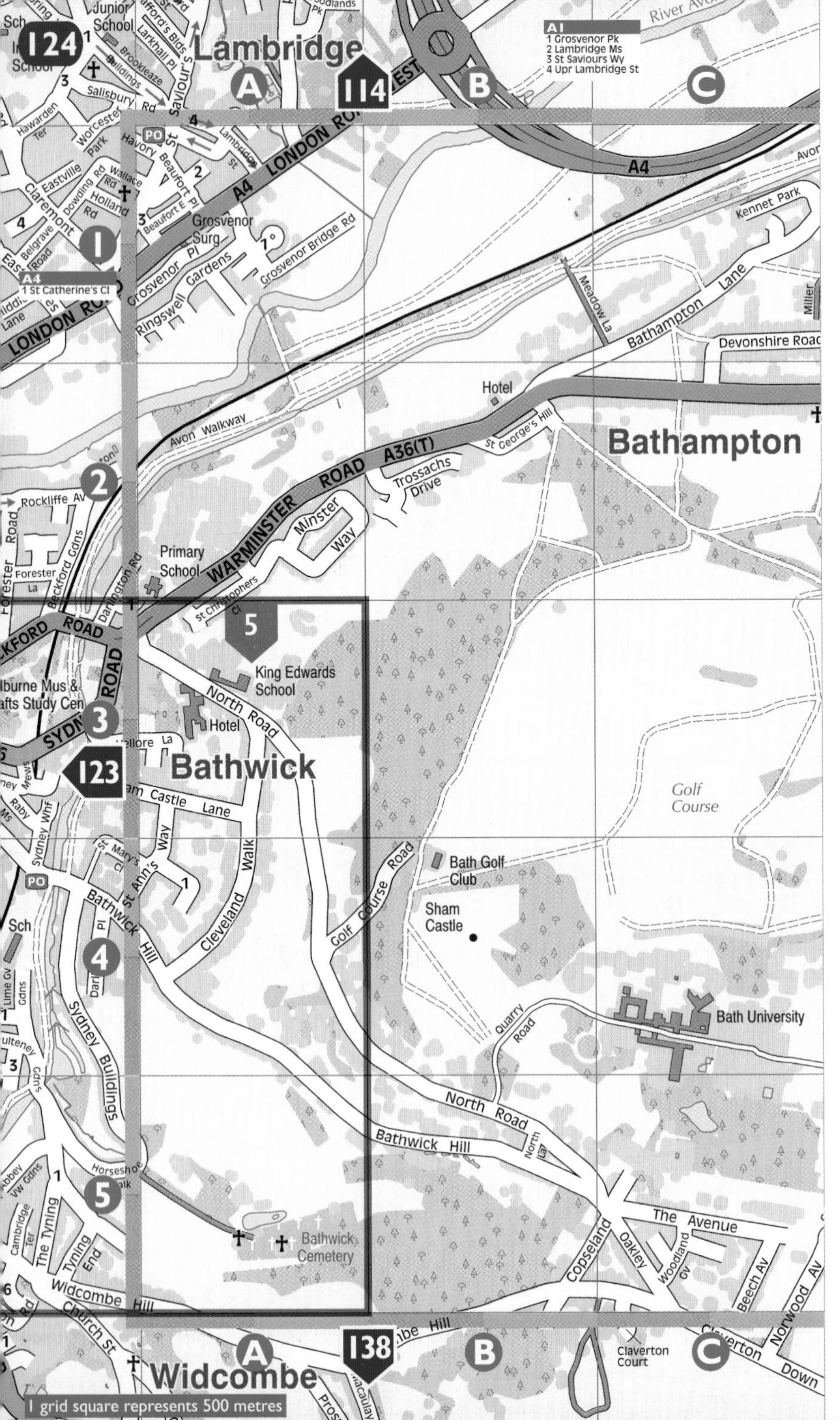

124
114
Lambridge
A
B
C
A1
1 Grosvenor Pk
2 Lambridge Ms
3 St Saviours Wy
4 Upr Lambridge St
River Avon
Junior School
Brookleaze Buildings
Larkhall Pl
Salisbury Rd
Hawarden Ter
Worcester Park
Eastville
Claremont
Belgrave Road
Dowding Rd
Wallace Rd
Holland Rd
Havory
Beaufort St
Beaufort E
Beaufort Pl
Lambridge St
A4 LONDON ROAD
Grosvenor Surg
Grosvenor Pl
Gardens
Ringswell
Grosvenor Bridge Rd
A4
1 St Catherine's Cl
LONDON ROAD
A4
Avon
Kennet Park
Meadow La
Bathampton Lane
Devonshire Road
Hotel
St George's Hill
Bathampton
Avon Walkway
WARMINSTER ROAD A36(T)
Trossachs Drive
Minster Way
Primary School
St Christophers Cl
Rockliffe Av
Forester Road
Forester La
Beckford Gdns
Darlington Rd
BECKFORD ROAD
SYDNEY ROAD
5
King Edwards School
North Road
Hotel
Vellore La
Bathwick
123
Golf Course
Castle Lane
Sydney Whf
St Mary's Cl
St Ann's Way
Cleveland Walk
Golf Course Road
Bath Golf Club
Sham Castle
Bathwick Hill
Sydney Buildings
Quarry Road
Bath University
North Road
Bathwick Hill
North La
Horseshoe Walk
The Tyning
Tyning End
Cambridge Ter
Bathwick Cemetery
The Avenue
Copseland
Oakley
Woodland Gv
Beech Av
Norwood Av
Widcombe Hill
Church St
138
Claverton Court
Claverton Down
Widcombe
1 grid square represents 500 metres

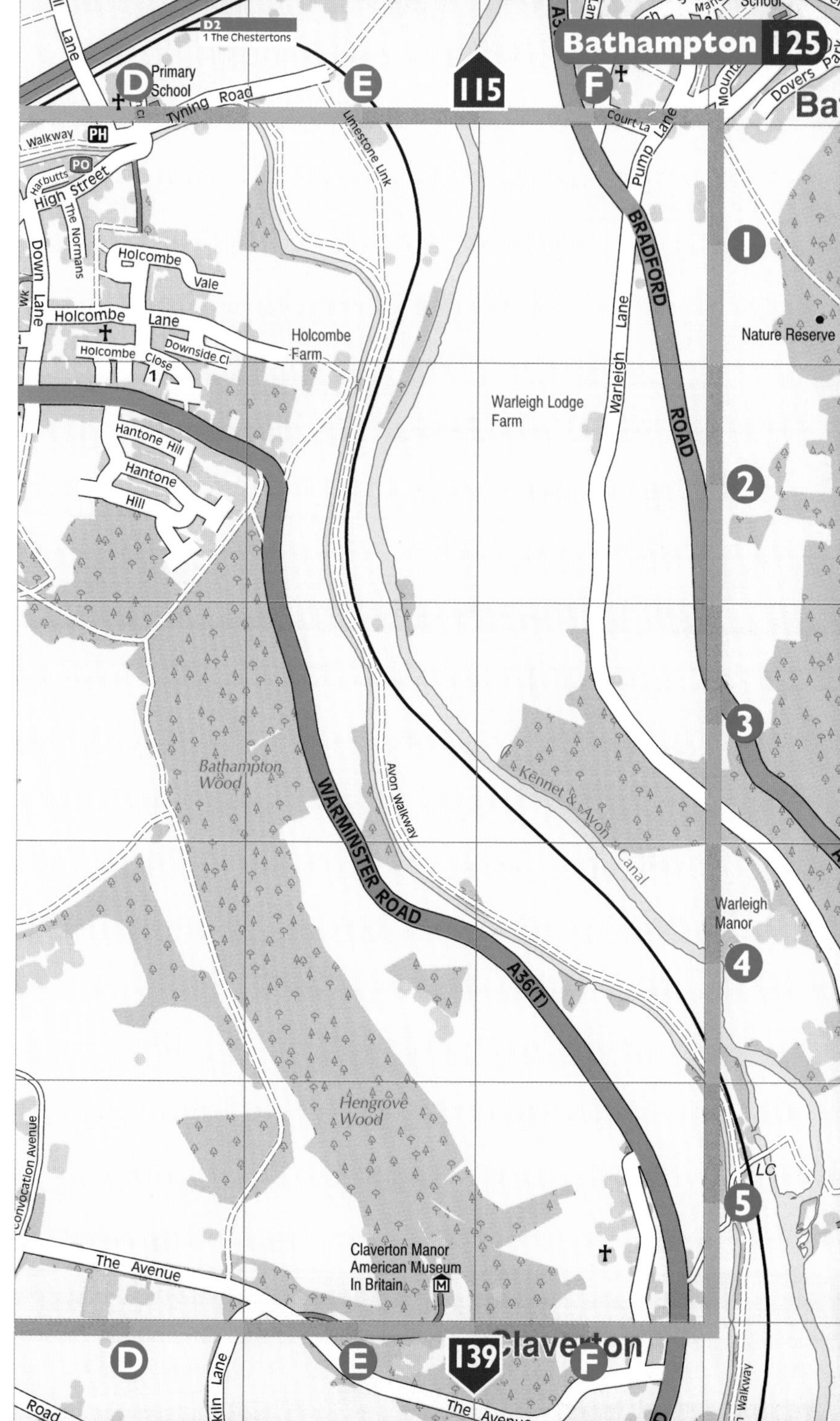
D2
1 The Chestertons
D
E
F
115
Primary School
Tyning Road
Walkway
PH
PO
Harbutts
High Street
The Normans
Down Lane
Holcombe Vale
Holcombe Lane
Holcombe Close
Downside Cl
Holcombe Farm
Limestone Link
Court La
Pump Lane
BRADFORD ROAD
Warleigh Lane
Warleigh Lodge Farm
Nature Reserve
School
Dovers Park
Hantone Hill
Hantone Hill
Bathampton Wood
WARMINSTER ROAD
A36(T)
Avon Walkway
Kennet & Avon Canal
Warleigh Manor
Hengrove Wood
LC
Convocation Avenue
The Avenue
Claverton Manor
American Museum
In Britain
Claverton
139
The Avenue
Road
1
2
3
4
5

A
B
C
1
2
3
4
5
Kewstoke Road
Life Boat
Station
Pier
College
Education
140
Birkett
Road
South Road
Road
1 grid square represents 500 metres

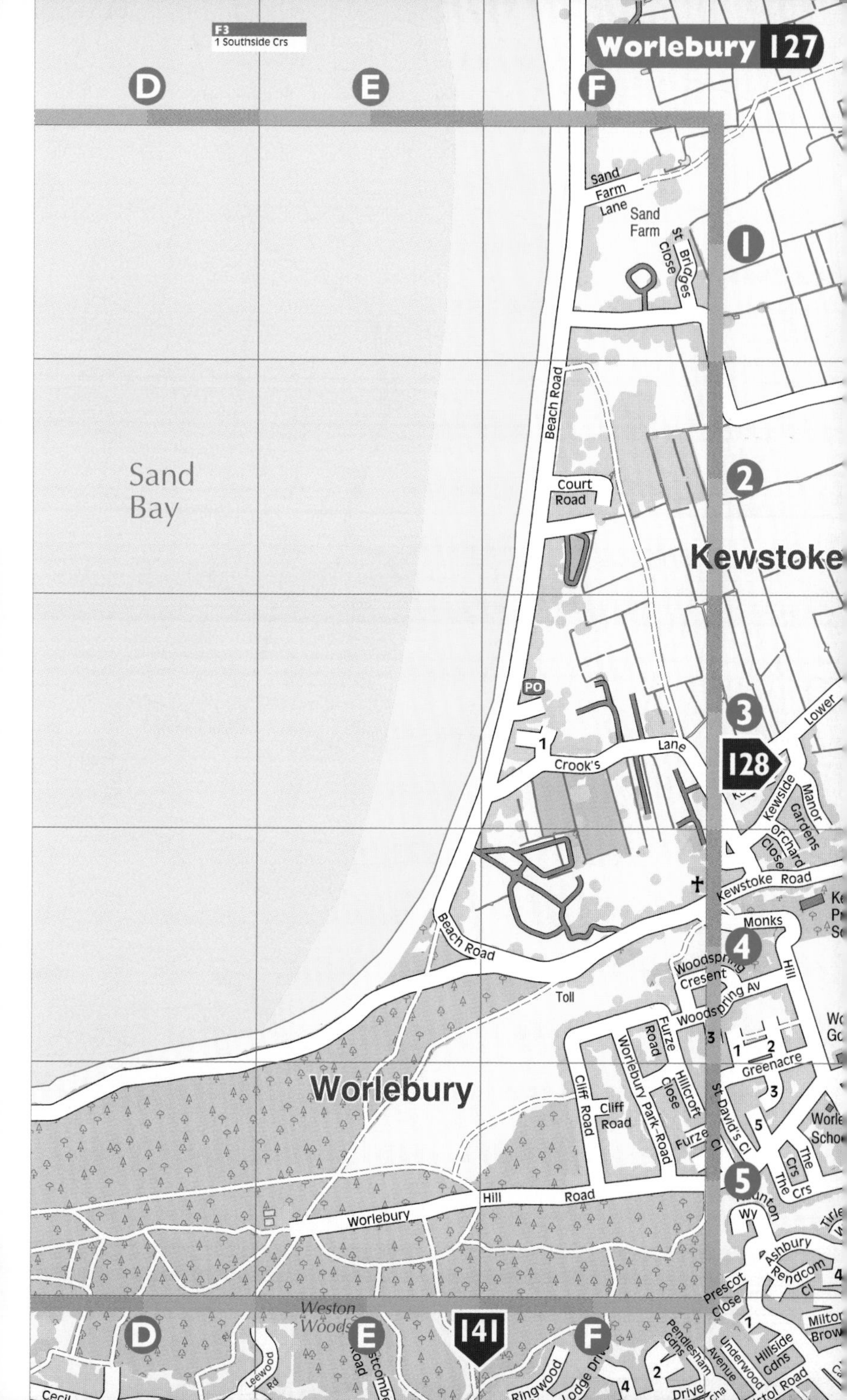
F3
1 Southside Crs
D
E
F
Sand Farm Lane
Sand Farm
St Bridges Close
1
2
Beach Road
Sand Bay
Court Road
Kewstoke
PO
1
Crook's Lane
3
Lower
128
Kewside
Manor Gardens
Orchard Close
Kewstoke Road
Beach Road
Monks Hill
4
Woodspring Cresent
Woodspring Av
Toll
Furze Road
Worlebury Park Road
Hillcroft Close
Greenacre
Cliff Road
Cliff Road
St David's Cl
Worlebury
Furze
5
The Crs
The Crs
Wy
Hill Road
Worlebury
Ashbury
Rendcomb Cl
Prescot Close
Weston Woods
141
Pendlesham Gdns
Underwood Avenue
Hillside Gdns
Ringwood
Lodge Drive
Leewood Rd
Drive
Cecil
D
E
F

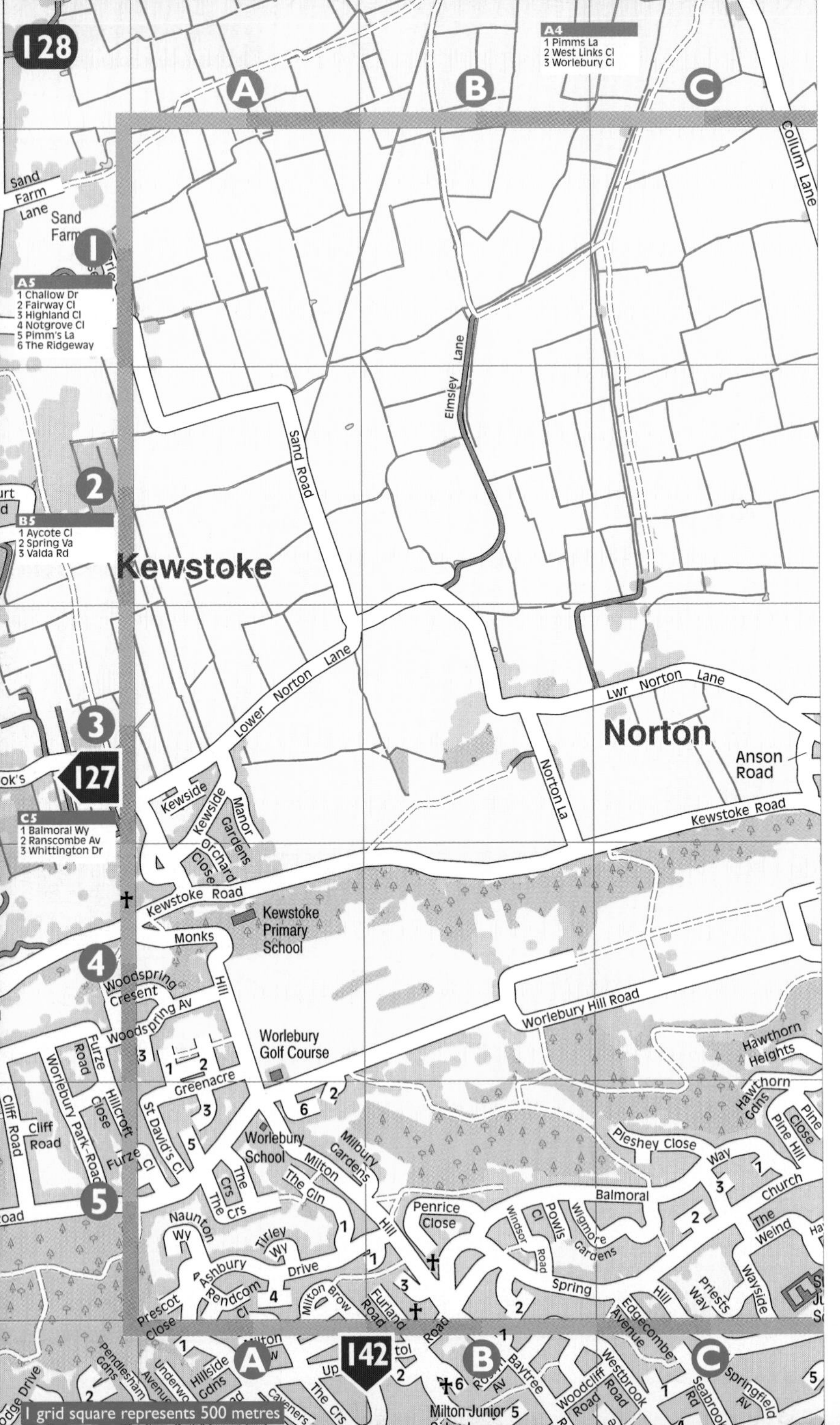
A
B
C
A4
1 Pimms La
2 West Links Cl
3 Worlebury Cl
Collum Lane
Sand Farm Lane
Sand Farm
1
A5
1 Challow Dr
2 Fairway Cl
3 Highland Cl
4 Notgrove Cl
5 Pimm's La
6 The Ridgeway
Elmsley Lane
Sand Road
2
B5
1 Aycote Cl
2 Spring Va
3 Valda Rd
Kewstoke
Lower Norton Lane
Lwr Norton Lane
Norton
3
127
Anson Road
Norton La
Kewside
Kewside
Manor Gardens
Orchard Close
C5
1 Balmoral Wy
2 Ranscombe Av
3 Whittington Dr
Kewstoke Road
Kewstoke Road
Kewstoke Primary School
Monks Hill
4
Woodspring Cresent
Woodspring Av
Worlebury Hill Road
Worlebury Golf Course
Hawthorn Heights
Furze Road
Worlebury Park Road
Hillcroft Close
Greenacre
St David's Cl
Cliff Road
Cliff Road
Furze Cl
Worlebury School
Milton Hill
Milbury Gardens
The Gln
The Crs
The Crs
Hawthorn Gdns
Pine Close
Pine Hill
Pleshey Close
Way
Church
5
Balmoral
Penrice Close
Windsor Road
Powis Cl
Wigmore Gardens
The Weind
Naunton Wy
Tirley Wy
Drive
Ashbury
Rendcom Cl
Prescot Close
Milton Brow
Furland Road
Road
Spring
Hill
Edgecombe Avenue
Priests Way
Wayside
142
A
B
C
Pendlesham Gdns
Hillside Gdns
Baytree
Woodcliff Road
Westbrook Road
Seabrook Rd
Springfield Av
Milton Junior
1 grid square represents 500 metres

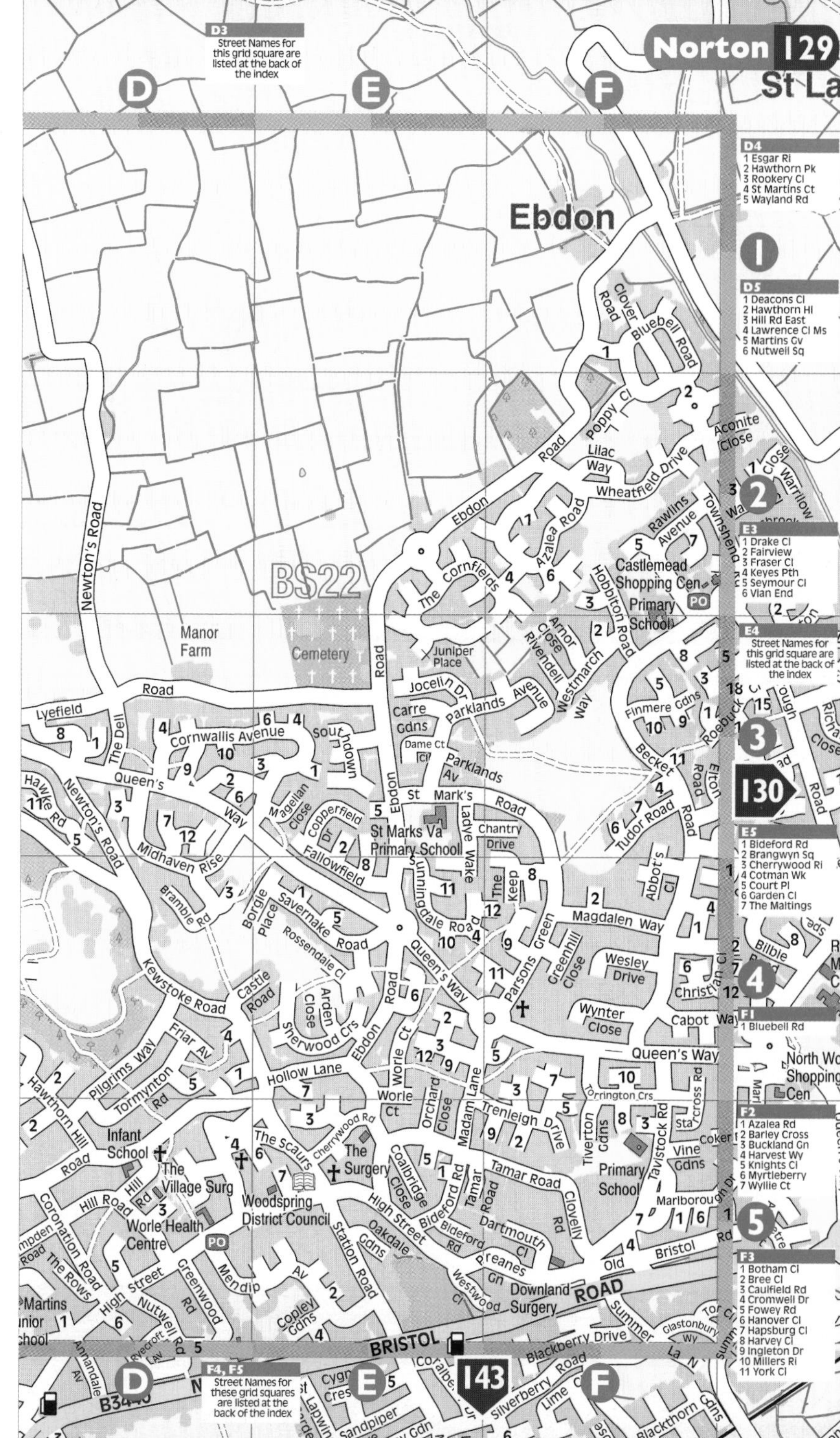
Norton 129
St Law
D3
Street Names for this grid square are listed at the back of the index
D
E
F
Ebdon
D4
1 Esgar Ri
2 Hawthorn Pk
3 Rookery Cl
4 St Martins Ct
5 Wayland Rd
1
D5
1 Deacons Cl
2 Hawthorn Hl
3 Hill Rd East
4 Lawrence Cl Ms
5 Martins Gv
6 Nutwell Sq
2
E3
1 Drake Cl
2 Fairview
3 Fraser Cl
4 Keyes Pth
5 Seymour Cl
6 Vian End
E4
Street Names for this grid square are listed at the back of the index
3
130
E5
1 Bideford Rd
2 Brangwyn Sq
3 Cherrywood Ri
4 Cotman Wk
5 Court Pl
6 Garden Cl
7 The Maltings
4
F1
1 Bluebell Rd
North Worle Shopping Cen
F2
1 Azalea Rd
2 Barley Cross
3 Buckland Gn
4 Harvest Wy
5 Knights Cl
6 Myrtleberry
7 Wyllie Ct
5
F3
1 Botham Cl
2 Bree Cl
3 Caulfield Rd
4 Cromwell Dr
5 Fowey Rd
6 Hanover Cl
7 Hapsburg Cl
8 Harvey Cl
9 Ingleton Dr
10 Millers Ri
11 York Cl
BS22
Newton's Road
Manor Farm
Cemetery
Lyefield Road
Ebdon Road
Clover Road
Bluebell Road
Poppy Cl
Aconite Close
Lilac Way
Wheatfield Drive
Azalea Road
The Cornfields
Rawlins Avenue
Townshend
Warrilow Close
Castlemead Shopping Cen
Primary School
PO
Hobbiton Road
Armor Close
Rivendell
Westmarch Way
Juniper Place
Jocelin Dr
Parklands Avenue
Carre Gdns
Dame Ct Cl
Parklands Av
Finmere Gdns
Roebuck
Becket Road
Elton Road
Tudor Road
The Dell
Cornwallis Avenue
Southdown
Queen's Way
Hawke Rd
Magellan Close
Copperfield Dr
St Mark's Road
St Marks Va Primary School
Ladye Wake
Chantry Drive
The Keep
Abbot's Cl
Midhaven Rise
Fallowfield
Bramble Rd
Borgie Place
Savernake Road
Sunningdale Road
Magdalen Way
Rossendale Cl
Greenhill Close
Wesley Drive
Christian Cl
Parsons Green
Kewstoke Road
Castle Road
Arden Close
Sherwood Crs
Wynter Close
Cabot Way
Friar Av
Pilgrims Way
Hollow Lane
Queen's Way
Tormynton Rd
Worle Ct
Orchard Close
Madam Lane
Torrington Crs
Hawthorn Hill
Infant School
The Village Surg
Hill Road
The Scaurs
Cherrywood Rd
The Surgery
Coalbridge Close
Trenleigh Drive
Tiverton Gdns
Tavistock Rd
Cross Rd
Vine Gdns
Coker
Primary School
Woodspring District Council
Tamar Road
Clovelly Rd
Marlborough Dr
Coronation Road
Worle Health Centre
High Street
Bideford Rd
Dartmouth Cl
Old Bristol Rd
The Rows
Greenwood Rd
Mendip Av
Station Road
Oakdale Gdns
Treanes Gn
Westwood Cl
Downland Surgery
ROAD
Martins Junior School
Nutwell Rd
Copley Gdns
Summer La
Glastonbury Wy
Ryecroft Av
Annandale Av
BRISTOL
Blackberry Drive
F4, F5
Street Names for these grid squares are listed at the back of the index
143
Silverberry Road
Lime
Blackthorn Gdns
B3440
Sandpiper Drive
Lapwing

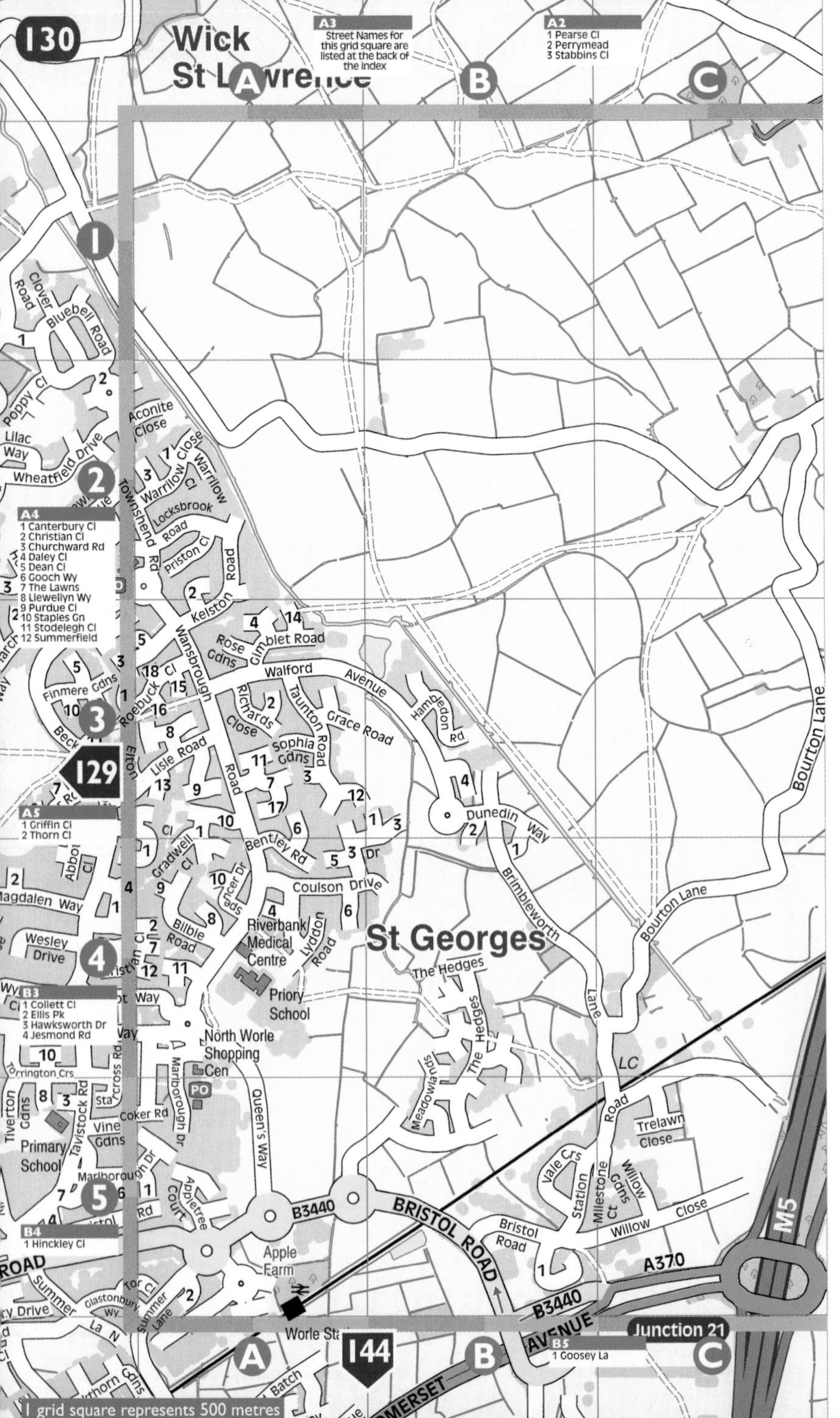
Wick St Lawrence
A3
Street Names for this grid square are listed at the back of the index
A2
1 Pearse Cl
2 Perrymead
3 Stabbins Cl
A4
1 Canterbury Cl
2 Christian Cl
3 Churchward Rd
4 Daley Cl
5 Dean Cl
6 Gooch Wy
7 The Lawns
8 Llewellyn Wy
9 Purdue Cl
10 Staples Gn
11 Stodelegh Cl
12 Summerfield
A5
1 Griffin Cl
2 Thorn Cl
B3
1 Collett Cl
2 Ellis Pk
3 Hawksworth Dr
4 Jesmond Rd
B4
1 Hinckley Cl
B5
1 Goosey La
Clover Road
Bluebell Road
Poppy Cl
Lilac Way
Wheatfield Drive
Aconite Close
Warrilow Close
Townshend Rd
Locksbrook Road
Priston Cl
Kelston Road
Wansbrough Road
Rose Gdns
Gimblet Road
Walford Avenue
Finmere Gdns
Roebuck Cl
Richards Close
Taunton Road
Grace Road
Hambledon Rd
Sophia Gdns
Lisle Road
Elton
Dunedin Way
Bentley Rd
Gradwell Cl
Coulson Drive
Brimbleworth Lane
Magdalen Way
Bilbie Road
Riverbank Medical Centre
Lyddon Road
St Georges
Wesley Drive
Priory School
The Hedges
North Worle Shopping Cen
PO
Torrington Crs
Tiverton Gdns
Tavistock Rd
Coker Rd
Marlborough Dr
Queen's Way
Meadowlands
Vine Gdns
Primary School
Marlborough Dr
Appletree Court
Road
Trelawn Close
Vale Crs
Station
Milestone Ct
Willow Gdns
Willow Close
B3440
BRISTOL ROAD
Bristol Road
Apple Farm
A370
M5
Bourton Lane
LC
Summer Lane
Glastonbury Wy
Tor Cl
Worle Sta
B3440
AVENUE
Junction 21
129
144
1 grid square represents 500 metres

D
E
F
M5
River
Yeo
1
Oldbridge River
St Annes
Primary S
Bourton
West
Hewish
2
A370
3
May's
4
Green
A370
Doubleton
Farm
5
Rolstone
Barn
Lane
West Rolstone Road
Balls
D
E
145
F

116
A
B
C
Congresbury Moor
1
WESTON
River Yeo
Old
Weston Rd
ROAD
A370
STATION ROAD
Stepstones Farm
Lane
Station
Close
St Andrews VC Junior School
2
Dolemoor
Dolemoor Lane
3
4
5
A
B
C
1 grid square represents 500 metres

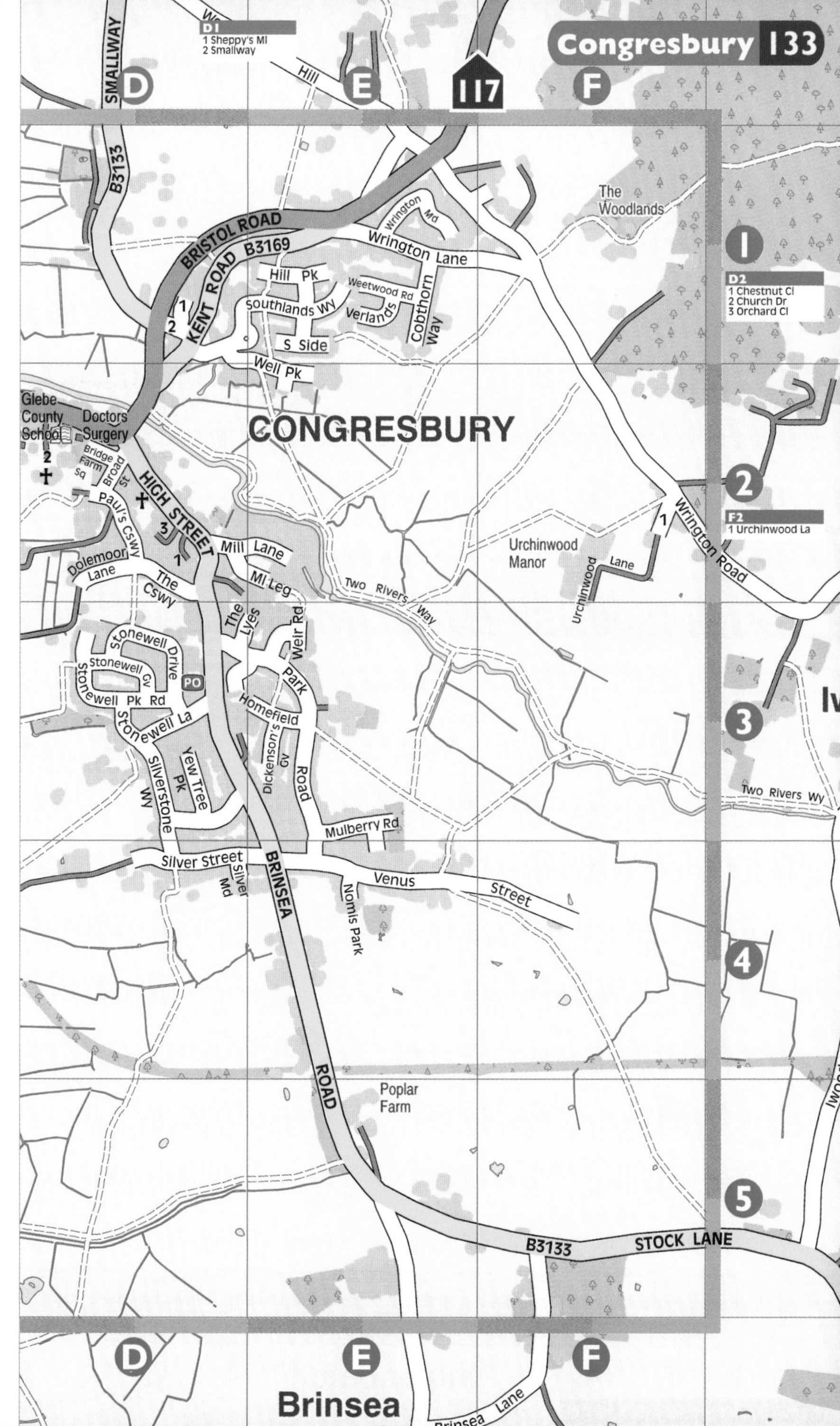
D1
1 Sheppy's Ml
2 Smallway
SMALLWAY
D
E
117
F
Hill
B3133
BRISTOL ROAD
KENT ROAD B3169
Wrington Md
Wrington Lane
The Woodlands
Hill Pk
Weetwood Rd
Southlands Wy
Verlands
Cobthorn Way
S Side
Well Pk
D2
1 Chestnut Cl
2 Church Dr
3 Orchard Cl
Glebe County School
Doctors Surgery
CONGRESBURY
Bridge Farm Sq
Broad St
HIGH STREET
Paul's Cswy
Mill Lane
Ml Leg
Dolemoor Lane
The Cswy
Two Rivers Way
Urchinwood Manor
Urchinwood Lane
Wrington Road
F2
1 Urchinwood La
The Lyes
Weir Rd
Stonewell Drive
Stonewell Gv
Stonewell Pk Rd
PO
Park
Homefield
Stonewell La
Dickenson's Gv
Road
Yew Tree Pk
Silverstone Wy
Mulberry Rd
Two Rivers Wy
Silver Street
Silver Md
BRINSEA
Venus
Street
Nomis Park
ROAD
Poplar Farm
Iwood La
B3133
STOCK LANE
Brinsea
Brinsea Lane
1
2
3
4
5

Newton Park
134
120
A
B
C
1
2
3
4
5
Newton Brook
Pennsylvania
Farm
Englishco
Inglesbatch
Stitch
Kilke
1 grid square represents 500 metres

Whiteway
Southdown
Rush Hill
Hycombe Farm
Haycombe Cemetery
Haycombe Drive
Blagdon Park
The Hollow
Roundhill Park
Wedmore Park
Mount Road
Sladebrook Road
Southdown Road
Hillcrest Drive
Glebe Road
Oriel Grove
Langon Rd
Elliston Drive
Parry Close
Lytton Gdns
Alderley Rd
Burford Cl
Southdown Av
Melrose Gv
Roundhill Gv
Mount Vw
Mount Gv
Belmore Gdns
Southdown Junior Sch
Whiteway Road
Whiteway Av
Haycombe La
Padleigh Hill
Washpool Lane
Innox Gv
Culverhay Boys Sch
Rowacres
Canons Cl
Marsden Road
Georgian View
Ambleside Road
Edgeworth Road
Rush Hill
Kingsway
Stirtingale
Kingsfield
Coronation Avenue
Ivy Avenue
Ivy Grove
Ivy Pl
Teddington Cl
Sladebrook Av
Chest Gv
Acacia
Somerdale View
Old Culverhaysian
Breach Wood
Middle Wood
Vernham Wood
Kilkenny Lane
Kelston View
West Cl
St Michaels Road
North Wy
Haycombe Dr
Rosewarn Cl
Windrush Cl
Poolmead
Garrick
Sheridan
Wedgwood Rd
F2
1 The Circle
Surg
PO
121
136
mbe
BA2
D E F
1 2 3 4 5

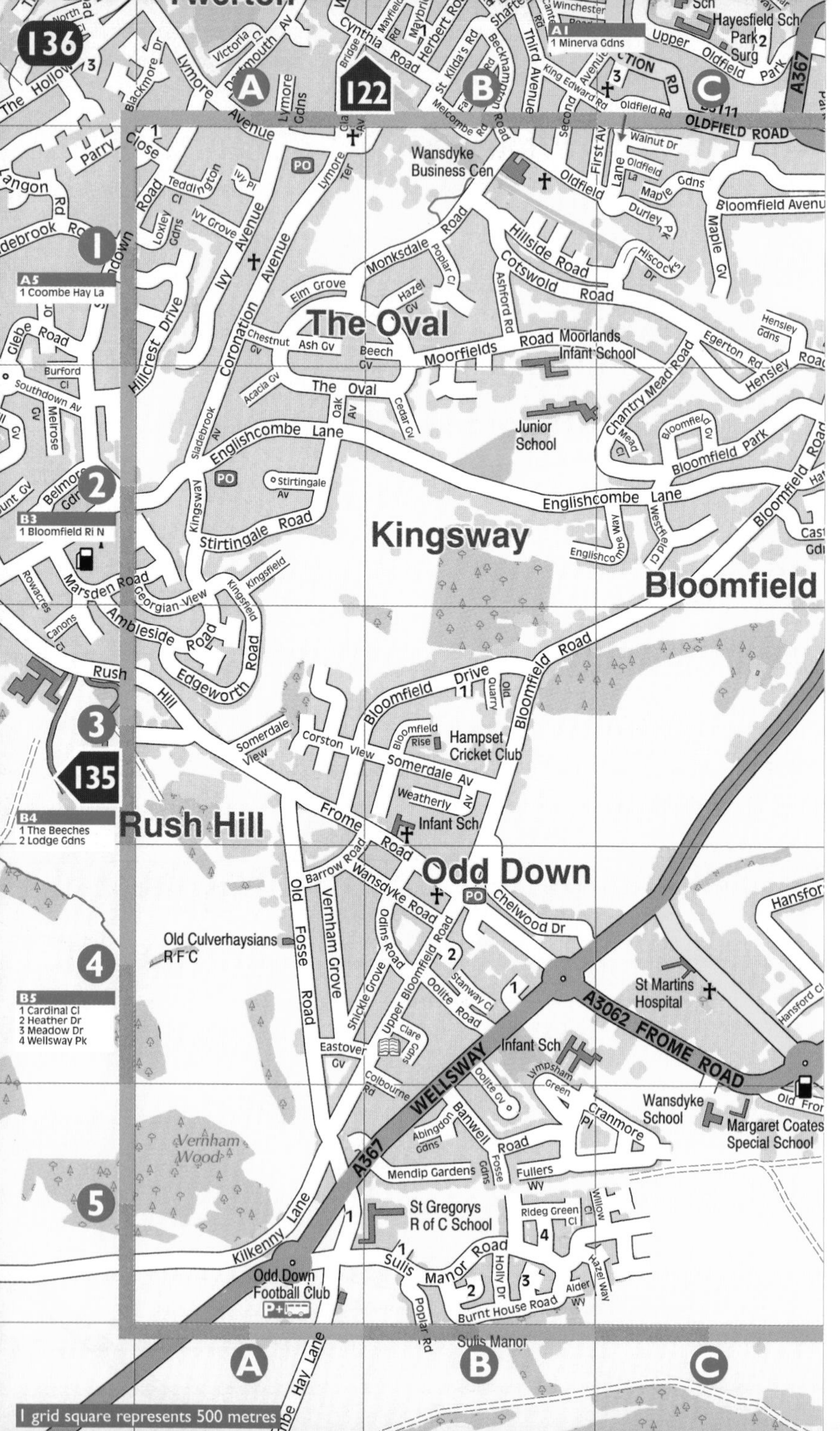
136
122
135
A
B
C
1
2
3
4
5
The Oval
Kingsway
Bloomfield
Rush Hill
Odd Down
A1
1 Minerva Gdns
A5
1 Coombe Hay La
B3
1 Bloomfield Ri N
B4
1 The Beeches
2 Lodge Gdns
B5
1 Cardinal Cl
2 Heather Dr
3 Meadow Dr
4 Wellsway Pk
Hayesfield Sch
Park Surg
Upper Oldfield Park
OLDFIELD ROAD
A367
Cynthia Road
Herbert Rd
St Kilda's Rd
Beckhampton Road
Third Avenue
Second Avenue
First Av
King Edward Rd
Oldfield Rd
Walnut Dr
Oldfield La
Maple Gdns
Bloomfield Avenue
Maple Gv
Durley Pk
Hiscocks Dr
Lymore Avenue
Dartmouth Av
Victoria Cl
Lymore Gdns
Lymore Ter
The Hollow
Blackmore Dr
Parry Close
Langon Rd
Teddington Cl
Ivy Pl
Ivy Grove
Ivy Avenue
Loxley Gdns
Coronation Avenue
Hillcrest Drive
Wansdyke Business Cen
Oldfield Lane
Monksdale Road
Poplar Cl
Hillside Road
Cotswold Road
Elm Grove
Hazel Gv
Ashford Rd
Chestnut Gv
Ash Gv
Beech Gv
Moorfields Road
Moorlands Infant School
Hensley Gdns
Egerton Rd
Hensley Road
Chantry Mead Road
Acacia Gv
The Oval
Oak Av
Cedar Gv
Junior School
Mead Cl
Bloomfield Gv
Bloomfield Park
Bloomfield Road
Glebe Road
Burford Cl
Southdown Av
Melrose Gv
Belmore Gdns
Sladebrook Av
Englishcombe Lane
Stirtingale Av
Stirtingale Road
Kingsway
Englishcombe Way
Westfield Cl
Marsden Road
Rowacres
Canons Cl
Georgian View
Kingsfield
Ambleside Road
Edgeworth Road
Rush Hill
Bloomfield Drive
Quarry Old
Bloomfield Road
Bloomfield Rise
Hampset Cricket Club
Somerdale View
Corston View
Somerdale Av
Weatherly Av
Frome Road
Infant Sch
Barrow Road
Wansdyke Road
Chelwood Dr
Old Fosse Road
Vernham Grove
Odins Road
Upper Bloomfield Road
Shickle Grove
Stanway Cl
Oolite Road
Old Culverhaysians R F C
St Martins Hospital
A3062 FROME ROAD
Hansford Cl
Eastover Gv
Clare Gdns
Colbourne Rd
WELLSWAY
Oolite Gv
Lympsham Green
Cranmore Pl
Wansdyke School
Margaret Coates Special School
Abingdon Gdns
Banwell Road
Fosse Gdns
Mendip Gardens
Fullers Wy
Vernham Wood
St Gregorys R of C School
Rideg Green Cl
Willow Cl
Hazel Way
Kilkenny Lane
Sulis Manor Road
Holly Dr
Alder Wy
Burnt House Road
Odd Down Football Club
P+
Poplar Rd
Sulis Manor
Coombe Hay Lane
1 grid square represents 500 metres

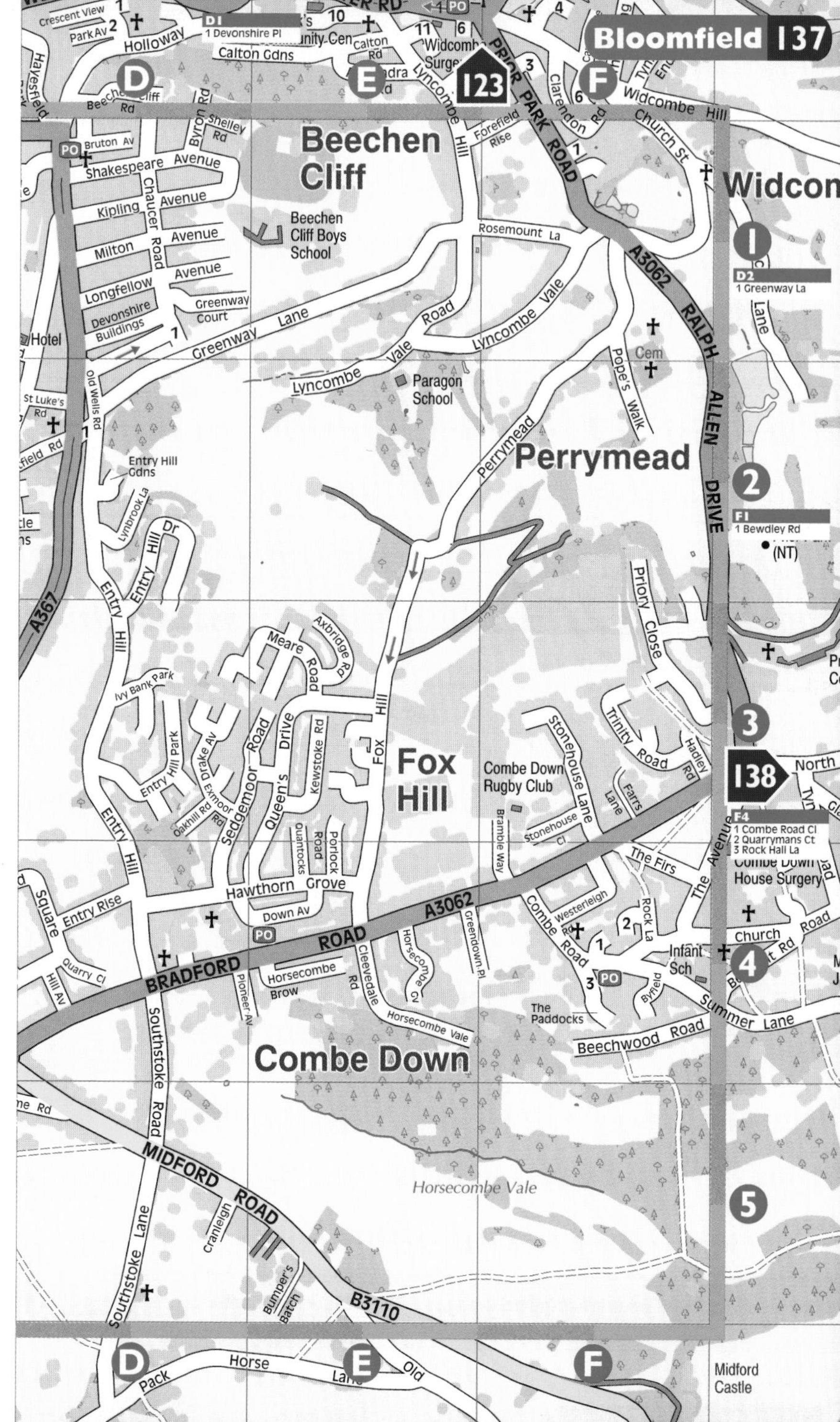

Beechen Cliff
Beechen Cliff Boys School
Perrymead
Paragon School
Fox Hill
Combe Down Rugby Club
Combe Down
Horsecombe Vale
Widcombe
Midford Castle
123
138
D1 1 Devonshire Pl
D2 1 Greenway La
F1 1 Bewdley Rd
F4 1 Combe Road Cl 2 Quarrymans Ct 3 Rock Hall La
Combe Down House Surgery
Infant Sch
Holloway
Calton Gdns
Crescent View
Park Av
Hayesfield
Shakespeare Avenue
Kipling Avenue
Milton Avenue
Longfellow Avenue
Chaucer Road
Devonshire Buildings
Greenway Court
Greenway Lane
Bruton Av
Byron Rd
Shelley Rd
Lyncombe Hill
Lyncombe Vale Road
Lyncombe Vale
Rosemount La
Forefield Rise
Prior Park Road
Clarendon Rd
Widcombe Hill
Church St
A3062 Ralph Allen Drive
Pope's Walk
Cem
Old Wells Rd
St Luke's Rd
Entry Hill Gdns
Lynbrook La
Entry Hill Dr
Entry Hill
A367
Perrymead
Priory Close
Meare Road
Axbridge Rd
Ivy Bank Park
Entry Hill Park
Drake Av
Exmoor Rd
Oakhill Rd
Sedgemoor Road
Queen's Drive
Kewstoke Rd
Quantocks
Porlock Road
Hawthorn Grove
Down Av
Fox Hill
Trinity Road
Hadley Rd
Stonehouse Lane
Stonehouse Cl
Farrs Lane
Bramble Way
The Firs
The Avenue
Westerleigh Rd
Rock La
Combe Road
Byfield
Summer Lane
The Paddocks
Beechwood Road
Church Road
North Road
Square
Entry Rise
Quarry Cl
Hill Av
Bradford Road A3062
Horsecombe Brow
Pioneer Av
Cleevedale Rd
Horsecombe Gv
Greendown Pl
Horsecombe Vale
Southstoke Road
Midford Road
B3110
Southstoke Lane
Cranleigh
Bumper's Batch
Horse Lane
Pack Horse Lane
Old
Hotel
PO

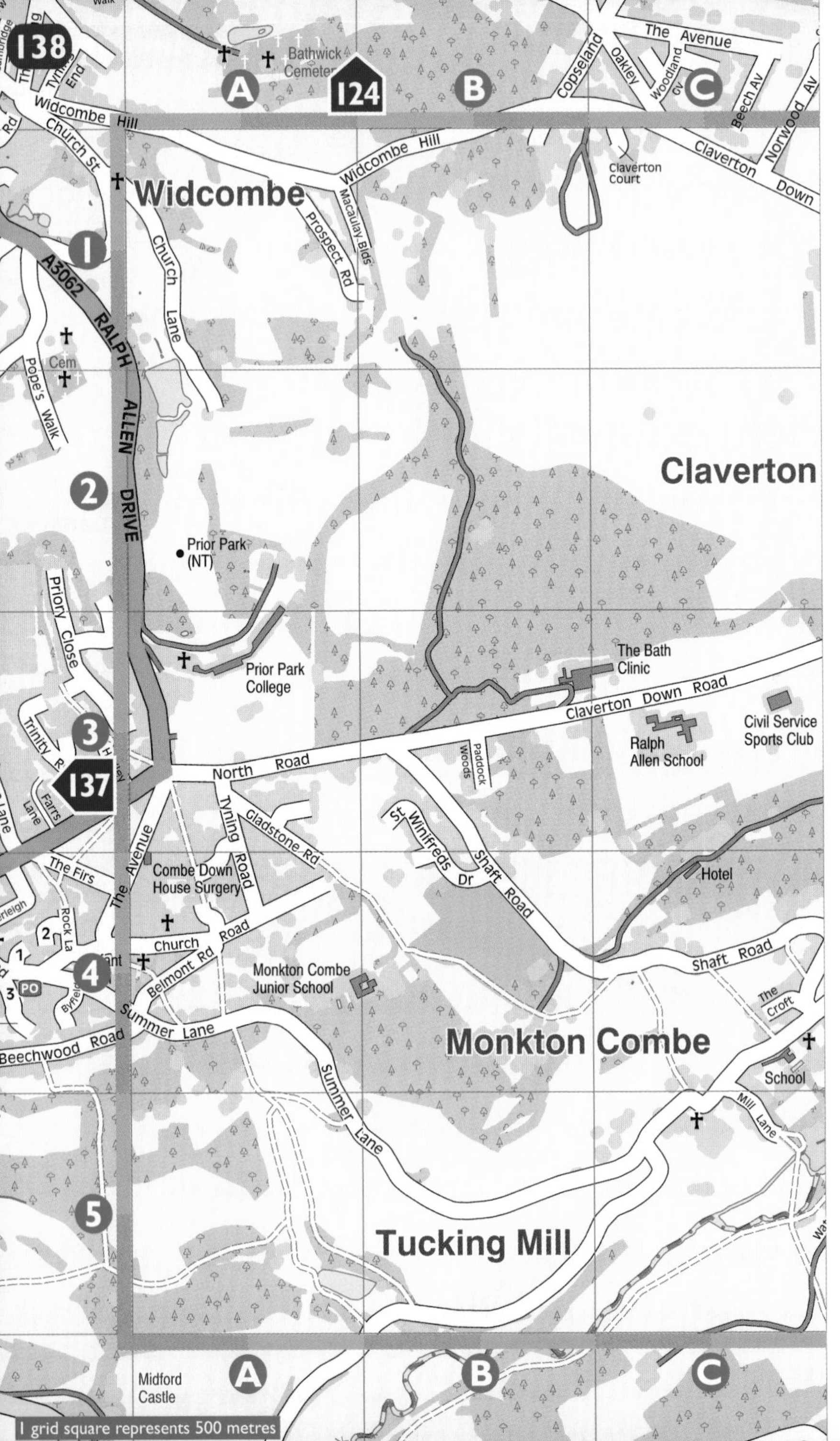
138
124
137
A
B
C
1
2
3
4
5
Bathwick Cemetery
The Avenue
Copseland
Oakley
Woodland Gv
Beech AV
Norwood AV
Widcombe Hill
Church St
A3062
RALPH ALLEN DRIVE
Widcombe
Macaulay Blds
Prospect Rd
Claverton Down
Claverton Court
Church Lane
Cem
Pope's Walk
Claverton
Prior Park (NT)
Priory Close
Prior Park College
The Bath Clinic
Claverton Down Road
Civil Service Sports Club
Ralph Allen School
Paddock Woods
North Road
Trinity R
Farrs Lane
Tyning Road
Gladstone Rd
St Winifreds Dr
Shaft Road
The Firs
The Avenue
Combe Down House Surgery
Hotel
Rock La
Church Road
Belmont Rd
Monkton Combe Junior School
PO
Summer Lane
Beechwood Road
The Croft
Monkton Combe
School
Mill Lane
Tucking Mill
Midford Castle
1 grid square represents 500 metres

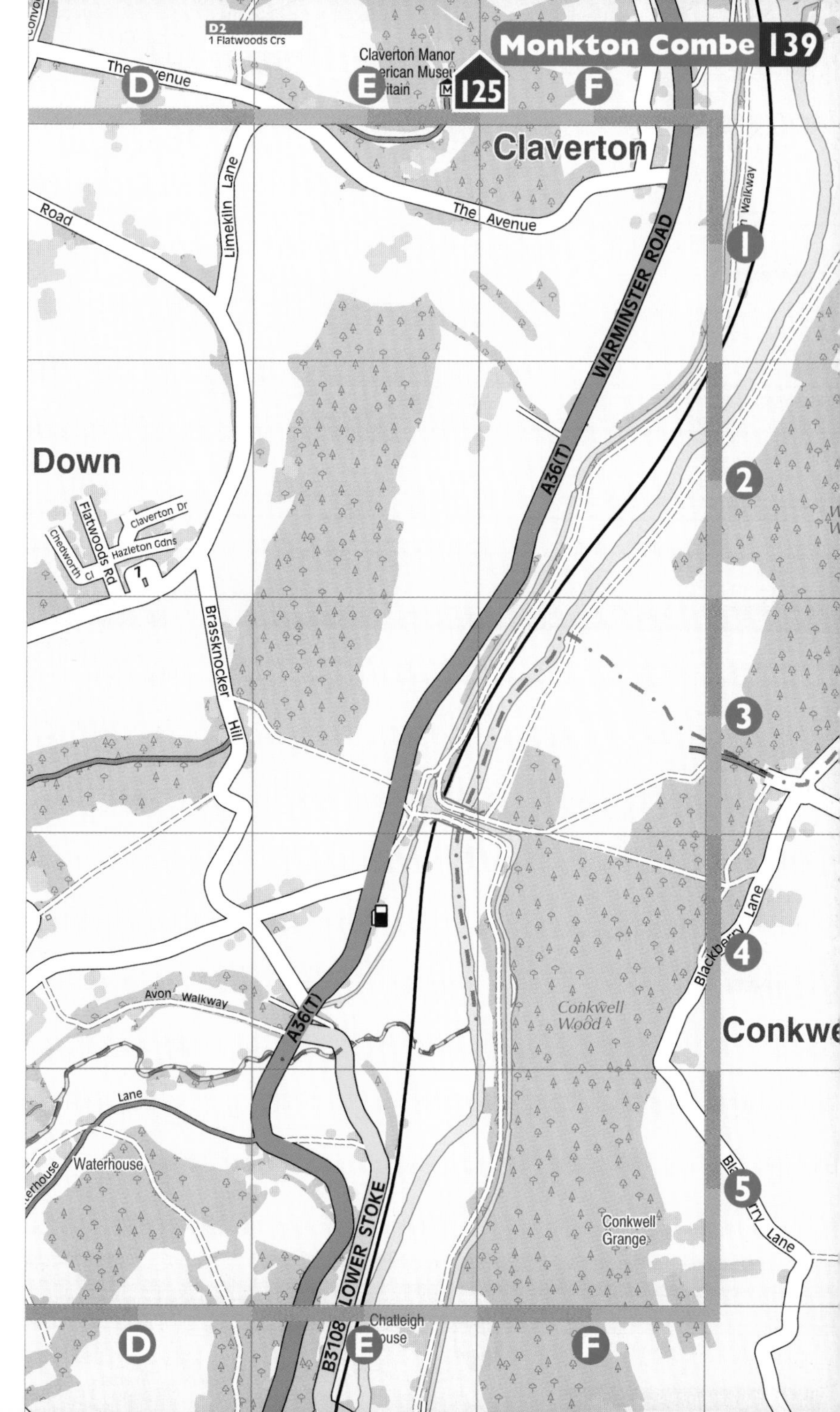
D2
1 Flatwoods Crs
The Avenue
Claverton Manor
American Museum
Britain
125
D
E
F
Claverton
Limekiln Lane
Road
The Avenue
WARMINSTER ROAD
Walkway
1
2
3
4
5
Down
A36(T)
Claverton Dr
Flatwoods Rd
Chedworth Cl
Hazleton Gdns
7
Brassknocker Hill
Blackberry Lane
Avon Walkway
Conkwell Wood
Conkwe
Lane
Waterhouse
LOWER STOKE
B3108
Conkwell Grange
Blackberry Lane
Chatleigh House
D
E
F

140
126
150
A
B
C
1
2
3
4
5
Life Boat Station
Pier
Anchor Head
Westcliff College of Further Education
B1
1 Camp Rd North
2 Hamilton Rd
3 Manilla Pl
4 Shrubbery Ter
B2
1 Raglan Pl
C1
1 St Matthew's Cl
2 Shrubbery Wk W
3 Tower Wk
C2
Street Names for this grid square are listed at the back of the index
C3
1 Gloucester St
2 High St
3 Richmond St
4 St James St
5 Union Pl
6 Union St
7 Victoria Sq
8 Wellington Pl
9 York St
C4
1 Wilton Gdns
Birkett Road
Trinity Road
South Road
Atlantic Road
Paragon
Madeira Rd
Birnbeck Road
Atlantic Rd S
Hotel
Manilla Crescent
Highbury Road
Shrubbery Avenue
Shrubbery Road
St Peter's Avenue
Victoria Park
St John's Close
Grove Pk Rd
Queen's Road
Upper Church Road
Marine Lake
Greenfield Pl
Park Pl
Royal Crs
Grove Lane
Old Knightstone Theatre
Knightstone Causeway
Knightstone Road
South Ter
Lwr Church Road
Knightstone
Weston College
Playhouse Theatre
Htl
Waterloo
Gals
High St
North
WESTON-SUPER-MARE
Model Yacht Pond
Royal Parade
North Somerset Council
Salisbury
Frame Ga
Leisure Pavillion
Grand Pier
A370
Regent
Co Court
OXFORD ST
AMF Bowling
CARLTON ST
Salvation Army
Prima Scho
Hotel
Ashbrooke Ho Sch
Ellenborough
Sea Life Centre
ROAD
Corpus Christi RC Va Primary School
Tropicana Leisure Complex
Clevedon Road
Clifton
Model Yacht Pond
Parade
BEACH
A370
Wallscote
Clarence Road No
Rd
Clarence Park
Marine
Quantock Road
Clarence Road South
Weston Bay
Quantock Road
Marine Parade
Wyncroft School
PO
1 grid square represents 500 metres

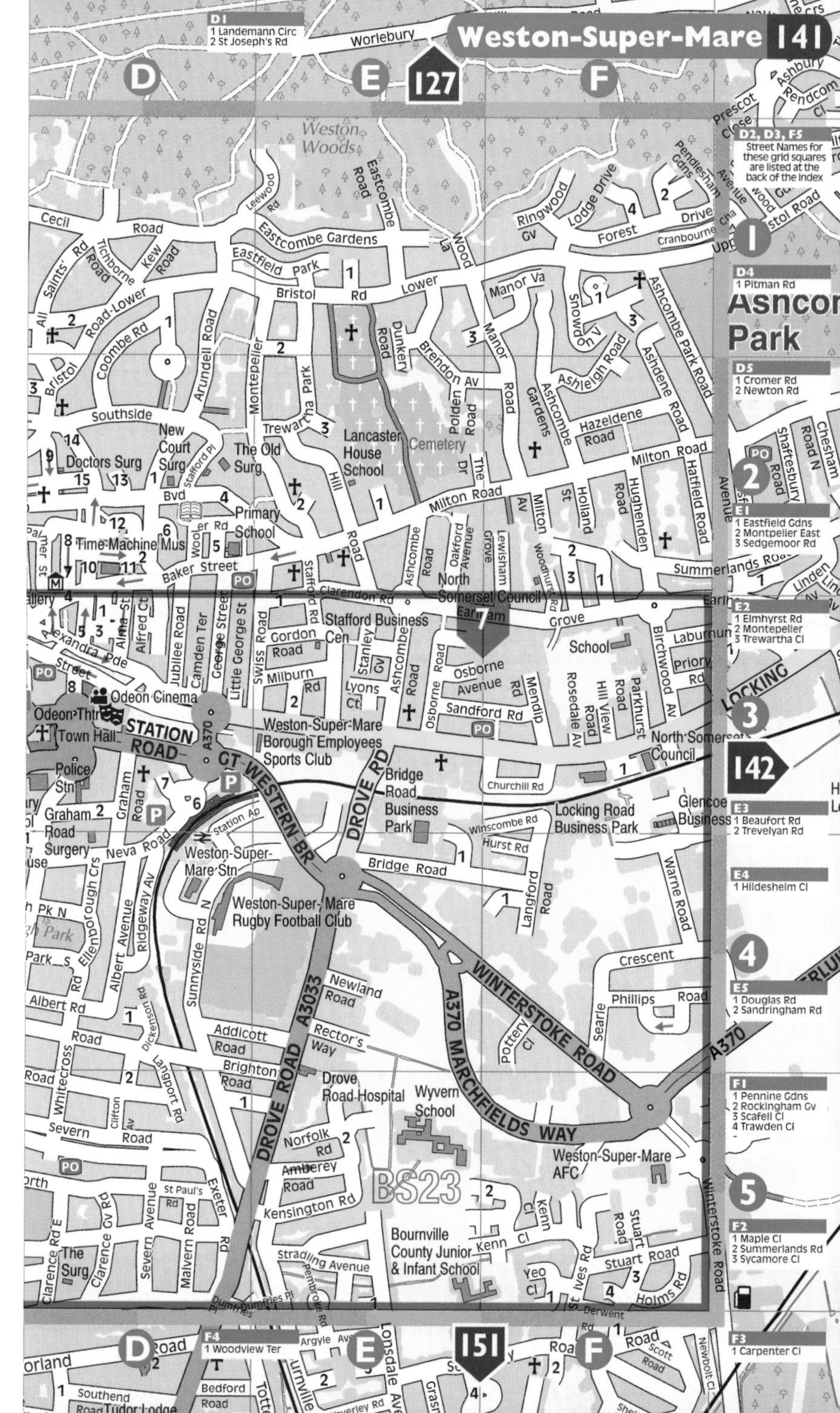
D1
1 Landemann Circ
2 St Joseph's Rd
Worlebury
127
D
E
F
Weston Woods
Eastcombe Road
Leewood Rd
Cecil Road
Eastcombe Gardens
Eastfield Park
Ringwood Gv
Lodge Drive
Pendlesham Gdns
Forest Drive
Cranbourne Cha
Tichborne Road
Kew Road
All Saints' Rd
Bristol Rd Lower
La Wood
Manor Va
Snowdon V
Ashcombe Park Road
Road-Lower
Coombe Rd
Arundell Road
Montepelier
Trewartha Park
Dunkery Road
Brendon Av
Manor Road
Ashleigh Road
Ashdene Road
Bristol
Southside
New Court Surg
Stafford Pl
The Old Surg
Lancaster House School
Cemetery
Polden Road
The Dr
Ashcombe Gardens
Hazeldene Road
Milton Road
Hatfield Road
Hughenden Road
Holland St
Milton Av
Doctors Surg
Bvd
Primary School
Hill Road
Milton Road
Oakford Avenue
Lewisham Grove
Woodhurst Rd
Summerlands Road
Time Machine Mus
Wooler Rd
Baker Street
Stafford Rd
Clarendon Rd
Ashcombe Road
North Somerset Council
Earlham Grove
Alexandra Pde
Alma St
Alfred Ct
Jubilee Road
Camden Ter
George Street
Little George St
Swiss Road
Gordon Road
Stafford Business Cen
Stanley Gv
Osborne Road
Osborne Avenue
School
Birchwood Av
Laburnum
Priory Rd
Street
Milburn Rd
Lyons Ct
Mendip Rd
Rosedale Av
Hill View Road
Parkhurst Road
Odeon Cinema
Odeon Thtr
Town Hall
STATION ROAD
A370
Sandford Rd
Weston-Super-Mare Borough Employees Sports Club
North Somerset Council
LOCKING
Police Stn
GT WESTERN BR
DROVE RD
Bridge Road Business Park
Churchill Rd
142
Graham Road
Graham Road Surgery
Station Ap
Neva Road
Weston-Super-Mare Stn
Winscombe Rd
Hurst Rd
Locking Road Business Park
Glencoe Business
Bridge Road
Langford Road
Warne Road
Ellenborough Crs
Ridgeway Av
Albert Avenue
Sunnyside Rd N
Weston-Super-Mare Rugby Football Club
Park
Albert Rd
Dickenson Rd
A3033
Newland Road
WINTERSTOKE ROAD
Crescent
Phillips Road
Searle
Pottery Cl
Addicott Road
Rector's Way
A370 MARCHFIELDS WAY
A370
Whitecross Road
Langport Rd
Brighton Road
DROVE ROAD
Drove Road Hospital
Wyvern School
Severn Road
Clifton Av
Norfolk Rd
Amberey Road
BS23
Weston-Super-Mare AFC
Kensington Rd
St Paul's Rd
Exeter Rd
Clarence Gv Rd
Severn Avenue
Malvern Road
Clarence Rd E
The Surg
Stradling Avenue
Pembroke Rd
Bournville County Junior & Infant School
Kenn Cl
Yeo Cl
St Ives Rd
Stuart Road
Holms Rd
Derwent Rd
Winterstoke Road
Dumfries Pl
F4
1 Woodview Ter
Argyle Av
Lonsdale Ave
151
Scott Road
Newbolt Cl
Southend Road
Tudor Lodge
Bedford Road
Waverley Rd
Prescot Close
Ashbury
Rendcomb Cl
D2, D3, F5
Street Names for these grid squares are listed at the back of the index
Upper Bristol Road
D4
1 Pitman Rd
Ashcombe Park
D5
1 Cromer Rd
2 Newton Rd
Shaftesbury Road
Road N
Chesham
E1
1 Eastfield Gdns
2 Montpelier East
3 Sedgemoor Rd
E2
1 Elmhyrst Rd
2 Montepelier
3 Trewartha Cl
E3
1 Beaufort Rd
2 Trevelyan Rd
E4
1 Hildesheim Cl
E5
1 Douglas Rd
2 Sandringham Rd
F1
1 Pennine Gdns
2 Rockingham Gv
3 Scafell Cl
4 Trawden Cl
F2
1 Maple Cl
2 Summerlands Rd
3 Sycamore Cl
F3
1 Carpenter Cl

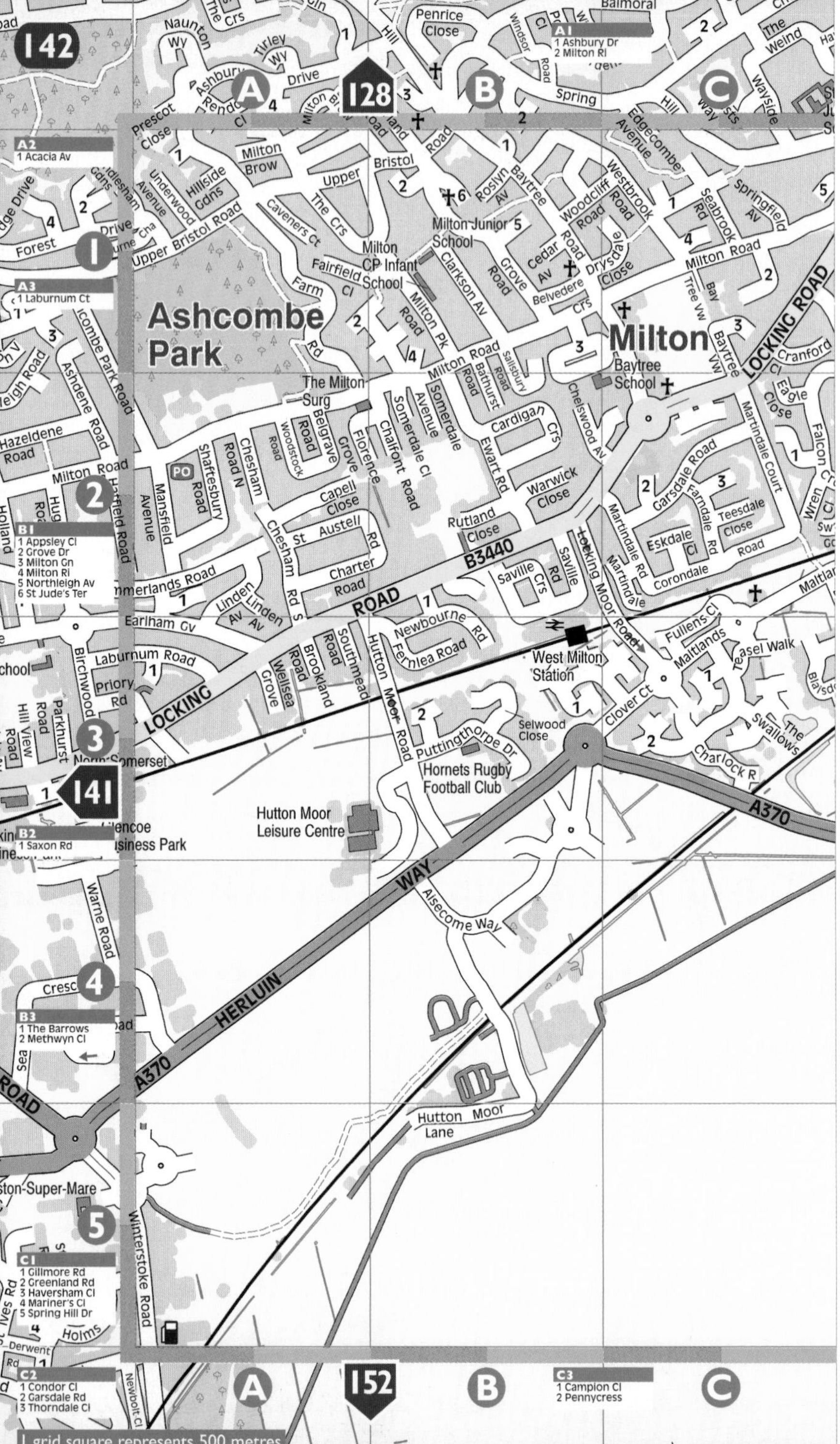

142
128
141
152
A
B
C
1
2
3
4
5
A1
1 Ashbury Dr
2 Milton Ri
A2
1 Acacia Av
A3
1 Laburnum Ct
B1
1 Appsley Cl
2 Grove Dr
3 Milton Gn
4 Milton Ri
5 Northleigh Av
6 St Jude's Ter
B2
1 Saxon Rd
B3
1 The Barrows
2 Methwyn Cl
C1
1 Gillmore Rd
2 Greenland Rd
3 Haversham Cl
4 Mariner's Cl
5 Spring Hill Dr
C2
1 Condor Cl
2 Garsdale Rd
3 Thorndale Cl
C3
1 Campion Cl
2 Pennycress
Ashcombe Park
Milton
Naunton Wy
Tirley Wy
Penrice Close
Balmoral
The Weind
Windsor Road
Spring Hill
Edgecombe Avenue
Wayside
Prescot Close
Milton Brow
Upper Bristol Road
Hillside Gdns
Underwood Avenue
Caveners Ct
The Crs
Roslyn Av
Baytree Road
Westbrook Road
Woodcliff Road
Seabrook Rd
Springfield Av
Milton Junior School
Milton CP Infant School
Fairfield Cl
Farm Rd
Clarkson Av
Grove Road
Cedar Av
Drysdale Close
Belvedere Crs
Milton Road
Tree Vw
Bay Tree Vw
LOCKING ROAD
Cranford Cl
Eagle Close
Falcon Cr
Wren Cl
Forest Drive
Ashdene Road
Hazeldene Road
Milton Pk
Bathurst Road
Salisbury Road
Baytree School
The Milton Surg
Belgrave Road
Woodstock Road
Somerdale Avenue
Somerdale Cl
Chalfont Road
Florence Grove
Cardigan Crs
Ewart Rd
Chelswood Av
Martindale Court
Garsdale Road
Farndale Rd
Teesdale Close
Eskdale Cl
Corondale Road
Martindale Rd
PO
Shaftesbury Road
Road N
Chesham Road
Mansfield Avenue
Capell Close
St Austell Rd
Charter Road
Warwick Close
Rutland Close
B3440
Saville Crs
Saville Rd
Locking Moor Road
Maltlands
Fullens Cl
Teasel Walk
Summerlands Road
Linden Av
Earlham Gv
ROAD
Newbourne Rd
Fernlea Road
West Milton Station
Clover Ct
Laburnum Road
Priory Rd
Birchwood
School
Wellsea Grove
Brookland Road
Southmead Road
Hutton Moor Road
LOCKING
Parkhurst Road
Hill View Road
Selwood Close
Puttingthorpe Dr
Hornets Rugby Football Club
The Swallows
Charlock R
A370
North Somerset
Hutton Moor Leisure Centre
Glencoe Business Park
WAY
Aisecombe Way
Warne Road
HERLUIN
A370
ROAD
Hutton Moor Lane
Winterstoke Road
Weston-Super-Mare
St Ives Rd
Holms
Derwent
Newbolt Cl
1 grid square represents 500 metres

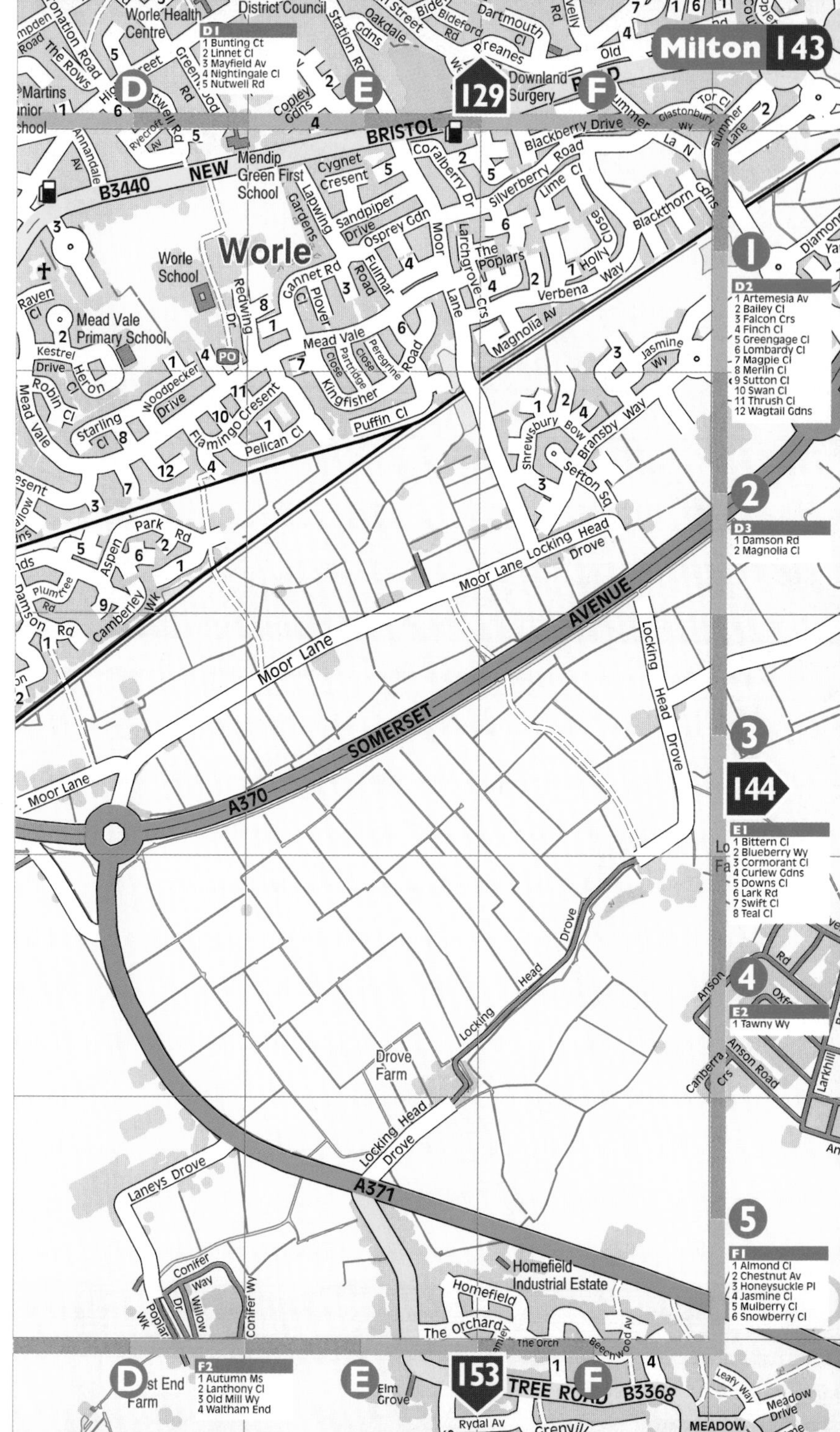
Milton 143
129
144
153
D
E
F
D
E
F
1
2
3
4
5
Worle
Worle Health Centre
District Council
St Martins Junior School
Mendip Green First School
Worle School
Mead Vale Primary School
Downland Surgery
Drove Farm
Homefield Industrial Estate
West End Farm
BRISTOL
NEW
B3440
SOMERSET
AVENUE
A370
A371
TREE ROAD
B3368
MEADOW
Moor Lane
Locking Head Drove
Laneys Drove
Mead Vale
Kingfisher Road
Flamingo Cresent
Woodpecker Drive
Starling Cl
Robin Cl
Heron Cl
Kestrel Drive
Raven Cl
Pelican Cl
Puffin Cl
Partridge Close
Peregrine Close
Plover Cl
Gannet Rd
Fulmar Road
Redwing Dr
Osprey Gdn
Sandpiper Drive
Lapwing Gardens
Cygnet Cresent
Coralberry Dr
Moor Lane
Larchgrove Crs
Silverberry Road
Blackberry Drive
Lime Cl
Holly Close
Blackthorn Gdns
The Poplars
Verbena Way
Magnolia Av
Jasmine Wy
Bransby Way
Shrewsbury Bow
Sefton Sq
Park Rd
Aspen
Plumtree Rd
Damson Rd
Camberley Wk
Annandale Av
Ryecroft Av
Nutwell Rd
Greenwood Rd
Copley Gdns
Station Rd
Oakdale Gdns
Bideford Rd
Dartmouth Cl
Preanes
Old
Summer Lane
Glastonbury Wy
Tor Cl
Diamond
Anson Road
Canberra Crs
Oxford
Larkhill
Conifer Way
Conifer Wy
Willow Dr
Poplar Wk
Homefield
The Orchard
The Orch
Beechwood Av
Leafy Way
Meadow Drive
Rydal Av
Grenville
Elm Grove
D1
1 Bunting Ct
2 Linnet Cl
3 Mayfield Av
4 Nightingale Cl
5 Nutwell Rd
D2
1 Artemesia Av
2 Bailey Cl
3 Falcon Crs
4 Finch Cl
5 Greengage Cl
6 Lombardy Cl
7 Magpie Cl
8 Merlin Cl
9 Sutton Cl
10 Swan Cl
11 Thrush Cl
12 Wagtail Gdns
D3
1 Damson Rd
2 Magnolia Cl
E1
1 Bittern Cl
2 Blueberry Wy
3 Cormorant Cl
4 Curlew Gdns
5 Downs Cl
6 Lark Rd
7 Swift Cl
8 Teal Cl
E2
1 Tawny Wy
F1
1 Almond Cl
2 Chestnut Av
3 Honeysuckle Pl
4 Jasmine Cl
5 Mulberry Cl
6 Snowberry Cl
F2
1 Autumn Ms
2 Lanthony Cl
3 Old Mill Wy
4 Waltham End

144
130
143
A
B
C
1
2
3
4
5
Junction 21
West Wick
Worle Station
Apple Farm
BRISTOL ROAD
Bristol Road
B3440
A370
M5
SOMERSET AVENUE
Somerset Avenue
Summer Lane
West Wick
Wolvers Hill Road
Diamond Batch
Yarbury Way
Blackthorn Gdns
Glastonbury Wy
Tor Cl
Holly Close
Jasmine Wy
Bransby Way
Locking Head Drove
Summer Lane
Eton
Wolvers Hill Road
Wolvershill Manor
Locking Head Farm
Varsity Way
Woolvers Way
Anson Rd
Oxford Square
Larkhill Road
Anson Road
Canberra Crs
Russell Road
Leedham Road
Lower Pde Gnd Rd
Mc Crae Road
Parkes Road
Bowen Road
Post Office Road
Cranwell Road
Cranwell Rd
Farnborough Rd
Spinney Road
Beechwood Av
Leafy Way
Meadow Drive
ROAD B3368
A1
1 Darmead
2 Rowan Pl
3 Summer La
Close
1 grid square represents 500 metres

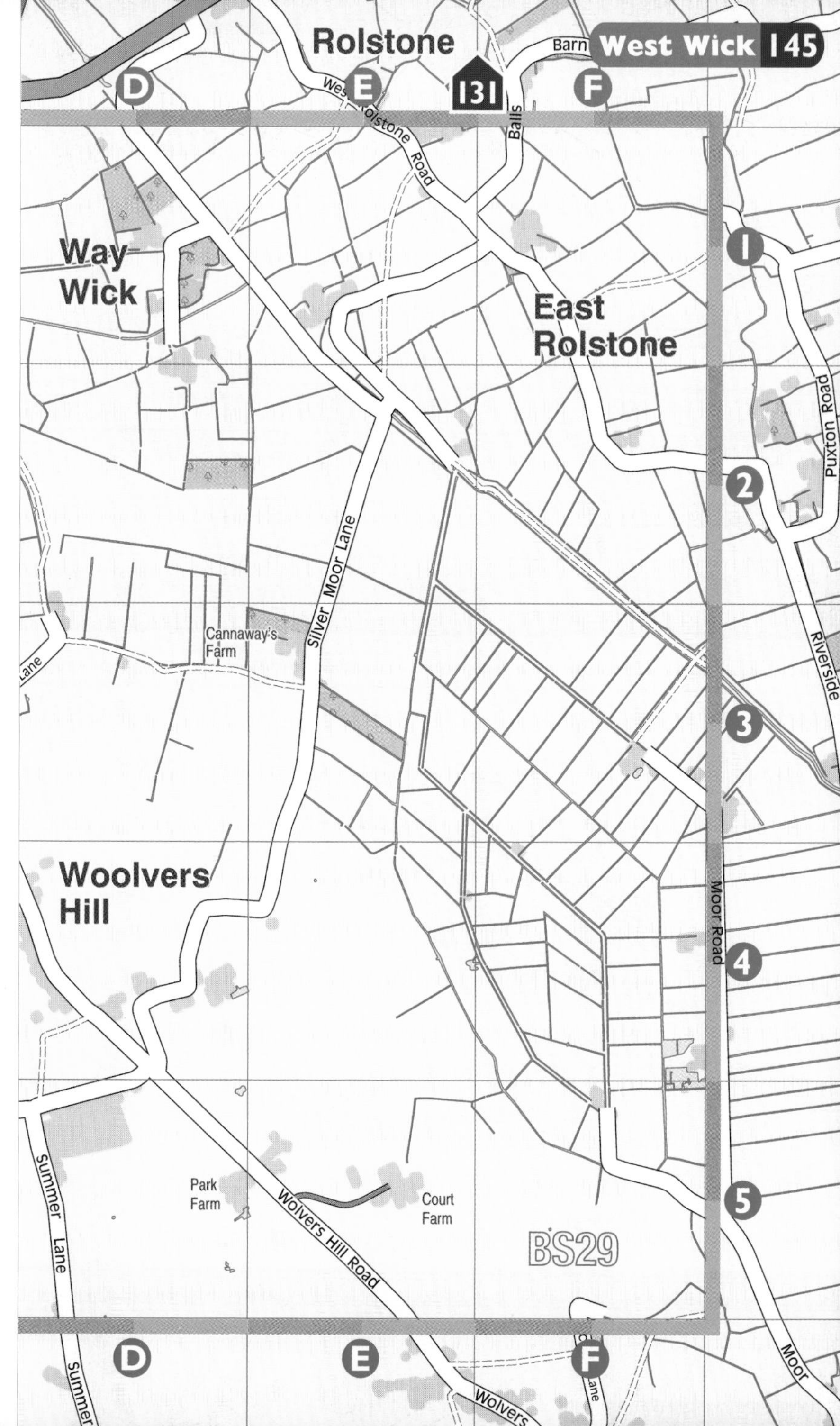
Rolstone
D
E
F
131
Barn
West Rolstone Road
Balls
Way Wick
East Rolstone
1
2
3
4
5
Puxton Road
Riverside
Silver Moor Lane
Cannaway's Farm
Lane
Woolvers Hill
Moor Road
Summer Lane
Park Farm
Court Farm
Wolvers Hill Road
BS29
Moor
Summer
Wolvers
Lane

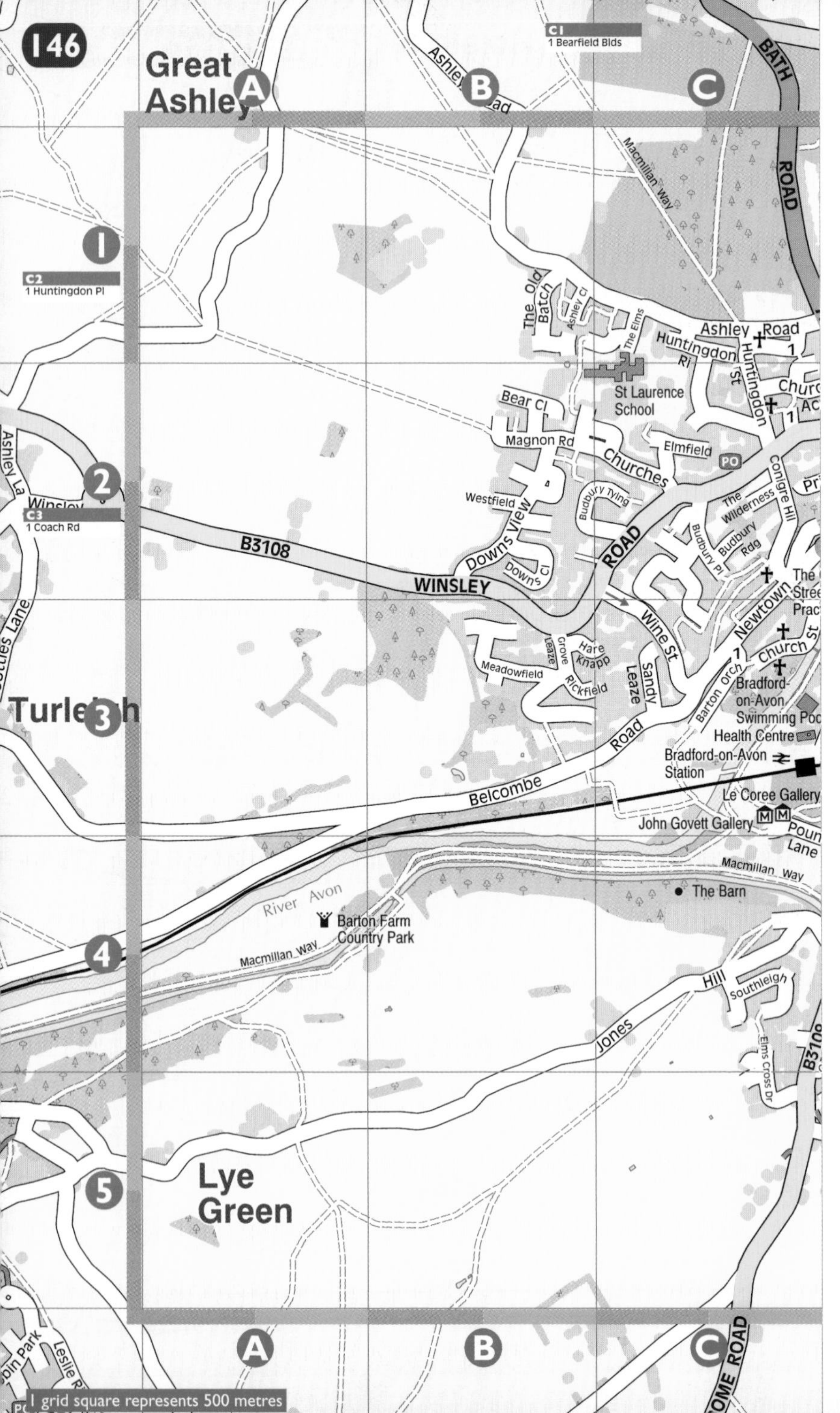
Great Ashley
A
B
C
Ashley Road
C1
1 Bearfield Blds
BATH ROAD
Macmillan Way
1
C2
1 Huntingdon Pl
The Old Batch
Ashley Cl
The Elms
Ashley Road
Huntingdon Ri
Huntingdon St
St Laurence School
Bear Cl
Magnon Rd
Churches
Elmfield
PO
2
Ashley La
Winsley
C3
1 Coach Rd
Westfield
Downs View
Budbury Tying
ROAD
The Wilderness
Conigre Hill
Budbury Pl
Budbury Rdg
B3108
WINSLEY
Downs Cl
Wine St
Newtown
Church St
Leaze
Grove
Hare Knapp
Meadowfield
Rickfield
Sandy Leaze
Barton Orch
Bradford-on-Avon Swimming Poo
Health Centre
Bradford-on-Avon Station
Turleigh
3
Road
Belcombe
Le Coree Gallery
John Govett Gallery
Pound Lane
Macmillan Way
The Barn
River Avon
Barton Farm Country Park
4
Macmillan Way
Hill
Southleigh
Jones
Elms Cross Dr
B3109
Lye Green
5
A
B
C
Leslie Ri
ROAD
1 grid square represents 500 metres

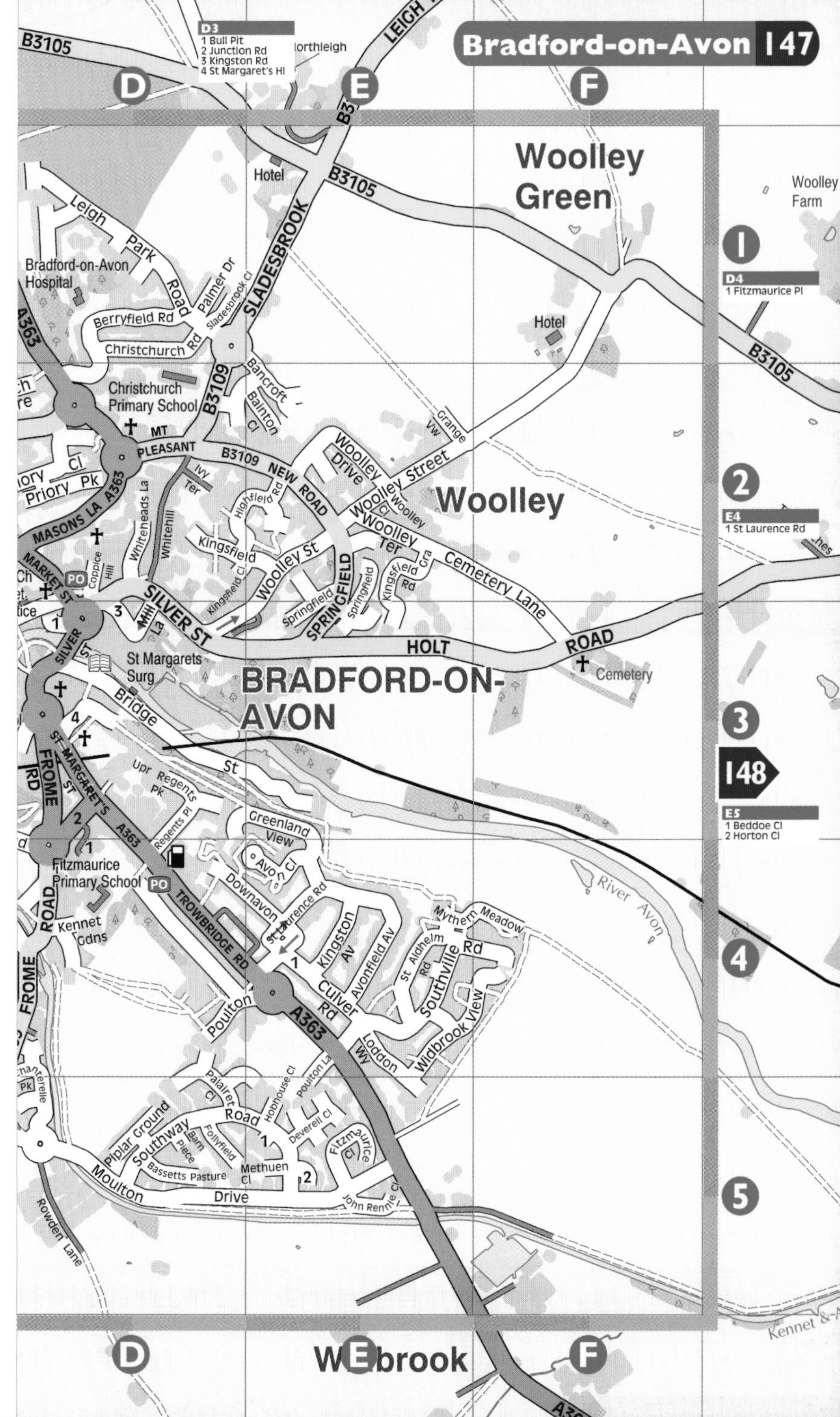
D3
1 Bull Pit
2 Junction Rd
3 Kingston Rd
4 St Margaret's Hl
D4
1 Fitzmaurice Pl
E4
1 St Laurence Rd
E5
1 Beddoe Cl
2 Horton Cl
148
Woolley Green
Woolley
BRADFORD-ON-AVON
Woolley Farm
Hotel
B3105
B3109
A363
SLADESBROOK
Leigh Park Road
Bradford-on-Avon Hospital
Berryfield Rd
Christchurch Rd
Palmer Dr
Sladesbrook Cl
Christchurch Primary School
Bancroft
Bainton Cl
Grange Vw
PLEASANT
MT
NEW ROAD
Woolley Drive
Woolley Street
Woolley Ter
Cemetery Lane
Priory Cl
Priory Pk
MASONS LA
Whiteheads La
Whitehill
Ivy Ter
Highfield Rd
Kingsfield
Kingsfield Cl
Woolley St
Springfield
SPRINGFIELD
Kingsfield Gra
Kingsfield Rd
MARKET ST
Coppice Hill
SILVER ST
Mill La
HOLT ROAD
Cemetery
St Margarets Surg
Bridge St
ST MARGARET'S ST
FROME RD
Upr Regents Pk
Regents Pl
Greenland View
Avon Cl
Downavon
St Laurence Rd
Kingston Av
Avonfield Av
Mythern Meadow
River Avon
St Aldhelm Rd
Southville Rd
Southville
Widbrook View
Fitzmaurice Primary School
PO
TROWBRIDGE RD
Kennet Gdns
ROAD
FROME
Poulton
Culver Rd
Loddon Wy
Chanterelle
Pk
Palairet Cl
Hobhouse Cl
Poulton La
Road
Deverell Cl
Fitzmaurice Cl
Piplar Ground
Southway
Barn Piece
Follyfield
Bassetts Pasture
Methuen Cl
Moulton Drive
John Rennie Cl
Rowden Lane
Kennet & A
Widbrook
D
E
F
1
2
3
4
5

1 grid square represents 500 metres

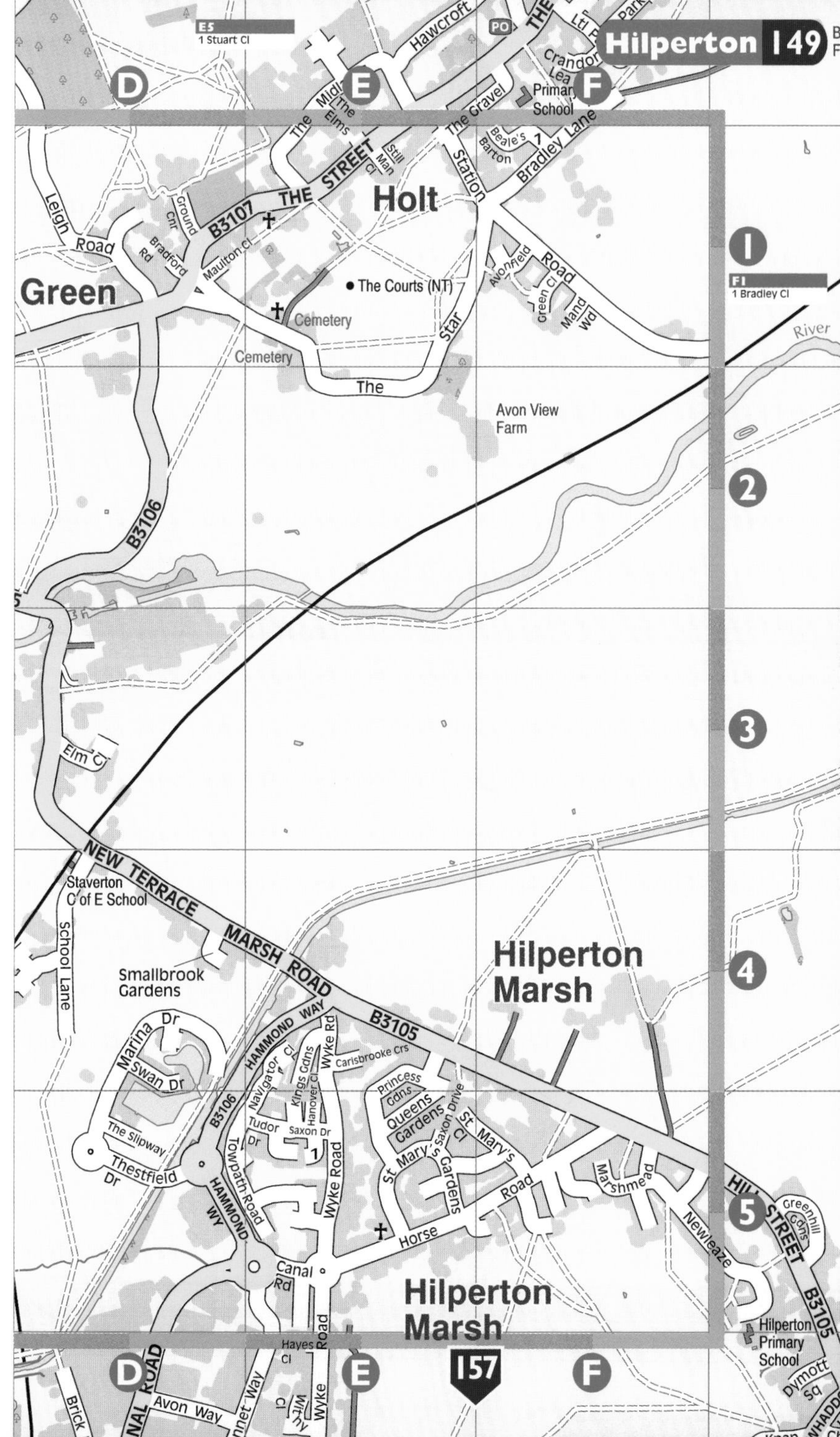
E5
1 Stuart Cl
F1
1 Bradley Cl
Holt
Green
Hilperton Marsh
Hilperton Marsh
THE STREET
B3107
Leigh Road
Bradford Rd
Ground Cnr
Maulton Cl
The Courts (NT)
Cemetery
Cemetery
Station Road
Star
The
Bradley Lane
Beale's Barton
The Gravel
Primary School
Crandon Lea
Hawcroft
Avonfield
Green Cl
Mand Wd
Still Man Cl
The Elms
Avon View Farm
River
B3106
Elm Cl
NEW TERRACE
MARSH ROAD
B3105
Staverton C of E School
School Lane
Smallbrook Gardens
Marina Dr
Swan Dr
The Slipway
Thestfield Dr
HAMMOND WAY
Navigator Cl
Kings Gdns
Hanover Cl
Wyke Rd
Carisbrooke Crs
Tudor Dr
Saxon Dr
Towpath Road
Wyke Road
Princess Gdns
Queens Gardens
Saxon Drive
St Mary's Cl
St Mary's Gardens
Horse Road
Marshmead
Newleaze
Canal Rd
Hayes Cl
HILL STREET
Greenhill Gdns
B3105
Hilperton Primary School
Dymott Sq
Avon Way
Wyke
157
D
E
F
1
2
3
4
5

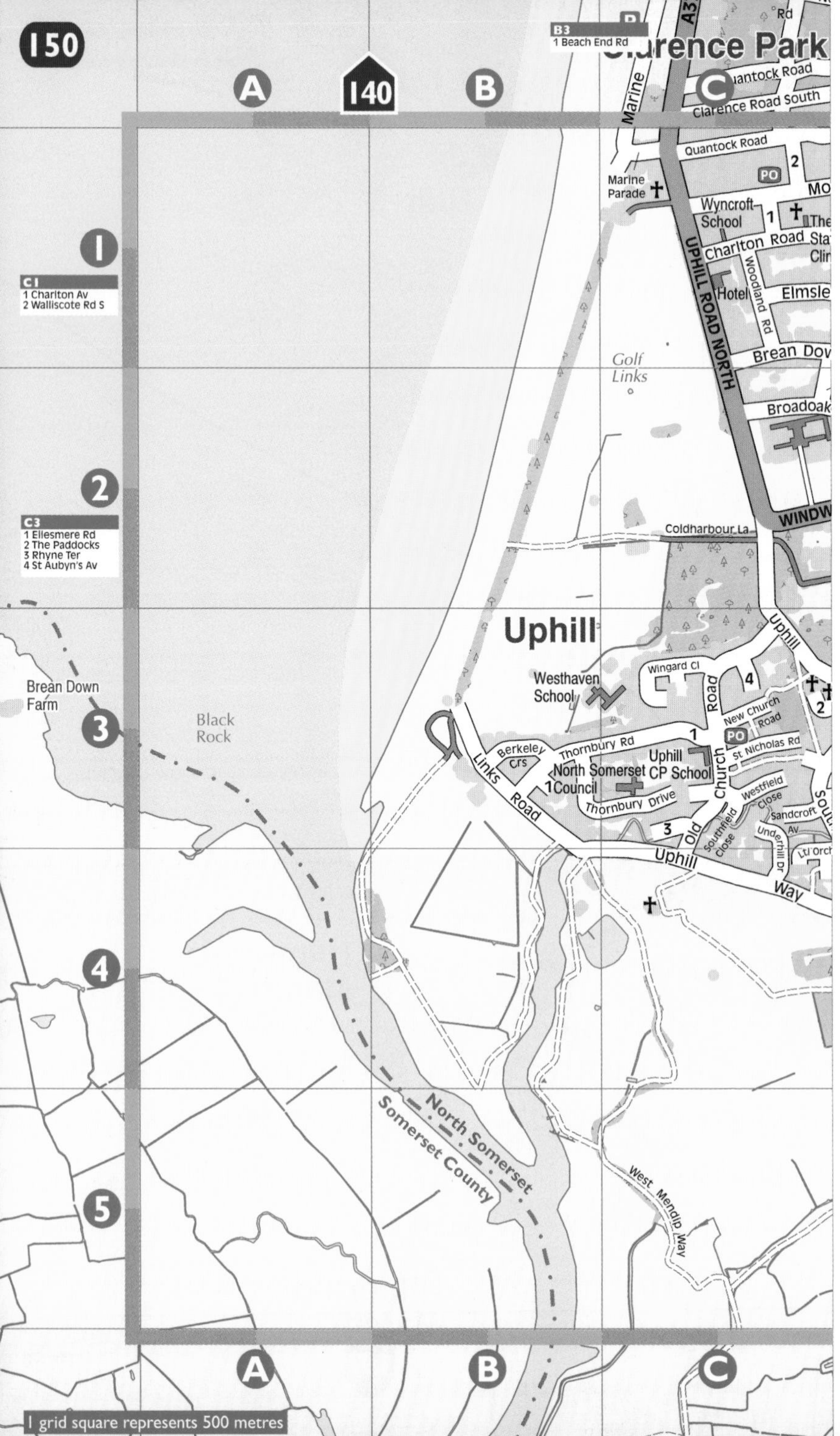

140
A
B
C
1
2
3
4
5
B3
1 Beach End Rd
C1
1 Charlton Av
2 Walliscote Rd S
C3
1 Ellesmere Rd
2 The Paddocks
3 Rhyne Ter
4 St Aubyn's Av
Clarence Park
Quantock Road
Clarence Road South
Marine
Marine Parade
Wyncroft School
Charlton Road
Woodland Rd
Hotel
UPHILL ROAD NORTH
Brean Dow
Broadoak
Golf Links
Coldharbour La
WINDW
Uphill
Brean Down Farm
Black Rock
Westhaven School
Wingard Cl
Road
New Church Road
St Nicholas Rd
Berkeley Crs
Thornbury Rd
Uphill CP School
North Somerset Council
Church
Thornbury Drive
Links Road
Westfield Close
Sandcroft Av
Southfield Close
Underhill Dr
Old
Uphill Way
North Somerset
Somerset County
West Mendip Way
1 grid square represents 500 metres

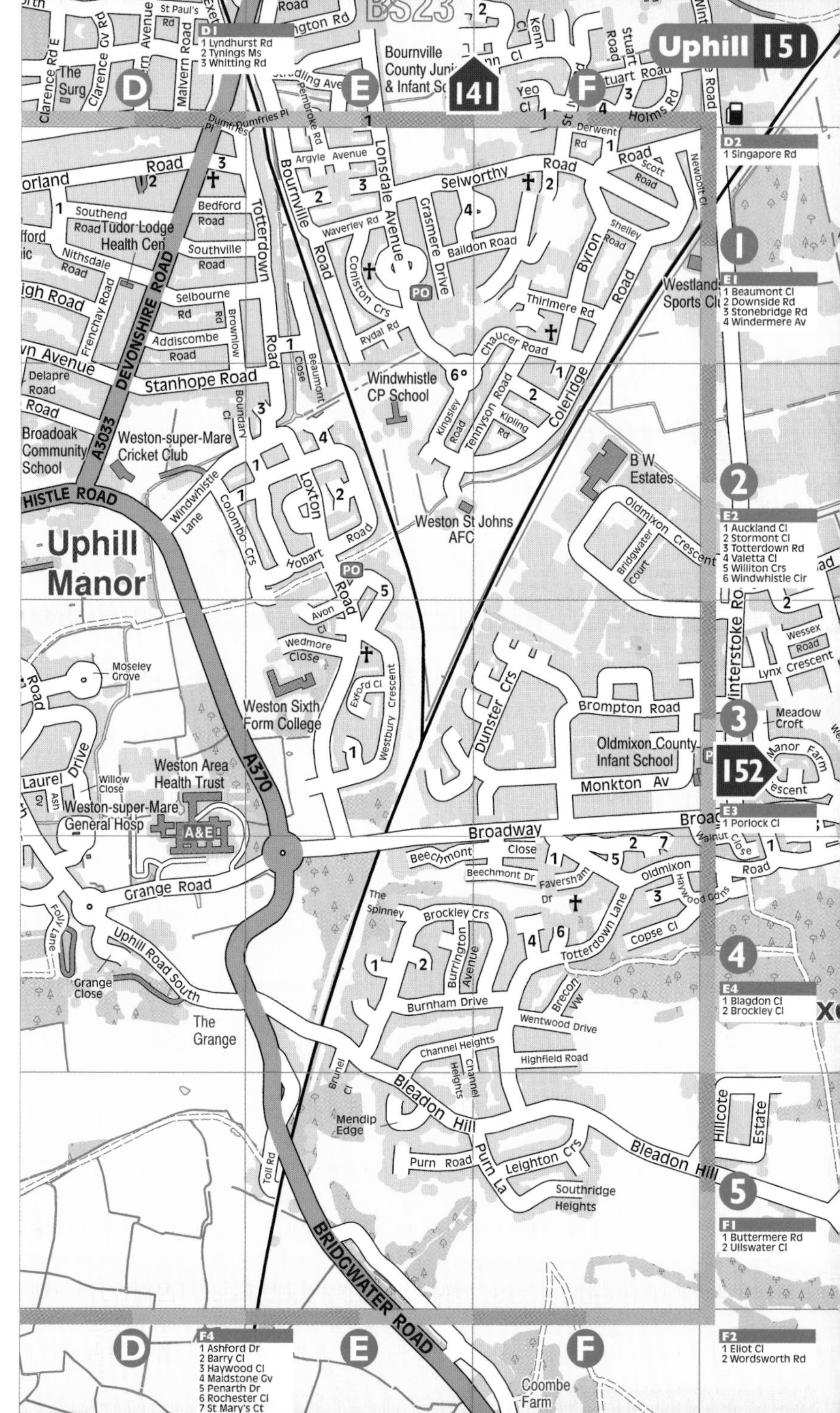
BS23
D1
1 Lyndhurst Rd
2 Tynings Ms
3 Whitting Rd
D2
1 Singapore Rd
E1
1 Beaumont Cl
2 Downside Rd
3 Stonebridge Rd
4 Windermere Av
E2
1 Auckland Cl
2 Stormont Cl
3 Totterdown Rd
4 Valetta Cl
5 Williton Crs
6 Windwhistle Cir
E3
1 Porlock Cl
E4
1 Blagdon Cl
2 Brockley Cl
F1
1 Buttermere Rd
2 Ullswater Cl
F2
1 Eliot Cl
2 Wordsworth Rd
F4
1 Ashford Dr
2 Barry Cl
3 Haywood Cl
4 Maidstone Gv
5 Penarth Dr
6 Rochester Cl
7 St Mary's Ct
141
152
D
E
F
1
2
3
4
5
Uphill Manor
Bournville County Junior & Infant School
Windwhistle CP School
Weston St Johns AFC
B W Estates
Westlands Sports Club
Oldmixon County Infant School
Weston Sixth Form College
Weston Area Health Trust
Weston-super-Mare General Hosp
A&E
Weston-super-Mare Cricket Club
Broadoak Community School
Tudor Lodge Health Cen
The Surg
The Grange
The Spinney
Mendip Edge
Southridge Heights
Hillcote Estate
Coombe Farm
DEVONSHIRE ROAD
A3033
A370
BRIDGWATER ROAD
Broadway
Bleadon Hill
Stanhope Road
Totterdown Road
Bournville Road
Lonsdale Avenue
Selworthy Road
Argyle Avenue
Waverley Rd
Coniston Crs
Rydal Rd
Grasmere Drive
Baildon Road
Byron Road
Shelley Road
Scott Road
Newbolt Cl
Thirlmere Rd
Chaucer Road
Coleridge
Kingsley Road
Tennyson Road
Kipling Rd
Loxton Road
Hobart Road
Colombo Crs
Windwhistle Lane
Boundary Cl
Beaumont Close
Avon Cl
Wedmore Close
Exford Cl
Westbury Crescent
Dunster Crs
Brompton Road
Monkton Av
Oldmixon Crescent
Bridgwater Court
Winterstoke Road
Wessex Road
Lynx Crescent
Meadow Croft
Manor Farm Crescent
Walnut Close
Oldmixon Road
Beechmont Close
Beechmont Dr
Faversham Dr
Haywood Gdns
Copse Cl
Totterdown Lane
Brockley Crs
Burrington Avenue
Burnham Drive
Brecon Vw
Wentwood Drive
Highfield Road
Channel Heights
Brunel Cl
Purn Road
Purn La
Leighton Crs
Toll Rd
Grange Road
Uphill Road South
Folly Lane
Grange Close
Moseley Grove
Laurel Drive
Willow Close
Ash Gv
Southend Road
Nithsdale Road
Frenchay Road
Bedford Road
Southville Road
Selbourne Rd
Brownlow Rd
Addiscombe Road
Delapre Road
Dumfries Pl
Stradling Ave
Pembroke Rd
Clarence Rd E
Clarence Gv Rd
Malvern Road
St Paul's Rd
Derwent Rd
Stuart Road
Holms Rd
Yeo Cl
Kenn Cl
PO

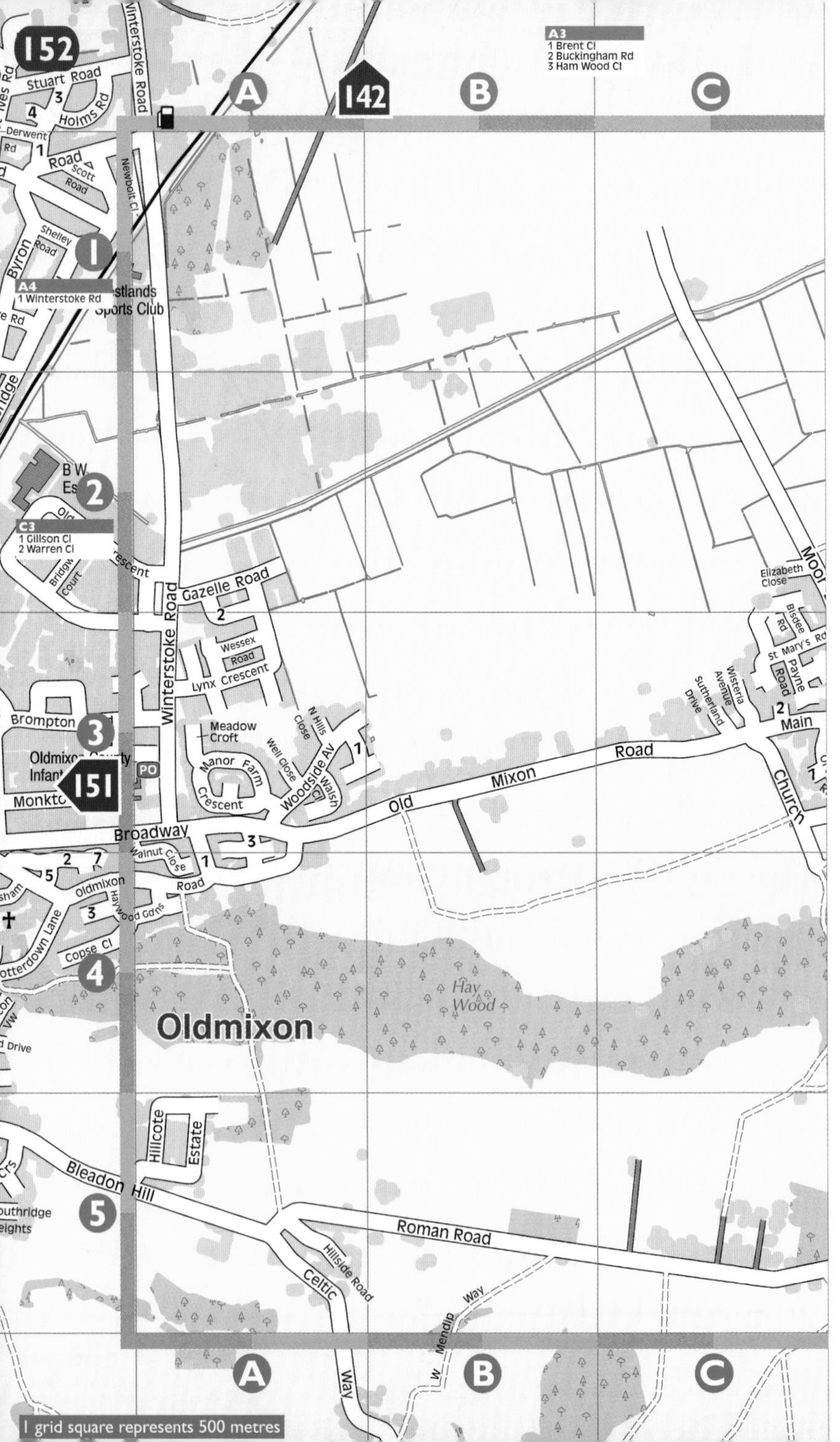

152
142
151
A3
1 Brent Cl
2 Buckingham Rd
3 Ham Wood Cl
A4
1 Winterstoke Rd
C3
1 Gillson Cl
2 Warren Cl
A
B
C
1
2
3
4
5
Stuart Road
Holms Rd
Derwent Rd
Scott Road
Shelley Road
Byron
Winterstoke Road
Newbolt Cl
Sports Club
Gazelle Road
Wessex Road
Lynx Crescent
Meadow Croft
Manor Farm Crescent
Well Close
N Hills Close
Woodside Av
Walsh Cl
Old Mixon Road
Broadway
Walnut Close
Oldmixon Road
Haywood Gdns
Brompton
Monkton
Copse Cl
Totterdown Lane
Elizabeth Close
Bisdee Rd
St Mary's Rd
Payne Road
Wisteria Avenue
Sutherland Drive
Main
Church
Moor
Hay Wood
Oldmixon
Hillcote Estate
Bleadon Hill
Roman Road
Hillside Road
Celtic Way
W Mendip Way
Southridge Heights
1 grid square represents 500 metres

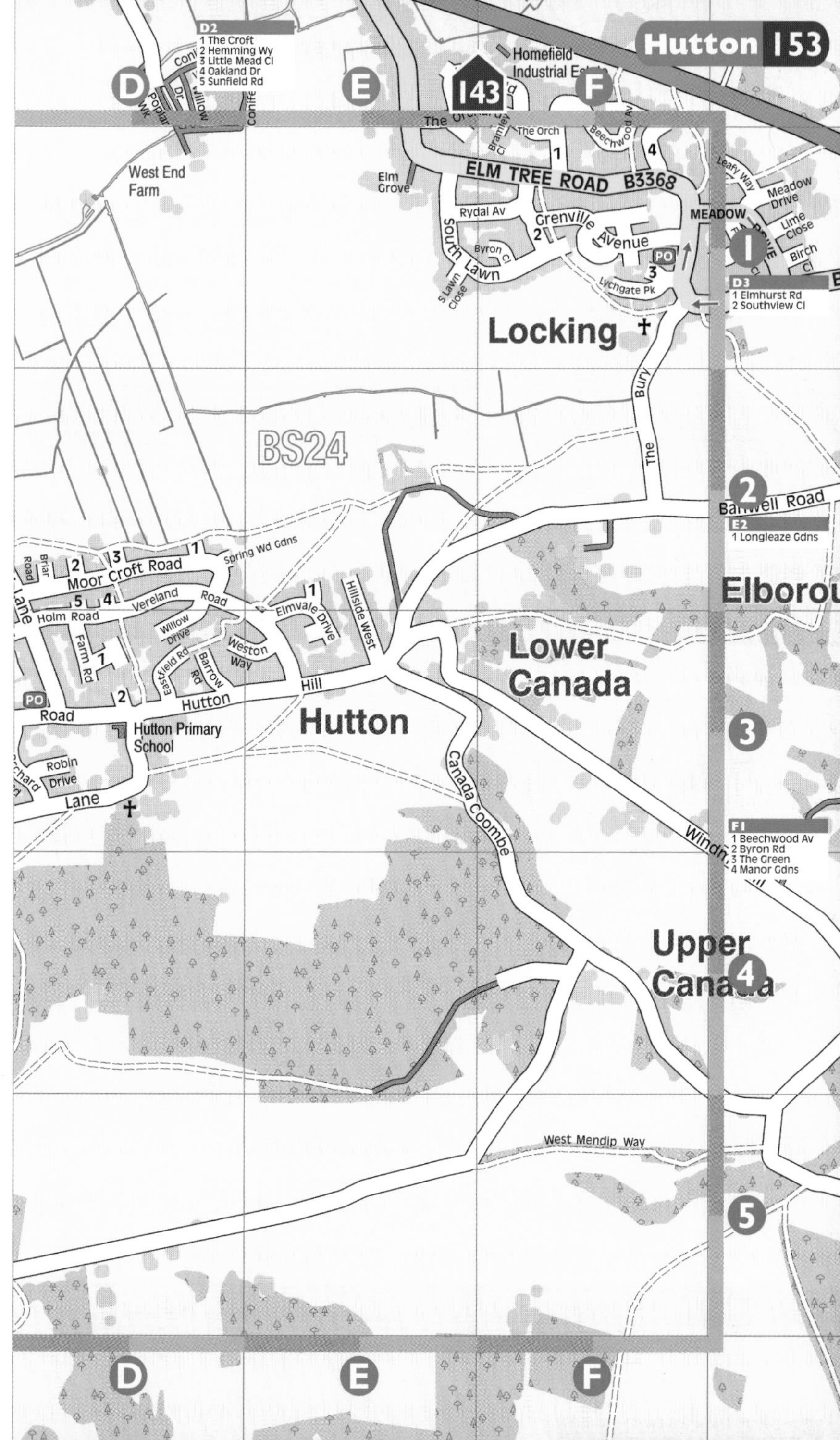
D2
1 The Croft
2 Hemming Wy
3 Little Mead Cl
4 Oakland Dr
5 Sunfield Rd
D
E
F
143
Homefield
Industrial Estate
West End
Farm
Elm
Grove
ELM TREE ROAD B3368
The Orch
Beechwood Av
Leafy Way
Meadow
Drive
Lime
Close
Birch
Cl
MEADOW
Rydal Av
Grenville Avenue
Byron Cl
South Lawn
S Lawn Close
Lychgate Pk
PO
1
D3
1 Elmhurst Rd
2 Southview Cl
Locking
The Bury
BS24
2
Banwell Road
E2
1 Longleaze Gdns
Elborou
Spring Wd Gdns
Moor Croft Road
Briar
Road
Vereland Road
Holm Road
Willow Drive
Elmvale Drive
Hillside West
Weston Way
Farm Rd
Eastfield Rd
Barrow Rd
Lower
Canada
Hill
Hutton
Road
PO
Hutton
Hutton Primary
School
Robin
Drive
Orchard
Lane
Canada Coombe
3
F1
1 Beechwood Av
2 Byron Rd
3 The Green
4 Manor Gdns
Upper
Canada
4
West Mendip Way
5
D
E
F

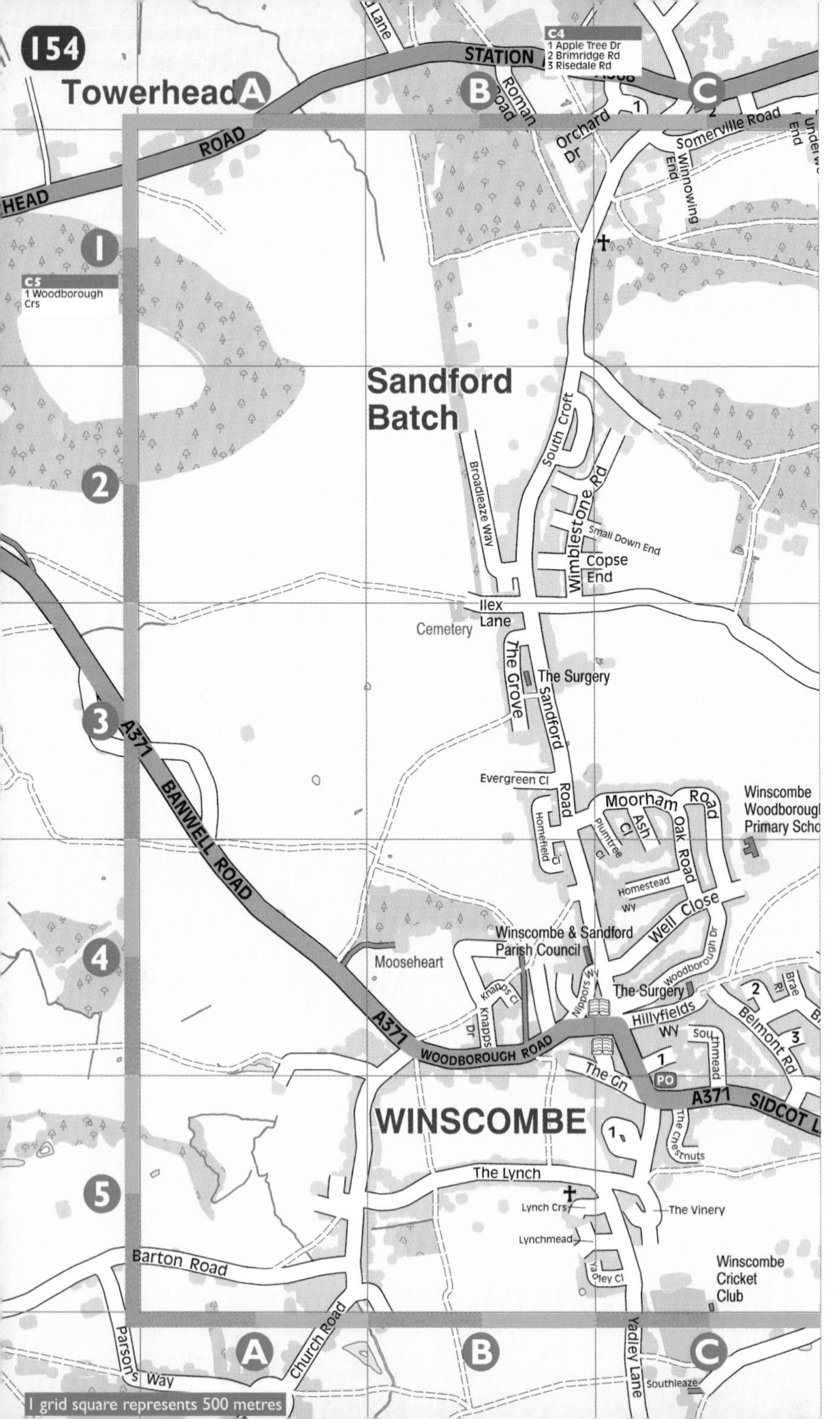
Towerhead
A
B
C
STATION
C4
1 Apple Tree Dr
2 Brimridge Rd
3 Risedale Rd
Roman Road
Orchard Dr
Somerville Road
Winnowing End
ROAD
HEAD
1
C5
1 Woodborough Crs
2
Sandford Batch
South Croft
Broadleaze Way
Wimblestone Rd
Small Down End
Copse End
Ilex Lane
Cemetery
The Grove
The Surgery
Sandford Road
3
A371
BANWELL ROAD
Evergreen Cl
Moorham Road
Ash Cl
Oak Road
Homefield Cl
Plumtree Cl
Homestead Wy
Well Close
Winscombe Woodborough Primary School
4
Winscombe & Sandford Parish Council
Mooseheart
Knapps Cl
Knapps Dr
Nippors Wy
Woodborough Dr
The Surgery
Hillyfields Wy
Belmont Rd
Brae Rd
Southmead
WOODBOROUGH ROAD
The Gn
PO
A371
SIDCOT L
WINSCOMBE
The Chestnuts
5
The Lynch
Lynch Crs
The Vinery
Lynchmead
Barton Road
Yadley Cl
Winscombe Cricket Club
Church Road
Parsons Way
Yadley Lane
Southleaze
1 grid square represents 500 metres

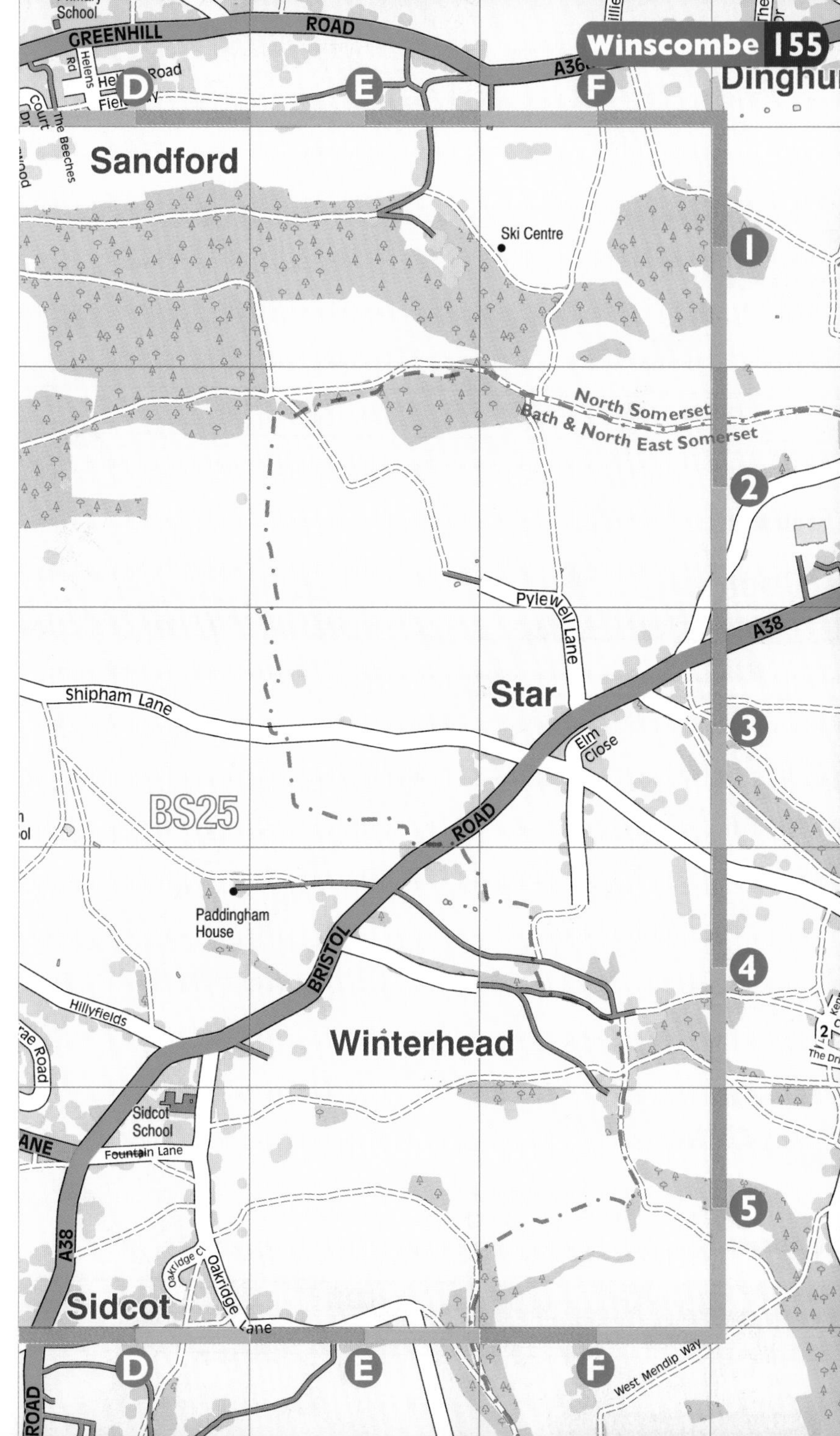
School
GREENHILL
ROAD
A368
Dinghurst
Helens Rd
Helens Road
Fieldway
Court Dr
The Beeches
D
E
F
Sandford
Ski Centre
1
2
3
4
5
North Somerset
Bath & North East Somerset
Pylewell Lane
A38
Star
Shipham Lane
Elm Close
BS25
BRISTOL ROAD
Paddingham House
Hillyfields
Winterhead
Sidcot School
Fountain Lane
LANE
A38
Oakridge Cl
Oakridge Lane
Sidcot
West Mendip Way
The Dri
ROAD

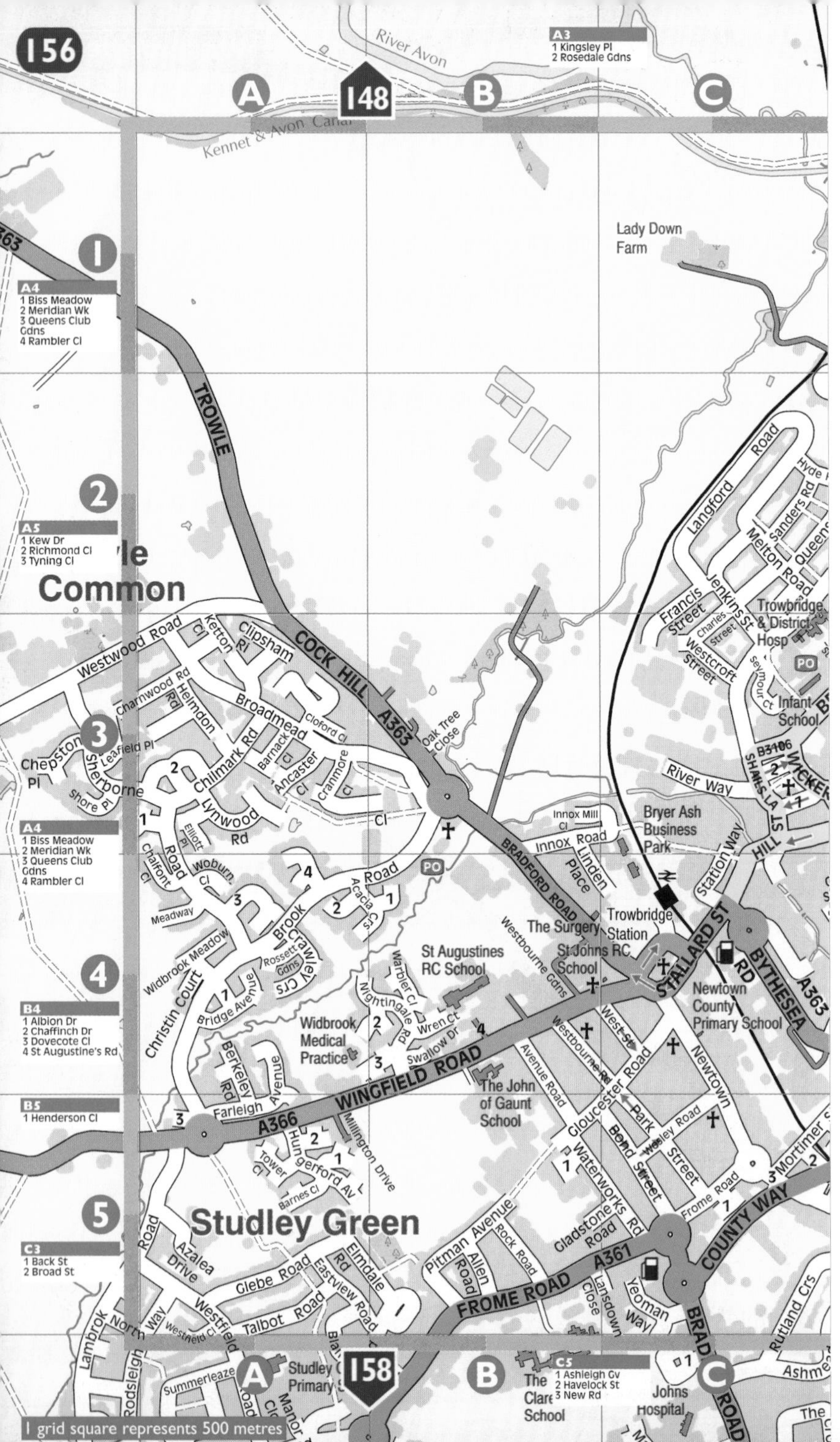

148
A
B
C
River Avon
A3
1 Kingsley Pl
2 Rosedale Gdns
Kennet & Avon Canal
Lady Down Farm
A363
A4
1 Biss Meadow
2 Meridian Wk
3 Queens Club Gdns
4 Rambler Cl
A5
1 Kew Dr
2 Richmond Cl
3 Tyning Cl
Common
TROWLE
COCK HILL
A363
Westwood Road
Ketton Cl
Clipsham Ri
Charnwood Rd
Helmdon Rd
Broadmead
Cloford Cl
Oak Tree Close
Chepstow Pl
Leafield Pl
Sherborne
Shore Pl
Chilmark Rd
Barnack Cl
Ancaster Cl
Cranmore Cl
Lynwood Rd
Elliott Pl
Chalfont Cl
Road
Woburn Cl
Meadway
Brook
Crawley Crs
Acacia Crs
Road
Widbrook Meadow
Rossett Gdns
Christin Court
Bridge Avenue
B4
1 Albion Dr
2 Chaffinch Dr
3 Dovecote Cl
4 St Augustine's Rd
B5
1 Henderson Cl
Berkeley Rd
Talbot Avenue
Farleigh
A366
WINGFIELD ROAD
Hungerford Av
Tower Cl
Barnes Cl
Millington Drive
Studley Green
C3
1 Back St
2 Broad St
Azalea Drive
Glebe Road
Eastview Road
Elmdale Rd
Westfield
Westfield Cl
Talbot Road
North Way
Lambrok
Rodsleigh
Summerleaze
Studley Primary
Manor
158
Warbler Cl
Nightingale Rd
Wren Ct
Swallow Dr
St Augustines RC School
Widbrook Medical Practice
The John of Gaunt School
Avenue Road
Westbourne Gdns
Westbourne Rd
West St
Gloucester Road
Park
Bond Street
Wesley Road
Street
Waterworks Rd
Gladstone Road
Pitman Avenue
Rock Road
Allen Road
FROME ROAD
A361
Lansdown Close
Yeoman Way
Frome Road
COUNTY WAY
Newtown
Mortimer St
Rutland Crs
Ashmead
BRADFORD ROAD
C5
1 Ashleigh Gv
2 Havelock St
3 New Rd
The Clarendon School
Johns Hospital
Innox Mill Cl
Innox Road
Linden Place
BRADFORD ROAD
The Surgery
St Johns RC School
Trowbridge Station
Bryer Ash Business Park
Station Way
STALLARD ST
BYTHESEA RD
A363
Newtown County Primary School
River Way
B3106
SHAILS LA
HILL ST
WICKER
Langford Road
Hyde
Sanders Rd
Melton Road
Queens
Francis Street
Jenkins St
Charles Street
Westcroft Street
Seymour Ct
Trowbridge & District Hosp
PO
Infant School
1 grid square represents 500 metres

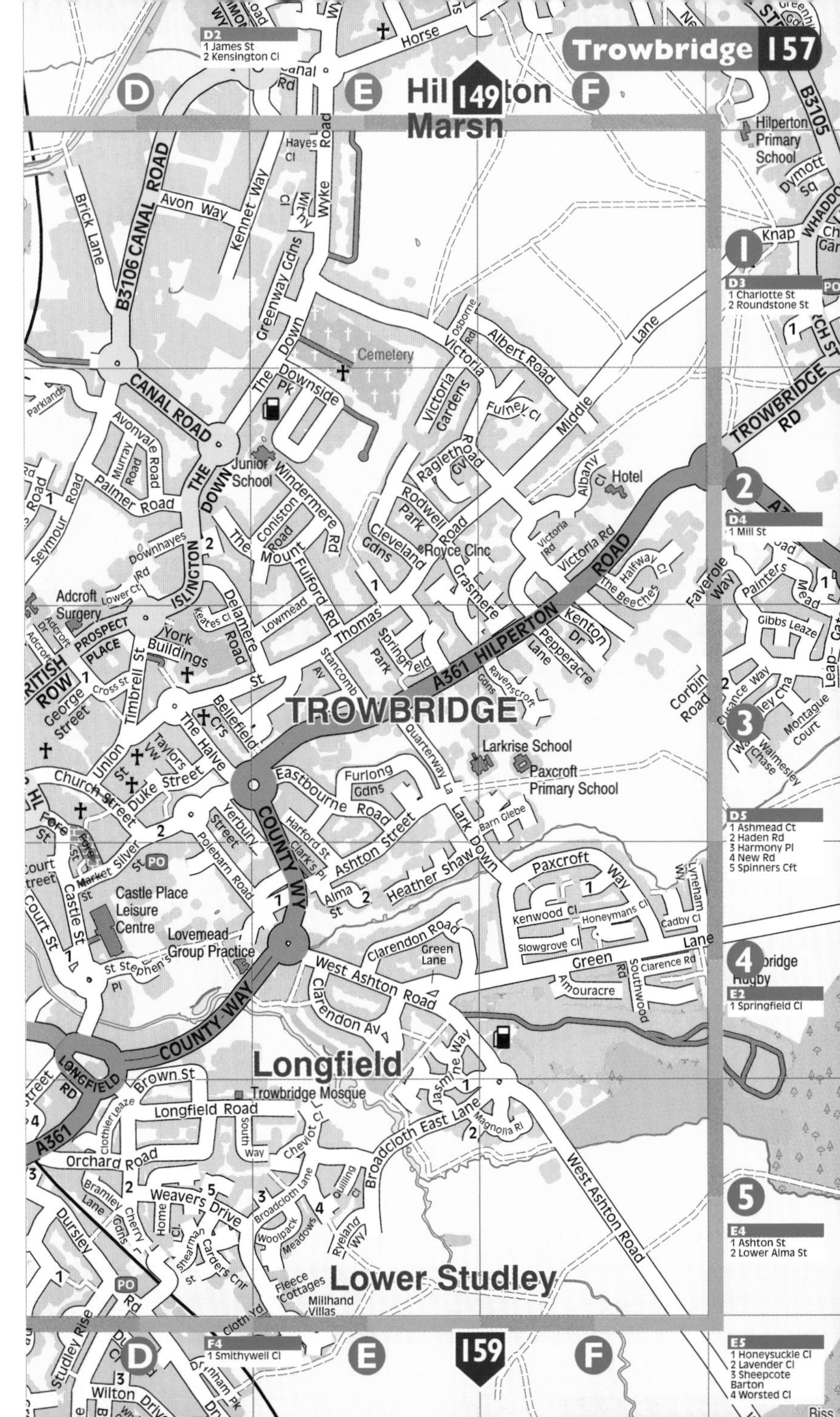
D2
1 James St
2 Kensington Cl
Hilperton Marsh
149
D
E
F
Hilperton Primary School
B3105
Dymott Sq
Knap
D3
1 Charlotte St
2 Roundstone St
TROWBRIDGE RD
D4
1 Mill St
D5
1 Ashmead Ct
2 Haden Rd
3 Harmony Pl
4 New Rd
5 Spinners Cft
E2
1 Springfield Cl
E4
1 Ashton St
2 Lower Alma St
E5
1 Honeysuckle Cl
2 Lavender Cl
3 Sheepcote Barton
4 Worsted Cl
F4
1 Smithywell Cl
159
Horse
Canal Rd
Hayes Cl
Wyke Road
Brick Lane
B3106 CANAL ROAD
Avon Way
Kennet Way
Greenway Gdns
The Down
Cemetery
Osborne Rd
Victoria
Albert Road
Lane
Middle
CANAL ROAD
Parklands
Avonvale Road
Murray Road
The Downside Pk
Victoria Gardens
Fulney Cl
Raglethorpe Road
Ragleth Gv
Albany Cl
Hotel
Junior School
Windermere Rd
Palmer Road
THE DOWN
Seymour Road
Coniston Road
The Mount
Fulford Rd
Cleveland Gdns
Rodwell Park Road
Royce Clnc
Victoria Rd
ROAD
Halfway Cl
The Beeches
Downhayes Rd
Lower Ct
ISLINGTON
Adcroft Surgery
Adcroft Dr
PROSPECT PLACE
Keates Cl
Delamere Road
Lowmead
Thomas St
Springfield Park
Grasmere
A361 HILPERTON
Kenton Dr
Pepperacre Lane
Faverole Way
Painters Mead
Gibbs Leaze
York Buildings
Timbrell St
Cross St
George Street
BRITISH ROW
Stancomb Av
Ravenscroft Gdns
TROWBRIDGE
Corbin Road
Walmesley Chase
Montague Court
Bellefield Crs
The Halve
Taylors Vw
Union St
Church Street
Duke Street
Quarterway La
Larkrise School
Paxcroft Primary School
Furlong Gdns
Eastbourne Road
COUNTY WAY
Lark Down
Barn Glebe
Fore St
Market St
Silver St
PO
Yerbury Street
Polebarn Road
Harford St
Clark's Pl
Ashton Street
Heather Shaw
Paxcroft Way
Lyneham Wy
Court Street
Castle St
Castle Place Leisure Centre
Lovemead Group Practice
Alma St
Kenwood Cl
Honeymans Cl
Cadby Cl
Clarendon Road
Green Lane
Slowgrove Cl
Green Lane
Clarence Rd
Southwood Rd
Amouracre
St Stephen's Pl
West Ashton Road
Clarendon Av
COUNTY WAY
LONGFIELD RD
A361
Longfield
Jasmine Way
Trowbridge Mosque
Brown St
Longfield Road
Clothier Leaze
South Way
Cheviot Cl
Broadcloth East Lane
Magnolia Ri
West Ashton Road
Orchard Road
Bramley Lane
Weavers Drive
Home Cl
Cherry Gdns
Broadcloth Lane
Quilling Cl
Woolpack Meadows
Ryeland Wy
Dursley Rd
Shearman St
Carders Cnr
Fleece Cottages
Lower Studley
Millhand Villas
Cloth Yd
Studley Rise
Wilton Drive
Drynham Pk
Biss

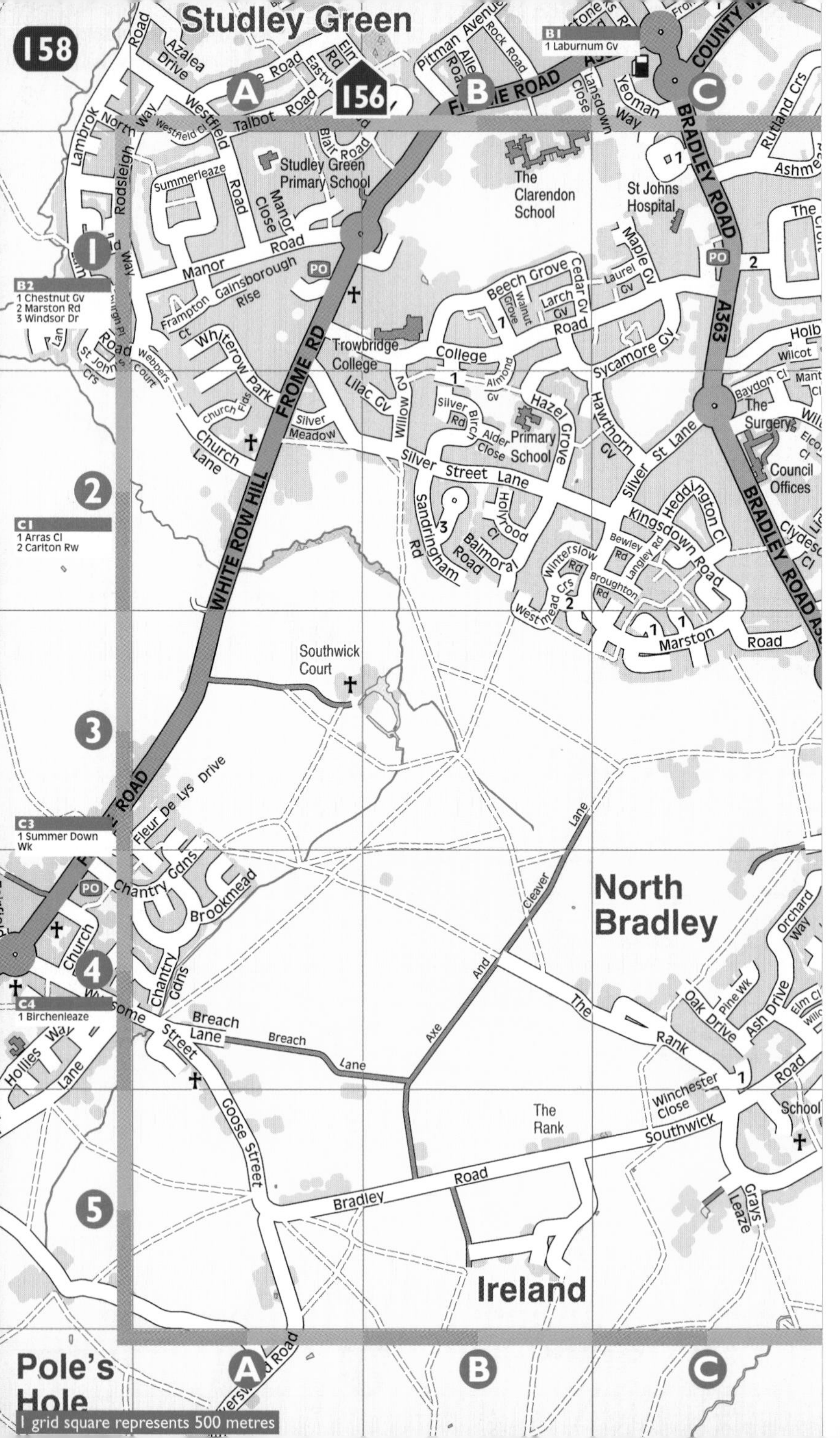
Studley Green
156
North Bradley
Ireland
Pole's Hole
B1
1 Laburnum Gv
B2
1 Chestnut Gv
2 Marston Rd
3 Windsor Dr
C1
1 Arras Cl
2 Carlton Rw
C3
1 Summer Down Wk
C4
1 Birchenleaze
FROME ROAD
BRADLEY ROAD
A363
COUNTY WAY
FROME RD
WHITE ROW HILL
Studley Green Primary School
The Clarendon School
St Johns Hospital
Trowbridge College
Primary School
The Surgery
Council Offices
Southwick Court
The Rank
Azalea Drive
Westfield Road
Talbot Road
Lambrok
North Way
Rodsleigh Way
Summerleaze
Manor Close
Manor Road
Gainsborough Rise
Frampton Ct
Whiterow Park
Webbers Court
Church Flds
Church Lane
Silver Meadow
Lilac Gv
Willow Gv
College Road
Beech Grove
Walnut Grove
Larch Gv
Cedar Gv
Laurel Gv
Maple Gv
Sycamore Gv
Almond Gv
Silver Birch Rd
Alder Close
Hazel Grove
Hawthorn Gv
Silver Street Lane
Silver St Lane
Sandringham Rd
Holyrood Cl
Balmoral Road
Kingsdown Road
Heddington Cl
Bewley Rd
Langley Rd
Wintersloe Rd
Westmead Crs
Broughton Rd
Marston Road
Yeoman Way
Lansdown Close
Pitman Avenue
Rock Road
Rutland Crs
Ashmead
Wilcot
Baydon Cl
Clydesdale Cl
Fleur De Lys Drive
Chantry Gdns
Brookmead
Church Lane
Breach Lane
Goose Street
Cleaver Lane
Axe And Cleaver Lane
The Rank
Winchester Close
Southwick Road
Bradley Road
Orchard Way
Oak Drive
Pine Wk
Ash Drive
Elm Cl
Grays Leaze
School
Hollies Way
PO
A
B
C
1
2
3
4
5
1 grid square represents 500 metres

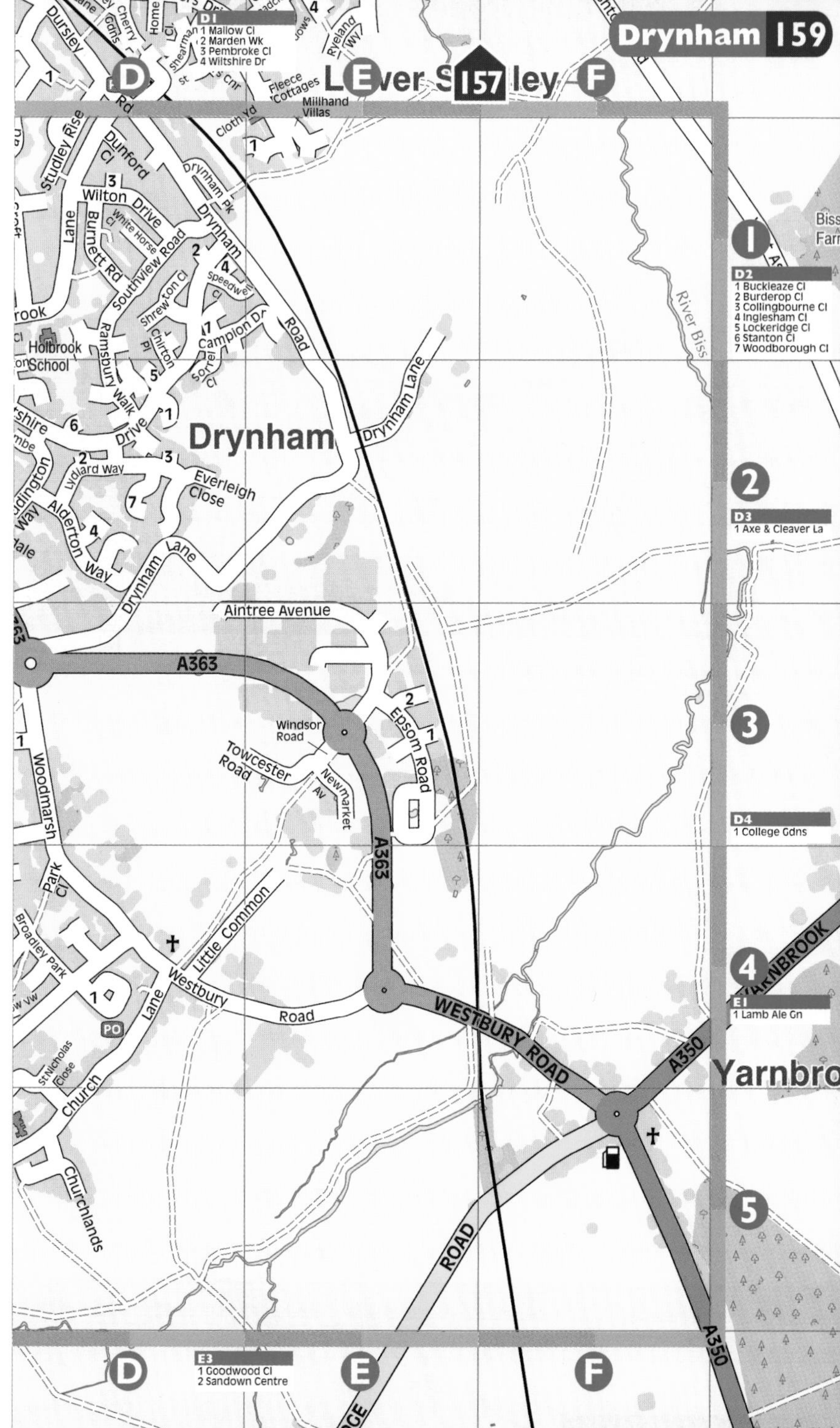
D1
1 Mallow Cl
2 Marden Wk
3 Pembroke Cl
4 Wiltshire Dr
D2
1 Buckleaze Cl
2 Burderop Cl
3 Collingbourne Cl
4 Inglesham Cl
5 Lockeridge Cl
6 Stanton Cl
7 Woodborough Cl
D3
1 Axe & Cleaver La
D4
1 College Gdns
E1
1 Lamb Ale Gn
E3
1 Goodwood Cl
2 Sandown Centre
Drynham
Yarnbro
Studley Rise
Dunford Cl
Wilton Drive
Burnett Rd
Southview Road
Drynham Road
Drynham Lane
Holbrook School
Ramsbury Walk
Campion Dr
Lydiard Way
Everleigh Close
Alderton Way
Aintree Avenue
A363
Windsor Road
Towcester Road
Epsom Road
Newmarket Av
Woodmarsh
Little Common
Westbury Road
WESTBURY ROAD
A350
River Biss
Biss Farm
Church Lane
Churchlands
Broadley Park
St Nicholas Close
Millhand Villas
Fleece Cottages
Cloth Yd
ROAD

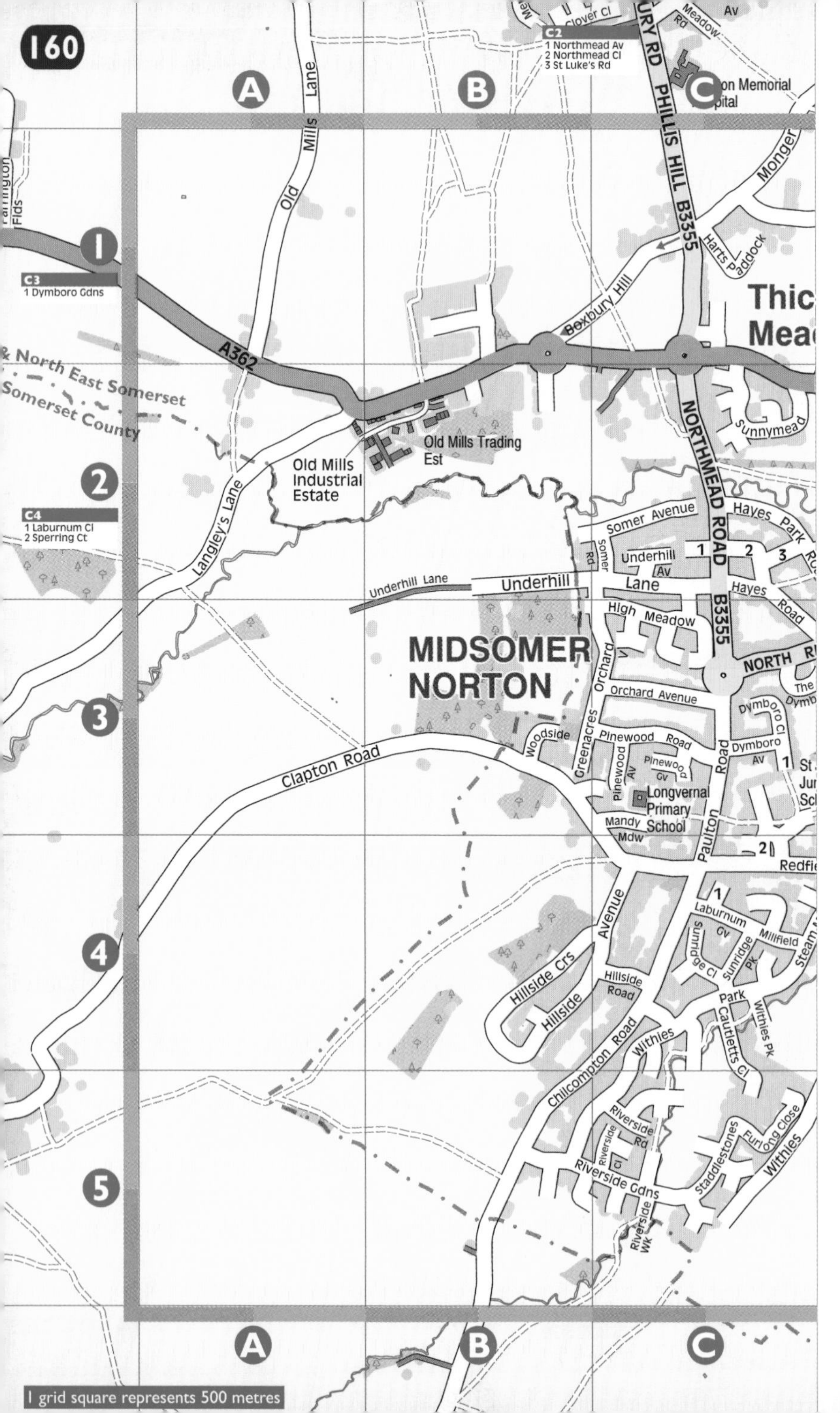
C2
1 Northmead Av
2 Northmead Cl
3 St Luke's Rd
C3
1 Dymboro Gdns
C4
1 Laburnum Cl
2 Sperring Ct
A
B
C
1
2
3
4
5
Old Mills Lane
A362
Boxbury Hill
PHILLIS HILL B3355
NORTHMEAD ROAD
Harts Paddock
Monger
Thic
Mea
Sunnymead
North East Somerset
Somerset County
Old Mills Trading Est
Old Mills Industrial Estate
Langley's Lane
Somer Avenue
Hayes Park
Underhill Lane
Underhill Av
Hayes Road
High Meadow
B3355
MIDSOMER NORTON
Orchard Avenue
NORTH
Greenacres
Pinewood Road
Woodside
Dymboro Cl
Dymboro Av
Clapton Road
Pinewood Av
Pinewood Gv
Longvernal Primary School
Mandy Mdw
Paulton Road
Laburnum Gv
Sunridge Cl
Sunridge Pk
Millfield
Avenue
Hillside Crs
Hillside Road
Hillside
Park
Withies Pk
Chilcompton Road
Withies
Cautletts Cl
Riverside Rd
Riverside Cl
Riverside Gdns
Staddlestones
Furlong Close
Withies
Riverside Wk
Redfie
1 grid square represents 500 metres

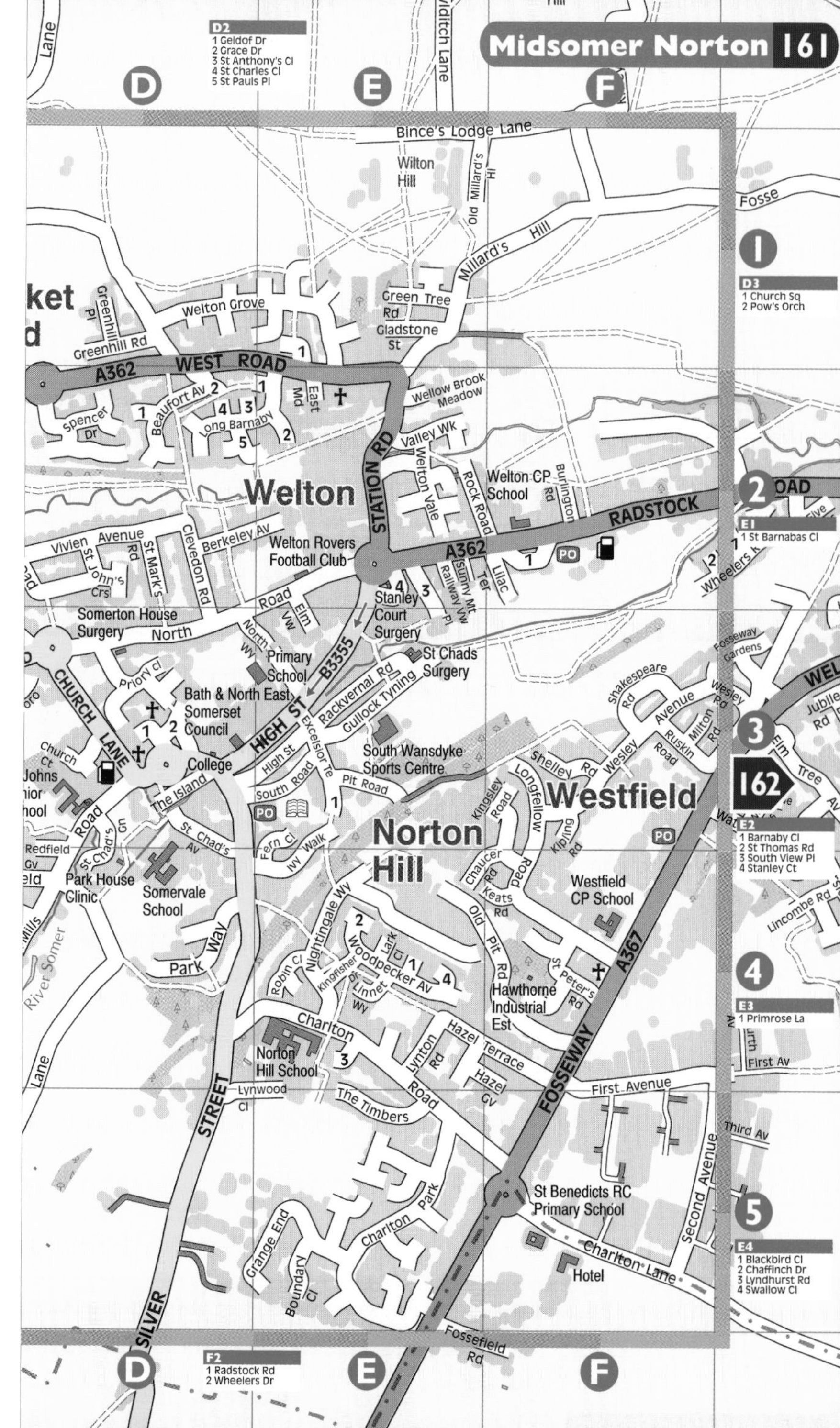
D2
1 Geldof Dr
2 Grace Dr
3 St Anthony's Cl
4 St Charles Cl
5 St Pauls Pl
D3
1 Church Sq
2 Pow's Orch
E1
1 St Barnabas Cl
E2
1 Barnaby Cl
2 St Thomas Rd
3 South View Pl
4 Stanley Ct
E3
1 Primrose La
E4
1 Blackbird Cl
2 Chaffinch Dr
3 Lyndhurst Rd
4 Swallow Cl
F2
1 Radstock Rd
2 Wheelers Dr
Welton
Norton Hill
Westfield
Bince's Lodge Lane
Wilton Hill
Old Millard's Hl
Millard's Hill
Fosse
Green Tree Rd
Gladstone St
Welton Grove
Greenhill Rd
Greenhill Pl
A362 WEST ROAD
Spencer Dr
Beaufort Av
Long Barnaby
East Md
Wellow Brook Meadow
Valley Wk
Welton Vale
Rock Road
Welton CP School
Burlington Rd
RADSTOCK ROAD
A362
STATION RD
Welton Rovers Football Club
Vivien Avenue
St John's Crs
St Mark's Rd
Clevedon Rd
Berkeley Av
North Road
Elm Vw
Stanley Court Surgery
Railway Vw
Sunny Mt Ter
Lilac Ter
Wheelers Rd
Somerton House Surgery
North Wy
Primary School
B3355
St Chads Surgery
Rackvernal Rd
Gullock Tyning
Fosseway Gardens
Shakespeare Rd
Wesley Avenue
Wesley Rd
Ruskin Road
Milton Rd
Jubilee Rd
Elm Tree Av
CHURCH LANE
Priory Cl
Bath & North East Somerset Council
HIGH ST
Excelsior Te
High St
College
Church Ct
St Johns Junior School
South Wansdyke Sports Centre
Pit Road
South Road
The Island
Shelley Rd
Wesley
Longfellow Road
Kingsley Road
Kipling Rd
St Chad's Av
St Chad's Gn
Fern Cl
Ivy Walk
Redfield Gv
Park House Clinic
Somervale School
Chaucer Rd
Keats Rd
Westfield CP School
Lincombe Rd
River Somer
Park Way
Nightingale Wy
Robin Cl
Kingfisher Dr
Lark Cl
Woodpecker Av
Linnet Wy
Old Pit Rd
Hawthorne Industrial Est
St Peter's Rd
A367
Charlton Road
Norton Hill School
Lynton Rd
Hazel Terrace
Hazel Gv
FOSSEWAY
First Av
Lynwood Cl
The Timbers
First Avenue
Third Av
STREET
SILVER
Lane
Grange End
Boundary Cl
Charlton Park
St Benedicts RC Primary School
Second Avenue
Charlton Lane
Hotel
Fossefield Rd
162

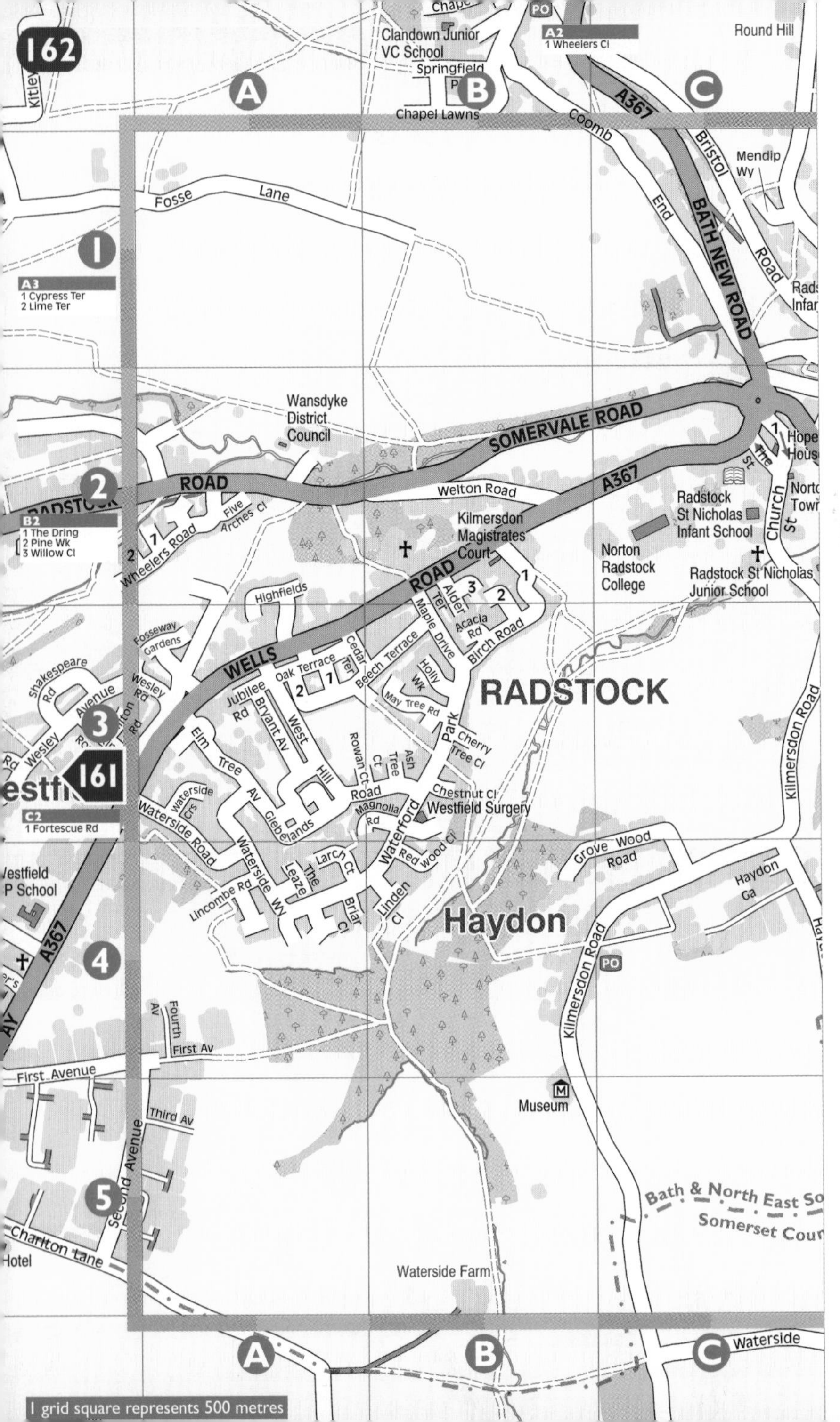
A
B
C
1
2
3
4
5
A2
1 Wheelers Cl
A3
1 Cypress Ter
2 Lime Ter
B2
1 The Dring
2 Pine Wk
3 Willow Cl
C2
1 Fortescue Rd
161
Clandown Junior VC School
Springfield
Chapel Lawns
Round Hill
Coomb End
A367
Bristol Road
BATH NEW ROAD
Mendip Wy
Fosse Lane
Wansdyke District Council
SOMERVALE ROAD
RADSTOCK ROAD
Welton Road
Wheelers Road
Five Arches Cl
Kilmersdon Magistrates Court
Radstock St Nicholas Infant School
Norton Radstock College
Radstock St Nicholas Junior School
Church St
The St
Hope House
Highfields
Fosseway Gardens
WELLS ROAD
Alder Ter
Acacia Rd
Birch Road
Maple Drive
Beech Terrace
Cedar Ter
Oak Terrace
Holly Wk
May Tree Rd
Park Road
Cherry Tree Cl
Chestnut Cl
Westfield Surgery
RADSTOCK
Shakespeare Rd
Wesley Avenue
Wesley Rd
Jubilee Rd
Bryant Av
West Hill Road
Rowan Ct
Ash Tree Ct
Elm Tree Av
Glebelands
Magnolia Rd
Waterford Park
Red Wood Cl
Waterside Crs
Waterside Road
Waterside Wy
The Leaze
Larch Ct
Lincombe Rd
Briar Cl
Linden Cl
Haydon
Grove Wood Road
Haydon Ga
Kilmersdon Road
Westfield P School
Fourth Av
First Av
First Avenue
Third Av
Second Avenue
Charlton Lane
Hotel
Museum
Waterside Farm
Bath & North East Somerset
Somerset County
Waterside

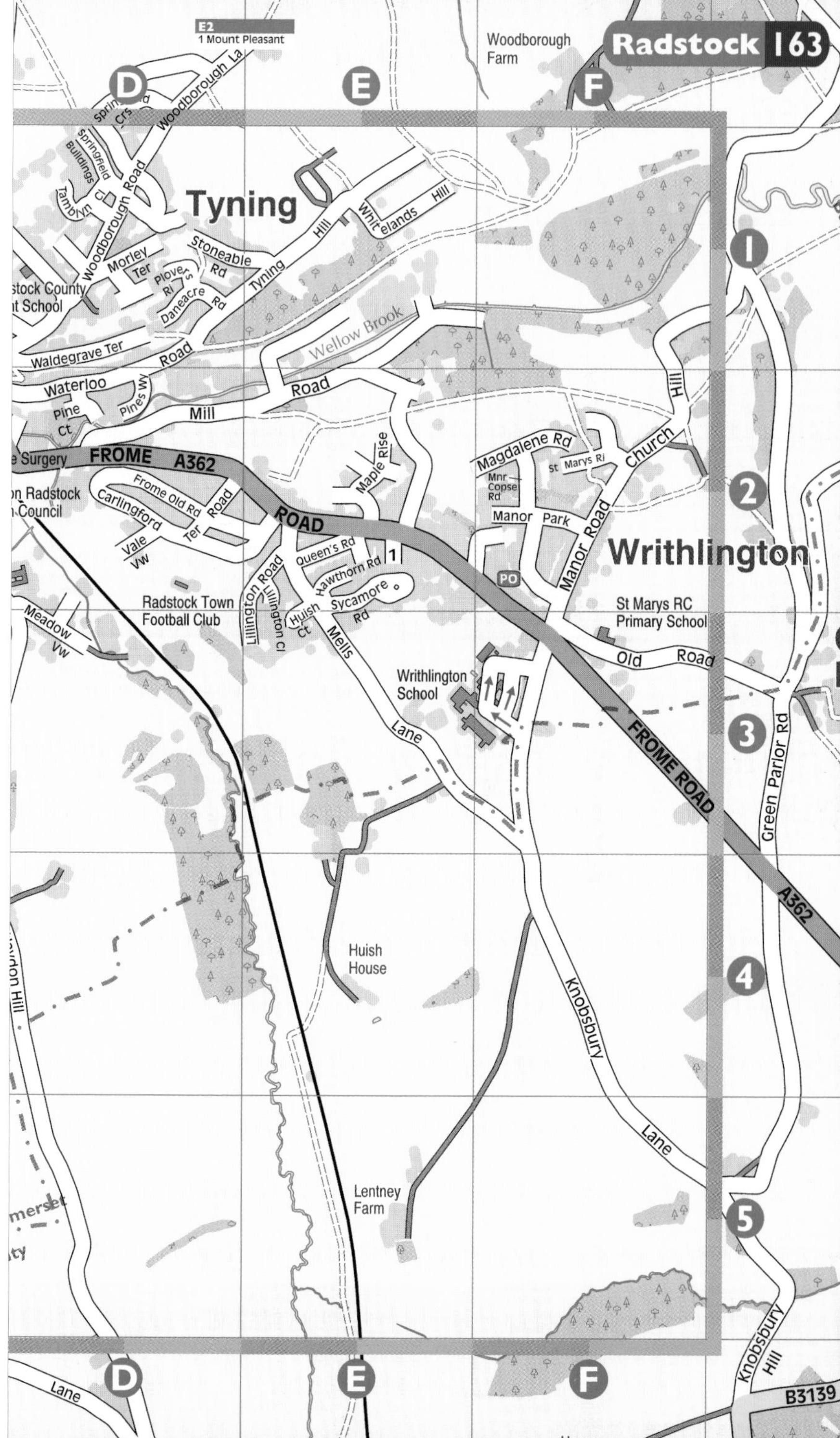
E2
1 Mount Pleasant
Woodborough Farm
Tyning
Woodborough La
Springfield Crs
Springfield Buildings
Tamblyn Cl
Woodborough Road
Morley Ter
Plovers Ri
Stoneable Rd
Daneacre Rd
Tyning Hill
Whitelands Hill
Waldegrave Ter
Road
Wellow Brook
Waterloo
Pine Ct
Pines Wy
Mill
Road
FROME A362
ROAD
Frome Old Rd
Carlingford Ter
Road
Vale Vw
Maple Rise
Queen's Rd
Hawthorn Rd
Sycamore Rd
Huish Ct
Lillington Road
Lillington Cl
Mells
Lane
Radstock Town Football Club
Meadow Vw
Magdalene Rd
St Marys Ri
Mnr Copse Rd
Manor Park
Manor Road
Church
Hill
Writhlington
PO
St Marys RC Primary School
Old Road
Writhlington School
FROME ROAD
A362
Green Parlor Rd
Huish House
Knobsbury Lane
Lentney Farm
Knobsbury Hill
B3139
Lane
Home

Abbots Leigh 73 E1
Almondsbury 13 D1
Arno's Vale 77 F5
Ashcombe Park 142 A1
Ashley Down 65 D2
Ashton Gate 75 D5
Ashton Vale 91 D2
Avonmouth 42 C1
Aztec West 12 B3
Backwell Common 87 F4
Bailbrook 114 B4
Barton Hill 78 A3
The Batch 81 F4
Bath 122 C3
Bathampton 124 C2
Batheaston 115 F3
Bathwick 5 F2
Beacon Hill 123 D1
Bedminster 91 F1
Bedminster Down 91 F4
Beechen Cliff 4 C6
Berwick 25 E2
Bishopston 64 B2
Bishopsworth 101 D2
Bitton 99 D4
Blackhorse 52 A4
Blaise Hamlet 45 E1
Bloomfield 136 C2
Bourton 131 D2
Bower Ashton 74 B5
Bradford-on-Avon 147 D3
Bradley Stoke 13 F5
Brentry 46 C1
Bridge Yate 82 C2
Brislington 94 C1
Bristol 3 G4
Bristol 77 E1
Bromley Heath 51 D1
Broomhill 49 F5
Broom Hill 79 E5
Cadbury Heath 81 E4
Cambridge Batch 88 A4
Catbrain 26 C2
Charlcombe 113 D4
Chewton Keynsham 107 D5
Chipping Sodbury 21 E4
Clapton in Gordano 56 B5
Clarence Park 6 B6
Claverham 117 E2
Claverton 139 F1
Claverton Down 138 C2
Clay Hill 67 D4
Clays End 120 B4
Clevedon 70 B5
Clifton 75 D1
Coalpit Heath 33 E2
Colt's Green 21 F5
Combe Down 137 E4
Congresbury 133 D2
Conham 79 E4
Coombe Dingle 45 D3
Corston 119 E2
Cotham 64 A5
Cowhorn Hill 82 A5
Crew's Hole 79 D2
Cribbs Causeway 26 A2
Crossways 9 F2
Dodington 37 F3
Dolemeads 4 D5
Downend 51 E4
Drynham 159 D2
Dundry 100 B5
East Clevedon 85 F1
Eastfield 46 C4
Easton 78 A1
Easton-in-Gordano 59 D2
East Rolstone 145 F1
Eastville 66 A3
Ebdon 129 F1
Emerson's Green 53 D5
Englishcombe 134 C3
Failand 72 A5
Fairfield Park 113 E5
Filton 28 C5
Filwood Park 93 D4
Fishponds 67 D1
Forewoods Common 148 B2
Fox Hill 137 E3
Frampton Cotterell 32 B1
Frampton End 17 D5
Frenchay 50 C3
Frogland Cross 15 D1
Frost Hill 116 C5
Golden Hill 47 E5
Goose Green 19 E2
Great Stoke 30 B3
Grovesend 9 F5
The Hacket 9 F4
Hallen 25 D3
Hambrook 51 D1
Ham Green 60 C2
Ham Green 148 C1
Hangstone Hill 84 C1
Hanham 80 A4
Hanham Green 96 A1
Harry Stoke 49 F1
Hartcliffe 102 B3
Haydon 162 B4
Headley Park 101 E1
Henbury 45 F1
Henfield 33 E5
Hengrove 103 E1
Hengrove Park 102 C1
Henleaze 47 D5
Hicks Gate 95 F4
Highridge 100 B3
Highridge 100 C1
Hillfields 67 F3
Hilperton Marsh 149 E5
Holbrook Common 83 E2
Holt 149 E1
Horfield 48 A4
Hotwells 75 E4
Hutton 153 E3
Ireland 158 B5
Iron Acton 17 E1
Kelston 110 A4
Kendleshire 32 B5
Kenn 85 F5
Kewstoke 127 F2
Keynsham 107 E2
Kingsway 136 B2
Kingswood 80 C1
The Knapp 9 F1
Knowle 93 E3
Lambridge 114 A5
Lansdown 111 F1
Lansdown 122 C1
Larkhall 113 F5
Lawrence Weston 44 B1
Leigh Woods 74 A3
Little Sodbury End 21 F1
Little Stoke 29 E1
Locking 153 F1
Lockleaze 49 D4
Locksbrook 122 A4
Lodway 59 F1
Long Ashton 89 E3
Longfield 157 D4
Longwell Green 96 C1
Lower Canada 153 F3
Lower Knowle 92 C3
Lower Studley 157 E5
Lower Swainswick 114 A4
Lower Weston 122 A3
Lyde Green 53 F3
Lye Green 146 A5
Mangotsfield 69 D1
Mayshill 17 F4
Mead Riding 21 D2
Middle Bridge 57 D3
Midsomer Norton 160 B3
Milton 142 C1
Monkton Combe 138 B4
Montpelier 64 C4
Moorend 51 F1
Morton 9 D2
Mount Hill 80 C3
Nailsea 87 D3
Netham 78 A3
Newbridge 121 E2
New Cheltenham 69 D5
New Passage 10 B1
Newton St Loe 120 B4
Nibley 18 B4
North Bradley 158 C4
North Common 82 B3
North Corner 16 A4
Northend 115 E2
North Weston 56 B3
Norton 128 C3
Norton Hill 161 E3
Novers Park 92 B4
Odd Down 136 B4
Oldfield Park 122 C5
Oldland 97 E1
Oldland Common 98 B1
Oldmixon 152 A4
The Oval 136 A1
Patchway 12 B4
Perrymead 137 F2
Pill 60 A2
Pilning 11 E3
Portbury 58 A3
Portishead 55 F2
Primrose Hill 112 B5
Pye Corner 31 E5
Queen Charlton 105 F5
Radstock 162 B3
Ram Hill 33 E4
Redcliff Bay 54 A3
Redland 64 A3
Redwick 10 C2
Ridgeway 67 D3
Rolstone 131 E5
Rush Hill 135 F3
St Anne's Park 78 C3
St George 79 E2
St Georges 130 A4
Saltford 108 B5
Sandford 155 D1
Sandford Batch 154 B2
Sea Mills 62 A1
Severn Beach 10 C4
Sheepway 58 A1
Shirehampton 43 F4
Sidcot 155 D5
Sion Hill 122 C2
Siston Common 69 E5
Sneyd Park 62 B2
Somerdale 96 C5
Soundwell 68 C3
Southdown 135 E2
Southmead 46 C2
South Twerton 122 A5
Speedwell 67 E4
Staple Hill 68 C2
Stapleton 66 A1
Star 155 F3
Staverton 148 C3
Stockwood 104 B1
Stockwood Vale 105 F1
Stoke Bishop 45 E5
Stoke Gifford 29 E3
Stone Hill 80 C5
Stub Riding 20 C2
Studley Green 156 A5
Swineford 99 E5
Thicket Mead 160 C1
Thornbury 8 B3
Trowbridge 157 E3
Tucking Mill 138 B5
Twerton 121 E5
Two Mile Hill 67 F5
Tyning 163 D1
Uphill 150 B3
Uphill Manor 151 D2
Upper Canada 153 F4
Upper Swainswick 113 E2
Upper Weston 111 F4
Upton Cheyney 99 F4
Vinney Green 52 B4
Walcot 123 E2
Walton St Mary 71 E3
Wapley 35 F4
Warmley 81 F2
Warmley Hill 81 D1
Warmley Tower 81 F3
Watley's End 32 B1
Way Wick 145 D1
Webb's Heath 82 C1
Welton 161 D2
Westbury on Trym 45 F5
Westbury Park 63 F2
West End 84 A2
Westerleigh 34 B4
Westerleigh Hill 35 E5
Westfield 161 F3
West Hewish 131 F2
West Hill 55 E1
Weston 121 E1
Weston-in-Gordano 55 E5
Weston Park 122 A1
Weston-Super-Mare 140 A2
West Wick 144 B1
Whitchurch 104 B3
Whitehall 66 A5
Whiteshill 31 D5
Whiteway 135 E1
Widcombe 138 A1
Willsbridge 97 F2
Windmill Hill 92 C1
Winscombe 154 B5
Winterbourne 31 E2
Winterbourne Down 32 A4
Winterhead 155 E4
Withywood 101 D3
Woodhill 39 D4
Woolley 113 D1
Woolley 147 E2
Woolley Green 147 F1
Woolvers Hill 145 D4
Worle 143 D1
Worlebury 127 E5
Writhlington 163 F2
Yanley 90 A4
Yate 19 E4
Yatton 116 C3

USING THE STREET INDEX

Street names are listed alphabetically. Each street name is followed by its postal town or area locality, the Postcode District, the page number, and the reference to the square in which the name is found.

Example: **Abbey Ct** *BRSG/KWL/STAPK* BS4 ....**79** D4

Some entries are followed by a number in a blue box. This number indicates the location of the street within the referenced grid square. The full street name is listed at the side of the map page.

GENERAL ABBREVIATIONS

ACC	ACCESS
ALY	ALLEY
AP	APPROACH
AR	ARCADE
ASS	ASSOCIATION
AV	AVENUE
BCH	BEACH
BLDS	BUILDINGS
BND	BEND
BNK	BANK
BR	BRIDGE
BRK	BROOK
BTM	BOTTOM
BUS	BUSINESS
BVD	BOULEVARD
BY	BYPASS
CATH	CATHEDRAL
CEM	CEMETERY
CEN	CENTRE
CFT	CROFT
CH	CHURCH
CHA	CHASE
CHYD	CHURCHYARD
CIR	CIRCLE
CIRC	CIRCUS
CL	CLOSE
CLFS	CLIFFS
CMP	CAMP
CNR	CORNER
CO	COUNTY
COLL	COLLEGE
COM	COMMON
COMM	COMMISSION
CON	CONVENT
COT	COTTAGE
COTS	COTTAGES
CP	CAPE
CPS	COPSE
CR	CREEK
CREM	CREMATORIUM
CRS	CRESCENT
CSWY	CAUSEWAY
CT	COURT
CTRL	CENTRAL
CTS	COURTS
CTYD	COURTYARD
CUTT	CUTTINGS
CV	COVE
CYN	CANYON
DEPT	DEPARTMENT
DL	DALE
DM	DAM
DR	DRIVE
DRO	DROVE
DRY	DRIVEWAY
DWGS	DWELLINGS
E	EAST
EMB	EMBANKMENT
EMBY	EMBASSY
ESP	ESPLANADE
EST	ESTATE
EX	EXCHANGE
EXPY	EXPRESSWAY
EXT	EXTENSION
F/O	FLYOVER
FC	FOOTBALL CLUB
FK	FORK
FLD	FIELD
FLDS	FIELDS
FLS	FALLS
FLS	FLATS
FM	FARM
FT	FORT
FWY	FREEWAY
FY	FERRY
GA	GATE
GAL	GALLERY
GDN	GARDEN
GDNS	GARDENS
GLD	GLADE
GLN	GLEN
GN	GREEN
GND	GROUND
GRA	GRANGE
GRG	GARAGE
GT	GREAT
GTWY	GATEWAY
GV	GROVE
HGR	HIGHER
HL	HILL
HLS	HILLS
HO	HOUSE
HOL	HOLLOW
HOSP	HOSPITAL
HRB	HARBOUR
HTH	HEATH
HTS	HEIGHTS
HVN	HAVEN
HWY	HIGHWAY
IMP	IMPERIAL
IN	INLET
IND EST	INDUSTRIAL ESTATE
INF	INFIRMARY
INFO	INFORMATION
INT	INTERCHANGE
IS	ISLAND
JCT	JUNCTION
JTY	JETTY
KG	KING
KNL	KNOLL
L	LAKE
LA	LANE
LDG	LODGE
LGT	LIGHT
LK	LOCK
LKS	LAKES
LNDG	LANDING
LTL	LITTLE
LWR	LOWER
MAG	MAGISTRATE
MAN	MANSIONS
MD	MEAD
MDW	MEADOWS
MEM	MEMORIAL
MKT	MARKET
MKTS	MARKETS
ML	MALL
ML	MILL
MNR	MANOR
MS	MEWS
MSN	MISSION
MT	MOUNT
MTN	MOUNTAIN
MTS	MOUNTAINS
MUS	MUSEUM
MWY	MOTORWAY
N	NORTH
NE	NORTH EAST
NW	NORTH WEST
O/P	OVERPASS
OFF	OFFICE
ORCH	ORCHARD
OV	OVAL
PAL	PALACE
PAS	PASSAGE
PAV	PAVILION
PDE	PARADE
PH	PUBLIC HOUSE
PK	PARK
PKWY	PARKWAY
PL	PLACE
PLN	PLAIN
PLNS	PLAINS
PLZ	PLAZA
POL	POLICE STATION
PR	PRINCE
PREC	PRECINCT
PREP	PREPARATORY
PRIM	PRIMARY
PROM	PROMENADE
PRS	PRINCESS
PRT	PORT
PT	POINT
PTH	PATH
PZ	PIAZZA
QD	QUADRANT
QU	QUEEN
QY	QUAY
R	RIVER
RBT	ROUNDABOUT
RD	ROAD
RDG	RIDGE
REP	REPUBLIC
RES	RESERVOIR
RFC	RUGBY FOOTBALL CLUB
RI	RISE
RP	RAMP
RW	ROW
S	SOUTH
SCH	SCHOOL
SE	SOUTH EAST
SER	SERVICE AREA
SH	SHORE
SHOP	SHOPPING
SKWY	SKYWAY
SMT	SUMMIT
SOC	SOCIETY
SP	SPUR
SPR	SPRING
SQ	SQUARE
ST	STREET
STN	STATION
STR	STREAM
STRD	STRAND
SW	SOUTH WEST
TDG	TRADING
TER	TERRACE
THWY	THROUGHWAY
TNL	TUNNEL
TOLL	TOLLWAY
TPK	TURNPIKE
TR	TRACK
TRL	TRAIL
TWR	TOWER
U/P	UNDERPASS
UNI	UNIVERSITY
UPR	UPPER
V	VALE
VA	VALLEY
VIAD	VIADUCT
VIL	VILLA
VIS	VISTA
VLG	VILLAGE
VLS	VILLAS
VW	VIEW
W	WEST
WD	WOOD
WHF	WHARF
WK	WALK
WKS	WALKS
WLS	WELLS
WY	WAY
YD	YARD
YHA	YOUTH HOSTEL

POSTCODE TOWNS AND AREA ABBREVIATIONS

ALMDB .... Almondsbury
AVONM .... Avonmouth
BATHSE .... Bath south & east
BMSTR .... Bedminster
BMSTRD/HC/WWD .... Bedminster Down/Hartcliffe/Withywood
BNWL .... Banwell
BOAV .... Bradford-on-Avon
BOS .... Burnham-on-Sea
BRSG/KWL/STAPK .... Brislington/Knowle/St Anne's Park
BRSTK/PCHW .... Bradley Stoke/Patchway
CBATH/BATHN .... Central Bath/Bath north
CBRIS/FH ... Central Bristol/Floating Harbour
CBRISNE .... Central Bristol north & east
CFTN/FAIL .... Clifton/Failand
CLVDN .... Clevedon
EVILLE/WHL .... Eastville/Whitehall
FRCTL/WBN .... Frampton Cotterell/Winterbourne
HGRV/WHIT .... Hengrove/Whitchurch
HNBRY/STHM .... Henbury/Southmead
HNLZ/SM/SNYPK/WT .... Henleaze/Sea Mills/Sneyd Park/Westbury-on-Trym
HORF/LLZ .... Horfield/Lockleaze
KEYN .... Keynsham
KGWD/HNM .... Kingswood/Hanham
LGASH .... Long Ashton
MANG/FISH .... Mangotsfield/Fishponds
MTN/WRL .... Milton/Worle
NAIL .... Nailsea
OLD/WMLY/WICK .... Oldland/Warmley/Wick
OMX/HUT/LCK ...... Oldmixon/Hutton/Locking
PLTN/PENS .... Paulton/Pensford
PTSHD/EG ..... Portishead/Easton-in-Gordano
RDLND/MONT .... Redland/Montpelier
RDSTK/MIDN ...... Radstock/Midsomer Norton
THNB/SVB .... Thornbury/Severn Beach
TRWBR .... Trowbridge

Abb - Aps

Index - streets

A

Abbey Ct *BRSG/KWL/STAPK* BS4 .... **79** D4 1
Abbeydale *FRCTL/WBN* BS36 .... **31** F2
Abbeygate St *CBATH/BATHN* BA1 .... **4** C4 1
Abbey Gn *CBATH/BATHN* BA1 .... **4** C4 2
Abbey Pk *KEYN* BS31 .... **107** D1
Abbey Rd *HNLZ/SM/SNYPK/WT* BS9 .. **46** A5
Abbey St *CBATH/BATHN* BA1 .... **4** C3 1
Abbey Vw *BATHSE* BA2 .... **5** F5
Abbey View Gdns *BATHSE* BA2 .... **5** E5
Abbeywood Dr
HNLZ/SM/SNYPK/WT BS9 .... **62** A1 1
Abbots Av *KGWD/HNM* BS15 .... **80** A5
Abbotsbury Rd *NAIL* BS48 .... **86** C3 1
Abbots Cl *HGRV/WHIT* BS14 .... **103** E4
MTN/WRL BS22 .... **129** F4
Abbotsford Rd *RDLND/MONT* BS6 .... **63** F5
Abbots Horn *NAIL* BS48 .... **86** C2 1
Abbots Leigh Rd *CFTN/FAIL* BS8 .... **73** F2
Abbots Rd *KGWD/HNM* BS15 .... **96** A2
Abbots Wy
HNLZ/SM/SNYPK/WT BS9 .... **47** E5
Abbotswood *KGWD/HNM* BS15 .... **80** B2 1
YATE/CS BS37 .... **35** E1 1
Abbott Rd *THNB/SVB* BS35 .... **10** B5
Aberdeen Rd *RDLND/MONT* BS6 .... **63** F5
Abingdon Gdns *BATHSE* BA2 .... **136** B5
Abingdon Rd *MANG/FISH* BS16 .... **67** E3
Ableton La *THNB/SVB* BS35 .... **10** B4
Ableton Wk
HNLZ/SM/SNYPK/WT BS9 .... **62** A1 2
Abraham Cl *EVILLE/WHL* BS5 .... **77** F1 1
Acacia Av *MANG/FISH* BS16 .... **68** A2
WSM BS23 .... **142** A2 1
Acacia Cl *MANG/FISH* BS16 .... **68** A3 1
Acacia Ct *KEYN* BS31 .... **106** A3 1
Acacia Crs *TRWBR* BA14 .... **156** A4
Acacia Gv *BATHSE* BA2 .... **136** A2
Acacia Rd *MANG/FISH* BS16 .... **68** B3
RDSTK/MIDN BA3 .... **162** B3
Aconite Cl *MTN/WRL* BS22 .... **129** F2
Acorn Gv *BMSTRD/HC/WWD* BS13 .. **100** C1
Acraman's Rd *BMSTR* BS3 .... **76** A5
Acresbush Cl
BMSTRD/HC/WWD BS13 .... **101** E2
Acton Rd *MANG/FISH* BS16 .... **67** E3 1
Adams Hay
BRSG/KWL/STAPK BS4 .... **94** B3 1
Adcroft Dr *TRWBR* BA14 .... **157** D3
Adcroft St *TRWBR* BA14 .... **157** D3
Adderly Ga *MANG/FISH* BS16 .... **52** C4
Addicott Rd *WSM* BS23 .... **6** D4
Addiscombe Rd *HGRV/WHIT* BS14 .. **103** F2
WSM BS23 .... **151** D1
Addison Rd *BMSTR* BS3 .... **92** C1
Adelaide Pl *EVILLE/WHL* BS5 .... **77** F1 2
MANG/FISH BS16 .... **67** D2 1
Agate St *BMSTR* BS3 .... **91** F1
Aiken St *EVILLE/WHL* BS5 .... **77** F3
Aintree Av *TRWBR* BA14 .... **159** D3
Aintree Dr *MANG/FISH* BS16 .... **52** A2
Air Balloon Rd *EVILLE/WHL* BS5 .... **79** E2
Airport Rd *HGRV/WHIT* BS14 .... **93** E4
Aisecome Wy *WSM* BS23 .... **142** B4
Akeman Wy *AVONM* BS11 .... **43** D3
Alard Rd *BRSG/KWL/STAPK* BS4 .... **93** D5
Albany Cl *TRWBR* BA14 .... **157** F2
Albany Ga *BRSTK/PCHW* BS34 .... **29** F3
Albany Rd *BATHSE* BA2 .... **121** F4
RDLND/MONT BS6 .... **65** D5 1
Albany St *KGWD/HNM* BS15 .... **80** A1
Albany Wy *OLD/WMLY/WICK* BS30 .... **82** A4
Albermarle Rw *CFTN/FAIL* BS8 ...... **75** D3 1
Albert Av *WSM* BS23 .... **6** C4
Albert Crs *CBRISNE* BS2 .... **77** E4
Albert Gv *EVILLE/WHL* BS5 .... **79** D1 1
Alberton Rd *MANG/FISH* BS16 .... **50** A5
Albert Pde *EVILLE/WHL* BS5 .... **78** A1
Albert Pk *RDLND/MONT* BS6 .... **65** D5 2
Albert Park Pl *RDLND/MONT* BS6 ...... **64** C5
Albert Pl *HNLZ/SM/SNYPK/WT* BS9 .. **46** B4
Albert Qd *WSM* BS23 .... **141** D2 1
Albert Rd *CBRISNE* BS2 .... **77** F5
CLVDN BS21 .... **84** C1 1
KEYN BS31 .... **106** C2
KGWD/HNM BS15 .... **80** B4
MANG/FISH BS16 .... **68** C2
PTSHD/EG BS20 .... **56** B1
THNB/SVB BS35 .... **10** B4
TRWBR BA14 .... **157** F1
WSM BS23 .... **6** C4
Albert Ter *MANG/FISH* BS16 .... **67** D2 2
Albion Cl *MANG/FISH* BS16 .... **69** D1
Albion Dr *TRWBR* BA14 .... **156** B4 1
Albion Rd *EVILLE/WHL* BS5 .... **65** F5
Albion St *EVILLE/WHL* BS5 .... **78** A1 1
Alcove Rd *MANG/FISH* BS16 .... **66** C3
Alder Cl *TRWBR* BA14 .... **158** B2
Aldercombe Rd
HNLZ/SM/SNYPK/WT BS9 .... **45** D3
Alderdown Cl *AVONM* BS11 .... **44** B3 1
Alder Dr *EVILLE/WHL* BS5 .... **66** C5
Alderley Rd *BATHSE* BA2 .... **135** E1
Aldermoor Wy
OLD/WMLY/WICK BS30 .... **80** C5
Alderney Av *BRSG/KWL/STAPK* BS4 .. **79** D5
Alder Ter *RDSTK/MIDN* BA3 .... **162** B2
Alderton Rd *HORF/LLZ* BS7 .... **47** F3
Alderton Wy *TRWBR* BA14 .... **159** D2
Alder Wy *BATHSE* BA2 .... **136** B5
Aldwick Av
BMSTRD/HC/WWD BS13 .... **102** A4
Alec Ricketts Cl *BATHSE* BA2 .... **121** D5 1
Alexander Wy *YTN/CONG* BS49 .... **116** B4 1
Alexandra Cl *MANG/FISH* BS16 .... **68** B2 1
Alexandra Gdns *MANG/FISH* BS16 .... **68** B2
Alexandra Pde *WSM* BS23 .... **6** C1 1
Alexandra Pk *MANG/FISH* BS16 .... **67** D2
RDLND/MONT BS6 .... **64** A4
Alexandra Pl *MANG/FISH* BS16 .... **68** B2
Alexandra Rd *BATHSE* BA2 .... **4** D6
BMSTRD/HC/WWD BS13 .... **91** D5
CFTN/FAIL BS8 .... **75** F1
CLVDN BS21 .... **70** C5
FRCTL/WBN BS36 .... **33** E1
HNBRY/STHM BS10 .... **47** D3 1
KGWD/HNM BS15 .... **80** B4 1
Alexandra Wy *THNB/SVB* BS35 .... **8** B1
Alford Rd *BRSG/KWL/STAPK* BS4 .... **94** A2
Alfred Ct *WSM* BS23 .... **6** C1 2
Alfred Hl *CBRISNE* BS2 .... **76** B1
Alfred Pde *CBRISNE* BS2 .... **76** B1
Alfred Pl *CBRISNE* BS2 .... **76** A1
Alfred Rd *BMSTR* BS3 .... **92** B1
RDLND/MONT BS6 .... **63** E2 1
Alfred St *CBATH/BATHN* BA1 .... **4** B1
CBRISNE BS2 .... **77** E3
EVILLE/WHL BS5 .... **78** A1 2
WSM BS23 .... **6** D1
Algiers St *BMSTR* BS3 .... **92** B1
Alison Gdns *NAIL* BS48 .... **87** F5
Allanmead Rd *HGRV/WHIT* BS14 .... **93** F4 1
Allen Rd *TRWBR* BA14 .... **156** B5
Allerton Crs *HGRV/WHIT* BS14 .... **103** F3
Allerton Gdns *HGRV/WHIT* BS14 .... **103** F2
Allerton Rd *HGRV/WHIT* BS14 .... **103** E3
Allfoxton Rd *HORF/LLZ* BS7 .... **65** E3
All Hallows Rd *EVILLE/WHL* BS5 .... **77** F1 3
Allington Dr *OLD/WMLY/WICK* BS30 .. **81** D5
Allington Gdns *NAIL* BS48 .... **86** B4
Allington Rd *BMSTR* BS3 .... **2** A6
Allison Av *BRSG/KWL/STAPK* BS4 ...... **78** C5
Allison Rd *BRSG/KWL/STAPK* BS4 ...... **94** C1
All Saints' La *CBRIS/FH* BS1 .... **2** D3 1
CLVDN BS21 .... **71** F5
All Saints Rd *CBATH/BATHN* BA1 .. **123** D2 1
CFTN/FAIL BS8 .... **75** E1
WSM BS23 .... **141** D1
All Saints' St *CBRIS/FH* BS1 .... **2** D2
Alma Cl *KGWD/HNM* BS15 .... **80** C1
Alma Rd *CFTN/FAIL* BS8 .... **75** E1
KGWD/HNM BS15 .... **68** C5
Alma Road Av *CFTN/FAIL* BS8 .... **75** F1 1
Alma St *TRWBR* BA14 .... **157** E4
WSM BS23 .... **6** C1 3
Alma Vale Rd *CFTN/FAIL* BS8 .... **75** E1
Almeda Rd *EVILLE/WHL* BS5 .... **79** E3
Almond Cl *MTN/WRL* BS22 .... **143** F1 1
Almond Gv *TRWBR* BA14 .... **158** B2
Almond Wy *MANG/FISH* BS16 .... **69** D1
Almorah Rd *BMSTR* BS3 .... **92** C1 1
Alpha Rd *BMSTR* BS3 .... **76** A5
Alpine Gdns *CBATH/BATHN* BA1 .. **123** E2 1
Alpine Rd *EVILLE/WHL* BS5 .... **66** A5
Alsop Rd *KGWD/HNM* BS15 .... **80** B1
Alton Rd *HORF/LLZ* BS7 .... **48** A5
Altringham Rd *EVILLE/WHL* BS5 .... **78** B1 1
Alverstoke *HGRV/WHIT* BS14 .... **93** D5
Alveston Wk
HNLZ/SM/SNYPK/WT BS9 .... **44** C4
Alwins Ct *OLD/WMLY/WICK* BS30 .. **81** D5 1
Amberey Rd *WSM* BS23 .... **7** E5 1
Amberlands Cl *NAIL* BS48 .... **87** F5
Amberley Cl *KEYN* BS31 .... **106** C3
MANG/FISH BS16 .... **51** F4
Amberley Rd *BRSTK/PCHW* BS34 ...... **12** C5
MANG/FISH BS16 .... **51** E4
Amble Cl *KGWD/HNM* BS15 .... **81** D2
Ambleside Av *HNBRY/STHM* BS10 .... **46** C2
Ambleside Rd *BATHSE* BA2 .... **135** F3
Ambra V *CFTN/FAIL* BS8 .... **75** E3 1
Ambra V East *CFTN/FAIL* BS8 .... **75** E3
Ambra V South *CFTN/FAIL* BS8 ...... **75** E3 2
Ambra V West *CFTN/FAIL* BS8 .... **75** E3 3
Ambrose Rd *CFTN/FAIL* BS8 .... **75** E3
Ambury *BATHSE* BA2 .... **4** B5
Amercombe Wk *HGRV/WHIT* BS14 .... **94** B5
Amery La *CBATH/BATHN* BA1 .... **4** C4 3
Amouracre *TRWBR* BA14 .... **157** F4
Ancaster Cl *TRWBR* BA14 .... **156** A3
Anchor Rd *CBATH/BATHN* BA1 .... **121** F1
CBRIS/FH BS1 .... **2** A4
KGWD/HNM BS15 .... **69** E5
Anchor Wy *PTSHD/EG* BS20 .... **60** B2
Andereach Cl *HGRV/WHIT* BS14 .... **93** F4
Andover Rd *BRSG/KWL/STAPK* BS4 .. **93** D2
Andruss Dr *LGASH* BS41 .... **100** B5
Angels Gnd
BRSG/KWL/STAPK BS4 .... **79** D3 1
Angers Rd *BRSG/KWL/STAPK* BS4 .. **77** E5 1
Anglesea Pl *CFTN/FAIL* BS8 .... **63** E4 1
Annandale Av *MTN/WRL* BS22 .... **143** D1
Anson Cl *KEYN* BS31 .... **108** B5
Anson Rd *MTN/WRL* BS22 .... **128** C3
OMX/HUT/LCK BS24 .... **144** A4
Anstey's Rd *KGWD/HNM* BS15 .... **79** F4
Anstey St *EVILLE/WHL* BS5 .... **65** F5
Anthea Rd *EVILLE/WHL* BS5 .... **66** C4
Antona Ct *AVONM* BS11 .... **43** E4 1
Antona Dr *AVONM* BS11 .... **43** E4 2
Antrim Rd
HNLZ/SM/SNYPK/WT BS9 .... **46** C5
Anvil Rd *YTN/CONG* BS49 .... **117** F2 1
Anvil St *CBRISNE* BS2 .... **3** H3
Apperley Cl *YATE/CS* BS37 .... **19** E5
Appleby Wk
BRSG/KWL/STAPK BS4 .... **92** B5 1
Appledore Cl *HGRV/WHIT* BS14 .... **93** F4
Applegate *HNBRY/STHM* BS10 .... **26** C5
Appletree Ct *MTN/WRL* BS22 .... **130** A5
Apple Tree Dr *WNSC* BS25 .... **154** C4 1
Appsley Cl *MTN/WRL* BS22 .... **142** B1 1
Apseleys Md *ALMDB* BS32 .... **13** D3
Apsley Rd *CBATH/BATHN* BA1 .... **121** E3
CFTN/FAIL BS8 .... **63** E5
Apsley St *EVILLE/WHL* BS5 .... **66** A4 1

Arbutus Dr
HNLZ/SM/SNYPK/WT BS9 45 D4
Archer Ct *OLD/WMLY/WICK* BS30 97 D1
Archer Wk *HGRV/WHIT* BS14 104 C1
Archfield Rd *RDLND/MONT* BS6 64 A5
Archway St *BATHSE* BA2 5 E5
Arden Cl *ALMDB* BS32 29 F2
MTN/WRL BS22 129 E4
Ardenton Wk
HNBRY/STHM BS10 26 B5 1
Ardern Cl *HNLZ/SM/SNYPK/WT* BS9 44 C3
Argus Rd *BMSTR* BS3 92 A1
Argyle Av *WSM* BS23 151 E1
Argyle Dr *YATE/CS* BS37 19 F1
Argyle Pl *CFTN/FAIL* BS8 75 E3
Argyle Rd *CBRISNE* BS2 76 C1
CLVDN BS21 71 D4
MANG/FISH BS16 67 F4
Argyle St *BATHSE* BA2 4 D3 1
BMSTR BS3 76 A5 1
EVILLE/WHL BS5 66 A4 2
Arley Cottages
RDLND/MONT BS6 64 B5 1
Arley Hl *RDLND/MONT* BS6 64 B5
Arley Pk *RDLND/MONT* BS6 64 B5 2
Arley Ter *EVILLE/WHL* BS5 66 C5 1
Arlington Rd *BATHSE* BA2 122 B5
BRSG/KWL/STAPK BS4 78 B3
Arlington Vls *CFTN/FAIL* BS8 75 E2
Armada Pl *CBRIS/FH* BS1 76 C1
Armidale Av *RDLND/MONT* BS6 64 C5 1
Armoury Sq *EVILLE/WHL* BS5 77 E1 1
Armstrong Cl *THNB/SVB* BS35 9 D5 1
Armstrong Dr
OLD/WMLY/WICK BS30 81 F4 1
Armstrong Wy *YATE/CS* BS37 19 D2
Arnall Dr *HNBRY/STHM* BS10 46 A2
Arneside Rd *HNBRY/STHM* BS10 47 D2
Arnor Cl *MTN/WRL* BS22 129 F3
Arno's St *BRSG/KWL/STAPK* BS4 77 E5
Arras Cl *TRWBR* BA14 158 C1 1
Arrowfield Cl *HGRV/WHIT* BS14 103 E5
Artemesia Av *MTN/WRL* BS22 143 D2 1
Arthur Skemp Cl
EVILLE/WHL BS5 77 F2 1
Arthur St *CBRISNE* BS2 77 E4
EVILLE/WHL BS5 78 A1 3
Arthurswood Rd
BMSTRD/HC/WWD BS13 101 E3
Arundel Cl
BMSTRD/HC/WWD BS13 101 F3
Arundell Rd *WSM* BS23 141 D2
Arundel Rd *CBATH/BATHN* BA1 123 E1
HORF/LLZ BS7 64 B3
Ascot Cl *MANG/FISH* BS16 52 A2
Ascot Rd *HNBRY/STHM* BS10 47 E1
Ashbourne Cl
OLD/WMLY/WICK BS30 82 A3 1
Ashburton Rd *HNBRY/STHM* BS10 47 D2
Ashbury Dr *MTN/WRL* BS22 142 A1 1
Ash Cl *BRSTK/PCHW* BS34 29 E1
WNSC BS25 154 C3
YATE/CS BS37 19 E2
Ashcombe Cl
OLD/WMLY/WICK BS30 82 A3 2
Ashcombe Crs
OLD/WMLY/WICK BS30 82 B3 1
Ashcombe Gdns *WSM* BS23 141 F2
Ashcombe Park Rd *WSM* BS23 141 F1
Ashcombe Rd *WSM* BS23 7 F1
Ashcott *HGRV/WHIT* BS14 103 D1
Ashcroft Av *KEYN* BS31 106 B2
Ashcroft Rd
HNLZ/SM/SNYPK/WT BS9 45 D4
Ashdene Av *EVILLE/WHL* BS5 66 B3
Ashdene Rd *WSM* BS23 141 F1
Ashdown Rd *PTSHD/EG* BS20 38 B5
Ash Dr *TRWBR* BA14 158 C4
Asher La *CBRISNE* BS2 3 G1
Ashfield Pl *RDLND/MONT* BS6 65 D5 3
Ashfield Rd *BMSTR* BS3 91 F1
Ashford Dr *OMX/HUT/LCK* BS24 151 F4 1
Ashford Rd *BATHSE* BA2 136 B1
BRSTK/PCHW BS34 28 B1
Ashgrove *THNB/SVB* BS35 8 C3
Ash Gv *BATHSE* BA2 136 A1
CLVDN BS21 71 E5
MANG/FISH BS16 68 A3
WSM BS23 151 D3
Ashgrove Av *CFTN/FAIL* BS8 73 F2
HORF/LLZ BS7 65 D2
Ashgrove Rd *BMSTR* BS3 91 F1
HORF/LLZ BS7 65 D2
Ash Hayes Dr *NAIL* BS48 87 D3
Ash Hayes Rd *NAIL* BS48 87 D3
Ashland Rd
BMSTRD/HC/WWD BS13 101 E3
Ashleigh Crs *YTN/CONG* BS49 116 B3
Ashleigh Gv *TRWBR* BA14 156 C5 1
Ashleigh Rd *WSM* BS23 141 F2
YTN/CONG BS49 116 B3
Ashley *KGWD/HNM* BS15 81 D1
Ashley Av *CBATH/BATHN* BA1 122 A3
Ashley Cl *BOAV* BA15 146 B1
HORF/LLZ BS7 65 D2
Ashley Court Rd
RDLND/MONT BS6 65 D4 1
Ashley Down Rd *HORF/LLZ* BS7 64 C1
Ashley Grove Rd *CBRISNE* BS2 65 D4 2
CBRISNE BS2 65 E5 1
Ashley Hl *RDLND/MONT* BS6 65 D3
Ashley Pde *CBRISNE* BS2 65 D4 3
Ashley Pk *RDLND/MONT* BS6 65 D3
Ashley Rd *CLVDN* BS21 84 B3
RDLND/MONT BS6 64 C5
Ashley St *CBRISNE* BS2 65 E5
Ashman Cl *EVILLE/WHL* BS5 77 E1 2
Ashmans Yd *CBATH/BATHN* BA1 121 F4
Ashmead *TRWBR* BA14 158 C1
Ashmead Ct *TRWBR* BA14 157 D5 1
Ashmead Rd *KEYN* BS31 107 F2
Ashmead Wy *CBRIS/FH* BS1 75 D4 1
Ash Ridge Rd *ALMDB* BS32 12 C2
Ash Rd *HORF/LLZ* BS7 64 C1
Ashton Av *CBRIS/FH* BS1 75 E4 1
Ashton Cl *CLVDN* BS21 84 B3
Ashton Crs *NAIL* BS48 86 C3
Ashton Dr *BMSTR* BS3 90 C3
Ashton Gate Rd *BMSTR* BS3 75 E5
Ashton Gate Ter *BMSTR* BS3 75 E5 1
Ashton Hl *BATHSE* BA2 119 E3
Ashton Rd *BMSTR* BS3 91 D1
LGASH BS41 90 A1
Ashton St *TRWBR* BA14 157 E4 1
Ashton Vale Rd *BMSTR* BS3 90 C1
Ashton Wy *KEYN* BS31 106 C1
Ash Tree Ct *RDSTK/MIDN* BA3 162 B3
Ashvale Cl *NAIL* BS48 87 F2
Ashville Rd *BMSTR* BS3 75 E5
Ash Wk *HNBRY/STHM* BS10 26 C5
Ashwell Cl *HGRV/WHIT* BS14 104 C1
Ashwicke *HGRV/WHIT* BS14 103 D1
Aspen Park Rd *MTN/WRL* BS22 143 D2
Aspley Cl *CBATH/BATHN* BA1 121 F3 1
Assembly Rooms La
CBRIS/FH BS1 2 C4 1
Astry Cl *AVONM* BS11 44 B2
Atchley St *EVILLE/WHL* BS5 77 F2 2
Atherston *OLD/WMLY/WICK* BS30 82 A4
Athlone Wk *BRSG/KWL/STAPK* BS4 92 C3
Atholl Cl *MTN/WRL* BS22 129 E4 1
Atkins Cl *HGRV/WHIT* BS14 104 C1
Atlantic Rd *AVONM* BS11 43 D3
WSM BS23 140 B1
Atlantic Rd South *WSM* BS23 140 B1
Atlas Cl *EVILLE/WHL* BS5 67 E4
Atlas Rd *BMSTR* BS3 92 C1
Atlas St *CBRISNE* BS2 77 F4
Atwell Dr *ALMDB* BS32 12 C4
Atwood Dr *AVONM* BS11 44 C1
Aubrey Meads
OLD/WMLY/WICK BS30 98 C4
Aubrey Rd *BMSTR* BS3 91 F1
Auburn Av *OLD/WMLY/WICK* BS30 97 F1
Auburn Rd *RDLND/MONT* BS6 63 F4
Auckland Cl *WSM* BS23 151 E2 1
Audley Av *CBATH/BATHN* BA1 122 A3
Audley Cl *CBATH/BATHN* BA1 122 B3
Audley Gv *CBATH/BATHN* BA1 122 A3
Audley Park Rd
CBATH/BATHN BA1 122 B3 1
Audrey Wk
HNLZ/SM/SNYPK/WT BS9 47 E5
Augustine's Cl *PTSHD/EG* BS20 54 C2
Austen Dr *MTN/WRL* BS22 130 A3 1
Austen Gv *HORF/LLZ* BS7 48 B3 1
Autumn Ms *OMX/HUT/LCK* BS24 143 F2 1
Avalon Cl *YTN/CONG* BS49 116 A2 1
Avalon Rd *EVILLE/WHL* BS5 79 F3
Avebury Rd *BMSTR* BS3 90 C2
Avening Cl *NAIL* BS48 87 E4
Avening Rd *KGWD/HNM* BS15 79 E1
Avenue Rd *TRWBR* BA14 156 B4
The Avenue *BATHSE* BA2 124 C5
BATHSE BA2 137 F4
BRSTK/PCHW BS34 12 C3
BRSTK/PCHW BS34 29 D2
CFTN/FAIL BS8 63 E5
CLVDN BS21 71 D4
EVILLE/WHL BS5 79 D2
HNLZ/SM/SNYPK/WT BS9 62 B4
KEYN BS31 96 C5
MANG/FISH BS16 49 F2
NAIL BS48 87 F5
RDLND/MONT BS6 64 C3
YATE/CS BS37 19 E4
YTN/CONG BS49 116 B3
Averay Rd *MANG/FISH* BS16 66 A2
Avon Cl *BOAV* BA15 147 E4
BRSG/KWL/STAPK BS4 79 D3
KEYN BS31 107 D1
WSM BS23 151 E3
Avon Ct *CBATH/BATHN* BA1 115 E3
Avon Crs *CBRIS/FH* BS1 75 E4
Avondale Buildings
CBATH/BATHN BA1 113 F5 1
Avondale Pl *CBATH/BATHN* BA1 115 D4 1
Avondale Rd *CBATH/BATHN* BA1 121 F3
Avondown Cl *HNBRY/STHM* BS10 47 E1 1
Avonfield *TRWBR* BA14 149 F1
Avonfield Av *BOAV* BA15 147 E4
Avon Gv *HNLZ/SM/SNYPK/WT* BS9 62 B4
Avon La *KEYN* BS31 109 D2
Avonlea *KGWD/HNM* BS15 80 A4 1
Avonleaze
HNLZ/SM/SNYPK/WT BS9 61 F1
Avonleigh Rd *BMSTR* BS3 91 F2
Avon Mill La *KEYN* BS31 107 D1
Avonmouth Rd *AVONM* BS11 42 C2
Avonmouth Wy *AVONM* BS11 43 D2
Avonmouth Wy West *AVONM* BS11 42 C1
Avon Pk *CBATH/BATHN* BA1 121 E3
EVILLE/WHL BS5 78 B2
Avon Rd
BMSTRD/HC/WWD BS13 101 E1 1
KEYN BS31 107 D2
PTSHD/EG BS20 60 A1
Avonside Rd *CBRISNE* BS2 78 A3
Avonside Wy
BRSG/KWL/STAPK BS4 79 D3 2
Avon St *BATHSE* BA2 4 B5
CBATH/BATHN BA1 4 B4
CBRISNE BS2 3 G3
Avon V *HNLZ/SM/SNYPK/WT* BS9 62 B2
Avonvale Rd *EVILLE/WHL* BS5 78 A2
TRWBR BA14 157 D2
Avon Vw *KGWD/HNM* BS15 95 F1
Avon Walkway *CBRISNE* BS2 77 D5
OLD/WMLY/WICK BS30 108 A1
PTSHD/EG BS20 60 B2
Avon Wy *HNBRY/STHM* BS10 47 E3
HNLZ/SM/SNYPK/WT BS9 62 A1
PTSHD/EG BS20 56 A1
THNB/SVB BS35 8 C4
TRWBR BA14 157 D1
Avonwood Cl *AVONM* BS11 43 F5
Awdelett Cl *AVONM* BS11 44 C2
Axbridge Cl *NAIL* BS48 87 D4 1
Axbridge Rd *BATHSE* BA2 137 E3
BRSG/KWL/STAPK BS4 93 D2
Axe And Cleaver La *TRWBR* BA14 158 B4
Axe & Cleaver La *TRWBR* BA14 159 D3 1
Axe Cl *WSM* BS23 7 G6
Aycote Cl *MTN/WRL* BS22 128 B5 1
Aylesbury Crs *BMSTR* BS3 91 F3
Aylesbury Rd *BMSTR* BS3 91 F3
Aylmer Crs *HGRV/WHIT* BS14 103 F1
Aylminton Wk *AVONM* BS11 44 C1
Ayr St *BATHSE* BA2 122 B4
Azalea Dr *TRWBR* BA14 156 A5
Azalea Rd *MTN/WRL* BS22 129 F2 1

B

Backfields *CBRISNE* BS2 76 C1 1
Backfields La *CBRISNE* BS2 76 C1 2
Back La *KEYN* BS31 106 C1
PTSHD/EG BS20 60 A2
Back of Kingsdown Pde
RDLND/MONT BS6 76 B1
Back Rd *BMSTR* BS3 75 E5
Back Stoke La
HNLZ/SM/SNYPK/WT BS9 46 A5
Back St *TRWBR* BA14 156 C3 1
WSM BS23 6 C1 4
Backwell Common *NAIL* BS48 87 F5
Backwell Wk
BMSTRD/HC/WWD BS13 91 D4 1
Badenham Gv *AVONM* BS11 44 A3
Baden Rd *EVILLE/WHL* BS5 78 A2
KGWD/HNM BS15 81 E2
Bader Cl *YATE/CS* BS37 19 E2
Badger Ri *PTSHD/EG* BS20 54 C3
Badgers Cl *ALMDB* BS32 13 E2 1
Badgers Wk
BRSG/KWL/STAPK BS4 94 B2 1
Badgeworth *YATE/CS* BS37 35 E2
Badmington Rd *MANG/FISH* BS16 52 A3
Badminton Gdns
CBATH/BATHN BA1 122 A2
Badminton Rd *CBRISNE* BS2 65 D5
FRCTL/WBN BS36 32 B5
MANG/FISH BS16 51 F4
YATE/CS BS37 18 C3
YATE/CS BS37 21 F5
Baglyn Av *KGWD/HNM* BS15 69 D3
Bagnell Cl *HGRV/WHIT* BS14 104 C2 1
Bagnell Rd *HGRV/WHIT* BS14 104 C2
Bagworth Dr
OLD/WMLY/WICK BS30 97 D1 1
Bailbrook Gv
CBATH/BATHN BA1 114 A4 1
Bailbrook La *CBATH/BATHN* BA1 114 C4
Baildon Rd *WSM* BS23 151 E1
Bailey Cl *MTN/WRL* BS22 143 D2 2
Baileys Court Rd *ALMDB* BS32 29 F2
Baileys Mead Rd
MANG/FISH BS16 66 A1 1
Bainton Cl *BOAV* BA15 147 E2
Baker Cl *CLVDN* BS21 84 B4 1
Bakersfield
OLD/WMLY/WICK BS30 97 E1 1

Bakers Gnd *BRSTK/PCHW* BS34 .... **30** A3 1
Baker St *WSM* BS23 .... **141** D2
Balaclava Rd *MANG/FISH* BS16 .... **67** D3 1
Baldwin St *CBRIS/FH* BS1 .... **2** D3
Balfour Rd *BMSTR* BS3 .... **91** F1
Ballance St *CBATH/BATHN* BA1 .... **123** D2 2
Ballast La *AVONM* BS11 .... **43** E1
Balls Barn La *OMX/HUT/LCK* BS24 .. **145** F1
Balmain St *BRSG/KWL/STAPK* BS4 .... **77** E5
Balmoral Cl *BRSTK/PCHW* BS34 .... **29** E4 1
Balmoral Ct *MANG/FISH* BS16 .... **69** E1 1
Balmoral Rd *KEYN* BS31 .... **106** C3
OLD/WMLY/WICK BS30 .... **97** D2
RDLND/MONT BS6 .... **65** D4
TRWBR BA14 .... **158** B2
Balmoral Wy *MTN/WRL* BS22 .... **128** C5 1
Baltic Pl *PTSHD/EG* BS20 .... **60** B2 1
Bamfield *HGRV/WHIT* BS14 .... **103** E1
Bampton Cl
BMSTRD/HC/WWD BS13 .... **91** F5
Bampton Dr *MANG/FISH* BS16 .... **51** E2 1
Bancroft *BOAV* BA15 .... **147** D1
Banfield Cl *AVONM* BS11 .... **44** B3
Bangor Gv *BRSG/KWL/STAPK* BS4 .... **79** D4
Bangrove Wk *AVONM* BS11 .... **43** F3 1
Bank Pl *PTSHD/EG* BS20 .... **60** B2
Bank Rd *AVONM* BS11 .... **23** E1
KGWD/HNM BS15 .... **80** B1 1
THNB/SVB BS35 .... **11** E3
Banks Cl *CLVDN* BS21 .... **85** D4
Bankside *MANG/FISH* BS16 .... **69** D2 1
Bankside Rd
BRSG/KWL/STAPK BS4 .... **94** B1 1
Bannerdown Cl
CBATH/BATHN BA1 .... **115** F3
Bannerdown Dr
CBATH/BATHN BA1 .... **115** E3
Bannerdown Rd
CBATH/BATHN BA1 .... **115** E4
Bannerleigh La *CFTN/FAIL* BS8 .... **74** C3 1
Bannerleigh Rd *CFTN/FAIL* BS8 .... **74** C2
Bannerman Rd *EVILLE/WHL* BS5 .... **77** F1
Banner Rd *RDLND/MONT* BS6 .... **64** C5
Bantry Rd *BRSG/KWL/STAPK* BS4 .... **92** C4
Banwell Cl *BMSTRD/HC/WWD* BS13 .. **91** E4
KEYN BS31 .... **107** E5
Banwell Rd *BATHSE* BA2 .... **136** B5
BMSTR BS3 .... **91** E1
WNSC BS25 .... **154** A3
Baptist St *EVILLE/WHL* BS5 .... **65** E5 2
Barberry Farm Rd
YTN/CONG BS49 .... **116** B2
Barbour Gdns
BMSTRD/HC/WWD BS13 .... **102** B4
Barbour Rd
BMSTRD/HC/WWD BS13 .... **102** B4
Barcroft Cl *KGWD/HNM* BS15 .... **80** A1 1
Barkers Md *YATE/CS* BS37 .... **20** A1 1
Barker Wk *EVILLE/WHL* BS5 .... **65** E5 3
Barkleys Hl *MANG/FISH* BS16 .... **66** A1
Barley Cl *FRCTL/WBN* BS36 .... **16** C5 1
MANG/FISH BS16 .... **52** B5
Barley Cft
HNLZ/SM/SNYPK/WT BS9 .... **63** D1
Barley Cross *MTN/WRL* BS22 .... **129** F2 2
Barnabas St *CBRISNE* BS2 .... **64** C5 2
Barnaby Cl *RDSTK/MIDN* BA3 .... **161** E2 1
Barnack Cl *TRWBR* BA14 .... **156** A3
Barnard's Cl *YTN/CONG* BS49 .... **116** C4
Barnard Wk *KEYN* BS31 .... **106** B3
Barnes Cl *TRWBR* BA14 .... **156** A5
Barnes St *EVILLE/WHL* BS5 .... **78** B2 1
Barnfield Wy *CBATH/BATHN* BA1 .... **115** F3
Barn Glebe *TRWBR* BA14 .... **157** F3
Barnhill Rd *YATE/CS* BS37 .... **20** C4
Barn Owl Wy *BRSTK/PCHW* BS34 .... **30** A3
Barn Piece *BOAV* BA15 .... **147** D5
Barns Cl *NAIL* BS48 .... **87** D2
Barnstaple Rd
BRSG/KWL/STAPK BS4 .... **92** C4
Barnstaple Wk
BRSG/KWL/STAPK BS4 .... **93** D4 1
Barnwood Ct *NAIL* BS48 .... **86** A3
Barnwood Rd *YATE/CS* BS37 .... **35** D1
Barossa Pl *CBRIS/FH* BS1 .... **2** D5
Barrack's La *AVONM* BS11 .... **43** E3
Barratt St *EVILLE/WHL* BS5 .... **65** F5
Barrington Cl *KGWD/HNM* BS15 .... **69** D4
Barrington Ct *KGWD/HNM* BS15 .... **68** C5
Barrow Hl *OLD/WMLY/WICK* BS30 .... **83** F3
Barrow Hill Crs *AVONM* BS11 .... **43** D4
Barrow Hill Rd *AVONM* BS11 .... **43** D5
Barrowmead Dr *AVONM* BS11 .... **44** A3
Barrow Rd *BATHSE* BA2 .... **136** A4
CBRISNE BS2 .... **77** E2
EVILLE/WHL BS5 .... **77** F2
OMX/HUT/LCK BS24 .... **153** D3
The Barrows *MTN/WRL* BS22 .... **142** B3 1
Barrs Court Av
OLD/WMLY/WICK BS30 .... **81** E4
Barrs Court Rd
OLD/WMLY/WICK BS30 .... **81** E4
Barry Cl *OLD/WMLY/WICK* BS30 .... **98** A3 1
OMX/HUT/LCK BS24 .... **151** F4 2
Barry Rd *OLD/WMLY/WICK* BS30 .... **98** A2
Bartlett's Rd *BMSTR* BS3 .... **92** A2
Bartlett St *CBATH/BATHN* BA1 .... **4** B2 1
Bartley St *BMSTR* BS3 .... **76** B5
Barton Cl *BRSG/KWL/STAPK* BS4 .... **79** D3 3
FRCTL/WBN BS36 .... **31** F3
Barton Ct *EVILLE/WHL* BS5 .... **78** A3 1
Barton Hill Rd *EVILLE/WHL* BS5 .... **77** F3
Bartonia Gv
BRSG/KWL/STAPK BS4 .... **94** B3 2
Barton Mnr *CBRISNE* BS2 .... **77** E3
Barton Orch *BOAV* BA15 .... **146** C3
Barton Rd *CBRISNE* BS2 .... **3** H3
Barton St *CBATH/BATHN* BA1 .... **4** B3 1
CBRIS/FH BS1 .... **76** B1 1
The Barton *BATHSE* BA2 .... **119** E3
KGWD/HNM BS15 .... **79** F5
Barton V *CBRISNE* BS2 .... **3** H3
CBRISNE BS2 .... **77** E3 1
Barwood Cl *KGWD/HNM* BS15 .... **81** D1 1
Bassetts Pasture *BOAV* BA15 .... **147** D5
The Batch *YTN/CONG* BS49 .... **116** B4
Bates Cl *EVILLE/WHL* BS5 .... **77** E1 3
Bathampton La *BATHSE* BA2 .... **124** C1
Bath Br *BRSG/KWL/STAPK* BS4 .... **3** G6
Bath Buildings
RDLND/MONT BS6 .... **64** C5 3
Bathford Hl *CBATH/BATHN* BA1 .... **115** F5
Bath Hl *KEYN* BS31 .... **107** D2
Bath New Rd *RDSTK/MIDN* BA3 .... **162** C1
Bath Rd *BRSG/KWL/STAPK* BS4 .... **3** H6
BRSG/KWL/STAPK BS4 .... **94** A1
KEYN BS31 .... **95** F4
KEYN BS31 .... **107** E2
OLD/WMLY/WICK BS30 .... **82** B3
OLD/WMLY/WICK BS30 .... **97** D1
OLD/WMLY/WICK BS30 .... **109** F2
THNB/SVB BS35 .... **8** B4
Bath Road Brislington Hl
BRSG/KWL/STAPK BS4 .... **94** C2
Bath St *BMSTR* BS3 .... **75** E5
CBATH/BATHN BA1 .... **4** B4 1
CBRIS/FH BS1 .... **3** E3
MANG/FISH BS16 .... **68** C2
Bathurst Pde *CBRIS/FH* BS1 .... **2** C6
Bathurst Rd *MTN/WRL* BS22 .... **142** B1
Bathwell Rd
BRSG/KWL/STAPK BS4 .... **93** E1 1
Bathwick Hl *BATHSE* BA2 .... **5** F3
Bathwick Ri *BATHSE* BA2 .... **5** F1 1
Bathwick St *BATHSE* BA2 .... **123** E2
Batley Ct *OLD/WMLY/WICK* BS30 .. **82** B5 1
Batstone Cl *CBATH/BATHN* BA1 .... **113** E5
Battenburg Rd *EVILLE/WHL* BS5 .... **79** E1
Batten Ct *YATE/CS* BS37 .... **21** D4
Batten's La *EVILLE/WHL* BS5 .... **79** E3
Battens Rd *EVILLE/WHL* BS5 .... **79** F2 1
Battersby Wy *HNBRY/STHM* BS10 .... **45** F1
Battersea Rd *EVILLE/WHL* BS5 .... **78** A1
Battery La *PTSHD/EG* BS20 .... **39** E5
Battson Rd *HGRV/WHIT* BS14 .... **104** C3
Baugh Gdns *MANG/FISH* BS16 .... **51** F2
Baxter Cl *KGWD/HNM* BS15 .... **81** D1 2
Baydon Cl *TRWBR* BA14 .... **158** C2
Bay Gdns *EVILLE/WHL* BS5 .... **66** A4 3
Bayham Rd *BRSG/KWL/STAPK* BS4 .... **93** D1
Bayleys Dr *KGWD/HNM* BS15 .... **80** A3
Baynton Rd *BMSTR* BS3 .... **75** E5 2
Bay Rd *CLVDN* BS21 .... **71** D3
Bayswater Av *RDLND/MONT* BS6 .... **63** F2
Bayswater Rd *HORF/LLZ* BS7 .... **48** A4
Bay Tree Cl *BRSTK/PCHW* BS34 .... **28** A1
Bay Tree Rd *CBATH/BATHN* BA1 .... **113** F5
CLVDN BS21 .... **85** E2
Baytree Rd *MTN/WRL* BS22 .... **142** B1
Baytree Vw *MTN/WRL* BS22 .... **142** C1
Beach Av *CLVDN* BS21 .... **84** C2
THNB/SVB BS35 .... **10** B3
Beach End Rd *WSM* BS23 .... **150** B3 1
Beachgrove Gdns *MANG/FISH* BS16.. **68** A2
Beachgrove Rd *MANG/FISH* BS16 .... **67** F2
Beach Hl *OLD/WMLY/WICK* BS30 .... **99** D1
PTSHD/EG BS20 .... **39** D5
Beachley Wk *AVONM* BS11 .... **43** E4
Beach Rd *THNB/SVB* BS35 .... **10** A3
WSM BS23 .... **6** A5
Beach Rd East *PTSHD/EG* BS20 .... **39** E5
Beach Rd West *PTSHD/EG* BS20 .... **39** D5
The Beach *CLVDN* BS21 .... **70** C5
Beacon La *MANG/FISH* BS16 .... **30** C3
Beaconlea *KGWD/HNM* BS15 .... **80** B3
Beacon Rd *CBATH/BATHN* BA1 .... **123** E1
Beaconsfield Rd
BRSG/KWL/STAPK BS4 .... **93** F1
CFTN/FAIL BS8 .... **63** E5 1
CLVDN BS21 .... **85** E2
EVILLE/WHL BS5 .... **78** C1
WSM BS23 .... **6** C2
Beaconsfield St *EVILLE/WHL* BS5 .. **77** F3 1
Beale Cl *HGRV/WHIT* BS14 .... **104** C1 1
Beale's Barton *TRWBR* BA14 .... **149** F1
Beam St *EVILLE/WHL* BS5 .... **78** A2 1
The Bean Acre *AVONM* BS11 .... **43** E3
Bean St *EVILLE/WHL* BS5 .... **65** E5 4
Bearbridge Rd
BMSTRD/HC/WWD BS13 .... **101** D3
Bear Cl *BOAV* BA15 .... **146** B2
Bearfield Buildings *BOAV* BA15 .. **146** C1 1
Beauchamp Rd *HORF/LLZ* BS7 .... **64** B2
Beaufort Sq *CBATH/BATHN* BA1 .... **4** B3 2
Beaufort Av *RDSTK/MIDN* BA3 .... **161** D2
Beaufort Cl *EVILLE/WHL* BS5 .... **78** B2 2
Beaufort Crs *BRSTK/PCHW* BS34 .... **29** F4
Beaufort East *CBATH/BATHN* BA1 .. **124** A1
Beaufort Pl *CBATH/BATHN* BA1 .... **124** A1
MANG/FISH BS16 .... **50** C2 1
Beaufort Rd *CFTN/FAIL* BS8 .... **63** E5
EVILLE/WHL BS5 .... **78** B2
FRCTL/WBN BS36 .... **16** B5
HORF/LLZ BS7 .... **48** A5
KGWD/HNM BS15 .... **67** F5 1
MANG/FISH BS16 .... **52** B4
MANG/FISH BS16 .... **68** C2
WSM BS23 .... **7** E1
YATE/CS BS37 .... **19** E3
Beaufort St *BMSTR* BS3 .... **92** A2 1
EVILLE/WHL BS5 .... **77** E1 4
Beaufort Wy *HNBRY/STHM* BS10 .... **47** E3
Beauley Rd *BMSTR* BS3 .... **75** F5
Beaumont Cl
OLD/WMLY/WICK BS30 .... **97** E1 2
WSM BS23 .... **151** E1 1
Beaumont St *EVILLE/WHL* BS5 .... **77** E1 5
Beaumont Ter *EVILLE/WHL* BS5 .... **77** E1 6
Beau St *CBATH/BATHN* BA1 .... **4** B4 2
Beaver Cl *FRCTL/WBN* BS36 .... **32** A1
Beazer Cl *MANG/FISH* BS16 .... **68** B3 1
Becket Dr *MTN/WRL* BS22 .... **129** F4 1
Becket Rd *MTN/WRL* BS22 .... **129** F3
Becket's La *NAIL* BS48 .... **87** D4
Beckford Gdns
HGRV/WHIT BS14 .... **103** E4 1
Beckford Rd *BATHSE* BA2 .... **5** E1
Beckhampton Rd *BATHSE* BA2 .... **122** B5
Beckington Rd *BMSTR* BS3 .... **93** D2
Beckington Wk *BMSTR* BS3 .... **93** D2 1
Beckspool Rd *MANG/FISH* BS16 .... **51** D3 1
Beddoe Cl *BOAV* BA15 .... **147** E5 1
Bedford Crs *HORF/LLZ* BS7 .... **65** D1
Bedford Rd *WSM* BS23 .... **151** D1
Bedford St *CBATH/BATHN* BA1 .... **123** E2 2
Bedminster Down Rd
BMSTR BS3 .... **91** F2 1
BMSTRD/HC/WWD BS13 .... **91** E3
Bedminster Pde *BMSTR* BS3 .... **76** B5
Bedminster Pl *BMSTR* BS3 .... **76** B5 1
Bedminster Rd *BMSTR* BS3 .... **92** A2
Bedwin Cl *PTSHD/EG* BS20 .... **55** D2 1
Beech Av *BATHSE* BA2 .... **138** C1
Beech Cl *OLD/WMLY/WICK* BS30 .... **81** E4
Beechcroft *LGASH* BS41 .... **100** B5 1
Beechcroft Wk *HORF/LLZ* BS7 .... **48** B3
Beech Dr *NAIL* BS48 .... **87** F2
Beechen Cliff Rd *BATHSE* BA2 .... **4** A6
Beechen Dr *MANG/FISH* BS16 .... **67** F4
Beeches Gv
BRSG/KWL/STAPK BS4 .... **94** B2 2
The Beeches *ALMDB* BS32 .... **13** E5
BATHSE BA2 .... **136** B4 1
BOAV BA15 .... **148** A2
BRSG/KWL/STAPK BS4 .... **78** C4 1
OLD/WMLY/WICK BS30 .... **98** A2
TRWBR BA14 .... **157** F2
Beechfield Cl *LGASH* BS41 .... **90** A2 1
Beech Gv *BATHSE* BA2 .... **136** A1
TRWBR BA14 .... **158** B1
Beechmont Cl
OMX/HUT/LCK BS24 .... **151** E4
Beechmont Dr
OMX/HUT/LCK BS24 .... **151** E4
Beechmount Gv *HGRV/WHIT* BS14 .... **93** F4
Beech Rd *HORF/LLZ* BS7 .... **64** C1
KEYN BS31 .... **108** C4
YTN/CONG BS49 .... **116** C3
Beech Ter *RDSTK/MIDN* BA3 .... **162** A3
Beechwood Av *KGWD/HNM* BS15 .... **80** B4
OMX/HUT/LCK BS24 .... **153** F1 1
Beechwood Cl *HGRV/WHIT* BS14 .... **94** A4
Beechwood Rd *BATHSE* BA2 .... **137** F4
MANG/FISH BS16 .... **67** E2
NAIL BS48 .... **86** C2
PTSHD/EG BS20 .... **54** C2
PTSHD/EG BS20 .... **59** E2
Beehive Yd *CBATH/BATHN* BA1 .... **4** C2 1
Beesmoor Rd *FRCTL/WBN* BS36 .... **32** C1
Begbrook Dr *MANG/FISH* BS16 .... **50** A5
Begbrook La *MANG/FISH* BS16 .... **50** A5
Begbrook Pk *MANG/FISH* BS16 .... **50** B4
Beggar Bush La *CFTN/FAIL* BS8 .... **72** B5
Beggarswell Cl *CBRISNE* BS2 .... **77** D1 1
Belcombe Rd *BOAV* BA15 .... **146** B3
Belfast Wk
BRSG/KWL/STAPK BS4 .... **92** C4 1
Belgrave Crs *CBATH/BATHN* BA1 .... **123** E2
Belgrave Hl *CFTN/FAIL* BS8 .... **63** E4 2
Belgrave Pl *CFTN/FAIL* BS8 .... **75** E2 1
Belgrave Rd *CBATH/BATHN* BA1 .... **123** F1
CFTN/FAIL BS8 .... **75** F1
MTN/WRL BS22 .... **142** A2
Bellamy Av
BMSTRD/HC/WWD BS13 .... **102** A3

Bellamy Cl *KGWD/HNM* BS15 79 E4
Belland Dr *HGRV/WHIT* BS14 103 D3
Bella Vista Rd
CBATH/BATHN BA1 123 D2 3
Bell Barn Rd
HNLZ/SM/SNYPK/WT BS9 45 E5
Bell Cl *HNBRY/STHM* BS10 47 F4
Bellefield Crs *TRWBR* BA14 157 D3
Bellevue *CFTN/FAIL* BS8 75 F3
Bellevue Cl *KGWD/HNM* BS15 80 C2 1
Bellevue Cottages
CFTN/FAIL BS8 75 F3 1
Bellevue Crs *CFTN/FAIL* BS8 75 F3
Bellevue Pk
BRSG/KWL/STAPK BS4 94 B2 3
Belle Vue Rd *EVILLE/WHL* BS5 66 A5
Bellevue Rd *BRSG/KWL/STAPK* BS4 77 D5
CLVDN BS21 71 D5
EVILLE/WHL BS5 79 E1
KGWD/HNM BS15 81 D2
Bellevue Ter
BRSG/KWL/STAPK BS4 77 D5 1
BRSG/KWL/STAPK BS4 94 B2 4
Bell Hl *MANG/FISH* BS16 66 A2
Bell Hill Rd *EVILLE/WHL* BS5 79 D1
Bellhouse Wk *AVONM* BS11 44 C2 1
Bell La *CBRIS/FH* BS1 2 D2
Bellotts Rd *BATHSE* BA2 122 A4
Bell Rd *FRCTL/WBN* BS36 33 D2
Belluton Rd *BRSG/KWL/STAPK* BS4 93 E1
Belmont Dr *BRSTK/PCHW* BS34 29 F3
CFTN/FAIL BS8 88 A1 1
Belmont Rd *BATHSE* BA2 138 A4
BRSG/KWL/STAPK BS4 94 A1 1
RDLND/MONT BS6 64 C4
WNSC BS25 154 C4
Belmont St *EVILLE/WHL* BS5 65 F5
Belmore Gdns *BATHSE* BA2 135 F2
Beloe Rd *HORF/LLZ* BS7 64 B1
Belroyal Av *BRSG/KWL/STAPK* BS4 95 D1
Belsher Dr *KGWD/HNM* BS15 81 E3
Belstone Wk *BRSG/KWL/STAPK* BS4 92 A5
Belton Rd *EVILLE/WHL* BS5 65 F5
PTSHD/EG BS20 38 B5
Belvedere Crs *MTN/WRL* BS22 142 B1
Belvedere Rd *RDLND/MONT* BS6 63 E3
Belvoir Rd *BATHSE* BA2 122 B5 1
RDLND/MONT BS6 64 C4
Bence Ct *KGWD/HNM* BS15 79 F4 1
Benford Cl *MANG/FISH* BS16 51 D5
Bennett La *CBATH/BATHN* BA1 123 E1
Bennett Rd *EVILLE/WHL* BS5 78 C2 1
Bennett's Ct *YATE/CS* BS37 20 A4
Bennett's Rd *CBATH/BATHN* BA1 114 A4
Bennett St *CBATH/BATHN* BA1 4 B1 1
Bennetts Wy *CLVDN* BS21 71 E4
Bensaunt Gv *HNBRY/STHM* BS10 27 E4
Bentley Cl *HGRV/WHIT* BS14 103 D4 1
Bentley Rd *MTN/WRL* BS22 130 A4
Benville Av
HNLZ/SM/SNYPK/WT BS9 45 D3
Berenda Dr *OLD/WMLY/WICK* BS30 97 F1
Beresford Cl *KEYN* BS31 108 C5
Beresford Gdns
CBATH/BATHN BA1 111 E4 1
Berkeley Av *CFTN/FAIL* BS8 2 A2
HORF/LLZ BS7 64 B3
RDSTK/MIDN BA3 161 D2
Berkeley Cl *MANG/FISH* BS16 52 A3
Berkeley Crs *WSM* BS23 150 B3
Berkeley Gdns *KEYN* BS31 106 B3
Berkeley Gn *EVILLE/WHL* BS5 66 A4 4
MANG/FISH BS16 50 C2 2
Berkeley Gv *EVILLE/WHL* BS5 66 B4 1
Berkeley Md *ALMDB* BS32 30 A2
Berkeley Rd *HORF/LLZ* BS7 64 B3
KGWD/HNM BS15 80 C2 2
MANG/FISH BS16 67 E4
RDLND/MONT BS6 63 E2
TRWBR BA14 156 A4
Berkeley St *EVILLE/WHL* BS5 66 A3
Berkeley Wy *MANG/FISH* BS16 52 C4
Berkley Av *CFTN/FAIL* BS8 75 F2 1
Berkshire Rd *HORF/LLZ* BS7 64 B3
Berrow Wk *BMSTR* BS3 92 C2
Berryfield Rd *BOAV* BA15 147 D1
Berry La *HORF/LLZ* BS7 48 B5
Berwick La *HNBRY/STHM* BS10 25 D3
Berwick Rd *EVILLE/WHL* BS5 65 F4
Beryl Gv *HGRV/WHIT* BS14 94 A4
Beryl Rd *BMSTR* BS3 91 F1
Besom La *YATE/CS* BS37 35 D3
Bethel Rd *EVILLE/WHL* BS5 79 D1
Betjeman Ct
OLD/WMLY/WICK BS30 81 E4 1
Bevan Ct *BRSTK/PCHW* BS34 48 A1
Beverley Av *MANG/FISH* BS16 52 A2
Beverley Cl *EVILLE/WHL* BS5 79 F3 1
Beverley Gdns
HNLZ/SM/SNYPK/WT BS9 45 E4
Beverstone *KGWD/HNM* BS15 80 A1 2
Beverston Gdns *AVONM* BS11 44 C1 1
Bewdley Rd *BATHSE* BA2 137 F1 1
Bewley Rd *TRWBR* BA14 158 C2
Bexley Rd *MANG/FISH* BS16 67 F3
Bibstone *KGWD/HNM* BS15 81 E1
Bibury Av *BRSTK/PCHW* BS34 12 C5
Bibury Cl *HNLZ/SM/SNYPK/WT* BS9 47 E4
NAIL BS48 87 F3
Bibury Crs
HNLZ/SM/SNYPK/WT BS9 47 E4
KGWD/HNM BS15 80 A4
Bickerton Cl *HNBRY/STHM* BS10 26 A5
Bickford Cl *OLD/WMLY/WICK* BS30 81 E3
Bickley Cl *KGWD/HNM* BS15 96 A2 1
Biddestone Rd *HORF/LLZ* BS7 47 F3
Biddisham Cl *NAIL* BS48 87 D3 1
Biddle St *YTN/CONG* BS49 116 A4
Bideford Crs *BRSG/KWL/STAPK* BS4 93 D4
Bideford Rd *MTN/WRL* BS22 129 E5 1
Bidwell Cl *HNBRY/STHM* BS10 26 C5
Bifield Cl *HGRV/WHIT* BS14 105 D2
Bifield Gdns *HGRV/WHIT* BS14 104 C2
Bifield Rd *HGRV/WHIT* BS14 105 D2
Bigwood La *CBRIS/FH* BS1 2 A3
Bilberry Cl
HNLZ/SM/SNYPK/WT BS9 45 D3 1
Bilbie Cl *HNBRY/STHM* BS10 47 E5
Bilbie Rd *MTN/WRL* BS22 130 A4
Bilbury La *CBATH/BATHN* BA1 4 B4 3
Billand Cl *BMSTRD/HC/WWD* BS13 100 C4
Bince's Lodge La
RDSTK/MIDN BA3 161 E1
Bindon Dr *HNBRY/STHM* BS10 27 E4
Binhay Rd *YTN/CONG* BS49 116 C4
Binley Gv *HGRV/WHIT* BS14 104 B2
Binmead Gdns
BMSTRD/HC/WWD BS13 101 F3 1
Birbeck Rd
HNLZ/SM/SNYPK/WT BS9 62 C1
Birchall Rd *RDLND/MONT* BS6 64 A2
Birch Av *CLVDN* BS21 71 E5
Birch Cl *BRSTK/PCHW* BS34 27 F1
Birch Ct *KEYN* BS31 106 A3
Birch Cft *HGRV/WHIT* BS14 103 F4 1
Birchdale Rd *HGRV/WHIT* BS14 93 E4
Birch Dene *NAIL* BS48 87 F2 1
Birchenleaze *TRWBR* BA14 158 C4 1
The Birches *NAIL* BS48 87 F2 2
Birch Gv *PTSHD/EG* BS20 56 A2
Birch Rd *BMSTR* BS3 75 F5
KGWD/HNM BS15 68 C3
RDSTK/MIDN BA3 162 B3
YATE/CS BS37 19 E3
Birchwood Av *WSM* BS23 7 H1
Birchwood Rd
BRSG/KWL/STAPK BS4 78 C5
Birdale Cl *HNBRY/STHM* BS10 25 F5
Birdcombe Cl *NAIL* BS48 87 D1 1
Birdlip Cl *NAIL* BS48 87 E4
Birdwell La *LGASH* BS41 89 D3 1
Birdwell Rd *LGASH* BS41 89 D3
Birdwood *KGWD/HNM* BS15 80 B3
Birkbeck Ct *WSM* BS23 6 B2 1
Birkdale *OLD/WMLY/WICK* BS30 81 F3
YATE/CS BS37 19 F5
Birkett Rd *WSM* BS23 140 A1
Birkin St *CBRISNE* BS2 3 H3
Birnbeck Rd *WSM* BS23 140 A1
Bisdee Rd *OMX/HUT/LCK* BS24 152 C2
Bishop Av *MTN/WRL* BS22 129 F4 2
Bishop Manor Rd
HNBRY/STHM BS10 47 E4
Bishop Rd *HORF/LLZ* BS7 64 A2
Bishops Cl
HNLZ/SM/SNYPK/WT BS9 62 C3
Bishops Cove
BMSTRD/HC/WWD BS13 101 D2 1
Bishops Knoll
HNLZ/SM/SNYPK/WT BS9 62 A3
Bishops Rd *YTN/CONG* BS49 117 F3
Bishop St *CBRISNE* BS2 76 C1
Bishopsworth Rd
BMSTRD/HC/WWD BS13 91 E3
Bishopthorpe Rd
HNBRY/STHM BS10 47 E4
Bishport Av
BMSTRD/HC/WWD BS13 101 E3
Bishport Cl
BMSTRD/HC/WWD BS13 101 F3
Bisley *YATE/CS* BS37 35 D1
Bissex Md *MANG/FISH* BS16 69 F1
Biss Meadow *TRWBR* BA14 156 A4 1
Bittern Cl *MTN/WRL* BS22 143 E1 1
Bitterwell Cl *FRCTL/WBN* BS36 33 E5
Blackacre *HGRV/WHIT* BS14 104 A4
Blackberry Av *MANG/FISH* BS16 66 C1 1
Blackberry Dr *MTN/WRL* BS22 143 F1
Blackberry Hl *MANG/FISH* BS16 66 C1
Blackberry La *PTSHD/EG* BS20 54 C4
Blackbird Cl *RDSTK/MIDN* BA3 161 E4 1
Blackdown Ct *HGRV/WHIT* BS14 103 F2 1
Blackdown Rd *PTSHD/EG* BS20 55 E1 1
PTSHD/EG BS20 55 F1 1
Blackfriars *CBRIS/FH* BS1 2 D1 1
Blackfriars Rd *NAIL* BS48 86 A4
Blackhorse La *MANG/FISH* BS16 52 B3
Blackhorse Pl *MANG/FISH* BS16 52 B5 1
Blackhorse Rd *KGWD/HNM* BS15 80 B1
MANG/FISH BS16 52 B5
Blackmoor *CLVDN* BS21 84 C3
Blackmoor Rd *CFTN/FAIL* BS8 60 C4
Blackmoors La *BMSTR* BS3 90 C1
Blackmore Dr *BATHSE* BA2 121 F5
Blacksmith La *CBATH/BATHN* BA1 113 F1
Blackswarth Rd *EVILLE/WHL* BS5 78 B2
Blackthorn Cl
BMSTRD/HC/WWD BS13 102 B2
Blackthorn Dr *ALMDB* BS32 29 E1 1
Blackthorn Gdns *MTN/WRL* BS22 143 F1
Blackthorn Rd
BMSTRD/HC/WWD BS13 102 B2
Blackthorn Sq *CLVDN* BS21 85 D3
Blackthorn Wk *KGWD/HNM* BS15 68 C4 1
Blackthorn Wy *NAIL* BS48 87 E2
Bladen Cl *PTSHD/EG* BS20 56 C2 1
Blagdon Cl *OMX/HUT/LCK* BS24 151 E4 1
Blagdon Pk *BATHSE* BA2 135 E1
Blagrove Cl
BMSTRD/HC/WWD BS13 102 A4
Blagrove Crs
BMSTRD/HC/WWD BS13 102 A4
Blair Rd *TRWBR* BA14 156 A5
Blaisdon *MTN/WRL* BS22 142 C3
YATE/CS BS37 35 F1
Blaisdon Cl *HNBRY/STHM* BS10 46 A2
Blaise Wk *HNLZ/SM/SNYPK/WT* BS9 45 D5
Blake End *MTN/WRL* BS22 129 D3 1
Blakeney Gv *NAIL* BS48 86 B4
Blakeney Mills *YATE/CS* BS37 19 E4 1
Blakeney Rd *HORF/LLZ* BS7 48 B4
Blake Rd *HORF/LLZ* BS7 48 C5
Blakes Rd *THNB/SVB* BS35 8 B3
Blanchards *YATE/CS* BS37 21 D5
Blandford Cl
HNLZ/SM/SNYPK/WT BS9 46 C5 1
NAIL BS48 87 D3 2
Bleadon Hl *OMX/HUT/LCK* BS24 151 E5
Blenheim Cl *MTN/WRL* BS22 129 F5 1
Blenheim Dr *BRSTK/PCHW* BS34 28 C4
YATE/CS BS37 19 D2
Blenheim Gdns
CBATH/BATHN BA1 113 E5
Blenheim Rd *RDLND/MONT* BS6 63 F3
Blenheim St *EVILLE/WHL* BS5 65 E5 5
Blenheim Wy *PTSHD/EG* BS20 56 C1 1
Blenman Cl *MANG/FISH* BS16 50 B4 1
Blethwin Cl *HNBRY/STHM* BS10 46 A2
Blind La *CBATH/BATHN* BA1 112 A5
YTN/CONG BS49 117 F4
Bloomfield Av *BATHSE* BA2 136 C1
Bloomfield Dr *BATHSE* BA2 136 B3
Bloomfield Gv *BATHSE* BA2 136 C2
Bloomfield Pk *BATHSE* BA2 136 C2
Bloomfield Ri *BATHSE* BA2 136 B3
Bloomfield Ri North
BATHSE BA2 136 B3 1
Bloomfield Rd *BATHSE* BA2 136 B3
BRSG/KWL/STAPK BS4 78 A5
Bloomfield Road Link
BRSG/KWL/STAPK BS4 78 A5
Bloy St *EVILLE/WHL* BS5 66 A5
Bluebell Cl *THNB/SVB* BS35 9 D2
Bluebell Rd *MTN/WRL* BS22 129 F1 1
The Bluebells *ALMDB* BS32 29 F1 1
ALMDB BS32 30 A1 1
Blueberry Wy *MTN/WRL* BS22 143 E1 2
Blythe Gdns *MTN/WRL* BS22 129 F4 3
Boat Stall La *CBATH/BATHN* BA1 4 C3 2
Bockenem Cl *THNB/SVB* BS35 9 D5 2
Bodey Cl *OLD/WMLY/WICK* BS30 81 E4
Bodmin Wk *BRSG/KWL/STAPK* BS4 93 D4
Bolton Rd *HORF/LLZ* BS7 64 C3
Bond St *CBRIS/FH* BS1 76 C1
TRWBR BA14 156 C5
Bonnington Wk *HORF/LLZ* BS7 48 C4
Bonville Rd *BRSG/KWL/STAPK* BS4 94 C3
Booth Rd *BMSTR* BS3 76 A5
Boot La *BMSTR* BS3 76 B5 2
Bordesley Rd *HGRV/WHIT* BS14 103 E4
Borgie Pl *MTN/WRL* BS22 129 D4
Borleyton Wk
BMSTRD/HC/WWD BS13 101 D3 1
Borver Gv
BMSTRD/HC/WWD BS13 101 F3
Boscombe Crs *MANG/FISH* BS16 52 A4 1
Boswell St *EVILLE/WHL* BS5 66 A4 5
Botham Cl *MTN/WRL* BS22 129 F3 1
Botham Dr
BRSG/KWL/STAPK BS4 94 C3 1
Bottom Cl *HGRV/WHIT* BS14 103 E1
Boucher Pl *CBRISNE* BS2 65 E4 1
Boulevard *WSM* BS23 141 D2
Boulters Rd
BMSTRD/HC/WWD BS13 102 A3 1
Boulton's Rd *KGWD/HNM* BS15 80 B1
Boundary Cl *RDSTK/MIDN* BA3 161 E5
WSM BS23 151 D2
Boundary Rd *AVONM* BS11 23 E4
FRCTL/WBN BS36 33 E1
Bourchier Gdns
BMSTRD/HC/WWD BS13 101 F4
Bourne Cl *FRCTL/WBN* BS36 31 F1
KGWD/HNM BS15 79 F1
Bourne Rd *KGWD/HNM* BS15 79 E1

Bourneville Rd *EVILLE/WHL* BS5 .... **78** B1 2
Bournville Rd *WSM* BS23 .... **151** E1
Boursland Cl *ALMDB* BS32 .... **13** E3 1
Bourton Av *BRSTK/PCHW* BS34 .... **13** D5
Bourton Cl *BRSTK/PCHW* BS34 .... **13** D5
Bourton La *MTN/WRL* BS22 .... **130** C4
Bourton Wk
BMSTRD/HC/WWD BS13 .... **91** E4 1
Boverton Rd *BRSTK/PCHW* BS34 .... **28** C5
Bowden Cl
HNLZ/SM/SNYPK/WT BS9 .... **45** D3
Bowden Pl *MANG/FISH* BS16 .... **52** A4 2
Bowden Rd *EVILLE/WHL* BS5 .... **66** C5 2
Bowen Rd *OMX/HUT/LCK* BS24 .... **144** B5
Bowerleaze
HNLZ/SM/SNYPK/WT BS9 .... **61** F1
Bower Rd *BMSTR* BS3 .... **91** E1
Bower Wk *BMSTR* BS3 .... **92** C1
Bowling Hl *YATE/CS* BS37 .... **20** B4
Bowling Rd *YATE/CS* BS37 .... **20** C5
Bowring Cl
BMSTRD/HC/WWD BS13 .... **102** A4
Bowsland Wy *ALMDB* BS32 .... **13** E3
Boxbury Hl *RDSTK/MIDN* BA3 .... **160** B1
Boxhedge Farm La
FRCTL/WBN BS36 .... **33** F5
Boyce Cl *BATHSE* BA2 .... **121** D5
Boyce Dr *CBRISNE* BS2 .... **65** E4 2
Boyce's Av *CFTN/FAIL* BS8 .... **75** E2 2
Boyd Cl *OLD/WMLY/WICK* BS30 .... **83** F2
Boyd Rd *KEYN* BS31 .... **108** B4
Brabazon Rd *BRSTK/PCHW* BS34 .... **48** C1
Bracewell Gdns *HNBRY/STHM* BS10 .. **27** D4
Bracey Dr *MANG/FISH* BS16 .... **51** D5 1
Brackenbury Dr
BRSTK/PCHW BS34 .... **29** F3
Brackendene *ALMDB* BS32 .... **13** D4 1
Brackenwood Rd *CLVDN* BS21 .... **71** E3
Bracton Dr *HGRV/WHIT* BS14 .... **103** E3
Bradeston Gv *MANG/FISH* BS16 .... **50** B4
Bradford Cl *CLVDN* BS21 .... **84** C3 1
Bradford Rd *BATHSE* BA2 .... **137** D4
CBATH/BATHN BA1 .... **125** F1
TRWBR BA14 .... **148** C2
Bradhurst St *EVILLE/WHL* BS5 .... **77** F3 2
Bradley Av *AVONM* BS11 .... **43** F5
FRCTL/WBN BS36 .... **31** F3
Bradley Cl *TRWBR* BA14 .... **149** F1 1
Bradley Crs *AVONM* BS11 .... **43** F5
Bradley La *TRWBR* BA14 .... **149** F1
Bradley Rd *BRSTK/PCHW* BS34 .... **12** A5
PTSHD/EG BS20 .... **58** C1
TRWBR BA14 .... **156** C5
TRWBR BA14 .... **158** A5
Bradley Stoke Wy *ALMDB* BS32 .... **13** D3
Bradstone Rd *FRCTL/WBN* BS36 .... **31** E3 1
Bradville Gdns *LGASH* BS41 .... **89** D4
Bradwell Gv *HNBRY/STHM* BS10 .... **47** D3
Braemar Av *HORF/LLZ* BS7 .... **48** A2
Braemar Crs *HORF/LLZ* BS7 .... **48** A2
Brae Ri *WNSC* BS25 .... **154** C4
Brae Rd *WNSC* BS25 .... **154** C4
Bragg's La *CBRISNE* BS2 .... **3** H1
Braikenridge Cl *CLVDN* BS21 .... **84** C3 2
Braikenridge Rd
BRSG/KWL/STAPK BS4 .... **78** B5
Brainsfield
HNLZ/SM/SNYPK/WT BS9 .... **46** A5
Brake Cl *ALMDB* BS32 .... **29** F2
KGWD/HNM BS15 .... **81** D2 1
The Brake *FRCTL/WBN* BS36 .... **33** D3
Bramble Dr
HNLZ/SM/SNYPK/WT BS9 .... **62** A3
Bramble La
HNLZ/SM/SNYPK/WT BS9 .... **62** A3
Bramble Rd *MTN/WRL* BS22 .... **129** D4
The Brambles *KEYN* BS31 .... **106** B4
Bramble Wy *BATHSE* BA2 .... **137** F3
Bramblewood *YTN/CONG* BS49 .... **116** B2
Brambling Wk *MANG/FISH* BS16 .... **50** A5
Bramley Cl *OMX/HUT/LCK* BS24 .... **153** F1
PTSHD/EG BS20 .... **60** A2
YTN/CONG BS49 .... **116** B4
Bramley Ct
OLD/WMLY/WICK BS30 .... **81** D5 2
Bramley La *TRWBR* BA14 .... **157** D5
The Bramleys *NAIL* BS48 .... **86** A4
Brampton Wy *PTSHD/EG* BS20 .... **56** C1
Branche Gv
BMSTRD/HC/WWD BS13 .... **102** B4
Brandash Rd *YATE/CS* BS37 .... **21** D4
Brandon Steep *CBRIS/FH* BS1 .... **2** A3 1
Brandon St *CBRIS/FH* BS1 .... **2** A4
Brangwyn Gv *HORF/LLZ* BS7 .... **48** C5
Brangwyn Sq *MTN/WRL* BS22 .... **129** E5 2
Branksome Crs
BRSTK/PCHW BS34 .... **28** C5 1
Branksome Dr *BRSTK/PCHW* BS34 .... **28** C5
FRCTL/WBN BS36 .... **31** F2
Branksome Rd
RDLND/MONT BS6 .... **63** F3 1
Bransby Wy *OMX/HUT/LCK* BS24 .... **143** F2
Branscombe Rd
HNLZ/SM/SNYPK/WT BS9 .... **62** A2
Branscombe Wk
PTSHD/EG BS20 .... **55** D3 1
Branwhite Cl *HORF/LLZ* BS7 .... **48** C4 1
Brassknocker Hl *BATHSE* BA2 .... **139** D3
Brassmill La *CBATH/BATHN* BA1 .... **121** E3
Bratton Rd
BRSG/KWL/STAPK BS4 .... **92** B5 2
Braunton Rd *BMSTR* BS3 .... **92** A1
Braydon Av *BRSTK/PCHW* BS34 .... **13** E5
Brayne Ct *OLD/WMLY/WICK* BS30 .... **97** D1
Breaches Ga *ALMDB* BS32 .... **30** A2
The Breaches *PTSHD/EG* BS20 .... **59** F2
Breach La *TRWBR* BA14 .... **158** A4
Breach Rd *BMSTR* BS3 .... **91** E1
Brean Down Av
HNLZ/SM/SNYPK/WT BS9 .... **63** F1
WSM BS23 .... **150** C1
Brecknock Rd
BRSG/KWL/STAPK BS4 .... **93** E1
Brecon Rd
HNLZ/SM/SNYPK/WT BS9 .... **46** B5
Brecon Vw *OMX/HUT/LCK* BS24 .... **151** F4
Bredon *YATE/CS* BS37 .... **35** E1
Bredon Cl *KGWD/HNM* BS15 .... **81** D2 2
Bredon Nook Rd
HNBRY/STHM BS10 .... **47** D4 1
Bree Cl *MTN/WRL* BS22 .... **129** F3 2
Brendon Av *WSM* BS23 .... **141** E1
Brendon Cl
OLD/WMLY/WICK BS30 .... **82** A5 1
Brendon Rd *BMSTR* BS3 .... **92** B1 1
PTSHD/EG BS20 .... **55** E1
Brenner St *EVILLE/WHL* BS5 .... **65** F4
Brent Cl *OMX/HUT/LCK* BS24 .... **152** A3 1
Brent Rd *HORF/LLZ* BS7 .... **65** D1
Brentry Av *EVILLE/WHL* BS5 .... **77** F2
Brentry La *HNBRY/STHM* BS10 .... **46** B1
Brentry Rd *MANG/FISH* BS16 .... **66** C2
Brereton Wy
OLD/WMLY/WICK BS30 .... **81** F5
Brewerton Cl *HNBRY/STHM* BS10 .... **27** D5
Brewery Hl *OLD/WMLY/WICK* BS30 .. **99** D4
Briar Cl *NAIL* BS48 .... **87** F2
RDSTK/MIDN BA3 .... **162** A4
Briarfield Av *KGWD/HNM* BS15 .... **80** A4 2
Briar Md *YTN/CONG* BS49 .... **116** A2
Briar Rd *OMX/HUT/LCK* BS24 .... **153** D2
Briarside Rd *HNBRY/STHM* BS10 .... **27** D5
The Briars *NAIL* BS48 .... **87** E5 1
Briar Wk *MANG/FISH* BS16 .... **68** A3
Briar Wy *MANG/FISH* BS16 .... **67** F2
Briarwood
HNLZ/SM/SNYPK/WT BS9 .... **46** A5
Briary Rd *PTSHD/EG* BS20 .... **56** A1
Briavels Gv *RDLND/MONT* BS6 .... **65** D4
Brick La *TRWBR* BA14 .... **157** D1
Brick St *CBRISNE* BS2 .... **3** H1
Bridewell La *CBATH/BATHN* BA1 .... **4** B3 3
Bridewell St *CBRIS/FH* BS1 .... **2** D1 2
Bridge Av *TRWBR* BA14 .... **156** A4
Bridge Cl *HGRV/WHIT* BS14 .... **104** A3 1
Bridge Farm Cl
HGRV/WHIT BS14 .... **103** E4 2
Bridge Farm Sq *YTN/CONG* BS49 .... **133** D2
Bridgeleap Rd *MANG/FISH* BS16 .... **52** A3
Bridge Rd *BATHSE* BA2 .... **122** A5
CFTN/FAIL BS8 .... **74** B3
EVILLE/WHL BS5 .... **65** F3 1
KGWD/HNM BS15 .... **69** D3
WSM BS23 .... **7** F3
YATE/CS BS37 .... **18** B3
Bridges Ct *MANG/FISH* BS16 .... **67** F2 1
Bridges Dr *MANG/FISH* BS16 .... **51** D5 2
Bridge St *BOAV* BA15 .... **147** D3
CBRIS/FH BS1 .... **2** D3
EVILLE/WHL BS5 .... **66** B4 2
Bridge Valley Rd *CFTN/FAIL* BS8 .... **74** C1
Bridge Wk *HORF/LLZ* BS7 .... **48** B3
Bridge Wy *FRCTL/WBN* BS36 .... **16** C5
Bridgman Gv *BRSTK/PCHW* BS34 .... **28** C5
Bridgwater Ct
OMX/HUT/LCK BS24 .... **151** F2
Bridgwater Rd
BMSTRD/HC/WWD BS13 .... **91** D4
OMX/HUT/LCK BS24 .... **151** E5
WSM BS23 .... **151** D3
Briercliffe Rd
HNLZ/SM/SNYPK/WT BS9 .... **45** E4
Brierly Furlong *BRSTK/PCHW* BS34 .. **29** E5
Briery Leaze Rd *HGRV/WHIT* BS14 .. **103** E2
Brighton Crs *BMSTR* BS3 .... **91** F2
Brighton Pk *EVILLE/WHL* BS5 .... **77** F1 1
Brighton Pl *KGWD/HNM* BS15 .... **68** B5 1
Brighton Rd *BRSTK/PCHW* BS34 .... **12** A5
RDLND/MONT BS6 .... **64** A5
WSM BS23 .... **6** D4
Brighton St *CBRISNE* BS2 .... **64** C5
Brighton Ter *BMSTR* BS3 .... **91** F2 2
Bright St *EVILLE/WHL* BS5 .... **77** F2 3
KGWD/HNM BS15 .... **80** B1
Brigstocke Rd *CBRISNE* BS2 .... **64** C5
Brimbles *HORF/LLZ* BS7 .... **48** C1
Brimbleworth La *MTN/WRL* BS22 .... **130** B4
Brimridge Rd *WNSC* BS25 .... **154** C4 2
Brinkworthy Rd *MANG/FISH* BS16 .... **49** E5
Brinmead Wk
BMSTRD/HC/WWD BS13 .... **101** D4 1
Brins Cl *BRSTK/PCHW* BS34 .... **30** A4
Brinsea Rd *YTN/CONG* BS49 .... **133** E4
Briscoes Av
BMSTRD/HC/WWD BS13 .... **102** A3
Bristol Br *CBRIS/FH* BS1 .... **3** E3
Bristol Hl *BRSG/KWL/STAPK* BS4 .... **94** B2
Bristol Rd *BATHSE* BA2 .... **119** F2
FRCTL/WBN BS36 .... **16** A5
HGRV/WHIT BS14 .... **104** A4
KEYN BS31 .... **106** B1
MANG/FISH BS16 .... **31** E5
MTN/WRL BS22 .... **130** A5
OMX/HUT/LCK BS24 .... **130** B5
PTSHD/EG BS20 .... **56** B2
RDSTK/MIDN BA3 .... **162** C1
THNB/SVB BS35 .... **8** B5
WNSC BS25 .... **155** E4
YTN/CONG BS49 .... **133** D1
Bristol Road-Lower *WSM* BS23 .... **141** D2
Bristow Broadway *AVONM* BS11 .... **43** D2
Britannia Crs *BRSTK/PCHW* BS34 .... **29** E3
Britannia Rd *BRSTK/PCHW* BS34 .... **27** E1
EVILLE/WHL BS5 .... **65** F5
KGWD/HNM BS15 .... **80** A1
Britannia Wy *CLVDN* BS21 .... **84** C3 3
British Rd *BMSTR* BS3 .... **92** A1
British Rw *TRWBR* BA14 .... **156** C3
Brittan Pl *PTSHD/EG* BS20 .... **58** C3
Britten Ct *OLD/WMLY/WICK* BS30 .. **81** D5 3
Brixham Rd *BMSTR* BS3 .... **92** A2
Brixton Rd *EVILLE/WHL* BS5 .... **77** F1
Broadbury Rd
BRSG/KWL/STAPK BS4 .... **92** C4
Broadcloth East La *TRWBR* BA14 .... **157** E5
Broadcloth La *TRWBR* BA14 .... **157** E5
Broad Cft *ALMDB* BS32 .... **13** D3 1
Broadcroft Av *YTN/CONG* BS49 .... **117** F2
Broadcroft Cl *YTN/CONG* BS49 .... **117** F2
Broadfield Av *KGWD/HNM* BS15 .... **80** A1
Broadfield Rd
BRSG/KWL/STAPK BS4 .... **93** E3
Broadlands *CLVDN* BS21 .... **85** F1 1
Broadlands Av *KEYN* BS31 .... **106** B1
Broadlands Dr *AVONM* BS11 .... **44** B2
Broad La *FRCTL/WBN* BS36 .... **33** E3
YATE/CS BS37 .... **19** E1
YATE/CS BS37 .... **34** B4
Broadleas *BMSTRD/HC/WWD* BS13 .. **91** F5
Broadleaze *AVONM* BS11 .... **43** F4 1
Broadleaze Wy *WNSC* BS25 .... **154** B2
Broadley Pk *TRWBR* BA14 .... **159** D4
Broadleys Av
HNLZ/SM/SNYPK/WT BS9 .... **46** C4
Broadmead *CBRIS/FH* BS1 .... **3** E1
TRWBR BA14 .... **156** A3
Broadmead La *KEYN* BS31 .... **107** E1
Broadmoor La *CBATH/BATHN* BA1 .. **111** D3
Broadmoor Pk
CBATH/BATHN BA1 .... **111** F5 1
Broadmoor V *CBATH/BATHN* BA1 .... **111** E4
Broadoak Hl *LGASH* BS41 .... **101** D5
Broad Oak Rd
BMSTRD/HC/WWD BS13 .... **101** D3
Broadoak Rd *WSM* BS23 .... **150** C2
Broad Oaks *CFTN/FAIL* BS8 .... **74** C3 2
Broadoak Wk *MANG/FISH* BS16 .... **67** F2
Broad Quay *BATHSE* BA2 .... **4** B5
CBRIS/FH BS1 .... **2** C3
Broad Rd *KGWD/HNM* BS15 .... **68** A5
Broadstone Wk
BMSTRD/HC/WWD BS13 .... **102** B2
Broad St *CBATH/BATHN* BA1 .... **4** B2
CBRIS/FH BS1 .... **2** D2
MANG/FISH BS16 .... **68** C2
TRWBR BA14 .... **156** C3 2
YATE/CS BS37 .... **20** C4
YTN/CONG BS49 .... **133** D2
Broad Wk *BRSG/KWL/STAPK* BS4 .... **93** D2
Broadway *BATHSE* BA2 .... **5** E5
KEYN BS31 .... **108** B4 1
OMX/HUT/LCK BS24 .... **151** E4
YATE/CS BS37 .... **20** A3 1
Broadway Av
HNLZ/SM/SNYPK/WT BS9 .... **47** E5
Broadway Rd
BMSTRD/HC/WWD BS13 .... **101** D2 2
HORF/LLZ BS7 .... **64** B3
Broadways Dr *MANG/FISH* BS16 .... **50** A4 1
Broad Weir *CBRIS/FH* BS1 .... **3** F2
Brock End *PTSHD/EG* BS20 .... **54** C3
Brockhurst Gdns *KGWD/HNM* BS15 .. **79** E1
Brockhurst Rd *KGWD/HNM* BS15 .... **79** E1
Brockley Cl *BRSTK/PCHW* BS34 .... **29** D1 1
NAIL BS48 .... **86** C3 2
OMX/HUT/LCK BS24 .... **151** E4 2
Brockley Crs *OMX/HUT/LCK* BS24 .... **151** E4
Brockley Rd *KEYN* BS31 .... **108** B4
Brockley Wk
BMSTRD/HC/WWD BS13 .... **91** E4 2
Brockridge La *FRCTL/WBN* BS36 .... **33** D1
Brocks Rd
BMSTRD/HC/WWD BS13 .... **102** A4
Brock St *CBATH/BATHN* BA1 .... **4** A1 1

Brockway NAIL BS48 87 E2
Brockworth YATE/CS BS37 35 D2
Brockworth Crs MANG/FISH BS16 50 A5
Bromfield Wk MANG/FISH BS16 52 C4 1
Bromley Dr MANG/FISH BS16 51 E3
Bromley Heath Av
MANG/FISH BS16 51 E3
Bromley Heath Rd
MANG/FISH BS16 51 E3 1
Bromley Rd HORF/LLZ BS7 65 D1
Brompton Cl KGWD/HNM BS15 81 D1
Brompton Rd OMX/HUT/LCK BS24 151 F3
Broncksea Rd HORF/LLZ BS7 48 A2
Brook Cl LGASH BS41 89 F3
Brookcote Dr BRSTK/PCHW BS34 29 E2
Brookdale Rd
BMSTRD/HC/WWD BS13 101 F1
Brookfield Av HORF/LLZ BS7 64 B3 1
Brookfield Cl YATE/CS BS37 21 D4
Brookfield La RDLND/MONT BS6 64 B4 1
Brookfield Pk CBATH/BATHN BA1 111 F5
Brookfield Rd BRSTK/PCHW BS34 12 C5
RDLND/MONT BS6 64 B4 2
Brookfield Wk CLVDN BS21 85 F1
OLD/WMLY/WICK BS30 98 A1 1
Brook Ga BMSTR BS3 90 C3
Brook Hl RDLND/MONT BS6 64 C5
Brookland Rd MTN/WRL BS22 142 A3
RDLND/MONT BS6 64 B1 1
Brook La MANG/FISH BS16 49 F5
RDLND/MONT BS6 65 D5 4
Brooklea OLD/WMLY/WICK BS30 81 F5
Brookleaze
HNLZ/SM/SNYPK/WT BS9 62 A1
Brookleaze Buildings
CBATH/BATHN BA1 113 F5
Brook Lintons
BRSG/KWL/STAPK BS4 94 B1 2
Brooklyn Rd
BMSTRD/HC/WWD BS13 91 F4
CBATH/BATHN BA1 114 A5
Brookmead THNB/SVB BS35 9 D5 3
TRWBR BA14 158 A4
Brook Rd BATHSE BA2 122 B4 1
BMSTR BS3 76 B5 3
EVILLE/WHL BS5 66 C5
KGWD/HNM BS15 81 E1 1
MANG/FISH BS16 52 A5
RDLND/MONT BS6 65 D5
TRWBR BA14 156 A4
Brookside PTSHD/EG BS20 60 B3
Brookside Cl CBATH/BATHN BA1 115 D2
Brookside Dr FRCTL/WBN BS36 16 C5
Brookside Rd
BRSG/KWL/STAPK BS4 94 C2
Brook St EVILLE/WHL BS5 78 A2 2
YATE/CS BS37 20 B4
Brookthorpe YATE/CS BS37 19 E5
Brookthorpe Av AVONM BS11 44 B3
Brookview Wk
BMSTRD/HC/WWD BS13 91 F5
Brook Wy ALMDB BS32 13 D4
Broom Farm Cl NAIL BS48 87 D4 2
Broom Hl MANG/FISH BS16 66 C1
Broomhill Rd
BRSG/KWL/STAPK BS4 95 D1
The Brooms MANG/FISH BS16 52 B1
Brougham Hayes BATHSE BA2 122 B4
Broughton Rd TRWBR BA14 158 B2
Brow Hl CBATH/BATHN BA1 115 D4
Browning Ct HORF/LLZ BS7 48 C3 1
Brownlow Rd WSM BS23 151 D1
Brown St TRWBR BA14 157 D5
The Brow BATHSE BA2 121 F5
Broxholme Wk AVONM BS11 44 A3 1
Bruce Av EVILLE/WHL BS5 66 A5
Bruce Rd EVILLE/WHL BS5 66 A5
Brue Cl WSM BS23 7 G6
Brunel Cl OLD/WMLY/WICK BS30 82 A2
OMX/HUT/LCK BS24 151 E5
Brunel Lock Rd CBRIS/FH BS1 75 D4
Brunel Rd BMSTRD/HC/WWD BS13 91 D4
NAIL BS48 86 A3
Brunel Wy BMSTR BS3 75 D4
THNB/SVB BS35 8 B5
Brunswick Pl CBRIS/FH BS1 75 D4 2
Brunswick Sq CBRISNE BS2 76 C1 3
Brunswick St
CBATH/BATHN BA1 123 F2 1
CBRISNE BS2 76 C1
EVILLE/WHL BS5 78 A2 3
Bruton Av BATHSE BA2 137 D1
PTSHD/EG BS20 55 E1 2
Bruton Cl EVILLE/WHL BS5 79 D1 2
NAIL BS48 87 D4 3
Bryansons Cl MANG/FISH BS16 49 E5 1
Bryant Av RDSTK/MIDN BA3 162 A3
Bryant Gdns CLVDN BS21 84 C3 4
Bryants Cl MANG/FISH BS16 51 D2 1
Bryant's Hl EVILLE/WHL BS5 79 F3
Brynland Av HORF/LLZ BS7 64 C2
Buckingham Dr BRSTK/PCHW BS34 29 E4
Buckingham Gdns
MANG/FISH BS16 51 F5
Buckingham Pl MANG/FISH BS16 51 F5 1
Buckingham Rd
BRSG/KWL/STAPK BS4 78 B4 1
OMX/HUT/LCK BS24 152 A3 2
Buckingham St BMSTR BS3 92 A2 2
Buckingham V CFTN/FAIL BS8 75 E1 1
Buckland Gn MTN/WRL BS22 129 F2 3
Bucklands Batch NAIL BS48 87 E4
Bucklands Dr NAIL BS48 87 E4
Bucklands Gv NAIL BS48 87 E4
Bucklands La NAIL BS48 87 E4
Bucklands Vw NAIL BS48 87 F4
Buckleaze Cl TRWBR BA14 159 D2 1
Budbury Pl BOAV BA15 146 C2
Budbury Rdg BOAV BA15 146 C2
Budbury Tyning BOAV BA15 146 B2
Bude Av EVILLE/WHL BS5 79 E1
Bude Cl NAIL BS48 87 F3
Bude Rd BRSTK/PCHW BS34 28 C5
Buller Rd BRSG/KWL/STAPK BS4 94 A2
Bull La EVILLE/WHL BS5 79 D3
PTSHD/EG BS20 60 A2
Bull Pit BOAV BA15 147 D3 1
Bunting Ct MTN/WRL BS22 143 D1 1
Burbank Cl OLD/WMLY/WICK BS30 97 E1
Burchells Green Cl
KGWD/HNM BS15 79 F1
Burchells Green Rd
KGWD/HNM BS15 67 F5
Burcombe Cl FRCTL/WBN BS36 33 E1
Burcott Rd AVONM BS11 23 D3
Burden Cl ALMDB BS32 29 F2
Burderop Cl TRWBR BA14 159 D2 2
Burfoote Gdns HGRV/WHIT BS14 104 C3
Burfoot Rd HGRV/WHIT BS14 104 C3
Burford Cl BATHSE BA2 135 F2
PTSHD/EG BS20 56 C2
Burford Gv AVONM BS11 61 D1
Burgage Cl YATE/CS BS37 20 C5 1
Burgess Green Cl
BRSG/KWL/STAPK BS4 78 C2 2
Burghill Rd HNBRY/STHM BS10 46 B2
Burghley Ct FRCTL/WBN BS36 31 F3 1
Burghley Rd RDLND/MONT BS6 64 C4
Burgis Rd HGRV/WHIT BS14 104 B1 1
Burleigh Gdns CBATH/BATHN BA1 121 E2
Burley Av MANG/FISH BS16 69 D1
Burley Crest MANG/FISH BS16 52 A5
Burley Gv MANG/FISH BS16 52 A5
Burlington Rd RDLND/MONT BS6 63 F4
RDSTK/MIDN BA3 161 F2
Burlington St
CBATH/BATHN BA1 123 D2 4
WSM BS23 141 D2 2
Burnbush Cl HGRV/WHIT BS14 104 C1
Burnell Dr CBRISNE BS2 77 D1
Burneside Cl HNBRY/STHM BS10 47 D1 1
Burnett Rd TRWBR BA14 159 D1
Burney Wy OLD/WMLY/WICK BS30 97 E1
Burnham Cl KGWD/HNM BS15 69 D5 1
Burnham Dr KGWD/HNM BS15 69 D5
OMX/HUT/LCK BS24 151 E4
Burnham Rd AVONM BS11 43 E5
BATHSE BA2 122 A4
Burnt House Rd BATHSE BA2 136 B5
Burrington Av
OMX/HUT/LCK BS24 151 E4
Burrington Cl NAIL BS48 87 D3 3
Burrington Wk
BMSTRD/HC/WWD BS13 91 E4 3
Burrough Wy FRCTL/WBN BS36 31 F3
Burton Cl CBRIS/FH BS1 3 E6
Burwalls Rd CFTN/FAIL BS8 74 C3
Burycourt Cl AVONM BS11 44 B2 1
Bury Hl MANG/FISH BS16 31 F5
The Bury OMX/HUT/LCK BS24 153 F2
Bush Av BRSTK/PCHW BS34 29 D3
Bushy Pk BRSG/KWL/STAPK BS4 77 D5 2
Butcombe Wk HGRV/WHIT BS14 103 F2
Butlers Cl EVILLE/WHL BS5 79 D2
Butterfield Cl HNBRY/STHM BS10 47 F4
Butterfield Pk CLVDN BS21 84 C3
Butterfield Rd HNBRY/STHM BS10 47 F4
Buttermere Rd WSM BS23 7 H6
WSM BS23 151 F1 1
Butterworth Ct
BRSG/KWL/STAPK BS4 92 B5 3
Butt La THNB/SVB BS35 8 C1
Buxton Wk HORF/LLZ BS7 48 B3
Bye Md MANG/FISH BS16 52 B3
Byfield BATHSE BA2 137 F4
Byfields CLVDN BS21 84 C4
Byron Cl OMX/HUT/LCK BS24 153 E1
Byron Pl CFTN/FAIL BS8 75 F2 2
MANG/FISH BS16 68 C2 1
Byron Rd BATHSE BA2 137 D1
OMX/HUT/LCK BS24 153 F1 2
WSM BS23 151 F1
Byron St CBRISNE BS2 65 E5 6
EVILLE/WHL BS5 78 A2 4
Bythesea Rd TRWBR BA14 156 C4

C

Cabot Cl KEYN BS31 108 B5 1
YATE/CS BS37 20 A4
Cabot Ri PTSHD/EG BS20 55 E1 3
Cabot Wy CFTN/FAIL BS8 75 D3
MTN/WRL BS22 129 F4
PTSHD/EG BS20 60 B3
Cabstand PTSHD/EG BS20 39 E5
Cadbury Farm Rd
YTN/CONG BS49 116 C4
Cadbury Heath Rd
OLD/WMLY/WICK BS30 81 F4
Cadbury La PTSHD/EG BS20 55 D5
Cadbury Rd KEYN BS31 107 E5
PTSHD/EG BS20 56 B2
Cadby Cl TRWBR BA14 157 F4
Caddick Cl KGWD/HNM BS15 69 D4
Cade Cl BRSTK/PCHW BS34 29 F3
KGWD/HNM BS15 81 D3
Cadogan Rd HGRV/WHIT BS14 93 E4
Caen Rd BMSTR BS3 92 B1
Caernarvon Rd KEYN BS31 106 A3
Caine Rd HORF/LLZ BS7 48 A4 1
Cains Cl KGWD/HNM BS15 80 C3
Cairn Cl NAIL BS48 87 F3 1
Cairn Gdns FRCTL/WBN BS36 31 F4 1
Cairns' Crs CBRISNE BS2 65 D5 5
Cairns Rd RDLND/MONT BS6 63 F1
Calcott Rd BRSG/KWL/STAPK BS4 93 E1
Caldbeck Cl HNBRY/STHM BS10 47 E1 2
Calder Cl KEYN BS31 107 E3
Caldicot Cl AVONM BS11 45 D1 1
OLD/WMLY/WICK BS30 97 F2
Caledonian Rd BATHSE BA2 122 B4
Caledonia Pl CFTN/FAIL BS8 75 D3
California Rd
OLD/WMLY/WICK BS30 81 F5 1
Callicroft Rd BRSTK/PCHW BS34 28 B1
Callington Rd
BRSG/KWL/STAPK BS4 94 B3
HGRV/WHIT BS14 94 A3
Callowhill Ct CBRIS/FH BS1 3 E1
Calton Gdns BATHSE BA2 4 B6
Calton Rd BATHSE BA2 4 C6
Camberley Dr FRCTL/WBN BS36 16 A5
Camberley Rd
BRSG/KWL/STAPK BS4 92 B4 1
Camberley Wk MTN/WRL BS22 143 D3
Camborne Rd HORF/LLZ BS7 48 B4
Cambrian Dr YATE/CS BS37 19 F2
Cambridge Crs
HNLZ/SM/SNYPK/WT BS9 46 B4
Cambridge Gv CLVDN BS21 71 D4
Cambridge Pk RDLND/MONT BS6 63 F3
Cambridge Pl WSM BS23 140 C2 1
Cambridge Rd CLVDN BS21 71 D4
HORF/LLZ BS7 64 B2
Cambridge St BMSTR BS3 77 D5
EVILLE/WHL BS5 78 A2 5
Cambridge Ter BATHSE BA2 5 E6
Camden Crs CBATH/BATHN BA1 123 D2
Camden Rd BMSTR BS3 75 F4 1
CBATH/BATHN BA1 123 E1
Camden Rw CBATH/BATHN BA1 123 D2
Camden Ter CFTN/FAIL BS8 75 E3 4
WSM BS23 6 D1 1
Cameley Gn BATHSE BA2 121 D4
Camelford Rd EVILLE/WHL BS5 66 B5 1
Cameron Wk HORF/LLZ BS7 49 D5 1
Cameroons Cl KEYN BS31 106 C2
Camerton Cl KEYN BS31 108 C4 1
Camerton Rd EVILLE/WHL BS5 66 B5 2
Campbell Farm Dr AVONM BS11 44 A2
Campbell St CBRISNE BS2 64 C5
Campion Cl MTN/WRL BS22 142 C3 1
THNB/SVB BS35 9 D2 1
Campion Dr ALMDB BS32 13 E3 2
TRWBR BA14 159 D1
Camp Rd CFTN/FAIL BS8 75 D2
Camp Rd North WSM BS23 140 B1 1
Camp Vw FRCTL/WBN BS36 31 F4
NAIL BS48 86 C2 2
Camwal Rd CBRISNE BS2 77 E4
Canada Coombe
OMX/HUT/LCK BS24 153 E3
Canada Wy CBRIS/FH BS1 75 E4
Canal Rd TRWBR BA14 149 E5
Canberra Crs OMX/HUT/LCK BS24 143 F4
Canberra Gv BRSTK/PCHW BS34 28 C4
Canford La
HNLZ/SM/SNYPK/WT BS9 45 F4
Canford Rd
HNLZ/SM/SNYPK/WT BS9 46 A4
Cannans Cl FRCTL/WBN BS36 31 F1
Cann La OLD/WMLY/WICK BS30 82 C3
Cannons Ga CLVDN BS21 84 C4
Cannon St CBRIS/FH BS1 2 D1
Canons Cl BATHSE BA2 135 F3
Canons Rd CBRIS/FH BS1 2 B5
CBRIS/FH BS1 75 F4
Canon's Wk KGWD/HNM BS15 68 C4

Canons Wy CBRIS/FH BS1 2 A4
Canowie Rd RDLND/MONT BS6 63 F3
Cantell Gv HGRV/WHIT BS14 105 D2 1
Canterbury Cl MTN/WRL BS22 130 A4 1
YATE/CS BS37 19 F2
Canterbury Rd BATHSE BA2 122 B5
Canterbury St EVILLE/WHL BS5 77 F3 3
Canvey Cl HNBRY/STHM BS10 47 F4 1
Canynge Rd CFTN/FAIL BS8 75 D1
Canynge Sq CFTN/FAIL BS8 75 D1
Canynge St CBRIS/FH BS1 3 E4
Capel Cl KGWD/HNM BS15 81 F1
Capell Cl MTN/WRL BS22 142 A2
Capel Rd AVONM BS11 44 C2
Capenor Cl PTSHD/EG BS20 56 A2
Capgrave Cl BRSG/KWL/STAPK BS4 95 E1
Capgrave Crs
BRSG/KWL/STAPK BS4 95 E1
Caraway Gdns EVILLE/WHL BS5 66 A4 6
Carders Cnr TRWBR BA14 157 D5
Cardigan Crs MTN/WRL BS22 142 B2
Cardigan Rd
HNLZ/SM/SNYPK/WT BS9 46 C5
Cardill Cl BMSTRD/HC/WWD BS13 91 E4
Cardinal Cl BATHSE BA2 136 B5 1
Carey's Cl CLVDN BS21 71 F5
Carice Gdns CLVDN BS21 85 D4
Carisbrooke Crs TRWBR BA14 149 E4
Carisbrooke Rd
BRSG/KWL/STAPK BS4 92 B4
Carlingford Terrace Rd
RDSTK/MIDN BA3 163 D2
Carlow Rd BRSG/KWL/STAPK BS4 92 C4
Carlton Pk EVILLE/WHL BS5 78 A1
Carlton Rw TRWBR BA14 158 C1 2
Carlton St WSM BS23 6 B2
Carlyle Rd EVILLE/WHL BS5 66 A5
Carmarthen Cl YATE/CS BS37 20 A1 2
Carmarthen Gv
OLD/WMLY/WICK BS30 97 F3 1
Carmarthen Rd
HNLZ/SM/SNYPK/WT BS9 63 E1 1
Carnarvon Rd RDLND/MONT BS6 64 A4
Caroline Cl KEYN BS31 106 A3
YATE/CS BS37 20 C3 1
Carpenter Cl WSM BS23 7 H2 1
Carpenters La KEYN BS31 106 C2
Carre Gdns MTN/WRL BS22 129 E3
Carrington Rd BMSTR BS3 75 E5
Carsons Rd MANG/FISH BS16 69 F3
Carter Wk ALMDB BS32 13 E5 1
Cartledge Rd EVILLE/WHL BS5 66 A5 1
Cassell Rd MANG/FISH BS16 68 A1
Cassey Bottom La
EVILLE/WHL BS5 79 E2 1
Castle Cl HNBRY/STHM BS10 45 F1
Castle Coombe THNB/SVB BS35 8 C2
Castle Ct BRSG/KWL/STAPK BS4 78 A5
THNB/SVB BS35 8 B3
Castle Farm Rd KGWD/HNM BS15 95 F2
Castle Gdns BATHSE BA2 136 C2
Castle Rd CLVDN BS21 71 D3
KGWD/HNM BS15 68 A4
MTN/WRL BS22 129 D4
OLD/WMLY/WICK BS30 98 A1
Castle St CBRISNE BS2 3 F2
THNB/SVB BS35 8 A2
TRWBR BA14 157 D4
Castle View Rd CLVDN BS21 71 D4
Castlewood Cl CLVDN BS21 71 D5
Caswell La PTSHD/EG BS20 57 D5
Catbrain Hl HNBRY/STHM BS10 26 C2
Catbrain La HNBRY/STHM BS10 26 C2
Catemead CLVDN BS21 84 C4
Cater Rd BMSTRD/HC/WWD BS13 101 F1
Catharine Pl CBATH/BATHN BA1 4 A1 2
Catherine Mead St BMSTR BS3 76 A5
Catherine St AVONM BS11 43 D4
Catherine Wy CBATH/BATHN BA1 115 D2
Catley Gv LGASH BS41 89 F3
Cattistock Dr EVILLE/WHL BS5 79 E3
Cattle Market Rd CBRIS/FH BS1 3 G5
Cattybrook Rd MANG/FISH BS16 53 E5
Cattybrook St EVILLE/WHL BS5 77 F1 5
Caulfield Rd MTN/WRL BS22 129 F3 3
Causeway CLVDN BS21 86 A1
The Causeway FRCTL/WBN BS36 33 D1
YTN/CONG BS49 133 D2
Causeway Vw NAIL BS48 86 B2
Causley Dr OLD/WMLY/WICK BS30 81 D4
Cautletts Cl RDSTK/MIDN BA3 160 C4
Cavan Wk BRSG/KWL/STAPK BS4 92 B3
Cave Dr MANG/FISH BS16 51 E5
Cave Gv MANG/FISH BS16 52 C4
Cavell Ct CLVDN BS21 84 C3
Cavendish Cl KEYN BS31 108 B5
Cavendish Crs
CBATH/BATHN BA1 122 C2 1
Cavendish Gdns
HNLZ/SM/SNYPK/WT BS9 62 A2
Cavendish Rd BRSTK/PCHW BS34 12 A5
CBATH/BATHN BA1 122 C2
HNLZ/SM/SNYPK/WT BS9 63 E1
Caveners Ct MTN/WRL BS22 142 A1
Caversham Dr NAIL BS48 87 F2
Cave St CBRISNE BS2 76 C1
Cecil Av EVILLE/WHL BS5 67 D5
Cecil Rd CFTN/FAIL BS8 75 D1
KGWD/HNM BS15 80 B1
WSM BS23 141 D1
Cedar Av MTN/WRL BS22 142 B1
Cedar Cl BRSTK/PCHW BS34 28 A1
LGASH BS41 89 D3
OLD/WMLY/WICK BS30 81 F5 2
Cedar Dr KEYN BS31 106 B3
Cedar Gv BATHSE BA2 136 B2
HNLZ/SM/SNYPK/WT BS9 62 B1
TRWBR BA14 158 B1
Cedarhurst Rd PTSHD/EG BS20 54 C3
Cedar Pk HNLZ/SM/SNYPK/WT BS9 62 B1
Cedar Ter RDSTK/MIDN BA3 162 A3
Cedar Wy BATHSE BA2 122 C5
FRCTL/WBN BS36 31 E3
NAIL BS48 87 F2
PTSHD/EG BS20 55 F2
Cedric Rd CBATH/BATHN BA1 122 A2
Celandine Cl THNB/SVB BS35 9 D2
Celestine Rd YATE/CS BS37 19 D2
Celia Ter BRSG/KWL/STAPK BS4 79 D3 4
Celtic Wy OMX/HUT/LCK BS24 152 A5
Cemetery La BOAV BA15 147 E2
Cemetery Rd
BRSG/KWL/STAPK BS4 93 E1
Cennick Av KGWD/HNM BS15 68 C5
Centaurus Rd BRSTK/PCHW BS34 27 D1
Central Av KGWD/HNM BS15 80 A4
Central Wy CLVDN BS21 85 D3
Ceres Cl OLD/WMLY/WICK BS30 97 D2
Cerimon Ga BRSTK/PCHW BS34 29 F3 1
Cerney Gdns NAIL BS48 87 F2 3
Cerney La AVONM BS11 60 C1
Cesson Cl YATE/CS BS37 21 D4
Chadleigh Gv
BRSG/KWL/STAPK BS4 92 A5
Chaffinch Dr RDSTK/MIDN BA3 161 E4 2
TRWBR BA14 156 B4 2
The Chaffins CLVDN BS21 85 E2
Chakeshill Cl HNBRY/STHM BS10 27 D5
Chakeshill Dr HNBRY/STHM BS10 27 D5
Chalcombe Cl BRSTK/PCHW BS34 13 D5
Chalcroft Wk
BMSTRD/HC/WWD BS13 100 C3
Chalfield Cl KEYN BS31 107 E5
Chalfont Cl TRWBR BA14 156 A3
Chalfont Rd MTN/WRL BS22 142 B2
Chalford Cl YATE/CS BS37 19 E5
Chalks Rd EVILLE/WHL BS5 78 B1
Challender Av HNBRY/STHM BS10 46 A1
Challoner Ct CBRIS/FH BS1 2 C6
Challow Dr MTN/WRL BS22 128 A5 1
Champion Rd KGWD/HNM BS15 69 E4
Champneys Av
HNBRY/STHM BS10 26 A5 1
Chancel Cl
HNLZ/SM/SNYPK/WT BS9 62 B3
NAIL BS48 86 C3
Chancery St EVILLE/WHL BS5 77 F2
Chandag Rd KEYN BS31 107 E3
Chandler Cl CBATH/BATHN BA1 121 F1
Chandos Rd KEYN BS31 96 C5
RDLND/MONT BS6 63 F5
Channel Hts OMX/HUT/LCK BS24 151 E4
Channell's Hl
HNLZ/SM/SNYPK/WT BS9 46 B3
Channel Rd CLVDN BS21 71 D3
Channel View Crs
PTSHD/EG BS20 55 F1 2
Channel View Rd
PTSHD/EG BS20 55 F1 3
Channon's Hl MANG/FISH BS16 67 D2
Chanterelle Pk BOAV BA15 146 C5
Chantry Cl NAIL BS48 86 B3 1
Chantry Dr MTN/WRL BS22 129 E3
Chantry Gdns TRWBR BA14 158 A4
Chantry Gv AVONM BS11 45 D1 2
Chantry La MANG/FISH BS16 52 A2 1
Chantry Mead Rd BATHSE BA2 136 C2
Chantry Rd CFTN/FAIL BS8 63 F5 1
THNB/SVB BS35 8 B2
Chapel Barton NAIL BS48 86 B3 2
Chapel Cl NAIL BS48 87 D2 1
Chapel Gdns HNBRY/STHM BS10 46 B2
Chapel Green La RDLND/MONT BS6 63 F4
Chapel Hl CLVDN BS21 85 D1
Chapel La AVONM BS11 44 C1
EVILLE/WHL BS5 66 C4
KGWD/HNM BS15 81 F1
MANG/FISH BS16 51 D4
YTN/CONG BS49 117 F3
Chapel Rd
BMSTRD/HC/WWD BS13 101 E1
EVILLE/WHL BS5 65 F5 1
KGWD/HNM BS15 80 A4
Chapel Rw CBATH/BATHN BA1 4 A3
PTSHD/EG BS20 60 A2 1
Chapel St CBRISNE BS2 77 E4
THNB/SVB BS35 8 B4
Chapel Wy BRSG/KWL/STAPK BS4 78 C3
Chaplin Rd EVILLE/WHL BS5 65 F5
Chapter St CBRISNE BS2 76 C1 4
Charbon Ga BRSTK/PCHW BS34 29 F3 2
Charborough Rd
BRSTK/PCHW BS34 48 A1
Chard Cl NAIL BS48 87 E4
Chard Rd CLVDN BS21 85 D3
Chardstock Av
HNLZ/SM/SNYPK/WT BS9 45 D3
Charfield KGWD/HNM BS15 81 E1 2
Charfield Rd HNBRY/STHM BS10 47 D2
Chargrove
OLD/WMLY/WICK BS30 82 A3 3
YATE/CS BS37 35 E1
Charis Av HNBRY/STHM BS10 47 D4
Charlcombe La
CBATH/BATHN BA1 113 D5
Charlcombe View Rd
CBATH/BATHN BA1 113 E5 1
Charlcombe Wy
CBATH/BATHN BA1 113 D5
Charlecombe Rd
HNLZ/SM/SNYPK/WT BS9 46 A5
Charles Av BRSTK/PCHW BS34 29 F4 1
Charles Cl THNB/SVB BS35 8 C1
Charles Pl CFTN/FAIL BS8 75 E3
Charles Rd BRSTK/PCHW BS34 28 C5
Charles St CBATH/BATHN BA1 4 A3 1
CBRIS/FH BS1 76 B1
TRWBR BA14 156 C3
Charlock Rd MTN/WRL BS22 142 C3
Charlotte St CBATH/BATHN BA1 4 A3
CBRIS/FH BS1 2 A3
CBRISNE BS2 77 D1 2
TRWBR BA14 157 D3 1
Charlotte St South CBRIS/FH BS1 2 A3
Charlton Av BRSTK/PCHW BS34 48 A1
WSM BS23 150 C1 1
Charlton Gdns HNBRY/STHM BS10 27 E4
Charlton La HNBRY/STHM BS10 26 B5
RDSTK/MIDN BA3 161 F5
Charlton Mead Dr
HNBRY/STHM BS10 27 E4
Charlton Pk KEYN BS31 106 B2
RDSTK/MIDN BA3 161 E5
Charlton Pl HNBRY/STHM BS10 27 E4 1
Charlton Rd HNBRY/STHM BS10 27 D5
KGWD/HNM BS15 67 F5
RDSTK/MIDN BA3 161 E4
WSM BS23 150 C1
Charlton St EVILLE/WHL BS5 77 F2 4
Charlton Vw PTSHD/EG BS20 56 A1 1
Charminster Rd MANG/FISH BS16 67 F3
Charmouth Rd CBATH/BATHN BA1 121 F3
Charnell Rd MANG/FISH BS16 68 C2
Charnhill Brow MANG/FISH BS16 69 E2
Charnhill Crs MANG/FISH BS16 69 D2
Charnhill Dr MANG/FISH BS16 69 D2
Charnhill Rdg MANG/FISH BS16 69 E2
Charnhill V MANG/FISH BS16 69 D2
Charnwood MANG/FISH BS16 69 E2
Charnwood Rd HGRV/WHIT BS14 103 F4
Charterhouse Cl NAIL BS48 87 E3 1
Charterhouse Rd
EVILLE/WHL BS5 78 B1 3
Charter Rd MTN/WRL BS22 142 A2
Chasefield La MANG/FISH BS16 67 F2 2
Chase Rd KGWD/HNM BS15 68 B4
The Chase MANG/FISH BS16 68 A3 2
Chatcombe YATE/CS BS37 35 F1 1
Chatham Rw CBATH/BATHN BA1 4 C1
Chatsworth Pk THNB/SVB BS35 8 C2
Chatsworth Rd
BRSG/KWL/STAPK BS4 78 A5
MANG/FISH BS16 67 F3
Chatterton Gn
HGRV/WHIT BS14 103 D4 2
Chatterton Rd YATE/CS BS37 19 E4
Chatterton Sq CBRIS/FH BS1 3 F6
Chaucer Rd BATHSE BA2 137 D1
RDSTK/MIDN BA3 161 E4
WSM BS23 151 F1
Chaundey Gv
BMSTRD/HC/WWD BS13 101 F2
Cheapside CBRISNE BS2 77 D1 3
Cheapside St BMSTR BS3 77 D5 3
Cheap St CBATH/BATHN BA1 4 C3 3
Cheddar Cl NAIL BS48 87 E4
Cheddar Gv
BMSTRD/HC/WWD BS13 91 E4
Chedworth KGWD/HNM BS15 68 C3
YATE/CS BS37 34 C1
Chedworth Cl BATHSE BA2 139 D2
Chedworth Rd HORF/LLZ BS7 48 B5
Cheese La CBRISNE BS2 3 F3
Chelford Gv BRSTK/PCHW BS34 12 C5 1
Chelmer Gv KEYN BS31 107 D3
Chelmsford Wk
BRSG/KWL/STAPK BS4 79 D4 2
Chelsea Cl KEYN BS31 107 E2 1
Chelsea Pk EVILLE/WHL BS5 78 A1
Chelsea Rd CBATH/BATHN BA1 122 A3
EVILLE/WHL BS5 65 F5
Chelston Rd BRSG/KWL/STAPK BS4 92 B5
Chelswood Av MTN/WRL BS22 142 B2
Cheltenham La
RDLND/MONT BS6 64 C4 1

Cheltenham Rd *RDLND/MONT* BS6 **64** B5
Cheltenham St *BATHSE* BA2 **122** C5 1
Chelvey Ri *NAIL* BS48 **87** F4
Chelvy Cl *BMSTRD/HC/WWD* BS13 **102** B4
Chelwood Dr *BATHSE* BA2 **136** B4
Chelwood Rd *AVONM* BS11 **43** E4
KEYN BS31 **108** C3
Chepstow Pk *MANG/FISH* BS16 **52** A2 2
Chepstow Rd
BRSG/KWL/STAPK BS4 **92** B4
Chequers Cl
OLD/WMLY/WICK BS30 **98** A1 2
Cherington *KGWD/HNM* BS15 **79** F4
YATE/CS BS37 **35** E2
Cherington Rd *HNBRY/STHM* BS10 **47** D4
NAIL BS48 **87** F3
Cheriton Pl
HNLZ/SM/SNYPK/WT BS9 **46** C4
OLD/WMLY/WICK BS30 **82** A3
Cherry Av *CLVDN* BS21 **85** E2
Cherry Cl *YTN/CONG* BS49 **116** B3
Cherry Garden La
OLD/WMLY/WICK BS30 **97** F2
Cherry Garden Rd
OLD/WMLY/WICK BS30 **98** A3
Cherry Gdns
OLD/WMLY/WICK BS30 **98** A3
TRWBR BA14 **157** D5
Cherry Gv *MANG/FISH* BS16 **52** B5
YTN/CONG BS49 **116** B3
Cherry Hay *CLVDN* BS21 **85** D3
Cherry La *CBRIS/FH* BS1 **76** B1 2
Cherry Rd *LGASH* BS41 **89** D2
NAIL BS48 **86** C3 3
YATE/CS BS37 **20** B4 1
Cherry Tree Cl *KEYN* BS31 **106** A3 2
RDSTK/MIDN BA3 **162** B3
Cherrytree Crs *MANG/FISH* BS16 **68** A4
Cherrytree Rd *KGWD/HNM* BS15 **68** A4
Cherry Wd *OLD/WMLY/WICK* BS30 **97** F2
Cherrywood Ri *MTN/WRL* BS22 **129** E5 3
Cherrywood Rd *MTN/WRL* BS22 **129** E5
Chertsey Rd *RDLND/MONT* BS6 **63** F5
Cherwell Cl *THNB/SVB* BS35 **8** C5 1
Cherwell Rd *KEYN* BS31 **107** E3
Chescombe Rd *YTN/CONG* BS49 **116** B4
Chesham Rd North
MTN/WRL BS22 **142** A2
Chesham Rd South
MTN/WRL BS22 **142** A2
Chesham Wy *KGWD/HNM* BS15 **68** B5 2
Cheshire Cl *YATE/CS* BS37 **19** F2
Chesle Cl *PTSHD/EG* BS20 **54** C3 1
Cheslefield *PTSHD/EG* BS20 **54** C3
Chesle Wy *PTSHD/EG* BS20 **54** C3
Chesley Hl *OLD/WMLY/WICK* BS30 **83** D2
Chessel Cl *ALMDB* BS32 **13** D3
Chessell Av *THNB/SVB* BS35 **11** D3 1
Chessel St *BMSTR* BS3 **91** F1
Chessington Av *HGRV/WHIT* BS14 **103** F2
Chesterfield Av
RDLND/MONT BS6 **64** C4 2
Chesterfield Rd *MANG/FISH* BS16 **68** C1
RDLND/MONT BS6 **64** C4
Chester Park Rd *MANG/FISH* BS16 **67** F4
Chester Rd *EVILLE/WHL* BS5 **66** C5 3
Chesters *OLD/WMLY/WICK* BS30 **81** E5 1
Chester St *EVILLE/WHL* BS5 **65** F4 1
Chesterton Dr *NAIL* BS48 **87** F2 4
The Chestertons *BATHSE* BA2 **125** D2 1
Chestnut Av *MTN/WRL* BS22 **143** F1 2
Chestnut Cha *NAIL* BS48 **87** F2 5
Chestnut Cl *HGRV/WHIT* BS14 **104** C2
RDSTK/MIDN BA3 **162** B3
YTN/CONG BS49 **133** D2 1
Chestnut Ct *MANG/FISH* BS16 **69** E1
Chestnut Dr *THNB/SVB* BS35 **8** C3 1
YATE/CS BS37 **20** B4 2
YTN/CONG BS49 **117** E2
Chestnut Gv *BATHSE* BA2 **136** A1
CLVDN BS21 **71** E5
TRWBR BA14 **158** B2 1
Chestnut Rd *KGWD/HNM* BS15 **69** D3 1
LGASH BS41 **89** F2
MANG/FISH BS16 **51** E5 1
The Chestnuts *WNSC* BS25 **154** C5
Chestnut Wk
BMSTRD/HC/WWD BS13 **101** E1
KEYN BS31 **108** C4
Chestnut Wy *KGWD/HNM* BS15 **69** D3
Chetwode Cl *HNBRY/STHM* BS10 **27** E5
Chevening Cl *BRSTK/PCHW* BS34 **29** E4 2
Cheviot Cl *TRWBR* BA14 **157** E5
Cheviot Dr *THNB/SVB* BS35 **9** E4
Cheviot Wy *OLD/WMLY/WICK* BS30 **82** A4
Chewton Cl *MANG/FISH* BS16 **67** F3
Cheyne Rd
HNLZ/SM/SNYPK/WT BS9 **45** E5
Chichester Wy *YATE/CS* BS37 **19** E2 1
Chilcompton Rd
RDSTK/MIDN BA3 **160** B5
Chillwood Cl *YATE/CS* BS37 **17** F2
Chilmark Rd *TRWBR* BA14 **156** A3
Chiltern Cl *HGRV/WHIT* BS14 **103** F3
OLD/WMLY/WICK BS30 **82** A4
Chiltern Pk *THNB/SVB* BS35 **9** E4
Chilton Rd *BRSG/KWL/STAPK* BS4 **93** E4
CBATH/BATHN BA1 **123** F1
The Chimes *NAIL* BS48 **86** B4
The Chine *MANG/FISH* BS16 **66** B1
Chine Vw *MANG/FISH* BS16 **52** A3
Chiphouse Rd *KGWD/HNM* BS15 **68** C4
Chipperfield Dr *KGWD/HNM* BS15 **69** D5
Chipping Cross *CLVDN* BS21 **84** C4
The Chippings *MANG/FISH* BS16 **66** B1
Chirton Pl *TRWBR* BA14 **159** D1
Chisbury St *EVILLE/WHL* BS5 **66** A3 1
Chittening Rd *AVONM* BS11 **23** F1
Chock La *HNLZ/SM/SNYPK/WT* BS9 **46** B4
Christchurch Av
MANG/FISH BS16 **68** B1 1
Christchurch Cl *NAIL* BS48 **87** D2 2
Christchurch La
MANG/FISH BS16 **68** B1 2
Christchurch Rd *BOAV* BA15 **147** D1
CFTN/FAIL BS8 **75** E2
Christian Cl *MTN/WRL* BS22 **130** A4 2
Christin Ct *TRWBR* BA14 **156** A4
Christmas St *CBRIS/FH* BS1 **2** C2 1
Chubb Cl *OLD/WMLY/WICK* BS30 **81** D4
Church Acre *BOAV* BA15 **146** C2
Church Av *EVILLE/WHL* BS5 **65** F5 2
HNLZ/SM/SNYPK/WT BS9 **62** C2
OLD/WMLY/WICK BS30 **82** A2
Church Cl *BATHSE* BA2 **115** D5
CBATH/BATHN BA1 **115** F5 1
CLVDN BS21 **84** A2
FRCTL/WBN BS36 **16** C5
PTSHD/EG BS20 **56** B1
YTN/CONG BS49 **116** C4
Church Ct *RDSTK/MIDN* BA3 **161** D3
Church Dr *YTN/CONG* BS49 **133** D2 2
Churches *BOAV* BA15 **146** C2
Churchfarm Cl *YATE/CS* BS37 **20** A2
Church Farm Rd *MANG/FISH* BS16 **53** D5
Church Flds *TRWBR* BA14 **158** A2
Church Hayes Cl *NAIL* BS48 **87** D4 4
Church Hayes Dr *NAIL* BS48 **87** D4
Church Hl *BRSG/KWL/STAPK* BS4 **94** C2
RDSTK/MIDN BA3 **163** F2
Churchill Av *CLVDN* BS21 **84** C2
Churchill Cl *CLVDN* BS21 **85** D2 1
OLD/WMLY/WICK BS30 **81** E4 2
Churchill Dr
HNLZ/SM/SNYPK/WT BS9 **45** E4
Churchill Rd *BRSG/KWL/STAPK* BS4 **78** A5
WSM BS23 **7** G2
Churchlands *TRWBR* BA14 **159** D5
Church La *BATHSE* BA2 **138** A1
BMSTR BS3 **92** B1 2
CBATH/BATHN BA1 **115** D3
CBRIS/FH BS1 **3** F4
CFTN/FAIL BS8 **75** F3
FRCTL/WBN BS36 **31** D2
FRCTL/WBN BS36 **33** D2 1
HNBRY/STHM BS10 **45** F1
LGASH BS41 **90** A2
MANG/FISH BS16 **51** F1
NAIL BS48 **86** B3
OLD/WMLY/WICK BS30 **98** C5
OMX/HUT/LCK BS24 **152** C3
PTSHD/EG BS20 **58** C3
RDSTK/MIDN BA3 **161** D3
TRWBR BA14 **158** A2
TRWBR BA14 **159** D5
YTN/CONG BS49 **116** C4
Church Leaze *AVONM* BS11 **43** E5
Church Pde
BRSG/KWL/STAPK BS4 **94** C2 1
Churchpath Rd *PTSHD/EG* BS20 **60** A2
Church Pl *PTSHD/EG* BS20 **60** A2 2
Church Rd *BATHSE* BA2 **138** A4
BMSTR BS3 **76** A5
BMSTRD/HC/WWD BS13 **101** E2
BRSTK/PCHW BS34 **28** B5
BRSTK/PCHW BS34 **29** F5
CBATH/BATHN BA1 **122** A1
CFTN/FAIL BS8 **61** F5
CFTN/FAIL BS8 **73** E1
CFTN/FAIL BS8 **74** B3
EVILLE/WHL BS5 **78** B1
FRCTL/WBN BS36 **16** B4
FRCTL/WBN BS36 **31** F4
HGRV/WHIT BS14 **103** F4
HNLZ/SM/SNYPK/WT BS9 **46** B4
HNLZ/SM/SNYPK/WT BS9 **62** B3
HORF/LLZ BS7 **47** F5
KGWD/HNM BS15 **79** F4
KGWD/HNM BS15 **80** C1
LGASH BS41 **100** B5
MANG/FISH BS16 **50** C4
MANG/FISH BS16 **68** B4
MTN/WRL BS22 **128** C5
OLD/WMLY/WICK BS30 **83** F3
OLD/WMLY/WICK BS30 **98** C4
PTSHD/EG BS20 **59** E2
THNB/SVB BS35 **8** B2
THNB/SVB BS35 **10** B4
YATE/CS BS37 **19** F2
YTN/CONG BS49 **116** C4
Church Rd North *PTSHD/EG* BS20 **56** B1
Church Rd South *PTSHD/EG* BS20 **56** B2
Churchside *MANG/FISH* BS16 **50** C4 1
Church Sq *RDSTK/MIDN* BA3 **161** D3 1
Church St *BATHSE* BA2 **5** F6
BOAV BA15 **146** C3
CBATH/BATHN BA1 **4** C4 4
CBATH/BATHN BA1 **113** D1
CBATH/BATHN BA1 **115** F5
CBRIS/FH BS1 **3** F4
EVILLE/WHL BS5 **65** F5
EVILLE/WHL BS5 **77** F2 5
RDSTK/MIDN BA3 **162** C2
TRWBR BA14 **157** D3
Church Vw *ALMDB* BS32 **12** A1
Church Wk *PTSHD/EG* BS20 **60** A2 3
Churchward Cl *KGWD/HNM* BS15 **79** F4 2
Churchward Rd *MTN/WRL* BS22 **130** A4 3
YATE/CS BS37 **18** C2 1
Churchways *HGRV/WHIT* BS14 **104** A3
Churchways Av *HORF/LLZ* BS7 **47** F5
Churchways Crs *HORF/LLZ* BS7 **47** F5
Churclands Rd *BMSTR* BS3 **91** F2 3
Churston Cl *HGRV/WHIT* BS14 **103** E4 3
The Circle *BATHSE* BA2 **135** F2 1
Circular Rd
HNLZ/SM/SNYPK/WT BS9 **62** C4
Circus Ms *CBATH/BATHN* BA1 **4** B1 2
Circus Pl *CBATH/BATHN* BA1 **4** A1 3
City Rd *CBRISNE* BS2 **76** C1
The Clamp
OLD/WMLY/WICK BS30 **98** A1 3
Clanage Rd *BMSTR* BS3 **74** C5
Clapton Dro *PTSHD/EG* BS20 **56** B5
Clapton La *PTSHD/EG* BS20 **56** B3
Clapton Rd *RDSTK/MIDN* BA3 **160** A3
Clapton Wk
HNLZ/SM/SNYPK/WT BS9 **61** F1
Clare Av *HORF/LLZ* BS7 **64** A3
Clare Gdns *BATHSE* BA2 **136** B4
Claremont Av *HORF/LLZ* BS7 **64** A3
Claremont Buildings
CBATH/BATHN BA1 **123** E1
Claremont Gdns *CLVDN* BS21 **85** E3 1
Claremont Rd *CBATH/BATHN* BA1 **123** F1
HORF/LLZ BS7 **64** B3
Claremont St *EVILLE/WHL* BS5 **65** E5
Claremont Wk
CBATH/BATHN BA1 **123** E1 1
Clarence Av *MANG/FISH* BS16 **68** C1
Clarence Gdns *MANG/FISH* BS16 **68** C1 1
Clarence Grove Rd *WSM* BS23 **6** C6
Clarence Pl *CBATH/BATHN* BA1 **121** F3
CBRISNE BS2 **76** A1 1
Clarence Rd *CBRIS/FH* BS1 **76** C5
CBRISNE BS2 **77** E2
KGWD/HNM BS15 **67** F5
MANG/FISH BS16 **68** B1
TRWBR BA14 **157** F4
Clarence Rd East *WSM* BS23 **6** C6
Clarence Rd North *WSM* BS23 **6** B5
Clarence Rd South *WSM* BS23 **6** A6
Clarence St *CBATH/BATHN* BA1 **123** E2 3
Clarendon Av *TRWBR* BA14 **157** E4
Clarendon Rd *BATHSE* BA2 **5** E6
RDLND/MONT BS6 **64** A4
TRWBR BA14 **157** E4
Clare Rd *EVILLE/WHL* BS5 **65** F4 2
KGWD/HNM BS15 **68** A4
RDLND/MONT BS6 **64** B5
Clare St *EVILLE/WHL* BS5 **78** A1 4
Clare Wk *THNB/SVB* BS35 **8** B2
Clark Cl *NAIL* BS48 **87** F2
Clark Dr *MANG/FISH* BS16 **50** A5
Clarken Cl *NAIL* BS48 **87** D3
Clarken Coombe *LGASH* BS41 **89** E1
Clarke St *BMSTR* BS3 **76** B5 4
Clarkson Av *MTN/WRL* BS22 **142** B1
Clark's Pl *TRWBR* BA14 **157** E4
Clark St *EVILLE/WHL* BS5 **77** E1 7
Clatworthy Dr *HGRV/WHIT* BS14 **93** E5
Claude Av *BATHSE* BA2 **136** A1
Clavell Rd *HNBRY/STHM* BS10 **46** A1
Claverham Cl *YTN/CONG* BS49 **117** D3
Claverham Pk *YTN/CONG* BS49 **117** F2
Claverham Rd *MANG/FISH* BS16 **67** E1 1
YTN/CONG BS49 **117** F3
Claverton Ct *BATHSE* BA2 **138** C1
Claverton Down Rd *BATHSE* BA2 **138** C1
Claverton Dr *BATHSE* BA2 **139** D2
Claverton Rd *KEYN* BS31 **108** B5
Claverton Rd West *KEYN* BS31 **108** B4
Claverton St *BATHSE* BA2 **4** D6
Clay Bottom *EVILLE/WHL* BS5 **66** B4
Clayfield Rd *BRSG/KWL/STAPK* BS4 **94** C1
Clay Hl *EVILLE/WHL* BS5 **66** C4
Clay La *BRSTK/PCHW* BS34 **29** D1
OLD/WMLY/WICK BS30 **98** B4
THNB/SVB BS35 **9** E3
Claymore Crs *KGWD/HNM* BS15 **67** F5 2
Claypiece Rd
BMSTRD/HC/WWD BS13 **101** D3
Claypit Hl *YATE/CS* BS37 **36** C1
Clay Pit Rd
HNLZ/SM/SNYPK/WT BS9 **63** E3

Claypool Rd *KGWD/HNM* BS15 ...... **80** B2
Clayton Cl *PTSHD/EG* BS20 ...... **56** C2 2
Clayton St *AVONM* BS11 ...... **42** B2
EVILLE/WHL BS5 ...... **77** F1 6
Cleave St *CBRISNE* BS2 ...... **65** E4 3
Cleeve Av *MANG/FISH* BS16 ...... **51** F4
Cleevedale Rd *BATHSE* BA2 ...... **137** E4
Cleeve Gdns *MANG/FISH* BS16 ...... **51** E4
Cleeve Gn *BATHSE* BA2 ...... **121** D4
Cleeve Gv *KEYN* BS31 ...... **106** B2
Cleeve Hl *MANG/FISH* BS16 ...... **51** E4
Cleeve Hill Extension
MANG/FISH BS16 ...... **51** F5
Cleeve Lawns *MANG/FISH* BS16 ...... **51** E4
Cleeve Lodge Rd *MANG/FISH* BS16 ...... **51** F4
Cleeve Park Rd *MANG/FISH* BS16 ...... **51** E4
Cleeve Pl *NAIL* BS48 ...... **87** F3 2
Cleeve Rd *BRSG/KWL/STAPK* BS4 ...... **93** F1
MANG/FISH BS16 ...... **51** F5
YATE/CS BS37 ...... **19** F4
Cleeve Wood Rd
MANG/FISH BS16 ...... **51** E4 1
Clement St *CBRISNE* BS2 ...... **77** D1
Clevedale *MANG/FISH* BS16 ...... **51** E4
Clevedon Rd *HORF/LLZ* BS7 ...... **64** B2
PTSHD/EG BS20 ...... **56** A3
RDSTK/MIDN BA3 ...... **161** D2
WSM BS23 ...... **6** B4
Clevedon Ter *RDLND/MONT* BS6 ...... **76** B1 3
Cleveland Cl *THNB/SVB* BS35 ...... **9** E3 1
Cleveland Gdns *TRWBR* BA14 ...... **157** E2
Cleve Rd *BRSTK/PCHW* BS34 ...... **28** B4
Clewson Ri *HGRV/WHIT* BS14 ...... **103** D4 3
Cliff Court Dr *MANG/FISH* BS16 ...... **50** C4
Clifford Gdns *AVONM* BS11 ...... **43** F5
Clifford Rd *MANG/FISH* BS16 ...... **68** A2
Cliff Rd *MTN/WRL* BS22 ...... **127** F5
Clift House Rd *BMSTR* BS3 ...... **75** E5
Clifton Down *CFTN/FAIL* BS8 ...... **75** D1
Clifton Down Rd *CFTN/FAIL* BS8 ...... **75** D2 1
Clifton Gv
HNLZ/SM/SNYPK/WT BS9 ...... **62** C1 1
Clifton Hl *CFTN/FAIL* BS8 ...... **75** E3 5
Clifton Pk *CFTN/FAIL* BS8 ...... **75** E1 2
Clifton Park Rd *CFTN/FAIL* BS8 ...... **75** D1
Clifton Pl *EVILLE/WHL* BS5 ...... **77** E1
Clifton Rd *CFTN/FAIL* BS8 ...... **75** E3
WSM BS23 ...... **6** B5
Clifton St *BMSTR* BS3 ...... **92** A1 1
PTSHD/EG BS20 ...... **56** A4
Clifton V *CFTN/FAIL* BS8 ...... **75** E3
Clifton Vale Cl *CFTN/FAIL* BS8 ...... **75** E3 6
Cliftonwood Crs *CFTN/FAIL* BS8 ...... **75** F3 2
Clifton Wood Rd *CFTN/FAIL* BS8 ...... **75** F3
Cliftonwood Ter *CFTN/FAIL* BS8 ...... **75** E3 7
Clift Pl *CBRIS/FH* BS1 ...... **2** D5
Clift Rd *BMSTR* BS3 ...... **75** E5
Clinton Rd *BMSTR* BS3 ...... **92** A2
Clipsham Ri *TRWBR* BA14 ...... **156** A3
Clive Rd *HGRV/WHIT* BS14 ...... **94** A5
Cloford Cl *TRWBR* BA14 ...... **156** A3
Cloisters Rd *FRCTL/WBN* BS36 ...... **31** F2
Clonmel Rd *BRSG/KWL/STAPK* BS4 ...... **92** B3
Closemead *CLVDN* BS21 ...... **85** D3 1
The Close *BRSTK/PCHW* BS34 ...... **13** D4
FRCTL/WBN BS36 ...... **33** D2
HNBRY/STHM BS10 ...... **26** A3
MANG/FISH BS16 ...... **68** B3
PTSHD/EG BS20 ...... **55** D5
Clothier Leaze *TRWBR* BA14 ...... **157** D5
Clothier Rd
BRSG/KWL/STAPK BS4 ...... **95** D2 1
Cloth Yd *TRWBR* BA14 ...... **159** D1
Clouds Hill Av *EVILLE/WHL* BS5 ...... **78** C1
Clouds Hill Rd *EVILLE/WHL* BS5 ...... **79** D1
Clovelly Cl *EVILLE/WHL* BS5 ...... **79** D1
Clovelly Rd *EVILLE/WHL* BS5 ...... **79** D1
MTN/WRL BS22 ...... **129** F5
Clover Cl *CLVDN* BS21 ...... **85** F1
Clover Ct *MTN/WRL* BS22 ...... **142** C3
Cloverdale Dr
OLD/WMLY/WICK BS30 ...... **97** E1
Clover Gnd
HNLZ/SM/SNYPK/WT BS9 ...... **46** C3
Cloverlea Rd
OLD/WMLY/WICK BS30 ...... **82** A4
Clover Leaze *BRSTK/PCHW* BS34 ...... **29** E2
Clover Rd *MTN/WRL* BS22 ...... **129** F1
Clyde Av *KEYN* BS31 ...... **107** D3
Clyde Gdns *BATHSE* BA2 ...... **121** F4
EVILLE/WHL BS5 ...... **79** F3 2
Clyde Gv *BRSTK/PCHW* BS34 ...... **48** A1
Clyde La *RDLND/MONT* BS6 ...... **63** F4
Clyde Rd *BRSG/KWL/STAPK* BS4 ...... **93** E1
FRCTL/WBN BS36 ...... **16** C5
RDLND/MONT BS6 ...... **63** F4
Clydesdale Cl *HGRV/WHIT* BS14 ...... **93** D5
TRWBR BA14 ...... **158** C2
Clyde Ter *BMSTR* BS3 ...... **92** A1
BRSG/KWL/STAPK BS4 ...... **93** E1 2
Clynder Gv *CLVDN* BS21 ...... **71** E3
Coach Rd *BOAV* BA15 ...... **146** C3 1
Coalbridge Cl *MTN/WRL* BS22 ...... **129** E5
Coaley Rd *AVONM* BS11 ...... **60** B1
Coalpit Rd *CBATH/BATHN* BA1 ...... **115** E3
Coalsack La *FRCTL/WBN* BS36 ...... **32** C5
Coalville Rd *FRCTL/WBN* BS36 ...... **33** E1
Coape Rd *HGRV/WHIT* BS14 ...... **105** D2
Coates Gv *NAIL* BS48 ...... **87** F2 6
Cobblestone Ms *CFTN/FAIL* BS8 ...... **75** E2
Cobden St *EVILLE/WHL* BS5 ...... **78** A2
Coberley *KGWD/HNM* BS15 ...... **80** A3
Cobhorn Dr
BMSTRD/HC/WWD BS13 ...... **101** D3
Cobley Cft *CLVDN* BS21 ...... **84** C4
Cobourg Rd *RDLND/MONT* BS6 ...... **65** D5
Cobthorn Wy *YTN/CONG* BS49 ...... **133** E1
Cock Hl *TRWBR* BA14 ...... **156** A3
Cock Rd *KGWD/HNM* BS15 ...... **80** C3
Codrington Pl *CFTN/FAIL* BS8 ...... **75** E2 3
Codrington Rd *HORF/LLZ* BS7 ...... **64** B3
Cogan Rd *MANG/FISH* BS16 ...... **68** C3
Cogsall Rd *HGRV/WHIT* BS14 ...... **105** D1 1
Coker Rd *MTN/WRL* BS22 ...... **129** F5
Colbourne Rd *BATHSE* BA2 ...... **136** B4
Colchester Crs
BRSG/KWL/STAPK BS4 ...... **92** B5
Coldharbour La *BRSTK/PCHW* BS34 .. **49** F2
MANG/FISH BS16 ...... **49** F3
Coldharbour Rd *RDLND/MONT* BS6 .. **63** F3
Coldpark Gdns
BMSTRD/HC/WWD BS13 ...... **100** C2
Coldpark Rd
BMSTRD/HC/WWD BS13 ...... **100** C2
Coldrick Cl *HGRV/WHIT* BS14 ...... **103** D4
Colebrook Rd *KGWD/HNM* BS15 ...... **80** A1
Coleford Rd *HNBRY/STHM* BS10 ...... **47** E3
Colehouse La *CLVDN* BS21 ...... **84** C4
Colemead
BMSTRD/HC/WWD BS13 ...... **101** F2
Coleridge Rd *CLVDN* BS21 ...... **84** C1 2
EVILLE/WHL BS5 ...... **66** A3 2
WSM BS23 ...... **151** F2
Coleridge Vale Rd East
CLVDN BS21 ...... **85** D2 2
Coleridge Vale Rd North
CLVDN BS21 ...... **84** C2
Coleridge Vale Rd South
CLVDN BS21 ...... **84** C2
Coleridge Vale Rd West
CLVDN BS21 ...... **84** C2 1
Cole Rd *CBRISNE* BS2 ...... **77** F3
Colesborne Cl *YATE/CS* BS37 ...... **19** F5 1
Coleshill Dr
BMSTRD/HC/WWD BS13 ...... **101** F2
Colin Cl *THNB/SVB* BS35 ...... **8** B3
College Av *MANG/FISH* BS16 ...... **67** E1 2
College Ct *MANG/FISH* BS16 ...... **67** E1
College Flds *CFTN/FAIL* BS8 ...... **75** D1
College Gdns *TRWBR* BA14 ...... **159** D4 1
College Gn *CBRIS/FH* BS1 ...... **2** B3
College Park Dr
HNBRY/STHM BS10 ...... **46** A2
College Rd *CBATH/BATHN* BA1 ...... **122** C1
CFTN/FAIL BS8 ...... **75** D1
HNLZ/SM/SNYPK/WT BS9 ...... **46** B4
MANG/FISH BS16 ...... **67** E1
TRWBR BA14 ...... **158** B1
College Sq *CBRIS/FH* BS1 ...... **2** A4
College St *CBRIS/FH* BS1 ...... **2** A3
Collett Cl *KGWD/HNM* BS15 ...... **79** F4 3
MTN/WRL BS22 ...... **130** B3 1
Collett Wy *YATE/CS* BS37 ...... **19** D2
Colliers Break *MANG/FISH* BS16 ...... **69** F1
Colliers La *CBATH/BATHN* BA1 ...... **113** D3
Collingbourne Cl *TRWBR* BA14 .... **159** D2 3
Collingwood Av
KGWD/HNM BS15 ...... **68** C5 1
Collingwood Cl *KEYN* BS31 ...... **108** C5
MTN/WRL BS22 ...... **129** D3 2
Collingwood Rd
RDLND/MONT BS6 ...... **63** F5 2
Collin Rd *BRSG/KWL/STAPK* BS4 ...... **78** B5
Collins Av *BRSTK/PCHW* BS34 ...... **29** D2
Collinson Rd
BMSTRD/HC/WWD BS13 ...... **101** F2
Collins St *AVONM* BS11 ...... **42** C3
Colliter Crs *BMSTR* BS3 ...... **91** E2
Coln Sq *THNB/SVB* BS35 ...... **8** C4
Colombo Crs *WSM* BS23 ...... **151** D2
Colston Av *CBRIS/FH* BS1 ...... **2** C3
Colston Cl *FRCTL/WBN* BS36 ...... **31** F4
MANG/FISH BS16 ...... **68** B3 2
Colston Dl *MANG/FISH* BS16 ...... **66** C2
Colston Hl *MANG/FISH* BS16 ...... **66** B2
Colston Pde *CBRIS/FH* BS1 ...... **3** E5
Colston Rd *EVILLE/WHL* BS5 ...... **66** A5
Colston St *CBRIS/FH* BS1 ...... **2** C2
MANG/FISH BS16 ...... **68** B3
Colthurst Dr *KGWD/HNM* BS15 ...... **80** B4
Colts Gn *YATE/CS* BS37 ...... **21** F5
Colwyn Rd *EVILLE/WHL* BS5 ...... **66** A5 2
Combe Av *PTSHD/EG* BS20 ...... **39** D5
Combe Cross Wk
BMSTRD/HC/WWD BS13 ...... **101** F4 1
Combe Flds *PTSHD/EG* BS20 ...... **39** D5
Combe Gv *CBATH/BATHN* BA1 ...... **121** F3
Combe Pk *CBATH/BATHN* BA1 ...... **122** A2
Combermere *THNB/SVB* BS35 ...... **9** D4
Combe Rd *BATHSE* BA2 ...... **137** F4
PTSHD/EG BS20 ...... **56** B1
Combe Road Cl *BATHSE* BA2 ...... **137** F4 1
Combe Side *NAIL* BS48 ...... **87** F5 1
Combfactory La *EVILLE/WHL* BS5 .. **77** F1 7
Comb Paddock
HNLZ/SM/SNYPK/WT BS9 ...... **46** C4
Commercial Rd *CBRIS/FH* BS1 ...... **2** C6
The Common (East) *ALMDB* BS32 ...... **13** D4
Commonfield Rd *AVONM* BS11 ...... **44** C2
Common La *PTSHD/EG* BS20 ...... **59** F5
Common Mead La
MANG/FISH BS16 ...... **50** B2
Common Rd *FRCTL/WBN* BS36 ...... **32** A1 1
KGWD/HNM BS15 ...... **95** F1
The Common *BRSTK/PCHW* BS34 ...... **12** C4
MANG/FISH BS16 ...... **50** C4
Compton Gn *KEYN* BS31 ...... **106** C3
Compton St *EVILLE/WHL* BS5 ...... **78** A2
Comyn Wk *MANG/FISH* BS16 ...... **67** E1
Concorde Dr *CLVDN* BS21 ...... **84** B3 1
HNBRY/STHM BS10 ...... **46** C1 1
Condor Cl *MTN/WRL* BS22 ...... **142** C2 1
Condover Rd
BRSG/KWL/STAPK BS4 ...... **95** D1
Conduit Pl *CBRISNE* BS2 ...... **65** E5 7
Conduit Rd *CBRISNE* BS2 ...... **65** E5
Conference Av *PTSHD/EG* BS20 ...... **56** C1
Congleton Rd *EVILLE/WHL* BS5 ...... **78** B1 4
Conham Hl *KGWD/HNM* BS15 ...... **79** E4
Conham Rd *KGWD/HNM* BS15 ...... **79** D4
Conham V *KGWD/HNM* BS15 ...... **79** D4
Conifer Cl *FRCTL/WBN* BS36 ...... **16** B4
MANG/FISH BS16 ...... **51** E5 2
Conifer Wy *OMX/HUT/LCK* BS24 ...... **143** E5
Conigre Hl *BOAV* BA15 ...... **146** C2
Coniston Av
HNLZ/SM/SNYPK/WT BS9 ...... **45** F5
Coniston Cl
OLD/WMLY/WICK BS30 ...... **82** B3 2
Coniston Crs *WSM* BS23 ...... **151** E1
Coniston Rd *TRWBR* BA14 ...... **157** E2
Connaught Pl *WSM* BS23 ...... **140** C2 2
Connaught Rd
BRSG/KWL/STAPK BS4 ...... **92** C4
Connection Rd *BATHSE* BA2 ...... **121** E4 1
Constable Cl *KEYN* BS31 ...... **107** D1 1
Constable Dr *MTN/WRL* BS22 ...... **129** E4 2
Constable Rd *HORF/LLZ* BS7 ...... **48** B5
Constantine Av *BRSTK/PCHW* BS34 .. **29** F3
Constitution Hl *CFTN/FAIL* BS8 ...... **75** E3
Convent Cl *HNBRY/STHM* BS10 ...... **25** E5
Conway Gn *KEYN* BS31 ...... **107** E4
Conway Rd *BRSG/KWL/STAPK* BS4 .... **78** A5
Conygar Cl *CLVDN* BS21 ...... **71** F4
Conygre Gv *BRSTK/PCHW* BS34 .... **29** D5 1
Conygre Rd *BRSTK/PCHW* BS34 ...... **28** C5
Cook Cl *OLD/WMLY/WICK* BS30 ...... **82** A5
Cooks Cl *ALMDB* BS32 ...... **13** D2
Cook's Folly Rd
HNLZ/SM/SNYPK/WT BS9 ...... **62** B3 1
Cooks La *FRCTL/WBN* BS36 ...... **33** E5
Cooksley Rd *EVILLE/WHL* BS5 ...... **78** A1
Cook St *AVONM* BS11 ...... **42** C3
Cookworthy Cl *EVILLE/WHL* BS5 .... **77** F3 4
Coombe Av *THNB/SVB* BS35 ...... **8** B2 1
Coombe Bridge Av
HNLZ/SM/SNYPK/WT BS9 ...... **45** E5
Coombe Cl *HNBRY/STHM* BS10 ...... **25** E5 1
Coombe Dl
HNLZ/SM/SNYPK/WT BS9 ...... **45** D5
Coombe Gdns
HNLZ/SM/SNYPK/WT BS9 ...... **45** F5
Coombe Hay La *BATHSE* BA2 ...... **136** A5 1
Coombe La *CFTN/FAIL* BS8 ...... **59** D5
HNLZ/SM/SNYPK/WT BS9 ...... **45** E5
Coombe Rd *EVILLE/WHL* BS5 ...... **66** A4 7
NAIL BS48 ...... **86** C3
WSM BS23 ...... **141** D2
Coombes Wy
OLD/WMLY/WICK BS30 ...... **82** B5
Coombe Wy *HNBRY/STHM* BS10 ...... **46** A2
Cooperage La *BMSTR* BS3 ...... **75** F4
Cooperage Rd *EVILLE/WHL* BS5 ...... **78** A2
Co-operation Rd *EVILLE/WHL* BS5 .... **66** A5
Cooper Rd
HNLZ/SM/SNYPK/WT BS9 ...... **46** A4
THNB/SVB BS35 ...... **8** B5
The Coots *HGRV/WHIT* BS14 ...... **104** C1
Copeland Dr *HGRV/WHIT* BS14 .... **103** F2 2
Copford La *LGASH* BS41 ...... **89** F3
Copley Ct *KGWD/HNM* BS15 ...... **80** C4 1
Copley Gdns *HORF/LLZ* BS7 ...... **48** C5 1
MTN/WRL BS22 ...... **129** E5
Copperfield Dr *MTN/WRL* BS22 ...... **129** E3
Coppice Hl *BOAV* BA15 ...... **147** D2
The Coppice *ALMDB* BS32 ...... **29** F1
BMSTRD/HC/WWD BS13 ...... **100** C3
Copse Cl *OMX/HUT/LCK* BS24 ...... **151** F4
Copse End *WNSC* BS25 ...... **154** B2
Copseland *BATHSE* BA2 ...... **124** B5
Copse Rd *BRSG/KWL/STAPK* BS4 ...... **93** F1
CLVDN BS21 ...... **70** C5
KEYN BS31 ...... **108** A3
Copthorne Cl *HGRV/WHIT* BS14 ...... **103** F2
Coralberry Dr *MTN/WRL* BS22 ...... **143** E1

Corbet Cl *AVONM* BS11 44 C1
Corbin Rd *TRWBR* BA14 157 F3
Cordwell Wk *HNBRY/STHM* BS10 47 E4 1
Corey Cl *CBRISNE* BS2 65 D5 6
Corfe Cl *NAIL* BS48 86 C3 4
Corfe Crs *KEYN* BS31 106 C2
Corfe Pl *OLD/WMLY/WICK* BS30 97 F3
Corfe Rd *BRSG/KWL/STAPK* BS4 92 B5 4
Coriander Dr *ALMDB* BS32 30 B1
Coriander Wk *EVILLE/WHL* BS5 66 A4 8
Cork St *CBATH/BATHN* BA1 122 B3
Cormorant Cl *MTN/WRL* BS22 143 E1 3
Corner Cft *CLVDN* BS21 85 D3 2
Cornfield Cl *ALMDB* BS32 13 D4
The Cornfields *MTN/WRL* BS22 129 E2
Cornhill Dr *HGRV/WHIT* BS14 93 E5
Cornish Gv *HGRV/WHIT* BS14 104 C1 2
Cornish Rd *HGRV/WHIT* BS14 104 C1
Cornish Wk *HGRV/WHIT* BS14 104 C1
Cornleaze
BMSTRD/HC/WWD BS13 101 E2 1
Corn St *CBATH/BATHN* BA1 4 B4
CBRIS/FH BS1 2 D3
Cornwall Crs *YATE/CS* BS37 20 A2
Cornwallis Av *CFTN/FAIL* BS8 75 D3 2
MTN/WRL BS22 129 D3
Cornwallis Crs *CFTN/FAIL* BS8 75 D3
Cornwall Rd *HORF/LLZ* BS7 64 B2
Coronation Av *BATHSE* BA2 136 A2
KEYN BS31 106 B3
MANG/FISH BS16 67 E2
Coronation Cl
OLD/WMLY/WICK BS30 81 E4 3
Coronation Pl *CBRIS/FH* BS1 2 D3 2
Coronation Rd *BMSTR* BS3 75 E5
CBATH/BATHN BA1 122 B3 2
KGWD/HNM BS15 81 E2
MANG/FISH BS16 68 C1
MTN/WRL BS22 129 D5
OLD/WMLY/WICK BS30 81 F4
Corondale Rd *MTN/WRL* BS22 142 C2
Corsley Wk
BRSG/KWL/STAPK BS4 93 D4 2
Corston La *BATHSE* BA2 119 E2
Corston Vw *BATHSE* BA2 136 A3
Corston Wk *AVONM* BS11 43 E4
Cossham Cl *THNB/SVB* BS35 8 C2 1
Cossham Rd *EVILLE/WHL* BS5 78 B1
Cossham St *MANG/FISH* BS16 69 F1
Cossham Wk *EVILLE/WHL* BS5 67 E5
Cossington Rd
BRSG/KWL/STAPK BS4 93 D4
Cossins Rd *RDLND/MONT* BS6 63 F3
Costiland Dr
BMSTRD/HC/WWD BS13 101 D1 1
Cote Dr *HNLZ/SM/SNYPK/WT* BS9 63 E2
Cote House La
HNLZ/SM/SNYPK/WT BS9 63 E1
Cote La *HNLZ/SM/SNYPK/WT* BS9 63 E1
Cote Lea Pk
HNLZ/SM/SNYPK/WT BS9 46 B4 1
Cote Paddock
HNLZ/SM/SNYPK/WT BS9 63 E2
Cote Pk *HNLZ/SM/SNYPK/WT* BS9 45 F5
Cote Rd *HNLZ/SM/SNYPK/WT* BS9 63 E2
Cotham Brow *RDLND/MONT* BS6 64 B4 3
Cotham Gdns *RDLND/MONT* BS6 63 F5 3
Cotham Gv *RDLND/MONT* BS6 64 B5
Cotham Hl *RDLND/MONT* BS6 63 F5 4
Cotham Lawn Rd
RDLND/MONT BS6 76 A1
Cotham Pk *RDLND/MONT* BS6 64 A5
Cotham Pk North
RDLND/MONT BS6 64 A5
Cotham Rd *RDLND/MONT* BS6 76 A1
Cotham Rd South
RDLND/MONT BS6 76 B1
Cotham Side *RDLND/MONT* BS6 64 B5
Cotham V *RDLND/MONT* BS6 64 A5
Cotman Wk *HORF/LLZ* BS7 48 C5
MTN/WRL BS22 129 E5 4
Cotrith Gv *HNBRY/STHM* BS10 25 F5
Cotswold Cl *PTSHD/EG* BS20 56 C2 3
Cotswold Rd *BATHSE* BA2 136 B1
BMSTR BS3 92 B1
YATE/CS BS37 20 C5
Cotswold Vw *BATHSE* BA2 121 F5
KGWD/HNM BS15 68 B4
Cottage Pl *CBRISNE* BS2 76 B1 4
Cottington Ct *KGWD/HNM* BS15 80 C4 2
Cottisford Rd *EVILLE/WHL* BS5 65 F2
Cottle Gdns *HGRV/WHIT* BS14 105 D1
Cottle Rd *HGRV/WHIT* BS14 105 D1
Cottonwood Dr
OLD/WMLY/WICK BS30 97 E1
Cottrell Av *KGWD/HNM* BS15 67 F4
Cottrell Rd *EVILLE/WHL* BS5 66 A3
Coulson Dr *MTN/WRL* BS22 130 A4
Coulson's Cl *HGRV/WHIT* BS14 103 E4 4
Coulson's Rd *HGRV/WHIT* BS14 103 D4
Coulson Wk *KGWD/HNM* BS15 68 A4 1
Counterpool Rd *KGWD/HNM* BS15 80 A2
Counterslip *CBRIS/FH* BS1 3 E3
Counterslip Gdns
HGRV/WHIT BS14 104 A1
Countess Wk *MANG/FISH* BS16 49 E5 2
County St *BRSG/KWL/STAPK* BS4 77 E5
County Wy *TRWBR* BA14 156 C5
Court Av *BRSTK/PCHW* BS34 30 A3 2
YTN/CONG BS49 116 B4
Court Cl *HORF/LLZ* BS7 47 F4
PTSHD/EG BS20 56 B2
Courtenay Rd *KEYN* BS31 107 E5
Courteney Crs
BRSG/KWL/STAPK BS4 92 B5 5
Court Farm Rd *HGRV/WHIT* BS14 103 D4
OLD/WMLY/WICK BS30 96 B3
Courtfield Gv *MANG/FISH* BS16 67 E2
Court Gdns *CBATH/BATHN* BA1 115 E4
Courtlands *ALMDB* BS32 13 D4
KEYN BS31 106 C2
Courtlands La *BMSTR* BS3 74 C5
Court La *CBATH/BATHN* BA1 115 F5
OLD/WMLY/WICK BS30 83 F4
Courtney Rd *KGWD/HNM* BS15 80 C2
Courtney Wy *KGWD/HNM* BS15 81 E2
Court Pl *MTN/WRL* BS22 129 E5 5
Court Rd *FRCTL/WBN* BS36 16 A5
HORF/LLZ BS7 48 A5
KGWD/HNM BS15 80 B2
MTN/WRL BS22 127 F2
OLD/WMLY/WICK BS30 97 F1
Courtside Ms *RDLND/MONT* BS6 64 A5 1
Court St *TRWBR* BA14 156 C4
Cousins Cl *HNBRY/STHM* BS10 25 E5 2
Cousins Ms
BRSG/KWL/STAPK BS4 79 D3 5
Cousins Wy *MANG/FISH* BS16 52 B3
Couzens Cl *YATE/CS* BS37 20 C3
Couzens Pl *BRSTK/PCHW* BS34 30 A3 3
Coventry Wk
BRSG/KWL/STAPK BS4 79 D3 6
Cowdray Rd
BRSG/KWL/STAPK BS4 92 B5 6
Cowhorn Hl *OLD/WMLY/WICK* BS30 82 A5
Cowler Wk
BMSTRD/HC/WWD BS13 101 D3 2
Cowling Dr *HGRV/WHIT* BS14 104 A2
Cowling Rd *HGRV/WHIT* BS14 104 A2
Cowper Rd *RDLND/MONT* BS6 63 F5
Cowper St *EVILLE/WHL* BS5 78 A2 6
Cox Ct *OLD/WMLY/WICK* BS30 81 D5
Coxley Dr *CBATH/BATHN* BA1 113 F5
Coxway *CLVDN* BS21 85 E2
Crabtree Wk *EVILLE/WHL* BS5 66 B4 3
Cradock Cl
OLD/WMLY/WICK BS30 81 F5 3
Cranberry Wk
HNLZ/SM/SNYPK/WT BS9 45 D3 2
Cranbourne Cha *WSM* BS23 141 F1
Cranbourne Rd *BRSTK/PCHW* BS34 28 A1
Cranbrook Rd *RDLND/MONT* BS6 64 A3
Crandale Rd *BATHSE* BA2 122 B5
Crandell Cl *HNBRY/STHM* BS10 26 A4
Crane Cl *KGWD/HNM* BS15 81 F1 1
Cranford Cl *MTN/WRL* BS22 142 C1
Cranham *YATE/CS* BS37 35 D1 1
Cranham Cl *KGWD/HNM* BS15 69 D4 1
Cranham Dr *BRSTK/PCHW* BS34 13 D4
Cranham Rd *HNBRY/STHM* BS10 47 D3
Cranhill Rd *CBATH/BATHN* BA1 122 B2
Cranleigh *BATHSE* BA2 137 D5
Cranleigh Court Rd
YATE/CS BS37 19 E3 1
Cranleigh Gdns
HNLZ/SM/SNYPK/WT BS9 62 C2
Cranleigh Rd *HGRV/WHIT* BS14 103 F2 3
Cranmoor Gn *THNB/SVB* BS35 11 E3
Cranmore Av *KEYN* BS31 106 C1
Cranmore Cl *TRWBR* BA14 156 B3
Cranmore Crs *HNBRY/STHM* BS10 47 E2
Cranmore Pl *BATHSE* BA2 136 B5
Cranside Av *RDLND/MONT* BS6 64 A3
Cransley Crs
HNLZ/SM/SNYPK/WT BS9 47 D4
Crantock Av
BMSTRD/HC/WWD BS13 91 F4
Crantock Rd *YATE/CS* BS37 19 E4
Cranwell Gv *HGRV/WHIT* BS14 103 E2
Cranwell Rd *OMX/HUT/LCK* BS24 144 B5
Cranwells Pk *CBATH/BATHN* BA1 122 B2
Craven Cl *OLD/WMLY/WICK* BS30 81 D4
Craven Wy *OLD/WMLY/WICK* BS30 81 D4
Crawford Cl *CLVDN* BS21 84 B3 2
Crawley Crs *TRWBR* BA14 156 A4
Craydon Gv *HGRV/WHIT* BS14 104 B3
Craydon Rd *HGRV/WHIT* BS14 104 B2
Craydon Wk *HGRV/WHIT* BS14 104 B2 1
Crediton Crs *BRSG/KWL/STAPK* BS4 93 D3
Crescent La *CBATH/BATHN* BA1 122 C2
Crescent Rd *MANG/FISH* BS16 51 D5
The Crescent
HNLZ/SM/SNYPK/WT BS9 45 D5
HNLZ/SM/SNYPK/WT BS9 47 D5
MANG/FISH BS16 50 A2
MANG/FISH BS16 68 B3
MTN/WRL BS22 128 A5
OLD/WMLY/WICK BS30 83 F2
Crescent Vw *BATHSE* BA2 4 A6
Cresswell Cl *MTN/WRL* BS22 129 F5 2
The Crest *BRSG/KWL/STAPK* BS4 94 A2
Creswicke Av *KGWD/HNM* BS15 80 A4 3
Creswicke Rd
BRSG/KWL/STAPK BS4 92 C5
Crew's Hole Rd *EVILLE/WHL* BS5 79 D3 7
Cribbs Cswy *HNBRY/STHM* BS10 26 C1
Cricklade Ct *NAIL* BS48 87 F3 3
Cricklade Rd *HORF/LLZ* BS7 64 C2
Cripps Rd *BMSTR* BS3 92 A1
Crispin La *THNB/SVB* BS35 8 B3 1
Crispin Wy *KGWD/HNM* BS15 69 D4
Crockerne Dr *PTSHD/EG* BS20 60 A3
Croft Av *MANG/FISH* BS16 66 A2 1
Croft Cl *OLD/WMLY/WICK* BS30 98 B4
Crofters Wk *ALMDB* BS32 13 E5
Crofton Av *HORF/LLZ* BS7 48 A5 1
Croft Rd *CBATH/BATHN* BA1 123 F1
Crofts End Rd *EVILLE/WHL* BS5 66 C5
The Croft *BATHSE* BA2 138 C4
CLVDN BS21 71 F5
MANG/FISH BS16 69 D1
NAIL BS48 87 F5
OLD/WMLY/WICK BS30 98 A1 4
OMX/HUT/LCK BS24 153 D2 1
TRWBR BA14 158 C1
Croft Vw
HNLZ/SM/SNYPK/WT BS9 47 D5 1
Crokeswood Wk *AVONM* BS11 44 B2 2
Crome Rd *HORF/LLZ* BS7 48 C4
Cromer Rd *EVILLE/WHL* BS5 66 A4
WSM BS23 6 D5
Cromwell Ct *KGWD/HNM* BS15 80 C4 3
Cromwell Dr *MTN/WRL* BS22 129 F3 4
Cromwell Rd *EVILLE/WHL* BS5 79 E1
RDLND/MONT BS6 64 B4
Cromwells Hide
MANG/FISH BS16 66 C1 2
Crook's La *MTN/WRL* BS22 127 F3
Croomes Hl *MANG/FISH* BS16 51 E5
Cropthorne Rd *HORF/LLZ* BS7 48 B2 1
Cropthorne Rd South
HORF/LLZ BS7 48 B3 2
Crosby Rw *CFTN/FAIL* BS8 75 E3
Crosscombe Dr
BMSTRD/HC/WWD BS13 101 F4
Cross Elms La
HNLZ/SM/SNYPK/WT BS9 62 C1
Crossfield Rd *MANG/FISH* BS16 68 C3
Cross Hands Rd *THNB/SVB* BS35 11 E3
Cross La *PTSHD/EG* BS20 59 F2
Crossleaze Rd *KGWD/HNM* BS15 96 A1
Crossley Cl *FRCTL/WBN* BS36 32 A1 2
Crossman Av *FRCTL/WBN* BS36 31 F3
Crossman Wk *CLVDN* BS21 85 F2 1
Cross St *KEYN* BS31 97 D5
KGWD/HNM BS15 68 A5
TRWBR BA14 157 D3
WSM BS23 6 C1 5
Cross Tree Gv *ALMDB* BS32 13 E5
Crossways Rd
BRSG/KWL/STAPK BS4 93 E3
THNB/SVB BS35 9 D3
Crow La *CBRIS/FH* BS1 2 D3
HNBRY/STHM BS10 46 A1
Crowley Wy *AVONM* BS11 42 C2
Crowndale Rd
BRSG/KWL/STAPK BS4 93 E1
Crown Gdns *OLD/WMLY/WICK* BS30 81 F2
Crown Hl *CBATH/BATHN* BA1 122 A1
EVILLE/WHL BS5 79 D1
Crown Hill Wk *EVILLE/WHL* BS5 79 D1
Crownleaze *MANG/FISH* BS16 68 B3
Crown Rd *CBATH/BATHN* BA1 121 F1
KGWD/HNM BS15 68 B4
OLD/WMLY/WICK BS30 82 A3
Crows Gv *ALMDB* BS32 13 E2
Crowther Pk *HORF/LLZ* BS7 65 E2
Crowther Rd *HORF/LLZ* BS7 65 E2
Crowthers Av *YATE/CS* BS37 19 F2
Crowther St *BMSTR* BS3 91 F1 1
Croydon St *EVILLE/WHL* BS5 77 F1
The Crunnis *ALMDB* BS32 29 F2
Crusty La *PTSHD/EG* BS20 60 A1 1
Cuckoo La *FRCTL/WBN* BS36 32 A5
Cuffington Av
BRSG/KWL/STAPK BS4 78 B5
Culverhill Rd *YATE/CS* BS37 20 B4
Culver Rd *BOAV* BA15 147 E4
Culvers Rd *KEYN* BS31 106 C1
Culver St *CBRIS/FH* BS1 2 B3
The Culvert *ALMDB* BS32 13 E5 2
Culverwell Rd
BMSTRD/HC/WWD BS13 101 E3
Cumberland Basin Rd
CFTN/FAIL BS8 75 D4
Cumberland Cl *CBRIS/FH* BS1 75 E4
Cumberland Gv
RDLND/MONT BS6 65 D4 4
Cumberland Pl *CFTN/FAIL* BS8 75 D3 3
Cumberland Rd *CBRIS/FH* BS1 75 D4 3
Cumberland Rw
CBATH/BATHN BA1 4 A3 2
Cumberland St *CBRISNE* BS2 76 C1 5
Cumbria Cl *THNB/SVB* BS35 9 E3

Cunningham Gdns
MANG/FISH BS16 .... 67 F1 1
Curland Gv *HGRV/WHIT* BS14 ...... 103 F2 4
Curlew Cl *MANG/FISH* BS16 .... 50 A5 1
Curlew Gdns *MTN/WRL* BS22 ...... 143 E1 4
Curtis La *BRSTK/PCHW* BS34 .... 30 B5
Custom Cl *HGRV/WHIT* BS14 .... 93 E5
Cutler Rd *BMSTRD/HC/WWD* BS13 .. 101 D1
Cygnet Crs *MTN/WRL* BS22 .... 143 E1
Cylde Pk *RDLND/MONT* BS6 .... 63 F4
Cynder Wy *MANG/FISH* BS16 .... 52 B2
Cynthia Rd *BATHSE* BA2 .... 122 A5
Cypress Gdns *CFTN/FAIL* BS8 .... 74 C3
Cypress Gv
HNLZ/SM/SNYPK/WT BS9 .... 47 D5
Cypress Ter *RDSTK/MIDN* BA3 ...... 162 A3 1
Cyrus Ct *MANG/FISH* BS16 .... 52 C4 2

D

Dafford's Buildings
CBATH/BATHN BA1 .... 113 F5
Dafford St *CBATH/BATHN* BA1 .... 114 A5
Daisy Rd *EVILLE/WHL* BS5 .... 66 A4
Dakota Dr *HGRV/WHIT* BS14 .... 103 E3
Dalby Av *BMSTR* BS3 .... 92 B1
Dale St *CBRISNE* BS2 .... 77 D1
EVILLE/WHL BS5 .... 79 D1
Daley Cl *MTN/WRL* BS22 .... 130 A4 4
Dalkeith Av *KGWD/HNM* BS15 .... 68 A5 1
Dalrymple Rd *CBRISNE* BS2 .... 64 C5 4
Dalston Rd *BMSTR* BS3 .... 75 F5 1
Dalton Sq *CBRISNE* BS2 .... 76 C1 6
Dame Court Cl *MTN/WRL* BS22 .... 129 E3
Dampier Rd *BMSTR* BS3 .... 91 E1
Damson Rd *MTN/WRL* BS22 .... 143 D3 1
Danbury Crs *HNBRY/STHM* BS10 .... 47 D2
Danbury Wk *HNBRY/STHM* BS10 .. 47 D2 1
Dancey Md
BMSTRD/HC/WWD BS13 .... 100 C1
Dandy's Meadow
PTSHD/EG BS20 .... 56 C2 4
Daneacre Rd *RDSTK/MIDN* BA3 ...... 163 D1
Dangerfield Av
BMSTRD/HC/WWD BS13 .... 100 C1
Daniel Cl *CLVDN* BS21 .... 85 F1
Daniel Ms *BATHSE* BA2 .... 5 E1
Daniel St *BATHSE* BA2 .... 5 E1
Dano View Gdns *PTSHD/EG* BS20 .. 56 A1 2
Dapps Hl *KEYN* BS31 .... 107 D2
Darley Cl *HNBRY/STHM* BS10 .... 25 E5
Darlington Pl *BATHSE* BA2 .... 5 F4
Darlington Rd *BATHSE* BA2 .... 5 F1
Darlington St *BATHSE* BA2 .... 5 E2
Darmead *OMX/HUT/LCK* BS24 ...... 144 A1 1
Darnley Av *HORF/LLZ* BS7 .... 48 A5
Dart Cl *THNB/SVB* BS35 .... 8 B4 1
Dartmoor St *BMSTR* BS3 .... 91 F1 2
Dartmouth Av *BATHSE* BA2 .... 122 A5
Dartmouth Cl *MTN/WRL* BS22 .... 129 E5
Dart Rd *CLVDN* BS21 .... 85 D3
Daubeny Cl *MANG/FISH* BS16 .... 67 F1
Daventry Rd *BRSG/KWL/STAPK* BS4 .. 93 D3
Davey St *CBRISNE* BS2 .... 65 D5
David's Rd *HGRV/WHIT* BS14 .... 104 A1
David St *CBRISNE* BS2 .... 3 G2
Davies Dr *BRSG/KWL/STAPK* BS4 .. 79 D4 3
Davin Crs *PTSHD/EG* BS20 .... 60 A3
Davis Cl *OLD/WMLY/WICK* BS30 .... 81 D4 1
Davis Ct *THNB/SVB* BS35 .... 8 C2
Davis La *CLVDN* BS21 .... 85 D4
Davis St *AVONM* BS11 .... 42 C3
Dawes Cl *CLVDN* BS21 .... 85 D3 3
Dawley Cl *FRCTL/WBN* BS36 .... 31 F1 1
Dawlish Rd *BMSTR* BS3 .... 92 B2
Dawn Ri *KGWD/HNM* BS15 .... 69 E5
Daws Ct *MANG/FISH* BS16 .... 67 F2 3
Day Crs *BATHSE* BA2 .... 121 D4
Day's Rd *CBRISNE* BS2 .... 77 E3
Deacon Cl *FRCTL/WBN* BS36 .... 31 F3
Deacons Cl *MTN/WRL* BS22 .... 129 D5 1
Deadmill La *CBATH/BATHN* BA1 ...... 114 A4
Dean Av *THNB/SVB* BS35 .... 8 C2
Dean Cl *KGWD/HNM* BS15 .... 79 E5
MTN/WRL BS22 .... 130 A4 5
Dean Crs *BMSTR* BS3 .... 76 B5 5
Deanery Rd *CBRIS/FH* BS1 .... 2 A4
KGWD/HNM BS15 .... 81 F1
Deanhill La *CBATH/BATHN* BA1 .... 111 D5
Dean La *BMSTR* BS3 .... 76 A5
Dean Rd *AVONM* BS11 .... 23 D3
YATE/CS BS37 .... 19 D2
Dean's Dr *EVILLE/WHL* BS5 .... 67 E4 1
Deans Md *AVONM* BS11 .... 44 B3
The Deans *PTSHD/EG* BS20 .... 55 F2
Dean St *BMSTR* BS3 .... 76 A5 2
CBRISNE BS2 .... 76 C1
Debecca's La *PTSHD/EG* BS20 .... 59 F2
De Clifford Rd *AVONM* BS11 .... 45 D1
Deep Coombe Rd *BMSTR* BS3 .... 91 E2 1
Deerhurst *KGWD/HNM* BS15 .... 68 C4 2
YATE/CS BS37 .... 19 D5
Deering Cl *AVONM* BS11 .... 44 C2
Deer Md *CLVDN* BS21 .... 84 B3
Deerswood *KGWD/HNM* BS15 .... 69 E4
Delabere Av *MANG/FISH* BS16 .... 67 F1
Delamere Rd *TRWBR* BA14 .... 157 D2
Delapre Rd *WSM* BS23 .... 151 D2
Delius Gv *BRSG/KWL/STAPK* BS4 .... 92 B5 7
The Dell *ALMDB* BS32 .... 29 F1
HNLZ/SM/SNYPK/WT BS9 .... 63 D1
MTN/WRL BS22 .... 129 D3 3
NAIL BS48 .... 86 C2
OLD/WMLY/WICK BS30 .... 82 A4 1
Delvin Rd *HNBRY/STHM* BS10 .... 47 D3
Denbigh St *CBRISNE* BS2 .... 64 C5
Dene Cl *KEYN* BS31 .... 107 D4
Dene Rd *HGRV/WHIT* BS14 .... 104 A3
Denleigh Cl *HGRV/WHIT* BS14 .... 103 E3
Denmark Pl *HORF/LLZ* BS7 .... 64 C3 1
Denmark Rd *BATHSE* BA2 .... 122 B4 2
Denmark St *CBRIS/FH* BS1 .... 2 B3
Denning Ct *MTN/WRL* BS22 .... 130 A3 2
Dennor Pk *HGRV/WHIT* BS14 .... 93 F5
Denny Cl *PTSHD/EG* BS20 .... 55 E1 4
Denny Isle Dr *THNB/SVB* BS35 .... 10 B5
Denny Vw *PTSHD/EG* BS20 .... 55 D1
Dennyview Rd *CFTN/FAIL* BS8 .... 73 D1
Denston Dr *PTSHD/EG* BS20 .... 56 C2
Denston Wk
BMSTRD/HC/WWD BS13 .... 91 E5
Denton Patch *MANG/FISH* BS16 .... 52 C4 3
Dentwood Gv
HNLZ/SM/SNYPK/WT BS9 .... 44 C4
Derby Rd *HORF/LLZ* BS7 .... 64 C3
Derby St *EVILLE/WHL* BS5 .... 78 B2
Derham Cl *YTN/CONG* BS49 .... 116 B3 1
Derham Pk *YTN/CONG* BS49 .... 116 C4 1
Derham Rd
BMSTRD/HC/WWD BS13 .... 101 E2
Dermot St *CBRISNE* BS2 .... 65 E5 8
Derricke Rd *HGRV/WHIT* BS14 .... 105 D1
Derrick Rd *KGWD/HNM* BS15 .... 80 B1
Derry Rd *BMSTR* BS3 .... 91 F2 4
Derwent Cl *BRSTK/PCHW* BS34 .... 12 B5
Derwent Gv *KEYN* BS31 .... 107 E2
Derwent Rd *EVILLE/WHL* BS5 .... 67 D5
WSM BS23 .... 7 G6
Deverell Cl *BOAV* BA15 .... 147 E5
De Verose Ct *KGWD/HNM* BS15 .... 80 C5
Devon Gv *EVILLE/WHL* BS5 .... 78 A1
Devon Rd *EVILLE/WHL* BS5 .... 66 A5
Devonshire Buildings
BATHSE BA2 .... 137 D1
Devonshire Dr *PTSHD/EG* BS20 .... 55 D1
Devonshire Pl *BATHSE* BA2 .... 137 D1 1
Devonshire Rd *BATHSE* BA2 .... 124 C1
RDLND/MONT BS6 .... 63 F2
WSM BS23 .... 151 D2
Dewfalls Dr *ALMDB* BS32 .... 13 E4
Dial Hill Rd *CLVDN* BS21 .... 71 D4
Dial La *MANG/FISH* BS16 .... 51 E5
Diamond Batch
OMX/HUT/LCK BS24 .... 144 A1
Diamond Rd *EVILLE/WHL* BS5 .... 79 D2
Diamond St *BMSTR* BS3 .... 92 A1 2
Diana Gdns *ALMDB* BS32 .... 13 F5
Dibden Cl *MANG/FISH* BS16 .... 52 B3
Dibden La *MANG/FISH* BS16 .... 52 B4
Dibden Rd *MANG/FISH* BS16 .... 52 B3
Dickens Cl *HORF/LLZ* BS7 .... 48 B3
Dickenson Rd *WSM* BS23 .... 6 D4
Dickenson's Gv *YTN/CONG* BS49 .... 133 E3
Didsbury Cl *HNBRY/STHM* BS10 .... 46 A2
Dighton Ga *BRSTK/PCHW* BS34 ...... 29 F3 3
Dighton St *CBRISNE* BS2 .... 76 B1
Dingle Cl *HNLZ/SM/SNYPK/WT* BS9 .. 45 D5
Dingle Rd *HNLZ/SM/SNYPK/WT* BS9.. 45 D4
The Dingle *FRCTL/WBN* BS36 .... 31 F5
HNLZ/SM/SNYPK/WT BS9 .... 45 D4
YATE/CS BS37 .... 20 A1
Dingle Vw
HNLZ/SM/SNYPK/WT BS9 .... 45 D4
Dinglewood Cl
HNLZ/SM/SNYPK/WT BS9 .... 45 E4 1
Dings Wk *CBRISNE* BS2 .... 77 E3 2
Dixon Gdns *CBATH/BATHN* BA1 .... 123 D1
Dixon Rd *BRSG/KWL/STAPK* BS4 .... 95 D2
Dock Gate La *CFTN/FAIL* BS8 .... 75 E4 2
Dodington La *YATE/CS* BS37 .... 36 C2
Dodington Rd *YATE/CS* BS37 .... 36 C1
Dodisham Wk *MANG/FISH* BS16 .... 50 C5
Dolemoor La *YTN/CONG* BS49 .... 132 A2
Dolman Cl *HNBRY/STHM* BS10 .... 26 A5 2
Dominion Rd *BATHSE* BA2 .... 121 E4
MANG/FISH BS16 .... 67 D3
Donald Rd *BMSTRD/HC/WWD* BS13 .. 91 D5
Doncaster Rd *HNBRY/STHM* BS10 .... 46 C2
Donegal Rd *BRSG/KWL/STAPK* BS4.... 92 B3
Dongola Av *HORF/LLZ* BS7 .... 64 C2
Dongola Rd *HORF/LLZ* BS7 .... 64 C2
Doone Rd *HORF/LLZ* BS7 .... 48 A3
Dorcas Av *BRSTK/PCHW* BS34 .... 30 A3
Dorchester Cl *NAIL* BS48 .... 86 C3 5
Dorchester Rd *HORF/LLZ* BS7 .... 48 B4
Dorchester St *CBATH/BATHN* BA1 ...... 4 C5
Dorester Cl *HNBRY/STHM* BS10 .... 27 D4
Dorian Cl *HORF/LLZ* BS7 .... 47 F4
Dorian Rd *HORF/LLZ* BS7 .... 47 F4
Dorian Wy *HNBRY/STHM* BS10 .... 47 F3
Dormer Cl *FRCTL/WBN* BS36 .... 33 E2
Dormer Rd *EVILLE/WHL* BS5 .... 65 E3
Dorset Cl *BATHSE* BA2 .... 122 B4 3
Dorset Gv *CBRISNE* BS2 .... 65 E4 4
Dorset Rd
HNLZ/SM/SNYPK/WT BS9 .... 46 C5
KGWD/HNM BS15 .... 68 B5
Dorset St *BATHSE* BA2 .... 122 B4 4
BMSTR BS3 .... 91 F1 3
Dorset Wy *YATE/CS* BS37 .... 20 B2
Douglas Rd *HORF/LLZ* BS7 .... 48 A4
KGWD/HNM BS15 .... 80 B2
Doulton Wy *HGRV/WHIT* BS14 .... 103 E2
Dovecote *YATE/CS* BS37 .... 35 F1
Dovecote Cl *TRWBR* BA14 .... 156 B4 3
Dovedale *THNB/SVB* BS35 .... 9 D5
Dove La *CBRISNE* BS2 .... 77 D1
Dovercourt Rd *HORF/LLZ* BS7 .... 65 E1
Dove St *CBRISNE* BS2 .... 76 B1
Dove St South *CBRISNE* BS2 .... 76 B1
Dovey Ct *OLD/WMLY/WICK* BS30 ...... 82 A4
Dowdeswell Cl
HNBRY/STHM BS10 .... 26 A5 3
Dowding Cl *YATE/CS* BS37 .... 21 D3 1
Dowding Rd *CBATH/BATHN* BA1 ...... 123 F1
Dowling Rd
BMSTRD/HC/WWD BS13 .... 102 B4
Down Av *BATHSE* BA2 .... 137 E4
Downavon *BOAV* BA15 .... 147 D4
Down Cl *PTSHD/EG* BS20 .... 55 D1 1
Downend Pk *HORF/LLZ* BS7 .... 65 D1
Downend Park Rd
MANG/FISH BS16 .... 68 B1 3
Downend Rd *HORF/LLZ* BS7 .... 65 D1
KGWD/HNM BS15 .... 68 B5
MANG/FISH BS16 .... 68 A1
Downfield Dr *FRCTL/WBN* BS36 .... 16 C5 2
Downfield Rd *CFTN/FAIL* BS8 .... 63 E5
Downhayes Rd *TRWBR* BA14 .... 157 D2
Down La *BATHSE* BA2 .... 125 D1
Downleaze
HNLZ/SM/SNYPK/WT BS9 .... 63 D3
MANG/FISH BS16 .... 51 E3
PTSHD/EG BS20 .... 55 E1
Downman Rd *HORF/LLZ* BS7 .... 65 E1
Down Rd *FRCTL/WBN* BS36 .... 31 F4
PTSHD/EG BS20 .... 54 C3
Downs Cl *BOAV* BA15 .... 146 B2
MTN/WRL BS22 .... 143 E1 5
Downs Cote Av
HNLZ/SM/SNYPK/WT BS9 .... 46 A5
Downs Cote Dr
HNLZ/SM/SNYPK/WT BS9 .... 46 A5
Downs Cote Gdns
HNLZ/SM/SNYPK/WT BS9 .... 46 A5
Downs Cote Pk
HNLZ/SM/SNYPK/WT BS9 .... 46 B5
Downs Cote Vw
HNLZ/SM/SNYPK/WT BS9 .... 46 B5
Downside *PTSHD/EG* BS20 .... 56 A1
Downside Close
OLD/WMLY/WICK BS30 .... 81 D4 2
Downside Cl *BATHSE* BA2 .... 125 D1
Downside Pk *TRWBR* BA14 .... 157 E2
Downside Rd *CFTN/FAIL* BS8 .... 63 E5 2
WSM BS23 .... 151 E1 2
Downs Pk East *RDLND/MONT* BS6 .... 63 E1
Downs Pk West
HNLZ/SM/SNYPK/WT BS9 .... 63 E1
Downs Rd
HNLZ/SM/SNYPK/WT BS9 .... 46 B5
LGASH BS41 .... 100 B5
The Downs *PTSHD/EG* BS20 .... 55 E2
Downs Vw *BOAV* BA15 .... 146 B2
The Down *TRWBR* BA14 .... 157 E2
Downton Rd *BRSG/KWL/STAPK* BS4.. 92 B4
Dowry Rd *CFTN/FAIL* BS8 .... 75 E3 3
Dowry Sq *CFTN/FAIL* BS8 .... 75 D3 4
Dragon Rd *FRCTL/WBN* BS36 .... 31 E4
Dragons Hill Cl *KEYN* BS31 .... 107 D2
Dragons Hill Ct *KEYN* BS31 .... 107 D2
Dragons Hill Gdns *KEYN* BS31 ...... 107 D2 1
Dragonswell Rd
HNBRY/STHM BS10 .... 46 B1
Dragon Wk *EVILLE/WHL* BS5 .... 67 D5 1
Drake Av *BATHSE* BA2 .... 137 D3
Drake Cl *KEYN* BS31 .... 108 B5
MTN/WRL BS22 .... 129 E3 1
Drake Rd *BMSTR* BS3 .... 91 E1
Drakes Wy *PTSHD/EG* BS20 .... 55 E1
Draycot Pl *CBRIS/FH* BS1 .... 2 C6
Draycott Rd *HORF/LLZ* BS7 .... 65 D1 1
Draydon Rd *BRSG/KWL/STAPK* BS4 .... 92 A5
Drayton Cl *HGRV/WHIT* BS14 .... 93 F4 2
Drayton Rd
HNLZ/SM/SNYPK/WT BS9 .... 45 D3 3
The Dring *RDSTK/MIDN* BA3 .... 162 B2 1
The Drive *HGRV/WHIT* BS14 .... 104 A2
HNLZ/SM/SNYPK/WT BS9 .... 63 F1
WSM BS23 .... 141 E2
Drove Rd *WSM* BS23 .... 7 E2
Druetts Cl *HNBRY/STHM* BS10 .... 47 F5 1

Druid Cl *HNLZ/SM/SNYPK/WT* BS9 **62** C1
Druid Hl *HNLZ/SM/SNYPK/WT* BS9 **62** C1
Druid Rd *HNLZ/SM/SNYPK/WT* BS9 **62** B2
Druid Stoke Av
HNLZ/SM/SNYPK/WT BS9 **62** A1
Druid Woods
HNLZ/SM/SNYPK/WT BS9 **62** A1 3
Drummond Ct
OLD/WMLY/WICK BS30 **81** D5 4
Drummond Rd *CBRISNE* BS2 **64** C5 5
MANG/FISH BS16 **67** D3 2
Dryleaze *KEYN* BS31 **96** C5
Dryleaze Rd *MANG/FISH* BS16 **50** A5
Drynham La *TRWBR* BA14 **159** D3
Drynham Pk *TRWBR* BA14 **159** D1
Drynham Rd *TRWBR* BA14 **159** D1
Drysdale Cl *MTN/WRL* BS22 **142** B1
Dubbers La *EVILLE/WHL* BS5 **66** C4
Dublin Crs
HNLZ/SM/SNYPK/WT BS9 **46** C5
Duchess Rd *CFTN/FAIL* BS8 **63** E5
Duchess Wy *MANG/FISH* BS16 **66** B1
Ducie Rd *EVILLE/WHL* BS5 **77** F2
MANG/FISH BS16 **68** C2
Duckmoor Rd *BMSTR* BS3 **91** E1
Dudley Cl *KEYN* BS31 **106** C3
Dudley Ct *OLD/WMLY/WICK* BS30 **81** D5 5
Dudley Gv *HORF/LLZ* BS7 **48** A3
Dugar Wk *RDLND/MONT* BS6 **64** A3
Duke St *BATHSE* BA2 **4** D4
TRWBR BA14 **157** D3
Dulverton Rd *HORF/LLZ* BS7 **64** B2 1
Dumaine Av *BRSTK/PCHW* BS34 **29** F3
Dumfries Pl *WSM* BS23 **151** D1
Duncan Gdns *CBATH/BATHN* BA1 **111** E4
Duncombe La *KGWD/HNM* BS15 **67** E4
Duncombe Rd *KGWD/HNM* BS15 **67** F5 3
Dundas Cl *HNBRY/STHM* BS10 **45** F1 1
Dundonald Rd *RDLND/MONT* BS6 **63** F3
Dundridge Gdns *EVILLE/WHL* BS5 **79** E3 1
Dundridge La *EVILLE/WHL* BS5 **79** E3
Dundry Cl *KGWD/HNM* BS15 **80** B3 1
Dundry Vw *BRSG/KWL/STAPK* BS4 **93** E3
Dunedin Wy *MTN/WRL* BS22 **130** B3
Dunford Cl *TRWBR* BA14 **159** D1
Dunford Rd *BMSTR* BS3 **92** B1
Dunkeld Av *BRSTK/PCHW* BS34 **48** A1
Dunkerry Rd *BMSTR* BS3 **92** B1
Dunkery Cl *NAIL* BS48 **87** D3 4
Dunkery Rd *WSM* BS23 **141** E1
Dunkirk Rd *MANG/FISH* BS16 **67** D3
Dunmail Rd *HNBRY/STHM* BS10 **47** D1
Dunmore St *BMSTR* BS3 **77** D5 4
Dunster Crs *OMX/HUT/LCK* BS24 **151** F3
Dunster Gdns
OLD/WMLY/WICK BS30 **97** F2 1
Dunster Rd
BRSG/KWL/STAPK BS4 **93** D4 3
KEYN BS31 **106** C3
Dunsters Rd *YTN/CONG* BS49 **117** F2
Durban Rd *BRSTK/PCHW* BS34 **12** A5
Durban Wy *YTN/CONG* BS49 **116** B2
Durbin Park Rd *CLVDN* BS21 **70** C4
Durbin Wk *EVILLE/WHL* BS5 **77** E1 8
Durdham Pk *RDLND/MONT* BS6 **63** E3
Durham Gv *KEYN* BS31 **106** B3
Durham Rd *CBRISNE* BS2 **65** E4 5
Durleigh Cl
BMSTRD/HC/WWD BS13 **101** E1
Durley Hl *KEYN* BS31 **95** F4
Durley La *KEYN* BS31 **96** B5
Durley Pk *BATHSE* BA2 **136** C1
Durnford Av *BMSTR* BS3 **75** E5
Durnford St *BMSTR* BS3 **75** E5
Dursley Cl *YATE/CS* BS37 **19** F4
Dursley Rd *AVONM* BS11 **60** C1
TRWBR BA14 **157** D5
Durville Rd
BMSTRD/HC/WWD BS13 **101** F1
Durweston Wk *HGRV/WHIT* BS14 **94** A4
Dutton Cl *HGRV/WHIT* BS14 **104** B1 2
Dutton Rd *HGRV/WHIT* BS14 **104** B2
Dutton Wk *HGRV/WHIT* BS14 **104** B1 3
Dyers Cl *BMSTRD/HC/WWD* BS13 **102** B3
Dyer's La *YATE/CS* BS37 **18** B2
Dylan Thomas Ct
OLD/WMLY/WICK BS30 **81** E4 4
Dymboro Av *RDSTK/MIDN* BA3 **160** C3
Dymboro Cl *RDSTK/MIDN* BA3 **160** C3
Dymboro Gdns
RDSTK/MIDN BA3 **160** C3 1
The Dymboro *RDSTK/MIDN* BA3 **160** C3
Dyrham Cl
HNLZ/SM/SNYPK/WT BS9 **47** E5
KGWD/HNM BS15 **81** D1 3
THNB/SVB BS35 **8** C1
Dyrham Pde *BRSTK/PCHW* BS34 **13** D5
Dyrham Rd *KGWD/HNM* BS15 **81** D1
Dyson Cl *YTN/CONG* BS49 **116** B3 2

E

Eagle Cl *MTN/WRL* BS22 **142** C2
Eagle Pk *CBATH/BATHN* BA1 **115** D2
Eagle Rd *BRSG/KWL/STAPK* BS4 **94** B2
CBATH/BATHN BA1 **115** D2
The Eagles *YTN/CONG* BS49 **116** B3 3
Earlesfield *NAIL* BS48 **86** B3
Earl Russell Wy *EVILLE/WHL* BS5 **77** F2 6
Earlsmead *MANG/FISH* BS16 **66** B2
Earlstone Cl *OLD/WMLY/WICK* BS30 **81** E5
Earlstone Crs
OLD/WMLY/WICK BS30 **81** E4 5
Earl St *CBRIS/FH* BS1 **76** B1 5
Early Wy *HNBRY/STHM* BS10 **47** F3
Easedale Cl *HNBRY/STHM* BS10 **47** E1 3
Eastbourne Rd *EVILLE/WHL* BS5 **77** F1 8
TRWBR BA14 **157** E3
Eastbury Cl *THNB/SVB* BS35 **8** C3
Eastbury Rd *MANG/FISH* BS16 **67** E2
East Cl *BATHSE* BA2 **121** E5
Eastcombe Gdns *WSM* BS23 **141** E1
Eastcombe Rd *WSM* BS23 **141** E1
Eastcote Pk *HGRV/WHIT* BS14 **103** F2
East Cft *HNLZ/SM/SNYPK/WT* BS9 **47** D4
East Dundry La *LGASH* BS41 **101** D5
East Dundry Rd *HGRV/WHIT* BS14 **103** D5
Eastfield *HNLZ/SM/SNYPK/WT* BS9 **46** C4
Eastfield Av *CBATH/BATHN* BA1 **111** F5
Eastfield Dr *YATE/CS* BS37 **19** F1
Eastfield Gdns *WSM* BS23 **141** E1 1
Eastfield Pk *WSM* BS23 **141** D1
Eastfield Rd
HNLZ/SM/SNYPK/WT BS9 **46** B4
OMX/HUT/LCK BS24 **153** D3
RDLND/MONT BS6 **64** B4
East Gv *RDLND/MONT* BS6 **65** D5
East Hill Eastfield Rd
HNLZ/SM/SNYPK/WT BS9 **46** B4 2
Eastlake Cl *HORF/LLZ* BS7 **48** C4
Eastland Av *THNB/SVB* BS35 **8** C2
Eastland Rd *THNB/SVB* BS35 **8** C2
Eastlea *CLVDN* BS21 **84** B3
East Lea Rd *CBATH/BATHN* BA1 **121** E2
Eastleigh Cl *MANG/FISH* BS16 **68** C2 2
Eastleigh Rd *HNBRY/STHM* BS10 **47** E2
MANG/FISH BS16 **68** C2
Eastlyn Rd *BMSTRD/HC/WWD* BS13 **91** F4
East Md *RDSTK/MIDN* BA3 **161** E2
Eastmead La
HNLZ/SM/SNYPK/WT BS9 **62** C2
Eastnor Rd *HGRV/WHIT* BS14 **103** E4
Easton Hill Rd *THNB/SVB* BS35 **9** D2
Easton Rd *CBRISNE* BS2 **77** E2
EVILLE/WHL BS5 **77** F1
PTSHD/EG BS20 **60** A2
Easton Wy *EVILLE/WHL* BS5 **65** E5
Eastover Cl
HNLZ/SM/SNYPK/WT BS9 **46** B3
Eastover Gv *BATHSE* BA2 **136** A4
East Pde *HNLZ/SM/SNYPK/WT* BS9 **45** D5
East Pk *EVILLE/WHL* BS5 **66** A4
East Park Dr *EVILLE/WHL* BS5 **66** A4 9
East Priory Cl
HNLZ/SM/SNYPK/WT BS9 **46** B4
East Ridge Dr
BMSTRD/HC/WWD BS13 **101** D2
East Shrubbery
RDLND/MONT BS6 **63** F4 1
East St *AVONM* BS11 **42** B2 1
BMSTR BS3 **76** B5
CBRISNE BS2 **77** D1 4
East Vw *MANG/FISH* BS16 **52** A5
Eastview Rd *TRWBR* BA14 **156** A5
Eastville *CBATH/BATHN* BA1 **123** F1
East Wy *BATHSE* BA2 **121** E5
Eastway *NAIL* BS48 **86** C1
Eastway Cl *NAIL* BS48 **86** C2 3
Eastway Sq *NAIL* BS48 **87** D1
Eastwood Crs
BRSG/KWL/STAPK BS4 **79** D5
East Wood Pl *PTSHD/EG* BS20 **39** E4
Eastwood Rd
BRSG/KWL/STAPK BS4 **79** D5
Eaton Cl *HGRV/WHIT* BS14 **104** C2
MANG/FISH BS16 **67** F2
Eaton Crs *CFTN/FAIL* BS8 **75** E1 3
Eaton St *BMSTR* BS3 **92** A1 3
Ebdon Rd *MTN/WRL* BS22 **129** E3
Ebenezer La
HNLZ/SM/SNYPK/WT BS9 **45** E5 1
HNLZ/SM/SNYPK/WT BS9 **62** C1 2
Ebenezer St *EVILLE/WHL* BS5 **78** B2 3
Eden Gv *HORF/LLZ* BS7 **48** B2
Eden Park Cl *CBATH/BATHN* BA1 **115** E3
Eden Park Dr *CBATH/BATHN* BA1 **115** E3
Edgecombe Av *MTN/WRL* BS22 **128** C5
Edgecumbe Rd
RDLND/MONT BS6 **64** B4 4
Edgefield Cl *HGRV/WHIT* BS14 **103** D4
Edgefield Rd *HGRV/WHIT* BS14 **103** D4
Edgehill Rd *CLVDN* BS21 **71** D3
Edgeware Rd *BMSTR* BS3 **76** A5
MANG/FISH BS16 **68** A2 1
Edgewood Cl *HGRV/WHIT* BS14 **93** F4 3
OLD/WMLY/WICK BS30 **97** E1
Edgeworth *YATE/CS* BS37 **35** D2
Edgeworth Rd *BATHSE* BA2 **136** A3
Edinburgh Pl *WSM* BS23 **141** D2 3
Edinburgh Rd *KEYN* BS31 **106** C3
Edington Gv *HNBRY/STHM* BS10 **46** B1
Edmund Cl *MANG/FISH* BS16 **51** E5 3
Edna Av *BRSG/KWL/STAPK* BS4 **94** C1
Edward Rd
BRSG/KWL/STAPK BS4 **77** F5 1
CLVDN BS21 **71** E4
KGWD/HNM BS15 **80** C1
Edward Rd South *CLVDN* BS21 **71** E4
Edward Rd West *CLVDN* BS21 **71** E3
Edward St *BATHSE* BA2 **5** E2
CBATH/BATHN BA1 **122** A3
EVILLE/WHL BS5 **66** B4 4
EVILLE/WHL BS5 **78** A1 5
Edwin Short Cl
OLD/WMLY/WICK BS30 **98** C4
Effingham Rd *RDLND/MONT* BS6 **64** C4
Egerton Brow *HORF/LLZ* BS7 **64** B2 2
Egerton Rd *BATHSE* BA2 **136** C1
HORF/LLZ BS7 **64** B2
Eggshill La *YATE/CS* BS37 **19** E4
Eighth Av *HORF/LLZ* BS7 **48** C3
Eirene Ter *PTSHD/EG* BS20 **60** B2
Elberton *KGWD/HNM* BS15 **81** E1 3
Elberton Rd
HNLZ/SM/SNYPK/WT BS9 **44** C4
Elborough Av *YTN/CONG* BS49 **116** B3
Elbury Av *KGWD/HNM* BS15 **68** A4
Elcombe Cl *TRWBR* BA14 **158** C2
Elderberry Wk *HNBRY/STHM* BS10 **47** D1
Elderwood Dr
OLD/WMLY/WICK BS30 **97** E1
Elderwood Rd *HGRV/WHIT* BS14 **93** F5 1
Eldon Pl *CBATH/BATHN* BA1 **113** F5
Eldon Ter *BMSTR* BS3 **92** B1
Eldon Wy *BRSG/KWL/STAPK* BS4 **78** A4
Eldred Cl *HNLZ/SM/SNYPK/WT* BS9 **62** A1
Eleanor Cl *BATHSE* BA2 **121** E5
Eleventh Av *HORF/LLZ* BS7 **48** C2 1
Elfin Rd *MANG/FISH* BS16 **67** E1
Elgar Cl *BRSG/KWL/STAPK* BS4 **102** B1 1
CLVDN BS21 **85** E3
Elgin Av *HORF/LLZ* BS7 **48** A2
Elgin Pk *RDLND/MONT* BS6 **63** F4
Elgin Rd *MANG/FISH* BS16 **67** F4
Eliot Cl *HORF/LLZ* BS7 **48** B3
WSM BS23 **151** F2 1
Elizabeth Cl *OMX/HUT/LCK* BS24 **152** C2
THNB/SVB BS35 **9** D4
Elizabeth Crs *BRSTK/PCHW* BS34 **29** F4
Elizabeths Ms
BRSG/KWL/STAPK BS4 **79** D3 8
Ellacombe Rd
OLD/WMLY/WICK BS30 **96** C2
Ellan Hay Rd *ALMDB* BS32 **30** B2
Ellbridge Cl
HNLZ/SM/SNYPK/WT BS9 **62** B1 1
Ellenborough Crs *WSM* BS23 **6** C4
Ellenborough Pk North *WSM* BS23 **6** B3
Ellenborough Park Rd *WSM* BS23 **6** C3
Ellenborough Pk South *WSM* BS23 **6** B3
Ellesmere *THNB/SVB* BS35 **8** C4
Ellesmere Rd
BRSG/KWL/STAPK BS4 **94** B3 3
KGWD/HNM BS15 **80** B1 2
WSM BS23 **150** C3 1
Ellfield Cl *BMSTRD/HC/WWD* BS13 **101** D1
Ellicks Cl *ALMDB* BS32 **13** F3
Ellicott Rd *HORF/LLZ* BS7 **48** A5
Ellinghurst Cl
HNBRY/STHM BS10 **46** B1 1
Elliott Av *MANG/FISH* BS16 **51** D2
Elliott Pl *TRWBR* BA14 **156** A3
Ellis Av *BMSTRD/HC/WWD* BS13 **91** E4
Ellis Pk *MTN/WRL* BS22 **130** B3 2
Elliston Dr *BATHSE* BA2 **135** F1
Elliston La *RDLND/MONT* BS6 **64** A4
Elliston Rd *RDLND/MONT* BS6 **64** A4
Ellsbridge Cl *KEYN* BS31 **107** F2
Ellsworth Rd *HNBRY/STHM* BS10 **46** A1
Elm Cl *BRSTK/PCHW* BS34 **29** E1
NAIL BS48 **86** B3 3
TRWBR BA14 **149** D3
TRWBR BA14 **158** C4
WNSC BS25 **155** F3
YATE/CS BS37 **20** B4
YTN/CONG BS49 **116** B4
Elmcroft Crs *HORF/LLZ* BS7 **65** E2
Elmdale Crs *THNB/SVB* BS35 **8** C3
Elmdale Rd *BMSTR* BS3 **91** F2
CFTN/FAIL BS8 **75** F2
TRWBR BA14 **156** A5
Elmfield *BOAV* BA15 **146** C2
KGWD/HNM BS15 **80** C3
Elmfield Cl *KGWD/HNM* BS15 **80** C3 1
Elmfield Rd
HNLZ/SM/SNYPK/WT BS9 **46** B3 1
Elm Gv *BATHSE* BA2 **136** A1
CBATH/BATHN BA1 **114** A5

OMX/HUT/LCK BS24 153 E1
Elmgrove Av *EVILLE/WHL* BS5 77 F1 9
Elmgrove Dr *YATE/CS* BS37 20 A3 2
Elmgrove Pk *RDLND/MONT* BS6 64 B5 3
Elmgrove Rd *MANG/FISH* BS16 66 C3
RDLND/MONT BS6 64 B5
Elm Hayes
BMSTRD/HC/WWD BS13 101 D1
Elmhirst Gdns *YATE/CS* BS37 20 B3 1
Elmhurst Av *EVILLE/WHL* BS5 66 B3
Elmhurst Rd
OMX/HUT/LCK BS24 153 D3 1
Elmhyrst Rd *WSM* BS23 141 E2 1
Elming Down Cl *ALMDB* BS32 29 E2 1
Elm La *RDLND/MONT* BS6 63 F4
Elmlea Av
HNLZ/SM/SNYPK/WT BS9 63 D1
Elmleigh Av *MANG/FISH* BS16 69 F1
Elmleigh Cl *MANG/FISH* BS16 69 E1 2
Elmleigh Rd *MANG/FISH* BS16 69 E1
Elm Lodge Rd *NAIL* BS48 87 F1
Elmore *KGWD/HNM* BS15 69 D4 2
YATE/CS BS37 19 E5 1
Elmore Rd *BRSTK/PCHW* BS34 12 A4
HORF/LLZ BS7 48 B5
Elm Pk *BRSTK/PCHW* BS34 48 B1
Elm Rd *HORF/LLZ* BS7 64 C1
KGWD/HNM BS15 80 C3
Elms Cross Dr *BOAV* BA15 146 C4
Elms Gv *BRSTK/PCHW* BS34 12 C4
Elmsleigh Rd *WSM* BS23 150 C1
Elmsley La *MTN/WRL* BS22 128 B2
The Elms *BOAV* BA15 146 C1
Elm Tree Av *MANG/FISH* BS16 52 B4
RDSTK/MIDN BA3 162 A3
Elmtree Cl *KGWD/HNM* BS15 68 B5
Elmtree Dr
BMSTRD/HC/WWD BS13 101 D2
Elm Tree Rd *CLVDN* BS21 85 D2 3
OMX/HUT/LCK BS24 153 E1
Elmvale Dr *OMX/HUT/LCK* BS24 153 E3
Elm Vw *RDSTK/MIDN* BA3 161 E2
Elm Wk *PTSHD/EG* BS20 56 A2
YTN/CONG BS49 116 B4
Elm Wd *YATE/CS* BS37 19 F5
Elsbert Dr
BMSTRD/HC/WWD BS13 100 C1
Elstree Rd *EVILLE/WHL* BS5 66 C5
Elton La *HORF/LLZ* BS7 64 B4
Elton Rd *CFTN/FAIL* BS8 75 F2
CLVDN BS21 84 C1
HORF/LLZ BS7 64 B3
KGWD/HNM BS15 67 F5
MTN/WRL BS22 129 F3
Elton St *CBRISNE* BS2 77 D1 5
Elvard Cl *BMSTRD/HC/WWD* BS13 101 E3
Elvard Rd *BMSTRD/HC/WWD* BS13 101 E2
Elvaston Rd *BMSTR* BS3 92 C1
Ely Gv *HNLZ/SM/SNYPK/WT* BS9 44 C4
Embassy Rd *EVILLE/WHL* BS5 66 C5
Embassy Wk *EVILLE/WHL* BS5 66 C5
Embleton Rd *HNBRY/STHM* BS10 46 C1
Emersons Green La
MANG/FISH BS16 52 C5
Emerson Sq *HORF/LLZ* BS7 48 B3
Emersons Wy *MANG/FISH* BS16 53 D4 1
Emery Rd *BRSG/KWL/STAPK* BS4 95 D3 1
Emet Gv *MANG/FISH* BS16 52 C5
Emet La *MANG/FISH* BS16 52 C5
Emlyn Rd *EVILLE/WHL* BS5 66 A4
Emma-chris Wy *BRSTK/PCHW* BS34 49 D1
Emmett Wd *HGRV/WHIT* BS14 103 F4
Emra Cl *EVILLE/WHL* BS5 67 D5 2
Enfield Rd *MANG/FISH* BS16 67 E3
Engine La *NAIL* BS48 86 A4
England's Crs *FRCTL/WBN* BS36 31 F1
Englishcombe La *BATHSE* BA2 136 A2
Englishcombe Rd
BMSTRD/HC/WWD BS13 102 A4
Englishcombe Wy *BATHSE* BA2 136 B2
Ennerdale Cl *WSM* BS23 7 H6 1
Ennerdale Rd *HNBRY/STHM* BS10 47 E1
Entry Hl *BATHSE* BA2 137 D2
Entry Hill Dr *BATHSE* BA2 137 D3
Entry Hill Gdns *BATHSE* BA2 137 D2
Entry Hill Pk *BATHSE* BA2 137 D3
Entry Ri *BATHSE* BA2 137 D4
Epney Cl *BRSTK/PCHW* BS34 12 A4
Epsom Cl *MANG/FISH* BS16 52 A2
Epsom Rd *TRWBR* BA14 159 E3
Epworth Rd *HNBRY/STHM* BS10 46 B1
Erin Wk *BRSG/KWL/STAPK* BS4 92 B4
Ermine Wy *AVONM* BS11 43 D4
Ermleet Rd *RDLND/MONT* BS6 64 A4 1
Ernest Barker Cl *EVILLE/WHL* BS5 77 F2 7
Ernestville Rd *MANG/FISH* BS16 67 D3
Ervine Ter *CBRISNE* BS2 77 D1
Esgar Ri *MTN/WRL* BS22 129 D4 1
Eskdale *THNB/SVB* BS35 9 D5
Eskdale Cl *MTN/WRL* BS22 142 C2
Esmond Gv *CLVDN* BS21 71 D5
Esplanade Rd *PTSHD/EG* BS20 39 D4
Essery Rd *EVILLE/WHL* BS5 66 A4
Esson Rd *KGWD/HNM* BS15 67 F5
Estoril *YATE/CS* BS37 20 A4
Estune Wk *LGASH* BS41 89 E3
Etloe Rd *RDLND/MONT* BS6 63 E2
Eton La *BNWL* BS29 144 C3
Eton Rd *BRSG/KWL/STAPK* BS4 94 B1
Ettlingen Wy *CLVDN* BS21 85 E2
Ettricke Dr *MANG/FISH* BS16 50 C5
Eugene St *CBRISNE* BS2 76 B1
EVILLE/WHL BS5 77 D1 6
Evans Cl *BRSG/KWL/STAPK* BS4 79 D4
Evans Rd *RDLND/MONT* BS6 63 F4 2
Evelyn Rd *CBATH/BATHN* BA1 121 F2
HNBRY/STHM BS10 47 D4 2
Evenlode Gdns *AVONM* BS11 61 D1
Evenlode Wy *KEYN* BS31 107 E4
Evercreech Rd *HGRV/WHIT* BS14 103 E3
Everest Av *MANG/FISH* BS16 66 C2
Everest Rd *MANG/FISH* BS16 66 C2
Evergreen Cl *WNSC* BS25 154 B3
Everleigh Cl *TRWBR* BA14 159 D2
Eve Rd *EVILLE/WHL* BS5 65 F5
Ewart Rd *MTN/WRL* BS22 142 B2
Excelsior St *BATHSE* BA2 4 D5
Excelsior Ter *RDSTK/MIDN* BA3 161 E3
Exeter Buildings
RDLND/MONT BS6 63 F4
Exeter Rd *BMSTR* BS3 75 F5
PTSHD/EG BS20 56 C2
WSM BS23 6 D5
Exford Cl *WSM* BS23 151 E3
Exley Cl *OLD/WMLY/WICK* BS30 82 A4
Exmoor Rd *BATHSE* BA2 137 D3
Exmoor St *BMSTR* BS3 75 F5
Exmouth Rd *BRSG/KWL/STAPK* BS4 93 D3
Eyer's La *CBRISNE* BS2 3 G1

F

Faber Gv
BMSTRD/HC/WWD BS13 102 A3 2
Fabian Dr *BRSTK/PCHW* BS34 29 F3
Factory Rd *FRCTL/WBN* BS36 32 A1
Failand Crs
HNLZ/SM/SNYPK/WT BS9 62 A1
Failand La *CFTN/FAIL* BS8 59 D5
Failand Wk
HNLZ/SM/SNYPK/WT BS9 45 D5 1
Fairacre Cl *HORF/LLZ* BS7 65 F1
Fairacres Cl *KEYN* BS31 106 C3
Fairfax St *CBRIS/FH* BS1 3 E2
Fairfield Av *CBATH/BATHN* BA1 113 E5
Fairfield Cl *MTN/WRL* BS22 142 A1
Fairfield Park Rd
CBATH/BATHN BA1 113 E5
Fairfield Pl *BMSTR* BS3 75 F5 2
Fairfield Rd *BMSTR* BS3 76 A5 3
CBATH/BATHN BA1 123 E1
RDLND/MONT BS6 65 D4
Fairfoot Rd
BRSG/KWL/STAPK BS4 93 E1 3
Fairford Cl *KGWD/HNM* BS15 69 D4 3
Fairford Crs *BRSTK/PCHW* BS34 12 C5
Fairford Rd *AVONM* BS11 43 D4
Fair Furlong
BMSTRD/HC/WWD BS13 101 E3
Fairhaven *YATE/CS* BS37 20 A4 1
Fairhaven Rd *RDLND/MONT* BS6 64 A2 1
Fair Lawn *OLD/WMLY/WICK* BS30 81 E5
Fairlawn Rd *RDLND/MONT* BS6 65 D4 5
Fairlyn Dr *KGWD/HNM* BS15 69 D3
Fairoaks *OLD/WMLY/WICK* BS30 97 E1 3
Fairview *MTN/WRL* BS22 129 E3 2
Fair View Dr *RDLND/MONT* BS6 64 A4
Fairview Rd *KGWD/HNM* BS15 81 D1
Fairway *BRSG/KWL/STAPK* BS4 94 B3
Fairway Cl *MTN/WRL* BS22 128 A5 2
OLD/WMLY/WICK BS30 81 F5
Fairways *KEYN* BS31 108 C5
Falcon Cl *HNLZ/SM/SNYPK/WT* BS9 46 A3
PTSHD/EG BS20 56 B2
Falcon Crs *MTN/WRL* BS22 143 D2 3
Falcondale Rd
HNLZ/SM/SNYPK/WT BS9 46 A3
Falcondale Wk
HNLZ/SM/SNYPK/WT BS9 46 B3
Falconer Rd *CBATH/BATHN* BA1 111 E4
Falcon Wy *THNB/SVB* BS35 9 D2
Falfield Rd
BRSG/KWL/STAPK BS4 94 A1 2
Falfield Wk *HNBRY/STHM* BS10 47 D3 2
Falkland Rd *RDLND/MONT* BS6 65 D4 6
Fallodon Ct
HNLZ/SM/SNYPK/WT BS9 63 F1 1
Fallodon Wy
HNLZ/SM/SNYPK/WT BS9 63 F1
Fallowfield *MTN/WRL* BS22 129 E3
OLD/WMLY/WICK BS30 82 A5
Falmouth Cl *NAIL* BS48 87 F3 4
Falmouth Rd *HORF/LLZ* BS7 64 B2
Fane Cl *HNBRY/STHM* BS10 26 B5 2
Fanshawe Rd *HGRV/WHIT* BS14 93 E5
Far Handstones
OLD/WMLY/WICK BS30 81 E5
Farington Rd
HNLZ/SM/SNYPK/WT BS9 47 E4
Farleigh Av *TRWBR* BA14 156 A5
Farleigh Rd *CLVDN* BS21 84 A3
KEYN BS31 106 B3
Farleigh Wk
BMSTRD/HC/WWD BS13 91 E4
Farler's End *NAIL* BS48 87 E4
Farley Cl *BRSTK/PCHW* BS34 29 D1
Farm Cl *MANG/FISH* BS16 52 C5 1
Farm Ct *MANG/FISH* BS16 51 F4
Farmer Rd
BMSTRD/HC/WWD BS13 100 C3
Farmhouse Cl *NAIL* BS48 87 D3 5
Farmhouse Ct *NAIL* BS48 87 D3 6
Farm Rd *MANG/FISH* BS16 51 F4
MTN/WRL BS22 142 A1
OMX/HUT/LCK BS24 153 D3
Farmwell Cl
BMSTRD/HC/WWD BS13 101 F2 1
Farnborough Rd
OMX/HUT/LCK BS24 144 B5
Farndale *EVILLE/WHL* BS5 79 E3
Farndale Rd *MTN/WRL* BS22 142 C2
Farne Cl *HNLZ/SM/SNYPK/WT* BS9 63 F1
Farrant Cl *BRSG/KWL/STAPK* BS4 102 B1
Farr's La *CBRIS/FH* BS1 2 C4
Farr St *AVONM* BS11 42 C3
Faulkland Rd *BATHSE* BA2 122 B5
Faverole Wy *TRWBR* BA14 157 F3
Faversham Dr *OMX/HUT/LCK* BS24 151 F4
Fawkes Cl *KGWD/HNM* BS15 81 F1
Fearnville Est *CLVDN* BS21 84 C2 2
Featherstone Rd
MANG/FISH BS16 67 D2 3
Feeder Rd *CBRISNE* BS2 77 E4
Felix Rd *EVILLE/WHL* BS5 77 F1
Felstead Rd *HNBRY/STHM* BS10 47 F2
Felton Gv *BMSTRD/HC/WWD* BS13 91 D4
Fennel Dr *ALMDB* BS32 30 B1
Fennell Gv *HNBRY/STHM* BS10 46 B1 2
Fenners *MTN/WRL* BS22 130 A3 3
Fenshurst Gdns *LGASH* BS41 89 D4
Fenswood Md *LGASH* BS41 88 C3
Fenswood Rd *LGASH* BS41 88 C3
Fenton Cl *KEYN* BS31 108 B4
Fenton Rd *HORF/LLZ* BS7 64 B2
Fermaine Av *BRSG/KWL/STAPK* BS4 95 D1
Fernbank Rd *RDLND/MONT* BS6 64 A4
Fernbrook Cl *MANG/FISH* BS16 50 C2
Fern Cl *HNBRY/STHM* BS10 26 C5
RDSTK/MIDN BA3 161 E4
Ferndale Av *OLD/WMLY/WICK* BS30 97 D1
Ferndale Rd *CBATH/BATHN* BA1 114 A4
HORF/LLZ BS7 48 B1
PTSHD/EG BS20 39 E5
Ferndene *ALMDB* BS32 13 D3
Ferndown *YATE/CS* BS37 19 F4
Ferndown Cl *AVONM* BS11 44 B4 1
Fern Gv *BRSTK/PCHW* BS34 29 E1
NAIL BS48 86 B4
Fernhill La *AVONM* BS11 44 C2
Fernhurst Rd *EVILLE/WHL* BS5 67 D5 3
Fernlea Gdns *PTSHD/EG* BS20 59 F2 1
Fernlea Rd *MTN/WRL* BS22 142 B3
Fernleaze *FRCTL/WBN* BS36 33 D2
Fern Rd *MANG/FISH* BS16 68 B1
Fernsteed Rd
BMSTRD/HC/WWD BS13 101 D1
Fern St *CBRISNE* BS2 65 D5
Ferry La *BATHSE* BA2 4 D4
Ferry Rd *KGWD/HNM* BS15 96 B3
Ferry St *CBRIS/FH* BS1 3 E4 1
Fiddes Rd *RDLND/MONT* BS6 64 A2
The Fielders *MTN/WRL* BS22 130 A3 4
Field Farm Cl *BRSTK/PCHW* BS34 30 A4
Fielding's Rd *BATHSE* BA2 122 A4 1
Field La *OLD/WMLY/WICK* BS30 96 C1
Field Rd *KGWD/HNM* BS15 68 A5
Field View Dr *MANG/FISH* BS16 51 D5
Fiennes Cl *MANG/FISH* BS16 68 C2 3
Fifth Av *HORF/LLZ* BS7 48 B2
Filby Dr *BRSTK/PCHW* BS34 13 D5 1
Filton Av *BRSTK/PCHW* BS34 28 C5
HORF/LLZ BS7 47 F5
Filton Gv *HORF/LLZ* BS7 48 A5
Filton La *BRSTK/PCHW* BS34 49 E1
Filton Rd *BRSTK/PCHW* BS34 49 E1
HORF/LLZ BS7 48 A4
MANG/FISH BS16 50 A2
Filwood Broadway
BRSG/KWL/STAPK BS4 92 C4
Filwood Ct *MANG/FISH* BS16 67 F3 1
Filwood Dr *KGWD/HNM* BS15 81 D1
Filwood Rd *MANG/FISH* BS16 67 E3
Finch Cl *MTN/WRL* BS22 143 D2 4
THNB/SVB BS35 8 C2
Finch Rd *YATE/CS* BS37 20 A5
Finmere Gdns *MTN/WRL* BS22 129 F3
Fircliff Pk *PTSHD/EG* BS20 39 E4
Fire Engine La *FRCTL/WBN* BS36 33 E1 1
Firework Cl *KGWD/HNM* BS15 81 F1
Firfield St *BRSG/KWL/STAPK* BS4 77 E5 2
Firgrove Crs *YATE/CS* BS37 20 B3
Fir Leaze *NAIL* BS48 86 A3 1

First Av BATHSE BA2 136 C1
BRSG/KWL/STAPK BS4 78 C4
RDSTK/MIDN BA3 161 F5
The Firs BATHSE BA2 137 F4
First Wy AVONM BS11 43 D2
Fir Tree Cl BRSTK/PCHW BS34 27 F1
Fir Tree La EVILLE/WHL BS5 79 E3
Fisher Av KGWD/HNM BS15 69 E5
Fisher Rd KGWD/HNM BS15 69 E5
Fishponds Rd EVILLE/WHL BS5 66 A4
Fishpool Hl HNBRY/STHM BS10 26 C4
Fitchett Wk HNBRY/STHM BS10 26 A5
Fitzgerald Rd BMSTR BS3 93 D1
Fitzmaurice Cl BOAV BA15 147 E5
Fitzmaurice Pl BOAV BA15 147 D4 1
Fitzroy Rd MANG/FISH BS16 67 F4
Fitzroy St BRSG/KWL/STAPK BS4 77 E5 3
Five Acre Dr MANG/FISH BS16 50 A4
Five Arches Cl RDSTK/MIDN BA3 162 A2
Flamingo Crs MTN/WRL BS22 143 D2
Flatwoods Crs BATHSE BA2 139 D2 1
Flatwoods Rd BATHSE BA2 139 D2
Flaxman Cl HORF/LLZ BS7 48 C5
Flaxpits La FRCTL/WBN BS36 31 E2
Fleece Cottages TRWBR BA14 157 E5
Fleur De Lys Dr TRWBR BA14 158 A3
Florence Gv MTN/WRL BS22 142 A2
Florence Pk RDLND/MONT BS6 63 F2
Florence Rd MANG/FISH BS16 68 C3
Flowers Hl BRSG/KWL/STAPK BS4 94 C3
Flowers Hill Cl
BRSG/KWL/STAPK BS4 94 C3 2
Flowerwell Rd
BMSTRD/HC/WWD BS13 101 F2 2
Folleigh Cl LGASH BS41 89 F2
Folleigh Dr LGASH BS41 89 F2
Folleigh La LGASH BS41 89 F2
Folliot Cl MANG/FISH BS16 50 B3
Folly Bridge Cl YATE/CS BS37 19 E3 2
Folly Brook Rd MANG/FISH BS16 52 B1
Follyfield BOAV BA15 147 D5
Folly La CBRISNE BS2 77 E3
WSM BS23 151 D4
Folly Rd YATE/CS BS37 16 A1
The Folly KEYN BS31 109 D5
MANG/FISH BS16 52 A4
Fontana Cl OLD/WMLY/WICK BS30 97 F1
Fonthill Rd CBATH/BATHN BA1 112 C5
HNBRY/STHM BS10 47 E1
Fontmell Ct HGRV/WHIT BS14 94 B5 1
Fontwell Dr MANG/FISH BS16 52 A2
Footes La FRCTL/WBN BS36 32 C1
Footshill Cl KGWD/HNM BS15 80 A3
Footshill Dr KGWD/HNM BS15 80 A2
Footshill Rd KGWD/HNM BS15 80 A3
Forde Cl OLD/WMLY/WICK BS30 81 D4 3
Fordell Pl BRSG/KWL/STAPK BS4 93 E1 4
Ford La MANG/FISH BS16 52 C5
Ford St EVILLE/WHL BS5 78 A3 2
Forefield Pl BATHSE BA2 4 D6
Forefield Ri BATHSE BA2 137 E1
Forest Av MANG/FISH BS16 67 F3
Forest Dr HNBRY/STHM BS10 27 D5
WSM BS23 141 F1
Forest Edge KGWD/HNM BS15 80 A5
Forester Av BATHSE BA2 123 F2
Forester La BATHSE BA2 123 F2
Forester Rd BATHSE BA2 5 E1
PTSHD/EG BS20 56 B2
Fore St TRWBR BA14 157 D3
Forest Rd KGWD/HNM BS15 80 B2
MANG/FISH BS16 67 F3
Forest Wk KGWD/HNM BS15 80 A2
MANG/FISH BS16 67 F4 1
Forge End PTSHD/EG BS20 58 C3
Fortescue Rd RDSTK/MIDN BA3 162 C2 1
Fortfield Rd HGRV/WHIT BS14 103 F2
Fosse Barton NAIL BS48 86 C2 4
Fosse Cl NAIL BS48 86 B2 1
Fossedale Av HGRV/WHIT BS14 103 F1
Fosse Gdns BATHSE BA2 136 B5
Fosse La CBATH/BATHN BA1 115 E3
NAIL BS48 86 B2
RDSTK/MIDN BA3 162 A1
Fosse Wy NAIL BS48 86 B2
Fosseway CLVDN BS21 85 D3
RDSTK/MIDN BA3 161 F5
Fosseway Gdns RDSTK/MIDN BA3 161 F3
The Fosseway CFTN/FAIL BS8 75 E3
Foster St EVILLE/WHL BS5 65 F4
Foundry La EVILLE/WHL BS5 67 D4
Fountaine Ct EVILLE/WHL BS5 66 A4 10
Fountain La WNSC BS25 155 D5
Fountains Dr
OLD/WMLY/WICK BS30 81 D3
Four Acre Av MANG/FISH BS16 51 F3
Four Acre Crs MANG/FISH BS16 51 F2
Four Acre Rd MANG/FISH BS16 51 F2
Four Acres
BMSTRD/HC/WWD BS13 100 C3
Four Acres Cl
BMSTRD/HC/WWD BS13 101 D3
NAIL BS48 87 D4
Fourth Av HORF/LLZ BS7 48 B1
Fowey Cl NAIL BS48 87 F4
Fowey Rd MTN/WRL BS22 129 F3 5
Fox & Hounds La KEYN BS31 107 D2 2
Fox Av YATE/CS BS37 19 E3
Foxborough Gdns ALMDB BS32 13 E3 3
Foxcombe Rd CBATH/BATHN BA1 121 F3
HGRV/WHIT BS14 103 F3 1
Foxcote KGWD/HNM BS15 81 D2
Foxcote Rd BMSTR BS3 91 E1
Fox Ct OLD/WMLY/WICK BS30 97 D1
Foxcroft Cl ALMDB BS32 30 A2
Foxcroft Rd EVILLE/WHL BS5 78 B1
Fox Den Rd BRSTK/PCHW BS34 29 E5
Foxe Rd FRCTL/WBN BS36 16 B5
Foxfield Av ALMDB BS32 13 E2
Foxglove Cl MANG/FISH BS16 66 C2 1
THNB/SVB BS35 9 D2 2
Fox Hl BATHSE BA2 137 E3
Fraley Rd HNLZ/SM/SNYPK/WT BS9 46 B4
Frampton Ct
OLD/WMLY/WICK BS30 81 D5 6
TRWBR BA14 158 A1
Frampton Crs MANG/FISH BS16 68 A2
Frampton End Rd FRCTL/WBN BS36 17 D4
Francis Fox Rd WSM BS23 6 D2 1
Francis Pl OLD/WMLY/WICK BS30 81 D5
Francis Rd BMSTR BS3 92 A2 3
HNBRY/STHM BS10 47 D3 3
Francis St TRWBR BA14 156 C3
Francis Wy OLD/WMLY/WICK BS30 82 B3
Francombe Gv HNBRY/STHM BS10 47 F5
Frankland Cl CBATH/BATHN BA1 121 E1
Frankley Buildings
CBATH/BATHN BA1 123 F1 1
Franklin's Wy YTN/CONG BS49 117 F2
Franklyn La CBRISNE BS2 65 D5 7
Franklyn St CBRISNE BS2 65 D5
Fraser Cl MTN/WRL BS22 129 E3 3
Fraser St BMSTR BS3 92 B1
Frayne Rd BMSTR BS3 75 E5
Frederick Pl CFTN/FAIL BS8 75 F2
Fredrick St BRSG/KWL/STAPK BS4 77 E5 4
Freeland Buildings
EVILLE/WHL BS5 66 A4 11
Freeland Pl CFTN/FAIL BS8 75 D3 5
Freelands CLVDN BS21 84 C4
Freemantle Gdns EVILLE/WHL BS5 66 A3 3
Freemantle Rd EVILLE/WHL BS5 66 A3 4
Freestone Rd CBRISNE BS2 77 E3 3
Free Tank CBRISNE BS2 3 H4
Freeview Rd BATHSE BA2 121 E4
Fremantle La RDLND/MONT BS6 64 B5 4
Fremantle Rd RDLND/MONT BS6 64 B5 5
Frenchay Hl MANG/FISH BS16 50 C4
Frenchay Rd MANG/FISH BS16 51 D4
WSM BS23 151 D1
French Cl NAIL BS48 87 E1
Freshland Wy KGWD/HNM BS15 79 F1
Freshmoor CLVDN BS21 85 F1
Friar Av MTN/WRL BS22 129 D4
Friary Cl CLVDN BS21 70 C4
Friary Grange Pk FRCTL/WBN BS36 31 F2
Friary Rd HORF/LLZ BS7 64 B3
PTSHD/EG BS20 55 F1
Friendly Rw PTSHD/EG BS20 60 A1
Friendship Gv NAIL BS48 87 E2 1
Friendship Rd
BRSG/KWL/STAPK BS4 93 D2
NAIL BS48 87 E1
Friezewood Rd BMSTR BS3 75 E5
Fripp Cl EVILLE/WHL BS5 77 F3 5
Frobisher Av PTSHD/EG BS20 55 E1
Frobisher Cl MTN/WRL BS22 129 D3 4
PTSHD/EG BS20 55 E1 5
Frobisher Rd BMSTR BS3 91 E1
Frog La CBRIS/FH BS1 2 A3
FRCTL/WBN BS36 17 F5
Frogmore St CBRIS/FH BS1 2 B3 1
Frome Ct THNB/SVB BS35 8 C4
Frome Gln FRCTL/WBN BS36 31 F4
Frome Old Rd RDSTK/MIDN BA3 163 D2
Frome Pl MANG/FISH BS16 66 C1 3
Frome Rd BATHSE BA2 136 C4
BOAV BA15 147 D3
RDSTK/MIDN BA3 163 D2
TRWBR BA14 156 C5
YATE/CS BS37 21 D4
Frome St CBRISNE BS2 77 D1 7
Frome Valley Rd MANG/FISH BS16 50 A5
Frome Valley Walkway
FRCTL/WBN BS36 17 F3
FRCTL/WBN BS36 31 F5
MANG/FISH BS16 51 D4
YATE/CS BS37 19 D2
Frome Valley Wy YATE/CS BS37 21 F5
Frome Vw FRCTL/WBN BS36 32 C1
Frome Wy FRCTL/WBN BS36 31 F3
Froomshaw Rd MANG/FISH BS16 50 B4
Frost Hl YTN/CONG BS49 117 D4
Fry's Cl MANG/FISH BS16 66 B2 1
Frys Hl KGWD/HNM BS15 68 C4 3
KGWD/HNM BS15 68 C5 2
Fryth Wy NAIL BS48 86 B2
Fulford Rd
BMSTRD/HC/WWD BS13 101 F2 3
TRWBR BA14 157 E2
Fulford Wk
BMSTRD/HC/WWD BS13 101 F2 4
Fullens Cl MTN/WRL BS22 142 C3
Fuller Rd CBATH/BATHN BA1 114 A5
Fullers Wy BATHSE BA2 136 B5
Fulmar Cl THNB/SVB BS35 9 D2 3
Fulmar Rd MTN/WRL BS22 143 E1
Fulney Cl TRWBR BA14 157 F2
Furber Ct EVILLE/WHL BS5 79 F3
Furber Rdg EVILLE/WHL BS5 79 F3
Furber Rd EVILLE/WHL BS5 79 F3
Furber V EVILLE/WHL BS5 79 F3
Furland Rd MTN/WRL BS22 128 B5
Furlong Cl RDSTK/MIDN BA3 160 C5
Furlong Gdns TRWBR BA14 157 E3
The Furlong
HNLZ/SM/SNYPK/WT BS9 64 A1
Furnwood EVILLE/WHL BS5 79 E3
Furze Cl MTN/WRL BS22 127 F5
Furze Rd MANG/FISH BS16 68 A3
MTN/WRL BS22 127 F4
Furzewood Rd KGWD/HNM BS15 81 D1
Fylton Cft HGRV/WHIT BS14 103 F4

G

Gable Rd EVILLE/WHL BS5 65 E5 9
Gadshill Dr BRSTK/PCHW BS34 29 F3
Gadshill Rd EVILLE/WHL BS5 66 A3
Gages Cl KGWD/HNM BS15 81 D2
Gages Rd KGWD/HNM BS15 81 D2
Gainsborough Dr
MTN/WRL BS22 129 E4 3
Gainsborough Gdns
CBATH/BATHN BA1 122 A2
Gainsborough Ri TRWBR BA14 158 A1
Gainsborough Rd KEYN BS31 107 D2
Galingale Wy PTSHD/EG BS20 57 D1
Gallivan Cl BRSTK/PCHW BS34 28 C1
Galway Rd BRSG/KWL/STAPK BS4 92 C3
Gander Cl
BMSTRD/HC/WWD BS13 101 F2 5
Gannet Rd MTN/WRL BS22 143 E1
Garden Cl HNLZ/SM/SNYPK/WT BS9 62 A1
MTN/WRL BS22 129 E5 6
Gardeners Wk LGASH BS41 89 F3 1
Gardens Rd CLVDN BS21 70 C5
The Gardens MANG/FISH BS16 50 A2
Gardner Av
BMSTRD/HC/WWD BS13 91 D5
Gardner Rd PTSHD/EG BS20 39 E5
Garfield Rd EVILLE/WHL BS5 79 E1
Garnet St BMSTR BS3 91 F2
Garnett Pl MANG/FISH BS16 52 A4
Garrett Dr ALMDB BS32 29 E1 2
Garrick Rd BATHSE BA2 121 D5
Garsdale Rd MTN/WRL BS22 142 C2 2
Garstons CLVDN BS21 84 B4
The Garstons PTSHD/EG BS20 56 A2
Garth Rd BMSTRD/HC/WWD BS13 91 E4
Gasferry Rd CBRIS/FH BS1 75 F3 3
The Gaskins HORF/LLZ BS7 65 E1
Gas La CBRISNE BS2 77 E3
Gaston Av KEYN BS31 107 D2
The Gastons AVONM BS11 44 B3
Gatcombe Dr BRSTK/PCHW BS34 29 F4
Gatcombe Rd
BMSTRD/HC/WWD BS13 101 F2
Gatehouse Av
BMSTRD/HC/WWD BS13 101 E2
Gatehouse Cl
BMSTRD/HC/WWD BS13 101 E2 2
Gatehouse Ct
BMSTRD/HC/WWD BS13 101 F2 6
Gatehouse Wy
BMSTRD/HC/WWD BS13 101 E2
Gatesby Md BRSTK/PCHW BS34 29 F3
Gathorne Rd BMSTR BS3 75 F5
Gatton Rd CBRISNE BS2 65 E5
Gaunts Cl PTSHD/EG BS20 55 D2 2
Gaunt's La CBRIS/FH BS1 2 B3 2
Gaunts Rd YATE/CS BS37 20 C5
Gay Elms Rd
BMSTRD/HC/WWD BS13 101 E3
Gayner Rd HORF/LLZ BS7 48 B2
Gay's Hl CBATH/BATHN BA1 123 E2 4
Gays Rd KGWD/HNM BS15 79 F5
Gay St CBATH/BATHN BA1 4 B2 2
Gaythorne Crs YATE/CS BS37 19 E3
Gazelle Rd OMX/HUT/LCK BS24 152 A2
Gazzard Cl FRCTL/WBN BS36 31 F1
Gee Moors KGWD/HNM BS15 81 D2 3
Gefle Cl CBRIS/FH BS1 75 F4 2
Geldof Dr RDSTK/MIDN BA3 161 D2 1
Geoffrey Cl
BMSTRD/HC/WWD BS13 100 C1
George's Rd CBATH/BATHN BA1 123 E1
George St CBATH/BATHN BA1 4 B2
EVILLE/WHL BS5 78 A1 6
PTSHD/EG BS20 56 A4
TRWBR BA14 157 D3
WSM BS23 6 D1

George Whitefield Ct
CBRIS/FH BS1 3 F1 1
Georgian Vw *BATHSE* BA2 135 F2
Gerald Rd *BMSTR* BS3 91 E1
Gerard Rd *WSM* BS23 141 D2 4
Gerrard Cl *BRSG/KWL/STAPK* BS4 92 B5
Gerrish Av *EVILLE/WHL* BS5 78 A1
MANG/FISH BS16 69 D1
Gibbsfold Rd
BMSTRD/HC/WWD BS13 102 A4
Gibson Rd *RDLND/MONT* BS6 64 B5
Gifford Rd *HNBRY/STHM* BS10 26 A4
Giffords Pl *BMSTRD/HC/WWD* BS13 91 E5
Gilbeck Rd *NAIL* BS48 86 B2 2
Gilbert Rd *EVILLE/WHL* BS5 78 A1
KGWD/HNM BS15 68 B5
Gilberyn Dr *MTN/WRL* BS22 129 F4 4
Gilda Cl *HGRV/WHIT* BS14 103 F2
Gilda Crs *HGRV/WHIT* BS14 103 F1
Gilda Sq West *HGRV/WHIT* BS14 103 F2
Gillard Cl *KGWD/HNM* BS15 79 F1
Gillard Rd *KGWD/HNM* BS15 79 F1
Gill Av *MANG/FISH* BS16 50 C5
Gillebank Cl *HGRV/WHIT* BS14 104 B2 2
Gillingham Hl *EVILLE/WHL* BS5 79 F4 4
Gillingham Ter
CBATH/BATHN BA1 123 F1 3
Gillingstool *THNB/SVB* BS35 8 C4
Gill Ms *MTN/WRL* BS22 130 A3 5
Gillmore Rd *MTN/WRL* BS22 142 C1 1
Gillray Cl *HORF/LLZ* BS7 48 C5
Gillson Cl *OMX/HUT/LCK* BS24 152 C3 1
Gilpin Cl *KGWD/HNM* BS15 69 D5 2
Gilroy Cl *OLD/WMLY/WICK* BS30 97 F1
Gilslake Av *HNBRY/STHM* BS10 26 C5
Gimblet Rd *MTN/WRL* BS22 130 A3
Gipsy Patch La *BRSTK/PCHW* BS34 28 C2
The Glades *EVILLE/WHL* BS5 66 C4
Gladstone Dr *MANG/FISH* BS16 68 C3 1
Gladstone La *FRCTL/WBN* BS36 33 D1 1
Gladstone Rd *BATHSE* BA2 138 A3
HGRV/WHIT BS14 103 F1
KGWD/HNM BS15 68 B5 3
TRWBR BA14 156 B5
Gladstone St *BMSTR* BS3 91 F1
EVILLE/WHL BS5 78 B2 4
MANG/FISH BS16 68 B3
RDSTK/MIDN BA3 161 E1
Glaisdale Rd *MANG/FISH* BS16 67 E1
Glanville Gdns *KGWD/HNM* BS15 80 C2
Glass House La *CBRISNE* BS2 77 F4 1
Glastonbury Cl
OLD/WMLY/WICK BS30 81 D4 4
Glastonbury Wy *MTN/WRL* BS22 129 F5
Glebe Av *PTSHD/EG* BS20 56 C2
Glebe Cl *LGASH* BS41 89 F2
Glebelands *RDSTK/MIDN* BA3 162 A3
Glebelands Rd
BRSTK/PCHW BS34 28 B5 1
Glebe Rd *BATHSE* BA2 135 F1
CLVDN BS21 84 C2
EVILLE/WHL BS5 78 C1
LGASH BS41 90 A3
PTSHD/EG BS20 56 C2
TRWBR BA14 156 A5
WSM BS23 141 D2 5
The Glebe *THNB/SVB* BS35 11 D3
Gledemoor Dr *FRCTL/WBN* BS36 33 E1
Glena Av *BRSG/KWL/STAPK* BS4 93 F2
Glenarm Rd *BRSG/KWL/STAPK* BS4 94 C2
Glenarm Wk *BRSG/KWL/STAPK* BS4 94 C2
Glen Av *CFTN/FAIL* BS8 73 D1
Glenavon Pk
HNLZ/SM/SNYPK/WT BS9 62 A2 1
Glen Brook
HNLZ/SM/SNYPK/WT BS9 62 B2
Glenburn Rd *KGWD/HNM* BS15 67 F5
Glencoyne Sq *HNBRY/STHM* BS10 47 D1
Glendale *CFTN/FAIL* BS8 75 D3 6
MANG/FISH BS16 51 F3
MANG/FISH BS16 68 A3 3
Glendare St *EVILLE/WHL* BS5 78 A3
Glendevon Rd *HGRV/WHIT* BS14 103 E4 5
Glen Dr *HNLZ/SM/SNYPK/WT* BS9 62 B1
Gleneagles *YATE/CS* BS37 19 F4
Gleneagles Cl *MTN/WRL* BS22 129 E4 4
NAIL BS48 87 F3 5
Gleneagles Dr
HNBRY/STHM BS10 25 E5 3
Gleneagles Rd
OLD/WMLY/WICK BS30 81 F3 1
Glenfall *YATE/CS* BS37 35 E1
Glenfrome Rd *CBRISNE* BS2 65 F3
EVILLE/WHL BS5 65 F3
Glen La *BRSG/KWL/STAPK* BS4 94 B2
Glen Pk *EVILLE/WHL* BS5 66 A4
EVILLE/WHL BS5 79 E1
Glen Park Gdns *EVILLE/WHL* BS5 79 E1
Glenroy Av *KGWD/HNM* BS15 67 F5
Glenside Cl *MANG/FISH* BS16 51 D4
Glenside Pk *MANG/FISH* BS16 66 C1 4
The Glen *KEYN* BS31 119 D1
KGWD/HNM BS15 79 F5
MTN/WRL BS22 128 A5
RDLND/MONT BS6 63 F3
YATE/CS BS37 19 F3
Glentworth Rd *CFTN/FAIL* BS8 75 F3 4
RDLND/MONT BS6 64 A4 2
Glenwood *MANG/FISH* BS16 68 A3 4
Glenwood Dr
OLD/WMLY/WICK BS30 81 F5
Glenwood Ri *PTSHD/EG* BS20 55 D1
Glenwood Rd *HNBRY/STHM* BS10 47 D4
Gloster Av *EVILLE/WHL* BS5 66 B3 1
Gloucester Cl *BRSTK/PCHW* BS34 29 E3
Gloucester La *CBRISNE* BS2 3 H1 1
Gloucester Rd *AVONM* BS11 42 B2
BRSTK/PCHW BS34 12 C4
CBATH/BATHN BA1 113 F2
HORF/LLZ BS7 64 B4
MANG/FISH BS16 68 C3 2
THNB/SVB BS35 8 C2
TRWBR BA14 156 B5
Gloucester Rd North
BRSTK/PCHW BS34 28 B3
HORF/LLZ BS7 48 A2
Gloucester St *CBATH/BATHN* BA1 4 A1 4
CBRISNE BS2 76 C1 7
CFTN/FAIL BS8 75 D2 2
EVILLE/WHL BS5 66 B3
WSM BS23 6 B1
Glyn V *BMSTR* BS3 92 B3
Goddard Dr *MTN/WRL* BS22 130 A3 6
Godfrey Ct
OLD/WMLY/WICK BS30 81 D5 7
Godwin Dr *NAIL* BS48 86 B2
Goffenton Dr *MANG/FISH* BS16 50 C5
Goldcrest Rd *YATE/CS* BS37 36 A1
Golden Valley La
OLD/WMLY/WICK BS30 99 D3
Goldney Av *CFTN/FAIL* BS8 75 E3
OLD/WMLY/WICK BS30 82 A2
Goldney Rd *CFTN/FAIL* BS8 75 E3
Goldsbury Wk *AVONM* BS11 44 B2
Golf Club La *KEYN* BS31 108 C5 1
Golf Course La *BRSTK/PCHW* BS34 28 A5
Golf Course Rd *BATHSE* BA2 5 H3
Gooch Ct *OLD/WMLY/WICK* BS30 98 A1
Gooch Wy *MTN/WRL* BS22 130 A4 6
Goodeve Rd
HNLZ/SM/SNYPK/WT BS9 62 B4
Goodhind St *EVILLE/WHL* BS5 77 E1
Goodneston Rd *MANG/FISH* BS16 67 E3
Goodring Hl *AVONM* BS11 44 B2
Good Shepherd Cl *HORF/LLZ* BS7 64 A2 2
Goodwin Dr *HGRV/WHIT* BS14 103 D3
Goodwood Cl *TRWBR* BA14 159 E3 1
Goodwood Gdns
MANG/FISH BS16 52 A2 3
Goold Cl *BATHSE* BA2 119 E2
Goolden St
BRSG/KWL/STAPK BS4 93 E1 5
ALMDB BS32 30 A2 1
Goose Acre *ALMDB* BS32 30 B2 1
Goosegreen *FRCTL/WBN* BS36 16 C5
Goose Gn *YATE/CS* BS37 19 F2
Goose Green Wy *YATE/CS* BS37 19 D1
Gooseland Cl *HGRV/WHIT* BS14 103 D4 4
Goose St *TRWBR* BA14 158 A5
Goosey La *MTN/WRL* BS22 130 B5 1
Gordano Gdns *PTSHD/EG* BS20 59 F2
Gordano Rd *PTSHD/EG* BS20 41 E4
Gordano Wy *PTSHD/EG* BS20 59 D1
Gordon Av *EVILLE/WHL* BS5 66 C5
Gordon Cl *EVILLE/WHL* BS5 66 C5
Gordon Rd *BATHSE* BA2 5 E6
CBRISNE BS2 65 D5
CFTN/FAIL BS8 75 F2
EVILLE/WHL BS5 66 B4
WSM BS23 7 E1
Gore Rd *BMSTR* BS3 91 E1
Gore's Marsh Rd *BMSTR* BS3 91 E2
Gorham Cl *AVONM* BS11 45 D1 3
Gorlands Rd *YATE/CS* BS37 21 D4
Gorlangton Cl *HGRV/WHIT* BS14 93 E5
Gorse Cover Rd *THNB/SVB* BS35 10 B3
Gorse Hl *MANG/FISH* BS16 68 A3
Gorse La *CFTN/FAIL* BS8 75 F3 5
Gosforth Rd *HNBRY/STHM* BS10 46 C2
Goslet Rd *HGRV/WHIT* BS14 104 C2
Goss Barton *NAIL* BS48 86 C3 6
Goss Cl *NAIL* BS48 86 B3 4
Goss La *NAIL* BS48 86 B3
Goss Vw *NAIL* BS48 86 B3 5
Gotley Rd *BRSG/KWL/STAPK* BS4 94 B2
Gott Dr *BRSG/KWL/STAPK* BS4 78 B4
Goulston Rd
BMSTRD/HC/WWD BS13 101 E2
Goulston Wk
BMSTRD/HC/WWD BS13 101 E2 3
Goulter St *EVILLE/WHL* BS5 77 F3 6
Gourney Cl *AVONM* BS11 44 C1
Gover Rd *KGWD/HNM* BS15 96 A1
Grace Cl *YATE/CS* BS37 21 D4
YTN/CONG BS49 116 B3
Grace Ct *MANG/FISH* BS16 51 E5
Grace Dr *KGWD/HNM* BS15 69 E5
RDSTK/MIDN BA3 161 D2 2
Grace Park Rd
BRSG/KWL/STAPK BS4 94 B3
Grace Rd *MANG/FISH* BS16 68 A1
MTN/WRL BS22 130 A3
Gradwell Cl *MTN/WRL* BS22 130 A4
Graeme Cl *MANG/FISH* BS16 67 E2
Graham Rd *BMSTR* BS3 92 A1 4
EVILLE/WHL BS5 65 F5 3
MANG/FISH BS16 52 A5
WSM BS23 6 C3
Grainger Ct *AVONM* BS11 43 F4 2
Grampian Cl *OLD/WMLY/WICK* BS30 82 A5
Granby Hl *CFTN/FAIL* BS8 75 D3
Grand Pde *CBATH/BATHN* BA1 4 C3 4
Grange Av *BRSTK/PCHW* BS34 29 D2
KGWD/HNM BS15 80 B4
Grange Cl *ALMDB* BS32 13 D3
WSM BS23 151 D4
Grange Cl North
HNLZ/SM/SNYPK/WT BS9 46 C5 2
Grange Ct *KGWD/HNM* BS15 80 B4 2
Grange Court Rd
HNLZ/SM/SNYPK/WT BS9 46 B5
Grange Dr *MANG/FISH* BS16 51 D5
Grange End *RDSTK/MIDN* BA3 161 D5
Grange Pk
HNLZ/SM/SNYPK/WT BS9 46 C5
MANG/FISH BS16 51 D3
Grange Rd
BMSTRD/HC/WWD BS13 101 E2
CFTN/FAIL BS8 75 E2
KEYN BS31 108 A4
WSM BS23 151 D4
The Grange
HNLZ/SM/SNYPK/WT BS9 45 E4
Grange Vw *BOAV* BA15 147 E2
Grangeville Cl
OLD/WMLY/WICK BS30 97 F1
Grangewood Cl
MANG/FISH BS16 51 D5 3
Granny's La *KGWD/HNM* BS15 80 C3 2
Grantham La *KGWD/HNM* BS15 80 A1 3
Grantham Rd *KGWD/HNM* BS15 68 A5
Grantson Cl *BRSG/KWL/STAPK* BS4 94 C2
Granville Cl *KGWD/HNM* BS15 95 F1
Granville Rd *CBATH/BATHN* BA1 112 C4
Granville St *EVILLE/WHL* BS5 78 A3
Grasington Dr *YATE/CS* BS37 20 B4
Grasmere *TRWBR* BA14 157 E2
Grasmere Cl *HNBRY/STHM* BS10 46 B3
Grasmere Dr *WSM* BS23 151 E1
Grass Meers Dr *HGRV/WHIT* BS14 103 E3
Grassmere Gdns
OLD/WMLY/WICK BS30 82 B3
Grassmere Rd *YTN/CONG* BS49 116 B3
Gratitude Rd *EVILLE/WHL* BS5 66 A5
Gravel Hill Rd *YATE/CS* BS37 20 A1
The Gravel *TRWBR* BA14 149 E1
Gravel Wk *CBATH/BATHN* BA1 4 A1
Graveney Cl
BRSG/KWL/STAPK BS4 94 B3 4
Grayle Rd *HNBRY/STHM* BS10 26 A5
Gray's Cl *HNBRY/STHM* BS10 45 F1 2
Grays Leaze *TRWBR* BA14 158 C5
Great Ann St *CBRISNE* BS2 3 H1
Great Bedford St
CBATH/BATHN BA1 123 D2 5
Great Brockeridge
HNLZ/SM/SNYPK/WT BS9 46 A5
Great Dowles
OLD/WMLY/WICK BS30 81 E5
Great George St *CBRIS/FH* BS1 75 F3
CBRISNE BS2 3 G1
Great Hayles Rd *HGRV/WHIT* BS14 93 E5
Great Leaze *OLD/WMLY/WICK* BS30 81 E5
Great Meadow Rd *ALMDB* BS32 30 A1
Great Park Rd *ALMDB* BS32 13 D2
Great Pulteney St *BATHSE* BA2 4 D2
Great Stanhope St
CBATH/BATHN BA1 122 C4 1
Great Stoke Wy *BRSTK/PCHW* BS34 29 E5
Great Western Br *WSM* BS23 7 E2
Great Western La
EVILLE/WHL BS5 78 A3 3
Great Western Rd *CLVDN* BS21 85 D1
Greenacre *MTN/WRL* BS22 128 A5
Greenacre Rd *HGRV/WHIT* BS14 103 E4
Greenacres *CBATH/BATHN* BA1 111 F4
RDSTK/MIDN BA3 160 B3
Greenbank Av *EVILLE/WHL* BS5 66 A5
Greenbank Av West
EVILLE/WHL BS5 65 F5 4
Greenbank Gdns
CBATH/BATHN BA1 121 F1
Greenbank Rd *BMSTR* BS3 75 E5
EVILLE/WHL BS5 66 A5
KGWD/HNM BS15 80 B4
Greenbank Vw *EVILLE/WHL* BS5 66 A4
Green Cl *TRWBR* BA14 149 F1
Green Cft *EVILLE/WHL* BS5 67 E5
Greendale Rd *BMSTR* BS3 92 C1
RDLND/MONT BS6 63 F2
Green Dell Cl *HNBRY/STHM* BS10 25 E5 4
Greenditch Av
BMSTRD/HC/WWD BS13 102 A2
Greendown *EVILLE/WHL* BS5 79 E2
Greendown Pl *BATHSE* BA2 137 E4

Green Dragon Rd *FRCTL/WBN* BS36.. **31** E3
Greenfield Av
HNBRY/STHM BS10 .... **47** E3 1
Greenfield Crs *NAIL* BS48 .... **87** D1
Greenfield Pk *PTSHD/EG* BS20 .... **56** A3
Greenfield Pl *WSM* BS23 .... **140** B2
Greenfield Rd
HNBRY/STHM BS10 .... **47** E2 1
Greengage Cl *MTN/WRL* BS22 ...... **143** D2 5
Green Hayes *YATE/CS* BS37 .... **21** D5
Greenhill Cl *MTN/WRL* BS22 .... **129** F4
NAIL BS48 .... **86** C2 5
Greenhill Gv *BMSTR* BS3 .... **91** E2
Greenhill La *AVONM* BS11 .... **45** D2 1
Greenhill Pl *RDSTK/MIDN* BA3 .... **161** D1
Greenhill Rd *RDSTK/MIDN* BA3 .... **161** D1
Greenland Rd *MTN/WRL* BS22 .... **142** C1 2
Greenlands Wy *HNBRY/STHM* BS10.. **25** F4
Greenland Vw *BOAV* BA15 .... **147** E3
Green La *AVONM* BS11 .... **42** C3
CFTN/FAIL BS8 .... **72** A5
FRCTL/WBN BS36 .... **31** D1
THNB/SVB BS35 .... **10** C2
TRWBR BA14 .... **157** E4
Greenleaze *BRSG/KWL/STAPK* BS4 .... **93** F3
Greenleaze Av *MANG/FISH* BS16 .... **51** E2
Greenmore Rd
BRSG/KWL/STAPK BS4 .... **93** F2
Greenore *KGWD/HNM* BS15 .... **80** A2
Green Park Rd *BATHSE* BA2 .... **4** A4
Greenpark Rd
HNBRY/STHM BS10 .... **47** F2 1
Greenridge Cl
BMSTRD/HC/WWD BS13 .... **100** C3 1
Green Side *MANG/FISH* BS16 .... **52** B5
Greenside Cl *HNBRY/STHM* BS10 .. **25** E5 5
Greenslade Gdns *NAIL* BS48 .... **86** C1
Greensplott Rd *AVONM* BS11 .... **23** E1
Green St *BMSTR* BS3 .... **77** D5
CBATH/BATHN BA1 .... **4** C3 5
The Green *BRSTK/PCHW* BS34 .... **29** F4
KGWD/HNM BS15 .... **68** C4
OMX/HUT/LCK BS24 .... **153** F1 3
WNSC BS25 .... **154** B4
Green Tree Rd *RDSTK/MIDN* BA3 .... **161** E1
Greenview
OLD/WMLY/WICK BS30 .... **97** E2 1
Green Wk *BRSG/KWL/STAPK* BS4 .. **93** E3 1
Greenway Bush La *BMSTR* BS3 .... **75** E5
Greenway Ct *BATHSE* BA2 .... **137** D1
Greenway Dr *HNBRY/STHM* BS10 .. **47** E3 2
Greenway Gdns *TRWBR* BA14 .... **157** E1
Greenway La *BATHSE* BA2 .... **137** D2 1
Greenway Pk *CLVDN* BS21 .... **85** F1 2
HNBRY/STHM BS10 .... **47** E3 3
Greenway Rd *RDLND/MONT* BS6 ...... **63** F4
Greenways *KGWD/HNM* BS15 .... **69** E5 1
Greenways Rd *YATE/CS* BS37 .... **19** E2
The Greenway *MANG/FISH* BS16 .. **68** A3 5
Greenwood Cl *HORF/LLZ* BS7 .... **47** F4 2
Greenwood Rd
BRSG/KWL/STAPK BS4 .... **93** E3 2
MTN/WRL BS22 .... **129** D5
Gregory Ct
OLD/WMLY/WICK BS30 .... **81** E3 1
Gregory Md *YTN/CONG* BS49 .... **116** A2
Grenville Av *OMX/HUT/LCK* BS24 .... **153** F1
Grenville Cl *EVILLE/WHL* BS5 .... **79** D1
Grenville Pl *CBRIS/FH* BS1 .... **75** D4 4
Grenville Rd *RDLND/MONT* BS6 .... **64** C3
Greve Ct *OLD/WMLY/WICK* BS30 .... **81** D5 8
Greville Rd *BMSTR* BS3 .... **75** F5
Greville St *BMSTR* BS3 .... **76** A5
Greylands Rd
BMSTRD/HC/WWD BS13 .... **91** D5
Greystoke Av *HNBRY/STHM* BS10 .... **46** B3
Greystoke Gdns
HNLZ/SM/SNYPK/WT BS9 .... **46** B3 2
Greystones *MANG/FISH* BS16 .... **51** F2 1
Griffin Cl *MTN/WRL* BS22 .... **130** A5 1
Griffin Rd *CLVDN* BS21 .... **85** D1
Griggfield Wk *HGRV/WHIT* BS14 .... **93** D5 1
Grimsbury Rd *KGWD/HNM* BS15 .... **81** E1
Grindell Rd *EVILLE/WHL* BS5 .... **78** B2
Grinfield Av
BMSTRD/HC/WWD BS13 .... **102** A3
Grinfield Cl
BMSTRD/HC/WWD BS13 .... **102** A3 3
Grinfield Ct
BMSTRD/HC/WWD BS13 .... **102** A3 4
Grittleton Rd *HORF/LLZ* BS7 .... **47** F3
Grosvenor Bridge Rd
CBATH/BATHN BA1 .... **124** A1
Grosvenor Pk
CBATH/BATHN BA1 .... **124** A1 1
Grosvenor Pl *CBATH/BATHN* BA1 .... **123** F1
Grosvenor Rd *CBRISNE* BS2 .... **76** C1
Ground Cnr *TRWBR* BA14 .... **149** D1
Grove Av *CBRIS/FH* BS1 .... **2** D5
HNLZ/SM/SNYPK/WT BS9 .... **45** D4
Grove Bank *MANG/FISH* BS16 .... **51** D2
Grove Dr *MTN/WRL* BS22 .... **142** B1 2
Grove La *WSM* BS23 .... **140** C2
Grove Leaze *AVONM* BS11 .... **43** E5
BOAV BA15 .... **146** B3
Grove Pk *BRSG/KWL/STAPK* BS4 .... **94** B2 5
RDLND/MONT BS6 .... **64** A4
Grove Park Av
BRSG/KWL/STAPK BS4 .... **94** B2
Grove Park Rd
BRSG/KWL/STAPK BS4 .... **94** B2
WSM BS23 .... **140** C1
Grove Rd *HNLZ/SM/SNYPK/WT* BS9 .. **45** E3
MANG/FISH BS16 .... **66** C2
MTN/WRL BS22 .... **142** B1
RDLND/MONT BS6 .... **63** F4
WSM BS23 .... **140** C2 3
Grovesend Rd *THNB/SVB* BS35 .... **8** C4
Grove St *CBATH/BATHN* BA1 .... **4** C2
The Grove *CBRIS/FH* BS1 .... **2** C5
OLD/WMLY/WICK BS30 .... **81** E5
WNSC BS25 .... **154** B3
Grove Vw *MANG/FISH* BS16 .... **49** F5 1
Grove Wood Rd *RDSTK/MIDN* BA3 .. **162** B4
Guernsey Av *BRSG/KWL/STAPK* BS4.. **79** D5
Guest Av *MANG/FISH* BS16 .... **52** C5
Guildford Rd *BRSG/KWL/STAPK* BS4.. **78** C4
Guinea La *CBATH/BATHN* BA1 .... **4** B1
MANG/FISH BS16 .... **67** E1 3
Guinea St *CBRIS/FH* BS1 .... **2** D6
Gulliford's Bank *CLVDN* BS21 .... **85** E2
Gullimores Gdns
BMSTRD/HC/WWD BS13 .... **101** F3 2
Gullivers Pl *YATE/CS* BS37 .... **20** B5
Gullock Tyning *RDSTK/MIDN* BA3 .... **161** E3
Gullons Cl
BMSTRD/HC/WWD BS13 .... **101** E1 2
Gullon Wk
BMSTRD/HC/WWD BS13 .... **101** D2
The Gully *FRCTL/WBN* BS36 .... **32** A1
Gunning Cl *KGWD/HNM* BS15 .... **80** B3
Gunter's Hl *EVILLE/WHL* BS5 .... **79** E3 2
Guthrie Rd *CFTN/FAIL* BS8 .... **75** E1
Gwilliam St *BMSTR* BS3 .... **92** B1
Gwyn St *CBRISNE* BS2 .... **64** C5

H

Haberfield Hl *PTSHD/EG* BS20 .... **60** B4
Hacket Hl *THNB/SVB* BS35 .... **9** F4
Hacket La *THNB/SVB* BS35 .... **9** E4
Haden Rd *TRWBR* BA14 .... **157** D5 2
Hadley Ct *OLD/WMLY/WICK* BS30 .. **81** F3 2
Hadley Rd *BATHSE* BA2 .... **137** F3
Hadrian Cl
HNLZ/SM/SNYPK/WT BS9 .... **62** A2 2
Halbrow Crs *MANG/FISH* BS16 .... **68** A1
Haldon Cl *BMSTR* BS3 .... **92** B3
Hale Cl *KGWD/HNM* BS15 .... **80** B5 1
Hales Horn Cl *ALMDB* BS32 .... **29** E2
Halfacre Cl *HGRV/WHIT* BS14 .... **103** E4
Halfacre La *HGRV/WHIT* BS14 .... **103** F4
Halfway Cl *TRWBR* BA14 .... **157** F2
Halifax Rd *YATE/CS* BS37 .... **19** E1
Hallam Rd *CLVDN* BS21 .... **84** C1
Hallards Cl *AVONM* BS11 .... **44** A3
Hallen Cl *HNBRY/STHM* BS10 .... **25** E5
Hallen Dr *HNLZ/SM/SNYPK/WT* BS9 .. **45** D4
Hallen Rd *HNBRY/STHM* BS10 .... **25** D4
Halletts Wy *PTSHD/EG* BS20 .... **56** B1 1
Halliwell Rd *PTSHD/EG* BS20 .... **54** B2
Halls Rd *KGWD/HNM* BS15 .... **80** B1 3
Hall St *BMSTR* BS3 .... **91** F2
Halsbury Rd *RDLND/MONT* BS6 .... **63** F2
Halstock Av *MANG/FISH* BS16 .... **67** D3 3
Halston Dr *CBRISNE* BS2 .... **77** D1
Halswell Gdns
BMSTRD/HC/WWD BS13 .... **101** F3
Halswell Rd *CLVDN* BS21 .... **85** D3
Halt End *HGRV/WHIT* BS14 .... **104** A4
The Halve *TRWBR* BA14 .... **157** D3
Halwyn Cl
HNLZ/SM/SNYPK/WT BS9 .... **62** B1 2
Hamble Cl *THNB/SVB* BS35 .... **8** C4
Hambledon Rd *MTN/WRL* BS22 ...... **130** B3
Hambrook La *BRSTK/PCHW* BS34 ...... **30** A4
Ham Farm La *MANG/FISH* BS16 .... **52** C5
Ham Gn *PTSHD/EG* BS20 .... **60** B2
Hamilton Rd *BMSTR* BS3 .... **75** F5
CBATH/BATHN BA1 .... **112** C5
EVILLE/WHL BS5 .... **77** E1 9
WSM BS23 .... **140** B1 2
Ham La *LGASH* BS41 .... **100** B4
MANG/FISH BS16 .... **49** F5
The Hamlet *NAIL* BS48 .... **87** F1
Hammersmith Rd
EVILLE/WHL BS5 .... **78** B1 5
Hammond Cl
BRSG/KWL/STAPK BS4 .... **94** B3 5
Hammond Gdns
HNLZ/SM/SNYPK/WT BS9 .... **45** F4 1
Hammond Wy *TRWBR* BA14 .... **149** D5
Hampden Cl *YATE/CS* BS37 .... **19** E1
Hampden Rd
BRSG/KWL/STAPK BS4 .... **93** F1 1
MTN/WRL BS22 .... **128** C5
Hampshire Wy *YATE/CS* BS37 .... **20** A1 3
Hampstead Rd
BRSG/KWL/STAPK BS4 .... **94** A1
Hampton Cl *OLD/WMLY/WICK* BS30 .. **81** E4
Hampton La *RDLND/MONT* BS6 .... **63** F5
Hampton Pk *RDLND/MONT* BS6 .... **63** F5 5
Hampton Rd *RDLND/MONT* BS6 .... **63** F4
Hampton Rw *BATHSE* BA2 .... **123** F2
Hampton St *KGWD/HNM* BS15 .... **68** B5 4
Hampton Vw *CBATH/BATHN* BA1 .... **123** F1
Hams Rd *KEYN* BS31 .... **97** D5
Ham Wood Cl
OMX/HUT/LCK BS24 .... **152** A3 3
Hanbury Cl *KGWD/HNM* BS15 .... **80** B4
Hanbury Rd *CFTN/FAIL* BS8 .... **75** E1
Handel Av *EVILLE/WHL* BS5 .... **78** B2 5
Handel Rd *KEYN* BS31 .... **106** B2
Handford Wy
OLD/WMLY/WICK BS30 .... **97** F1 1
Hanford Ct *HGRV/WHIT* BS14 .... **94** B5 2
Hanham Rd *KGWD/HNM* BS15 .... **80** B2
Hanham Wy *NAIL* BS48 .... **86** A2
Hannah More Rd *NAIL* BS48 .... **86** B3
Hanover Cl *MTN/WRL* BS22 .... **129** F3 6
TRWBR BA14 .... **149** E5
Hanover Ct *CBRIS/FH* BS1 .... **3** F1 2
Hanover Pl *CBRIS/FH* BS1 .... **75** F4 3
Hanover St *CBATH/BATHN* BA1 .... **123** F1 3
EVILLE/WHL BS5 .... **78** A2 7
Hansford Cl *BATHSE* BA2 .... **136** C4
Hansford Sq *BATHSE* BA2 .... **136** C4
Hanson's Wy *CLVDN* BS21 .... **84** C2 3
Hans Price Cl *WSM* BS23 .... **141** D2 6
Hantone Hl *BATHSE* BA2 .... **125** D2
Happerton La *PTSHD/EG* BS20 .... **60** A4
Hapsburg Cl *MTN/WRL* BS22 .... **129** F3 7
Harbour Rd *PTSHD/EG* BS20 .... **39** F5
Harbour Wall
HNLZ/SM/SNYPK/WT BS9 .... **62** A2 3
Harbour Wy *CBRIS/FH* BS1 .... **2** A5
Harbury Rd
HNLZ/SM/SNYPK/WT BS9 .... **47** D4
Harbutts *BATHSE* BA2 .... **125** D1
Harcombe Hl *FRCTL/WBN* BS36 .... **31** F4
Harcombe Rd *FRCTL/WBN* BS36 .... **31** E3
Harcourt Av *EVILLE/WHL* BS5 .... **79** E3 3
Harcourt Cl *KEYN* BS31 .... **108** C5 2
Harcourt Gdns
CBATH/BATHN BA1 .... **111** F5 2
Harcourt Hl *RDLND/MONT* BS6 .... **64** A3
Harcourt Rd *RDLND/MONT* BS6 .... **63** F2
Hardenhuish Rd
BRSG/KWL/STAPK BS4 .... **78** B4
Harden Rd *HGRV/WHIT* BS14 .... **104** C2
Hardington Dr *KEYN* BS31 .... **107** E5
Hardwick Cl *BRSG/KWL/STAPK* BS4 .. **94** C1
OLD/WMLY/WICK BS30 .... **82** B4 1
Hardwicke *YATE/CS* BS37 .... **35** D1
Hardwick Rd *PTSHD/EG* BS20 .... **60** A2
Hardy Av *BMSTR* BS3 .... **91** E1
Hardy Ct *OLD/WMLY/WICK* BS30 .... **81** D4
Hardy Rd *BMSTR* BS3 .... **91** F2 5
Hareclive Rd
BMSTRD/HC/WWD BS13 .... **101** F2
Harefield Cl *KGWD/HNM* BS15 ...... **96** A2 2
Hare Knapp *BOAV* BA15 .... **146** B3
Harescombe *YATE/CS* BS37 .... **35** F1
Harewood Rd *EVILLE/WHL* BS5 .... **67** E5
Harford Cl
HNLZ/SM/SNYPK/WT BS9 .... **45** D4 1
Harford Dr *MANG/FISH* BS16 .... **51** D2
Harford St *TRWBR* BA14 .... **157** E3
Harington Pl *CBATH/BATHN* BA1 .... **4** B3 4
Harlech Wy *OLD/WMLY/WICK* BS30 .. **97** F2
Harleston St *EVILLE/WHL* BS5 .... **77** E1 10
Harley St *CBATH/BATHN* BA1 .... **123** D2 6
Harmer Cl *HNBRY/STHM* BS10 .... **26** A5
Harmony Dr *PTSHD/EG* BS20 .... **55** D2
Harmony Pl *TRWBR* BA14 .... **157** D5 3
Harnhill Cl
BMSTRD/HC/WWD BS13 .... **101** F3 3
Harolds Wy *KGWD/HNM* BS15 .... **80** A3
Harptree Cl *NAIL* BS48 .... **86** C4
Harptree Ct
OLD/WMLY/WICK BS30 .... **81** E5 2
Harptree Gv *BMSTR* BS3 .... **91** F2 6
Harrington Av *HGRV/WHIT* BS14 .... **104** C1
Harrington Cl
OLD/WMLY/WICK BS30 .... **98** C4
Harrington Gv
HGRV/WHIT BS14 .... **104** C1 3
Harrington Rd *HGRV/WHIT* BS14 .... **104** C1
Harrington Wk
HGRV/WHIT BS14 .... **104** C1 4
Harris Barton *FRCTL/WBN* BS36 .... **32** B1
Harris Ct *OLD/WMLY/WICK* BS30 .... **81** D5 9
Harris La *CFTN/FAIL* BS8 .... **73** D1
Harrison Cl *MANG/FISH* BS16 .... **52** C5 2
Harrowdene Rd
BRSG/KWL/STAPK BS4 .... **93** F1
Harrow Rd *BRSG/KWL/STAPK* BS4 .... **94** B1
Harry Stoke Rd *BRSTK/PCHW* BS34 .. **29** F5
Hartcliffe Rd *BRSG/KWL/STAPK* BS4.. **92** C4
Hartcliffe Wk
BRSG/KWL/STAPK BS4 .... **93** D4 4
Hartcliffe Wy *BMSTR* BS3 .... **92** A3

BRSG/KWL/STAPK BS4 .... **92** A5
Hartfield Av *RDLND/MONT* BS6 .... **76** A1
Hartgill Cl
BMSTRD/HC/WWD BS13 .... **101** F4
Hartington Pk
RDLND/MONT BS6 .... **63** F4 5
Hartley Cl *YATE/CS* BS37........................ **21** D4
Harts Cft *YATE/CS* BS37........................ **20** A1 4
Harts Paddock *RDSTK/MIDN* BA3.... **160** C1
Harvest Cl *ALMDB* BS32 .... **13** E4
Harvest Wy *MTN/WRL* BS22 .... **129** F2 4
Harvey Cl *MTN/WRL* BS22 .... **129** F3 3
Harwood Gdns *MTN/WRL* BS22 .. **129** D3 5
Haselbury Gv *KEYN* BS31 .... **108** C5
Haskins Ct
OLD/WMLY/WICK BS30 .... **81** E5 3
Hassell Dr *CBRISNE* BS2 .... **77** E2
Hastings Cl *BMSTR* BS3 .... **92** A3 1
Hastings Rd *BMSTR* BS3....................... **92** A3
Hatchet La *BRSTK/PCHW* BS34 .... **29** F4
Hatchet Rd *BRSTK/PCHW* BS34.......... **29** E3
Hatchmere *THNB/SVB* BS35 .... **9** D4
Hatfield Buildings *BATHSE* BA2 .... **5** E6
Hatfield Rd *BATHSE* BA2 .... **136** C2
WSM BS23 .... **141** F2
Hatherley *YATE/CS* BS37 .... **35** F1
Hatherley Rd *HORF/LLZ* BS7 .... **64** C2
Hathway Wk *EVILLE/WHL* BS5 .... **77** E1
Hatters' La *YATE/CS* BS37..................... **21** D4
Havelock St *TRWBR* BA14 .... **156** C5 2
The Haven *KGWD/HNM* BS15 .... **68** C5
Haversham Cl *MTN/WRL* BS22 .... **142** C1 3
Haverstock Rd
BRSG/KWL/STAPK BS4....................... **93** E1
Haviland Gv *CBATH/BATHN* BA1 ...... **111** E4
Haviland Pk *CBATH/BATHN* BA1 .. **111** F5 3
Havory *CBATH/BATHN* BA1 .... **123** F1
Hawarden Ter *CBATH/BATHN* BA1 .. **123** F1
Hawburn Cl *BRSG/KWL/STAPK* BS4 .. **94** B2
Haweswater Cl
OLD/WMLY/WICK BS30 .... **82** B3 3
Hawke Rd *MTN/WRL* BS22................ **129** D3
Hawkesbury Rd *MANG/FISH* BS16 .... **66** C3
Hawkesley Dr *BRSTK/PCHW* BS34 .... **29** E2
Hawkfield Cl
BMSTRD/HC/WWD BS13 .... **102** B2
Hawkfield Rd
BMSTRD/HC/WWD BS13 .... **102** B2
Hawkfield Wy
BMSTRD/HC/WWD BS13 .... **102** B2 1
Hawkins Cl
OLD/WMLY/WICK BS30 .... **82** A5 2
Hawkins Crs *ALMDB* BS32 .... **13** E5
Hawkins St *CBRISNE* BS2 .... **3** G2
Hawkley Dr *ALMDB* BS32 .... **13** E2
Hawksmoor Cl *HGRV/WHIT* BS14 .... **103** E1
Hawksworth Dr *KGWD/HNM* BS15.... **79** F5
MTN/WRL BS22 .... **130** B3 3
Hawthorn Av *KGWD/HNM* BS15 .... **79** F4 5
Hawthorn Cl *BRSTK/PCHW* BS34 ...... **27** F1
PTSHD/EG BS20 .... **55** D1
Hawthorn Crs *THNB/SVB* BS35 .... **8** C2 2
YTN/CONG BS49 .... **116** A2
The Hawthornes *MANG/FISH* BS16 .. **69** D2
Hawthorne St
BRSG/KWL/STAPK BS4........................ **93** E1
Hawthorn Gdns *MTN/WRL* BS22...... **128** C5
Hawthorn Gv *BATHSE* BA2................ **137** D4
TRWBR BA14...................................... **158** B2
Hawthorn Hts *MTN/WRL* BS22 .... **128** C4
Hawthorn Hl *MTN/WRL* BS22 ...... **129** D5 2
Hawthorn Pk *MTN/WRL* BS22 ...... **129** D4 2
Hawthorn Rd *RDSTK/MIDN* BA3...... **163** E2
Hawthorns La *KEYN* BS31 .... **106** C2
Hawthorn Wy *BRSTK/PCHW* BS34 .... **29** F3
NAIL BS48 .... **87** E2
Haycombe *HGRV/WHIT* BS14 ...... **103** D1 1
Haycombe Dr *BATHSE* BA2 .... **121** E5
Haycombe La *BATHSE* BA2 .... **135** E2
Hay Ct *PTSHD/EG* BS20......................... **59** E2
Hayden Cl *BATHSE* BA2 .... **122** C5 2
Haydock Cl *MANG/FISH* BS16 .... **52** A2 4
Haydon Gdns *HORF/LLZ* BS7 .... **65** F1 1
Haydon Ga *RDSTK/MIDN* BA3 .... **162** C4
Haydon Hl *RDSTK/MIDN* BA3............ **162** C4
Hayeley Dr *BRSTK/PCHW* BS34 .... **29** F2
Hayes Cl *CBRISNE* BS2.......................... **77** E2
TRWBR BA14....................................... **157** E1
Hayesfield Pk *BATHSE* BA2 .... **4** A6
Hayes Park Rd *RDSTK/MIDN* BA3 .... **160** C2
Hayes Rd *RDSTK/MIDN* BA3............. **160** C2
Hay Hl *CBATH/BATHN* BA1 .... **4** B1
Hay Leaze *YATE/CS* BS37 .... **19** E1 1
The Haymarket *CBRIS/FH* BS1 .... **2** D1
Haynes La *MANG/FISH* BS16 .... **68** B1
Haythorn Ct *MANG/FISH* BS16 .... **69** D1
Haytor Pk
HNLZ/SM/SNYPK/WT BS9 .... **45** E5
Hayward Cl *CLVDN* BS21....................... **84** C3
Hayward Rd *EVILLE/WHL* BS5 .... **78** A2
MANG/FISH BS16 .... **68** B3
Haywood Cl
OMX/HUT/LCK BS24 .... **151** F4 3
Haywood Gdns
OMX/HUT/LCK BS24.......................... **151** F4
Hazel Av *RDLND/MONT* BS6................ **63** F4
Hazelbury Dr
OLD/WMLY/WICK BS30 .... **82** A3
Hazelbury Rd *HGRV/WHIT* BS14 .... **94** A4
NAIL BS48 .... **86** C3
Hazel Cote Rd *HGRV/WHIT* BS14...... **103** F3
Hazel Cresent *THNB/SVB* BS35 .... **9** D3
Hazeldene Rd *BRSTK/PCHW* BS34 .... **28** B1
WSM BS23 .... **141** F2
Hazel Gv *BATHSE* BA2 .... **136** B1
Hazelgrove *FRCTL/WBN* BS36 .... **31** E3 2
Hazel Gv *HORF/LLZ* BS7 .... **48** B3
RDSTK/MIDN BA3 .... **161** E4
TRWBR BA14...................................... **158** B2
Hazell Cl *CLVDN* BS21 .... **85** E3
Hazel Ter *RDSTK/MIDN* BA3............. **161** E4
Hazelton Rd *HORF/LLZ* BS7 .... **64** B3
Hazel Wy *BATHSE* BA2 .... **136** B5
Hazelwood Rd
HNLZ/SM/SNYPK/WT BS9 .... **62** B3
Hazleton Gdns *BATHSE* BA2 .... **139** D2
Headford Av *EVILLE/WHL* BS5............ **79** F2
Headford Rd
BRSG/KWL/STAPK BS4....................... **92** B3
Headington Cl *KGWD/HNM* BS15 .. **80** B5 2
Headley Ct
BMSTRD/HC/WWD BS13 .... **101** F1
Headley La
BMSTRD/HC/WWD BS13 .... **101** F1
Headley Park Av
BMSTRD/HC/WWD BS13 .... **91** F5
Headley Park Rd
BMSTRD/HC/WWD BS13 .... **91** E5
Headley Rd
BMSTRD/HC/WWD BS13 .... **101** E1
Headley Wk
BMSTRD/HC/WWD BS13 .... **91** F5
Heart Meers *HGRV/WHIT* BS14 .... **103** F2 5
Heath Cl *FRCTL/WBN* BS36................ **31** F2
Heathcote Dr *FRCTL/WBN* BS36 .... **33** E1
Heathcote Rd *MANG/FISH* BS16 .... **67** F4
MANG/FISH BS16 .... **68** C1 2
Heathcote Wk *KGWD/HNM* BS15 ...... **68** A4
Heath Ct *MANG/FISH* BS16 .... **51** E4 2
Heather Av *FRCTL/WBN* BS36 .... **32** C2
Heather Cl *KGWD/HNM* BS15............. **79** F1
Heatherdene *HGRV/WHIT* BS14 .... **93** D5
Heather Dr *BATHSE* BA2 .... **136** B5 2
Heather Shaw *TRWBR* BA14 .... **157** E4
Heathfield Cl *CBATH/BATHN* BA1 .... **111** E4
KEYN BS31... **106** A2
Heathfield Crs *HGRV/WHIT* BS14 .... **103** E3
Heathfield Rd *NAIL* BS48 .... **87** D2
Heathfields *MANG/FISH* BS16 .... **51** E3
Heathfield Wy *NAIL* BS48 .... **87** D2 3
Heath Gdns *FRCTL/WBN* BS36........... **33** D2
MANG/FISH BS16 .... **51** E3
Heathgate *YTN/CONG* BS49............. **116** B3
Heath House La
MANG/FISH BS16 .... **66** A1 2
Heath Rdg *LGASH* BS41 .... **89** E2
Heath Ri *OLD/WMLY/WICK* BS30 .... **81** F4 2
Heath Rd *EVILLE/WHL* BS5.................. **65** F3
KGWD/HNM BS15................................. **79** F5
MANG/FISH BS16 .... **51** E4
NAIL BS48 .... **87** E2 2
Heath St *EVILLE/WHL* BS5 .... **66** A4
Heath Wk *MANG/FISH* BS16................ **51** E4
Heber St *EVILLE/WHL* BS5 .... **78** A2
Hebron Rd *BMSTR* BS3 .... **92** A1 5
Heddington Cl *TRWBR* BA14 .... **158** C2
Hedgemead Vw *MANG/FISH* BS16 .... **66** B1
Hedges Cl *CLVDN* BS21 .... **84** B3 3
The Hedges *MTN/WRL* BS22 .... **130** B4
Hedwick St *EVILLE/WHL* BS5 .... **78** C2
Heggard Cl
BMSTRD/HC/WWD BS13 .... **101** E2 4
Hellier Wk
BMSTRD/HC/WWD BS13 .... **102** A4 1
Helmdon Rd *TRWBR* BA14.................. **156** A3
Helston Rd *NAIL* BS48.......................... **87** F3
Helting Ct *CBATH/BATHN* BA1 .... **4** B4 4
Hemming Wy
OMX/HUT/LCK BS24 .... **153** D2 2
Hemplow Cl *HGRV/WHIT* BS14 .... **94** B5
Hempton La *ALMDB* BS32 .... **12** B3
Henacre Rd *AVONM* BS11...................... **44** A3
Henbury Rd *HNBRY/STHM* BS10 .... **45** F1 3
HNLZ/SM/SNYPK/WT BS9 .... **46** B3
KGWD/HNM BS15 .... **79** F4 6
Henbury Road Henbury Hl
HNLZ/SM/SNYPK/WT BS9 .... **46** A3
Hencliffe Rd *HGRV/WHIT* BS14 .... **104** B1
Hencliffe Wy *KGWD/HNM* BS15 .... **95** F1
Henderson Cl *TRWBR* BA14 .... **156** B5 1
Henderson Rd *KGWD/HNM* BS15 ...... **79** F4
Hendre Rd *BMSTR* BS3........................ **91** E2
Henfield Crs *OLD/WMLY/WICK* BS30.. **81** F5
Henfield Rd *FRCTL/WBN* BS36............ **33** D4
Hengaston St *BMSTR* BS3 .... **91** F2 7
Hengrove Av *HGRV/WHIT* BS14......... **93** F4
Hengrove La *HGRV/WHIT* BS14.......... **93** F4
Hengrove Rd
BRSG/KWL/STAPK BS4........................ **93** E2
Hengrove Wy
BMSTRD/HC/WWD BS13 .... **101** F2
BRSG/KWL/STAPK BS4...................... **102** C1
Henleaze Av
HNLZ/SM/SNYPK/WT BS9 .... **63** E1
Henleaze Gdns
HNLZ/SM/SNYPK/WT BS9 .... **63** E1
Henleaze Pk
HNLZ/SM/SNYPK/WT BS9 .... **64** A1
Henleaze Park Dr
HNLZ/SM/SNYPK/WT BS9 .... **47** D5
Henleaze Rd
HNLZ/SM/SNYPK/WT BS9 .... **63** E1
Henleaze Ter
HNLZ/SM/SNYPK/WT BS9 .... **46** C4
Henley Gv
HNLZ/SM/SNYPK/WT BS9 .... **63** F1
Henley La *YTN/CONG* BS49............... **117** D4
Henley Ldg *YTN/CONG* BS49 .... **117** D4 1
Henley Pk *YTN/CONG* BS49 .... **116** C4
Hennessy Cl *HGRV/WHIT* BS14 .... **102** C4
Henrietta Gdns *BATHSE* BA2 .... **4** D1
Henrietta Ms *BATHSE* BA2 .... **4** D2
Henrietta Pl *BATHSE* BA2 .... **4** C2 2
Henrietta Rd *BATHSE* BA2 .... **4** D1
Henrietta St *BATHSE* BA2...................... **4** D2
CBRISNE BS2 .... **76** B1 6
EVILLE/WHL BS5 .... **65** F5 5
Henry St *BMSTR* BS3........................... **77** D5
CBATH/BATHN BA1 .... **4** C4 5
Henry Williamson Ct
OLD/WMLY/WICK BS30 .... **81** E4 6
Henshaw Cl *KGWD/HNM* BS15 ...... **68** A4 2
Henshaw Rd *KGWD/HNM* BS15.......... **68** A4
Henshaw Wk *KGWD/HNM* BS15 .... **68** A4
Hensley Gdns *BATHSE* BA2 .... **136** C1
Hensley Rd *BATHSE* BA2................... **136** C2
Hensman's Hl *CFTN/FAIL* BS8 .... **75** E3
Hepburn Rd *CBRIS/FH* BS1 .... **76** C1
Herald Cl *HNLZ/SM/SNYPK/WT* BS9 .. **62** B1
Herapath St *EVILLE/WHL* BS5 .... **78** A3
Herbert Crs *EVILLE/WHL* BS5 .... **66** B3 2
Herbert Rd *BATHSE* BA2.................... **122** B5
CLVDN BS21... **71** D5
Herbert St *BMSTR* BS3 .... **76** A5
EVILLE/WHL BS5 .... **78** A1
Hercules Cl *BRSTK/PCHW* BS34.......... **29** E2
Hereford Rd *CBRISNE* BS2 .... **65** E4 6
Hereford St *BMSTR* BS3 .... **92** B1 3
Herkomer Cl *HORF/LLZ* BS7............... **48** C4
Herluin Wy *WSM* BS23 .... **142** A4
Hermes Cl *KEYN* BS31........................ **108** A5
Hermitage Cl *AVONM* BS11 .... **43** F4
Hermitage Rd *CBATH/BATHN* BA1 .. **122** C1
MANG/FISH BS16 .... **68** B1
Heron Cl *MTN/WRL* BS22 .... **143** D1
Heron Gdns *PTSHD/EG* BS20 .... **56** C2
Heron Rd *EVILLE/WHL* BS5.................. **65** F5
Heron Wy *YATE/CS* BS37 .... **36** A1
Herridge Cl
BMSTRD/HC/WWD BS13 .... **101** F3
Herridge Rd
BMSTRD/HC/WWD BS13 .... **101** F3
Hersey Gdns
BMSTRD/HC/WWD BS13 .... **100** C4
Hesding Cl *KGWD/HNM* BS15 .... **96** A1 1
Hestercombe Rd
BMSTRD/HC/WWD BS13 .... **101** F1 1
Hewland Ct *AVONM* BS11 .... **45** D1 4
Heyford Av *EVILLE/WHL* BS5.............. **65** F3
Heyron Wk
BMSTRD/HC/WWD BS13 .... **101** F3
Heywood Rd *PTSHD/EG* BS20 .... **60** A2
Heywood Ter *PTSHD/EG* BS20 ...... **60** A2 4
Hicks Av *MANG/FISH* BS16 .... **52** C3
Hicks Common Rd
FRCTL/WBN BS36 .... **31** F2
Hicks Ct *OLD/WMLY/WICK* BS30 .. **81** D5 10
Higham St *BRSG/KWL/STAPK* BS4 .. **77** D5 5
High Bannerdown
CBATH/BATHN BA1.......................... **115** F3
Highbury Pl *CBATH/BATHN* BA1 ...... **123** E1
Highbury Rd *BMSTR* BS3 .... **92** A3
HORF/LLZ BS7 .... **48** A4
WSM BS23 .... **140** B1
Highbury Vls *CBRISNE* BS2 .... **76** A1 2
Highcroft *OLD/WMLY/WICK* BS30 .. **82** A3 4
Highdale Av *CLVDN* BS21 .... **85** D1
Highdale Cl *HGRV/WHIT* BS14 .... **103** F3
Highdale Rd *CLVDN* BS21 .... **85** D1
High Elm *KGWD/HNM* BS15 .... **80** C3 3
Highett Dr *EVILLE/WHL* BS5 .... **65** E5 10
Highfield Av *KGWD/HNM* BS15 .... **80** B4
Highfield Cl *BATHSE* BA2 .... **121** F5 1
Highfield Dr *PTSHD/EG* BS20............... **54** C3
Highfield Gdns
OLD/WMLY/WICK BS30 .... **98** A2
Highfield Gv *HORF/LLZ* BS7 .... **64** B1
Highfield Rd *BOAV* BA15 .... **147** D2
KEYN BS31 .... **107** D5 1
OMX/HUT/LCK BS24.......................... **151** F4
YATE/CS BS37 .... **20** B4
Highfields *RDSTK/MIDN* BA3 .... **162** A2
Highfields Cl *BRSTK/PCHW* BS34........ **30** A5
High Gv *HNLZ/SM/SNYPK/WT* BS9 .... **44** C4

Highgrove St
BRSG/KWL/STAPK BS4 77 E5 5
Highland Cl *MTN/WRL* BS22 128 A5 3
Highland Crs *CFTN/FAIL* BS8 63 E4 3
Highland Rd *BATHSE* BA2 121 F5
Highland Sq *CFTN/FAIL* BS8 63 E4 4
Highlands Rd *LGASH* BS41 89 E2
PTSHD/EG BS20 55 F1 4
Highleaze Rd
OLD/WMLY/WICK BS30 82 A5
Highmead Gdns
BMSTRD/HC/WWD BS13 100 C3
High Mdw *RDSTK/MIDN* BA3 160 C3
Highmore Gdns *HORF/LLZ* BS7 49 D4
Highnam Cl *BRSTK/PCHW* BS34 12 C4
High Pk *HGRV/WHIT* BS14 93 F3
Highridge Crs
BMSTRD/HC/WWD BS13 101 D2
Highridge Gn
BMSTRD/HC/WWD BS13 100 C1
Highridge Pk
BMSTRD/HC/WWD BS13 101 D2 3
Highridge Rd *BMSTR* BS3 91 F2 8
LGASH BS41 100 A4
Highridge Wk
BMSTRD/HC/WWD BS13 90 C5
High St *AVONM* BS11 43 E4
BATHSE BA2 121 F4
BATHSE BA2 125 D1
CBATH/BATHN BA1 4 C3 6
CBATH/BATHN BA1 111 F5
CBATH/BATHN BA1 113 D2
CBATH/BATHN BA1 115 D4
CBRIS/FH BS1 2 D2
CFTN/FAIL BS8 63 E4
EVILLE/WHL BS5 65 F5
FRCTL/WBN BS36 31 E2
HNLZ/SM/SNYPK/WT BS9 46 B3
KEYN BS31 106 C1
KEYN BS31 108 C4
KGWD/HNM BS15 80 A4
KGWD/HNM BS15 80 C1
KGWD/HNM BS15 81 F1
MANG/FISH BS16 68 A2
MTN/WRL BS22 129 D5
NAIL BS48 87 D2
OLD/WMLY/WICK BS30 82 B2
OLD/WMLY/WICK BS30 82 B5
OLD/WMLY/WICK BS30 83 F3
OLD/WMLY/WICK BS30 98 C4
PTSHD/EG BS20 56 B1
PTSHD/EG BS20 58 B3
RDSTK/MIDN BA3 161 E3
THNB/SVB BS35 8 B3
WSM BS23 6 B1 1
WSM BS23 140 C2 4
YATE/CS BS37 17 E1
YATE/CS BS37 20 C4
YTN/CONG BS49 116 B3
YTN/CONG BS49 117 F2
YTN/CONG BS49 133 D2
High Vw *PTSHD/EG* BS20 55 E2
Highview Rd *KGWD/HNM* BS15 68 C4
Highway *YATE/CS* BS37 20 A3
Highwood La *BRSTK/PCHW* BS34 27 F1
HNBRY/STHM BS10 27 E1
Highwood Rd *BRSTK/PCHW* BS34 27 F1
Highworth Crs *YATE/CS* BS37 19 E5
Highworth Rd
BRSG/KWL/STAPK BS4 78 B4
Hildesheim Cl *WSM* BS23 7 F3 1
Hill Av *BATHSE* BA2 137 D4
BMSTR BS3 92 C1
Hillbrook Rd *THNB/SVB* BS35 9 D4 1
Hill Burn *HNLZ/SM/SNYPK/WT* BS9 47 D5
Hillburn Rd *EVILLE/WHL* BS5 79 E1
Hillcote Est *OMX/HUT/LCK* BS24 152 A5
Hill Crest *BRSG/KWL/STAPK* BS4 93 F3
Hillcrest *THNB/SVB* BS35 8 B3
Hillcrest Cl *NAIL* BS48 87 D3
Hillcrest Dr *BATHSE* BA2 135 F2
Hillcrest Rd *NAIL* BS48 87 D3
PTSHD/EG BS20 54 C2
Hillcroft Cl *MTN/WRL* BS22 127 F5
Hill Dr *CFTN/FAIL* BS8 88 A1
Hill End Dr *HNBRY/STHM* BS10 25 E5
Hillfields Av *MANG/FISH* BS16 68 A3
Hill Frost *YTN/CONG* BS49 116 C5
Hill Gay Cl *PTSHD/EG* BS20 55 D2 3
Hill Gv *HNLZ/SM/SNYPK/WT* BS9 47 D5
Hillgrove St *CBRISNE* BS2 76 C1 8
Hillgrove St North *CBRISNE* BS2 76 B1 7
Hill House Rd *MANG/FISH* BS16 69 D1
Hill La *PTSHD/EG* BS20 55 D5
Hill Lawn *BRSG/KWL/STAPK* BS4 94 B1
Hill Moor *CLVDN* BS21 85 E2
Hill Pk *YTN/CONG* BS49 133 E1
Hill Rd *CLVDN* BS21 70 C5
LGASH BS41 100 B5
MTN/WRL BS22 129 D5
WSM BS23 141 E2
Hill Rd East *MTN/WRL* BS22 129 D5 3
Hillsborough Rd
BRSG/KWL/STAPK BS4 78 A5
Hills Cl *KEYN* BS31 107 E2
Hillsdon Rd
HNLZ/SM/SNYPK/WT BS9 46 A3
Hillside *MANG/FISH* BS16 69 D1
PTSHD/EG BS20 58 B3
Hillside Av *KGWD/HNM* BS15 80 A1
RDSTK/MIDN BA3 160 B4
Hillside Cl *FRCTL/WBN* BS36 33 D1
Hillside Crs *RDSTK/MIDN* BA3 160 B4
Hillside Gdns *MTN/WRL* BS22 142 A1
Hillside La *FRCTL/WBN* BS36 33 D1 2
Hillside Rd *BATHSE* BA2 136 B1
CLVDN BS21 85 D1
EVILLE/WHL BS5 79 E2
LGASH BS41 89 F2
OMX/HUT/LCK BS24 152 A5
PTSHD/EG BS20 54 B2
RDSTK/MIDN BA3 160 C4
Hillside St *BRSG/KWL/STAPK* BS4 77 E5 6
Hillside West *OMX/HUT/LCK* BS24 153 E2
Hill St *BMSTR* BS3 77 D5
CBRIS/FH BS1 2 A3
EVILLE/WHL BS5 79 D1
TRWBR BA14 156 C4
The Hill *ALMDB* BS32 12 C1
Hilltop Gdns *EVILLE/WHL* BS5 79 E2
Hilltop Rd *MANG/FISH* BS16 68 B4
Hilltop Vw *EVILLE/WHL* BS5 79 E2
Hill Vw *CFTN/FAIL* BS8 75 F3
HNLZ/SM/SNYPK/WT BS9 47 D5
MANG/FISH BS16 68 B4
Hillview Av *CLVDN* BS21 85 D2 4
Hill View Cl *OLD/WMLY/WICK* BS30 82 A5
Hill View Rd
BMSTRD/HC/WWD BS13 91 E5
CBATH/BATHN BA1 113 F5
WSM BS23 7 H1
Hillyfield Rd
BMSTRD/HC/WWD BS13 101 E1
Hillyfields *WNSC* BS25 155 D4
Hillyfields Wy *WNSC* BS25 154 C4
Hilperton Rd *TRWBR* BA14 157 F3
Hinckley Cl *MTN/WRL* BS22 130 B4 1
Hinton Cl *KEYN* BS31 108 C4
Hinton Dr *OLD/WMLY/WICK* BS30 82 A3
Hinton Rd *EVILLE/WHL* BS5 66 A5
MANG/FISH BS16 67 E2 1
Hiscocks Dr *BATHSE* BA2 136 C1
Hither Gn *CLVDN* BS21 85 F2
Hobart Rd *WSM* BS23 151 E2
Hobbiton Rd *MTN/WRL* BS22 129 F2
Hobb's La *CBRIS/FH* BS1 2 B3 3
KGWD/HNM BS15 69 F5
Hobhouse Cl *BOAV* BA15 147 E5
Hobwell La *LGASH* BS41 90 A2 2
Hockey's La *MANG/FISH* BS16 67 E2 2
Hogarth Ms *MTN/WRL* BS22 129 F4 5
Hogarth Wk *HORF/LLZ* BS7 48 C4
Hogues Wk
BMSTRD/HC/WWD BS13 101 F3 4
Holbeach Wy *HGRV/WHIT* BS14 103 E4
Holbrook Crs
BMSTRD/HC/WWD BS13 102 B3
Holbrook La *OLD/WMLY/WICK* BS30 83 E2
TRWBR BA14 158 C1
Holcombe *HGRV/WHIT* BS14 103 D1 2
Holcombe Cl *BATHSE* BA2 125 D1
Holcombe Gn *CBATH/BATHN* BA1 111 F5
Holcombe Gv *KEYN* BS31 106 B2
Holcombe La *BATHSE* BA2 125 D1
Holcombe V *BATHSE* BA2 125 D1
Holdenhurst Rd *KGWD/HNM* BS15 68 A5
Holders Wk *LGASH* BS41 89 D3
Holford Cl *NAIL* BS48 87 D3
Holford Ct *HGRV/WHIT* BS14 103 F2
Holland Rd *CBATH/BATHN* BA1 123 F1
CLVDN BS21 84 B3
Holland St *WSM* BS23 141 F2
Hollies La *CBATH/BATHN* BA1 115 E1
Hollis Av *PTSHD/EG* BS20 56 A3
Hollis Cl *LGASH* BS41 89 D4
Hollis Crs *PTSHD/EG* BS20 56 A3 1
Hollister's Dr
BMSTRD/HC/WWD BS13 102 B4
Holloway *BATHSE* BA2 4 B6
Hollow La *MTN/WRL* BS22 129 E4
Hollowmead Cl *YTN/CONG* BS49 117 F3
Hollow Rd *ALMDB* BS32 12 B1
KGWD/HNM BS15 80 C1
The Hollows *FRCTL/WBN* BS36 53 D1
The Hollow *BATHSE* BA2 135 E1
Hollway Cl *HGRV/WHIT* BS14 104 C2 2
Hollway Rd *HGRV/WHIT* BS14 104 C2
Hollybush La
HNLZ/SM/SNYPK/WT BS9 62 C1
Holly Cl *EVILLE/WHL* BS5 67 E4
MTN/WRL BS22 143 F1
NAIL BS48 87 F1 1
Holly Crs *KGWD/HNM* BS15 68 C5 3
Holly Dr *BATHSE* BA2 136 B5
Holly Gn *KGWD/HNM* BS15 69 E5
Holly Gv *MANG/FISH* BS16 68 A3
Hollyguest Rd *KGWD/HNM* BS15 80 C3
Holly Hl *YATE/CS* BS37 17 F2
Holly Hill Rd *KGWD/HNM* BS15 81 D1
Holly La *CLVDN* BS21 71 F3
Hollyleigh Av *BRSTK/PCHW* BS34 48 A1
Holly Lodge Rd *EVILLE/WHL* BS5 67 D4
Hollyman Wk *CLVDN* BS21 85 F1 3
Hollymead La
HNLZ/SM/SNYPK/WT BS9 62 C2
Hollyridge *HGRV/WHIT* BS14 104 A1
Holly Rdg *PTSHD/EG* BS20 55 E1
Holly Wk *KEYN* BS31 106 B4
RDSTK/MIDN BA3 162 B3
Hollywood La *THNB/SVB* BS35 26 B1
Hollywood Rd
BRSG/KWL/STAPK BS4 94 B1
Holmdale Rd *BRSTK/PCHW* BS34 28 C5
Holmesdale Rd *BMSTR* BS3 92 C1
Holmes Gv
HNLZ/SM/SNYPK/WT BS9 63 F1
Holmes Hill Rd *EVILLE/WHL* BS5 79 D1
Holmes St *EVILLE/WHL* BS5 77 F3 7
Holmoak Rd *KEYN* BS31 106 A3
Holm Rd *OMX/HUT/LCK* BS24 153 D3
Holms Rd *WSM* BS23 7 H6
Holmwood *KGWD/HNM* BS15 80 A4
Holmwood Cl *FRCTL/WBN* BS36 31 E2 1
Holmwood Gdns
HNLZ/SM/SNYPK/WT BS9 46 B3
Holsom Cl *HGRV/WHIT* BS14 104 C1
Holsom Rd *HGRV/WHIT* BS14 105 D1 2
Holst Gdns *BRSG/KWL/STAPK* BS4 92 A5
Holton Rd *HORF/LLZ* BS7 48 B5
Holt Rd *BOAV* BA15 147 E3
Holyrood Cl *BRSTK/PCHW* BS34 29 E4 3
TRWBR BA14 158 B2
Holy Well Cl
BRSG/KWL/STAPK BS4 78 C3 1
Homeapple Hl
OLD/WMLY/WICK BS30 82 C2
Home Cl *HNBRY/STHM* BS10 47 F1
TRWBR BA14 157 D5
Home Farm Rd *CFTN/FAIL* BS8 73 E2
Homefield *OMX/HUT/LCK* BS24 143 E5
THNB/SVB BS35 9 D4 2
YATE/CS BS37 19 F2
YTN/CONG BS49 133 D3
Home Field Cl *MANG/FISH* BS16 52 C5
Homefield Cl *KEYN* BS31 108 C4
WNSC BS25 154 B3
Homefield Rd *KEYN* BS31 108 C4
Homeground *CLVDN* BS21 85 E2
Home Gnd *AVONM* BS11 43 E4
HNLZ/SM/SNYPK/WT BS9 46 C4
Homelea Pk East
CBATH/BATHN BA1 121 E3
Homelea Pk West
CBATH/BATHN BA1 121 E3 1
Homeleaze Rd *HNBRY/STHM* BS10 27 E5
Home Md *OLD/WMLY/WICK* BS30 81 E5
Homemead Dr
BRSG/KWL/STAPK BS4 94 B3 6
Home Orch *YATE/CS* BS37 19 E3
Homestead *PTSHD/EG* BS20 54 C3 2
Homestead Gdns *MANG/FISH* BS16 50 C2
Homestead Rd *BRSTK/PCHW* BS34 28 A5
The Homestead *CLVDN* BS21 84 C1
KEYN BS31 107 D5
Homestead Wy *WNSC* BS25 154 C4
Honey Garston Cl
BMSTRD/HC/WWD BS13 101 F3 5
Honey Garston Rd
BMSTRD/HC/WWD BS13 101 F3
Honey Hill Rd *KGWD/HNM* BS15 81 D1
Honeylands *PTSHD/EG* BS20 56 A3
Honeymans Cl *TRWBR* BA14 157 F4
Honeymead *HGRV/WHIT* BS14 104 A1 1
Honeysuckle Cl *ALMDB* BS32 13 F3 1
TRWBR BA14 157 E5 1
Honey Suckle La
MANG/FISH BS16 66 C2 2
Honeysuckle Pl
OMX/HUT/LCK BS24 143 F1 3
Honiton Rd *CLVDN* BS21 85 E3 2
MANG/FISH BS16 67 E3
Hooper Rd *HGRV/WHIT* BS14 104 B2
Hopechapel Hl *CFTN/FAIL* BS8 75 D3 7
Hope Rd *BMSTR* BS3 92 A2
YATE/CS BS37 18 B3
Hope Sq *CFTN/FAIL* BS8 75 D3 8
Hopetoun Rd *CBRISNE* BS2 65 D3 1
Hopewell Gdns *AVONM* BS11 44 A4
Hopkin Cl *THNB/SVB* BS35 9 D5
Hopkins St *WSM* BS23 141 D2 7
Hopland Cl *OLD/WMLY/WICK* BS30 97 F1
Hopp's Rd *KGWD/HNM* BS15 80 B2
Horesham Gv
BMSTRD/HC/WWD BS13 102 A2 1
Horfield Rd *CBRISNE* BS2 2 C1
Horley Rd *CBRISNE* BS2 65 E5
Horsecastle Cl *YTN/CONG* BS49 116 A2
Horsecombe Brow *BATHSE* BA2 137 E4
Horsecombe Gv *BATHSE* BA2 137 E4
Horsecombe V *BATHSE* BA2 137 E4
Horsecroft Gdns
OLD/WMLY/WICK BS30 81 E3 2
The Horsefair *CBRIS/FH* BS1 3 E1
Horsepool Rd
BMSTRD/HC/WWD BS13 100 C3

Horse Rd *TRWBR* BA14 149 E5
Horseshoe Dr
HNLZ/SM/SNYPK/WT BS9 62 A2
Horseshoe La *YATE/CS* BS37 20 C4
Horseshoe Wk *BATHSE* BA2 5 F5
Horse St *YATE/CS* BS37 21 D5
Horton Cl *BOAV* BA15 147 E5 2
Horton Rd *YATE/CS* BS37 21 D3
Horton St *CBRISNE* BS2 3 H3
Horwood Ct
OLD/WMLY/WICK BS30 81 E5 4
Horwood Rd *NAIL* BS48 87 E3
Hosey Wk
BMSTRD/HC/WWD BS13 101 E2
Host St *CBRIS/FH* BS1 2 C2
Hottom Gdns *HORF/LLZ* BS7 48 B4
Hot Water La *KGWD/HNM* BS15 69 D3
Hotwell Rd *CFTN/FAIL* BS8 75 D3 9
Houlton St *CBRISNE* BS2 77 D1
Hounds Rd *YATE/CS* BS37 20 C5
Howard Av *EVILLE/WHL* BS5 78 C1
Howard Cl *KEYN* BS31 108 A4
Howard Rd *BMSTR* BS3 75 F5
MANG/FISH BS16 68 B2
RDLND/MONT BS6 63 F2
THNB/SVB BS35 8 C2 3
Howard St *EVILLE/WHL* BS5 66 C5
Howecroft Gdns
HNLZ/SM/SNYPK/WT BS9 62 C2 1
Howells Md *MANG/FISH* BS16 52 C4 4
Howes Cl *OLD/WMLY/WICK* BS30 81 E3
Howett Rd *EVILLE/WHL* BS5 78 A2 8
How Hl *BATHSE* BA2 121 E4
Howsmoor La *MANG/FISH* BS16 52 C3
Hoylake Dr *OLD/WMLY/WICK* BS30 81 F3
Huckford La *FRCTL/WBN* BS36 32 B4
Huckford Rd *FRCTL/WBN* BS36 31 F3
Huckley Wy *ALMDB* BS32 30 A2
Hudd's Hill Rd *EVILLE/WHL* BS5 79 D1
Hudd's Vale Rd *EVILLE/WHL* BS5 78 C1 1
Hudson Cl *YATE/CS* BS37 20 A5
Hughenden Rd *CFTN/FAIL* BS8 63 E4 5
HORF/LLZ BS7 64 C1
WSM BS23 141 F2
Huish Ct *RDSTK/MIDN* BA3 163 E3
Hulbert Cl *BRSG/KWL/STAPK* BS4 95 E2 1
Hulse Rd *BRSG/KWL/STAPK* BS4 94 B3
Humberstan Wk *AVONM* BS11 43 F3 2
Humber Wy *AVONM* BS11 23 E3
Humphrys Barton
BRSG/KWL/STAPK BS4 79 D4
Hungerford Av *TRWBR* BA14 156 A5
Hungerford Cl
BRSG/KWL/STAPK BS4 94 C4
Hungerford Crs
BRSG/KWL/STAPK BS4 94 C4
Hungerford Gdns
BRSG/KWL/STAPK BS4 94 C4
Hungerford Rd
BRSG/KWL/STAPK BS4 94 C4
CBATH/BATHN BA1 122 A3
Hungerford Wk
BRSG/KWL/STAPK BS4 94 C3
Hung Rd *AVONM* BS11 43 F5
Hunters Cl *KGWD/HNM* BS15 80 A4 4
Hunters Dr *KGWD/HNM* BS15 69 D5
Hunters Rd *KGWD/HNM* BS15 80 A4
Hunters Rd East *KGWD/HNM* BS15 80 A4
Hunter's Wy *BRSTK/PCHW* BS34 28 C5
Huntingdon Pl *BOAV* BA15 146 C2 1
Huntingdon Ri *BOAV* BA15 146 C1
Huntingdon St *BOAV* BA15 146 C1
Huntingham Rd
BMSTRD/HC/WWD BS13 100 C3
Huntley Gv *NAIL* BS48 87 F3
Hunt's La *YTN/CONG* BS49 117 E3
Hurle Crs *CFTN/FAIL* BS8 63 E5
Hurle Rd *CFTN/FAIL* BS8 63 F5
Hurlingham Rd *RDLND/MONT* BS6 65 D4
Hurn La *KEYN* BS31 107 D3
Hurn Rd *CLVDN* BS21 85 E2
Hurston Rd *BRSG/KWL/STAPK* BS4 92 B4
Hurst Rd *BRSG/KWL/STAPK* BS4 93 D4
WSM BS23 7 G3
Hurst Wk *BRSG/KWL/STAPK* BS4 92 C4
Hurstwood Rd *MANG/FISH* BS16 68 B1
Hutton Cl *HNLZ/SM/SNYPK/WT* BS9 45 F4
KEYN BS31 107 E5
Hutton Hl *OMX/HUT/LCK* BS24 153 D3
Hutton Moor La
OMX/HUT/LCK BS24 142 B5
Hutton Moor Rd *MTN/WRL* BS22 142 A3
Huyton Rd *EVILLE/WHL* BS5 66 C3 1
Hyde Av *THNB/SVB* BS35 8 B1
Hyde Rd *TRWBR* BA14 156 C2
The Hyde *CLVDN* BS21 84 C4
Hyland Gv
HNLZ/SM/SNYPK/WT BS9 46 A3

I

Ida Rd *EVILLE/WHL* BS5 78 A1 2
Iddesleigh Rd *RDLND/MONT* BS6 63 F3 2
Idstone Rd *MANG/FISH* BS16 67 F2
Iford Cl *KEYN* BS31 108 C4
Ilchester Crs
BMSTRD/HC/WWD BS13 91 F3
Ilchester Rd
BMSTRD/HC/WWD BS13 91 F4
Iles Cl *KGWD/HNM* BS15 80 B5
Ilex Av *CLVDN* BS21 85 E2 1
Ilex Cl *BMSTRD/HC/WWD* BS13 101 D1
Ilex La *WNSC* BS25 154 B3
Ilminster Av *BRSG/KWL/STAPK* BS4 92 C3
Ilminster Cl *CLVDN* BS21 85 E2 2
NAIL BS48 86 C4 1
Ilsyn Gv *HGRV/WHIT* BS14 94 B5
Imber Court Cl *HGRV/WHIT* BS14 93 F4
Imperial Rd *HGRV/WHIT* BS14 94 A4
RDLND/MONT BS6 63 F5 6
Imperial Wk *HGRV/WHIT* BS14 93 F3
Inglesham Cl *TRWBR* BA14 159 D2 4
Ingleside Rd *KGWD/HNM* BS15 68 A5
Ingleton Dr *MTN/WRL* BS22 129 F3 9
Ingmire Rd *EVILLE/WHL* BS5 65 F3
Inkerman Cl *HORF/LLZ* BS7 47 F4
Innox Gdns
BMSTRD/HC/WWD BS13 101 E2 5
Innox Gv *BATHSE* BA2 135 D3
Innox La *CBATH/BATHN* BA1 113 F2
Innox Mill Cl *TRWBR* BA14 156 B3
Innox Rd *BATHSE* BA2 121 F5
TRWBR BA14 156 B3
Inns Court Av
BRSG/KWL/STAPK BS4 92 B5
Inns Court Dr
BRSG/KWL/STAPK BS4 102 B1 2
Instow Rd *BRSG/KWL/STAPK* BS4 92 C4
Instow Wk
BRSG/KWL/STAPK BS4 92 C4 2
Inverness Rd *BATHSE* BA2 122 A4
Ipswich Dr *BRSG/KWL/STAPK* BS4 78 C3
Irby Rd *BMSTR* BS3 91 E1
Irena Rd *MANG/FISH* BS16 67 D4 1
Ireton Rd *BMSTR* BS3 91 F1
Iron Acton Wy *YATE/CS* BS37 18 B2
Ironchurch Rd *AVONM* BS11 22 C3
Ironmould La
BRSG/KWL/STAPK BS4 95 E2
Irving Cl *CLVDN* BS21 85 F1
MANG/FISH BS16 68 C2 4
The Island *RDSTK/MIDN* BA3 161 D3
Isleys Ct *OLD/WMLY/WICK* BS30 97 D1 2
Islington *TRWBR* BA14 157 D3
Islington Rd *BMSTR* BS3 75 F5
Ison Hill Rd *HNBRY/STHM* BS10 25 E5 6
Ivo Peters Rd *BATHSE* BA2 122 C4 2
Ivor Rd *EVILLE/WHL* BS5 78 A1
Ivy Av *BATHSE* BA2 136 A1
Ivy Bank Pk *BATHSE* BA2 137 D3
Ivy Ct *PTSHD/EG* BS20 55 D1 2
Ivy Gv *BATHSE* BA2 136 A1
Ivy La *MANG/FISH* BS16 67 E3 2
Ivy Pl *BATHSE* BA2 136 A1
Ivy Ter *BOAV* BA15 147 D2
Ivy Wk *RDSTK/MIDN* BA3 161 E4
Ivywell Rd
HNLZ/SM/SNYPK/WT BS9 62 C3

J

Jackson Cl *THNB/SVB* BS35 11 E3 1
Jacob St *CBRISNE* BS2 3 F2
Jacob's Well Rd *CFTN/FAIL* BS8 75 F3
Jamaica St *CBRISNE* BS2 76 B1
James Cl *MANG/FISH* BS16 68 C2 5
James Rd *MANG/FISH* BS16 68 C3
James St *CBRISNE* BS2 65 E4
EVILLE/WHL BS5 77 D1
TRWBR BA14 157 D2 1
James St West *CBATH/BATHN* BA1 122 C4
Jane St *EVILLE/WHL* BS5 77 F2
Jarvis St *EVILLE/WHL* BS5 77 F3
Jasmine Cl *MTN/WRL* BS22 143 F1 4
Jasmine Gv *AVONM* BS11 45 D1 5
Jasmine La *YTN/CONG* BS49 117 F1
Jasmine Wy *OMX/HUT/LCK* BS24 143 F1
TRWBR BA14 157 E5
Jasper St *BMSTR* BS3 91 F1 4
Jean Rd *BRSG/KWL/STAPK* BS4 94 C2
Jefferies Hill Bottom
KGWD/HNM BS15 79 F4
Jeffery Ct *OLD/WMLY/WICK* BS30 81 F3
Jellicoe Ct *MTN/WRL* BS22 129 D3 6
Jena Ct *KEYN* BS31 108 B4
Jenkins St *TRWBR* BA14 156 C2
Jenner Cl *YATE/CS* BS37 21 E5
Jersey Av *BRSG/KWL/STAPK* BS4 79 D5
Jesmond Rd *CLVDN* BS21 84 C1 3
MTN/WRL BS22 130 B3 4
Jesse Hughes Ct
CBATH/BATHN BA1 114 A5 1
Jessop Under/pass *BMSTR* BS3 75 D5
Jews La *BATHSE* BA2 122 A4
Jocelin Dr *MTN/WRL* BS22 129 E3
Jocelyn Rd *HORF/LLZ* BS7 48 A4
Jockey La *EVILLE/WHL* BS5 79 E2
John Carr's Ter *CFTN/FAIL* BS8 75 F3 6
John Rennie Cl *BOAV* BA15 147 E5
Johnson Dr *OLD/WMLY/WICK* BS30 81 D4
Johnsons La *EVILLE/WHL* BS5 66 B5
Johnsons Rd *EVILLE/WHL* BS5 78 B1
Johnstone St *BATHSE* BA2 4 D3
John St *CBATH/BATHN* BA1 4 B2
CBRIS/FH BS1 2 D2 1
CBRISNE BS2 65 E4 7
KGWD/HNM BS15 80 A1
John Wesley Rd *EVILLE/WHL* BS5 79 F3
Jones Hl *BOAV* BA15 146 C4
Jordan Wk *ALMDB* BS32 13 E5
Joy Hl *CFTN/FAIL* BS8 75 D3 10
Jubilee Crs *MANG/FISH* BS16 52 B5
Jubilee Dr *THNB/SVB* BS35 9 D4
Jubilee Gdns *YATE/CS* BS37 20 B3 2
Jubilee Pl *CBRIS/FH* BS1 2 D5 1
CLVDN BS21 85 D3
Jubilee Rd *BRSG/KWL/STAPK* BS4 94 A3
CBRISNE BS2 65 E5
EVILLE/WHL BS5 79 D2
KGWD/HNM BS15 68 C3
RDSTK/MIDN BA3 162 A3
WSM BS23 6 D1
Jubilee St *CBRISNE* BS2 3 H3
Julian Cl *HNLZ/SM/SNYPK/WT* BS9 62 B3
Julian Rd *CBATH/BATHN* BA1 123 D2
HNLZ/SM/SNYPK/WT BS9 62 C3
Julius Rd *HORF/LLZ* BS7 64 B3
Junction Av *BATHSE* BA2 122 C5 3
Junction Rd *BATHSE* BA2 122 C5
BOAV BA15 147 D3 2
BRSG/KWL/STAPK BS4 78 A5
Juniper Ct *EVILLE/WHL* BS5 66 A4 12
Juniper Pl *MTN/WRL* BS22 129 E3
Juniper Wy *ALMDB* BS32 30 A1
Jupiter Rd *BRSTK/PCHW* BS34 27 E1
Justice Av *KEYN* BS31 108 C4
Justice Rd *MANG/FISH* BS16 67 E3 3
Jutland Rd *AVONM* BS11 42 C2

K

Kathdene Gdns *HORF/LLZ* BS7 65 D3
Kaynton Md *CBATH/BATHN* BA1 121 F3
Keates Cl *TRWBR* BA14 157 D3
Keats Rd *RDSTK/MIDN* BA3 161 E4
Keble Av *BMSTRD/HC/WWD* BS13 101 D2
Keeds La *LGASH* BS41 89 D3
Keedwell Hl *LGASH* BS41 89 D3
Keene's Wy *CLVDN* BS21 84 B2
Keen's Gv *THNB/SVB* BS35 11 D3
The Keep *MTN/WRL* BS22 129 F4
OLD/WMLY/WICK BS30 82 B4
Keinton Wk *HNBRY/STHM* BS10 46 B1
Kelbra Crs *FRCTL/WBN* BS36 32 C2
Kellaway Av *HNBRY/STHM* BS10 47 F5 2
RDLND/MONT BS6 64 B1
Kellaway Crs *HORF/LLZ* BS7 47 E5
Kelston Cl *KEYN* BS31 108 B4
Kelston Gdns *HNBRY/STHM* BS10 47 E3 4
Kelston Gv *KGWD/HNM* BS15 80 C3
Kelston Rd *CBATH/BATHN* BA1 120 C1
HNBRY/STHM BS10 47 D3
KEYN BS31 106 B3
MTN/WRL BS22 130 A3
Kelston Vw *BATHSE* BA2 121 E5
Kelston Wk *MANG/FISH* BS16 68 A2
Kelting Gv *CLVDN* BS21 85 F2
Kemble Cl *KGWD/HNM* BS15 80 C3 4
NAIL BS48 87 F3 6
Kemperleye Wy *ALMDB* BS32 29 E1 3
Kempe's Cl *LGASH* BS41 89 E2
Kempton Cl *THNB/SVB* BS35 8 B1 1
Kencot Wk
BMSTRD/HC/WWD BS13 101 F4
Kendall Gdns *MANG/FISH* BS16 68 B2
Kendall Rd *MANG/FISH* BS16 68 B2
Kendal Rd *HORF/LLZ* BS7 48 B4
Kendon Dr *HNBRY/STHM* BS10 47 E4
Kendon Wy *HNBRY/STHM* BS10 47 E3
Kenilworth *YATE/CS* BS37 20 A5
Kenilworth Cl *KEYN* BS31 106 B3
Kenilworth Dr
OLD/WMLY/WICK BS30 97 F3 2
Kenilworth Rd
RDLND/MONT BS6 64 A5 2
Kenmare Rd *BRSG/KWL/STAPK* BS4 92 C4
Kenmore Crs *HORF/LLZ* BS7 47 F2
Kenmore Dr *HORF/LLZ* BS7 47 F2
Kenmore Gv *HORF/LLZ* BS7 47 F2 2
Kennard Ri *KGWD/HNM* BS15 80 A2
Kennard Rd *KGWD/HNM* BS15 80 A1
Kennaway Rd *CLVDN* BS21 85 D2
Kenn Cl *WSM* BS23 7 G6
Kennedy Wy *YATE/CS* BS37 19 F4
Kennel Lodge Rd *BMSTR* BS3 74 C5
Kennet Gdns *BOAV* BA15 147 D4

Kenneth Rd BRSG/KWL/STAPK BS4 94 B2
Kennet Pk BATHSE BA2 124 C1
Kennet Rd KEYN BS31 107 D3
Kennet Wy THNB/SVB BS35 9 D4
TRWBR BA14 157 D1
Kennington Av HORF/LLZ BS7 64 C2
KGWD/HNM BS15 68 B5 5
Kennington Rd
CBATH/BATHN BA1 121 F3
Kennion Rd EVILLE/WHL BS5 79 E2 2
Kennmoor Cl
OLD/WMLY/WICK BS30 81 E3
Kenn Moor Dr CLVDN BS21 85 E3
Kenn Moor Rd YTN/CONG BS49 116 B2
Kenn Rd CLVDN BS21 85 E5
EVILLE/WHL BS5 79 E2
Kenn St CLVDN BS21 85 F5
Kensal Av BMSTR BS3 92 C1
Kensal Rd BMSTR BS3 92 C1
Kensington Cl THNB/SVB BS35 8 B2 2
TRWBR BA14 157 D2 2
Kensington Gdns
CBATH/BATHN BA1 123 F1
Kensington Pk EVILLE/WHL BS5 65 E5 11
Kensington Park Rd
BRSG/KWL/STAPK BS4 94 A2
Kensington Pl CFTN/FAIL BS8 75 E2
Kensington Rd EVILLE/WHL BS5 79 E1 1
MANG/FISH BS16 68 B2 2
RDLND/MONT BS6 64 A5
WSM BS23 7 E6
Kent Av YATE/CS BS37 20 A2
Kent Cl BRSTK/PCHW BS34 29 E4
Kenton Dr TRWBR BA14 157 F3
Kenton Ms
HNLZ/SM/SNYPK/WT BS9 64 A1
Kent Rd HORF/LLZ BS7 64 C3
YTN/CONG BS49 133 D1
Kents Gn KGWD/HNM BS15 68 C4
Kent St BMSTR BS3 92 A1 6
Kent Wy MTN/WRL BS22 130 A3 7
Kenwood Cl TRWBR BA14 157 F4
Keppel Cl KEYN BS31 108 B5 2
Kerry Rd BRSG/KWL/STAPK BS4 92 C3
Kersteman Rd
RDLND/MONT BS6 64 B3 2
Kestrel Cl THNB/SVB BS35 9 D2 4
YATE/CS BS37 20 A5
Kestrel Dr MTN/WRL BS22 143 D1
Keswick Wk HNBRY/STHM BS10 47 D1 2
Ketch Rd BMSTR BS3 93 D1
Ketton Cl TRWBR BA14 156 A3
Kew Dr TRWBR BA14 156 A5 1
Kew Rd WSM BS23 141 D1
Kewside MTN/WRL BS22 128 A3
Kewstoke Rd BATHSE BA2 137 E3
HNLZ/SM/SNYPK/WT BS9 62 C2
WSM BS23 126 C5
Kew Wk BRSG/KWL/STAPK BS4 94 A4
Keyes Pth MTN/WRL BS22 129 E3 4
Keynsham By-pass KEYN BS31 96 C5
Keynsham Rd
OLD/WMLY/WICK BS30 97 D5
Keys Av HORF/LLZ BS7 48 A4
Kielder Dr MTN/WRL BS22 129 E4 5
Kilbirnie Rd HGRV/WHIT BS14 103 E4
Kildare Rd BRSG/KWL/STAPK BS4 92 B4
Kilkenny St CBRISNE BS2 3 H3
Kilmersdon Rd
BMSTRD/HC/WWD BS13 101 F3
RDSTK/MIDN BA3 162 B4
Kilminster Rd AVONM BS11 43 E4 3
Kiln Cl KGWD/HNM BS15 67 F5
Kilnhurst Cl OLD/WMLY/WICK BS30 97 D2
Kilvert Cl BRSG/KWL/STAPK BS4 78 B4
Kimberley Av MANG/FISH BS16 68 A1
Kimberley Cl MANG/FISH BS16 52 A4 5
Kimberley Crs MANG/FISH BS16 68 A1
Kimberley Rd CLVDN BS21 84 C2
KGWD/HNM BS15 68 B5 6
MANG/FISH BS16 68 A1
Kinber Cl CBATH/BATHN BA1 111 E4
King Edward Rd BATHSE BA2 122 B5
Kingfisher Cl ALMDB BS32 13 F3 2
THNB/SVB BS35 9 D2 5
Kingfisher Dr MANG/FISH BS16 49 F5 2
RDSTK/MIDN BA3 161 E4
Kingfisher Rd MTN/WRL BS22 143 E2
YATE/CS BS37 20 B5
King George's Rd BATHSE BA2 122 A4
BMSTRD/HC/WWD BS13 101 D2
King John's Rd KGWD/HNM BS15 67 F4
King Rd BRSG/KWL/STAPK BS4 93 F3
King Road Av AVONM BS11 42 B1
Kingrove Crs YATE/CS BS37 21 D5
Kingrove La YATE/CS BS37 37 D1
Kings Av KGWD/HNM BS15 79 F5
RDLND/MONT BS6 64 A2
Kingscote YATE/CS BS37 35 E2
Kingscote Pk EVILLE/WHL BS5 79 F3
Kingscourt Cl HGRV/WHIT BS14 103 E2
Kingsdown Pde RDLND/MONT BS6 76 B1
Kingsdown Rd TRWBR BA14 158 C2
King's Dr HORF/LLZ BS7 64 A1
KGWD/HNM BS15 79 F5
Kingsfield BATHSE BA2 136 A2
BOAV BA15 147 D2
Kingsfield Cl BOAV BA15 147 D3
Kingsfield Grange Rd BOAV BA15 147 E3
Kingsfield La KGWD/HNM BS15 80 C4
OLD/WMLY/WICK BS30 80 C5
Kings Gdns TRWBR BA14 149 E5
King's Head La
BMSTRD/HC/WWD BS13 90 C5
Kingshill NAIL BS48 86 B2
Kingshill Rd BRSG/KWL/STAPK BS4 93 F3
Kingsholme Rd KGWD/HNM BS15 68 B5
Kingsholm Rd HNBRY/STHM BS10 47 E3
Kingsland Rd CBRISNE BS2 77 E3
Kingsland Road Br CBRISNE BS2 77 E3
King's La WSM BS23 141 D2 8
Kingsleigh Ct KGWD/HNM BS15 81 D2 4
Kingsleigh Gdns
KGWD/HNM BS15 81 D2 5
Kingsley Pl TRWBR BA14 156 A3 1
Kingsley Rd CLVDN BS21 85 D2 5
EVILLE/WHL BS5 66 A5
RDLND/MONT BS6 64 B4
RDSTK/MIDN BA3 161 E3
WSM BS23 151 E2
Kingsmead NAIL BS48 86 B2
Kingsmead North
CBATH/BATHN BA1 4 A4
Kingsmead Rd EVILLE/WHL BS5 67 E5
Kingsmead Sq CBATH/BATHN BA1 4 B3 5
Kingsmead St CBATH/BATHN BA1 4 B3 6
Kingsmead Wk EVILLE/WHL BS5 67 E5
Kingsmead West
CBATH/BATHN BA1 4 A4 1
Kingsmill HNLZ/SM/SNYPK/WT BS9 62 B1
King's Parade Av CFTN/FAIL BS8 63 F5 7
King's Parade Ms CFTN/FAIL BS8 63 E5 3
Kings Park Av CBRISNE BS2 78 A3 4
King Sq CBRISNE BS2 76 B1 8
King Square Av CBRISNE BS2 76 B1 9
King's Rd BRSG/KWL/STAPK BS4 94 A1
CFTN/FAIL BS8 75 E2 4
CLVDN BS21 71 D4
PTSHD/EG BS20 55 D2
Kings Sq OLD/WMLY/WICK BS30 98 B4
Kingston Av BOAV BA15 147 E4
CLVDN BS21 85 E1
KEYN BS31 108 A5
Kingston Cl MANG/FISH BS16 52 B4 1
Kingston Dr MANG/FISH BS16 52 B4
Kingston Rd BMSTR BS3 76 A5 4
BOAV BA15 147 D3 3
CBATH/BATHN BA1 4 C4 6
Kingston Wy NAIL BS48 86 B4
Kingstree St
BRSG/KWL/STAPK BS4 77 E5 7
King St AVONM BS11 42 B2
CBRIS/FH BS1 2 C4
EVILLE/WHL BS5 66 A5
KGWD/HNM BS15 79 F1
Kings Wk BMSTRD/HC/WWD BS13 90 C5
Kingsway BATHSE BA2 136 A2
BRSTK/PCHW BS34 29 D2
EVILLE/WHL BS5 79 F2
PTSHD/EG BS20 55 D2 4
Kingsway Av KGWD/HNM BS15 79 F1
Kingsway Crs KGWD/HNM BS15 79 F1
Kingswear Rd BMSTR BS3 92 B3
Kings Weston Av AVONM BS11 43 E4
Kings Weston La AVONM BS11 23 D4
Kings Weston Rd AVONM BS11 45 E1 1
King William Av CBRIS/FH BS1 2 D4 1
King William St BMSTR BS3 75 F5 3
Kinsale Rd HGRV/WHIT BS14 94 A5
Kinsale Wk
BRSG/KWL/STAPK BS4 92 C3 1
Kinvara Rd
BRSG/KWL/STAPK BS4 92 C4 3
Kipling Av BATHSE BA2 137 D1
Kipling Rd HORF/LLZ BS7 48 C2
RDSTK/MIDN BA3 161 F4
WSM BS23 151 F2
Kirkby Rd AVONM BS11 44 B2
Kirtlington Rd EVILLE/WHL BS5 65 F3 2
Kite Hay Cl MANG/FISH BS16 66 C1 5
Kites Cl ALMDB BS32 13 D3 2
Knapp Rd THNB/SVB BS35 9 F2
Knapps Cl WNSC BS25 154 B4
Knapps Dr WNSC BS25 154 B4
Knapps La EVILLE/WHL BS5 66 C4
Knightcott Rd CFTN/FAIL BS8 73 D1
Knighton Rd HNBRY/STHM BS10 47 F2
Knights Cl MTN/WRL BS22 129 F2 5
Knightstone Cswy WSM BS23 140 B2
Knightstone Rd WSM BS23 140 C2 5
Knightwood Rd BRSTK/PCHW BS34 30 A3
Knobsbury La RDSTK/MIDN BA3 163 F4
Knole Cl ALMDB BS32 12 A1
Knole La HNBRY/STHM BS10 26 B5
Knole Pk ALMDB BS32 12 A2
Knoll Hl HNLZ/SM/SNYPK/WT BS9 62 B3
The Knoll PTSHD/EG BS20 39 E4
Knovill Cl AVONM BS11 44 C2
Knowle Rd
BRSG/KWL/STAPK BS4 93 E1 6
Knowles Rd CLVDN BS21 84 C2
Knowsley Rd MANG/FISH BS16 66 C3 2
Kyght Cl KGWD/HNM BS15 81 E1
Kylross Av HGRV/WHIT BS14 103 F2
Kynges Mill Cl MANG/FISH BS16 50 B4

L

The Labbott KEYN BS31 106 C2
Laburnum Cl RDSTK/MIDN BA3 160 C4 1
Laburnum Ct WSM BS23 142 A3 1
Laburnum Gv MANG/FISH BS16 67 F2
RDSTK/MIDN BA3 160 C4
TRWBR BA14 158 B1 1
Laburnum Rd KGWD/HNM BS15 80 A4 5
WSM BS23 7 H1
Lacey Rd HGRV/WHIT BS14 104 C1
Lacock Dr OLD/WMLY/WICK BS30 81 D4
Ladd Cl KGWD/HNM BS15 81 D2 6
Ladden Ct THNB/SVB BS35 8 C4 1
Ladies Mile
HNLZ/SM/SNYPK/WT BS9 63 D5
Ladman Gv HGRV/WHIT BS14 104 C1
Ladman Rd HGRV/WHIT BS14 104 C2
Ladycroft CLVDN BS21 84 B3 4
Ladye Bay CLVDN BS21 71 D3
Ladye Wake MTN/WRL BS22 129 E3
Ladysmith Rd RDLND/MONT BS6 63 F2 1
Laggan Gdns CBATH/BATHN BA1 122 C1
Lakemead Gv
BMSTRD/HC/WWD BS13 101 D1
Lake Rd HNBRY/STHM BS10 47 D4
PTSHD/EG BS20 39 D5
Lakeside MANG/FISH BS16 66 C3
Lake View Rd EVILLE/WHL BS5 78 B1
Lakewood Crs HNBRY/STHM BS10 46 C3
Lakewood Rd HNBRY/STHM BS10 46 C3
Lamb Ale Gn TRWBR BA14 159 E1 1
Lambert Cl BRSG/KWL/STAPK BS4 102 B1
Lambley Rd EVILLE/WHL BS5 78 C1
Lambourne Wy PTSHD/EG BS20 57 D2
Lambourn Rd KEYN BS31 107 E3
Lambridge Ms
CBATH/BATHN BA1 124 A1 2
Lambridge St CBATH/BATHN BA1 124 A1
Lambrook Rd MANG/FISH BS16 67 E2
Lamb St CBRISNE BS2 3 H1
Lamord Ga BRSTK/PCHW BS34 29 F3
Lampeter Rd
HNLZ/SM/SNYPK/WT BS9 46 A4
Lampton Av
BMSTRD/HC/WWD BS13 102 C4
Lampton Gv
BMSTRD/HC/WWD BS13 102 C4
Lampton Rd LGASH BS41 89 D3
Lanaway Rd MANG/FISH BS16 50 C5 1
Lancashire Rd HORF/LLZ BS7 64 C3
Lancaster Cl BRSTK/PCHW BS34 29 E4 4
Lancaster Rd CBRISNE BS2 65 E4 8
YATE/CS BS37 19 F2
Lancaster St EVILLE/WHL BS5 78 A2 9
Landemann Circ WSM BS23 141 D1 1
Landseer Av HORF/LLZ BS7 48 C4
Landseer Cl MTN/WRL BS22 129 E4 6
Landseer Rd BATHSE BA2 121 F4
The Land FRCTL/WBN BS36 33 D1
Lanercost Rd HNBRY/STHM BS10 47 D1
Lanesborough Ri HGRV/WHIT BS14 94 B5
Laneys Dro OMX/HUT/LCK BS24 143 D5
Langdale Rd MANG/FISH BS16 67 D2 4
Langdon Rd BATHSE BA2 135 F1
Langfield Cl HNBRY/STHM BS10 26 A5 4
Langford Rd
BMSTRD/HC/WWD BS13 91 D4
TRWBR BA14 156 C2
WSM BS23 7 G2 1
Langford Wy KGWD/HNM BS15 80 C2
Langham Rd
BRSG/KWL/STAPK BS4 93 F2 1
Langhill Av
BRSG/KWL/STAPK BS4 92 B5 8
Langley Crs BMSTR BS3 90 C3
Langley Mow MANG/FISH BS16 52 C4 5
Langley Rd TRWBR BA14 158 C2
Langley's La PLTN/PENS BS39 160 A2
Langport Gdns NAIL BS48 87 D4 5
Langport Rd WSM BS23 6 D4
Langthorn Cl FRCTL/WBN BS36 32 C1
Langton Court Rd
BRSG/KWL/STAPK BS4 78 B4
Langton Pk BMSTR BS3 76 A5
Langton Rd BRSG/KWL/STAPK BS4 78 B4
Langton Wy BRSG/KWL/STAPK BS4 78 C3
Lansdown YATE/CS BS37 19 F5 2
Lansdown Cl KGWD/HNM BS15 68 B4
TRWBR BA14 156 B5
Lansdown Crs CBATH/BATHN BA1 123 D2
Lansdown Gv CBATH/BATHN BA1 123 D2
Lansdown Hts CBATH/BATHN BA1 123 D1
Lansdown La CBATH/BATHN BA1 111 F4
OLD/WMLY/WICK BS30 99 F4
Lansdown Pk CBATH/BATHN BA1 112 C4

Lansdown Pl East
CBATH/BATHN BA1 .... **123** D2 7
Lansdown Pl West
CBATH/BATHN BA1 .... **123** D2 8
Lansdown Rd *CBATH/BATHN* BA1 .... **112** B3
CBATH/BATHN BA1 .... **123** D2
CFTN/FAIL BS8 .... **75** E2
KEYN BS31 .... **108** C4
KGWD/HNM BS15 .... **68** B4
RDLND/MONT BS6 .... **64** A5
Lansdown Ter *RDLND/MONT* BS6 .. **64** B1 2
Lansdown Vw *BATHSE* BA2 .... **122** A5
KGWD/HNM BS15 .... **80** C1
Lanthony Cl
OMX/HUT/LCK BS24 .... **143** F2 2
Laphams Ct
OLD/WMLY/WICK BS30 .... **81** D5 11
Lapwing Cl *ALMDB* BS32 .... **13** E3
Lapwing Gdns *MANG/FISH* BS16 .... **50** A5 2
MTN/WRL BS22 .... **143** E1
Larch Cl *NAIL* BS48 .... **87** F2
Larch Ct *RDSTK/MIDN* BA3 .... **162** A4
The Larches *MTN/WRL* BS22 .... **129** F4 6
Larch Gv *TRWBR* BA14 .... **158** B1
Larchgrove Crs *MTN/WRL* BS22 ...... **143** E1
Larch Rd *KGWD/HNM* BS15 .... **68** C3
Larch Wy *BRSTK/PCHW* BS34 .... **27** F1
Lark Cl *RDSTK/MIDN* BA3 .... **161** E4
Lark Down *TRWBR* BA14 .... **157** E3
Larkfield *FRCTL/WBN* BS36 .... **33** E1 2
Larkhall Pl *CBATH/BATHN* BA1 .... **114** A5
Larkhill Rd *OMX/HUT/LCK* BS24 ...... **144** A4
Lark Rd *MTN/WRL* BS22 .... **143** E1 6
Lark's Fld *MANG/FISH* BS16 .... **66** C1 6
Larksleaze Rd
OLD/WMLY/WICK BS30 .... **96** C2
Larkspur Cl *THNB/SVB* BS35 .... **9** D2
Lasbury Gv
BMSTRD/HC/WWD BS13 .... **102** A2 2
Latimer Cl *BRSG/KWL/STAPK* BS4 ...... **78** C5
Latteridge Rd *YATE/CS* BS37 .... **17** E1
Latton Rd *HORF/LLZ* BS7 .... **48** A3
Launceston Av *KGWD/HNM* BS15 ...... **79** F4
Launceston Rd *KGWD/HNM* BS15 .. **67** F5 4
Laurel Dr *NAIL* BS48 .... **87** E2
WSM BS23 .... **151** D3
Laurel Gdns *YTN/CONG* BS49 .... **116** B2 1
Laurel Gv *TRWBR* BA14 .... **158** C1
The Laurels *HNBRY/STHM* BS10 .... **26** B2
MANG/FISH BS16 .... **52** B5
Laurel St *KGWD/HNM* BS15 .... **80** B1
Laurel Ter *YTN/CONG* BS49 .... **116** B2
Laurie Crs
HNLZ/SM/SNYPK/WT BS9 .... **47** E5
Laurie Lee Ct
OLD/WMLY/WICK BS30 .... **81** E4 7
Lavender Cl *THNB/SVB* BS35 .... **9** D3
TRWBR BA14 .... **157** E5 2
Lavender Wy *ALMDB* BS32 .... **30** A1
Lavenham Rd *YATE/CS* BS37 .... **18** C3
Lavers Cl *KGWD/HNM* BS15 .... **80** C3
Lavington Cl *CLVDN* BS21 .... **84** A3
Lavington Rd *EVILLE/WHL* BS5 .... **79** F3
Lawfield Av *BRSTK/PCHW* BS34 .... **29** D2
Lawfords Ga *CBRISNE* BS2 .... **3** H1
Lawn Av *MANG/FISH* BS16 .... **67** F1
Lawn Rd *MANG/FISH* BS16 .... **67** F1
Lawns Rd *YATE/CS* BS37 .... **19** F3
The Lawns *MTN/WRL* BS22 .... **130** A4 7
YTN/CONG BS49 .... **116** A2 2
Lawrence Av *EVILLE/WHL* BS5 .... **65** F5 6
Lawrence Cl *KGWD/HNM* BS15 .... **69** E4
Lawrence Close Ms
MTN/WRL BS22 .... **129** D5 4
Lawrence Dr *YATE/CS* BS37 .... **18** C3
Lawrence Gv
HNLZ/SM/SNYPK/WT BS9 .... **63** F1
Lawrence Hl *EVILLE/WHL* BS5 .... **77** F2
Lawrence Weston Rd *AVONM* BS11 .. **23** F4
AVONM BS11 .... **45** D2 2
Lawson Cl *KEYN* BS31 .... **108** A5
Laxey Rd *HORF/LLZ* BS7 .... **48** A4
Lays Dr *KEYN* BS31 .... **106** A3
Leach Cl *CLVDN* BS21 .... **85** D3 4
Lea Grove Rd *CLVDN* BS21 .... **70** C5
Leaholme Gdns *HGRV/WHIT* BS14 .. **103** E4
Leaman Cl *YATE/CS* BS37 .... **20** C4 1
Leap V *MANG/FISH* BS16 .... **52** B3
Leap Valley Crs *MANG/FISH* BS16 ...... **52** A3
The Leaze *RDSTK/MIDN* BA3 .... **162** A4
YATE/CS BS37 .... **19** E3
Leda Av *HGRV/WHIT* BS14 .... **93** E5
Ledbury Rd *MANG/FISH* BS16 .... **68** A2
Lee Cl *BRSTK/PCHW* BS34 .... **12** A5
Leedham Rd *OMX/HUT/LCK* BS24 .... **144** B5
Leeming Wy *AVONM* BS11 .... **43** D3
Lees Hl *KGWD/HNM* BS15 .... **68** C4
Leeside *PTSHD/EG* BS20 .... **56** A1
Lees La *OLD/WMLY/WICK* BS30 .... **82** B4
Leewood Rd *WSM* BS23 .... **141** D1
Leicester Sq *MANG/FISH* BS16 .... **68** B3 3
Leicester St *BMSTR* BS3 .... **76** B5 6
Leicester Wk
BRSG/KWL/STAPK BS4 .... **79** D4
Leigh Cl *CBATH/BATHN* BA1 .... **113** E5
Leigh Park Rd *BOAV* BA15 .... **147** D1
Leigh Rd *CFTN/FAIL* BS8 .... **75** F1
Leigh St *BMSTR* BS3 .... **75** E5 3
Leighton Crs *OMX/HUT/LCK* BS24.... **151** F5
Leighton Rd *BMSTR* BS3 .... **75** F5
BRSG/KWL/STAPK BS4 .... **93** F2
CBATH/BATHN BA1 .... **111** E4
Leigh View Rd *PTSHD/EG* BS20 .... **39** E4
Leighwood Dr *NAIL* BS48 .... **86** A3
Leinster Av *BRSG/KWL/STAPK* BS4 .... **92** B4
Lemon La *CBRISNE* BS2 .... **76** C1
Lena Av *EVILLE/WHL* BS5 .... **66** A5
Lena St *EVILLE/WHL* BS5 .... **65** F5
Lenover Gdns
BMSTRD/HC/WWD BS13 .... **101** F3 6
Leonard La *CBRIS/FH* BS1 .... **2** C2
Leonard Rd *EVILLE/WHL* BS5 .... **78** A2
Leonards Av *EVILLE/WHL* BS5 .... **66** A5 3
Leopold Rd *RDLND/MONT* BS6 .... **64** C4
Lester Dr *MTN/WRL* BS22 .... **129** F4 7
Lewington Rd *MANG/FISH* BS16 .... **68** A2
Lewins Md *CBRIS/FH* BS1 .... **2** D1
Lewin St *EVILLE/WHL* BS5 .... **78** B2 6
Lewis Cl *OLD/WMLY/WICK* BS30 .... **82** B4
Lewisham Gv *WSM* BS23 .... **7** G1
Lewis Rd *BMSTRD/HC/WWD* BS13 .... **91** E4
Lewis St *CBRISNE* BS2 .... **77** F4
Lewton La *FRCTL/WBN* BS36 .... **31** F1
Leyland Wk
BMSTRD/HC/WWD BS13 .... **101** D3
The Leys *CLVDN* BS21 .... **84** B3
Leyton Vls *RDLND/MONT* BS6 .... **63** F4
Lichfield Rd *BRSG/KWL/STAPK* BS4 .. **78** C3
Liddington Wy *TRWBR* BA14 .... **158** C2
Lilac Cl *HNBRY/STHM* BS10 .... **47** D2
Lilac Gv *TRWBR* BA14 .... **158** A2
Lilac Ter *RDSTK/MIDN* BA3 .... **161** F2
Lilac Wy *MTN/WRL* BS22 .... **129** F2
Lillian St *EVILLE/WHL* BS5 .... **78** A1 8
Lillington Cl *RDSTK/MIDN* BA3 .... **163** E2
Lillington Rd *RDSTK/MIDN* BA3 .... **163** E3
Lilliput Av *YATE/CS* BS37 .... **20** B5
Lilliput Ct *YATE/CS* BS37 .... **20** B5
Lilstock Av *HORF/LLZ* BS7 .... **65** D2
Lilton Wk
BMSTRD/HC/WWD BS13 .... **91** E3 1
Lilymead Av *BRSG/KWL/STAPK* BS4 .. **93** E1
Lime Cl *HNBRY/STHM* BS10 .... **26** C5
MTN/WRL BS22 .... **143** F1
Lime Cft *YATE/CS* BS37 .... **20** B1
Lime Gv *BATHSE* BA2 .... **5** E4
Lime Grove Gdns *BATHSE* BA2 .... **5** F4
Lime Kiln Cl *BRSTK/PCHW* BS34 .... **49** E1
Lime Kiln Gdns *ALMDB* BS32 .... **13** E2 2
Limekiln La *BATHSE* BA2 .... **139** D1
Lime Kiln La *CLVDN* BS21 .... **85** D1
Limerick Rd *RDLND/MONT* BS6 .... **64** A4
Lime Rd *BMSTR* BS3 .... **75** F5
KGWD/HNM BS15 .... **79** E4
Limestone Link *BATHSE* BA2 .... **115** E5
Lime Ter *RDSTK/MIDN* BA3 .... **162** A3 2
Lime Tree Gv *PTSHD/EG* BS20 .... **60** B3
Lincoln Cl *KEYN* BS31 .... **106** A3
Lincoln St *EVILLE/WHL* BS5 .... **77** F2
Lincombe Av *MANG/FISH* BS16 .... **51** E5
Lincombe Rd *MANG/FISH* BS16 .... **68** A1
RDSTK/MIDN BA3 .... **162** A4
Linden Av *WSM* BS23 .... **142** A2
Linden Cl *FRCTL/WBN* BS36 .... **31** F2
KGWD/HNM BS15 .... **67** F4
RDSTK/MIDN BA3 .... **162** B4
Linden Dr *ALMDB* BS32 .... **13** E5
Linden Gdns *CBATH/BATHN* BA1 ...... **122** B2
Linden Pl *TRWBR* BA14 .... **156** B3
Linden Rd *CLVDN* BS21 .... **71** D5
RDLND/MONT BS6 .... **63** F2
The Lindens *MTN/WRL* BS22 .... **129** D3 7
Lindrea St *BMSTR* BS3 .... **91** F1 5
Lindsay Rd *HORF/LLZ* BS7 .... **65** E2
Lindsey Cl *PTSHD/EG* BS20 .... **55** D2
Lines Wy *HGRV/WHIT* BS14 .... **104** A4
Lingfield Pk *FRCTL/WBN* BS36 .... **52** A2
Link Rd *BRSTK/PCHW* BS34 .... **28** A5
NAIL BS48 .... **87** E2 3
PTSHD/EG BS20 .... **56** A1 3
YATE/CS BS37 .... **20** A4
Linkside *CLVDN* BS21 .... **71** E3
Links Rd *WSM* BS23 .... **150** B3
Linley Cl *BATHSE* BA2 .... **121** E5
The Linleys *CBATH/BATHN* BA1 .... **122** A3
Linnell Cl *HORF/LLZ* BS7 .... **48** C5 2
Linnet Cl *MTN/WRL* BS22 .... **143** D1 2
Linnet Wy *RDSTK/MIDN* BA3 .... **161** E4
Lintern Crs *OLD/WMLY/WICK* BS30 .... **81** E3
Lintham Dr *KGWD/HNM* BS15 .... **81** D3
Lion Cl *NAIL* BS48 .... **86** B2
Lisburn Rd *BRSG/KWL/STAPK* BS4 .... **92** C4
Lisle Rd *MTN/WRL* BS22 .... **130** A3
Litfield Rd *CFTN/FAIL* BS8 .... **75** D1
Little Ann St *CBRISNE* BS2 .... **3** H1
Little Birch Cft *HGRV/WHIT* BS14 .... **103** E4
Little Bishop St *CBRISNE* BS2 .... **76** C1 9
Little Caroline Pl *CFTN/FAIL* BS8 .... **75** D4 5
Little Common *TRWBR* BA14 .... **159** D4
Littledean *YATE/CS* BS37 .... **35** F2
Little Dowles
OLD/WMLY/WICK BS30 .... **81** E5 5
Little George St *CBRISNE* BS2 .... **77** D1
WSM BS23 .... **6** D1 2
Little Green La *THNB/SVB* BS35 .... **10** B3
Little Halt *PTSHD/EG* BS20 .... **54** C2
Little Ham *CLVDN* BS21 .... **84** C4
Little Hayes *MANG/FISH* BS16 .... **50** C5 2
Little Headley Cl
BMSTRD/HC/WWD BS13 .... **91** F5
Little King St *CBRIS/FH* BS1 .... **2** D4 2
Little Md *AVONM* BS11 .... **44** C2
Little Mead Cl
OMX/HUT/LCK BS24 .... **153** D2 3
Little Meadow *ALMDB* BS32 .... **30** A2
Little Meadow End *NAIL* BS48 .... **87** D4
Little Orch *WSM* BS23 .... **150** C4
Little Paradise *BMSTR* BS3 .... **76** B5
Little Parr Cl *MANG/FISH* BS16 .... **66** A1 3
Little Paul St *CBRISNE* BS2 .... **76** A1
Little Stanhope St
CBATH/BATHN BA1 .... **122** C4 3
Little Stoke La *BRSTK/PCHW* BS34 .... **29** D1
Little Stoke Rd
HNLZ/SM/SNYPK/WT BS9 .... **62** C2
Littleton Rd *BMSTR* BS3 .... **92** B2
Little Withey Md
HNLZ/SM/SNYPK/WT BS9 .... **46** A5
Littlewood Cl *HGRV/WHIT* BS14 ...... **103** F4
Livingstone Rd *BATHSE* BA2 .... **122** B5
Llewellyn Wy *MTN/WRL* BS22 .... **130** A4 8
Lockemor Rd
BMSTRD/HC/WWD BS13 .... **103** D3
Lockeridge Cl *TRWBR* BA14 .... **159** D2 5
Lock Gdns *BMSTRD/HC/WWD* BS13 .. **90** C5
Locking Head Dro
OMX/HUT/LCK BS24 .... **143** E4
Locking Moor Rd *MTN/WRL* BS22 .. **142** B2
Locking Rd *MTN/WRL* BS22 .... **142** C2
WSM BS23 .... **6** D1 3
Lockingwell Rd *KEYN* BS31 .... **106** B2
Lockleaze Rd *HORF/LLZ* BS7 .... **48** B5
Locksbrook Rd
CBATH/BATHN BA1 .... **121** F4
MTN/WRL BS22 .... **130** A2
Loddon Wy *BOAV* BA15 .... **147** E4
Lodge Cswy *MANG/FISH* BS16 .... **67** E3
Lodge Cl *YTN/CONG* BS49 .... **116** B3
Lodge Dr *LGASH* BS41 .... **89** F2
OLD/WMLY/WICK BS30 .... **98** A2 1
WSM BS23 .... **141** F1
Lodge Gdns *BATHSE* BA2 .... **136** B4 2
Lodge Hl *KGWD/HNM* BS15 .... **68** A4
Lodge La *NAIL* BS48 .... **87** F1
Lodge Rd *KGWD/HNM* BS15 .... **68** A4
OLD/WMLY/WICK BS30 .... **83** E1
YATE/CS BS37 .... **18** B3
Lodgeside Av *KGWD/HNM* BS15 .... **68** A5 2
Lodgeside Gdns *KGWD/HNM* BS15 .... **68** A5
Lodge St *CBRIS/FH* BS1 .... **2** B2
Lodge Wk *MANG/FISH* BS16 .... **51** E5
Lodore Rd *MANG/FISH* BS16 .... **67** D3 4
Lodway *PTSHD/EG* BS20 .... **59** F2
Lodway Cl *PTSHD/EG* BS20 .... **60** A1
Lodway Gdns *PTSHD/EG* BS20 .... **60** A2
Lodway Rd *BRSG/KWL/STAPK* BS4 .... **94** A2
Logan Rd *HORF/LLZ* BS7 .... **64** B3
Logus Ct
OLD/WMLY/WICK BS30 .... **81** D5 12
Lombard St *BMSTR* BS3 .... **76** B5 7
Lombardy Cl *MTN/WRL* BS22 .... **143** D2 6
Lomond Rd *HORF/LLZ* BS7 .... **48** A2
London Rd *CBATH/BATHN* BA1 .... **123** F1
CBRISNE BS2 .... **65** D5 8
OLD/WMLY/WICK BS30 .... **82** A2
London Rd East
CBATH/BATHN BA1 .... **115** E4
London Rd West
CBATH/BATHN BA1 .... **114** B5
London St *KGWD/HNM* BS15 .... **80** B1
Longacre *CLVDN* BS21 .... **84** B4
Longacre Rd *HGRV/WHIT* BS14 .... **103** E4
Long Acres Cl
HNLZ/SM/SNYPK/WT BS9 .... **45** E4
Long Ashton Rd *LGASH* BS41 .... **89** E3
Long Av *CLVDN* BS21 .... **84** B2
Long Barnaby *RDSTK/MIDN* BA3 .... **161** D2
Long Beach Rd
OLD/WMLY/WICK BS30 .... **97** E2
Long Cl *ALMDB* BS32 .... **29** F2
MANG/FISH BS16 .... **51** D5
Long Cross *AVONM* BS11 .... **43** F3
Longden Rd *MANG/FISH* BS16 .... **52** A5
Longdown Dr *MTN/WRL* BS22 .... **130** A3 8
Long Eaton Dr *HGRV/WHIT* BS14 ...... **93** F4
Longfellow Av *BATHSE* BA2 .... **137** D1
Longfellow Rd *RDSTK/MIDN* BA3 .... **161** F3
Longfield Rd *HORF/LLZ* BS7 .... **64** C3
TRWBR BA14 .... **157** D5
Longford *YATE/CS* BS37 .... **19** D5
Longford Av *HNBRY/STHM* BS10 ...... **47** E3
Long Handstones
OLD/WMLY/WICK BS30 .... **81** E5
Long Hay Cl *BATHSE* BA2 .... **121** F5 2

Longleat Cl
HNLZ/SM/SNYPK/WT BS9 64 A1 1
Longleaze Gdns
OMX/HUT/LCK BS24 153 E2 1
Longmead Av HORF/LLZ BS7 64 B1
Long Meadow MANG/FISH BS16 66 B1
Longmeadow Rd KEYN BS31 106 A3
Longmoor Rd BMSTR BS3 91 E2
Longney Pl BRSTK/PCHW BS34 12 A4
Longreach Gv HGRV/WHIT BS14 94 B5
Long Rd MANG/FISH BS16 69 E1
Long Rw CBRIS/FH BS1 3 E4 2
Longs Dr YATE/CS BS37 19 D2 1
YATE/CS BS37 19 E3 3
Longton Grove Rd WSM BS23 141 D2 9
Longway Av HGRV/WHIT BS14 103 D3
Longwood BRSG/KWL/STAPK BS4 95 E2
Longwood La CFTN/FAIL BS8 72 C5
Lonsdale Av WSM BS23 7 F6
Lorain Wk HNBRY/STHM BS10 46 A1
Lorne Rd BATHSE BA2 122 B4
Lorton Rd HNBRY/STHM BS10 46 C2
Louisa St CBRISNE BS2 3 H3
Louise Av MANG/FISH BS16 69 E1 3
YATE/CS BS37 20 B1
Love La YATE/CS BS37 20 B5
Lovelinch Gdns LGASH BS41 89 D3 2
Lovell Av OLD/WMLY/WICK BS30 82 B5 2
Lovell's Hl KGWD/HNM BS15 79 F4 7
Loveringe Cl HNBRY/STHM BS10 26 A4
Lowbourne HGRV/WHIT BS14 103 D1
Lower Alma St TRWBR BA14 157 E4 2
Lower Ashley Rd
EVILLE/WHL BS5 65 E5 12
RDLND/MONT BS6 65 D5
Lower Borough Walls
CBATH/BATHN BA1 4 B4 5
Lower Bristol Rd BATHSE BA2 121 D3
BATHSE BA2 122 B4
Lower Castle St CBRIS/FH BS1 3 F1
Lower Chapel La FRCTL/WBN BS36 33 D1
Lower Chapel Rd
KGWD/HNM BS15 80 A4 6
Lower Cheltenham Pl
RDLND/MONT BS6 65 D5
Lower Church La CBRISNE BS2 2 B2
Lower Church Rd WSM BS23 140 C2
Lower Clifton Hl CFTN/FAIL BS8 75 E3
Lower Cock Rd KGWD/HNM BS15 81 D2
Lower College St CBRIS/FH BS1 2 A4 1
Lower Ct TRWBR BA14 157 D2
Lower Down Rd PTSHD/EG BS20 55 F1
Lower Fallow Cl
HGRV/WHIT BS14 103 D4 5
Lower Gay St CBRISNE BS2 76 B1 10
Lower Grove Rd
MANG/FISH BS16 66 C2 3
Lower Guinea St CBRIS/FH BS1 2 D6
Lower Hanham Rd
KGWD/HNM BS15 80 A4
Lower Hedgemead Rd
CBATH/BATHN BA1 123 E2 5
Lower High St AVONM BS11 43 E3
Lower House Crs
BRSTK/PCHW BS34 28 C4
Lower Knole La HNBRY/STHM BS10 26 B5
Lower Knowles Rd CLVDN BS21 84 C2 4
Lower Lamb St CBRIS/FH BS1 2 A4
Lower Linden Rd CLVDN BS21 85 D1
Lower Maudlin St CBRIS/FH BS1 2 D1 3
Lower Moor Rd YATE/CS BS37 19 F1
Lower Northend
CBATH/BATHN BA1 115 D2
Lower Norton La MTN/WRL BS22 128 A3
Lower Oldfield Pk BATHSE BA2 122 C5
Lower Parade Ground Rd
OMX/HUT/LCK BS24 144 A5
Lower Park Rw CBRIS/FH BS1 2 C2 2
Lower Queen's CLVDN BS21 85 D1 1
Lower Redland Rd
RDLND/MONT BS6 63 F4
Lower Sidney St BMSTR BS3 75 E5
Lower Station Approach Rd
CBRIS/FH BS1 3 G5 1
Lower Station Rd MANG/FISH BS16 67 D2
Lower Stone Cl FRCTL/WBN BS36 17 D5
Lower Strode Rd CLVDN BS21 84 A5
Lowlis Cl HNBRY/STHM BS10 26 A5 5
Lowmead TRWBR BA14 157 E3
Lowther Rd HNBRY/STHM BS10 47 D1 3
Loxley Gdns BATHSE BA2 136 A1
Loxton Dr BATHSE BA2 121 F4
Loxton Rd WSM BS23 151 E2
Loxton Sq HGRV/WHIT BS14 103 E1
Lucas Cl BRSG/KWL/STAPK BS4 94 B4
Luccombe Hl RDLND/MONT BS6 63 F4 4
Luckington Rd HORF/LLZ BS7 47 F3
Lucklands Rd CBATH/BATHN BA1 122 A1
Luckley Av
BMSTRD/HC/WWD BS13 102 A2 3
Luckwell Rd BMSTR BS3 91 F1
Lucky La BMSTR BS3 76 B5
Ludlow Cl CBRISNE BS2 65 D5
KEYN BS31 106 B2
OLD/WMLY/WICK BS30 97 F2
Ludlow Rd HORF/LLZ BS7 48 B4
Ludwell Cl FRCTL/WBN BS36 31 E3 3
Lullington Rd
BRSG/KWL/STAPK BS4 93 F2
Lulsgate Rd
BMSTRD/HC/WWD BS13 91 E4
Lulworth Crs MANG/FISH BS16 52 A3
Lulworth Rd KEYN BS31 106 C3
Lurgan Wk BRSG/KWL/STAPK BS4 92 B3
Lux Furlong
HNLZ/SM/SNYPK/WT BS9 44 C4
Luxton St EVILLE/WHL BS5 77 F1 10
Lychgate Pk OMX/HUT/LCK BS24 153 F1
Lydbrook Cl YATE/CS BS37 19 E5 2
Lyddington Rd HORF/LLZ BS7 47 F2
Lyddon Rd MTN/WRL BS22 130 A4
Lydford Wk BMSTR BS3 92 A2
Lydiard Cft KGWD/HNM BS15 80 A5
Lydiard Wy TRWBR BA14 159 D2
Lydney Rd HNBRY/STHM BS10 47 E3
MANG/FISH BS16 68 C2
Lydstep Ter BMSTR BS3 76 A5
Lyefield Rd MTN/WRL BS22 129 D3
The Lyes YTN/CONG BS49 133 D3
Lyme Gdns CBATH/BATHN BA1 121 F3 2
Lyme Rd CBATH/BATHN BA1 121 F3
Lymore Av BATHSE BA2 122 A5
Lymore Gdns BATHSE BA2 122 A5
Lymore Ter BATHSE BA2 136 A1
Lympsham Gn BATHSE BA2 136 B4
Lynbrook LGASH BS41 89 D3
Lynbrook La BATHSE BA2 137 D2
Lynch Cl MTN/WRL BS22 129 E4 7
Lynch Ct OLD/WMLY/WICK BS30 81 D5 13
Lynch Crs WNSC BS25 154 B5
Lynchmead WNSC BS25 154 B5
The Lynch WNSC BS25 154 B5
Lyncombe Hl BATHSE BA2 4 D6
Lyncombe V BATHSE BA2 137 E1
Lyncombe Vale Rd BATHSE BA2 137 E2
Lyncombe Wk MANG/FISH BS16 67 F4 2
Lyndale Av
HNLZ/SM/SNYPK/WT BS9 62 A1
Lyndale Rd EVILLE/WHL BS5 78 B1
YATE/CS BS37 19 E4
Lynde Cl BMSTRD/HC/WWD BS13 101 F3
Lyndhurst Rd BATHSE BA2 122 A4
HNLZ/SM/SNYPK/WT BS9 46 A4
KEYN BS31 107 D4
RDSTK/MIDN BA3 161 E4 3
WSM BS23 151 D1 1
Lyneham Wy TRWBR BA14 157 F4
Lynfield Pk CBATH/BATHN BA1 111 F5
Lynmouth Cl MTN/WRL BS22 129 F5 3
Lynmouth Rd CBRISNE BS2 65 E4 9
Lynn Rd MANG/FISH BS16 66 B1 1
Lynton Cl PTSHD/EG BS20 56 C2 5
Lynton Pl EVILLE/WHL BS5 78 A1
Lynton Rd BMSTR BS3 92 B3
RDSTK/MIDN BA3 161 E4
Lynton Wy MANG/FISH BS16 50 C2
Lynwood Cl RDSTK/MIDN BA3 161 D5
Lynwood Rd TRWBR BA14 156 A3
Lynx Crs OMX/HUT/LCK BS24 152 A3
Lyons Ct WSM BS23 7 E1
Lyons Court Rd HGRV/WHIT BS14 94 B5
Lyppiatt Rd EVILLE/WHL BS5 78 B1
Lyppincourt Rd HNBRY/STHM BS10 26 B5
Lysander Rd BRSTK/PCHW BS34 27 D2
HNBRY/STHM BS10 26 C2
Lysander Wk BRSTK/PCHW BS34 29 F3 4
Lytchet Dr MANG/FISH BS16 52 A3 1
Lytes Cary Rd KEYN BS31 107 E5
Lytton Gdns BATHSE BA2 135 F1
Lytton Gv HORF/LLZ BS7 48 B3
KEYN BS31 107 E2
Lyveden Gdns
BMSTRD/HC/WWD BS13 101 F2 7
Lyvedon Wy LGASH BS41 89 F3

M

Macaulay Buildings BATHSE BA2 138 A1
Macauley Rd HORF/LLZ BS7 48 B3
Macey's Rd
BMSTRD/HC/WWD BS13 102 B4 1
Machin Cl HNBRY/STHM BS10 26 A5
Machin Gdns HNBRY/STHM BS10 26 B5 3
Machin Rd HNBRY/STHM BS10 26 A5
The Macies CBATH/BATHN BA1 111 F4
Mackie Av BRSTK/PCHW BS34 48 C1
Mackie Gv BRSTK/PCHW BS34 48 C1
Mackie Rd BRSTK/PCHW BS34 48 C1
Macleod Cl CLVDN BS21 84 A2 1
Macmillan Wy BOAV BA15 146 A4
Macrae Ct KGWD/HNM BS15 80 C1 1
Madam La MTN/WRL BS22 129 E5
Madeira Rd CLVDN BS21 85 D1 2
WSM BS23 140 B1
Madeline Rd MANG/FISH BS16 67 D4 2
Madison Cl YATE/CS BS37 19 E3
Maesbury KGWD/HNM BS15 80 C3
Maesbury Rd KEYN BS31 107 E5
Maesknoll Rd
BRSG/KWL/STAPK BS4 93 E1
Magdalen Av BATHSE BA2 4 A6
Magdalene Pl CBRISNE BS2 65 D5
Magdalene Rd RDSTK/MIDN BA3 163 F2
Magdalen Rd BATHSE BA2 4 A6
Magdalen Wy MTN/WRL BS22 129 F4
Magellan Cl MTN/WRL BS22 129 E3
Maggs Cl HNBRY/STHM BS10 27 D5
Maggs La EVILLE/WHL BS5 66 C4
HGRV/WHIT BS14 103 F3
Magnolia Av MTN/WRL BS22 143 F1
Magnolia Cl MTN/WRL BS22 143 D3 2
Magnolia Ri TRWBR BA14 157 E5
Magnolia Rd RDSTK/MIDN BA3 162 A3
Magnon Rd BOAV BA15 146 B2
Magpie Bottom La
EVILLE/WHL BS5 79 F3
KGWD/HNM BS15 80 A3 1
Magpie Cl MTN/WRL BS22 143 D2 7
Maidenhead Rd
BMSTRD/HC/WWD BS13 102 B4
Maiden Wy AVONM BS11 43 D4 1
Maidstone Gv
OMX/HUT/LCK BS24 151 F4 4
Maidstone St BMSTR BS3 93 D1
Main Rd OMX/HUT/LCK BS24 152 C3
Main Vw FRCTL/WBN BS36 33 E1
Maisemore YATE/CS BS37 35 F2
Maisemore Av BRSTK/PCHW BS34 12 C4
Makin Cl OLD/WMLY/WICK BS30 82 A4 2
Malago Rd BMSTR BS3 92 A1
Malago Wk
BMSTRD/HC/WWD BS13 100 C3 2
Maldowers La EVILLE/WHL BS5 67 E5
Mallard Cl ALMDB BS32 13 E3
EVILLE/WHL BS5 67 D5
YATE/CS BS37 20 B5
Mallow Cl CLVDN BS21 85 E2 3
THNB/SVB BS35 9 D2
TRWBR BA14 159 D1 1
The Mall CFTN/FAIL BS8 75 D2
Malmains Dr MANG/FISH BS16 50 C2
Malmesbury Cl
OLD/WMLY/WICK BS30 81 D4 5
RDLND/MONT BS6 64 A2 3
The Maltings MTN/WRL BS22 129 E5 7
Maltlands MTN/WRL BS22 142 C2
Malvern Buildings
CBATH/BATHN BA1 113 E5
Malvern Ct EVILLE/WHL BS5 79 D2
Malvern Dr OLD/WMLY/WICK BS30 82 A4
THNB/SVB BS35 9 D4
Malvern Rd BRSG/KWL/STAPK BS4 94 B1
EVILLE/WHL BS5 79 D2
WSM BS23 6 D6
Mancroft Av AVONM BS11 44 A4
Mand Wd TRWBR BA14 149 F1
Mandy Mdw RDSTK/MIDN BA3 160 C3
Mangotsfield Rd MANG/FISH BS16 69 D2
Manilla Pl WSM BS23 140 B1 3
Manilla Rd CFTN/FAIL BS8 75 E2
Manor Cl FRCTL/WBN BS36 33 D2
PTSHD/EG BS20 59 E2
TRWBR BA14 158 A1
The Manor Cl CFTN/FAIL BS8 73 E1
Manor Copse Rd
RDSTK/MIDN BA3 163 F2
Manor Court Dr HORF/LLZ BS7 47 F4
Manor Dr CBATH/BATHN BA1 115 F5
Manor Farm Crs ALMDB BS32 13 E4
OMX/HUT/LCK BS24 152 A3
Manor Gdns MTN/WRL BS22 128 A3
OMX/HUT/LCK BS24 153 F1 4
Manor Gv ALMDB BS32 12 C3 1
MANG/FISH BS16 69 E2
Manor La CFTN/FAIL BS8 73 D1
FRCTL/WBN BS36 32 A1
Manor Pk CBATH/BATHN BA1 121 F2
RDLND/MONT BS6 63 F3
RDSTK/MIDN BA3 163 F2
Manor Pl MANG/FISH BS16 51 D2
Manor Rd
BMSTRD/HC/WWD BS13 101 D1
CBATH/BATHN BA1 122 A1
CFTN/FAIL BS8 73 D3
HORF/LLZ BS7 64 C2
KEYN BS31 107 E4
MANG/FISH BS16 67 D1
MANG/FISH BS16 69 E2
RDSTK/MIDN BA3 163 F2
TRWBR BA14 158 A1
WSM BS23 141 E1
Manor Va WSM BS23 141 F1
Manor Wk THNB/SVB BS35 8 B1
Manor Wy CFTN/FAIL BS8 72 A5
YATE/CS BS37 21 D3
Mansel Cl KEYN BS31 108 A4
Mansfield Av WSM BS23 142 A2
Mansfield St BMSTR BS3 91 F2
Manston Cl HGRV/WHIT BS14 94 A5
Manton Cl TRWBR BA14 158 C2
Manvers St CBATH/BATHN BA1 4 C4 7

Manworthy Rd
BRSG/KWL/STAPK BS4 94 B1
Manx Rd *HORF/LLZ* BS7 48 A4
Maple Av *MANG/FISH* BS16 68 A3
THNB/SVB BS35 8 C3
Maple Cl *BRSTK/PCHW* BS34 29 D1
HGRV/WHIT BS14 104 B2
OLD/WMLY/WICK BS30 81 F5
WSM BS23 141 F2 1
Maple Dr *RDSTK/MIDN* BA3 162 B2
Maple Gdns *BATHSE* BA2 136 C1
Maple Gv *BATHSE* BA2 136 C1
TRWBR BA14 158 C1
Mapleleaze *BRSG/KWL/STAPK* BS4 94 B1
Maplemeade *HORF/LLZ* BS7 64 A2 4
Maple Ri *RDSTK/MIDN* BA3 163 E2
Maple Rd *BRSG/KWL/STAPK* BS4 78 B4
HORF/LLZ BS7 64 B1
The Maples *NAIL* BS48 86 B3
Maplestone Rd *HGRV/WHIT* BS14 103 E4
Maple Wk *KEYN* BS31 106 B3
Marbeck Rd *HNBRY/STHM* BS10 46 C2
Marchfields Wy *WSM* BS23 7 F4
Marconi Rd *PTSHD/EG* BS20 55 D2
Mardale Cl *HNBRY/STHM* BS10 47 D1 4
Marden Rd *KEYN* BS31 107 E3
Marden Wk *TRWBR* BA14 159 D1 2
Mardon Rd *BRSG/KWL/STAPK* BS4 78 B3
Mardyke Ferry Rd *CBRIS/FH* BS1 75 F4 4
Margaret's Hl
CBATH/BATHN BA1 123 E2 6
Margate St *BMSTR* BS3 92 C1
Marguerite Rd
BMSTRD/HC/WWD BS13 91 D4
Marigold Wk *BMSTR* BS3 91 E2
Marina Dr *TRWBR* BA14 149 D4
Marina Gdns *MANG/FISH* BS16 66 C3
Marindrin Dr *MTN/WRL* BS22 130 A3 9
Marine Hl *CLVDN* BS21 70 C5
Marine Pde *CLVDN* BS21 70 C5
PTSHD/EG BS20 60 A1
WSM BS23 6 A6
Mariner's Cl *MTN/WRL* BS22 142 C1 4
Mariners Dr
HNLZ/SM/SNYPK/WT BS9 62 B2
Mariners' Pth
HNLZ/SM/SNYPK/WT BS9 62 B2
Mariner's Wy *PTSHD/EG* BS20 60 A1
Marion Rd *KGWD/HNM* BS15 95 F1
Marion Wk *EVILLE/WHL* BS5 79 E2
Marissal Cl *HNBRY/STHM* BS10 25 F5
Marissal Rd *HNBRY/STHM* BS10 25 F5
Mariston Wy
OLD/WMLY/WICK BS30 82 A3
Marjoram Pl *ALMDB* BS32 30 A1
Market La *WSM* BS23 140 C2 6
Market Sq *MANG/FISH* BS16 68 A3 6
Market St *BOAV* BA15 147 D2
TRWBR BA14 157 D4
Markham Cl *AVONM* BS11 43 D4 2
Mark La *CBRIS/FH* BS1 2 B3
Marksbury Rd *BMSTR* BS3 92 A2
Marlborough Av
EVILLE/WHL BS5 66 C3 3
Marlborough Buildings
CBATH/BATHN BA1 122 C3
Marlborough Dr *MANG/FISH* BS16 50 C2
MTN/WRL BS22 129 F5
Marlborough Hl *RDLND/MONT* BS6 76 B1
Marlborough Hill Pl
CBRISNE BS2 76 B1 11
Marlborough La
CBATH/BATHN BA1 122 C3
Marlborough St
CBATH/BATHN BA1 122 C2 2
CBRISNE BS2 2 C1
EVILLE/WHL BS5 66 C3 4
Marlepit Gv
BMSTRD/HC/WWD BS13 101 D1 2
Marlfield Wk
BMSTRD/HC/WWD BS13 90 C5
Marling Rd *EVILLE/WHL* BS5 79 E2 3
Marlwood Dr *HNBRY/STHM* BS10 26 B5
Marmaduke St *BMSTR* BS3 93 D1
Marmion Crs *HNBRY/STHM* BS10 26 A5
Marne Cl *HGRV/WHIT* BS14 104 B2
Marsden Rd *BATHSE* BA2 135 F2
Marsham Wy
OLD/WMLY/WICK BS30 80 C4
Marsh Cl *FRCTL/WBN* BS36 31 F4
Marsh Common *THNB/SVB* BS35 11 E4
Marshfield La
OLD/WMLY/WICK BS30 99 E3
Marshfield Rd *MANG/FISH* BS16 67 F2
Marshfield Wy *CBATH/BATHN* BA1 123 E1
Marsh La *EVILLE/WHL* BS5 78 A2
PTSHD/EG BS20 41 F5
Marshmead *TRWBR* BA14 149 F5
Marsh Rd *BMSTR* BS3 91 D1
TRWBR BA14 149 E4
YTN/CONG BS49 116 B4
Marsh St *AVONM* BS11 43 D3
CBRIS/FH BS1 2 C3
Marson Rd *CLVDN* BS21 85 D1
Marston Rd
BRSG/KWL/STAPK BS4 93 F2 2
TRWBR BA14 158 B2 2
Martcombe Rd *PTSHD/EG* BS20 59 F3
Martindale Ct *MTN/WRL* BS22 142 C2
Martindale Rd *MTN/WRL* BS22 142 C2
Martingale Rd
BRSG/KWL/STAPK BS4 78 B5
Martins Cl *KGWD/HNM* BS15 80 A4 7
Martins Gv *MTN/WRL* BS22 129 D5 5
Martin's Rd *KGWD/HNM* BS15 80 A4
Martin St *BMSTR* BS3 91 F1 6
Martlock Crs *BMSTR* BS3 92 A3
Martock Rd *BMSTR* BS3 92 A3
KEYN BS31 107 E4
Marwood Rd
BRSG/KWL/STAPK BS4 92 C4 4
Marybush La *CBRISNE* BS2 3 F2 1
Marygold Leaze
OLD/WMLY/WICK BS30 81 E5 6
Mary St *EVILLE/WHL* BS5 78 B1 6
Mascot Rd *BMSTR* BS3 92 B1
Masefield Wy *HORF/LLZ* BS7 48 B4 1
Maskelyne Av *HNBRY/STHM* BS10 47 E4
Masons La *BOAV* BA15 147 D2
Masons Vw *FRCTL/WBN* BS36 31 F1
Materman Rd *HGRV/WHIT* BS14 104 C2
Matford Cl *FRCTL/WBN* BS36 31 F3
HNBRY/STHM BS10 27 E4
Matthews Cl *HGRV/WHIT* BS14 105 D1
Matthew's Rd *EVILLE/WHL* BS5 78 A2 10
Maules La *MANG/FISH* BS16 50 A1
Maulton Cl *TRWBR* BA14 149 D1
Maunsell Rd *AVONM* BS11 44 C1
Maurice Rd *RDLND/MONT* BS6 64 C4
Mautravers Cl *ALMDB* BS32 29 E1
Maxse Rd *BRSG/KWL/STAPK* BS4 93 F1
Maybec Gdns *EVILLE/WHL* BS5 79 E3 4
Maybourne
BRSG/KWL/STAPK BS4 95 E2 2
Maybrick Rd *BATHSE* BA2 122 B5
Maycliffe Pk *RDLND/MONT* BS6 65 D4
Mayfair Av *NAIL* BS48 87 D3
Mayfield Av *MANG/FISH* BS16 67 E4
MTN/WRL BS22 143 D1 3
Mayfield Pk *MANG/FISH* BS16 67 E4
Mayfield Pk North
MANG/FISH BS16 67 E4
Mayfield Pk South
MANG/FISH BS16 67 E4
Mayfield Rd *BATHSE* BA2 122 B5
Mayfields *KEYN* BS31 106 C2
Mayflower Gdns *NAIL* BS48 87 F2
Maynard Cl
BMSTRD/HC/WWD BS13 102 A2
CLVDN BS21 85 F1 4
Maynard Rd
BMSTRD/HC/WWD BS13 102 A2
Maysfield Cl *PTSHD/EG* BS20 56 B3
May St *KGWD/HNM* BS15 68 A5
Maytree Av
BMSTRD/HC/WWD BS13 91 F5
Maytree Cl *BMSTRD/HC/WWD* BS13 91 F5
May Tree Cl *NAIL* BS48 86 B3 6
May Tree Rd *RDSTK/MIDN* BA3 162 B3
Mayville Av *BRSTK/PCHW* BS34 28 B5
Maywood Crs *MANG/FISH* BS16 67 F2
Maywood Rd *MANG/FISH* BS16 68 A2
Maze St *EVILLE/WHL* BS5 77 F3 8
Mc Crae Rd *OMX/HUT/LCK* BS24 144 A5
Mead Cl *AVONM* BS11 43 F5 1
BATHSE BA2 136 C2
Meadgate *MANG/FISH* BS16 52 C3
Mead Lands *BATHSE* BA2 119 E3
Mead La *KEYN* BS31 109 D3
Meadowbank *MTN/WRL* BS22 129 E4 8
Meadow Cl *MANG/FISH* BS16 52 A4
NAIL BS48 87 D1
PTSHD/EG BS20 55 D1 3
Meadow Court Dr
OLD/WMLY/WICK BS30 98 A1
Meadowcroft *MANG/FISH* BS16 52 B3 1
Meadow Cft *OMX/HUT/LCK* BS24 152 A3
Meadow Dr *BATHSE* BA2 136 B5 3
OMX/HUT/LCK BS24 153 F1
PTSHD/EG BS20 55 D5
Meadowfield *BOAV* BA15 146 B3
Meadow Gdns *CBATH/BATHN* BA1 121 E1
Meadow Gv *AVONM* BS11 43 E4
Meadowland *YTN/CONG* BS49 116 A2
Meadowland Rd
HNBRY/STHM BS10 25 F4
Meadowlands *MTN/WRL* BS22 130 B5
Meadow La *BATHSE* BA2 124 B1
Meadow Md *FRCTL/WBN* BS36 16 C5
Meadow Pk *CBATH/BATHN* BA1 115 F3
Meadow Rd *CLVDN* BS21 85 E1 1
YATE/CS BS37 20 B4 3
Meadowside *THNB/SVB* BS35 9 D4 3
Meadowside Dr *HGRV/WHIT* BS14 103 E4
The Meadows *KGWD/HNM* BS15 80 B5
Meadow St *AVONM* BS11 42 B2
CBRISNE BS2 3 F1 3
Meadowsweet Av
BRSTK/PCHW BS34 28 C5
Meadow V *EVILLE/WHL* BS5 67 E5
Meadow Vw *FRCTL/WBN* BS36 33 D1
RDSTK/MIDN BA3 163 D3
Meadow Wy *ALMDB* BS32 29 F1
Mead Ri *BMSTR* BS3 77 D5
Mead Rd *BRSTK/PCHW* BS34 30 A2
PTSHD/EG BS20 56 A3
YATE/CS BS37 21 D5
The Meads *MANG/FISH* BS16 52 A4
Mead St *BMSTR* BS3 77 D5
The Mead *BRSTK/PCHW* BS34 28 C4
LGASH BS41 100 B5
Mead V *MTN/WRL* BS22 143 D2
Meadway
HNLZ/SM/SNYPK/WT BS9 45 D5
TRWBR BA14 156 A4
Mead Wy *THNB/SVB* BS35 8 B5
Meadway Av *NAIL* BS48 86 C2
Meardon Rd *HGRV/WHIT* BS14 104 C1 5
Meare Rd *BATHSE* BA2 137 E3
Mede Cl *CBRIS/FH* BS1 3 E6 1
Medical Av *CFTN/FAIL* BS8 2 B2
Medina Cl *THNB/SVB* BS35 8 C5 2
Medway Cl *KEYN* BS31 107 D4
Medway Ct *THNB/SVB* BS35 9 D4
Medway Dr *FRCTL/WBN* BS36 32 C1
KEYN BS31 107 E4
Meere Bank *AVONM* BS11 44 C2
Meg Thatchers Cl
EVILLE/WHL BS5 79 F2 2
Melbourne Dr *YATE/CS* BS37 20 C4
Melbourne Rd *HORF/LLZ* BS7 64 B2
Melbourne Ter *CLVDN* BS21 85 D2 6
Melbury Rd *BRSG/KWL/STAPK* BS4 93 E2
Melcombe Rd *BATHSE* BA2 122 B5
Melita Rd *RDLND/MONT* BS6 64 C3
Mellent Av
BMSTRD/HC/WWD BS13 102 A4
Mells Cl *KEYN* BS31 107 E5
Mells La *RDSTK/MIDN* BA3 163 E3
Melrose Av *CFTN/FAIL* BS8 75 F1 2
YATE/CS BS37 20 A3
Melrose Cl *YATE/CS* BS37 20 B3
Melrose Gv *BATHSE* BA2 135 F2
Melrose Pl *CFTN/FAIL* BS8 75 F1
Melton Crs *HORF/LLZ* BS7 48 B4
Melton Rd *TRWBR* BA14 156 C2
Melville Rd *RDLND/MONT* BS6 63 F5
Melville Ter *BMSTR* BS3 92 A1
Melvin Sq *BRSG/KWL/STAPK* BS4 92 C3
Memorial Cl *KGWD/HNM* BS15 79 F5
Memorial Rd *KGWD/HNM* BS15 79 F4
Mendip Av *MTN/WRL* BS22 129 D5
Mendip Cl *KEYN* BS31 106 B2
NAIL BS48 87 D3 7
Mendip Crs *MANG/FISH* BS16 52 B4
Mendip Edge *OMX/HUT/LCK* BS24 151 E5
Mendip Gdns *BATHSE* BA2 136 B5
YTN/CONG BS49 116 B4
Mendip Rd *BMSTR* BS3 92 B1
PTSHD/EG BS20 55 E1
WSM BS23 7 G1
YTN/CONG BS49 116 B3
Mendip View Av *MANG/FISH* BS16 67 E3
Mendip Wy *RDSTK/MIDN* BA3 162 C1
Merchants Rd *CFTN/FAIL* BS8 75 E2
Merchant St *CBRIS/FH* BS1 3 E1
Mercia Dr *CBRISNE* BS2 65 E4
Mercier Cl *YATE/CS* BS37 20 A3
Merfield Rd
BRSG/KWL/STAPK BS4 93 F2 3
Meridian Pl *CFTN/FAIL* BS8 75 F2
Meridian Rd *RDLND/MONT* BS6 64 A5
Meridian V *CFTN/FAIL* BS8 75 F2
Meridian Wk *TRWBR* BA14 156 A4 2
Meriet Av *BMSTRD/HC/WWD* BS13 101 F3
Merioneth St *BMSTR* BS3 93 D1 1
Meriton St *CBRISNE* BS2 77 F4
Merlin Cl *HNLZ/SM/SNYPK/WT* BS9 46 A3
MTN/WRL BS22 143 D2 8
Merlin Pk *PTSHD/EG* BS20 55 D2
Merlin Rd *BRSTK/PCHW* BS34 27 D2
Merlin Wy *YATE/CS* BS37 36 A1
Merrimans Rd *AVONM* BS11 43 E3
Merryweather Cl *ALMDB* BS32 13 D5
Merrywood Cl *BMSTR* BS3 76 A5 3
Merrywood Rd *BMSTR* BS3 76 A5
Merstham Rd *CBRISNE* BS2 65 E4 10
Merton Rd *HORF/LLZ* BS7 64 C1
Mervyn Rd *HORF/LLZ* BS7 64 C2
Metford Gv *RDLND/MONT* BS6 63 F3
Metford Pl *RDLND/MONT* BS6 64 A3 1
Metford Rd *RDLND/MONT* BS6 63 F3
Methuen Cl *BOAV* BA15 147 D5
Methwyn Cl *WSM* BS23 142 B3 2
The Mews *CBATH/BATHN* BA1 121 E2
Middle Av *CBRIS/FH* BS1 2 C4 2
Middle La *CBATH/BATHN* BA1 123 F1
TRWBR BA14 157 F2
Middle Rd *KGWD/HNM* BS15 68 C3
Middleton Rd *AVONM* BS11 44 A3
Midford Rd *BATHSE* BA2 137 D5
Midhaven Ri *MTN/WRL* BS22 129 D3
Midland Bridge Rd *BATHSE* BA2 122 C4
Midland Rd *BATHSE* BA2 122 B4

CBRISNE BS2 3 H2
MANG/FISH BS16 68 B2
The Midlands TRWBR BA14 149 E1
Midland St CBRISNE BS2 3 H3
Midland Ter MANG/FISH BS16 67 D3 5
Midland Wy THNB/SVB BS35 8 B4
Midsummer Buildings
CBATH/BATHN BA1 123 E1
Milburn Rd WSM BS23 7 E1
Milbury Gdns MTN/WRL BS22 128 A5
Mildred St EVILLE/WHL BS5 78 A2
Miles Ct OLD/WMLY/WICK BS30 81 D5 14
Miles Rd CFTN/FAIL BS8 63 E5
Miles St BATHSE BA2 4 D5
Milestone Ct MTN/WRL BS22 130 C5
Milford Av OLD/WMLY/WICK BS30 83 F2
Milford St BMSTR BS3 76 A5
Milk St CBATH/BATHN BA1 4 B4
Millard Cl HNBRY/STHM BS10 47 D1 5
Millard's Hl RDSTK/MIDN BA3 161 E1
Mill Av CBRIS/FH BS1 2 D4
Millbank Cl BRSG/KWL/STAPK BS4 94 C1
Millbrook Av
BRSG/KWL/STAPK BS4 95 D1 1
Millbrook Cl OLD/WMLY/WICK BS30 82 A3
Millbrook Pl BATHSE BA2 4 D6
Millbrook Rd YATE/CS BS37 18 C3
Mill Cl FRCTL/WBN BS36 33 D1
PTSHD/EG BS20 58 B4
Mill Crs YATE/CS BS37 34 C4
Millcross CLVDN BS21 84 C4
Millers Cl PTSHD/EG BS20 60 A2 5
Millers Dr OLD/WMLY/WICK BS30 82 A4
Millers Ri MTN/WRL BS22 129 F3 10
Miller Wk BATHSE BA2 124 C1
Millfield RDSTK/MIDN BA3 160 C4
THNB/SVB BS35 8 C2
Millfield Dr OLD/WMLY/WICK BS30 82 A3
Millground Rd
BMSTRD/HC/WWD BS13 100 C3
Millhand Vls TRWBR BA14 157 E5
Milliman Cl
BMSTRD/HC/WWD BS13 102 A2
Millington Dr TRWBR BA14 156 A5
Mill La BATHSE BA2 115 D5
BATHSE BA2 121 F4 1
BATHSE BA2 138 C5
BMSTR BS3 76 B5
BOAV BA15 147 D3
FRCTL/WBN BS36 16 C5
OLD/WMLY/WICK BS30 82 A4
OLD/WMLY/WICK BS30 98 C4
PTSHD/EG BS20 58 C4
YTN/CONG BS49 133 D2
Mill Leg YTN/CONG BS49 133 E2
Millmead Rd BATHSE BA2 122 A5
Mill Rd FRCTL/WBN BS36 31 E4
RDSTK/MIDN BA3 163 D2
Mill St TRWBR BA14 157 D4 1
Millward Gv MANG/FISH BS16 68 A2
Milner Gn OLD/WMLY/WICK BS30 81 E4
Milner Rd HORF/LLZ BS7 65 D1
Milsom St CBATH/BATHN BA1 4 B2 3
EVILLE/WHL BS5 77 E1
Milton Av BATHSE BA2 137 D1
WSM BS23 141 F2
Milton Brow MTN/WRL BS22 128 A5
Milton Cl NAIL BS48 87 D1
YATE/CS BS37 19 E3
Milton Gn MTN/WRL BS22 142 B1 3
Milton Hl MTN/WRL BS22 128 A5
Milton Pk EVILLE/WHL BS5 78 A2 11
Milton Park Rd MTN/WRL BS22 142 B1
MTN/WRL BS22 142 A1 2
Milton Ri MTN/WRL BS22 142 B1 4
Milton Rd HORF/LLZ BS7 47 F5
RDSTK/MIDN BA3 161 F3
WSM BS23 141 E2
YATE/CS BS37 19 E3
Miltons Cl
BMSTRD/HC/WWD BS13 102 B3
Milverton Gdns
RDLND/MONT BS6 65 D4 7
Milward Rd KEYN BS31 106 C1
Mina Rd CBRISNE BS2 65 D3
Minehead Rd
BRSG/KWL/STAPK BS4 93 D3
Minerva Gdns BATHSE BA2 136 A1 1
Minsmere Rd KEYN BS31 107 E4
Minster Wy BATHSE BA2 124 A2
Minton Cl HGRV/WHIT BS14 103 F2
Minto Rd CBRISNE BS2 65 E4
Mission Rd YATE/CS BS37 18 B1
Mitchell La CBRIS/FH BS1 3 E4
Mitchell Wk
OLD/WMLY/WICK BS30 82 B3 4
Mivart St EVILLE/WHL BS5 65 F4
Mizzymead Cl NAIL BS48 86 C3 7
Mizzymead Ri NAIL BS48 86 C3
Mizzymead Rd NAIL BS48 87 D2 4
Modecombe Gv
HNBRY/STHM BS10 26 A5 6
Mogg St CBRISNE BS2 65 E4
Molesworth Cl
BMSTRD/HC/WWD BS13 101 E3
Molesworth Dr
BMSTRD/HC/WWD BS13 101 E3
Monarch's Wy EVILLE/WHL BS5 78 B3
LGASH BS41 88 C2
OLD/WMLY/WICK BS30 96 C3
YATE/CS BS37 37 D1
Monger La RDSTK/MIDN BA3 160 C1
Monk Rd HORF/LLZ BS7 64 B2
Monks Av KGWD/HNM BS15 79 F1 1
Monksdale Rd BATHSE BA2 136 B1
Monks Hl MTN/WRL BS22 128 A4
Monk's Park Av HORF/LLZ BS7 47 F2
Monks Park Wy
HNBRY/STHM BS10 47 F3
Monkton Av OMX/HUT/LCK BS24 151 F3
Monkton Rd KGWD/HNM BS15 79 F5
Monmouth Cl PTSHD/EG BS20 55 D2 5
Monmouth Pl CBATH/BATHN BA1 4 A3
Monmouth Rd HORF/LLZ BS7 64 B2
KEYN BS31 106 B2
PTSHD/EG BS20 60 A1
Monmouth St BMSTR BS3 93 D1 2
CBATH/BATHN BA1 4 A3 3
Monsdale Cl HNBRY/STHM BS10 46 B1
Monsdale Dr HNBRY/STHM BS10 26 B5
Montague Cl BRSTK/PCHW BS34 29 F3 5
Montague Hl CBRISNE BS2 76 B1 12
Montague Hl South
CBRISNE BS2 76 B1 13
Montague Rd KEYN BS31 108 B5
Montague St CBRISNE BS2 76 B1 14
Montepelier WSM BS23 141 E2 2
Montgomery St BMSTR BS3 93 D1 3
Montpelier East WSM BS23 141 E1 2
Montreal Av HORF/LLZ BS7 48 A3
Montrose Av RDLND/MONT BS6 64 A5
Montrose Dr
OLD/WMLY/WICK BS30 81 F3
Montrose Pk
BRSG/KWL/STAPK BS4 94 B2
Montroy Cl
HNLZ/SM/SNYPK/WT BS9 47 D5
Moon St CBRISNE BS2 76 C1
Moor Croft Dr
OLD/WMLY/WICK BS30 81 D5
Moor Croft Rd
OMX/HUT/LCK BS24 153 D2
Moordell Cl YATE/CS BS37 19 E4
Moorend Gdns AVONM BS11 44 A4
Moorend Rd MANG/FISH BS16 31 E5
Moor End Spout NAIL BS48 86 C2 6
Moorfield Rd NAIL BS48 87 E5
Moorfields Rd BATHSE BA2 136 B1
NAIL BS48 86 C2
Moor Gv AVONM BS11 44 A3
Moorham Rd WNSC BS25 154 C3
Moorhill St EVILLE/WHL BS5 65 F5 7
Moorhouse La AVONM BS11 24 A3
HNBRY/STHM BS10 24 C4
The Moorings PTSHD/EG BS20 60 A2
Moorland Rd BATHSE BA2 122 B5
WSM BS23 150 C1
YATE/CS BS37 19 E4
Moorlands Cl NAIL BS48 86 C2
Moorlands Rd MANG/FISH BS16 67 E4
Moor La CLVDN BS21 85 F2
MTN/WRL BS22 143 E1
NAIL BS48 87 E5
OMX/HUT/LCK BS24 143 D3
OMX/HUT/LCK BS24 152 C2
PTSHD/EG BS20 56 C5
Moor Pk CLVDN BS21 85 E2
Moorpark Av YATE/CS BS37 19 D4
Moorside YTN/CONG BS49 116 B2 2
Moravian Rd KGWD/HNM BS15 80 B1
Morden Wk HGRV/WHIT BS14 94 B5 3
Moreton Cl HGRV/WHIT BS14 103 E3
Morford St CBATH/BATHN BA1 4 B1
CBATH/BATHN BA1 123 D2 9
Morgan Cl KEYN BS31 108 B5
Morgans Hill Cl NAIL BS48 86 C4
Morgan St CBRISNE BS2 65 D5
Morley Av MANG/FISH BS16 69 E2
Morley Cl BRSTK/PCHW BS34 28 C1
MANG/FISH BS16 68 B3
Morley Rd BMSTR BS3 76 A5 6
MANG/FISH BS16 68 B3
Morley Sq HORF/LLZ BS7 64 C2 1
Morley St CBRISNE BS2 65 D5
EVILLE/WHL BS5 77 F2
Morley Ter KGWD/HNM BS15 68 B5 7
RDSTK/MIDN BA3 163 D1
Mornington Rd CFTN/FAIL BS8 63 E4 6
Morpeth Rd BRSG/KWL/STAPK BS4 92 B4
Morris La CBATH/BATHN BA1 115 F4
Morris Rd HORF/LLZ BS7 65 E1
Morse Rd EVILLE/WHL BS5 78 A2 12
Mortimer Cl CBATH/BATHN BA1 111 F5
Mortimer Rd BRSTK/PCHW BS34 48 C2
CFTN/FAIL BS8 75 E2
Mortimer St TRWBR BA14 156 C5
Morton St EVILLE/WHL BS5 77 F2 8
Morton Wy THNB/SVB BS35 9 E4
Moseley Gv WSM BS23 151 D3
Moulton Dr BOAV BA15 147 D5
Mountain Ash CBATH/BATHN BA1 122 B1
Mountbatten Cl
MTN/WRL BS22 129 D3 8
YATE/CS BS37 19 E2
Mount Cl FRCTL/WBN BS36 16 A5
Mount Crs FRCTL/WBN BS36 31 F3
Mount Gdns KGWD/HNM BS15 80 B3
Mount Gv BATHSE BA2 135 F2
Mount Hill Rd KGWD/HNM BS15 80 A3
Mount Pleasant BOAV BA15 147 D2
PTSHD/EG BS20 60 B2
RDSTK/MIDN BA3 163 E2 1
Mount Pleasant Ter BMSTR BS3 76 A5 7
Mount Rd BATHSE BA2 135 F2
CBATH/BATHN BA1 123 D2
The Mount TRWBR BA14 157 D2
Mount Vw BATHSE BA2 135 F1
Mow Barton
BMSTRD/HC/WWD BS13 100 C1
YATE/CS BS37 19 E3 4
Mowbray Rd HGRV/WHIT BS14 94 A5
Mowcroft Rd
BMSTRD/HC/WWD BS13 102 A3
Moxham Dr
BMSTRD/HC/WWD BS13 102 A3
Mud La YTN/CONG BS49 117 E1
Muirfield OLD/WMLY/WICK BS30 81 E3
Mulberry Av PTSHD/EG BS20 56 C1 2
Mulberry Cl KGWD/HNM BS15 80 C1
MTN/WRL BS22 143 F1 5
Mulberry Dr KGWD/HNM BS15 69 D5
Mulberry Rd YTN/CONG BS49 133 E3
Mulberry Wk
HNLZ/SM/SNYPK/WT BS9 45 D3 4
Muller Av HORF/LLZ BS7 65 D2
Muller Rd EVILLE/WHL BS5 66 A3 5
HORF/LLZ BS7 48 A5
Mulready Cl HORF/LLZ BS7 49 D5
Murford Av
BMSTRD/HC/WWD BS13 101 F3
Murford Wk
BMSTRD/HC/WWD BS13 101 F3
Murray Rd TRWBR BA14 157 D2
Murray St BMSTR BS3 76 A5 8
Musgrove Cl AVONM BS11 45 D1
Myrtleberry MTN/WRL BS22 129 F2 6
Myrtle Dr AVONM BS11 60 C1
Myrtle Gdns YTN/CONG BS49 116 B3
PTSHD/EG BS20 60 A2 6
Myrtle Hl PTSHD/EG BS20 60 B1 1
Myrtle Rd CBRISNE BS2 76 A1
Myrtle St BMSTR BS3 75 F5
Mythern Meadow BOAV BA15 147 E4

N

Nags Head Hl EVILLE/WHL BS5 79 E3
Nailsea Cl BMSTRD/HC/WWD BS13 91 E5
Nailsea Pk NAIL BS48 87 E2
Nailsea Park Cl NAIL BS48 87 E2 4
Nailsworth Av YATE/CS BS37 19 F4
Naish Hl PTSHD/EG BS20 57 D5
Napier Miles Rd AVONM BS11 44 B3
Napier Rd AVONM BS11 42 C2
CBATH/BATHN BA1 111 E4
EVILLE/WHL BS5 65 F4
RDLND/MONT BS6 63 F4
Napier Sq AVONM BS11 42 B2
Napier St EVILLE/WHL BS5 77 F3 9
Narroways Rd CBRISNE BS2 65 E3
Narrow La MANG/FISH BS16 68 C2
Narrow Pln CBRISNE BS2 3 F3
Narrow Quay CBRIS/FH BS1 2 C4
Naseby Wk EVILLE/WHL BS5 67 D5
Nash Cl KEYN BS31 107 E2 2
Nash Dr HORF/LLZ BS7 49 D4
Naunton Wy MTN/WRL BS22 128 A5
Navigator Cl TRWBR BA14 149 E5
Neads Dr OLD/WMLY/WICK BS30 82 A4 3
Neale Wy AVONM BS11 43 D2 1
Neath Rd EVILLE/WHL BS5 78 B1 7
Nelson Ct MTN/WRL BS22 129 D3 9
Nelson Pl CBATH/BATHN BA1 123 E2 7
Nelson Pl West
CBATH/BATHN BA1 122 C4 4
Nelson Rd MANG/FISH BS16 68 B1 4
MANG/FISH BS16 68 B2 3
Nelson St BMSTR BS3 91 E2 2
CBRIS/FH BS1 2 D2
Nelson Ter CBATH/BATHN BA1 123 E2 8
Nelson Vls CBATH/BATHN BA1 122 C3
Neston Wk
BRSG/KWL/STAPK BS4 93 D4 5
Netham Rd EVILLE/WHL BS5 78 B3
Netherways CLVDN BS21 84 B3
Nettlestone Cl
HNBRY/STHM BS10 25 F4 1
Nevalan Dr EVILLE/WHL BS5 79 E3
Neva Rd WSM BS23 6 C3
Neville Rd KGWD/HNM BS15 68 C4
Nevil Rd HORF/LLZ BS7 64 C2
Newark St CBATH/BATHN BA1 4 C5

Newbolt Cl WSM BS23 151 F1
New Bond St CBATH/BATHN BA1 4 C3 7
Newbourne Rd MTN/WRL BS22 142 B3
Newbrick Rd BRSTK/PCHW BS34 30 B3
New Br BATHSE BA2 121 D2
Newbridge Cl
BRSG/KWL/STAPK BS4 78 B3
Newbridge Gdns
CBATH/BATHN BA1 121 E2
Newbridge Hl CBATH/BATHN BA1 121 E2
Newbridge Rd
BRSG/KWL/STAPK BS4 78 B3
CBATH/BATHN BA1 121 E3
New Bristol Rd MTN/WRL BS22 143 D1
New Brunswick Av
EVILLE/WHL BS5 79 F2
New Buildings MANG/FISH BS16 67 D2
Newbury Rd HORF/LLZ BS7 48 B4
New Charlotte St BMSTR BS3 76 B5
New Cheltenham Rd
KGWD/HNM BS15 68 B5
New Church Rd WSM BS23 150 C3
Newcombe Dr
HNLZ/SM/SNYPK/WT BS9 62 A2 4
Newcombe Rd
HNLZ/SM/SNYPK/WT BS9 46 A4
Newent Av KGWD/HNM BS15 79 F2
New Fosseway Rd
HGRV/WHIT BS14 103 F1
Newfoundland Rd
CBRISNE BS2 65 E5 13
Newfoundland St CBRISNE BS2 76 C1
Newfoundland Wy CBRISNE BS2 77 D1
Newgate CBRIS/FH BS1 3 E2
Newhaven Pl PTSHD/EG BS20 54 C2
Newhaven Rd PTSHD/EG BS20 54 B3
New John St BMSTR BS3 92 A1 7
New Kingsley Rd CBRISNE BS2 3 G3 1
New King St CBATH/BATHN BA1 4 A3
Newland Dr
BMSTRD/HC/WWD BS13 101 E3 1
Newland Rd
BMSTRD/HC/WWD BS13 101 E3
WSM BS23 7 E4
Newlands Av FRCTL/WBN BS36 33 D1
Newlands Gn CLVDN BS21 85 D3 5
Newlands Hl PTSHD/EG BS20 56 A2
Newlands Rd KEYN BS31 106 B3
The Newlands MANG/FISH BS16 50 C4
Newland Wk
BMSTRD/HC/WWD BS13 101 E4
New Leaze ALMDB BS32 13 D2
Newleaze TRWBR BA14 149 F5
Newlyn Av
HNLZ/SM/SNYPK/WT BS9 62 B1
Newlyn Wk
BRSG/KWL/STAPK BS4 93 F3 1
Newlyn Wy YATE/CS BS37 20 A3
Newman Cl YATE/CS BS37 34 C4
Newmarket Av TRWBR BA14 159 E3
Newnham Cl HGRV/WHIT BS14 94 B5
Newnham Pl BRSTK/PCHW BS34 12 A4 1
New Orchard St
CBATH/BATHN BA1 4 C4 8
Newpit La OLD/WMLY/WICK BS30 99 D1
Newport Cl CLVDN BS21 84 C2 5
PTSHD/EG BS20 55 D2 6
Newport Rd PTSHD/EG BS20 60 A1 2
Newport St BMSTR BS3 92 C1 2
Newquay Rd
BRSG/KWL/STAPK BS4 93 D4
New Queen St BMSTR BS3 76 C5
KGWD/HNM BS15 67 F5
New Rd BOAV BA15 147 E2
BRSTK/PCHW BS34 28 A5
CLVDN BS21 85 D2 7
PTSHD/EG BS20 60 A2
TRWBR BA14 156 C5 3
TRWBR BA14 157 D5 4
Newry Wk BRSG/KWL/STAPK BS4 92 C3
Newsome Av PTSHD/EG BS20 60 A2
New Stadium Rd EVILLE/WHL BS5 65 F4
New Station Rd MANG/FISH BS16 67 E2
New St CBATH/BATHN BA1 4 B4 6
CBRISNE BS2 3 G1
New Ter TRWBR BA14 149 D4
New Thomas St CBRISNE BS2 3 G2
Newton Cl KGWD/HNM BS15 69 E5
Newton Gn NAIL BS48 86 B4
Newton Rd BATHSE BA2 121 D4
OLD/WMLY/WICK BS30 81 E4
WSM BS23 6 C5
Newton's Rd MTN/WRL BS22 129 D3
Newton St EVILLE/WHL BS5 77 E1
Newtown BOAV BA15 146 C3
TRWBR BA14 156 C4
New Wk KGWD/HNM BS15 79 F4
New Walls BRSG/KWL/STAPK BS4 77 D5
Niblett Cl KGWD/HNM BS15 81 D3 1
Niblett's Hl EVILLE/WHL BS5 79 E3
Nibley La YATE/CS BS37 18 A2
Nibley Rd AVONM BS11 60 C1
Nicholas La EVILLE/WHL BS5 79 E3
Nicholas Rd EVILLE/WHL BS5 65 F5
Nicholas St BMSTR BS3 76 C5 1
Nicholettes OLD/WMLY/WICK BS30 82 B4
Nicholls La FRCTL/WBN BS36 31 F1
Nichol's Rd PTSHD/EG BS20 38 A5
Nigel Pk AVONM BS11 43 F4
Nightingale Cl FRCTL/WBN BS36 32 B2
MTN/WRL BS22 143 D1 4
THNB/SVB BS35 9 D2 6
Nightingale Gdns NAIL BS48 86 B2
Nightingale La FRCTL/WBN BS36 32 B1 1
Nightingale Ri PTSHD/EG BS20 55 D3
Nightingale Rd TRWBR BA14 156 A4
Nightingale Wy RDSTK/MIDN BA3 161 E4
Nile St CBATH/BATHN BA1 122 C4 5
Nine Tree Hl CBRISNE BS2 64 B5
Ninth Av HORF/LLZ BS7 48 C2
Nippors Wy WNSC BS25 154 B4
Nithsdale Rd WSM BS23 151 D1
Noble Av OLD/WMLY/WICK BS30 82 A5
Nomis Pk YTN/CONG BS49 133 E4
Nore Gdns PTSHD/EG BS20 39 D5 1
Nore Park Dr PTSHD/EG BS20 55 D1
Nore Rd PTSHD/EG BS20 54 C2
Norfolk Av CBRISNE BS2 76 C1 10
RDLND/MONT BS6 64 C4 3
Norfolk Buildings
CBATH/BATHN BA1 122 C4 6
Norfolk Crs CBATH/BATHN BA1 122 C4 7
Norfolk Gv KEYN BS31 106 A3
Norfolk Pl BMSTR BS3 92 A1
Norfolk Rd PTSHD/EG BS20 56 C2
WSM BS23 7 E5
Norland Rd CFTN/FAIL BS8 75 D1 1
Norley Rd HORF/LLZ BS7 48 A4
Normanby Rd EVILLE/WHL BS5 65 F5 8
Norman Gv KGWD/HNM BS15 68 B4 1
Norman Rd CBRISNE BS2 65 E4 11
KEYN BS31 108 B4
OLD/WMLY/WICK BS30 81 F1
The Normans BATHSE BA2 125 D1
Normanton Rd CFTN/FAIL BS8 63 E4 7
Norrisville Rd RDLND/MONT BS6 64 C5 6
Northampton Buildings
CBATH/BATHN BA1 123 D2 10
Northampton St
CBATH/BATHN BA1 123 D2 11
Northcote Rd CFTN/FAIL BS8 63 D5
EVILLE/WHL BS5 78 C1
MANG/FISH BS16 52 A5
Northcote St EVILLE/WHL BS5 65 F5 9
North Cft OLD/WMLY/WICK BS30 82 B5 3
North Devon Rd MANG/FISH BS16 67 E1
North East Rd THNB/SVB BS35 8 C2 4
North End YTN/CONG BS49 116 A1
Northend Av KGWD/HNM BS15 68 B4
Northend Rd KGWD/HNM BS15 68 C4
Northern Wy CLVDN BS21 85 F1
Northfield YATE/CS BS37 19 E5
Northfield Av KGWD/HNM BS15 80 B4
Northfield Rd EVILLE/WHL BS5 79 F2
PTSHD/EG BS20 54 B3
Northfields CBATH/BATHN BA1 123 D1 1
Northfields Cl
CBATH/BATHN BA1 123 D1 2
Northgate St CBATH/BATHN BA1 4 C3 8
North Green St CFTN/FAIL BS8 75 D3 11
North Gv PTSHD/EG BS20 60 A2
North Hills Cl OMX/HUT/LCK BS24 152 A3
North La BATHSE BA2 124 B5
NAIL BS48 86 A3
Northleach Wk AVONM BS11 61 D1 1
North Leaze LGASH BS41 89 F2
Northleigh Av MTN/WRL BS22 142 B1 5
Northmead Av
RDSTK/MIDN BA3 160 C2 1
Northmead Cl
RDSTK/MIDN BA3 160 C2 2
Northmead Rd RDSTK/MIDN BA3 160 C2
Northover Rd
HNLZ/SM/SNYPK/WT BS9 46 A2
North Parade Rd CBATH/BATHN BA1 4 D4
North Pk KGWD/HNM BS15 68 C5
North Rd BATHSE BA2 5 G1
BATHSE BA2 138 A3
BMSTR BS3 75 E5 4
BRSTK/PCHW BS34 29 F4
CFTN/FAIL BS8 74 B3
FRCTL/WBN BS36 32 A1
RDLND/MONT BS6 64 B4
RDSTK/MIDN BA3 160 C3
THNB/SVB BS35 8 C2
YATE/CS BS37 19 D3
North Stoke La
OLD/WMLY/WICK BS30 99 E4
North St BMSTR BS3 75 E5
MANG/FISH BS16 68 B1
NAIL BS48 86 A3
OLD/WMLY/WICK BS30 82 A5
WSM BS23 140 C2
Northumberland Pl
CBATH/BATHN BA1 4 C3 9
Northumberland Rd
RDLND/MONT BS6 64 A4
Northumbria Dr
HNLZ/SM/SNYPK/WT BS9 63 F1
North Vw MANG/FISH BS16 68 B2 4
RDLND/MONT BS6 63 E2
North View Cl BATHSE BA2 121 F5
Northville Rd HORF/LLZ BS7 48 B2
Northway BRSTK/PCHW BS34 28 C4
North Wy BATHSE BA2 121 E5
RDSTK/MIDN BA3 161 D3
Northwick Rd HORF/LLZ BS7 48 A3
THNB/SVB BS35 11 E2
Northwoods Wk
HNBRY/STHM BS10 27 E5 1
Norton Cl KGWD/HNM BS15 81 D2 7
Norton La MTN/WRL BS22 128 B3
Norton Rd BRSG/KWL/STAPK BS4 93 E2
Norwich Dr BRSG/KWL/STAPK BS4 78 C3
Norwood Av BATHSE BA2 138 C1
Norwood Gv PTSHD/EG BS20 55 D1 4
Notgrove Cl MTN/WRL BS22 128 A5 4
Nottingham Rd HORF/LLZ BS7 64 C3
Nottingham St BMSTR BS3 93 D1 4
Nova Scotia Pl CBRIS/FH BS1 75 E4 3
Novers Crs BRSG/KWL/STAPK BS4 92 A4
Novers Hl BRSG/KWL/STAPK BS4 92 A4
Novers La BRSG/KWL/STAPK BS4 92 A5
Novers Park Dr
BRSG/KWL/STAPK BS4 92 A4
Novers Park Rd
BRSG/KWL/STAPK BS4 92 B4
Novers Rd BRSG/KWL/STAPK BS4 92 A4
Nugent Hl RDLND/MONT BS6 64 B5
Nunney Cl KEYN BS31 107 E5
Nursery Gdns HNBRY/STHM BS10 26 B5
The Nursery BMSTR BS3 91 F1 7
Nutfield Gv BRSTK/PCHW BS34 48 C1
Nutgrove Av BMSTR BS3 92 C1
Nuthatch Dr MANG/FISH BS16 50 A5
Nuthatch Gdns MANG/FISH BS16 50 B5
Nutwell Rd MTN/WRL BS22 143 D1 5
Nutwell Sq MTN/WRL BS22 129 D5 6
Nympsfield KGWD/HNM BS15 68 C4

O

Oak Av BATHSE BA2 136 A2
Oak Cl BRSTK/PCHW BS34 29 E1
YATE/CS BS37 19 E2
Oakdale Av MANG/FISH BS16 51 E3
Oakdale Cl MANG/FISH BS16 51 F3
Oakdale Ct MANG/FISH BS16 51 F4 1
Oakdale Gdns MTN/WRL BS22 129 E5
Oakdale Rd HGRV/WHIT BS14 93 E4
MANG/FISH BS16 51 F3
Oakdene Av EVILLE/WHL BS5 66 B3
Oak Dr PTSHD/EG BS20 55 F2
TRWBR BA14 158 C4
Oakenhill Rd BRSG/KWL/STAPK BS4 94 C2
Oakenhill Wk
BRSG/KWL/STAPK BS4 94 C2
Oakfield Cl CBATH/BATHN BA1 122 B2
Oakfield Gv CFTN/FAIL BS8 75 F1
Oakfield Pl CFTN/FAIL BS8 75 F1 3
Oakfield Rd CFTN/FAIL BS8 75 E1
KEYN BS31 107 D4
KGWD/HNM BS15 80 B2
Oakford Av WSM BS23 141 E2
Oak Gv PTSHD/EG BS20 60 A2
Oakhanger Dr AVONM BS11 44 C2
Oakhill HNBRY/STHM BS10 25 D4
Oakhill Av OLD/WMLY/WICK BS30 98 A2
Oakhill Rd BATHSE BA2 137 D3
Oakhurst Rd
HNLZ/SM/SNYPK/WT BS9 63 D1
Oakland Dr OMX/HUT/LCK BS24 153 D2 4
Oakland Rd EVILLE/WHL BS5 78 C1 2
RDLND/MONT BS6 63 F5 8
Oaklands Cl MANG/FISH BS16 69 F1 1
Oaklands Dr ALMDB BS32 12 B1
MANG/FISH BS16 50 B3
OLD/WMLY/WICK BS30 98 A2 2
Oaklands Rd MANG/FISH BS16 69 E1 4
Oak La EVILLE/WHL BS5 67 D4
Oakleaze FRCTL/WBN BS36 33 E1 3
Oakleaze Rd THNB/SVB BS35 8 C3
Oakleigh Av EVILLE/WHL BS5 78 B1 8
Oakleigh Gdns
OLD/WMLY/WICK BS30 98 A2
Oakley BATHSE BA2 124 C5
CLVDN BS21 84 B4
Oakley Rd HORF/LLZ BS7 48 A4
Oakmeade Pk
BRSG/KWL/STAPK BS4 93 F2 4
Oakridge Cl KGWD/HNM BS15 81 E2
WNSC BS25 155 D5
Oakridge La WNSC BS25 155 D5
Oak Rd HORF/LLZ BS7 64 C1
WNSC BS25 154 C3
Oaksey Gv NAIL BS48 87 F2
The Oaks NAIL BS48 87 F2 7
Oak St BATHSE BA2 4 A5
Oak Ter RDSTK/MIDN BA3 162 A3
Oak Tree Cl KGWD/HNM BS15 96 A1 2
TRWBR BA14 156 B3
Oaktree Ct AVONM BS11 43 F4

Oaktree Crs ALMDB BS32 ..... 12 C3
Oaktree Gdns
BMSTRD/HC/WWD BS13 ..... 100 C2
Oak Tree Wk KEYN BS31 ..... 106 B4
Oakwood Av
HNLZ/SM/SNYPK/WT BS9 ..... 46 C5
Oakwood Rd
HNLZ/SM/SNYPK/WT BS9 ..... 46 C5
Oatlands Av HGRV/WHIT BS14 ..... 103 E1
Oberon Av EVILLE/WHL BS5 ..... 66 C4
Odins Rd BATHSE BA2 ..... 136 B4
Okebourne Cl HNBRY/STHM BS10 ..... 26 C4
Okebourne Rd HNBRY/STHM BS10 ..... 26 C5
Oldacre Rd HGRV/WHIT BS14 ..... 103 E5
Old Ashley Hl RDLND/MONT BS6 ..... 65 D4 8
Old Barrow Hl AVONM BS11 ..... 43 E4
The Old Batch BOAV BA15 ..... 146 B1
Old Bond St CBATH/BATHN BA1 ..... 4 B3 7
Old Bread St CBRISNE BS2 ..... 3 G3
Oldbridge Rd HGRV/WHIT BS14 ..... 104 A4
Old Bristol Rd MTN/WRL BS22 ..... 129 F5
Oldbury Cha
OLD/WMLY/WICK BS30 ..... 97 E2
Oldbury Court Dr
MANG/FISH BS16 ..... 50 C5 3
Oldbury Court Rd MANG/FISH BS16 ..... 67 E1
Old Church Rd CLVDN BS21 ..... 84 B2
NAIL BS48 ..... 86 C4
WSM BS23 ..... 150 C3
Old Farm La EVILLE/WHL BS5 ..... 79 F3 3
Oldfield La BATHSE BA2 ..... 136 B1
Oldfield Pl CFTN/FAIL BS8 ..... 75 D4
Oldfield Rd BATHSE BA2 ..... 122 C5
CFTN/FAIL BS8 ..... 75 E4 4
Old Fosse Rd BATHSE BA2 ..... 136 A4
Old Frome Rd BATHSE BA2 ..... 136 C5
Old Gloucester Rd
FRCTL/WBN BS36 ..... 30 C1
MANG/FISH BS16 ..... 30 C4
Old King St CBATH/BATHN BA1 ..... 4 B2 4
Old King Street Ct CBRIS/FH BS1 ..... 3 E1 1
Oldlands Av FRCTL/WBN BS36 ..... 33 D2
Old Market St CBRISNE BS2 ..... 3 G2
Oldmead Wk
BMSTRD/HC/WWD BS13 ..... 90 C5
Old Millard's Hl RDSTK/MIDN BA3 ..... 161 E1
Old Mill Cl YATE/CS BS37 ..... 34 C4
Old Mill Rd PTSHD/EG BS20 ..... 56 B1
Old Mills La PLTN/PENS BS39 ..... 160 A1
Old Mill Wy OMX/HUT/LCK BS24 ..... 143 F2 3
Oldmixon Crs OMX/HUT/LCK BS24 ..... 151 F2
Oldmixon Rd OMX/HUT/LCK BS24 ..... 151 F4
Old Mixon Rd OMX/HUT/LCK BS24 ..... 152 B3
Old Newbridge Hl
CBATH/BATHN BA1 ..... 121 E2
Old Orch CBATH/BATHN BA1 ..... 4 C1
Old Pk CBRISNE BS2 ..... 2 B1 1
Old Park Hl CBRISNE BS2 ..... 2 B2
Old Park Rd AVONM BS11 ..... 43 E4
CLVDN BS21 ..... 71 D4
Old Pit Rd RDSTK/MIDN BA3 ..... 161 E4
Old Post Office La WSM BS23 ..... 140 C2 7
Old Priory Rd PTSHD/EG BS20 ..... 59 F2 2
Old Quarry BATHSE BA2 ..... 136 B3
Old Quarry Ri AVONM BS11 ..... 43 F4
Old Quarry Rd AVONM BS11 ..... 43 E4
Old Rd RDSTK/MIDN BA3 ..... 163 F3
Old Sneed Av
HNLZ/SM/SNYPK/WT BS9 ..... 62 B2
Old Sneed Pk
HNLZ/SM/SNYPK/WT BS9 ..... 62 B2
Old Sneed Rd
HNLZ/SM/SNYPK/WT BS9 ..... 62 B2
Old St CLVDN BS21 ..... 85 E1
Oldville Av CLVDN BS21 ..... 85 D2
Old Wells Rd BATHSE BA2 ..... 137 D2
Old Weston Rd YTN/CONG BS49 ..... 132 A1
Olveston Rd HORF/LLZ BS7 ..... 64 C1
Olympus Cl BRSTK/PCHW BS34 ..... 29 E2 2
Olympus Rd BRSTK/PCHW BS34 ..... 27 E1
Oolite Gv BATHSE BA2 ..... 136 B4
Oolite Rd BATHSE BA2 ..... 136 B4
Oram Ct OLD/WMLY/WICK BS30 ..... 81 D5
Orange Gv CBATH/BATHN BA1 ..... 4 C3 10
Orange St CBRISNE BS2 ..... 77 D1
Orchard Av CBRIS/FH BS1 ..... 2 B3 4
RDSTK/MIDN BA3 ..... 160 C3
THNB/SVB BS35 ..... 8 C3
Orchard Bvd
OLD/WMLY/WICK BS30 ..... 81 F5
Orchard Cl FRCTL/WBN BS36 ..... 31 F2
HNLZ/SM/SNYPK/WT BS9 ..... 63 D1
KEYN BS31 ..... 106 B1 1
KGWD/HNM BS15 ..... 80 C1
MTN/WRL BS22 ..... 128 A4
MTN/WRL BS22 ..... 129 E5
PTSHD/EG BS20 ..... 56 B1 2
YATE/CS BS37 ..... 20 A3
YTN/CONG BS49 ..... 133 D2 3
Orchard Ct YTN/CONG BS49 ..... 117 F2
Orchard Crs AVONM BS11 ..... 43 E4 4
Orchard Dr WNSC BS25 ..... 154 B1
Orchard Gdns KGWD/HNM BS15 ..... 81 D1
Orchard Gra THNB/SVB BS35 ..... 8 B2 3
Orchard La CBRIS/FH BS1 ..... 2 B3
Orchard Lea PTSHD/EG BS20 ..... 60 B2
Orchard Pl WSM BS23 ..... 6 C1 6
WSM BS23 ..... 141 D2 10
Orchard Rd CLVDN BS21 ..... 85 D3 6
EVILLE/WHL BS5 ..... 79 D1 3
FRCTL/WBN BS36 ..... 33 E1 4
HORF/LLZ BS7 ..... 64 C2
KGWD/HNM BS15 ..... 80 C1
LGASH BS41 ..... 89 D2
NAIL BS48 ..... 86 B3
OMX/HUT/LCK BS24 ..... 152 C3
TRWBR BA14 ..... 157 D5
Orchard Sq EVILLE/WHL BS5 ..... 78 B2 7
The Orchards KGWD/HNM BS15 ..... 81 D1
Orchard St CBRIS/FH BS1 ..... 2 B3
WSM BS23 ..... 6 C1 7
Orchard Ter BATHSE BA2 ..... 121 F4 2
The Orchard BRSTK/PCHW BS34 ..... 30 A3
OMX/HUT/LCK BS24 ..... 143 E5
PTSHD/EG BS20 ..... 60 A2 7
Orchard V KGWD/HNM BS15 ..... 81 D2
RDSTK/MIDN BA3 ..... 160 C3
Orchard Wy TRWBR BA14 ..... 158 C4
Oriel Gdns CBATH/BATHN BA1 ..... 114 A5
Oriel Gv BATHSE BA2 ..... 135 F1
Orion Dr BRSTK/PCHW BS34 ..... 29 E2
Orland Wy OLD/WMLY/WICK BS30 ..... 97 E1
Orlebar Gdns AVONM BS11 ..... 44 C1
Orme Dr CLVDN BS21 ..... 71 D4
Ormerod Rd
HNLZ/SM/SNYPK/WT BS9 ..... 62 C2
Ormonds Cl ALMDB BS32 ..... 13 F3
Ormsley Cl BRSTK/PCHW BS34 ..... 13 D5
Orpen Gdns HORF/LLZ BS7 ..... 65 F1
Orpheus Av BRSTK/PCHW BS34 ..... 29 E2
Orwell Dr KEYN BS31 ..... 107 D3
Orwell St BMSTR BS3 ..... 92 C1 3
Osborne Av HORF/LLZ BS7 ..... 65 D3 2
WSM BS23 ..... 7 F1
Osborne Cl BRSTK/PCHW BS34 ..... 29 E4 5
Osborne Rd BMSTR BS3 ..... 76 A5
CBATH/BATHN BA1 ..... 121 F4
CFTN/FAIL BS8 ..... 63 E5
THNB/SVB BS35 ..... 10 A3
TRWBR BA14 ..... 157 E1
WSM BS23 ..... 7 F1
Osborne Ter BMSTR BS3 ..... 91 F2 9
Osborne Vls CBRISNE BS2 ..... 76 A1 3
Oslings La CBATH/BATHN BA1 ..... 115 F5
Osprey Gdns MTN/WRL BS22 ..... 143 E1
Osprey Pk THNB/SVB BS35 ..... 9 D1
Osprey Rd EVILLE/WHL BS5 ..... 78 A2 13
Otterford Cl HGRV/WHIT BS14 ..... 103 F2 6
Otter Rd CLVDN BS21 ..... 85 E3 3
Ottery Cl AVONM BS11 ..... 44 B2
Ottrells Md ALMDB BS32 ..... 13 D2
The Oval BATHSE BA2 ..... 136 A2
Overhill PTSHD/EG BS20 ..... 60 A3
Over La ALMDB BS32 ..... 12 B1
Overndale Rd MANG/FISH BS16 ..... 68 A1
Overnhill Ct MANG/FISH BS16 ..... 68 A1
Overnhill Rd MANG/FISH BS16 ..... 68 A1
Overton Rd HORF/LLZ BS7 ..... 64 B4
Owen Gv HNLZ/SM/SNYPK/WT BS9 ..... 63 F1
Owen St EVILLE/WHL BS5 ..... 77 F1 11
Owls Head Rd KGWD/HNM BS15 ..... 80 C3
Oxbarton BRSTK/PCHW BS34 ..... 30 A3
Oxen Leaze ALMDB BS32 ..... 13 F3 3
Oxford Pl CFTN/FAIL BS8 ..... 75 D3 12
EVILLE/WHL BS5 ..... 65 E5 14
WSM BS23 ..... 6 B1 2
Oxford Sq OMX/HUT/LCK BS24 ..... 144 A4
Oxford St BMSTR BS3 ..... 77 D5
CBRISNE BS2 ..... 77 E3
EVILLE/WHL BS5 ..... 78 A2 14
RDLND/MONT BS6 ..... 76 A1
WSM BS23 ..... 6 B2
Oxleaze BMSTRD/HC/WWD BS13 ..... 102 B3
Oxleaze La LGASH BS41 ..... 100 C5
Ozleworth KGWD/HNM BS15 ..... 81 E1 4

P

Paddock Cl ALMDB BS32 ..... 13 E3
MANG/FISH BS16 ..... 53 D5 1
Paddock Gdns HGRV/WHIT BS14 ..... 103 E3
The Paddocks BATHSE BA2 ..... 137 F4
THNB/SVB BS35 ..... 9 D3
WSM BS23 ..... 150 C3 2
The Paddock CLVDN BS21 ..... 85 D3 7
PTSHD/EG BS20 ..... 56 B2
Paddock Woods BATHSE BA2 ..... 138 B3
Padfield Cl BATHSE BA2 ..... 121 F5 3
Padleigh Hl BATHSE BA2 ..... 135 E3
Padstow Rd BRSG/KWL/STAPK BS4 ..... 92 C4
Page Rd MANG/FISH BS16 ..... 68 B2
Pages Md AVONM BS11 ..... 43 D3
Painswick Av BRSTK/PCHW BS34 ..... 12 C5
Painswick Dr YATE/CS BS37 ..... 19 F4 1
Palace Yard Ms
CBATH/BATHN BA1 ..... 4 A3 4
Palairet Cl BOAV BA15 ..... 147 D4
Palmdale Cl
OLD/WMLY/WICK BS30 ..... 97 E2 2
Palmer Dr BOAV BA15 ..... 147 D1
Palmer Rd TRWBR BA14 ..... 157 D2
Palmers Cl OLD/WMLY/WICK BS30 ..... 81 E3
Palmers Leaze ALMDB BS32 ..... 30 B1
Palmerston Rd
RDLND/MONT BS6 ..... 63 F2 2
Palmerston St BMSTR BS3 ..... 91 F1
Palmer St WSM BS23 ..... 140 C2
Palmyra Rd BMSTR BS3 ..... 91 F2
Parade South CBATH/BATHN BA1 ..... 4 D4
The Parade AVONM BS11 ..... 43 F5 2
YATE/CS BS37 ..... 20 B4 4
Paragon Rd WSM BS23 ..... 140 B1
The Paragon CFTN/FAIL BS8 ..... 75 D3 13
Parish Brook Rd NAIL BS48 ..... 86 A2
Park Av ALMDB BS32 ..... 12 A3
BATHSE BA2 ..... 4 A6
BMSTR BS3 ..... 92 C1
EVILLE/WHL BS5 ..... 66 B3
EVILLE/WHL BS5 ..... 78 C1
FRCTL/WBN BS36 ..... 31 F2
FRCTL/WBN BS36 ..... 32 C1
YTN/CONG BS49 ..... 116 B2
Park Cl KEYN BS31 ..... 106 B2
KGWD/HNM BS15 ..... 80 C2
OLD/WMLY/WICK BS30 ..... 81 F4 3
TRWBR BA14 ..... 159 D4
Park Crs EVILLE/WHL BS5 ..... 78 B1
MANG/FISH BS16 ..... 51 D2
OLD/WMLY/WICK BS30 ..... 81 F4
Parkers Barton
EVILLE/WHL BS5 ..... 77 F3 10
Parkers Cl HNBRY/STHM BS10 ..... 27 F4
Parker St BMSTR BS3 ..... 91 F1 8
Parkes Rd OMX/HUT/LCK BS24 ..... 144 B5
Park Farm Ct
OLD/WMLY/WICK BS30 ..... 81 D5 15
Parkfield Av EVILLE/WHL BS5 ..... 78 B2 8
Park Gdns CBATH/BATHN BA1 ..... 122 B2
Park Gv RDLND/MONT BS6 ..... 64 A1
Park Hl AVONM BS11 ..... 43 F5
Parkhouse La KEYN BS31 ..... 106 A5
Parkhurst Av MANG/FISH BS16 ..... 67 F2 4
Parkhurst Rd WSM BS23 ..... 7 H1
Parklands KGWD/HNM BS15 ..... 80 B1 4
TRWBR BA14 ..... 157 D2
Parklands Av MTN/WRL BS22 ..... 129 E3
Parklands Rd BMSTR BS3 ..... 74 C5
Parkland Wy THNB/SVB BS35 ..... 8 B1
Park La CBATH/BATHN BA1 ..... 122 B3
FRCTL/WBN BS36 ..... 32 B4
Park Pl CBATH/BATHN BA1 ..... 122 C2
CBRISNE BS2 ..... 2 B1
EVILLE/WHL BS5 ..... 66 C3
WSM BS23 ..... 140 C2
Park Rd AVONM BS11 ..... 43 F5
BMSTR BS3 ..... 75 F5
CBATH/BATHN BA1 ..... 121 F3
CLVDN BS21 ..... 71 D5
HORF/LLZ BS7 ..... 48 A2
KEYN BS31 ..... 106 C2
KGWD/HNM BS15 ..... 68 B5
MANG/FISH BS16 ..... 66 B1
MANG/FISH BS16 ..... 68 C1
OLD/WMLY/WICK BS30 ..... 81 F4
THNB/SVB BS35 ..... 8 B2
YTN/CONG BS49 ..... 133 E3
Park Rw CBRIS/FH BS1 ..... 2 A2
FRCTL/WBN BS36 ..... 16 B5
Parkside Av FRCTL/WBN BS36 ..... 31 F2
Parkside Gdns EVILLE/WHL BS5 ..... 65 F2
Parkstone Av HORF/LLZ BS7 ..... 48 A5
Park St BRSG/KWL/STAPK BS4 ..... 77 E5
CBATH/BATHN BA1 ..... 122 C2
CBRIS/FH BS1 ..... 2 A2
EVILLE/WHL BS5 ..... 79 D1 4
TRWBR BA14 ..... 156 C5
YATE/CS BS37 ..... 17 E1
Park Street Av CBRIS/FH BS1 ..... 2 A2 1
Park Street Ms
CBATH/BATHN BA1 ..... 123 D2 12
The Park ALMDB BS32 ..... 13 D2
KEYN BS31 ..... 106 C1
KGWD/HNM BS15 ..... 80 C1
MANG/FISH BS16 ..... 50 C2
OLD/WMLY/WICK BS30 ..... 97 F3
YTN/CONG BS49 ..... 116 B2
Park Vw KGWD/HNM BS15 ..... 80 C2
Park View Av THNB/SVB BS35 ..... 8 C2
Parkwall Crs
OLD/WMLY/WICK BS30 ..... 81 D5
Parkwall Rd OLD/WMLY/WICK BS30 ..... 81 E5
Parkway BRSTK/PCHW BS34 ..... 30 B4
Park Wy OLD/WMLY/WICK BS30 ..... 81 F4
RDSTK/MIDN BA3 ..... 161 D4
Park Wood Cl HGRV/WHIT BS14 ..... 103 D3
Parnall Crs YATE/CS BS37 ..... 19 D3
Parnall Rd MANG/FISH BS16 ..... 67 E3
Parnell Rd CLVDN BS21 ..... 85 E1
Parry Cl BATHSE BA2 ..... 135 F1
Parry's Cl HNLZ/SM/SNYPK/WT BS9 ..... 62 C1
Parrys Gv HNLZ/SM/SNYPK/WT BS9 ..... 62 C1

Parry's La
HNLZ/SM/SNYPK/WT BS9 ... 63 D1
Parslow Barton EVILLE/WHL BS5 .. 79 E2 4
Parsonage La CBATH/BATHN BA1 .... 4 B3 8
Parsonage Rd LGASH BS41 ... 90 A2
Parsons Av BRSTK/PCHW BS34 ... 30 A3
Parsons Gn CLVDN BS21 ... 84 C4 1
MTN/WRL BS22 ... 129 F4 8
Parsons Paddock
HGRV/WHIT BS14 ... 93 E5 1
Parson St BMSTR BS3 ... 91 F3
Parsons Wk OLD/WMLY/WICK BS30 .. 82 B2
Partis Wy CBATH/BATHN BA1 ... 121 E2
Partition St CBRIS/FH BS1 ... 2 A4 2
Partridge Cl MTN/WRL BS22 ... 143 E1
Passage Leaze AVONM BS11 ... 43 E5
Passage Rd HNBRY/STHM BS10 .... 26 B5 4
HNLZ/SM/SNYPK/WT BS9 ... 46 B3
Passage Road Brentry Hl
HNBRY/STHM BS10 ... 26 B5
Passage St CBRIS/FH BS1 ... 3 F3
Patch Cft CLVDN BS21 ... 84 C4
Paulman Gdns LGASH BS41 ... 89 D4 1
Paul's Cswy YTN/CONG BS49 ... 133 D2
Paul St CBRISNE BS2 ... 76 A1
Paulton Dr HORF/LLZ BS7 ... 64 A2
Paulton Rd RDSTK/MIDN BA3 ... 160 C4
Paultow Av BMSTR BS3 ... 92 C1 4
Paultow Rd BMSTR BS3 ... 92 C1
Pavey Cl BMSTRD/HC/WWD BS13 .... 102 A3
Pavey Rd BMSTRD/HC/WWD BS13 .. 102 A3
Pawlett Rd
BMSTRD/HC/WWD BS13 ... 102 A4
Pawlett Wk
BMSTRD/HC/WWD BS13 ... 102 A4 2
Paxcroft Wy TRWBR BA14 ... 157 F4
Paybridge Rd
BMSTRD/HC/WWD BS13 ... 101 D3
Payne Dr EVILLE/WHL BS5 ... 77 F2 9
Payne Rd OMX/HUT/LCK BS24 ... 152 C3
Peache Rd MANG/FISH BS16 ... 51 F5
Peacocks La KGWD/HNM BS15 ... 80 A1
Pearces Hl MANG/FISH BS16 ... 50 C4
Pearl St BMSTR BS3 ... 91 F1
Pearsall Rd OLD/WMLY/WICK BS30 .. 96 C2
Pearse Cl MTN/WRL BS22 ... 130 A2 1
Peart Cl BMSTRD/HC/WWD BS13 .... 100 C2
Peart Dr BMSTRD/HC/WWD BS13 .... 100 C3
Peartree La EVILLE/WHL BS5 ... 79 F3
KGWD/HNM BS15 ... 69 D4 4
Pear Tree Rd ALMDB BS32 ... 13 D3
Pedder Rd CLVDN BS21 ... 85 D3 8
Peel St CBRISNE BS2 ... 77 D1
Pegasus Rd BRSTK/PCHW BS34 ... 27 E1
Pelican Cl MTN/WRL BS22 ... 143 D2
Pemberton Ct MANG/FISH BS16 .... 68 A1 1
Pembery Rd BMSTR BS3 ... 91 F1 9
Pembroke Av AVONM BS11 ... 43 F5 3
Pembroke Cl TRWBR BA14 ... 159 D1 3
Pembroke Gv CFTN/FAIL BS8 ... 75 E2
Pembroke Pl CFTN/FAIL BS8 ... 75 E4 5
Pembroke Rd AVONM BS11 ... 43 F5 4
BMSTR BS3 ... 76 A5
CFTN/FAIL BS8 ... 63 E5
KGWD/HNM BS15 ... 68 C4 4
PTSHD/EG BS20 ... 54 B3
WSM BS23 ... 7 E6
Pembroke St CBRISNE BS2 ... 76 C1 11
Pembroke V CFTN/FAIL BS8 ... 75 E1
Penard Wy KGWD/HNM BS15 ... 81 D2 8
Penarth Dr OMX/HUT/LCK BS24 .. 151 F4 5
Pendennis Av MANG/FISH BS16 .... 68 B2 5
Pendennis Pk
BRSG/KWL/STAPK BS4 ... 94 B2
Pendennis Rd MANG/FISH BS16 ... 68 B1
Pendlesham Gdns WSM BS23 ... 141 F1
Pendock Cl
OLD/WMLY/WICK BS30 ... 98 A3 2
Pendock Ct MANG/FISH BS16 ... 52 C4 6
Pendock Rd FRCTL/WBN BS36 ... 31 F3
MANG/FISH BS16 ... 50 C5
Penfield Rd CBRISNE BS2 ... 65 E4
Penlea Ct AVONM BS11 ... 43 E4
Pennard Ct HGRV/WHIT BS14 ... 103 F2
Pennard Gn BATHSE BA2 ... 121 E4
Penn Dr MANG/FISH BS16 ... 51 D2
Penn Gdns CBATH/BATHN BA1 ... 121 E2
Penngrove
OLD/WMLY/WICK BS30 ... 97 E1 4
Penn Hill Rd CBATH/BATHN BA1 ... 121 E1
Pennine Gdns WSM BS23 ... 141 F1 1
Pennine Rd OLD/WMLY/WICK BS30 .. 82 A5
Pennlea BMSTRD/HC/WWD BS13 ... 91 F5
Penn Lea Rd CBATH/BATHN BA1 ... 121 E1
The Penns CLVDN BS21 ... 85 E2
Penn St CBRIS/FH BS1 ... 3 F1
Pennycress MTN/WRL BS22 ... 142 C3 2
Pennyquick BATHSE BA2 ... 120 A4
Pennyroyal Gv MANG/FISH BS16 .. 66 C1 7
Pennywell Rd EVILLE/WHL BS5 ... 65 E5 15
Pen Park Rd HNBRY/STHM BS10 ... 27 D5
Penpole Av AVONM BS11 ... 43 F5
Penpole Cl AVONM BS11 ... 43 E4 5
Penpole La AVONM BS11 ... 43 F4
Penpole Pk AVONM BS11 ... 43 F4 3
Penpole Pl AVONM BS11 ... 43 F5
Penrice Cl MTN/WRL BS22 ... 128 B5
Penrose HGRV/WHIT BS14 ... 103 D1
Penrose Dr BRSTK/PCHW BS34 ... 29 E1 4
Pensfield Pk HNBRY/STHM BS10 ... 27 E4
Pensford Ct HGRV/WHIT BS14 .... 104 B2 3
Pentire Av BMSTRD/HC/WWD BS13 .. 91 E5
Pentland Av THNB/SVB BS35 ... 9 E4
Pepperacre La TRWBR BA14 ... 157 F3
Pepys Cl KEYN BS31 ... 108 B5
Pera Pl CBATH/BATHN BA1 ... 123 E2 9
Pera Rd CBATH/BATHN BA1 ... 123 E2
Percival Rd CFTN/FAIL BS8 ... 75 D2
Peregrine Cl MTN/WRL BS22 ... 143 E1
The Perrings NAIL BS48 ... 87 D3 8
Perrinpit Rd FRCTL/WBN BS36 ... 15 E2
Perrott Rd KGWD/HNM BS15 ... 69 E5 2
Perry Cl FRCTL/WBN BS36 ... 31 E4
Perrycroft Av
BMSTRD/HC/WWD BS13 ... 101 E1
Perrycroft Rd
BMSTRD/HC/WWD BS13 ... 101 E1
Perrymans Cl MANG/FISH BS16 ... 50 B5
Perrymead BATHSE BA2 ... 137 F2
MTN/WRL BS22 ... 130 A2 2
Perry Rd CBRIS/FH BS1 ... 2 B2
Perrys Lea ALMDB BS32 ... 13 E3 4
Perry St EVILLE/WHL BS5 ... 77 E1 11
Pesley Cl BMSTRD/HC/WWD BS13 .. 101 D3
Petercole Dr
BMSTRD/HC/WWD BS13 ... 101 E1
Peterson Sq
BMSTRD/HC/WWD BS13 ... 102 A4 3
Peter's Ter EVILLE/WHL BS5 ... 77 F2
Petersway Gdns EVILLE/WHL BS5 79 E3 5
Petherton Cl KGWD/HNM BS15 ... 80 C2
Petherton Gdns HGRV/WHIT BS14 .... 93 F5
Petherton Rd HGRV/WHIT BS14 ... 93 F4
Pettigrove Gdns KGWD/HNM BS15 .. 80 C2
Pettigrove Rd KGWD/HNM BS15 ... 80 C3
Pevensey Wk
BRSG/KWL/STAPK BS4 ... 92 B5 9
Peverell Cl HNBRY/STHM BS10 ... 26 A5
Peverell Dr HNBRY/STHM BS10 ... 26 A5
Philadelphia Ct CBRIS/FH BS1 ... 3 F1 4
Philippa Cl HGRV/WHIT BS14 ... 93 E5
Philip St BMSTR BS3 ... 76 B5
CBRISNE BS2 ... 77 F4
Phillips Rd WSM BS23 ... 7 H4
Phippen St CBRIS/FH BS1 ... 3 E5 1
Phipps St BMSTR BS3 ... 75 F5 4
Phoenix Gv RDLND/MONT BS6 ... 64 A1
Piccadilly Pl CBATH/BATHN BA1 .. 123 F2 2
Pickwick Rd CBATH/BATHN BA1 ... 113 E5
Picton La RDLND/MONT BS6 ... 64 C5
Picton St RDLND/MONT BS6 ... 64 C5
Pierrepont Pl CBATH/BATHN BA1 .... 4 C4 9
Pierrepont St CBATH/BATHN BA1 .. 4 C4 10
Pier Rd PTSHD/EG BS20 ... 39 E4
Pigeon House Dr
BMSTRD/HC/WWD BS13 ... 102 B3 1
Pigott Av BMSTRD/HC/WWD BS13 .. 101 E3
Pile Marsh EVILLE/WHL BS5 ... 78 B2
Pilgrims Wy AVONM BS11 ... 43 D4 3
MANG/FISH BS16 ... 51 E3 2
MTN/WRL BS22 ... 129 D5
Pilgrims Whf
BRSG/KWL/STAPK BS4 ... 78 C2 3
Pilkington Cl BRSTK/PCHW BS34 ... 49 D1
Pillingers Rd KGWD/HNM BS15 ... 80 A2
Pill Rd CFTN/FAIL BS8 ... 61 D5
PTSHD/EG BS20 ... 60 B3
Pill Wy CLVDN BS21 ... 84 B2
Pimms La MTN/WRL BS22 ... 128 A4 1
MTN/WRL BS22 ... 128 A5 5
Pimpernel Md ALMDB BS32 ... 29 F1 2
Pine Cl MTN/WRL BS22 ... 128 C5
THNB/SVB BS35 ... 8 C3
Pine Ct RDSTK/MIDN BA3 ... 163 D2
Pinecroft HGRV/WHIT BS14 ... 93 D5 2
Pine Gv HORF/LLZ BS7 ... 48 A2
Pine Grove Pl HORF/LLZ BS7 ... 64 B3 3
Pine Hl MTN/WRL BS22 ... 128 C5
Pine Ridge Cl
HNLZ/SM/SNYPK/WT BS9 ... 62 A2 5
Pine Rd HNBRY/STHM BS10 ... 26 C5
Pines Rd OLD/WMLY/WICK BS30 ... 98 A3
Pines Wy BATHSE BA2 ... 122 C4
RDSTK/MIDN BA3 ... 163 D2
Pine Wk RDSTK/MIDN BA3 ... 162 B2 2
TRWBR BA14 ... 158 C4
Pinewood KGWD/HNM BS15 ... 69 D5 3
Pinewood Av RDSTK/MIDN BA3 ... 160 C3
Pinewood Cl
HNLZ/SM/SNYPK/WT BS9 ... 46 C4
Pinewood Gv RDSTK/MIDN BA3 ... 160 C3
Pinewood Rd RDSTK/MIDN BA3 ... 160 C3
Pinhay Rd
BMSTRD/HC/WWD BS13 ... 101 F1 2
Pinkers Md MANG/FISH BS16 ... 53 D5
Pioneer Av BATHSE BA2 ... 137 D4
Pioneer Pk BRSG/KWL/STAPK BS4 .... 78 A4
Pipe La CBRIS/FH BS1 ... 2 B3
CBRIS/FH BS1 ... 3 F5
Piper Rd YATE/CS BS37 ... 19 F2 1
Piplar Gnd BOAV BA15 ... 147 D5
Pippin Ct
OLD/WMLY/WICK BS30 ... 81 D5 16
Pitch & Pay La
HNLZ/SM/SNYPK/WT BS9 ... 62 C3
Pitchcombe YATE/CS BS37 ... 35 D1 2
Pitchcombe Gdns
HNLZ/SM/SNYPK/WT BS9 ... 45 E4
Pitch La RDLND/MONT BS6 ... 64 B5
Pithay Ct CBRIS/FH BS1 ... 2 D2 2
Pitman Av TRWBR BA14 ... 156 B5
Pitman Rd WSM BS23 ... 6 C4 1
Pit Rd RDSTK/MIDN BA3 ... 161 E3
Pitt Rd HORF/LLZ BS7 ... 64 C1
Pittville Cl THNB/SVB BS35 ... 8 C1 1
Pixash La KEYN BS31 ... 107 F2
Pizey Av CLVDN BS21 ... 84 B2
Pizey Cl CLVDN BS21 ... 84 B2
Players Cl MANG/FISH BS16 ... 30 C4
Playford Gdns AVONM BS11 ... 43 F3
Pleasant Rd MANG/FISH BS16 ... 68 B1
Pleshey Cl MTN/WRL BS22 ... 128 C5
Ploughed Paddock NAIL BS48 ... 86 C3 8
Plover Cl MTN/WRL BS22 ... 143 E1
YATE/CS BS37 ... 19 D3
Plovers Ri RDSTK/MIDN BA3 ... 163 D1
Plumers Cl CLVDN BS21 ... 85 E3 4
Plummer's Hl EVILLE/WHL BS5 ... 78 C1
Plumpton Ct MANG/FISH BS16 ... 52 A2 5
Plumtree Cl WNSC BS25 ... 154 B3
Plumtree Rd MTN/WRL BS22 ... 143 D2
Podgers Dr CBATH/BATHN BA1 ... 111 F5
Poets' Cl EVILLE/WHL BS5 ... 78 B1 9
Polden Cl NAIL BS48 ... 87 D3
Polden Rd PTSHD/EG BS20 ... 55 E1 6
WSM BS23 ... 141 E2
Polebarn Rd TRWBR BA14 ... 157 D3
Polly Barnes Cl KGWD/HNM BS15 .. 79 F4 8
Polly Barnes Hl KGWD/HNM BS15 .... 79 F4
Polygon Rd CFTN/FAIL BS8 ... 75 E3 9
Pomfrett Gdns
HGRV/WHIT BS14 ... 104 C2 3
Ponsford Rd BRSG/KWL/STAPK BS4 .. 93 F3
Ponting Cl EVILLE/WHL BS5 ... 67 E5 1
Poole Court Dr YATE/CS BS37 ... 19 F3
Poole St AVONM BS11 ... 42 C3
Pooles Whf CFTN/FAIL BS8 ... 75 E4
Pooles Wharf Ct CFTN/FAIL BS8 .... 75 E4 6
Poolmead Rd BATHSE BA2 ... 121 D5
Pool Rd KGWD/HNM BS15 ... 68 C3
Pope's Wk BATHSE BA2 ... 137 F1
Poplar Av
HNLZ/SM/SNYPK/WT BS9 ... 45 E5 2
Poplar Cl BATHSE BA2 ... 136 B1
OLD/WMLY/WICK BS30 ... 82 A3 5
Poplar Pl MANG/FISH BS16 ... 67 E3 4
WSM BS23 ... 141 D2 11
Poplar Rd BATHSE BA2 ... 136 B5
BMSTRD/HC/WWD BS13 ... 91 D5
EVILLE/WHL BS5 ... 67 D5
KGWD/HNM BS15 ... 79 E4
OLD/WMLY/WICK BS30 ... 82 B3
The Poplars MTN/WRL BS22 ... 143 E1
PTSHD/EG BS20 ... 59 F2 3
Poplar Ter KGWD/HNM BS15 ... 81 D1 4
Poplar Wk OMX/HUT/LCK BS24 ... 143 D5
Poppy Cl MTN/WRL BS22 ... 129 F2
Poppy Md ALMDB BS32 ... 29 F1
Porlock Cl CLVDN BS21 ... 85 E3 5
WSM BS23 ... 151 E3 1
Porlock Gdns NAIL BS48 ... 87 D3
Porlock Rd BATHSE BA2 ... 137 E3
BMSTR BS3 ... 92 B1 4
Portbury Common
PTSHD/EG BS20 ... 56 C2
Portbury Gv AVONM BS11 ... 43 E5
The Portbury Hundred
PTSHD/EG BS20 ... 57 E3
Portbury La PTSHD/EG BS20 ... 58 C4
Portbury Wk AVONM BS11 ... 43 E5 1
Portbury Wy PTSHD/EG BS20 ... 58 B1
Portishead Rd MTN/WRL BS22 .. 130 A3 10
Portland Cl NAIL BS48 ... 86 C3
Portland Dr PTSHD/EG BS20 ... 56 C2
Portland Pl CBATH/BATHN BA1 ... 123 D2
MANG/FISH BS16 ... 68 B3 4
Portland Sq CBRISNE BS2 ... 76 C1 12
Portland St CBRISNE BS2 ... 76 A1
CFTN/FAIL BS8 ... 75 D2
MANG/FISH BS16 ... 68 B3
Portmeirion Cl
HGRV/WHIT BS14 ... 103 E2 1
Port Vw PTSHD/EG BS20 ... 60 A1 3
Portview Rd AVONM BS11 ... 42 C3
Portwall La CBRIS/FH BS1 ... 3 E5
Portwall La East CBRIS/FH BS1 ... 3 F5 1
Portway AVONM BS11 ... 43 D3
HNLZ/SM/SNYPK/WT BS9 ... 62 A3
Portway La YATE/CS BS37 ... 21 D3
Post Office Rd
OMX/HUT/LCK BS24 ... 144 A5
Pottery Cl WSM BS23 ... 7 C4
Poulton BOAV BA15 ... 147 D4
Poulton La BOAV BA15 ... 147 E5
Pound Dr MANG/FISH BS16 ... 67 D1

Pound La BOAV BA15 146 C3
MANG/FISH BS16 67 D2
NAIL BS48 86 C1
Pound Rd KGWD/HNM BS15 69 D4
Pountney Dr EVILLE/WHL BS5 77 F1 12
Powis Cl MTN/WRL BS22 128 B5
Powlett Ct BATHSE BA2 5 E1
Powlett Rd BATHSE BA2 123 F2
Pow's Orch RDSTK/MIDN BA3 161 D3 2
Pow's Rd KGWD/HNM BS15 80 B2
Poyntz Ct
OLD/WMLY/WICK BS30 97 D1 3
Poyntz Rd BRSG/KWL/STAPK BS4 93 D4
Preanes Gn MTN/WRL BS22 129 E5
Preddy's La EVILLE/WHL BS5 79 E3
Prescot Cl MTN/WRL BS22 142 A1
Prescott YATE/CS BS37 19 E5 3
Press Moor Dr
OLD/WMLY/WICK BS30 81 D5 17
Prestbury YATE/CS BS37 19 E5
Preston Wk
BRSG/KWL/STAPK BS4 93 E3 3
Prestwick Cl
BRSG/KWL/STAPK BS4 94 B3 7
Pretoria Rd BRSTK/PCHW BS34 12 A5
Prewett St CBRIS/FH BS1 3 E6
Priddy Cl BATHSE BA2 121 F5
Priddy Ct HGRV/WHIT BS14 103 F2
Priddy Dr HGRV/WHIT BS14 103 F2
Priests Wy MTN/WRL BS22 128 C5
Priestwood Cl
HNBRY/STHM BS10 26 B5 5
Primrose Cl ALMDB BS32 13 E3 5
KGWD/HNM BS15 67 F5
Primrose Dr THNB/SVB BS35 9 D2
Primrose Hl CBATH/BATHN BA1 122 B1
Primrose La KGWD/HNM BS15 80 A1
RDSTK/MIDN BA3 161 E3 1
Princes Ct OLD/WMLY/WICK BS30 81 D5
Princes' La CFTN/FAIL BS8 75 D3
Princes' Pl HORF/LLZ BS7 64 C3 2
Prince's Rd CLVDN BS21 85 D1
Princess Cl KEYN BS31 106 C2
Princess Gdns MANG/FISH BS16 49 E5 3
TRWBR BA14 149 E5
Princess Rw CBRISNE BS2 76 B1 15
Princess St BMSTR BS3 76 C5
CBRISNE BS2 77 E3
Princes St CBATH/BATHN BA1 4 B3 9
CBRISNE BS2 77 D1
Princess Victoria St CFTN/FAIL BS8 75 D3
Prince St CBRIS/FH BS1 2 C5
Prior Park Rd BATHSE BA2 5 E6
Priors Lea YATE/CS BS37 19 F4
Priory Av HNLZ/SM/SNYPK/WT BS9 46 B4
Priory Cl BATHSE BA2 137 F2
BOAV BA15 146 C2
RDSTK/MIDN BA3 161 D3
Priory Court Rd
HNLZ/SM/SNYPK/WT BS9 46 B4
Priory Dene
HNLZ/SM/SNYPK/WT BS9 46 B4 3
Priory Gdns AVONM BS11 43 E5 2
HORF/LLZ BS7 48 A3
PTSHD/EG BS20 59 F2
Priory Ms WSM BS23 7 H1
Priory Pk BOAV BA15 147 D2
Priory Rd AVONM BS11 43 E5
BRSG/KWL/STAPK BS4 93 F2
CFTN/FAIL BS8 75 F1
KEYN BS31 96 C5
PTSHD/EG BS20 58 B3
PTSHD/EG BS20 59 F2
WSM BS23 7 H1
Priston Cl MTN/WRL BS22 130 A2
Pritchard St CBRISNE BS2 76 C1
Probyn Cl MANG/FISH BS16 50 B4 2
Prospect Av KGWD/HNM BS15 67 F5 5
Prospect Cl FRCTL/WBN BS36 31 F4 2
Prospect Crs KGWD/HNM BS15 69 D4
Prospect Gdns CBATH/BATHN BA1 115 D2
Prospect La FRCTL/WBN BS36 16 A5 1
Prospect Pl EVILLE/WHL BS5 78 A1
TRWBR BA14 157 D3
WSM BS23 141 D2 12
Prospect Rd BATHSE BA2 138 A1
THNB/SVB BS35 10 B4
Providence La LGASH BS41 89 D2
Providence Pl CBRISNE BS2 3 G3 2
Providence Vw LGASH BS41 89 E3 1
Prudham St EVILLE/WHL BS5 66 A5 4
Puffin Cl MTN/WRL BS22 143 E2
Pullin Ct OLD/WMLY/WICK BS30 82 B5
Pulteney Av BATHSE BA2 5 E4 1
Pulteney Gdns BATHSE BA2 5 E4
Pulteney Gv BATHSE BA2 5 E5
Pulteney Ms BATHSE BA2 4 D2
Pulteney Rd BATHSE BA2 5 E3
Pump La CBATH/BATHN BA1 125 F1
CBRIS/FH BS1 3 E6
Pump Sq PTSHD/EG BS20 60 B1 2
Purcell Wk
BRSG/KWL/STAPK BS4 92 B5 10
Purdown Rd HORF/LLZ BS7 65 D1
Purdue Cl MTN/WRL BS22 130 A4 9
Purlewent Dr CBATH/BATHN BA1 122 A1
Purn La OMX/HUT/LCK BS24 151 F5
Purn Rd OMX/HUT/LCK BS24 151 E5
Pursey Dr ALMDB BS32 29 F2
Purton Cl KGWD/HNM BS15 80 C3
Purton Rd HORF/LLZ BS7 64 B4 5
Puttingthorpe Dr WSM BS23 142 B3
Puxley Cl HGRV/WHIT BS14 104 C1 6
Pye Cft ALMDB BS32 13 F2
Pyecroft Av
HNLZ/SM/SNYPK/WT BS9 46 C4
Pylewell La WNSC BS25 155 F2
Pylle Hill Crs BMSTR BS3 77 D5
Pyne Point CLVDN BS21 84 C1
Pynne Cl HGRV/WHIT BS14 104 C1
Pynne Rd HGRV/WHIT BS14 105 D2
The Quadrangle YATE/CS BS37 35 D4

Q

Quadrant East MANG/FISH BS16 68 A3 7
The Quadrant RDLND/MONT BS6 63 F3 3
Quadrant West MANG/FISH BS16 68 A3
Quaker La THNB/SVB BS35 8 B3 2
Quaker's Cl MANG/FISH BS16 51 E3 3
Quakers' Friars CBRIS/FH BS1 3 E1 2
Quaker's Rd MANG/FISH BS16 51 E3
Quantock Cl OLD/WMLY/WICK BS30 82 A4
Quantock Rd BMSTR BS3 92 B1
PTSHD/EG BS20 55 F1
WSM BS23 6 B6
Quantocks BATHSE BA2 137 E3
Quarrington Rd HORF/LLZ BS7 64 C1
Quarry Barton MANG/FISH BS16 31 D4
Quarry Cl BATHSE BA2 137 D4
Quarry La AVONM BS11 45 D2
FRCTL/WBN BS36 31 F4
Quarrymans Ct BATHSE BA2 137 F4 2
Quarry Rd KGWD/HNM BS15 80 B3
MANG/FISH BS16 51 D4 1
YATE/CS BS37 20 B4
Quarry Steps CFTN/FAIL BS8 63 E4 8
Quarry Wy MANG/FISH BS16 52 B2
MANG/FISH BS16 66 C1
NAIL BS48 86 C2
Quarterway La TRWBR BA14 157 E3
Quays Av PTSHD/EG BS20 56 C1
Quayside La EVILLE/WHL BS5 79 D3 9
Quay St CBRIS/FH BS1 2 D2 3
Quedgeley YATE/CS BS37 19 D5
Queen Ann Rd EVILLE/WHL BS5 77 F2
Queen Charlotte St CBRIS/FH BS1 2 D3 3
Queen Charlton La
HGRV/WHIT BS14 104 B4
Queen's Av CFTN/FAIL BS8 75 F2 3
PTSHD/EG BS20 56 A1
Queens Club Gdns TRWBR BA14 156 A4 3
Queenscote PTSHD/EG BS20 57 D1
Queensdale Crs
BRSG/KWL/STAPK BS4 93 E3
Queens Down Gdns
BRSG/KWL/STAPK BS4 93 F1
Queen's Dr BATHSE BA2 137 E3
HORF/LLZ BS7 64 A2
KGWD/HNM BS15 79 F5
Queens Gdns TRWBR BA14 149 E5
Queens Ga
HNLZ/SM/SNYPK/WT BS9 62 B1
Queenshill Rd
BRSG/KWL/STAPK BS4 93 E3
Queensholm Av
MANG/FISH BS16 51 F2 2
Queensholm Cl MANG/FISH BS16 51 F2
Queensholm Crs MANG/FISH BS16 51 E2
Queensholm Dr MANG/FISH BS16 51 F3
Queen's Pde CBATH/BATHN BA1 4 A2 1
CBRIS/FH BS1 75 F3
Queen's Parade Pl
CBATH/BATHN BA1 4 B2 5
Queen Sq CBRIS/FH BS1 2 C4
KEYN BS31 109 D4 1
Queen Square Av CBRIS/FH BS1 2 D4 3
Queen's Rd
BMSTRD/HC/WWD BS13 101 D3
BRSG/KWL/STAPK BS4 94 A3
CFTN/FAIL BS8 75 E2
CFTN/FAIL BS8 75 F2 4
CLVDN BS21 85 D1
EVILLE/WHL BS5 79 D2
HORF/LLZ BS7 65 D2
KEYN BS31 106 B3
LGASH BS41 101 D4
NAIL BS48 86 B3
NAIL BS48 87 D4
OLD/WMLY/WICK BS30 81 E5
RDSTK/MIDN BA3 163 E2
TRWBR BA14 156 C2
WSM BS23 140 C1
Queen St AVONM BS11 42 B2
CBATH/BATHN BA1 4 B3 10
CBRISNE BS2 3 F2
EVILLE/WHL BS5 66 B3 3
KGWD/HNM BS15 79 F2
Queens Wk THNB/SVB BS35 8 B1
Queensway BRSTK/PCHW BS34 29 D2
Queen's Wy MTN/WRL BS22 129 E4
PTSHD/EG BS20 54 C2
Queen Victoria Rd
RDLND/MONT BS6 63 E2
Queen Victoria St CBRISNE BS2 77 E3 4
Queenwood Av
CBATH/BATHN BA1 123 E1 2
Quickthorn Cl HGRV/WHIT BS14 103 E1
Quiet St CBATH/BATHN BA1 4 B3 11
Quilling Cl TRWBR BA14 157 E5

R

Raby Ms BATHSE BA2 5 E2
Rackfield Pl BATHSE BA2 121 F4 3
Rackham Cl HORF/LLZ BS7 48 C5
Rackhay CBRIS/FH BS1 2 D3 4
Rackvernal Rd RDSTK/MIDN BA3 161 E3
Radley Rd MANG/FISH BS16 67 F2
Radnor Rd
HNLZ/SM/SNYPK/WT BS9 63 F1
HORF/LLZ BS7 64 B1
Radstock Rd RDSTK/MIDN BA3 161 F2 1
Raeburn Rd EVILLE/WHL BS5 79 F2
Ragland La CBATH/BATHN BA1 123 E1
Ragland St CBATH/BATHN BA1 113 E5
Raglan Pl HORF/LLZ BS7 64 B3 4
THNB/SVB BS35 8 B4
WSM BS23 140 B2 1
Raglan Rd HORF/LLZ BS7 64 B3
Ragleth Gv TRWBR BA14 157 E2
Railton Jones Cl
BRSTK/PCHW BS34 29 F5
Railway Pl CBATH/BATHN BA1 4 D5
Railway St CBATH/BATHN BA1 4 C5
Railway Ter MANG/FISH BS16 68 A2
Railway View Pl RDSTK/MIDN BA3 161 E2
Raleigh Cl KEYN BS31 108 A5 1
Raleigh Ri PTSHD/EG BS20 38 C5
Raleigh Rd BMSTR BS3 75 F5
Ralph Allen Dr BATHSE BA2 137 F1
Ralph Rd HORF/LLZ BS7 65 D2
Rambler Cl TRWBR BA14 156 A4 4
Ram Hl FRCTL/WBN BS36 33 E4
Ramsay Cl MTN/WRL BS22 129 D3 10
Ramsbury Wk TRWBR BA14 159 D1
Ramscombe La
CBATH/BATHN BA1 115 D1
Ramsey Rd HORF/LLZ BS7 48 A4
Ranchways PTSHD/EG BS20 55 D2 7
Randall Cl KGWD/HNM BS15 69 D4
Randall Rd CFTN/FAIL BS8 75 E3
Randolph Av
BMSTRD/HC/WWD BS13 101 F2
YATE/CS BS37 19 E1
Randolph Cl
BMSTRD/HC/WWD BS13 101 F2
Rangers Wk KGWD/HNM BS15 80 A5
The Rank TRWBR BA14 158 B4
Rannoch Rd BRSTK/PCHW BS34 48 A1
Ransombe Av MTN/WRL BS22 128 C5 2
Ransford CLVDN BS21 84 B3
Ratcliffe Dr BRSTK/PCHW BS34 29 F3
Rathbone Cl FRCTL/WBN BS36 33 D3
Raven Cl MTN/WRL BS22 143 D1
Ravendale Dr
OLD/WMLY/WICK BS30 97 F1
Ravenglass Crs HNBRY/STHM BS10 47 D1
Ravenhead Dr HGRV/WHIT BS14 93 F4
Ravenhill Av BMSTR BS3 93 D2
Ravenhill Rd BMSTR BS3 93 D1
Ravenscroft Gdns TRWBR BA14 157 F3
Ravenswood Rd RDLND/MONT BS6 64 A5
Rawens Wd
OLD/WMLY/WICK BS30 97 F1 2
Rawlins Av MTN/WRL BS22 129 F2
Rayens Cross Rd LGASH BS41 89 D3
Rayleigh Rd
HNLZ/SM/SNYPK/WT BS9 45 E4
Raymend Rd BMSTR BS3 92 C1
Raymend Wk BMSTR BS3 92 C2
Raymill BRSG/KWL/STAPK BS4 95 E2 3
Raymore Ri LGASH BS41 89 D4
Raynes Rd BMSTR BS3 91 E1
Rector's Wy WSM BS23 7 E4
Rectory Cl NAIL BS48 87 F2
YATE/CS BS37 20 A2 1
Rectory Dr YTN/CONG BS49 116 C4
Rectory La BRSTK/PCHW BS34 28 B5
Rectory Rd FRCTL/WBN BS36 16 C5
PTSHD/EG BS20 59 F3
Rectory Wy YTN/CONG BS49 116 C4
Redcar Ct FRCTL/WBN BS36 52 A2 6
Redcatch Rd BMSTR BS3 93 D2
BRSG/KWL/STAPK BS4 93 E2
Redcliff Backs CBRIS/FH BS1 3 E4
Redcliffe Cl PTSHD/EG BS20 54 C3 3
Redcliffe Pde East CBRIS/FH BS1 2 D5
Redcliffe Pde West CBRIS/FH BS1 2 D5

Redcliffe Wy *CBRIS/FH* BS1 2 D5
Redcliff Hl *CBRIS/FH* BS1 3 E6
Redcliff Mead La *CBRIS/FH* BS1 3 F5
Redcliff St *CBRIS/FH* BS1 3 E3
Redcross St *CBRISNE* BS2 3 G2
The Reddings *KGWD/HNM* BS15 69 D4
Redfield Gv *RDSTK/MIDN* BA3 161 D4
Redfield Hl *OLD/WMLY/WICK* BS30 82 B5
Redfield Rd *BRSTK/PCHW* BS34 28 C1
RDSTK/MIDN BA3 160 C4
Redford Crs
BMSTRD/HC/WWD BS13 100 C4
Redford Wk
BMSTRD/HC/WWD BS13 101 D4 2
Redhill Cl *MANG/FISH* BS16 66 C3
Redhill Dr *MANG/FISH* BS16 66 C3
Red House La *ALMDB* BS32 12 C1
HNLZ/SM/SNYPK/WT BS9 45 F5
Redland Court Rd
RDLND/MONT BS6 64 A3
Redland Green Rd
RDLND/MONT BS6 63 F4
Redland Gv *RDLND/MONT* BS6 64 A4
Redland Hl *RDLND/MONT* BS6 63 E4
Redland Pk *BATHSE* BA2 121 D4
RDLND/MONT BS6 63 F5
Redland Rd *PTSHD/EG* BS20 42 A5
RDLND/MONT BS6 63 F3 4
Redland Ter *RDLND/MONT* BS6 63 E4 9
Redlynch La *KEYN* BS31 106 B5
Redshelf Wk *HNBRY/STHM* BS10 27 D5
Redwick Cl *AVONM* BS11 45 D1
Redwick Gdns *THNB/SVB* BS35 11 D3
Redwick Rd *THNB/SVB* BS35 10 C1
Redwing Dr *MTN/WRL* BS22 143 D1
Redwing Gdns *MANG/FISH* BS16 49 F5 3
Redwood Cl *NAIL* BS48 87 F2 8
OLD/WMLY/WICK BS30 97 E1 5
RDSTK/MIDN BA3 162 B4
Redwood La *NAIL* BS48 88 A5
Reed Cl *HNBRY/STHM* BS10 47 E4 2
Reed Ct *OLD/WMLY/WICK* BS30 97 D1 4
Reedley Rd
HNLZ/SM/SNYPK/WT BS9 63 D1
Reedling Cl *MANG/FISH* BS16 49 F5 4
Regency Dr
BRSG/KWL/STAPK BS4 95 E2 4
Regent Rd *BMSTR* BS3 76 B5 8
Regents Cl *THNB/SVB* BS35 8 B1
Regents Pl *BOAV* BA15 147 D4
Regent St *CFTN/FAIL* BS8 75 E3
KGWD/HNM BS15 80 A1
WSM BS23 6 B1 3
Remenham Dr
HNLZ/SM/SNYPK/WT BS9 63 F1 2
Remenham Pk
HNLZ/SM/SNYPK/WT BS9 63 F1
Rendcomb Cl *MTN/WRL* BS22 128 A5
Repton Rd *BRSG/KWL/STAPK* BS4 94 A1
Reubens Ct *MTN/WRL* BS22 129 E4 9
Reynolds Cl *KEYN* BS31 107 E2
Reynold's Wk *HORF/LLZ* BS7 48 B4
Rhode Cl *KEYN* BS31 107 E5
Rhodyate Hl *YTN/CONG* BS49 117 F5
Rhyne Ter *WSM* BS23 150 C3 3
Rhyne Vw *NAIL* BS48 86 A3
Ribblesdale *THNB/SVB* BS35 8 C4
Richards Cl *MTN/WRL* BS22 130 A3
Richeson Cl *HNBRY/STHM* BS10 46 A1
Richeson Wk *HNBRY/STHM* BS10 46 A1
Richmond Av *BRSTK/PCHW* BS34 29 F3
RDLND/MONT BS6 65 D4 9
Richmond Cl *KEYN* BS31 106 B3
PTSHD/EG BS20 56 C1 3
TRWBR BA14 156 A5 2
Richmond Dl *CFTN/FAIL* BS8 63 E4 10
Richmond Gn *NAIL* BS48 87 E3
Richmond Hts *CBATH/BATHN* BA1 123 D1
Richmond Hl *CBATH/BATHN* BA1 123 D1
CFTN/FAIL BS8 75 F2
Richmond Hill Av *CFTN/FAIL* BS8 75 F2 5
Richmond La
CBATH/BATHN BA1 123 D1 3
CFTN/FAIL BS8 75 E2 5
Richmond Park Rd *CFTN/FAIL* BS8 75 E2
Richmond Pl *CBATH/BATHN* BA1 123 D1
Richmond Rd *CBATH/BATHN* BA1 113 D5
EVILLE/WHL BS5 78 C1
MANG/FISH BS16 69 E1
RDLND/MONT BS6 64 C5
RDLND/MONT BS6 65 D4 10
Richmond St *BMSTR* BS3 77 D5
WSM BS23 6 B1 4
Richmond Ter *AVONM* BS11 42 B2
CFTN/FAIL BS8 75 E2
Ricketts La *MTN/WRL* BS22 129 F5 4
Rickfield *BOAV* BA15 146 B3
Rickford Rd *NAIL* BS48 87 E3
The Ride *KGWD/HNM* BS15 69 E4
Ridge Cl *PTSHD/EG* BS20 55 E2
Ridge Green Cl *BATHSE* BA2 136 B5
Ridgehill *HNLZ/SM/SNYPK/WT* BS9 47 D5
The Ridge *AVONM* BS11 43 F4
FRCTL/WBN BS36 33 D1
YTN/CONG BS49 116 B3
Ridgeview *LGASH* BS41 89 F2 1
Ridgeway *FRCTL/WBN* BS36 33 D1
NAIL BS48 86 B3
YATE/CS BS37 20 B3
Ridgeway Av *WSM* BS23 6 D4
Ridgeway Ct *HNBRY/STHM* BS10 46 A2
Ridgeway Gdns *HGRV/WHIT* BS14 104 A2
Ridgeway La *HGRV/WHIT* BS14 103 F3
Ridgeway Pde *EVILLE/WHL* BS5 66 C3 5
Ridgeway Rd *LGASH* BS41 89 E3
MANG/FISH BS16 66 C3
The Ridgeway *HNBRY/STHM* BS10 46 B2
MTN/WRL BS22 128 A5 6
Riding Barn Hl
OLD/WMLY/WICK BS30 83 D3
Ridingleaze *AVONM* BS11 44 B2
Ridings Cl *YATE/CS* BS37 21 D4
Ridings Rd *FRCTL/WBN* BS36 33 D2
The Ridings
BMSTRD/HC/WWD BS13 100 C3
FRCTL/WBN BS36 33 D2
Ringswell Gdns
CBATH/BATHN BA1 124 A1
Ringwood Crs *HNBRY/STHM* BS10 47 E2
Ringwood Gv *WSM* BS23 141 F1
Ringwood Rd *BATHSE* BA2 122 A4
Ripley Rd *EVILLE/WHL* BS5 67 E5
Ripon Ct *MANG/FISH* BS16 52 A2
Ripon Rd *BRSG/KWL/STAPK* BS4 78 C3
Rippleside *PTSHD/EG* BS20 56 A1
Rippleside Rd *CLVDN* BS21 71 E4
Risdale Rd *BMSTR* BS3 90 C3
Risedale Rd *WNSC* BS25 154 C4 3
Rivendell *MTN/WRL* BS22 129 F3
Riverland Dr
BMSTRD/HC/WWD BS13 101 D3
Riverleaze
HNLZ/SM/SNYPK/WT BS9 61 F1
PTSHD/EG BS20 38 A5
River Md *CLVDN* BS21 85 D4
River Rd *PTSHD/EG* BS20 41 F3
YATE/CS BS37 20 B4 5
Riverside Cl *AVONM* BS11 61 D1
CLVDN BS21 84 B3 5
RDSTK/MIDN BA3 160 C5
Riverside Ct *BRSG/KWL/STAPK* BS4 79 D3
Riverside Gdns *RDSTK/MIDN* BA3 160 B5
Riverside Pk *THNB/SVB* BS35 10 A4
Riverside Rd *BATHSE* BA2 4 A4
RDSTK/MIDN BA3 160 C5
Riverside Wk *EVILLE/WHL* BS5 79 D3 10
RDSTK/MIDN BA3 160 C5
Riverside Wy *KGWD/HNM* BS15 96 A1
Rivers St *CBATH/BATHN* BA1 4 A1
Rivers Street Ms
CBATH/BATHN BA1 4 A1 5
River St *CBRISNE* BS2 3 G1
River Vw *MANG/FISH* BS16 66 C1
Riverway *NAIL* BS48 87 E1
River Wy *TRWBR* BA14 156 C3
Riverwood Rd *MANG/FISH* BS16 51 D2
Riviera Crs *MANG/FISH* BS16 68 C2
Roath Rd *PTSHD/EG* BS20 56 B1
Robbins Cl *ALMDB* BS32 30 A2
Robbins Ct *MANG/FISH* BS16 52 C5
Robel Av *FRCTL/WBN* BS36 16 A5
Robert Ct *MANG/FISH* BS16 52 C4
Robertson Dr
BRSG/KWL/STAPK BS4 79 D3
Robertson Rd *EVILLE/WHL* BS5 66 A4
Robert St *EVILLE/WHL* BS5 65 F4 3
EVILLE/WHL BS5 77 F2 10
Robin Cl *HNBRY/STHM* BS10 46 C1
MTN/WRL BS22 143 D2
RDSTK/MIDN BA3 161 E4
Robin Dr *OMX/HUT/LCK* BS24 153 D3
Robin La *CLVDN* BS21 71 D4
Robinson Dr *EVILLE/WHL* BS5 77 E1 12
Robin Wy *YATE/CS* BS37 36 A1
Rochester Cl
OMX/HUT/LCK BS24 151 F4 6
Rochester Rd
BRSG/KWL/STAPK BS4 78 C4
Rock Av *NAIL* BS48 86 B2
Rock Cl *BRSG/KWL/STAPK* BS4 94 C2 2
Rock Hall La *BATHSE* BA2 137 F4 3
Rockingham Gdns *AVONM* BS11 44 B3 2
Rockingham Gv *WSM* BS23 141 F1 2
Rockland Gv *MANG/FISH* BS16 66 B1 2
Rockland Rd *MANG/FISH* BS16 51 D4
Rock La *BATHSE* BA2 137 F4
BRSTK/PCHW BS34 30 A4
Rockleaze
HNLZ/SM/SNYPK/WT BS9 62 C4
Rockleaze Av
HNLZ/SM/SNYPK/WT BS9 62 C3
Rockleaze Rd
HNLZ/SM/SNYPK/WT BS9 62 C4
Rockliffe Av *BATHSE* BA2 123 F2
Rockliffe Rd *BATHSE* BA2 123 F2
Rock Rd *KEYN* BS31 106 C2
RDSTK/MIDN BA3 161 E2
TRWBR BA14 156 B5
YTN/CONG BS49 116 C4
Rockside Av *MANG/FISH* BS16 52 A3
Rockside Dr
HNLZ/SM/SNYPK/WT BS9 46 C5
Rockside Gdns *FRCTL/WBN* BS36 17 D5
MANG/FISH BS16 52 A3 2
Rockstowes Wy
HNBRY/STHM BS10 27 E5
Rock St *THNB/SVB* BS35 8 B4
The Rock *BRSG/KWL/STAPK* BS4 94 C1
Rockwell Av *AVONM* BS11 44 C2
Rodborough *YATE/CS* BS37 35 D1
Rodfords Md *HGRV/WHIT* BS14 93 E5
Rodford Wy *YATE/CS* BS37 35 D1
Rodmead Wk
BMSTRD/HC/WWD BS13 101 E3 2
Rodmoor Rd *PTSHD/EG* BS20 39 E5
Rodney Av *KGWD/HNM* BS15 79 E1
Rodney Crs *BRSTK/PCHW* BS34 28 B4
Rodney Rd *KEYN* BS31 108 C5
KGWD/HNM BS15 67 E5
Rodney Wk *KGWD/HNM* BS15 67 E5
Rodway Hl *MANG/FISH* BS16 69 E2
Rodway Rd *BRSTK/PCHW* BS34 12 B5
MANG/FISH BS16 69 E1
Rodway Vw *KGWD/HNM* BS15 69 D3
Rodwell Pk *TRWBR* BA14 157 E2
Roebuck Cl *MTN/WRL* BS22 129 F3
Roegate Dr
BRSG/KWL/STAPK BS4 78 C3 2
Rogers Cl *OLD/WMLY/WICK* BS30 81 F4
Rokeby Av *RDLND/MONT* BS6 64 A5
Roman Farm Ct *AVONM* BS11 45 D1 6
Roman Rd *CBATH/BATHN* BA1 4 C1
OMX/HUT/LCK BS24 152 B5
Roman Wk *BRSG/KWL/STAPK* BS4 94 A1
BRSTK/PCHW BS34 29 F3 6
Roman Wy
HNLZ/SM/SNYPK/WT BS9 62 A2
Romney Av *HORF/LLZ* BS7 65 F1
Ronald Rd *MANG/FISH* BS16 50 A5 3
Ronayne Wk *MANG/FISH* BS16 51 D5
Rookery Cl *MTN/WRL* BS22 129 D4 3
Rookery Rd *BRSG/KWL/STAPK* BS4 93 E1
Rookery Wy *HGRV/WHIT* BS14 103 D3
Rose Acre *HNBRY/STHM* BS10 26 B5
Rosebay Md *MANG/FISH* BS16 66 C2 4
Roseberry Pk *EVILLE/WHL* BS5 78 B1
Roseberry Rd *BATHSE* BA2 122 A4 2
EVILLE/WHL BS5 78 A2
Rosebery Av *CBRISNE* BS2 65 E5 16
Rose Cl *FRCTL/WBN* BS36 31 F4
Rosedale Av *WSM* BS23 7 G2 2
Rosedale Gdns *TRWBR* BA14 156 A3 2
Rosedale Rd *MANG/FISH* BS16 67 F3
Rose Gdns *MTN/WRL* BS22 130 A3
Rose Green Rd *EVILLE/WHL* BS5 66 B4
Rose Hl *CBATH/BATHN* BA1 113 F5
Rose La *FRCTL/WBN* BS36 33 E1
Roselarge Gdns
HNBRY/STHM BS10 46 B1 3
Rosemary Cl *ALMDB* BS32 30 A1
Rosemary La *EVILLE/WHL* BS5 66 A4
Rose Md *HORF/LLZ* BS7 48 B4 2
Rosemount La *BATHSE* BA2 137 E1
Rose Oak Dr *FRCTL/WBN* BS36 33 E1 5
Rose Oak Gdns *FRCTL/WBN* BS36 33 E1 6
Rose Oak La *FRCTL/WBN* BS36 33 E1
Rose Rd *EVILLE/WHL* BS5 78 C2
Rosery Cl *HNLZ/SM/SNYPK/WT* BS9 46 B3
The Rosery *MANG/FISH* BS16 68 A3 8
Rose St *CBRIS/FH* BS1 3 F5
Roseville Av *OLD/WMLY/WICK* BS30 97 E2
Rose Wk *MANG/FISH* BS16 68 A3
Rosewarn Cl *BATHSE* BA2 135 E1
Rosling Rd *HORF/LLZ* BS7 47 F5
Roslyn Av *MTN/WRL* BS22 142 B1
Roslyn Rd *RDLND/MONT* BS6 64 A4
Rossall Av *BRSTK/PCHW* BS34 29 D2
Rossall Rd *BRSG/KWL/STAPK* BS4 94 B1
Ross Cl *YATE/CS* BS37 20 C3
Rossendale Cl *MTN/WRL* BS22 129 E4
Rossett Gdns *TRWBR* BA14 156 A4
Rossiter Rd *BATHSE* BA2 4 C5
Rossiter's La *EVILLE/WHL* BS5 79 E3
Rosslyn Rd *CBATH/BATHN* BA1 121 F3
Rosslyn Wy *THNB/SVB* BS35 8 C1
Roundhill Gv *BATHSE* BA2 135 F2
Roundhill Pk *BATHSE* BA2 135 E1
Roundmoor Cl *KEYN* BS31 108 B4
Roundmoor Gdns
HGRV/WHIT BS14 94 B5 4
Roundstone St *TRWBR* BA14 157 D3 2
Roundways *FRCTL/WBN* BS36 33 D2
Rousham Rd *EVILLE/WHL* BS5 65 E3
Rowacres *BATHSE* BA2 135 F2
HGRV/WHIT BS14 103 D1
Rowan Cl *MANG/FISH* BS16 67 E4
NAIL BS48 87 F2 9
Rowan Ct *RDSTK/MIDN* BA3 162 A3
Rowan Pl *OMX/HUT/LCK* BS24 144 A1 2
The Rowans *PTSHD/EG* BS20 55 F2
Rowan Wy *KGWD/HNM* BS15 95 F1 1
Rowberrow *HGRV/WHIT* BS14 93 D5
Rowberrow Wy *NAIL* BS48 87 D3 9
Rowden La *BOAV* BA15 147 D5
Rowland Av *MANG/FISH* BS16 66 A2 2

Rowlands Cl CBATH/BATHN BA1 115 F5 2
Rowlandson Gdns HORF/LLZ BS7 48 C5 3
Rowley St BMSTR BS3 92 A1 8
Rownham Cl BMSTR BS3 74 C5 1
Rownham Hl CFTN/FAIL BS8 74 C3 3
Rownham Md CFTN/FAIL BS8 75 E4 7
The Rows MTN/WRL BS22 129 D5
Royal Albert Rd RDLND/MONT BS6 63 E2
Royal Cl HNBRY/STHM BS10 25 E5
Royal Crs CBATH/BATHN BA1 122 C3
WSM BS23 140 C2
Royal Fort Rd CFTN/FAIL BS8 2 B1
Royal Pde WSM BS23 140 C2
Royal Pk CFTN/FAIL BS8 75 E2
Royal Portbury Dock Rd
PTSHD/EG BS20 41 F5
Royal Rd MANG/FISH BS16 52 B5
Royal York Crs CFTN/FAIL BS8 75 D3 14
Royal York Vls CFTN/FAIL BS8 75 E3 10
Royate Hl EVILLE/WHL BS5 66 B4
Roycroft Rd BRSTK/PCHW BS34 48 C1
Roy King Gdns
OLD/WMLY/WICK BS30 82 A4
Royston Wk HNBRY/STHM BS10 47 E1
Rozel Rd HORF/LLZ BS7 47 F5
Rubens Cl KEYN BS31 107 E2 3
Ruby St BMSTR BS3 91 F1
Ruddymead CLVDN BS21 85 D2
Rudford Cl BRSTK/PCHW BS34 12 C4
Rudge Cl KGWD/HNM BS15 69 D4
Rudgewood Cl
BMSTRD/HC/WWD BS13 102 B3 2
Rudgleigh Av PTSHD/EG BS20 60 A2 3
Rudgleigh Rd PTSHD/EG BS20 60 A2
Rudhall Gv HNBRY/STHM BS10 47 F4
Rudmore Pk CBATH/BATHN BA1 121 E3
Rudthorpe Rd HORF/LLZ BS7 64 C1
Ruffet Rd FRCTL/WBN BS36 32 C4
Rugby Rd BRSG/KWL/STAPK BS4 94 B1
Runnymead Av
BRSG/KWL/STAPK BS4 94 B3
Runnymede KGWD/HNM BS15 68 C5 4
Runswick Rd
BRSG/KWL/STAPK BS4 94 A1
Rupert St CBRIS/FH BS1 2 D2
EVILLE/WHL BS5 78 A2
Rush Cl ALMDB BS32 13 E3
Rush Hl BATHSE BA2 135 F3
Rushmoor CLVDN BS21 84 A3
Rushton Dr FRCTL/WBN BS36 33 E1
Rushy OLD/WMLY/WICK BS30 81 E5
Rushy Wy MANG/FISH BS16 52 B2
Ruskin Gv HORF/LLZ BS7 48 B3
Ruskin Rd RDSTK/MIDN BA3 161 F3
Russell Av KGWD/HNM BS15 80 B2
Russell Gv RDLND/MONT BS6 64 A1
Russell Rd CLVDN BS21 84 C1 4
MANG/FISH BS16 67 F4
OMX/HUT/LCK BS24 144 B4
RDLND/MONT BS6 63 F2
Russell St CBATH/BATHN BA1 4 B1
Russell Town Av EVILLE/WHL BS5 77 F1
Russett Gv NAIL BS48 86 B4 1
Russ St CBRISNE BS2 3 G3
Rutherford Cl
OLD/WMLY/WICK BS30 97 E1 6
Ruthven Rd BRSG/KWL/STAPK BS4 92 C4
Rutland Av OLD/WMLY/WICK BS30 97 E2
Rutland Cl MTN/WRL BS22 142 B2
Rutland Crs TRWBR BA14 158 C1
Rutland Rd HORF/LLZ BS7 64 C3 3
Rydal Av OMX/HUT/LCK BS24 153 E1
Rydal Rd WSM BS23 151 E1
Ryde Rd BRSG/KWL/STAPK BS4 93 F2 5
Rye Cl BMSTRD/HC/WWD BS13 100 C1
Ryecroft Av MTN/WRL BS22 143 D1
Ryecroft Ri LGASH BS41 89 F3
Ryecroft Rd FRCTL/WBN BS36 17 D5
Ryedown La
OLD/WMLY/WICK BS30 98 A3
Ryeland Wy TRWBR BA14 157 E5
Ryland Pl CBRISNE BS2 65 E4 12
Rylestone Cl FRCTL/WBN BS36 16 A5
Rylestone Gv
HNLZ/SM/SNYPK/WT BS9 63 D1
Rysdale Rd
HNLZ/SM/SNYPK/WT BS9 46 A5

S

Sabrina Wy
HNLZ/SM/SNYPK/WT BS9 62 A2
PTSHD/EG BS20 60 B2 2
Sadbury Cl MTN/WRL BS22 130 A3 11
Sadlier Cl AVONM BS11 44 A3
The Saffrons MTN/WRL BS22 130 A3 12
Sage Cl PTSHD/EG BS20 54 C2
Sages Md ALMDB BS32 13 F5 1
St Agnes Av BRSG/KWL/STAPK BS4 93 D2
St Agnes Cl
BRSG/KWL/STAPK BS4 93 D2 2
NAIL BS48 87 F3 7
St Agnes Wk
BRSG/KWL/STAPK BS4 93 D2 3
St Aidan's Cl EVILLE/WHL BS5 79 F3 4
St Aidan's Rd EVILLE/WHL BS5 79 E3
St Alban's Rd RDLND/MONT BS6 63 F2
St Aldhelm Rd BOAV BA15 147 E4
St Aldwyn's Cl HORF/LLZ BS7 48 A3 1
St Andrews OLD/WMLY/WICK BS30 81 F3
YATE/CS BS37 20 A4
St Andrews Cl MTN/WRL BS22 129 E4 10
NAIL BS48 87 F3 8
St Andrew's Dr CLVDN BS21 84 A2
St Andrew's Rd AVONM BS11 23 D3
AVONM BS11 42 C2
RDLND/MONT BS6 64 C4 4
RDLND/MONT BS6 65 D4 11
St Anne's Av KEYN BS31 106 B1
St Anne's Cl OLD/WMLY/WICK BS30 81 F5
St Anne's Dr FRCTL/WBN BS36 33 D3
OLD/WMLY/WICK BS30 83 F2
OLD/WMLY/WICK BS30 98 A2
St Anne's Park Rd
BRSG/KWL/STAPK BS4 78 C4
St Anne's Rd BRSG/KWL/STAPK BS4 78 B3
EVILLE/WHL BS5 79 F3
St Anne's Ter
BRSG/KWL/STAPK BS4 78 C4
St Ann's Wy BATHSE BA2 5 F3
St Anthony's Cl
RDSTK/MIDN BA3 161 D2 3
St Aubin's Av
BRSG/KWL/STAPK BS4 95 D1
St Aubyn's Av WSM BS23 150 C3 4
St Augustine's Pde CBRIS/FH BS1 2 C3
St Augustine's Pl CBRIS/FH BS1 2 C3 1
St Augustine's Rd TRWBR BA14 156 B4 4
St Austell Cl NAIL BS48 87 F4
St Austell Rd MTN/WRL BS22 142 A2
St Barnabas Cl
OLD/WMLY/WICK BS30 82 A2 1
RDSTK/MIDN BA3 161 E1 1
St Bartholomew's Rd
HORF/LLZ BS7 65 D3 3
St Bede's Rd KGWD/HNM BS15 68 A4
St Bernard's Rd AVONM BS11 43 F5
St Brelades Gv
BRSG/KWL/STAPK BS4 78 C4
St Brendan's Wy AVONM BS11 42 C2
St Briavels Dr YATE/CS BS37 19 E5
St Bridges Cl MTN/WRL BS22 127 F1
St Catherine's Cl BATHSE BA2 5 G3
St Catherine's Md
PTSHD/EG BS20 60 B3 1
St Chad's Av RDSTK/MIDN BA3 161 D3
St Chad's Gn RDSTK/MIDN BA3 161 D4
St Charles Cl RDSTK/MIDN BA3 161 D2 4
St Christophers Cl BATHSE BA2 5 G1
St Clements Ct KEYN BS31 106 C3
St Clements Rd KEYN BS31 106 C2
St David's Av
OLD/WMLY/WICK BS30 81 F4
St David's Cl MTN/WRL BS22 128 A5
St David's Crs
BRSG/KWL/STAPK BS4 78 C4
St David's Rd THNB/SVB BS35 8 C3
St Dunstan's Rd BMSTR BS3 92 A2
St Edward's Rd CFTN/FAIL BS8 75 F3 7
St Edyth's Rd
HNLZ/SM/SNYPK/WT BS9 44 C5
St Fagans Ct
OLD/WMLY/WICK BS30 97 F2 2
St Francis Dr FRCTL/WBN BS36 32 A2
OLD/WMLY/WICK BS30 83 F2
St Francis Rd BMSTR BS3 75 E5 5
KEYN BS31 106 A1
St Gabriel's Rd EVILLE/WHL BS5 77 E1 13
St Georges Av EVILLE/WHL BS5 79 D3 11
St George's Hl BATHSE BA2 124 B2
PTSHD/EG BS20 59 E3
St Georges Rd CBRIS/FH BS1 2 A4
KEYN BS31 106 B2
PTSHD/EG BS20 41 F4
St Gregory's Rd HORF/LLZ BS7 48 A3
St Gregory's Wk HORF/LLZ BS7 48 B3 3
St Helena Rd RDLND/MONT BS6 63 F2
St Helens Dr
OLD/WMLY/WICK BS30 98 A2
St Helen's Wk EVILLE/WHL BS5 67 E5
St Helier Av
BRSG/KWL/STAPK BS4 95 D1 2
St Hilary Cl
HNLZ/SM/SNYPK/WT BS9 62 B1
St Ivel Wy OLD/WMLY/WICK BS30 82 A3
St Ives Cl NAIL BS48 87 F3 9
St James's Pde
CBATH/BATHN BA1 4 B4 7
St James's Pk CBATH/BATHN BA1 123 D2
St James's Sq
CBATH/BATHN BA1 122 C2 3
St James's St MANG/FISH BS16 69 E1
St James St WSM BS23 6 B1 5
St John's Av CLVDN BS21 85 D1 3
St John's Br CBRIS/FH BS1 2 C1 1
St John's Cl WSM BS23 140 C1
St Johns Ct KEYN BS31 106 C1
St John's Crs BMSTR BS3 92 C2
RDSTK/MIDN BA3 161 D2
St John's La BMSTR BS3 92 B2
St John's Pl CBATH/BATHN BA1 4 B3 12
St John's Rd BATHSE BA2 4 C1
BMSTR BS3 92 A1 9
CBATH/BATHN BA1 122 A3
CFTN/FAIL BS8 63 E5
CLVDN BS21 84 C1
St John's St BMSTR BS3 92 A1 10
St John St THNB/SVB BS35 8 B3
St Johns Wy YATE/CS BS37 21 D3
St Joseph's Rd HNBRY/STHM BS10 26 C5
WSM BS23 141 D1 2
St Jude's Ter MTN/WRL BS22 142 B1 6
St Keyna Rd KEYN BS31 106 C2
St Kilda's Rd BATHSE BA2 122 B5
St Ladoc Rd KEYN BS31 106 B1
St Laud Cl
HNLZ/SM/SNYPK/WT BS9 62 A1
St Laurence Rd BOAV BA15 147 E4 1
St Leonard's Rd
EVILLE/WHL BS5 66 A4 13
HORF/LLZ BS7 47 F5
St Lucia Cl HORF/LLZ BS7 47 F3
St Lucia Crs HORF/LLZ BS7 47 F4
St Luke's Crs BMSTR BS3 77 D5
St Luke's Gdns
BRSG/KWL/STAPK BS4 94 C2
St Luke's Rd BATHSE BA2 137 D2
BMSTR BS3 76 C5
RDSTK/MIDN BA3 160 C2 3
St Luke St EVILLE/WHL BS5 77 F2 11
St Margaret's Cl KEYN BS31 106 B1 2
St Margaret's Dr
HNLZ/SM/SNYPK/WT BS9 64 A1 2
St Margaret's Hl BOAV BA15 147 D3 4
St Margaret's St BOAV BA15 147 D3
St Margaret's Ter WSM BS23 140 C2 8
St Marks Cl KEYN BS31 106 C1 1
St Mark's Rd BATHSE BA2 4 C6
EVILLE/WHL BS5 65 F5
MTN/WRL BS22 129 E3
RDSTK/MIDN BA3 161 D2
St Mark's Ter EVILLE/WHL BS5 65 F5 10
St Martins Ct MTN/WRL BS22 129 D4 4
St Martin's Gdns
BRSG/KWL/STAPK BS4 93 F3 2
St Martin's Rd
BRSG/KWL/STAPK BS4 93 F2
St Martin's Wk
BRSG/KWL/STAPK BS4 93 F3 3
St Mary's Cl BATHSE BA2 5 F3
TRWBR BA14 149 E5
St Mary's Ct
OMX/HUT/LCK BS24 151 F4 7
St Mary's Gdns TRWBR BA14 149 E5
St Mary's Gv NAIL BS48 86 B4
St Mary's Pk NAIL BS48 86 B4
St Marys Ri RDSTK/MIDN BA3 163 F2
St Mary's Rd AVONM BS11 43 E4
CFTN/FAIL BS8 74 B3 1
OMX/HUT/LCK BS24 152 C3
PTSHD/EG BS20 56 A2
St Mary St THNB/SVB BS35 8 B4 2
St Mary's Wk AVONM BS11 43 E5
St Mary's Wy YATE/CS BS37 20 A3
St Matthew's Av
RDLND/MONT BS6 64 B5 6
St Matthew's Cl WSM BS23 140 C1 1
St Matthew's Rd
RDLND/MONT BS6 76 B1
St Matthias Pk CBRISNE BS2 3 G1
St Michael's Av CLVDN BS21 85 D3
MTN/WRL BS22 129 F4 9
St Michael's Cl FRCTL/WBN BS36 31 F1
St Michaels Ct KGWD/HNM BS15 79 F1 2
St Michael's Hl CBRISNE BS2 76 A1
St Michael's Pk CFTN/FAIL BS8 76 A1
St Michael's Pl CBATH/BATHN BA1 4 B4 8
St Michaels Rd BATHSE BA2 121 E5
CBATH/BATHN BA1 122 B3 3
St Nicholas Cl TRWBR BA14 159 D4
St Nicholas Pk EVILLE/WHL BS5 65 F5 11
St Nicholas' Rd CBRISNE BS2 65 D5
HGRV/WHIT BS14 104 A3
WSM BS23 150 C3
St Nicholas St CBRIS/FH BS1 2 D3 5
St Oswald's Rd RDLND/MONT BS6 63 F3
St Pauls Pl RDSTK/MIDN BA3 161 D2 5
St Paul's Rd BMSTR BS3 76 B5 9
CFTN/FAIL BS8 75 F2
WSM BS23 6 C5
St Paul St CBRISNE BS2 76 C1
St Peter's Av WSM BS23 140 C1
St Peter's Crs FRCTL/WBN BS36 32 C1
St Peter's Ri
BMSTRD/HC/WWD BS13 91 E5
St Peters Rd PTSHD/EG BS20 56 B2
RDSTK/MIDN BA3 161 F4
St Peter's Wk
HNLZ/SM/SNYPK/WT BS9 63 F1
St Philips Cswy
BRSG/KWL/STAPK BS4 78 A5
CBRISNE BS2 77 F3

St Philips Rd *CBRISNE* BS2 .... 3 H2
St Phillips Rd *CBRISNE* BS2 .... 77 E2
St Pierre Dr
OLD/WMLY/WICK BS30 .... 81 F3 3
St Ronan's Av *RDLND/MONT* BS6 .... 64 A5
St Saviours Ri *FRCTL/WBN* BS36 .... 32 C2
St Saviour's Rd
CBATH/BATHN BA1 .... 124 A1
St Saviours Wy
CBATH/BATHN BA1 .... 124 A1 3
St Silas St *CBRISNE* BS2 .... 77 E4
St Stephen's Av *CBRIS/FH* BS1 .... 2 C3 2
St Stephen's Cl
CBATH/BATHN BA1 .... 123 D2 13
KGWD/HNM BS15 .... 68 C3 3
St Stephen's Pl *TRWBR* BA14 .... 157 D4
St Stephen's Rd
CBATH/BATHN BA1 .... 123 D2
MANG/FISH BS16 .... 68 B3
St Stephen's St *CBRIS/FH* BS1 .... 2 C2
St Thomas Rd *RDSTK/MIDN* BA3 .. 161 E2 2
TRWBR BA14 .... 157 E3
St Thomas St *CBRIS/FH* BS1 .... 3 E4
St Vincent's Hl
RDLND/MONT BS6 .... 63 E4 11
St Vincent's Rd *CFTN/FAIL* BS8 .... 75 E3 11
St Werburgh's Pk *CBRISNE* BS2 .... 65 E4
St Werburgh's Rd *CBRISNE* BS2 .. 65 D4 12
St Whytes Rd
BRSG/KWL/STAPK BS4 .... 92 B4
St Winifreds Dr *BATHSE* BA2 .... 138 B3
Salcombe Gdns *MTN/WRL* BS22 .. 129 F5 5
Salcombe Rd
BRSG/KWL/STAPK BS4 .... 93 E4
Salem Rd *FRCTL/WBN* BS36 .... 32 A1
Salisbury Av *KGWD/HNM* BS15 .... 79 F1
Salisbury Gdns *MANG/FISH* BS16 .... 68 C1
Salisbury Rd *BRSG/KWL/STAPK* BS4 .. 78 B4
CBATH/BATHN BA1 .... 113 F5
MANG/FISH BS16 .... 51 F5
MTN/WRL BS22 .... 142 B1
RDLND/MONT BS6 .... 64 B4
Salisbury St *EVILLE/WHL* BS5 .... 77 F3
EVILLE/WHL BS5 .... 78 C1
Salisbury Ter *WSM* BS23 .... 6 B1 6
WSM BS23 .... 140 C2
Sallybarn Cl *OLD/WMLY/WICK* BS30 .. 96 C2
Sallysmead Cl
BMSTRD/HC/WWD BS13 .... 101 F3 7
Sallys Wy *FRCTL/WBN* BS36 .... 32 A1
Salmons Wy *MANG/FISH* BS16 .... 52 B3
Salthouse Rd *CLVDN* BS21 .... 84 B1
Salthrop Rd *HORF/LLZ* BS7 .... 64 C3
Saltings Cl *CLVDN* BS21 .... 84 B2 1
Saltmarsh Dr *AVONM* BS11 .... 44 B2
Saltwell Av *HGRV/WHIT* BS14 .... 104 A2
Sambourne La *PTSHD/EG* BS20 .... 60 A1 4
Samian Wy *BRSTK/PCHW* BS34 .... 29 F3
Sampsons Rd
BMSTRD/HC/WWD BS13 .... 102 A3
Samuel St *EVILLE/WHL* BS5 .... 78 A1 9
Samuel White Rd
KGWD/HNM BS15 .... 96 A1
Samuel Wright Cl
OLD/WMLY/WICK BS30 .... 82 B4 2
Sandbach Rd
BRSG/KWL/STAPK BS4 .... 78 B5
Sandbed Rd *CBRISNE* BS2 .... 65 E4
Sandburrows Rd
BMSTRD/HC/WWD BS13 .... 100 C1
Sandburrows Wk
BMSTRD/HC/WWD BS13 .... 101 D1 3
Sandcroft *HGRV/WHIT* BS14 .... 103 D1
Sandcroft Av *WSM* BS23 .... 150 C3
Sanders Rd *TRWBR* BA14 .... 156 C2
Sand Farm La *MTN/WRL* BS22 .... 127 F1
Sandford Cl *CLVDN* BS21 .... 84 B3 6
Sandford Rd *CFTN/FAIL* BS8 .... 75 E4 8
WNSC BS25 .... 154 B3
WSM BS23 .... 7 F1
Sandgate Rd
BRSG/KWL/STAPK BS4 .... 94 B1
Sand Hl *BRSG/KWL/STAPK* BS4 .... 78 A5
Sandholme Cl *MANG/FISH* BS16 .... 51 F3 1
Sandholme Rd
BRSG/KWL/STAPK BS4 .... 78 A5
Sandhurst *YATE/CS* BS37 .... 19 E5 4
Sandhurst Cl *BRSTK/PCHW* BS34 .... 12 C4
Sandhurst Rd
BRSG/KWL/STAPK BS4 .... 78 B5 1
Sandling Av *HORF/LLZ* BS7 .... 48 B4
Sandown Centre *TRWBR* BA14 .... 159 E3 2
Sandown Cl *MANG/FISH* BS16 .... 52 A2
Sandown Rd *BRSG/KWL/STAPK* BS4.. 78 B5
BRSTK/PCHW BS34 .... 29 D5 2
Sandpiper Dr *MTN/WRL* BS22 .... 143 E1
Sandringham Av *MANG/FISH* BS16 .. 51 F3
Sandringham Pk
MANG/FISH BS16 .... 51 F3 2
Sandringham Rd
BRSG/KWL/STAPK BS4 .... 94 B1
BRSTK/PCHW BS34 .... 29 E4
TRWBR BA14 .... 158 B2
WSM BS23 .... 7 E5
Sand Rd *MTN/WRL* BS22 .... 128 A2
Sandstone Ri *FRCTL/WBN* BS36 .... 31 E4
Sandwich Rd
BRSG/KWL/STAPK BS4 .... 78 B5 2
Sandy Cl *ALMDB* BS32 .... 29 F2
Sandy La *EVILLE/WHL* BS5 .... 66 A3
Sandy Leaze *BOAV* BA15 .... 146 C3
Sandyleaze
HNLZ/SM/SNYPK/WT BS9 .... 45 F4
Sandy Ldg *YATE/CS* BS37 .... 19 F5
Sandy Park Rd
BRSG/KWL/STAPK BS4 .... 78 A5
Saracen St *CBATH/BATHN* BA1 .... 4 C2 3
Sarah St *EVILLE/WHL* BS5 .... 77 F2
Sargent St *BMSTR* BS3 .... 76 C5 2
Sarum Crs *HNBRY/STHM* BS10 .... 47 D2
Sassoon Ct
OLD/WMLY/WICK BS30 .... 81 D4 6
Satchfield Cl *HNBRY/STHM* BS10 .... 46 A1
Satchfield Crs *HNBRY/STHM* BS10 .... 46 A1
Sates Wy *HNLZ/SM/SNYPK/WT* BS9 .. 47 D5
Saunders Rd *MANG/FISH* BS16 .... 68 C2 6
Saunton Wk
BRSG/KWL/STAPK BS4 .... 92 C4 5
Savages Wood Rd *ALMDB* BS32 .... 13 E5
Savernake Rd *MTN/WRL* BS22 .... 129 E4
Saville Crs *MTN/WRL* BS22 .... 142 B2
Saville Gate Cl
HNLZ/SM/SNYPK/WT BS9 .... 63 D2 1
Saville Pl *CFTN/FAIL* BS8 .... 75 E3 12
Saville Rd *HNLZ/SM/SNYPK/WT* BS9.. 63 D3
MTN/WRL BS22 .... 142 B2
Saville Rw *CBATH/BATHN* BA1 .... 4 B1 3
Savoy Rd *BRSG/KWL/STAPK* BS4 .... 78 B5
Saw Cl *CBATH/BATHN* BA1 .... 4 B3 13
Saw Mill La *THNB/SVB* BS35 .... 8 B3 3
Sawyers Cl *NAIL* BS48 .... 87 F2 10
Sawyers Ct *CLVDN* BS21 .... 85 E1
Saxby Cl *CLVDN* BS21 .... 84 B3
MTN/WRL BS22 .... 130 A3 13
Saxon Dr *TRWBR* BA14 .... 149 E5
Saxon Rd *CBRISNE* BS2 .... 65 E4
MTN/WRL BS22 .... 142 B2 1
Saxon Wy *ALMDB* BS32 .... 13 D4
Say Wk *OLD/WMLY/WICK* BS30 .... 82 B2
Scafell Cl *WSM* BS23 .... 141 F1 3
Scandrett Cl *HNBRY/STHM* BS10 .. 25 F5 1
Scantleberry Cl *MANG/FISH* BS16 .. 51 E3 4
The Scaurs *MTN/WRL* BS22 .... 129 E5
School Cl *BRSTK/PCHW* BS34 .... 13 D5
EVILLE/WHL BS5 .... 66 B4
HGRV/WHIT BS14 .... 103 D3
School La *CBATH/BATHN* BA1 .... 115 D3
TRWBR BA14 .... 149 D4
School Rd *BRSG/KWL/STAPK* BS4 .... 93 E1
FRCTL/WBN BS36 .... 16 A5
KGWD/HNM BS15 .... 80 A1
OLD/WMLY/WICK BS30 .... 81 E5
OLD/WMLY/WICK BS30 .... 97 F1
School Wk *YATE/CS* BS37 .... 19 F3
School Wy *THNB/SVB* BS35 .... 10 B4 1
Scotch Horn Cl *NAIL* BS48 .... 87 E2 5
Scotch Horn Wy *NAIL* BS48 .... 87 E2
Scots Pine Av *NAIL* BS48 .... 87 E2 6
Scott Ct *OLD/WMLY/WICK* BS30 .... 81 D4 7
Scott Lawrence Cl
MANG/FISH BS16 .... 50 B4 3
Scott Rd *WSM* BS23 .... 151 F1
Scott Wk *OLD/WMLY/WICK* BS30 .... 82 B2
Scott Wy *YATE/CS* BS37 .... 20 A5
Sea Bank Rd *PTSHD/EG* BS20 .... 41 F3
Seabrook Rd *MTN/WRL* BS22 .... 142 C1
Seagry Cl *HNBRY/STHM* BS10 .... 47 F2
Sea Mills La
HNLZ/SM/SNYPK/WT BS9 .... 62 A2
Searle Court Av
BRSG/KWL/STAPK BS4 .... 78 C4
Searle Crs *WSM* BS23 .... 7 H4
Seaton Rd *EVILLE/WHL* BS5 .... 66 A5 5
Seavale Rd *CLVDN* BS21 .... 70 C5
Seaview Rd *PTSHD/EG* BS20 .... 38 A5
PTSHD/EG BS20 .... 54 C2
Seawalls Rd
HNLZ/SM/SNYPK/WT BS9 .... 62 B4
Second Av *BATHSE* BA2 .... 136 B1
RDSTK/MIDN BA3 .... 161 F5
Seddon Rd *CBRISNE* BS2 .... 65 E4 13
Sedgefield Gdns
MANG/FISH BS16 .... 52 A2 7
Sedgemoor Cl *NAIL* BS48 .... 87 D4
Sedgemoor Rd *BATHSE* BA2 .... 137 D4
WSM BS23 .... 141 E1 3
Sefton Park Rd *HORF/LLZ* BS7 .... 65 D3
Sefton Sq *OMX/HUT/LCK* BS24 .... 143 F2
Selborne Rd *HORF/LLZ* BS7 .... 65 D1
Selbourne Cl *CBATH/BATHN* BA1 .. 121 E2 1
Selbourne Rd *WSM* BS23 .... 151 D1
Selbrooke Crs *MANG/FISH* BS16 .... 51 D5
Selby Rd *EVILLE/WHL* BS5 .... 67 D5
Selden Rd *HGRV/WHIT* BS14 .... 104 C2
Selkirk Rd *KGWD/HNM* BS15 .... 68 A4
Selley Wk *BMSTRD/HC/WWD* BS13.. 101 E2
Selwood Cl *WSM* BS23 .... 142 B3
Selworthy *KGWD/HNM* BS15 .... 80 C2
Selworthy Cl *KEYN* BS31 .... 106 B2
Selworthy Rd
BRSG/KWL/STAPK BS4 .... 93 F2
WSM BS23 .... 151 E1
Seneca Pl *EVILLE/WHL* BS5 .... 78 B2 9
Seneca St *EVILLE/WHL* BS5 .... 78 B2
Serbert Rd *PTSHD/EG* BS20 .... 56 C1
Sercombe Pk *CLVDN* BS21 .... 85 E3
Seven Acres La
CBATH/BATHN BA1 .... 115 D2
Seventh Av *HORF/LLZ* BS7 .... 48 C2 2
Seven View Rd *THNB/SVB* BS35 .... 8 C2
Severn Av *WSM* BS23 .... 6 D6
Severn Dr *THNB/SVB* BS35 .... 8 B2
Severnmeade *PTSHD/EG* BS20 .... 55 D1 5
Severn Rd *AVONM* BS11 .... 43 E5 3
PTSHD/EG BS20 .... 56 A1
PTSHD/EG BS20 .... 60 A1
THNB/SVB BS35 .... 11 E1
WSM BS23 .... 6 B5
Severn Wy *BRSTK/PCHW* BS34 .... 12 A4
KEYN BS31 .... 107 D3
THNB/SVB BS35 .... 10 A4
Severnwood Gdns *THNB/SVB* BS35 .. 10 B5
Sevier St *CBRISNE* BS2 .... 65 E4
Seville Rd *PTSHD/EG* BS20 .... 39 F4
Seymour Av *HORF/LLZ* BS7 .... 64 C2 2
Seymour Cl *CLVDN* BS21 .... 85 E1
MTN/WRL BS22 .... 129 E3 5
Seymour Ct *TRWBR* BA14 .... 156 C3
Seymour Rd *CBATH/BATHN* BA1 .... 123 E2
EVILLE/WHL BS5 .... 65 E5
HORF/LLZ BS7 .... 64 C2
KGWD/HNM BS15 .... 68 A5 3
MANG/FISH BS16 .... 68 B2
TRWBR BA14 .... 157 D2
Seyton Wk *BRSTK/PCHW* BS34 .... 29 F3
Shackel Hendy Ms
MANG/FISH BS16 .... 69 F1 2
Shackleton Av *YATE/CS* BS37 .... 20 A5
Shadwell Rd *HORF/LLZ* BS7 .... 64 B3
Shaftesbury Av
CBATH/BATHN BA1 .... 122 A3 1
RDLND/MONT BS6 .... 64 C5
Shaftesbury Cl *NAIL* BS48 .... 86 C4
Shaftesbury Rd *BATHSE* BA2 .... 122 B5
WSM BS23 .... 142 A2
Shaft Rd *BATHSE* BA2 .... 138 B4
THNB/SVB BS35 .... 10 B2
Shails La *TRWBR* BA14 .... 156 C3
Shakespeare Av *BATHSE* BA2 .... 137 D1
HORF/LLZ BS7 .... 48 B3
Shakespeare Rd
RDSTK/MIDN BA3 .... 161 F3
Shaldon Rd *HORF/LLZ* BS7 .... 65 E2
The Shallows *KEYN* BS31 .... 109 D4
Sham Castle La *BATHSE* BA2 .... 5 F2
Shamrock Rd *EVILLE/WHL* BS5 .... 66 B3 4
Shanklin Dr *BRSTK/PCHW* BS34 .... 28 C5 2
Shannon Ct *THNB/SVB* BS35 .... 9 D4 4
Shapcott Cl
BRSG/KWL/STAPK BS4 .... 93 F3 4
Shaplands
HNLZ/SM/SNYPK/WT BS9 .... 63 D2
Shaws Wy *BATHSE* BA2 .... 121 D5
Shearman St *TRWBR* BA14 .... 157 D5
Shearmore Cl *HORF/LLZ* BS7 .... 48 B4 3
Sheene La *BMSTR* BS3 .... 92 A1
Sheepcote Barton *TRWBR* BA14 .. 157 E5 3
Sheeps Cft
BMSTRD/HC/WWD BS13 .... 101 E3
Sheepway *PTSHD/EG* BS20 .... 57 E2
Sheepwood Cl *HNBRY/STHM* BS10.... 46 B2
Sheepwood Rd *HNBRY/STHM* BS10.. 46 B1
Sheldare Barton
EVILLE/WHL BS5 .... 79 F2 3
Sheldon Cl *CLVDN* BS21 .... 85 F2 2
Shellard Rd *BRSTK/PCHW* BS34.......... 28 B5
Shellards Rd
OLD/WMLY/WICK BS30 .... 97 D1
Shelley Av *CLVDN* BS21 .... 85 D2
Shelley Cl *EVILLE/WHL* BS5.......... 79 D1
Shelley Rd *BATHSE* BA2 .... 4 B6
RDSTK/MIDN BA3 .... 161 F3
WSM BS23 .... 151 F1
Shelley Wy *HORF/LLZ* BS7 .... 48 B3
Shellmor Av *BRSTK/PCHW* BS34 .... 12 C4
Shellmor Cl *ALMDB* BS32 .... 13 E4 1
BRSTK/PCHW BS34 .... 13 D4
Shepherds Cl *MANG/FISH* BS16 .... 68 C1
Sheppard Rd *MANG/FISH* BS16 .... 51 D5
Sheppy's Ml *YTN/CONG* BS49 .... 133 D1 1
Shepton Wk *BMSTR* BS3 .... 92 A2
Sherbourne Av *ALMDB* BS32 .... 29 F1
Sherbourne Cl *KGWD/HNM* BS15 .... 69 D4
Sherbourne St *EVILLE/WHL* BS5 .... 78 C1
Sheridan Rd *BATHSE* BA2 .... 121 D5
HORF/LLZ BS7 .... 48 B2
Sheridan Wy
OLD/WMLY/WICK BS30 .... 97 E2
Sherrin Wy
BMSTRD/HC/WWD BS13 .... 100 C4
Sherston Cl *MANG/FISH* BS16 .... 67 F1
NAIL BS48 .... 87 F3 10
Sherston Rd *HORF/LLZ* BS7 .... 47 F3 1
Sherwell Rd *BRSG/KWL/STAPK* BS4 .. 94 C1

Sherwood Cl *KEYN* BS31 **106** C2
Sherwood Crs *MTN/WRL* BS22 **129** E4
Sherwood Rd *KEYN* BS31 **106** C2
KGWD/HNM BS15 **67** E5
Shetland Rd *HNBRY/STHM* BS10 **47** E2
Shetland Wy *NAIL* BS48 **87** F3
Shickle Gv *BATHSE* BA2 **136** A4
Shields Av *HORF/LLZ* BS7 **48** B1
Shiels Dr *ALMDB* BS32 **29** E1 5
Shilton Cl *KGWD/HNM* BS15 **81** D2 9
Shimsey Cl *MANG/FISH* BS16 **51** D5 4
Shiners Elms *YTN/CONG* BS49 **116** A3
Shipham Cl *HGRV/WHIT* BS14 **103** F2
NAIL BS48 **87** E4
Shipham La *WNSC* BS25 **155** D3
Ship La *CBRIS/FH* BS1 **3** E6
Shipley Mow *MANG/FISH* BS16 **52** C5
Shipley Rd
HNLZ/SM/SNYPK/WT BS9 **46** B3
Shipnran Ct *MANG/FISH* BS16 **68** C2 7
Shire Gdns *AVONM* BS11 **43** E3
Shirehampton Rd *AVONM* BS11 **44** A4
HNLZ/SM/SNYPK/WT BS9 **45** D5 2
Shire Wy *YATE/CS* BS37 **35** D2
Shockerwick La
CBATH/BATHN BA1 **115** F3
Shophouse Rd *BATHSE* BA2 **121** F5
Shorthill Rd *YATE/CS* BS37 **35** D4
Shortlands Rd *AVONM* BS11 **44** B2 3
Short La *LGASH* BS41 **89** D2
Short St *CBRISNE* BS2 **77** E4
Short Wy *THNB/SVB* BS35 **8** B5
Shortwood Rd
BMSTRD/HC/WWD BS13 **102** C4
Shortwood Vw
KGWD/HNM BS15 **81** D1 5
Shortwood Wk
BMSTRD/HC/WWD BS13 **102** C4 1
Showering Cl *HGRV/WHIT* BS14 **104** B2 4
Showering Rd *HGRV/WHIT* BS14 **104** B2
Shrewsbury Bow
OMX/HUT/LCK BS24 **143** F2
Shrewton Cl *TRWBR* BA14 **159** D1
Shrubbery Av *WSM* BS23 **140** B1
Shrubbery Cottages
RDLND/MONT BS6 **63** F4 5
Shrubbery Rd *MANG/FISH* BS16 **68** B1
WSM BS23 **140** C1
Shrubbery Ter *WSM* BS23 **140** B1 4
Shrubbery Wk West *WSM* BS23 **140** C1 2
Shuter Rd
BMSTRD/HC/WWD BS13 **101** D2 4
Sibland *THNB/SVB* BS35 **9** D4
Sibland Cl *THNB/SVB* BS35 **9** D4 5
Sibland Rd *THNB/SVB* BS35 **9** D3
Sibland Wy *THNB/SVB* BS35 **8** C4
Sidcot *BRSG/KWL/STAPK* BS4 **95** E2
Sidcot La *WNSC* BS25 **154** C5
Sideland Cl *HGRV/WHIT* BS14 **104** C1
Sidelands Rd *MANG/FISH* BS16 **51** D5
Sidmouth Gdns *BMSTR* BS3 **92** B2 1
Sidmouth Rd *BMSTR* BS3 **92** B2
Signal Rd *MANG/FISH* BS16 **68** C2
Silbury Ri *KEYN* BS31 **107** E5
Silbury Rd *BMSTR* BS3 **90** C2
Silcox Rd
BMSTRD/HC/WWD BS13 **102** A3 5
Silklands Gv
HNLZ/SM/SNYPK/WT BS9 **45** D5 3
Silverberry Rd *MTN/WRL* BS22 **143** F1
Silverbirch Cl *BRSTK/PCHW* BS34 **29** E1
Silver Birch Rd *TRWBR* BA14 **158** B2
Silverhill Rd *HNBRY/STHM* BS10 **25** F5
Silverlow Rd *NAIL* BS48 **86** C2
Silver Md *YTN/CONG* BS49 **133** D4
Silver Mdw *TRWBR* BA14 **158** A2
Silver Moor La *BNWL* BS29 **145** E3
Silverstone Wy *YTN/CONG* BS49 **133** D3
Silver St *BOAV* BA15 **147** D3
CBRIS/FH BS1 **2** D1 4
NAIL BS48 **86** C2
PTSHD/EG BS20 **54** C5
TRWBR BA14 **157** D4
YTN/CONG BS49 **133** D4
Silver Street La *TRWBR* BA14 **158** C2
Silverthorne La *CBRISNE* BS2 **77** E3
Silverton Ct
BRSG/KWL/STAPK BS4 **93** D3 1
Simmonds Vw *BRSTK/PCHW* BS34 **30** A4
Simons Cl *MTN/WRL* BS22 **129** F5 6
Singapore Rd *WSM* BS23 **151** D2 1
Sion Hl *CBATH/BATHN* BA1 **122** C1
CFTN/FAIL BS8 **75** D3
Sion Hill Pl *CBATH/BATHN* BA1 **122** C1
Sion La *CFTN/FAIL* BS8 **75** D2
Sion Pl *CFTN/FAIL* BS8 **75** D2
Sion Rd *BMSTR* BS3 **92** A1 11
CBATH/BATHN BA1 **122** C1
Sir John's La *EVILLE/WHL* BS5 **65** F2
HORF/LLZ BS7 **65** F2
Siston Cl *KGWD/HNM* BS15 **69** E4
Siston Pk *KGWD/HNM* BS15 **69** E4
Sixth Av *HORF/LLZ* BS7 **48** B2
Skippon Ct *KGWD/HNM* BS15 **80** C4 4
Sladebrook Av *BATHSE* BA2 **136** A2
Sladebrook Rd *BATHSE* BA2 **135** F1
Slade Rd *PTSHD/EG* BS20 **56** B1
Sladesbrook *BOAV* BA15 **147** E1
Sladesbrook Cl *BOAV* BA15 **147** D1
Sleep La *HGRV/WHIT* BS14 **104** B4
Slimbridge Cl *YATE/CS* BS37 **36** A1
The Slipway *TRWBR* BA14 **149** D5
Sloan St *EVILLE/WHL* BS5 **78** B1
Slowgrove Cl *TRWBR* BA14 **157** F4
Slymbridge Av *HNBRY/STHM* BS10 **26** B4
Smallbrook Gdns *TRWBR* BA14 **149** D4
Small Down End *WNSC* BS25 **154** B2
Small La *MANG/FISH* BS16 **66** C1
Small St *CBRIS/FH* BS1 **2** D2 4
CBRISNE BS2 **77** E4
Smallway *YTN/CONG* BS49 **133** D1 2
Smarts Gn *YATE/CS* BS37 **21** D5
Smeaton Rd *CBRIS/FH* BS1 **75** D4
Smithmead
BMSTRD/HC/WWD BS13 **101** F2
Smithywell Cl *TRWBR* BA14 **157** F4 1
Smoke La *AVONM* BS11 **23** E1
Smythe Cft *HGRV/WHIT* BS14 **103** E4
Smyth Rd *BMSTR* BS3 **91** E1
Smyths Cl *AVONM* BS11 **42** C2 1
Snowberry Cl *MTN/WRL* BS22 **143** F1 6
Snowberry Wk *EVILLE/WHL* BS5 **78** C1 3
Snowdon Cl *MANG/FISH* BS16 **67** D2
Snowdon Rd *MANG/FISH* BS16 **67** D1
Snowdon V *WSM* BS23 **141** F1
Snow Hl *CBATH/BATHN* BA1 **123** E1
Solent Wy *THNB/SVB* BS35 **9** D5 4
Solsbury La *CBATH/BATHN* BA1 **114** C3
Solsbury Wy *CBATH/BATHN* BA1 **113** E5
Somer Av *RDSTK/MIDN* BA3 **160** C2
Somerby Cl *ALMDB* BS32 **29** E1 6
Somerdale Av *BATHSE* BA2 **136** B3
BRSG/KWL/STAPK BS4 **93** E3
MTN/WRL BS22 **142** B2
Somerdale Cl *MTN/WRL* BS22 **142** B2
Somerdale Rd *KEYN* BS31 **97** D5
Somerdale Rd North *KEYN* BS31 **97** D5
Somerdale Vw *BATHSE* BA2 **136** A3
Somermead *BMSTR* BS3 **92** A3
Somer Rd *RDSTK/MIDN* BA3 **160** C2
Somerset Av *OMX/HUT/LCK* BS24 **143** E3
YATE/CS BS37 **20** A2
Somerset Crs *BRSTK/PCHW* BS34 **30** A3 4
Somerset La *CBATH/BATHN* BA1 **122** C1
Somerset Pl *CBATH/BATHN* BA1 **122** C1
Somerset Rd
BRSG/KWL/STAPK BS4 **93** E1
CLVDN BS21 **85** E1 2
PTSHD/EG BS20 **55** D1
Somerset Sq *CBRIS/FH* BS1 **3** E6
Somerset St *BATHSE* BA2 **4** B5
CBRIS/FH BS1 **3** F6
CBRISNE BS2 **76** B1
Somerset Ter *BMSTR* BS3 **92** C1
Somerton Cl *KGWD/HNM* BS15 **80** C2
Somerton Rd *CLVDN* BS21 **85** E3
HORF/LLZ BS7 **47** F5 3
Somervale Rd *RDSTK/MIDN* BA3 **162** B2
Somerville Cl *KEYN* BS31 **108** C5 3
Somerville Rd *WNSC* BS25 **154** C1
Sommerville Rd *RDLND/MONT* BS6 **64** C3
Sommerville Rd South
RDLND/MONT BS6 **65** D4 13
Sophia Gdns *MTN/WRL* BS22 **130** A3
Sorrel Cl *THNB/SVB* BS35 **9** D2
TRWBR BA14 **159** D2
Soundwell Rd *KGWD/HNM* BS15 **68** A5 4
South Av *BATHSE* BA2 **122** A5
PTSHD/EG BS20 **39** E5
YATE/CS BS37 **18** C4
Southbourne Gdns
CBATH/BATHN BA1 **123** F1 4
Southcot Pl *BATHSE* BA2 **4** D6 1
South Cft *HNLZ/SM/SNYPK/WT* BS9 **47** D4
WNSC BS25 **154** B2
South Dene
HNLZ/SM/SNYPK/WT BS9 **45** F5
Southdown *MTN/WRL* BS22 **129** E3
Southdown Av *BATHSE* BA2 **135** F2
Southdown Rd *BATHSE* BA2 **135** F1
HNLZ/SM/SNYPK/WT BS9 **46** A3
Southend Rd *WSM* BS23 **151** D1
Southernhay *CFTN/FAIL* BS8 **75** F3 8
MANG/FISH BS16 **68** A2
Southernhay Av *CFTN/FAIL* BS8 **75** F3 9
Southern Wy *CLVDN* BS21 **84** B2
Southey Av *KGWD/HNM* BS15 **68** B5
Southey Rd *CLVDN* BS21 **85** D2
Southey St *CBRISNE* BS2 **65** D5
Southfield Av *KGWD/HNM* BS15 **68** C5
Southfield Cl *NAIL* BS48 **87** D1 2
WSM BS23 **150** C4
Southfield Ct
HNLZ/SM/SNYPK/WT BS9 **46** B4 4
Southfield Rd
HNLZ/SM/SNYPK/WT BS9 **46** B4
NAIL BS48 **87** D1
RDLND/MONT BS6 **64** B5 7
Southgate *CBATH/BATHN* BA1 **4** C4 11
South Green St *CFTN/FAIL* BS8 **75** D3 15
South Gv *PTSHD/EG* BS20 **60** A2
RDLND/MONT BS6 **64** A1
South Hayes *EVILLE/WHL* BS5 **65** F2
Southlands *CBATH/BATHN* BA1 **111** F5
Southlands Wy *YTN/CONG* BS49 **133** D1
South Lawn *OMX/HUT/LCK* BS24 **153** E1
South Lawn Cl
OMX/HUT/LCK BS24 **153** E1
South Lea Rd
CBATH/BATHN BA1 **121** E2 2
Southleigh *BOAV* BA15 **146** C4
Southleigh Rd *CFTN/FAIL* BS8 **75** F1
South Liberty La *BMSTR* BS3 **90** C3
BMSTRD/HC/WWD BS13 **91** F2 10
Southmead *WNSC* BS25 **154** C4
Southmead Rd *BRSTK/PCHW* BS34 **47** F2
HNBRY/STHM BS10 **47** D3
HNLZ/SM/SNYPK/WT BS9 **46** C4
MTN/WRL BS22 **142** A3
Southmead Wy *HNBRY/STHM* BS10 **47** E3
Southover Cl
HNLZ/SM/SNYPK/WT BS9 **46** B3
Southridge Hts
OMX/HUT/LCK BS24 **151** F5
South Rd *BMSTR* BS3 **92** A1 12
KGWD/HNM BS15 **80** B1
PTSHD/EG BS20 **39** E5
RDLND/MONT BS6 **64** A4
RDSTK/MIDN BA3 **161** E3
WSM BS23 **140** B1
Southsea Rd *BRSTK/PCHW* BS34 **28** B1
Southside *WSM* BS23 **141** D2
South Side *YTN/CONG* BS49 **133** E1
Southside Cl *AVONM* BS11 **44** C4
Southside Crs *MTN/WRL* BS22 **127** F3 1
Southstoke Rd *BATHSE* BA2 **137** D4
South St *BMSTR* BS3 **91** F1
South Ter *WSM* BS23 **140** C2
South Vw *FRCTL/WBN* BS36 **32** C1
MANG/FISH BS16 **68** C1
PTSHD/EG BS20 **39** E4
Southview Cl
OMX/HUT/LCK BS24 **153** D3 2
South View Crs *FRCTL/WBN* BS36 **33** E2
South View Pl
RDSTK/MIDN BA3 **161** E2 3
South View Ri *FRCTL/WBN* BS36 **33** E2
South View Rd *BATHSE* BA2 **122** B4
Southview Rd *TRWBR* BA14 **159** D1
Southville Pl *BMSTR* BS3 **76** B5 10
Southville Rd *BMSTR* BS3 **76** A5
BOAV BA15 **147** E4
WSM BS23 **151** D1
South Wy *TRWBR* BA14 **157** D5
Southway Dr
OLD/WMLY/WICK BS30 **82** B4
Southway Rd *BOAV* BA15 **147** D5
Southwell St *CBRISNE* BS2 **76** A1 4
Southwick Rd *TRWBR* BA14 **158** C5
Southwood Av
HNLZ/SM/SNYPK/WT BS9 **45** D3
Southwood Dr
HNLZ/SM/SNYPK/WT BS9 **44** C3
Southwood Dr East
HNLZ/SM/SNYPK/WT BS9 **45** D3
Southwood Rd *TRWBR* BA14 **157** F4
Spalding Cl *CBRISNE* BS2 **65** E3
Spar Rd *YATE/CS* BS37 **19** E3
Spartley Dr
BMSTRD/HC/WWD BS13 **101** D1
Spartley Wk
BMSTRD/HC/WWD BS13 **101** D1 4
Speedwell Av *EVILLE/WHL* BS5 **78** B2 10
Speedwell Cl *THNB/SVB* BS35 **9** D2
TRWBR BA14 **159** D1
Speedwell Rd *KGWD/HNM* BS15 **67** F5
Spencer Dr *MTN/WRL* BS22 **130** A4
RDSTK/MIDN BA3 **161** D2
Sperring Ct *RDSTK/MIDN* BA3 **160** C4 2
Spey Cl *THNB/SVB* BS35 **8** C4
Spindleberry Gv *NAIL* BS48 **87** F2
Spinners Cft *TRWBR* BA14 **157** D5 5
Spinners End *MTN/WRL* BS22 **130** A3 14
The Spinney *ALMDB* BS32 **29** F1
FRCTL/WBN BS36 **32** C1 1
WSM BS23 **151** E4
Spires Vw *MANG/FISH* BS16 **66** C1 8
Spring Crs *BATHSE* BA2 **4** D5
Springfield *BOAV* BA15 **147** E3
THNB/SVB BS35 **8** C4 2
Springfield Av *AVONM* BS11 **43** E5 4
HORF/LLZ BS7 **65** D1
MANG/FISH BS16 **52** B5
MTN/WRL BS22 **142** C1
Springfield Buildings
RDSTK/MIDN BA3 **163** D1
Springfield Cl *BATHSE* BA2 **121** F5 4
MANG/FISH BS16 **52** B4 2
TRWBR BA14 **157** E2 1
Springfield Gv
HNLZ/SM/SNYPK/WT BS9 **63** F1
Springfield Pk *TRWBR* BA14 **157** E3
Springfield Rd *MANG/FISH* BS16 **52** B5 2
PTSHD/EG BS20 **55** F1
PTSHD/EG BS20 **60** A2 9

RDLND/MONT BS6 64 B5
Springfields *BRSTK/PCHW* BS34 48 B1
Spring Gdns *BRSG/KWL/STAPK* BS4 93 E3
Spring Gardens Rd
CBATH/BATHN BA1 4 C3 11
Spring Hl *CBRISNE* BS2 76 B1 16
KGWD/HNM BS15 68 C4
MTN/WRL BS22 128 B5
Spring Hill Dr *MTN/WRL* BS22 142 C1 5
Spring La *CBATH/BATHN* BA1 113 F5
Springleaze *BRSG/KWL/STAPK* BS4 93 E3
MANG/FISH BS16 52 B4
Spring Ri *PTSHD/EG* BS20 56 A3
Spring St *BMSTR* BS3 76 C5
Spring Street Pl *BMSTR* BS3 76 C5
Spring Va *MTN/WRL* BS22 128 B5 2
Springville Cl
OLD/WMLY/WICK BS30 97 E1 7
Springwood Dr *HNBRY/STHM* BS10 25 E5
Spring Wood Gdns
OMX/HUT/LCK BS24 153 D2
Spruce Wy *BRSTK/PCHW* BS34 27 F1 1
The Square
BRSG/KWL/STAPK BS4 93 E3 4
Squires Ct
OLD/WMLY/WICK BS30 97 D1 5
Squires Leaze *THNB/SVB* BS35 9 D2
Stabbins Cl *MTN/WRL* BS22 130 A2 3
Stackpool Rd *BMSTR* BS3 76 A5
Staddlestones *RDSTK/MIDN* BA3 160 C5
Stadium Rd *RDLND/MONT* BS6 64 A1
Stafford Crs *THNB/SVB* BS35 8 B3
Stafford Pl *WSM* BS23 141 D2
Stafford Rd *CBRISNE* BS2 65 E4 14
PTSHD/EG BS20 56 C2 6
WSM BS23 141 E2
Staffords Ct
OLD/WMLY/WICK BS30 81 E3 3
Stafford St *BMSTR* BS3 92 B1 5
Stainer Cl
BRSG/KWL/STAPK BS4 102 B1 3
Stallard St *TRWBR* BA14 156 C4
Stall St *CBATH/BATHN* BA1 4 C4 12
Stanbridge Cl *MANG/FISH* BS16 52 A5 1
Stanbridge Rd *MANG/FISH* BS16 52 A5
Stanbury Av *MANG/FISH* BS16 67 F1
Stanbury Rd *BMSTR* BS3 92 C1
Stancomb Av *TRWBR* BA14 157 E3
Standfast Rd *HNBRY/STHM* BS10 26 A5
Standish Av *BRSTK/PCHW* BS34 12 C4
Standish Cl *HNBRY/STHM* BS10 46 A2 1
Standon Wy *HNBRY/STHM* BS10 47 D1 6
Stane Wy *AVONM* BS11 43 D4 4
Stanfield Cl *HORF/LLZ* BS7 48 C5 4
Stanford Cl *FRCTL/WBN* BS36 16 A5
Stanhope Pl *CBATH/BATHN* BA1 122 C4 8
Stanhope Rd
OLD/WMLY/WICK BS30 97 D2
WSM BS23 151 D2
Stanhope St *CBRISNE* BS2 77 E4
Stanley Av *BRSTK/PCHW* BS34 48 C1
HORF/LLZ BS7 64 C3
Stanley Cha *EVILLE/WHL* BS5 66 B4
Stanley Ct *RDSTK/MIDN* BA3 161 E2 4
Stanley Crs *BRSTK/PCHW* BS34 48 C1
Stanley Gdns
OLD/WMLY/WICK BS30 81 F5
Stanley Gv *WSM* BS23 7 E1
Stanley Hl *BRSG/KWL/STAPK* BS4 77 E5
Stanley Md *ALMDB* BS32 13 F3 4
Stanley Pk *EVILLE/WHL* BS5 65 F5
Stanley Park Rd *MANG/FISH* BS16 68 C3
Stanley Rd *KGWD/HNM* BS15 69 F5
RDLND/MONT BS6 64 A4
WSM BS23 7 F1
Stanley Rd West *BATHSE* BA2 122 B5 2
Stanley St *BMSTR* BS3 92 A1 13
Stanley St North *BMSTR* BS3 91 F1 10
Stanley St South *BMSTR* BS3 92 A1
Stanley Ter *BMSTR* BS3 92 A2 4
Stanshawe Crs *YATE/CS* BS37 19 F4
Stanshawes Dr *YATE/CS* BS37 19 E4
Stanshaw Rd *MANG/FISH* BS16 50 B4
Stanshaws Cl *BRSTK/PCHW* BS34 12 C3
Stanton Cl *KGWD/HNM* BS15 69 D5
TRWBR BA14 159 D2 6
Stanton Rd *HNBRY/STHM* BS10 47 F2
Stanway *OLD/WMLY/WICK* BS30 97 F3
Stanway Cl *BATHSE* BA2 136 B4
Staple Gv *KEYN* BS31 106 B2
Staple Grove Crs
EVILLE/WHL BS5 79 E2 5
Staplehill Rd *MANG/FISH* BS16 67 F2
Staples Cl *CLVDN* BS21 85 E3 6
Staples Gn *MTN/WRL* BS22 130 A4 10
Staples Rd *YATE/CS* BS37 19 E3 5
Stapleton Cl *MANG/FISH* BS16 66 B1 3
Stapleton Rd *EVILLE/WHL* BS5 65 F4
Star Barn Rd *FRCTL/WBN* BS36 31 F1
Starcross Rd *MTN/WRL* BS22 129 F5
Star La *MANG/FISH* BS16 67 D3
PTSHD/EG BS20 60 B2 3
Starling Cl *MTN/WRL* BS22 143 D2
The Star *TRWBR* BA14 149 E2
Station Ap *WSM* BS23 6 D2 2
Station Av *MANG/FISH* BS16 67 E2
Station Cl *NAIL* BS48 87 E5
OLD/WMLY/WICK BS30 82 A1
YATE/CS BS37 21 E5
YTN/CONG BS49 132 C2
Station La *HORF/LLZ* BS7 65 E2
Station Rd *AVONM* BS11 60 B1
BRSG/KWL/STAPK BS4 94 B2
BRSTK/PCHW BS34 28 B5
BRSTK/PCHW BS34 29 D2
BRSTK/PCHW BS34 49 D1
CBATH/BATHN BA1 122 A3
CLVDN BS21 85 D1 4
FRCTL/WBN BS36 31 F4
FRCTL/WBN BS36 33 D3
HNBRY/STHM BS10 25 F5
HORF/LLZ BS7 65 D2
KEYN BS31 106 C1
KGWD/HNM BS15 69 D3
MANG/FISH BS16 67 E2
MTN/WRL BS22 129 E5
MTN/WRL BS22 130 B5
NAIL BS48 87 E3
OLD/WMLY/WICK BS30 82 A2
PTSHD/EG BS20 39 E5
PTSHD/EG BS20 58 A2
PTSHD/EG BS20 60 A2
RDLND/MONT BS6 64 B4
RDSTK/MIDN BA3 161 E2
THNB/SVB BS35 10 A4
TRWBR BA14 149 E1
WSM BS23 6 D2
YATE/CS BS37 17 E2
YATE/CS BS37 19 D3
YATE/CS BS37 19 F3
YATE/CS BS37 20 A4
YTN/CONG BS49 116 A2
YTN/CONG BS49 132 C2
Station Wy *MANG/FISH* BS16 67 E2
TRWBR BA14 156 C4
Staunton Flds *HGRV/WHIT* BS14 104 A4
Staunton La *HGRV/WHIT* BS14 104 A3
Staunton Wy *HGRV/WHIT* BS14 104 B3 1
Staveley Crs *HNBRY/STHM* BS10 47 D1
Stavordale Gv *HGRV/WHIT* BS14 103 F1
Staynes Crs *KGWD/HNM* BS15 80 C1 2
Steam Mills *RDSTK/MIDN* BA3 160 C4
Stean Bridge Rd *ALMDB* BS32 29 F2
Steel Ct *OLD/WMLY/WICK* BS30 97 D1
Steel Mills *KEYN* BS31 107 D3
Stella Gv *BMSTR* BS3 91 E2
Stephens Dr
OLD/WMLY/WICK BS30 81 D4
Stephen St *EVILLE/WHL* BS5 78 A1
Stepney Rd *EVILLE/WHL* BS5 66 A5
Stepney Wk *EVILLE/WHL* BS5 66 A5
Sterncourt Rd *MANG/FISH* BS16 50 B4
Stevens Crs *BMSTR* BS3 77 D5
Stevens Wk *ALMDB* BS32 13 E5
Steway La *CBATH/BATHN* BA1 115 E2
Stibbs Ct
OLD/WMLY/WICK BS30 81 D5 18
Stibbs Hl *EVILLE/WHL* BS5 79 E2
Stickland *CLVDN* BS21 84 C3 5
Stile Acres *AVONM* BS11 44 B2
Stillhouse La *BMSTR* BS3 76 B5
Stillingfleet Rd
BMSTRD/HC/WWD BS13 102 A2
Stillman Cl
BMSTRD/HC/WWD BS13 100 C3
Still Man Cl *TRWBR* BA14 149 E1
Stinchcombe *YATE/CS* BS37 19 F4 2
Stirling Cl *YATE/CS* BS37 19 E1 2
Stirling Rd *BRSG/KWL/STAPK* BS4 94 A1 3
Stirling Wy *KEYN* BS31 106 C3 1
Stirtingale Av *BATHSE* BA2 136 A2
Stirtingale Rd *BATHSE* BA2 136 A2
Stock La *YTN/CONG* BS49 133 F5
Stockton Cl *HGRV/WHIT* BS14 103 D3 1
OLD/WMLY/WICK BS30 97 F1 3
Stock Wy North *NAIL* BS48 87 D2
Stock Wy South *NAIL* BS48 87 D2 5
Stockwell Av *MANG/FISH* BS16 52 B5
Stockwell Cl *MANG/FISH* BS16 52 A4
Stockwell Dr *MANG/FISH* BS16 52 B5
Stockwood Crs
BRSG/KWL/STAPK BS4 93 D2
Stockwood Hl *KEYN* BS31 96 A5
Stockwood La *HGRV/WHIT* BS14 104 C2
Stockwood Ms
BRSG/KWL/STAPK BS4 79 D4 4
Stockwood Rd
BRSG/KWL/STAPK BS4 95 D3
HGRV/WHIT BS14 104 C2
Stodelegh Cl *MTN/WRL* BS22 130 A4 11
Stoke Bridge Av
BRSTK/PCHW BS34 29 E2
Stokefield Cl *THNB/SVB* BS35 8 B3
Stoke Gv *HNLZ/SM/SNYPK/WT* BS9 45 F5
Stoke Hamlet
HNLZ/SM/SNYPK/WT BS9 46 A5 1
Stoke Hl *HNLZ/SM/SNYPK/WT* BS9 62 C2
Stoke La *BRSTK/PCHW* BS34 13 D5
HNLZ/SM/SNYPK/WT BS9 46 A5 2
MANG/FISH BS16 49 F4
Stokeleigh Wk
HNLZ/SM/SNYPK/WT BS9 62 A1 4
Stokemead *BRSTK/PCHW* BS34 13 D5 2
Stoke Mdw *ALMDB* BS32 13 E4
Stoke Paddock Rd
HNLZ/SM/SNYPK/WT BS9 45 E5
Stoke Park Rd
HNLZ/SM/SNYPK/WT BS9 62 C2
Stoke Park Rd South
HNLZ/SM/SNYPK/WT BS9 62 C3
Stoke Rd *HNLZ/SM/SNYPK/WT* BS9 63 D3
PTSHD/EG BS20 56 B1
Stokes Ct *OLD/WMLY/WICK* BS30 81 E5 7
Stokes Cft *CBRIS/FH* BS1 76 C1
Stoke View Rd *MANG/FISH* BS16 67 D3 6
Stoneable Rd *RDSTK/MIDN* BA3 163 D1
Stoneberry Rd *HGRV/WHIT* BS14 103 E4
Stonebridge *CLVDN* BS21 85 D3 9
Stonebridge Pk *EVILLE/WHL* BS5 66 B4
Stonebridge Rd *WSM* BS23 151 E1 3
Stonechat Gdns *MANG/FISH* BS16 49 F5
Stonehill *OLD/WMLY/WICK* BS30 80 C5
Stonehouse Cl *BATHSE* BA2 137 F4
Stonehouse La *BATHSE* BA2 137 F3
Stone La *FRCTL/WBN* BS36 31 F4
Stoneleigh Crs
BRSG/KWL/STAPK BS4 93 E2
Stoneleigh Dr
OLD/WMLY/WICK BS30 81 D4
Stoneleigh Rd
BRSG/KWL/STAPK BS4 93 E2
Stoneleigh Wk
BRSG/KWL/STAPK BS4 93 E2 1
Stonewell Dr *YTN/CONG* BS49 133 D3
Stonewell Gv *YTN/CONG* BS49 133 D3
Stonewell La *YTN/CONG* BS49 133 D3
Stonewell Park Rd
YTN/CONG BS49 133 D3
Stoneyfield Cl *PTSHD/EG* BS20 59 F2
Stoneyfields *PTSHD/EG* BS20 59 F2
Stormont Cl *WSM* BS23 151 E2 2
Stothard Rd *HORF/LLZ* BS7 48 C4
Stottbury Rd *HORF/LLZ* BS7 65 E3
Stoulton Gv *HNBRY/STHM* BS10 26 B5 6
Stourden Cl *MANG/FISH* BS16 50 B4 4
Stourton Dr *OLD/WMLY/WICK* BS30 81 D5
Stover Rd *YATE/CS* BS37 18 B3
Stowey Pk *YTN/CONG* BS49 117 D4 2
Stowey Rd *YTN/CONG* BS49 116 B3
Stowick Crs *AVONM* BS11 45 D2
Stradbrook Av *EVILLE/WHL* BS5 79 F2
Stradling Av *WSM* BS23 7 E6
Stradling Rd *AVONM* BS11 45 D1
Straight St *CBRISNE* BS2 3 G3
Stratford Cl *HGRV/WHIT* BS14 103 D4 6
Strathmore Rd *HORF/LLZ* BS7 47 F5
Stratton Rd *KEYN* BS31 108 C4
Stratton St *CBRISNE* BS2 76 C1
Strawberry Cl *NAIL* BS48 86 C3 9
Strawberry Hl *CLVDN* BS21 71 E5
Strawbridge Rd
EVILLE/WHL BS5 77 F2 12
Stream Cl *HNBRY/STHM* BS10 27 E5
Streamcross *YTN/CONG* BS49 117 E1
Streamleaze *THNB/SVB* BS35 8 C4
Streamside *CLVDN* BS21 85 F1 5
Stream Side *MANG/FISH* BS16 52 A5
Streamside Rd *YATE/CS* BS37 20 B4 6
The Stream *MANG/FISH* BS16 50 C1
The Street *RDSTK/MIDN* BA3 162 C2
TRWBR BA14 149 E1
Stretford Av *EVILLE/WHL* BS5 78 B1 10
Stretford Rd *EVILLE/WHL* BS5 78 B1
Stride Cl *THNB/SVB* BS35 10 B4 2
Strode Rd *CLVDN* BS21 84 B4
Strode Wy *CLVDN* BS21 84 B3
Stroud Rd *AVONM* BS11 60 C1
Stuart Cl *TRWBR* BA14 149 E5 1
Stuart Pl *BATHSE* BA2 122 B4
Stuart Rd *WSM* BS23 7 H6
Stuart St *EVILLE/WHL* BS5 78 A2
Studley Ri *TRWBR* BA14 159 D1
Sturden La *MANG/FISH* BS16 31 D5
Sturdon Rd *BMSTR* BS3 91 E1
Sturmer Cl *YATE/CS* BS37 19 F1
Sturminster Cl *HGRV/WHIT* BS14 104 B1
Sturminster Rd *HGRV/WHIT* BS14 94 B5
Sulis Manor Rd *BATHSE* BA2 136 B5
Sumerlin Dr *CLVDN* BS21 85 F1
Summer Down Wk
TRWBR BA14 158 C3 1
Summerfield *MTN/WRL* BS22 130 A4 12
Summerfield Rd
CBATH/BATHN BA1 123 E1
Summerhayes
OLD/WMLY/WICK BS30 82 B4 3
Summer Hl *BRSG/KWL/STAPK* BS4 77 E5
Summerhill Rd *CBATH/BATHN* BA1 122 B1
EVILLE/WHL BS5 79 D1
Summerhill Ter *EVILLE/WHL* BS5 79 D2 1
Summerlands Rd *WSM* BS23 141 F2 2
Summer La *BATHSE* BA2 137 F4
BNWL BS29 144 C3
MTN/WRL BS22 144 A1
OMX/HUT/LCK BS24 144 A1 3

Summer La North MTN/WRL BS22 .. 129 F5
Summerleaze KEYN BS31 .... 96 C5 1
MANG/FISH BS16 .... 68 A3
TRWBR BA14 .... 158 A1
Summers Rd CBRISNE BS2 .... 65 E5 17
Summer St BMSTR BS3 .... 76 A5 9
Sundays Hl ALMDB BS32 .... 12 B1
Sunderland Pl CFTN/FAIL BS8 .... 75 F1
Sunderland St BATHSE BA2 .... 4 D2 1
Sundridge Pk YATE/CS BS37 .... 19 F5
Sunfield Rd
OMX/HUT/LCK BS24 .... 153 D2 5
Sunningdale YATE/CS BS37 .... 19 F5
Sunningdale Cl NAIL BS48 .... 87 F3 11
Sunningdale Dr
OLD/WMLY/WICK BS30 .... 81 F3
Sunningdale Rd MTN/WRL BS22 ...... 129 E4
Sunny Bank KGWD/HNM BS15 .... 67 F5
Sunnydene BRSG/KWL/STAPK BS4 .... 78 B5
Sunny Hl HNLZ/SM/SNYPK/WT BS9 .. 44 C4
Sunnyhill Dr AVONM BS11 .... 43 F5 5
Sunnymead KEYN BS31 .... 107 D4
RDSTK/MIDN BA3 .... 160 C2
Sunnymede Rd NAIL BS48 .... 86 C2
Sunnyside FRCTL/WBN BS36 .... 32 C1
HNLZ/SM/SNYPK/WT BS9 .... 62 C1 3
Sunnyside Crs CLVDN BS21 .... 85 D1 5
Sunnyside La MANG/FISH BS16 .... 50 C1
YATE/CS BS37 .... 19 D4
Sunnyside Rd CLVDN BS21 .... 85 D1
WSM BS23 .... 6 D4
Sunnyside Rd North WSM BS23 .... 6 D4
Sunnyvale CLVDN BS21 .... 84 A3
Sunnyvale Dr
OLD/WMLY/WICK BS30 .... 97 F1
Sunny Wk KGWD/HNM BS15 .... 67 F5
Sunridge MANG/FISH BS16 .... 51 E5
Sunridge Cl RDSTK/MIDN BA3 .... 160 C4
Sunridge Pk RDSTK/MIDN BA3 .... 160 C4
Sunrise Gv BRSG/KWL/STAPK BS4 ...... 78 B5
Surrey Rd HORF/LLZ BS7 .... 64 C3 4
Surrey St CBRISNE BS2 .... 76 C1
Suspension Br CFTN/FAIL BS8 .... 74 C2
Sussex St CBRISNE BS2 .... 77 E3
Sutherland Av MANG/FISH BS16 .... 51 F4
YATE/CS BS37 .... 19 E1 5
Sutherland Dr
OMX/HUT/LCK BS24 .... 152 C3
Sutherland Pl CFTN/FAIL BS8 .... 63 E4
Sutton Av BRSG/KWL/STAPK BS4 ...... 78 B5
Sutton Cl MTN/WRL BS22 .... 143 D2 9
Sutton St BATHSE BA2 .... 5 E2
Swainswick HGRV/WHIT BS14 .... 103 D1
Swainswick Gdns
CBATH/BATHN BA1 .... 114 A5
Swainswick La CBATH/BATHN BA1 .. 114 B4
Swaish Dr OLD/WMLY/WICK BS30 ...... 81 D5
Swallow Cl RDSTK/MIDN BA3 ...... 161 E4 4
Swallow Dr TRWBR BA14 .... 156 B4
Swallow Gdns MTN/WRL BS22 .... 142 C2
Swallow Pk THNB/SVB BS35 .... 8 C1
Swallows Ct BRSTK/PCHW BS34 .... 29 F4
The Swallows MTN/WRL BS22 .... 142 C3
Swallow St CBATH/BATHN BA1 ...... 4 C4 13
Swan Cl MTN/WRL BS22 .... 143 D2 10
Swan Dr TRWBR BA14 .... 149 D4
Swane Rd HGRV/WHIT BS14 .... 105 D1 3
Swan La FRCTL/WBN BS36 .... 15 D5
Swanmoor Crs HNBRY/STHM BS10 .. 26 B4
Sweets Cl KGWD/HNM BS15 .... 68 C4
Sweets Rd KGWD/HNM BS15 .... 68 B4
Swift Cl MTN/WRL BS22 .... 143 E1 7
Swiss Rd BMSTR BS3 .... 91 D2
WSM BS23 .... 7 E1
Sycamore Cl EVILLE/WHL BS5 .... 66 C5
KGWD/HNM BS15 .... 95 F1 2
NAIL BS48 .... 87 D2 6
WSM BS23 .... 141 F2 3
Sycamore Dr BRSTK/PCHW BS34 ...... 27 F1
THNB/SVB BS35 .... 8 C3 2
Sycamore Gv TRWBR BA14 .... 158 C2
Sycamore Rd RDSTK/MIDN BA3 ...... 163 E2
Sydenham Buildings BATHSE BA2 .. 122 C5
Sydenham Hl RDLND/MONT BS6 ...... 64 B5
Sydenham La RDLND/MONT BS6 ...... 64 B5
Sydenham Rd BATHSE BA2 .... 122 C4 9
BRSG/KWL/STAPK BS4 .... 93 E1
RDLND/MONT BS6 .... 64 B5
Sydenham Wy KGWD/HNM BS15 ...... 96 A1
Sydney Buildings BATHSE BA2 .... 5 F4
Sydney Ms BATHSE BA2 .... 5 E2
Sydney Pl BATHSE BA2 .... 5 E2
Sydney Rd BATHSE BA2 .... 5 F2
Sydney Rw CBRIS/FH BS1 .... 75 F4
Sydney Whf BATHSE BA2 .... 5 F3
Sylvan Wy
HNLZ/SM/SNYPK/WT BS9 .... 44 C5
Sylvia Av BMSTR BS3 .... 93 D1
Symes Av BMSTRD/HC/WWD BS13 .. 102 A4
Symes Pk CBATH/BATHN BA1 .... 111 E5
Symington Rd MANG/FISH BS16 .... 67 F1
Syston Wy KGWD/HNM BS15 .... 68 B5

T

Tabernacle Rd KGWD/HNM BS15 ...... 80 A3
Tackley Rd EVILLE/WHL BS5 .... 65 F3 3
Tadwick La CBATH/BATHN BA1 .... 113 F2
Talbot Av KGWD/HNM BS15 .... 67 F5
Talbot Rd BRSG/KWL/STAPK BS4 .... 93 F2
TRWBR BA14 .... 158 A1
Talgarth Rd HORF/LLZ BS7 .... 65 D2
Tallis Gv BRSG/KWL/STAPK BS4 .... 102 B1
Tamar Cl THNB/SVB BS35 .... 9 D5 5
Tamar Dr KEYN BS31 .... 107 E3
Tamar Rd CBRISNE BS2 .... 78 A3
MTN/WRL BS22 .... 129 F5
Tamblyn Cl RDSTK/MIDN BA3 .... 163 D1
Tamworth Rd KEYN BS31 .... 106 C3 2
Tankard's Cl CFTN/FAIL BS8 .... 2 B1
Tanner Cl OLD/WMLY/WICK BS30 ...... 81 D4
Tanners Wk BATHSE BA2 .... 121 D5
Tanorth Cl HGRV/WHIT BS14 .... 103 E4
Tanorth Rd HGRV/WHIT BS14 .... 103 D4
The Tanyard
OLD/WMLY/WICK BS30 .... 97 F2 5
Tapsters OLD/WMLY/WICK BS30 .... 81 E5 8
Tarnock Av HGRV/WHIT BS14 .... 93 E5
Tarragon Pl ALMDB BS32 .... 30 A1
Taunton Rd MTN/WRL BS22 .... 130 A3
Taunton Wk HORF/LLZ BS7 .... 48 B4 4
Taverner Cl
BRSG/KWL/STAPK BS4 .... 92 B5 11
Tavistock Rd BRSG/KWL/STAPK BS4 .. 93 D3
MTN/WRL BS22 .... 129 F5 7
Tavistock Wk
BRSG/KWL/STAPK BS4 .... 93 D3 2
Tawny Wy MTN/WRL BS22 .... 143 E2 1
Taylor Cl KGWD/HNM BS15 .... 81 D1 6
Taylor Ct MTN/WRL BS22 .... 130 A3 15
Taylor Gdns
BMSTRD/HC/WWD BS13 .... 101 D3 3
Taylors Vw TRWBR BA14 .... 157 D3
Tayman Cl HNBRY/STHM BS10 ...... 47 F5 4
Tayman Rdg
OLD/WMLY/WICK BS30 .... 98 B4
Taynton Cl OLD/WMLY/WICK BS30 .... 97 F2
Teal Cl ALMDB BS32 .... 13 E3 6
MTN/WRL BS22 .... 143 E1 8
Teasel Md ALMDB BS32 .... 29 F1 3
Teasel Wk MTN/WRL BS22 .... 142 C3
Teddington Cl BATHSE BA2 .... 136 A1
Teesdale Cl MTN/WRL BS22 .... 142 C2
Teewell Av MANG/FISH BS16 .... 68 C2
Teewell Cl MANG/FISH BS16 .... 68 C2 8
Teewell Hl MANG/FISH BS16 .... 68 C2
Teignmouth Rd
BRSG/KWL/STAPK BS4 .... 93 E3 5
CLVDN BS21 .... 85 E1
Telephone Av CBRIS/FH BS1 .... 2 C3
Telford Wk EVILLE/WHL BS5 .... 67 E5
Templar Rd YATE/CS BS37 .... 19 F2
Temple Back CBRIS/FH BS1 .... 3 F3
Temple Ga CBRIS/FH BS1 .... 3 F5
Templeland Rd
BMSTRD/HC/WWD BS13 .... 101 D2 5
Temple Rose St CBRIS/FH BS1 .... 3 F4
Temple St BMSTR BS3 .... 91 F2 11
CBRIS/FH BS1 .... 3 F4
KEYN BS31 .... 106 C2
Temple Wy CBRIS/FH BS1 .... 3 F4
Temple Way U/P CBRISNE BS2 .... 3 G2 1
Tenby Rd KEYN BS31 .... 106 B3
Tenby St EVILLE/WHL BS5 .... 77 F2
Tennessee Gv RDLND/MONT BS6 .. 64 A1 3
Tenniscourt Rd KGWD/HNM BS15 .... 69 E5
Tennis Rd BRSG/KWL/STAPK BS4 ...... 93 D2
Tennyson Av CLVDN BS21 .... 84 B2
Tennyson Cl KEYN BS31 .... 107 D1
Tennyson Rd CBATH/BATHN BA1 .... 122 B3
HORF/LLZ BS7 .... 64 C1 1
WSM BS23 .... 151 E2
Tenth Av HORF/LLZ BS7 .... 48 C2
Tereslake Gn HNBRY/STHM BS10 ...... 27 E4
Terrace Wk CBATH/BATHN BA1 ...... 4 C4 14
Terrell Gdns EVILLE/WHL BS5 ...... 78 B2 11
Terrell St CBRISNE BS2 .... 2 C1
CBRISNE BS2 .... 76 B1 17
Tetbury Cl BRSTK/PCHW BS34 .... 13 D5
Tetbury Gdns NAIL BS48 .... 87 F3
Tetbury Rd KGWD/HNM BS15 .... 79 F1
Teviot Rd KEYN BS31 .... 107 E3
Tewkesbury Rd CBRISNE BS2 ...... 65 E4 15
Tewther Rd
BMSTRD/HC/WWD BS13 .... 102 A4
Teyfant Rd
BMSTRD/HC/WWD BS13 .... 102 C4
Teyfant Wk
BMSTRD/HC/WWD BS13 .... 102 C3 1
Thackeray Av CLVDN BS21 .... 71 D5
Thackeray Rd CLVDN BS21 .... 71 E5
Thackeray Wk HORF/LLZ BS7 .... 48 B3 4
Thanet Rd BMSTR BS3 .... 91 F2
Thatcher Cl PTSHD/EG BS20 .... 56 B2 1
Thatchers Cl EVILLE/WHL BS5 .... 79 F2 4
There-and-back-again La
CFTN/FAIL BS8 .... 2 A2 2
Theresa Av HORF/LLZ BS7 .... 64 C2
Thestfield Dr TRWBR BA14 .... 149 D5
Theynes Cft LGASH BS41 .... 89 F3
Thicket Av MANG/FISH BS16 .... 68 A3
Thicket Rd MANG/FISH BS16 .... 68 A2
Thicket Wk THNB/SVB BS35 .... 8 C3 3
Thiery Rd BRSG/KWL/STAPK BS4 ...... 94 A2
Thingwall Pk MANG/FISH BS16 .... 66 C3
Third Av BATHSE BA2 .... 122 B5
HORF/LLZ BS7 .... 48 B2
Third Wy AVONM BS11 .... 43 D1
Thirlmere Ct
OLD/WMLY/WICK BS30 .... 82 B3
Thirlmere Rd BRSTK/PCHW BS34 .. 12 B5 1
WSM BS23 .... 151 F1
Thistle St BMSTR BS3 .... 91 F1 11
Thomas Av MANG/FISH BS16 .... 52 C3
Thomas Pring Wk
EVILLE/WHL BS5 .... 67 E5 2
Thomas St CBATH/BATHN BA1 .... 123 E2
CBRISNE BS2 .... 76 C1 13
Thomas St North
RDLND/MONT BS6 .... 64 B5
Thompson Rd HGRV/WHIT BS14 .. 104 C1 7
Thomson Rd EVILLE/WHL BS5 ...... 77 F1 13
Thornbank Pl BATHSE BA2 .... 122 C5
Thornbury Dr WSM BS23 .... 150 B3
Thornbury Rd WSM BS23 .... 150 B3
Thorn Cl MTN/WRL BS22 .... 130 A5 2
YATE/CS BS37 .... 19 E4
Thorndale CFTN/FAIL BS8 .... 75 E1
Thorndale Cl MTN/WRL BS22 ...... 142 C2 3
Thornhayes Cl FRCTL/WBN BS36 .. 16 B5 1
The Thornhills MANG/FISH BS16 .... 50 C5
Thornleigh Rd HORF/LLZ BS7 .... 64 C1
Thornmead Gv
HNBRY/STHM BS10 .... 46 B1 4
Thorns Farm YATE/CS BS37 .... 19 F4 3
Thornycroft Cl HORF/LLZ BS7 .... 48 C4
Three Queens' La CBRIS/FH BS1 .... 3 E4
Three Wells Rd
BMSTRD/HC/WWD BS13 .... 101 D3
Thrissell St EVILLE/WHL BS5 .... 77 E1
Throgmorton Rd
BRSG/KWL/STAPK BS4 .... 93 D5
Thrush Cl MTN/WRL BS22 .... 143 D2 11
Thurlestone HGRV/WHIT BS14 .... 103 D2
Thurlow Rd EVILLE/WHL BS5 .... 66 A4
Thurstons Barton
EVILLE/WHL BS5 .... 66 C5 4
Tibberton KGWD/HNM BS15 .... 81 E1
Tibbott Rd HGRV/WHIT BS14 .... 104 A2
Tibbott Wk HGRV/WHIT BS14 .... 104 A2
Tichborne Rd EVILLE/WHL BS5 .... 78 A2
WSM BS23 .... 141 D1
Tide Gv AVONM BS11 .... 44 B3
Tidenham Wy BRSTK/PCHW BS34 .... 12 A4
Tilley Cl KEYN BS31 .... 107 E5
Tilling Rd HNBRY/STHM BS10 .... 47 F4
Tilling Wk HNBRY/STHM BS10 .... 47 F4
Tilting Rd THNB/SVB BS35 .... 8 B2
Timber Dene MANG/FISH BS16 .... 66 B2
Timberscombe Wk
HGRV/WHIT BS14 .... 104 A2 1
The Timbers RDSTK/MIDN BA3 .... 161 E5
Timbrell St TRWBR BA14 .... 157 D3
Timsbury Rd BMSTR BS3 .... 92 C2
Tindell Ct
OLD/WMLY/WICK BS30 .... 81 D5 19
Tintern Av EVILLE/WHL BS5 .... 78 B1 11
Tintern Cl OLD/WMLY/WICK BS30 .. 81 D3 2
Tippetts Rd KGWD/HNM BS15 .... 80 B3
Tirley Wy MTN/WRL BS22 .... 128 A5
Tiverton Gdns MTN/WRL BS22 .... 129 F5
Tiverton Rd CLVDN BS21 .... 85 E3 7
Tiverton Wk MANG/FISH BS16 .... 67 E4
Tivoli La WSM BS23 .... 141 D2 13
Toll Bridge Rd CBATH/BATHN BA1 .. 114 C4
Toll Rd WSM BS23 .... 151 E5
Tone Rd CLVDN BS21 .... 85 D3 10
Tor Cl MTN/WRL BS22 .... 129 F5
Tormarton Crs HNBRY/STHM BS10 .. 26 A4
Tormynton Rd MTN/WRL BS22 .... 129 D5
Toronto Rd HORF/LLZ BS7 .... 48 B3
Torpoint Rd BMSTR BS3 .... 92 B3
Torrance Cl OLD/WMLY/WICK BS30 .. 82 B3
Torridge Rd KEYN BS31 .... 107 E3
Torrington Av
BRSG/KWL/STAPK BS4 .... 93 D4
Torrington Crs MTN/WRL BS22 .. 129 F4 10
Tortworth Rd HORF/LLZ BS7 .... 64 C1
Totnes Cl MTN/WRL BS22 .... 129 F5 8
Totshill Dr
BMSTRD/HC/WWD BS13 .... 102 C3
Totshill Gv
BMSTRD/HC/WWD BS13 .... 102 C3 2
Totterdown La
OMX/HUT/LCK BS24 .... 151 F4
Totterdown Rd WSM BS23 .... 151 E2 3
Touchstone Av BRSTK/PCHW BS34 .. 29 F3
Tovey Cl MTN/WRL BS22 .... 129 D3 11
Towcester Rd TRWBR BA14 .... 159 D3
Tower Cl TRWBR BA14 .... 156 A5

Tower Hl *CBRISNE* BS2 .... 3 F3
Tower La *CBRIS/FH* BS1 .... 2 D2
OLD/WMLY/WICK BS30 .... 81 E3
Tower Rd *KGWD/HNM* BS15 .... 68 A5
PTSHD/EG BS20 .... 55 E2
Tower Rd North *KGWD/HNM* BS15 .... 81 F1
Tower Rd South
OLD/WMLY/WICK BS30 .... 81 F3
Tower St *CBRIS/FH* BS1 .... 3 F4
Tower Wk *WSM* BS23 .... 140 C1 3
Townsend *ALMDB* BS32 .... 12 A1
Townsend Cl *HGRV/WHIT* BS14 .... 105 D2
Townsend Rd *HGRV/WHIT* BS14 .... 105 D2
Townshend Rd *MTN/WRL* BS22 .... 129 F2
Towpath Rd *TRWBR* BA14 .... 149 D5
Tozers Hl *BRSG/KWL/STAPK* BS4 .... 94 A2 1
Trafalgar Rd *CBATH/BATHN* BA1 .... 121 F1
Trafalgar Ter *BMSTR* BS3 .... 91 F2 12
Tralee Wk *BRSG/KWL/STAPK* BS4 .... 92 B3
Tramway Rd *BRSG/KWL/STAPK* BS4 .. 94 A1
Tranmere Av *HNBRY/STHM* BS10 .... 26 B4
Tranmere Gv *HNBRY/STHM* BS10 .... 26 B5
Tratman Wk *HNBRY/STHM* BS10 .. 26 A5 7
Travers Cl *BRSG/KWL/STAPK* BS4 102 B1 4
Travers Wk *BRSTK/PCHW* BS34 .... 29 F3
Trawden Cl *WSM* BS23 .... 141 F1 4
Tredegar Rd *MANG/FISH* BS16 .... 67 F3
Treefield Pl *CBRISNE* BS2 .... 65 E4 16
Treefield Rd *CLVDN* BS21 .... 85 D2
Tree Leaze *YATE/CS* BS37 .... 20 A3
Tregarth Rd *BMSTR* BS3 .... 91 D3
Trelawn Cl *MTN/WRL* BS22 .... 130 C5
Trelawney Av *EVILLE/WHL* BS5 .... 78 B1 12
Trelawney Pk
BRSG/KWL/STAPK BS4 .... 94 B1
Trelawney Rd *RDLND/MONT* BS6 .... 64 A5
Tremlett Ms *MTN/WRL* BS22 .... 130 A3 16
Trenchard Rd *KEYN* BS31 .... 108 B5
Trenchard St *CBRIS/FH* BS1 .... 2 B3
Trench La *ALMDB* BS32 .... 13 E2
FRCTL/WBN BS36 .... 14 A3
Trendlewood Pk *MANG/FISH* BS16 .... 66 C2
Trendlewood Wy *NAIL* BS48 .... 87 E4
Trenleigh Dr *MTN/WRL* BS22 .... 129 F5 9
Trent Dr *THNB/SVB* BS35 .... 9 D5
Trent Gv *KEYN* BS31 .... 107 E3
Trentham Cl *CBRISNE* BS2 .... 65 E4 17
Tresham Cl *ALMDB* BS32 .... 13 E3
Trevanna Rd *BMSTR* BS3 .... 91 D3
Trevelyan Rd *WSM* BS23 .... 7 E2
Trevelyan Wk
HNBRY/STHM BS10 .... 26 A5 8
Treverdowe Wk
HNBRY/STHM BS10 .... 25 E5
Trevethin Cl *KGWD/HNM* BS15 .... 80 A2 1
Trevisa Gv *HNBRY/STHM* BS10 .... 27 D4
Trewartha Cl *WSM* BS23 .... 141 E2 3
Trewartha Pk *WSM* BS23 .... 141 E2
Triangle East *BATHSE* BA2 .... 122 B5
Triangle North *BATHSE* BA2 .... 122 B4
Triangle South *CFTN/FAIL* BS8 .... 75 F2 6
Triangle West *BATHSE* BA2 .... 122 B5
CFTN/FAIL BS8 .... 75 F2 7
Trident Cl *MANG/FISH* BS16 .... 52 B2
Trim Br *CBATH/BATHN* BA1 .... 4 B3 14
Trim St *CBATH/BATHN* BA1 .... 4 B3 15
Trinder Rd *PTSHD/EG* BS20 .... 59 F2
Trinity Cl *CBATH/BATHN* BA1 .... 4 A4
Trinity Rd *BATHSE* BA2 .... 137 F3
CBRISNE BS2 .... 77 E2
NAIL BS48 .... 86 C3
WSM BS23 .... 140 B1
Trinity St *CBATH/BATHN* BA1 .... 4 B4 9
CBRISNE BS2 .... 77 E2
Trinity Wk *CBRISNE* BS2 .... 3 H1
Tripps Cnr *YTN/CONG* BS49 .... 117 D4 3
Troon *YATE/CS* BS37 .... 19 F5
Troon Dr *OLD/WMLY/WICK* BS30 .... 81 F3 4
Troopers' Hill Rd *EVILLE/WHL* BS5 .... 79 D3
Trossachs Dr *BATHSE* BA2 .... 124 B2
Trowbridge Rd *BOAV* BA15 .... 147 E4
HNBRY/STHM BS10 .... 47 D2
Trowbridge Wk
HNBRY/STHM BS10 .... 47 D2 2
Trowle *TRWBR* BA14 .... 156 A2
Truro Rd *BMSTR* BS3 .... 91 F1
NAIL BS48 .... 87 F3 12
Trym Cross Rd
HNLZ/SM/SNYPK/WT BS9 .... 62 A1
Trymleaze
HNLZ/SM/SNYPK/WT BS9 .... 62 A1 5
Trym Rd *HNLZ/SM/SNYPK/WT* BS9 .... 46 B4
Trym Side
HNLZ/SM/SNYPK/WT BS9 .... 62 A1
Trymwood Cl *HNBRY/STHM* BS10 .... 46 A1
Tuckett La *MANG/FISH* BS16 .... 51 D4 2
Tuckmill *CLVDN* BS21 .... 84 B3
Tudor Cl *OLD/WMLY/WICK* BS30 .... 98 A1
Tudor Dr *TRWBR* BA14 .... 149 E5
Tudor Rd *CBRISNE* BS2 .... 65 D5 9
EVILLE/WHL BS5 .... 66 A5
KGWD/HNM BS15 .... 80 A4
MTN/WRL BS22 .... 129 F3
PTSHD/EG BS20 .... 56 C2 7
Tuffley Rd *HNBRY/STHM* BS10 .... 47 D3
Tufton Av *AVONM* BS11 .... 44 B3
Tugela Rd *BMSTRD/HC/WWD* BS13 .. 91 D5
Tunstall Cl
HNLZ/SM/SNYPK/WT BS9 .... 62 C2
Turley Rd *EVILLE/WHL* BS5 .... 66 B5 3
Turnberry *OLD/WMLY/WICK* BS30 .. 81 F3 5
Turnbridge Rd *HNBRY/STHM* BS10 .... 27 D4
Turnbury *YATE/CS* BS37 .... 19 F5
Turnbury Av *NAIL* BS48 .... 87 F3
Turnbury Cl *MTN/WRL* BS22 .... 129 E4 11
Turner Cl *KEYN* BS31 .... 107 E2
Turner Ct *MTN/WRL* BS22 .... 129 E4 12
Turner Gdns *HORF/LLZ* BS7 .... 48 C5 5
Turners Ct
OLD/WMLY/WICK BS30 .... 81 D5 20
Turner Wy *CLVDN* BS21 .... 84 B3
Turnpike Cl *YATE/CS* BS37 .... 19 F3 1
Turtlegate Av
BMSTRD/HC/WWD BS13 .... 100 C3
Turtlegate Wk
BMSTRD/HC/WWD BS13 .... 100 C3
Turville Dr *HORF/LLZ* BS7 .... 48 B5
Tutton Wy *CLVDN* BS21 .... 85 D4
Tweed Cl *THNB/SVB* BS35 .... 8 C4
Tweed Rd *CLVDN* BS21 .... 84 C3
Tweeny La *OLD/WMLY/WICK* BS30 .... 82 B3
Twenty Acres Rd
HNBRY/STHM BS10 .... 47 D1 7
Twerton Farm Cl *BATHSE* BA2 .... 121 F4 4
Twickenham Rd
RDLND/MONT BS6 .... 64 A1 4
Two Acres Rd *HGRV/WHIT* BS14 .... 93 E5
Two Mile Ct *KGWD/HNM* BS15 .... 79 F1 3
Twomile Hill Rd *KGWD/HNM* BS15 .... 79 F1
Two Rivers Wy *YTN/CONG* BS49 .... 133 E2
The Twynings *KGWD/HNM* BS15 .... 68 C4
Tybalt Wy *BRSTK/PCHW* BS34 .... 29 F3
Tydeman Rd *PTSHD/EG* BS20 .... 57 D1
Tyler Cl *KGWD/HNM* BS15 .... 80 C3
Tyler's La *MANG/FISH* BS16 .... 68 B1 5
Tyndale Av *MANG/FISH* BS16 .... 67 E2
YATE/CS BS37 .... 19 E2
Tyndale Rd *KGWD/HNM* BS15 .... 68 C4 5
Tyndale Vw *THNB/SVB* BS35 .... 8 B4 3
Tyndall Av *CFTN/FAIL* BS8 .... 2 A1
Tyndall Rd *EVILLE/WHL* BS5 .... 77 F1 14
Tyndalls Park Ms *CBRISNE* BS2 .... 76 A1 5
Tyndall's Park Rd *CFTN/FAIL* BS8 .... 75 F1
Tyndalls Wy *HNBRY/STHM* BS10 .... 47 F3
Tyne Rd *HORF/LLZ* BS7 .... 64 B3
Tyne St *CBRISNE* BS2 .... 65 E4
Tyning Cl *HGRV/WHIT* BS14 .... 93 E5
TRWBR BA14 .... 156 A5 3
YATE/CS BS37 .... 19 F3
Tyning End *BATHSE* BA2 .... 5 F6
Tyning Hl *RDSTK/MIDN* BA3 .... 163 E1
Tyning La *CBATH/BATHN* BA1 .... 123 F1 5
Tyning Rd *BATHSE* BA2 .... 125 D1
BATHSE BA2 .... 138 A3
BMSTR BS3 .... 93 D1
KEYN BS31 .... 108 C5
Tynings Ms *WSM* BS23 .... 151 D1 2
The Tynings *CLVDN* BS21 .... 84 A3 1
The Tyning *BATHSE* BA2 .... 5 F6
Tynte Av *BMSTRD/HC/WWD* BS13 .. 102 B4
Tyntesfield Rd
BMSTRD/HC/WWD BS13 .... 91 E5
Tyrone Wk
BRSG/KWL/STAPK BS4 .... 92 C4 6
Tyrrel Wy *BRSTK/PCHW* BS34 .... 29 F2

U

Ullswater Cl
OLD/WMLY/WICK BS30 .... 82 B3 5
WSM BS23 .... 151 F1 2
YATE/CS BS37 .... 19 F2
Ullswater Dr *CBATH/BATHN* BA1 .... 113 E5
Ullswater Rd *HNBRY/STHM* BS10 .... 46 C2
Underbanks *PTSHD/EG* BS20 .... 60 B2
Underhill Av *RDSTK/MIDN* BA3 .... 160 C2
Underhill Dr *WSM* BS23 .... 150 C3
Underhill La *RDSTK/MIDN* BA3 .... 160 B2
Underwood Av *MTN/WRL* BS22 .... 142 A1
Underwood Rd *PTSHD/EG* BS20 .... 56 A3
Union Pl *WSM* BS23 .... 6 B1 7
Union Rd *CBRISNE* BS2 .... 3 H3
Union St *CBATH/BATHN* BA1 .... 4 C3 12
CBRIS/FH BS1 .... 2 D1
NAIL BS48 .... 86 B3
TRWBR BA14 .... 157 D3
WSM BS23 .... 6 B2 2
Unity Rd *KEYN* BS31 .... 107 E2
Unity St *CBRIS/FH* BS1 .... 2 B3 5
CBRISNE BS2 .... 3 G2
KGWD/HNM BS15 .... 80 A1
University Wk *CFTN/FAIL* BS8 .... 2 A1
Uphill Dr *CBATH/BATHN* BA1 .... 113 F5 2
Uphill Rd *HORF/LLZ* BS7 .... 65 D1 2
Uphill Rd North *WSM* BS23 .... 150 C1
Uphill Rd South *WSM* BS23 .... 150 C3
Uphill Wy *WSM* BS23 .... 150 C4
Upjohn Crs
BMSTRD/HC/WWD BS13 .... 102 B4
Uplands Dr *KEYN* BS31 .... 109 D5
Uplands Rd *KEYN* BS31 .... 108 C5
MANG/FISH BS16 .... 68 A3
The Uplands *NAIL* BS48 .... 86 B5
Upper Bath Rd *THNB/SVB* BS35 .... 8 B4 4
Upper Belgrave Rd *CFTN/FAIL* BS8 .... 63 E4
Upper Belmont Rd *HORF/LLZ* BS7 .... 64 C3
Upper Bloomfield Rd *BATHSE* BA2 .. 136 B4
Upper Borough Walls
CBATH/BATHN BA1 .... 4 C3 13
Upper Bristol Rd
CBATH/BATHN BA1 .... 122 B3
WSM BS23 .... 142 A1
Upper Broad St *TRWBR* BA14 .... 156 C3
Upper Byron Pl *CFTN/FAIL* BS8 .... 75 F2 8
Upper Chapel La *FRCTL/WBN* BS36 .. 33 D1
Upper Cheltenham Pl
RDLND/MONT BS6 .... 64 C5
Upper Church Rd *WSM* BS23 .... 140 B1
Upper Church St *CBATH/BATHN* BA1 .. 4 A1
Upper Cranbrook Rd
RDLND/MONT BS6 .... 63 F2
Upper East Hayes
CBATH/BATHN BA1 .... 123 F1
Upper Hedgemead Rd
CBATH/BATHN BA1 .... 123 D2
Upper Lambridge St
CBATH/BATHN BA1 .... 124 A1 4
Upper Lansdown Ms
CBATH/BATHN BA1 .... 123 D1
Upper Maudlin St *CBRISNE* BS2 .... 2 C1
Upper Oldfield Pk *BATHSE* BA2 .... 122 C5
Upper Perry Hl *BMSTR* BS3 .... 76 A5
Upper Regents Pk *BOAV* BA15 .... 147 D3
Upper Sandhurst Rd
BRSG/KWL/STAPK BS4 .... 78 B5
Upper Station Rd *MANG/FISH* BS16 .. 68 A2
Upper Stone Cl *FRCTL/WBN* BS36 .... 33 D1
Upper St *BRSG/KWL/STAPK* BS4 .... 77 E5
Upper Sydney St *BMSTR* BS3 .... 91 F1 12
Upper Wells St *CBRIS/FH* BS1 .... 2 B3 6
Upton Rd *BMSTR* BS3 .... 75 F5
Urchinwood La *YTN/CONG* BS49 .. 133 F2 1
Urfords Dr *MANG/FISH* BS16 .... 51 D5 5

V

Valda Rd *MTN/WRL* BS22 .... 128 B5 3
Vale Crs *MTN/WRL* BS22 .... 130 B5
Vale End *NAIL* BS48 .... 86 C3
Vale La *BMSTRD/HC/WWD* BS13 .... 92 A4
Valentine Cl *HGRV/WHIT* BS14 .... 103 F2
Valerian Cl *AVONM* BS11 .... 44 A5
Vale St *BRSG/KWL/STAPK* BS4 .... 93 E1 7
Valetta Cl *WSM* BS23 .... 151 E2 4
Vale Vw *RDSTK/MIDN* BA3 .... 163 D2
Vale View Ter *CBATH/BATHN* BA1 .... 115 D4
Valley Cl *NAIL* BS48 .... 87 D2
Valley Gdns *MANG/FISH* BS16 .... 52 A3
NAIL BS48 .... 87 D2
Valley Rd *BMSTRD/HC/WWD* BS13 .... 91 E4
CFTN/FAIL BS8 .... 74 A2
CLVDN BS21 .... 71 F4
MANG/FISH BS16 .... 69 E1
OLD/WMLY/WICK BS30 .... 82 B3
PTSHD/EG BS20 .... 55 E3
Valley View Cl *CBATH/BATHN* BA1 .. 113 F5
Valley View Rd *CBATH/BATHN* BA1 .. 114 A4
Valley Wk *RDSTK/MIDN* BA3 .... 161 E2
Valley Way Rd *NAIL* BS48 .... 87 D1
The Valls *ALMDB* BS32 .... 30 A2
Valma Rocks *EVILLE/WHL* BS5 .... 79 E3 6
Van Diemen's La
CBATH/BATHN BA1 .... 112 C5
Vandyck Av *KEYN* BS31 .... 107 D1
Vane St *BATHSE* BA2 .... 5 E2
Varsity Wy *OMX/HUT/LCK* BS24 .... 144 A4
Vassall Ct *MANG/FISH* BS16 .... 67 F1
Vassall Rd *MANG/FISH* BS16 .... 67 F1
Vaughan Cl *HNBRY/STHM* BS10 .... 26 A5
Vayre Cl *YATE/CS* BS37 .... 21 D4
Vellore La *BATHSE* BA2 .... 5 F2
Ventnor Rd *BRSTK/PCHW* BS34 .... 28 C5
EVILLE/WHL BS5 .... 67 D5
Venus St *YTN/CONG* BS49 .... 133 E4
Vera Rd *MANG/FISH* BS16 .... 67 D4
Verbena Wy *MTN/WRL* BS22 .... 143 F1
Vereland Rd *OMX/HUT/LCK* BS24 .... 153 D3
Verlands *YTN/CONG* BS49 .... 133 E1
Vernham Gv *BATHSE* BA2 .... 136 A4
Vernon Cl *KEYN* BS31 .... 108 B4
Vernon Pk *BATHSE* BA2 .... 122 A4
Vernon St *BRSG/KWL/STAPK* BS4 .. 77 D5 6
Vernslade *CBATH/BATHN* BA1 .... 111 E5
Verrier Rd *EVILLE/WHL* BS5 .... 78 A2 15
Verwood Dr *OLD/WMLY/WICK* BS30 .. 98 A3
Vian End *MTN/WRL* BS22 .... 129 E3 6
Vicarage Cl *MTN/WRL* BS22 .... 129 F4 11
Vicarage Ct *KGWD/HNM* BS15 .... 79 F4 9
Vicarage Rd *BMSTR* BS3 .... 75 F5

BMSTRD/HC/WWD BS13 ... 101 D1
CFTN/FAIL BS8 ... 74 B3
EVILLE/WHL BS5 ... 78 A1
FRCTL/WBN BS36 ... 33 D3
KGWD/HNM BS15 ... 79 F4
THNB/SVB BS35 ... 11 D3
Vicars Cl *MANG/FISH* BS16 ... 67 F2 5
Victoria Av *EVILLE/WHL* BS5 ... 78 A2
Victoria Bridge Rd *BATHSE* BA2 ... 122 C4
Victoria Cl *BATHSE* BA2 ... 122 A5
PTSHD/EG BS20 ... 56 B1 3
THNB/SVB BS35 ... 8 B1
Victoria Crs *THNB/SVB* BS35 ... 10 B4
Victoria Gdns *CBATH/BATHN* BA1 ... 115 D4
RDLND/MONT BS6 ... 64 B5 8
TRWBR BA14 ... 157 E2
Victoria Gv *BMSTR* BS3 ... 76 C5
Victoria Pde *EVILLE/WHL* BS5 ... 78 A1
Victoria Pk *KGWD/HNM* BS15 ... 80 B1
MANG/FISH BS16 ... 67 E1
WSM BS23 ... 140 C1
Victoria Pl *BMSTR* BS3 ... 92 A1 14
WSM BS23 ... 140 C2 9
Victoria Qd *WSM* BS23 ... 141 D2 14
Victoria Rd *AVONM* BS11 ... 42 C3
BATHSE BA2 ... 122 B4 5
CBRISNE BS2 ... 77 E4 1
CLVDN BS21 ... 84 C1
KEYN BS31 ... 108 B4
KGWD/HNM BS15 ... 80 A4
OLD/WMLY/WICK BS30 ... 82 B4
TRWBR BA14 ... 157 F2
Victoria Sq *CFTN/FAIL* BS8 ... 75 E2
PTSHD/EG BS20 ... 56 B1
WSM BS23 ... 6 A1 1
Victoria St *CBRIS/FH* BS1 ... 3 E3
MANG/FISH BS16 ... 68 B2
Victoria Ter *BATHSE* BA2 ... 122 B4 6
CBRISNE BS2 ... 77 F4
CFTN/FAIL BS8 ... 75 D3 16
Victoria Wk *RDLND/MONT* BS6 ... 64 B5
Victor Rd *BMSTR* BS3 ... 92 A1 15
Victor St *CBRISNE* BS2 ... 77 D5
EVILLE/WHL BS5 ... 77 F3 11
Vigor Rd
BMSTRD/HC/WWD BS13 ... 101 F2 8
Village Cl *YATE/CS* BS37 ... 19 E4 2
Villiers Rd *EVILLE/WHL* BS5 ... 65 F5
Vilner La *THNB/SVB* BS35 ... 8 B5
Vimpany Cl *HNBRY/STHM* BS10 ... 26 A5
Vincent Cl *AVONM* BS11 ... 45 D1
Vine Gdns *MTN/WRL* BS22 ... 129 F5
The Vinery *WNSC* BS25 ... 154 C5
Vining Wk *EVILLE/WHL* BS5 ... 77 F1 15
Vinny Av *MANG/FISH* BS16 ... 52 B4
Vintery Leys
HNLZ/SM/SNYPK/WT BS9 ... 46 C4
Virginia Cl *YATE/CS* BS37 ... 20 B4
Vivian St *BMSTR* BS3 ... 92 B1
Vivien Av *RDSTK/MIDN* BA3 ... 161 D2
Vowell Cl *BMSTRD/HC/WWD* BS13 ... 101 F3
Vowles Cl *NAIL* BS48 ... 87 F1
Vynes Cl *NAIL* BS48 ... 87 F3 13
Vyvyan Rd *CFTN/FAIL* BS8 ... 75 E2
Vyvyan Ter *CFTN/FAIL* BS8 ... 75 E2

W

Wade Rd *YATE/CS* BS37 ... 18 B2
Wades Rd *BRSTK/PCHW* BS34 ... 28 C5
Wade St *CBRISNE* BS2 ... 77 D1
Wadham Dr *MANG/FISH* BS16 ... 50 C2
Wadham Gv *MANG/FISH* BS16 ... 69 F1
Wadham St *WSM* BS23 ... 140 C2 10
Wagtail Gdns *MTN/WRL* BS22 ... 143 D2 12
Wainbridge Crs *THNB/SVB* BS35 ... 11 D3
Wainbrook Dr *EVILLE/WHL* BS5 ... 66 B4
Wains Cl *CLVDN* BS21 ... 84 C2 6
Wainwright Cl *MTN/WRL* BS22 ... 130 A3 17
Wakedean Gdns *YTN/CONG* BS49 ... 116 A2
Wakeford Rd *MANG/FISH* BS16 ... 52 B4 3
Walcot St *CBATH/BATHN* BA1 ... 4 C1
Waldegrave Rd
CBATH/BATHN BA1 ... 122 C1
Waldegrave Ter *RDSTK/MIDN* BA3 ... 163 D2
Walden Rd *KEYN* BS31 ... 107 E3
Walford Av *MTN/WRL* BS22 ... 130 A3
Walker Cl *EVILLE/WHL* BS5 ... 77 F2
MANG/FISH BS16 ... 52 B4
Walker St *CBRISNE* BS2 ... 76 A1
Walker Wy *THNB/SVB* BS35 ... 8 B5
Wallace Rd *CBATH/BATHN* BA1 ... 123 F1
Wallingford Rd
BRSG/KWL/STAPK BS4 ... 92 B5
Walliscote Av
HNLZ/SM/SNYPK/WT BS9 ... 47 D5
Walliscote Rd
HNLZ/SM/SNYPK/WT BS9 ... 47 D5
WSM BS23 ... 6 C2 1
Walliscote Rd South *WSM* BS23 ... 150 C1 2
Wallscourt Rd *BRSTK/PCHW* BS34 ... 48 C1
Wallscourt Rd South
BRSTK/PCHW BS34 ... 48 C2
Walnut Av *YATE/CS* BS37 ... 20 B3
Walnut Cl *KEYN* BS31 ... 106 A3
NAIL BS48 ... 87 D4
OMX/HUT/LCK BS24 ... 151 F3
PTSHD/EG BS20 ... 59 E3
THNB/SVB BS35 ... 9 D3
Walnut Crs *KGWD/HNM* BS15 ... 81 D1
Walnut Dr *BATHSE* BA2 ... 136 C1
Walnut Gv *TRWBR* BA14 ... 158 B1
Walnut La *KGWD/HNM* BS15 ... 81 E1 5
Walnut Wk
BMSTRD/HC/WWD BS13 ... 101 E1
Walsh Av *HGRV/WHIT* BS14 ... 93 E5
Walsh Cl *OMX/HUT/LCK* BS24 ... 152 A3
Walshe Av *YATE/CS* BS37 ... 21 D4
Walsingham Rd *RDLND/MONT* BS6 ... 64 C4
Walter St *BMSTR* BS3 ... 75 E5
Waltham End
OMX/HUT/LCK BS24 ... 143 F2 4
Walton Av *BRSG/KWL/STAPK* BS4 ... 78 B4
Walton Cl *KEYN* BS31 ... 106 B3
OLD/WMLY/WICK BS30 ... 98 A3 3
Walton Heath *YATE/CS* BS37 ... 20 A4
Walton Ri
HNLZ/SM/SNYPK/WT BS9 ... 46 B3
Walton Rd *AVONM* BS11 ... 43 E5
CLVDN BS21 ... 71 F4
Walton St *EVILLE/WHL* BS5 ... 65 F5
Walwyn Cl *BATHSE* BA2 ... 121 E4
Wansbeck Rd *KEYN* BS31 ... 107 E3 1
Wansbrough Rd *MTN/WRL* BS22 ... 130 A3
Wanscow Wk
HNLZ/SM/SNYPK/WT BS9 ... 46 C5
Wansdyke Rd *BATHSE* BA2 ... 136 A4
Wapley Hl *YATE/CS* BS37 ... 35 F4
Wapley Rd *YATE/CS* BS37 ... 36 B5
Wapping Rd *CBRIS/FH* BS1 ... 2 C5
Warbler Cl *TRWBR* BA14 ... 156 B4
Warden Rd *BMSTR* BS3 ... 76 A5
Wardour Rd *BRSG/KWL/STAPK* BS4 ... 92 B4
Wareham Cl *NAIL* BS48 ... 86 C3
Warleigh Dr *CBATH/BATHN* BA1 ... 115 E4
Warleigh La *CBATH/BATHN* BA1 ... 125 F2
Warman Cl *HGRV/WHIT* BS14 ... 105 D1
Warman Rd *HGRV/WHIT* BS14 ... 105 D1
Warmington Rd *HGRV/WHIT* BS14 ... 94 A4
Warminster Rd *BATHSE* BA2 ... 124 A2
CBRISNE BS2 ... 65 E4 18
Warner Cl *KGWD/HNM* BS15 ... 81 D3 3
Warne Rd *WSM* BS23 ... 7 H3
The Warns
OLD/WMLY/WICK BS30 ... 81 E5 9
Warren Cl *ALMDB* BS32 ... 13 E2 3
OMX/HUT/LCK BS24 ... 152 C3 2
Warren Gdns *HGRV/WHIT* BS14 ... 105 D2 2
Warren La *LGASH* BS41 ... 88 C4
Warren Rd *BRSTK/PCHW* BS34 ... 28 C5
Warren Wy *YATE/CS* BS37 ... 19 F2 2
Warrilow Cl *MTN/WRL* BS22 ... 130 A2
Warrington Rd
BRSG/KWL/STAPK BS4 ... 94 B2
Warwick Av *EVILLE/WHL* BS5 ... 65 F5 12
Warwick Cl *MTN/WRL* BS22 ... 142 B2
OLD/WMLY/WICK BS30 ... 97 F2 4
THNB/SVB BS35 ... 8 A3
Warwick Rd *CBATH/BATHN* BA1 ... 121 F3 3
EVILLE/WHL BS5 ... 65 F5 13
KEYN BS31 ... 106 B3
RDLND/MONT BS6 ... 63 F5 9
Washing Pound La
HGRV/WHIT BS14 ... 103 F3
Washington Av *EVILLE/WHL* BS5 ... 66 A5
Washpool La *BATHSE* BA2 ... 135 D2
Watch Elm Cl *ALMDB* BS32 ... 29 F2
Watchhouse Rd *PTSHD/EG* BS20 ... 60 B2
Watchill Av
BMSTRD/HC/WWD BS13 ... 101 D1
Watchill Cl
BMSTRD/HC/WWD BS13 ... 101 D1
Waterbridge Rd
BMSTRD/HC/WWD BS13 ... 101 D2
Watercress Rd *CBRISNE* BS2 ... 65 D3
Waterdale Cl *HNBRY/STHM* BS10 ... 47 D4
Waterdale Gdns
HNLZ/SM/SNYPK/WT BS9 ... 47 D4
Waterford Cl *THNB/SVB* BS35 ... 9 D4
Waterford Pk *RDSTK/MIDN* BA3 ... 162 B4
Waterford Rd
HNLZ/SM/SNYPK/WT BS9 ... 46 C5 3
Waterhouse La *BATHSE* BA2 ... 138 C5
Water La *BMSTR* BS3 ... 93 D1
BRSG/KWL/STAPK BS4 ... 94 B3
CBRIS/FH BS1 ... 3 F3
KGWD/HNM BS15 ... 95 F2
PTSHD/EG BS20 ... 60 A2
Waterloo Bldgs *BATHSE* BA2 ... 121 F4 5
Waterloo Pl *CBRISNE* BS2 ... 3 H2
Waterloo Rd *CBRISNE* BS2 ... 3 H2
RDSTK/MIDN BA3 ... 163 D2
Waterloo St *CBRISNE* BS2 ... 3 H1
CFTN/FAIL BS8 ... 75 D2
Watermore Cl *FRCTL/WBN* BS36 ... 33 D1
Waterside Crs *RDSTK/MIDN* BA3 ... 162 A3
Waterside Dr *ALMDB* BS32 ... 12 B4
Waterside Pk *PTSHD/EG* BS20 ... 54 B2 1
Waterside Rd *RDSTK/MIDN* BA3 ... 161 F3
Waterside Wy *RDSTK/MIDN* BA3 ... 162 A3
Water's La
HNLZ/SM/SNYPK/WT BS9 ... 46 B4
Waters Rd *KGWD/HNM* BS15 ... 80 A1
Waterworks Rd *TRWBR* BA14 ... 156 B5
Watery La *BATHSE* BA2 ... 121 E4
NAIL BS48 ... 86 A2
Wathen Rd *RDLND/MONT* BS6 ... 65 D3
Watkins Yd
HNLZ/SM/SNYPK/WT BS9 ... 46 B3 3
Watley's End Rd *FRCTL/WBN* BS36 ... 31 F1
Watling Wy *AVONM* BS11 ... 43 E4
Watson Av *BRSG/KWL/STAPK* BS4 ... 78 B5
Watson's Rd
OLD/WMLY/WICK BS30 ... 97 D1
Watters Cl *FRCTL/WBN* BS36 ... 33 E2
Wavell Cl *YATE/CS* BS37 ... 19 E1
Waveney Rd *KEYN* BS31 ... 107 E4
Waverley Rd *AVONM* BS11 ... 43 E5 5
NAIL BS48 ... 87 F5
RDLND/MONT BS6 ... 64 A5
WSM BS23 ... 151 E1
YATE/CS BS37 ... 18 C3
Waverley St *EVILLE/WHL* BS5 ... 65 E5 18
Wayfield Gdns *CBATH/BATHN* BA1 ... 115 D3
Wayford Cl *KEYN* BS31 ... 107 E4 1
Wayland Rd *MTN/WRL* BS22 ... 129 D4 5
Wayleaze *FRCTL/WBN* BS36 ... 33 E1
Wayside *MTN/WRL* BS22 ... 128 C5
Wayside Cl *FRCTL/WBN* BS36 ... 32 C1
Wayside Dr *CLVDN* BS21 ... 71 E4
The Weal *CBATH/BATHN* BA1 ... 111 F5
Weatherley Dr *PTSHD/EG* BS20 ... 55 D3
Weatherly Av *BATHSE* BA2 ... 136 B3
Weavers Dr *TRWBR* BA14 ... 157 D5
Webbers Ct *TRWBR* BA14 ... 158 A1
Webbs Heath
OLD/WMLY/WICK BS30 ... 82 B2
Webb St *EVILLE/WHL* BS5 ... 77 E1 14
Webbs Wood Rd *ALMDB* BS32 ... 30 A1
Wedgewood Rd *MANG/FISH* BS16 ... 51 E2
Wedgwood Cl *HGRV/WHIT* BS14 ... 103 F2 7
Wedgwood Rd *BATHSE* BA2 ... 121 D5
Wedmore Cl *KGWD/HNM* BS15 ... 81 D2
WSM BS23 ... 151 E3
Wedmore Pk *BATHSE* BA2 ... 135 E2
Wedmore Rd *CLVDN* BS21 ... 84 B3
KEYN BS31 ... 108 B3
NAIL BS48 ... 87 D4 6
Wedmore V *BMSTR* BS3 ... 92 C2 1
Weedon Cl *CBRISNE* BS2 ... 65 E4 19
Weetwood Rd *YTN/CONG* BS49 ... 133 E1
Weight Rd *EVILLE/WHL* BS5 ... 78 A2 16
The Weind *MTN/WRL* BS22 ... 128 C5
Weir La *CFTN/FAIL* BS8 ... 72 C4
Weir Rd *YTN/CONG* BS49 ... 133 E3
Welland Rd *KEYN* BS31 ... 107 D3
Wellard Cl *MTN/WRL* BS22 ... 130 A3 18
Well Cl *LGASH* BS41 ... 89 F3
OMX/HUT/LCK BS24 ... 152 A3
WNSC BS25 ... 154 C4
Wellgarth Rd
BRSG/KWL/STAPK BS4 ... 93 E2
Wellgarth Wk
BRSG/KWL/STAPK BS4 ... 93 E3
Well House Cl
HNLZ/SM/SNYPK/WT BS9 ... 62 C4
Wellington Av *RDLND/MONT* BS6 ... 64 C5
Wellington Buildings
CBATH/BATHN BA1 ... 111 F5
Wellington Crs *HORF/LLZ* BS7 ... 47 F5
Wellington Dr
HNLZ/SM/SNYPK/WT BS9 ... 47 E5
YATE/CS BS37 ... 18 C3
Wellington Hl *HORF/LLZ* BS7 ... 47 F5
Wellington Hl West
HNLZ/SM/SNYPK/WT BS9 ... 47 D4
Wellington La *RDLND/MONT* BS6 ... 64 C5
Wellington Ms *AVONM* BS11 ... 60 B1 3
Wellington Pk *CFTN/FAIL* BS8 ... 63 E5
Wellington Pl *WSM* BS23 ... 6 B1 8
Wellington Rd *CBRISNE* BS2 ... 3 F1 5
KGWD/HNM BS15 ... 68 B4 2
YATE/CS BS37 ... 19 F1
Wellington Ter *CLVDN* BS21 ... 70 C4
Wellington Wk *HNBRY/STHM* BS10 ... 47 D4
Well La *YTN/CONG* BS49 ... 116 C3
Wellow Brook Meadow
RDSTK/MIDN BA3 ... 161 E2
Well Pk *YTN/CONG* BS49 ... 133 E2
Wells Cl *HGRV/WHIT* BS14 ... 104 A2
Wellsea Gv *WSM* BS23 ... 142 A3
Wells Rd *BATHSE* BA2 ... 4 A6
BRSG/KWL/STAPK BS4 ... 77 D5
HGRV/WHIT BS14 ... 93 F4
RDSTK/MIDN BA3 ... 162 A3
Wells St *BMSTR* BS3 ... 75 E5 6
Wellstead Av *YATE/CS* BS37 ... 19 E4
Wellsway *BATHSE* BA2 ... 136 B5
KEYN BS31 ... 107 D3
Wellsway Pk *BATHSE* BA2 ... 136 B5 4
Welsford Av *MANG/FISH* BS16 ... 66 B2

Welsford Rd *MANG/FISH* BS16 .... **66** A2
Welsh Back *CBRIS/FH* BS1 .... **2** D5
Welton Gv *RDSTK/MIDN* BA3............ **161** D1
Welton Rd *RDSTK/MIDN* BA3............ **162** B2
Welton V *RDSTK/MIDN* BA3.............. **161** E2
Welton Wk *KGWD/HNM* BS15 .... **68** A4 3
Wemberham Crs *YTN/CONG* BS49 .. **116** A2
Wenmore Cl *MANG/FISH* BS16 .... **51** E2
Wentforth Dr *KGWD/HNM* BS15 .... **68** A4 4
Wentwood Dr
OMX/HUT/LCK BS24........................ **151** F4
Wentworth
OLD/WMLY/WICK BS30 .... **81** E3 4
YATE/CS BS37 .... **19** F4
Wentworth Cl *MTN/WRL* BS22 .. **129** F4 12
Wentworth Rd *HORF/LLZ* BS7........... **64** B3
Wesley Av *KGWD/HNM* BS15 .... **80** B4
RDSTK/MIDN BA3............................ **161** F3
Wesley Cl *MANG/FISH* BS16 .... **68** B3 5
Wesley Dr *MTN/WRL* BS22 .... **129** F4
Wesley Hl *KGWD/HNM* BS15 .... **68** B5 8
Wesley La *OLD/WMLY/WICK* BS30...... **81** F4
Wesley Pl *CFTN/FAIL* BS8 .... **63** E4
Wesley Rd *HORF/LLZ* BS7 .... **64** C2 3
RDSTK/MIDN BA3............................ **161** F3
TRWBR BA14.................................... **156** C5
Wesley St *BMSTR* BS3 .... **92** A1 16
Wessex Av *HORF/LLZ* BS7 .... **48** A4
Wessex Rd *OMX/HUT/LCK* BS24 ...... **152** A3
Westacre Cl *HNBRY/STHM* BS10 .... **46** B1
West Ashton Rd *TRWBR* BA14.......... **157** F5
West Av *BATHSE* BA2 .... **122** A5
Westaway Cl *YTN/CONG* BS49 ...... **116** C4 2
Westaway Pk *YTN/CONG* BS49 .... **117** D4
Westbourne Av *CLVDN* BS21 .... **84** C2 7
KEYN BS31 .... **106** C2 1
Westbourne Cl *MANG/FISH* BS16 .. **52** A4 4
Westbourne Crs *CLVDN* BS21 .... **84** C2 8
Westbourne Gdns *TRWBR* BA14........ **156** B4
Westbourne Pl *CFTN/FAIL* BS8 ...... **75** F1 4
Westbourne Rd
EVILLE/WHL BS5 .... **77** F1 16
MANG/FISH BS16 .... **52** A3
TRWBR BA14.................................... **156** B4
West Broadway
HNLZ/SM/SNYPK/WT BS9 .... **47** E5
Westbrook Pk *CBATH/BATHN* BA1 .. **111** E5
Westbrook Rd
BRSG/KWL/STAPK BS4 .... **94** B4
MTN/WRL BS22................................ **142** C1
Westbury Court Rd
HNLZ/SM/SNYPK/WT BS9 .... **46** A4
Westbury Crs *WSM* BS23 .... **151** E3
Westbury Hl
HNLZ/SM/SNYPK/WT BS9 .... **46** B4
Westbury La
HNLZ/SM/SNYPK/WT BS9 .... **44** C4
Westbury Pk *RDLND/MONT* BS6........ **63** E2
Westbury Rd *CFTN/FAIL* BS8 .... **63** E4 12
HNLZ/SM/SNYPK/WT BS9 .... **46** B5
HNLZ/SM/SNYPK/WT BS9 .... **63** E3
TRWBR BA14.................................... **159** D4
West Cl *BATHSE* BA2 .... **121** E5
West Coombe
HNLZ/SM/SNYPK/WT BS9 .... **45** E5
Westcourt Dr
OLD/WMLY/WICK BS30 .... **81** F5
West Cft *CLVDN* BS21 .... **84** B2
HNLZ/SM/SNYPK/WT BS9 .... **47** D4
Westcroft St *TRWBR* BA14................ **156** C3
West Dene
HNLZ/SM/SNYPK/WT BS9 .... **45** F5
West Dundry La *LGASH* BS41............ **100** C5
West End *CBRISNE* BS2...................... **76** B1
Westering Cl *MANG/FISH* BS16 ...... **69** E1 5
Westerleigh Cl *MANG/FISH* BS16 .. **52** A4 5
Westerleigh Rd *BATHSE* BA2 .... **137** F4
CLVDN BS21...................................... **84** B2
MANG/FISH BS16 .... **51** F5 2
YATE/CS BS37 .... **19** D5
Western Av *FRCTL/WBN* BS36 .... **16** B5
Western Dr *HGRV/WHIT* BS14 .... **92** C5
Western Rd *HORF/LLZ* BS7 .... **47** F5
Westfield *BOAV* BA15 .... **146** B2
CLVDN BS21...................................... **85** D4
Westfield Cl *BATHSE* BA2 .... **136** C2
KEYN BS31...................................... **106** A2
KGWD/HNM BS15............................ **80** B4
TRWBR BA14.................................... **156** A5
WSM BS23.. **150** C3
Westfield La *BRSTK/PCHW* BS34........ **29** F5
Westfield Pk *CBATH/BATHN* BA1...... **121** E3
RDLND/MONT BS6 .... **63** F5
Westfield Pl *CFTN/FAIL* BS8 .... **75** D2 3
Westfield Rd
HNLZ/SM/SNYPK/WT BS9 .... **46** B3
TRWBR BA14.................................... **156** A5
Westfield Wy *ALMDB* BS32 .... **13** E3
West Gdns *PTSHD/EG* BS20 .... **56** A1
Westgate Buildings
CBATH/BATHN BA1 .... **4** B3 16
Westgate St *CBATH/BATHN* BA1 .... **4** B3 17
West Gv *RDLND/MONT* BS6 .... **65** D5
Westhall Rd *CBATH/BATHN* BA1 ...... **122** B3
West Hl *PTSHD/EG* BS20...................... **56** A1
West Hill Rd *RDSTK/MIDN* BA3 .... **162** A3
Westland Av
OLD/WMLY/WICK BS30 .... **82** A5
West Lea Rd *CBATH/BATHN* BA1 ...... **121** E2
West Leaze Pl *ALMDB* BS32 .... **29** F2
Westleigh Cl *HNBRY/STHM* BS10 .. **47** E2 2
YATE/CS BS37 .... **19** D4
Westleigh Pk *HGRV/WHIT* BS14 .... **93** E4
Westleigh Rd *HNBRY/STHM* BS10...... **47** D2
West Links Cl *MTN/WRL* BS22 ...... **128** A4 2
West Ml *CFTN/FAIL* BS8........................ **75** D2
Westmarch Wy *MTN/WRL* BS22 ...... **129** F3
Westmead Crs *TRWBR* BA14 .... **158** B2
Westmead Gdns
CBATH/BATHN BA1 .... **111** E5 1
Westmead Rd *EVILLE/WHL* BS5 .... **79** F2
West Mendip Wy *WSM* BS23 .... **150** C5
Westminster Cl
HNLZ/SM/SNYPK/WT BS9 .... **46** B4 5
Westminster Rd
EVILLE/WHL BS5 .... **78** B1 13
Westmoreland Dr *BATHSE* BA2 .. **122** C4 10
Westmoreland Rd *BATHSE* BA2 .. **122** C5 4
RDLND/MONT BS6 .... **63** F3 5
Westmoreland Station Rd
BATHSE BA2 .... **122** C5 5
Westmoreland St *BATHSE* BA2 .... **122** C5 6
Weston Av *EVILLE/WHL* BS5 .... **78** B2 12
Weston Cl
HNLZ/SM/SNYPK/WT BS9 .... **45** D4
Weston Crs *HORF/LLZ* BS7 .... **47** F5
Weston Farm La
CBATH/BATHN BA1.......................... **111** F5
Weston La *CBATH/BATHN* BA1.......... **122** A1
Weston Pk *CBATH/BATHN* BA1 .... **122** A1
Weston Pk East
CBATH/BATHN BA1.......................... **122** B2
Weston Pk West
CBATH/BATHN BA1.......................... **122** A1
Weston Rd *CBATH/BATHN* BA1 .... **122** B2
CFTN/FAIL BS8.................................. **88** A1
LGASH BS41...................................... **89** D3
NAIL BS48 .... **88** B4
YTN/CONG BS49 .... **132** A1
Westons Brake *MANG/FISH* BS16 ...... **52** B2
Westons Hill Dr *MANG/FISH* BS16...... **52** B3
Westons Wy *KGWD/HNM* BS15.......... **81** D2
Weston Wy *OMX/HUT/LCK* BS24...... **153** D3
Weston Wood Rd *PTSHD/EG* BS20.... **56** A3
Westover Cl
HNLZ/SM/SNYPK/WT BS9 .... **46** A2
Westover Dr
HNLZ/SM/SNYPK/WT BS9 .... **46** B3
Westover Gdns
HNLZ/SM/SNYPK/WT BS9 .... **46** A3 1
Westover Ri
HNLZ/SM/SNYPK/WT BS9 .... **46** B2
Westover Rd
HNLZ/SM/SNYPK/WT BS9 .... **46** B3
West Pde *HNLZ/SM/SNYPK/WT* BS9.. **45** D4
West Pk *CFTN/FAIL* BS8 .... **75** F1
West Park Rd *MANG/FISH* BS16 .... **68** C1
West Priory Cl
HNLZ/SM/SNYPK/WT BS9 .... **46** B4 6
West Rdg *FRCTL/WBN* BS36................ **32** C1
West Rd *RDSTK/MIDN* BA3................ **161** D2
YTN/CONG BS49 .... **116** B4
West Rocke Av
HNLZ/SM/SNYPK/WT BS9 .... **45** E4
West Rolstone Rd
OMX/HUT/LCK BS24........................ **131** E5
West Shrubbery
RDLND/MONT BS6 .... **63** F4 6
West St *BMSTR* BS3............................ **91** F2
CBRISNE BS2 .... **3** H2
KGWD/HNM BS15 .... **80** B1 5
OLD/WMLY/WICK BS30 .... **82** A5
TRWBR BA14.................................... **156** B4
WSM BS23 .... **140** C2 11
West Town Dr
BRSG/KWL/STAPK BS4 .... **94** B3 3
West Town Gv
BRSG/KWL/STAPK BS4...................... **94** B4
West Town La
BRSG/KWL/STAPK BS4...................... **94** B3
HGRV/WHIT BS14.............................. **93** F4
West Town Pk
BRSG/KWL/STAPK BS4...................... **94** B4
West Town Rd *AVONM* BS11 .... **43** D4 5
West View Rd *BMSTR* BS3 .... **91** F1
CBATH/BATHN BA1.......................... **115** E4
KEYN BS31...................................... **106** C2
Westward Dr *PTSHD/EG* BS20............ **60** A2
Westward Gdns *LGASH* BS41 .... **89** F2 2
Westward Rd
BMSTRD/HC/WWD BS13 .... **91** D5
West Wy *CLVDN* BS21 .... **84** C1
Westway *NAIL* BS48 .... **86** C2
West Wick *OMX/HUT/LCK* BS24........ **144** B2
Westwood Cl *MTN/WRL* BS22 .... **129** E5
Westwood Crs
BRSG/KWL/STAPK BS4 .... **78** B4 2
Westwood Rd
BRSG/KWL/STAPK BS4...................... **94** B4
Westwoods *CBATH/BATHN* BA1 ...... **115** F4
Wetherby Ct *FRCTL/WBN* BS36 ...... **52** A2 3
Wetherell Pl *CFTN/FAIL* BS8 .... **75** F2 9
Wetlands La *PTSHD/EG* BS20 .... **56** A3
Wexford Rd *BRSG/KWL/STAPK* BS4 .. **92** B4
Weymouth Rd *BMSTR* BS3 .... **92** B2
Weymouth St
CBATH/BATHN BA1 .... **123** F2 3
Wharfedale *THNB/SVB* BS35 .... **9** D4
Wharf La *PTSHD/EG* BS20 .... **57** F1
Wharf Rd *MANG/FISH* BS16 .... **67** D2 5
Wharnecliffe Cl
HGRV/WHIT BS14 .... **103** F2 8
Wharnecliffe Gdns I
HGRV/WHIT BS14............................ **103** F2
Whatley Rd *CFTN/FAIL* BS8 .... **63** E5
Wheatfield Dr *ALMDB* BS32................ **13** E4
MTN/WRL BS22.............................. **129** F2
Wheathill Cl *KEYN* BS31 .... **106** A2
Wheelers Cl *RDSTK/MIDN* BA3 .... **162** A2 1
Wheelers Dr *RDSTK/MIDN* BA3 .... **161** F2 2
Wheelers Rd *RDSTK/MIDN* BA3.......... **161** F2
Whinchat Gdns *MANG/FISH* BS16 .. **50** A5 4
Whippington Ct *CBRIS/FH* BS1 .... **3** E1 3
Whitby Rd *BRSG/KWL/STAPK* BS4 .. **78** A5 1
Whitchurch La
BMSTRD/HC/WWD BS13 .... **101** E2
HGRV/WHIT BS14............................ **102** C2
Whitecross Av
HGRV/WHIT BS14 .... **104** A1 2
Whitecross Rd *WSM* BS23 .... **6** C5
Whitefield Av *EVILLE/WHL* BS5.......... **67** E5
KGWD/HNM BS15 .... **80** B4 3
Whitefield Cl
CBATH/BATHN BA1 .... **115** F3 1
Whitefield Rd *EVILLE/WHL* BS5.......... **67** E4
Whitefields *YATE/CS* BS37 .... **21** D4 1
Whitehall Av *EVILLE/WHL* BS5............ **66** C5
Whitehall Gdns
EVILLE/WHL BS5 .... **78** B1 14
Whitehall Rd *EVILLE/WHL* BS5............ **78** A1
Whiteheads La *BOAV* BA15 .... **147** D2
Whitehill *BOAV* BA15.......................... **147** D2
White Horse Cl *TRWBR* BA14............ **159** D1
Whitehouse La *BMSTR* BS3 .... **76** B5 11
Whitehouse Pl *BMSTR* BS3 .... **76** C5
Whitehouse Rd *THNB/SVB* BS35........ **11** D3
White House Rd
YTN/CONG BS49 .... **117** F3 1
Whitehouse St *BMSTR* BS3 .... **76** C5
Whiteladies Rd *CFTN/FAIL* BS8 .... **63** E4
Whitelands Hl *RDSTK/MIDN* BA3 .... **163** E1
Whiteleaze *HNBRY/STHM* BS10 .... **47** D4 3
White Lodge Rd *MANG/FISH* BS16 .... **69** D2
Whiteoak Wy *NAIL* BS48...................... **86** C4
White Park Ldg *PTSHD/EG* BS20.......... **39** E5
White Row Hl *TRWBR* BA14.............. **158** A3
Whiterow Pk *TRWBR* BA14 .... **158** A1
Whitesfield Rd *NAIL* BS48 .... **86** C3
Whites Hl *EVILLE/WHL* BS5.................. **79** E3
Whiteshill *MANG/FISH* BS16................ **31** E5
White St *EVILLE/WHL* BS5 .... **77** D1
White Tree Rd
HNLZ/SM/SNYPK/WT BS9 .... **63** F2
Whitewall La *THNB/SVB* BS35 .... **9** F2
Whiteway Av *BATHSE* BA2.................. **135** E2
Whiteway Cl
BRSG/KWL/STAPK BS4 .... **78** C3 3
EVILLE/WHL BS5 .... **79** E1
Whiteway Ms *EVILLE/WHL* BS5.......... **79** E1
Whiteway Rd *BATHSE* BA2 .... **121** D5
EVILLE/WHL BS5 .... **67** E5
Whitewells Rd *CBATH/BATHN* BA1 .. **113** E5
Whitewood Rd *EVILLE/WHL* BS5 .. **67** D5 4
Whitfield Cl *KGWD/HNM* BS15 ...... **68** B4 3
Whitfield Rd *THNB/SVB* BS35 .... **8** C2 5
Whiting Rd
BMSTRD/HC/WWD BS13 .... **101** E3
Whitland Av
BMSTRD/HC/WWD BS13 .... **101** F2 9
Whitland Rd
BMSTRD/HC/WWD BS13 .... **101** F2
Whitley Cl *YATE/CS* BS37 .... **19** D2
Whitley Md *BRSTK/PCHW* BS34.......... **29** F5
Whitmead Gdns
BMSTRD/HC/WWD BS13 .... **102** A3 6
Whitmore Av
BRSG/KWL/STAPK BS4 .... **95** E1
Whitson St *CBRIS/FH* BS1 .... **76** B1 18
Whitting Rd *WSM* BS23 .... **151** D1 3
Whittington Dr *MTN/WRL* BS22 .. **128** C5 3
Whittington Rd *MANG/FISH* BS16 .... **51** D5
Whittock Rd *HGRV/WHIT* BS14 .... **104** B2
Whittock Sq *HGRV/WHIT* BS14 .... **94** B5
Whittucks Rd *KGWD/HNM* BS15 .... **80** B4 4
Whitwell Rd *HGRV/WHIT* BS14 .... **93** F4
Whytes Cl
HNLZ/SM/SNYPK/WT BS9 .... **46** B3
Wick Crs *BRSG/KWL/STAPK* BS4 .... **94** B1
Wicker Hl *TRWBR* BA14 .... **156** C3
The Wickets *HORF/LLZ* BS7 .... **48** A2
KGWD/HNM BS15 .... **68** B4 4
Wickfield *CLVDN* BS21 .... **84** C3 6
Wickham Cl *YATE/CS* BS37 .... **21** E5
Wickham Gln *MANG/FISH* BS16.......... **66** B1
Wickham Hl *MANG/FISH* BS16............ **66** B1

Wickham Vw *MANG/FISH* BS16 66 B2 2
Wick House Cl *KEYN* BS31 108 B4
Wick La *OLD/WMLY/WICK* BS30 99 E3
Wicklow Rd *BRSG/KWL/STAPK* BS4 92 C4
Wick Rd *BRSG/KWL/STAPK* BS4 94 B1
THNB/SVB BS35 11 D3
Widbrook Meadow *TRWBR* BA14 156 A4
Widbrook Vw *BOAV* BA15 147 E4
Widcombe *HGRV/WHIT* BS14 103 E2
Widcombe Cl *EVILLE/WHL* BS5 79 E2 6
Widcombe Crs *BATHSE* BA2 5 E6 1
Widcombe Hl *BATHSE* BA2 5 E6
Wigmore Gdns *MTN/WRL* BS22 128 B5
Wigton Crs *HNBRY/STHM* BS10 47 D1
Wilbye Gv
BRSG/KWL/STAPK BS4 102 B1 5
Wilcot Cl *TRWBR* BA14 158 C1
Wilcox Cl *KGWD/HNM* BS15 80 A2
Wildcountry La *LGASH* BS41 88 C5
Wildcroft Rd
HNLZ/SM/SNYPK/WT BS9 63 F1
The Wilderness *BOAV* BA15 146 C2
Wilder St *CBRISNE* BS2 76 C1 14
Willada Cl *BMSTR* BS3 91 F2
William Mason Cl
EVILLE/WHL BS5 77 F2 13
Williams Cl *OLD/WMLY/WICK* BS30 97 D2
Williamson Rd *HORF/LLZ* BS7 65 D3
William St *BATHSE* BA2 4 D2
BMSTR BS3 76 C5
CBRISNE BS2 65 D5
CBRISNE BS2 77 E3 5
EVILLE/WHL BS5 78 A1 10
MANG/FISH BS16 67 F3 2
Willinton Rd *BRSG/KWL/STAPK* BS4 93 D5
Willis Rd *KGWD/HNM* BS15 69 D4
Williton Crs *WSM* BS23 151 E2 5
Willmott Cl *HGRV/WHIT* BS14 103 D4 7
Willoughby Cl
BMSTRD/HC/WWD BS13 91 E5
Willoughby Rd *HORF/LLZ* BS7 64 C1 2
Willow Bed Cl *MANG/FISH* BS16 50 C5
Willow Cl *BATHSE* BA2 136 B5
BRSTK/PCHW BS34 27 F1
CLVDN BS21 85 E1
LGASH BS41 89 D3
MTN/WRL BS22 130 C5
OLD/WMLY/WICK BS30 82 B3
OLD/WMLY/WICK BS30 83 F3
PTSHD/EG BS20 56 A2 1
RDSTK/MIDN BA3 162 B2 3
WSM BS23 151 D3
Willowdown *MTN/WRL* BS22 129 D3 12
Willow Dr *OMX/HUT/LCK* BS24 143 D5
OMX/HUT/LCK BS24 153 D3
The Willowfalls
CBATH/BATHN BA1 114 C4 1
Willow Gdns *MTN/WRL* BS22 130 C5
Willow Gv *MANG/FISH* BS16 68 A4 5
TRWBR BA14 158 B2
Willow Rd *KGWD/HNM* BS15 96 A1 3
The Willows *ALMDB* BS32 13 E5
NAIL BS48 87 E1
YATE/CS BS37 19 E3 6
Willow Vw *TRWBR* BA14 158 C4
Willow Wk *HNBRY/STHM* BS10 26 C5
KEYN BS31 106 B3
Willow Wy *FRCTL/WBN* BS36 33 D2 2
Willsbridge Hl
OLD/WMLY/WICK BS30 97 E2
Wills Dr *EVILLE/WHL* BS5 77 E1
Willway St *BMSTR* BS3 76 C5
CBRISNE BS2 3 H2
Wilmot Ct *OLD/WMLY/WICK* BS30 81 E3 5
Wilmots Wy *PTSHD/EG* BS20 60 B2 4
Wilshire Av *KGWD/HNM* BS15 80 B4
Wilson Pl *CBRISNE* BS2 77 D1 8
Wilson St *CBRISNE* BS2 77 D1
Wilton Cl *HNBRY/STHM* BS10 47 D3
Wilton Dr *TRWBR* BA14 159 D1
Wilton Gdns *WSM* BS23 6 C2 2
Wiltshire Av *YATE/CS* BS37 20 B2
Wiltshire Dr *TRWBR* BA14 159 D1 4
Wiltshire Pl *KGWD/HNM* BS15 68 C3 4
Wiltshire Wy *CBATH/BATHN* BA1 113 E5
Wimbledon Rd *RDLND/MONT* BS6 64 A1
Wimblestone Rd *WNSC* BS25 154 B2
Wimborne Rd *BMSTR* BS3 92 A3 2
Winash Cl *HGRV/WHIT* BS14 94 B5
Wincanton Cl *FRCTL/WBN* BS36 52 A2 9
Winchcombe Cl *NAIL* BS48 87 F4
Winchcombe Rd
FRCTL/WBN BS36 16 C5 3
Winchester Av
BRSG/KWL/STAPK BS4 94 B1 3
Winchester Cl *TRWBR* BA14 158 C5
Winchester Rd *BATHSE* BA2 122 B5
BRSG/KWL/STAPK BS4 94 B1
Wincroft *OLD/WMLY/WICK* BS30 82 A5
Windcliff Crs *AVONM* BS11 43 F3
Windermere Av *WSM* BS23 151 E1 4
Windermere Rd
BRSTK/PCHW BS34 12 B5
TRWBR BA14 157 E2
Windermere Wy
OLD/WMLY/WICK BS30 82 B3
Windmill Cl *BMSTR* BS3 76 C5
Windmill Hl *BMSTR* BS3 92 B1
OMX/HUT/LCK BS24 153 F3
Windmill La *HNBRY/STHM* BS10 25 E5
Windrush Cl *BATHSE* BA2 135 D1
Windrush Ct *THNB/SVB* BS35 8 C4
Windrush Rd *KEYN* BS31 107 E3
Windsor Av *EVILLE/WHL* BS5 79 F3
KEYN BS31 106 C3 3
Windsor Bridge Rd
CBATH/BATHN BA1 122 B3
Windsor Cl *BRSTK/PCHW* BS34 29 F4 2
CLVDN BS21 84 C2
Windsor Ct *MANG/FISH* BS16 51 F4
Windsor Crs *HNBRY/STHM* BS10 25 D4
Windsor Dr *TRWBR* BA14 158 B2 3
YATE/CS BS37 19 E2
Windsor Gv *EVILLE/WHL* BS5 77 F1 17
Windsor Pl *CFTN/FAIL* BS8 75 D3
MANG/FISH BS16 69 E1
Windsor Rd *MTN/WRL* BS22 128 B5
OLD/WMLY/WICK BS30 97 D2 1
RDLND/MONT BS6 64 C4
TRWBR BA14 159 E3
Windsor Ter *BMSTR* BS3 77 D5
CFTN/FAIL BS8 75 D3 17
Windwhistle Cir *WSM* BS23 151 E2 6
Windwhistle La *WSM* BS23 151 D2
Windwhistle Rd *WSM* BS23 150 C2
Wineberry Cl *EVILLE/WHL* BS5 66 B5
Wine St *BOAV* BA15 146 C3
CBRIS/FH BS1 2 D2
Winfield Rd *OLD/WMLY/WICK* BS30 82 A2
Winford Cl *PTSHD/EG* BS20 56 C2
Winford Gv
BMSTRD/HC/WWD BS13 91 E4
Wingard Cl *WSM* BS23 150 C3
Wingfield Rd *BMSTR* BS3 92 C2
TRWBR BA14 156 A5
Winifred's La *CBATH/BATHN* BA1 122 C1
Winkworth Pl *CBRISNE* BS2 65 D5 10
Winnowing End *WNSC* BS25 154 C1
Winsbury Wy *ALMDB* BS32 13 D5
Winscombe Cl *KEYN* BS31 106 B1
Winscombe Rd *WSM* BS23 7 G2 3
Winsford St *EVILLE/WHL* BS5 77 E1 15
Winsham Cl *HGRV/WHIT* BS14 103 F2 9
Winsley Rd *BOAV* BA15 146 B2
RDLND/MONT BS6 64 B5 9
Winterbourne Hl *FRCTL/WBN* BS36 31 E3
Winterbourne Rd
BRSTK/PCHW BS34 29 F2
Winterslow Rd *TRWBR* BA14 158 B2
Winterstoke Cl *BMSTR* BS3 91 F2 13
Winterstoke Rd *BMSTR* BS3 91 E2
OMX/HUT/LCK BS24 152 A4 1
WSM BS23 7 H5
Winton St *BRSG/KWL/STAPK* BS4 77 D5
Wistaria Av *YATE/CS* BS37 20 B4 7
Wisteria Av *OMX/HUT/LCK* BS24 152 C3
Witchell Rd *EVILLE/WHL* BS5 78 A2 17
Witch Hazel Rd
BMSTRD/HC/WWD BS13 102 C4
Witcombe *YATE/CS* BS37 35 D1
Witcombe Cl *KGWD/HNM* BS15 68 C5
Witham Rd *KEYN* BS31 107 E4
Witherlies Rd *MANG/FISH* BS16 50 A5 5
Withey Cl West
HNLZ/SM/SNYPK/WT BS9 62 C1
The Witheys *HGRV/WHIT* BS14 104 A3
Withies La *RDSTK/MIDN* BA3 160 C5
Withies Pk *RDSTK/MIDN* BA3 160 C4
Withington Cl
OLD/WMLY/WICK BS30 98 A2 3
Withleigh Rd
BRSG/KWL/STAPK BS4 93 F2
Withy Cl *NAIL* BS48 87 E1 1
TRWBR BA14 157 E1
Withy Cl East
HNLZ/SM/SNYPK/WT BS9 63 D1
Withypool Gdns
HGRV/WHIT BS14 103 F2 10
Withywood Rd
BMSTRD/HC/WWD BS13 101 D3
Witney Cl *KEYN* BS31 108 B4
Woburn Cl
OLD/WMLY/WICK BS30 81 D4 8
TRWBR BA14 156 A4
Woburn Rd *EVILLE/WHL* BS5 65 F3
Wolferton Rd *RDLND/MONT* BS6 65 D4
Wolfridge Gdns
HNBRY/STHM BS10 26 B4
Wolseley Rd *HORF/LLZ* BS7 64 B3
Wolvers Hill Rd
OMX/HUT/LCK BS24 144 B2
Woodbine Rd *EVILLE/WHL* BS5 78 B1 15
Woodborough Cl *TRWBR* BA14 159 D2 7
Woodborough Crs *WNSC* BS25 154 C5 1
Woodborough Dr *WNSC* BS25 154 C4
Woodborough La
RDSTK/MIDN BA3 163 D1
Woodborough Rd
RDSTK/MIDN BA3 163 D1
WNSC BS25 154 B4
Woodborough St
EVILLE/WHL BS5 65 F5 14
Woodbridge Rd
BRSG/KWL/STAPK BS4 93 E2
Woodchester *KGWD/HNM* BS15 68 C3 5
YATE/CS BS37 35 F2
Woodchester Rd
HNBRY/STHM BS10 47 D4 4
Woodcliff Rd *MTN/WRL* BS22 142 B1
Woodcote *KGWD/HNM* BS15 80 B3 2
Woodcote Rd *MANG/FISH* BS16 67 F4
Woodcote Wk *MANG/FISH* BS16 67 F4
Woodcroft Av *EVILLE/WHL* BS5 66 B5 4
Woodcroft Cl
BRSG/KWL/STAPK BS4 78 C5
Woodcroft Rd
BRSG/KWL/STAPK BS4 78 C5
Woodend *KGWD/HNM* BS15 80 B3 3
Woodend Rd *FRCTL/WBN* BS36 32 C1
Wood End Wk
HNLZ/SM/SNYPK/WT BS9 45 D5
Woodfield Rd *RDLND/MONT* BS6 63 F5
Woodford Cl *NAIL* BS48 87 F3 14
Woodgrove Rd *HNBRY/STHM* BS10 45 E1
Woodhall Cl *MANG/FISH* BS16 52 A5 2
Wood Hl *YTN/CONG* BS49 117 D5
Woodhill Av *PTSHD/EG* BS20 39 E5
Wood Hill Pk *PTSHD/EG* BS20 39 E4 1
Woodhill Rd *PTSHD/EG* BS20 39 E5
Woodhill Views *NAIL* BS48 87 E1
Woodhouse Gv *HORF/LLZ* BS7 47 F5
Woodhouse Rd *BATHSE* BA2 121 E4
Woodhurst Rd *WSM* BS23 141 F2
Woodington Ct
OLD/WMLY/WICK BS30 81 D5 21
Woodington Rd *CLVDN* BS21 84 C3 7
The Wood Kilns *YTN/CONG* BS49 116 A2
Woodland Av *KGWD/HNM* BS15 68 B4 5
Woodland Cl *MANG/FISH* BS16 68 A4 6
Woodland Gld *CLVDN* BS21 71 E4
Woodland Gv *BATHSE* BA2 124 C5
HNLZ/SM/SNYPK/WT BS9 45 E5
Woodland Rd *CFTN/FAIL* BS8 2 A1
NAIL BS48 87 D1
WSM BS23 150 C1
Woodlands *ALMDB* BS32 13 E2
CLVDN BS21 70 C5 1
MANG/FISH BS16 51 F5 3
Woodlands La *ALMDB* BS32 12 C3
Woodlands Pk *CBATH/BATHN* BA1 114 A5
Woodlands Ri *MANG/FISH* BS16 51 E5
Woodlands Rd *PTSHD/EG* BS20 39 E3
Woodland Ter *KGWD/HNM* BS15 80 B2
RDLND/MONT BS6 63 F4 7
Woodland Wy *KGWD/HNM* BS15 68 A4
Wood La *WSM* BS23 141 E1
Woodleaze
HNLZ/SM/SNYPK/WT BS9 44 C5
Woodleigh *THNB/SVB* BS35 8 C3
Woodleigh Gdns
HGRV/WHIT BS14 104 A1
Woodmancote *YATE/CS* BS37 19 E5
Woodmancote Rd
RDLND/MONT BS6 64 C5 7
Woodmans Cl *YATE/CS* BS37 20 C5
Woodmans Rd *YATE/CS* BS37 20 C5
Woodmans V *YATE/CS* BS37 21 D5 1
Woodmarsh *TRWBR* BA14 159 D3
Woodmarsh Cl *HGRV/WHIT* BS14 103 E3
Woodmead Gdns
BMSTRD/HC/WWD BS13 102 A3
Woodmill *YTN/CONG* BS49 116 A2 3
Woodpecker Av *RDSTK/MIDN* BA3 161 E4
Woodpecker Dr *MTN/WRL* BS22 143 D2
Wood Rd *KGWD/HNM* BS15 80 B1
Woodside *RDSTK/MIDN* BA3 160 B3
Woodside Av *OMX/HUT/LCK* BS24 152 A3
Woodside Gdns *PTSHD/EG* BS20 54 C1
Woodside Gv *HNBRY/STHM* BS10 25 E5
Woodside Rd
BRSG/KWL/STAPK BS4 78 C3
CLVDN BS21 71 E4
FRCTL/WBN BS36 33 E1
KGWD/HNM BS15 80 A1
MANG/FISH BS16 51 D4
Woodspring Av *MTN/WRL* BS22 127 F4
Woodspring Crs *MTN/WRL* BS22 127 F4
Woodstock Av
RDLND/MONT BS6 64 A5 3
Woodstock Cl *KGWD/HNM* BS15 81 D1 7
Woodstock Rd
KGWD/HNM BS15 81 D2 10
MTN/WRL BS22 142 A2
RDLND/MONT BS6 63 F4
Wood St *BATHSE* BA2 4 A5
CBATH/BATHN BA1 4 B3
EVILLE/WHL BS5 65 F4 4
Woodview *CLVDN* BS21 85 F1 6
Woodview Cl *AVONM* BS11 43 F4
Woodview Ter *NAIL* BS48 87 E2
WSM BS23 7 G3 1
Woodward Dr
OLD/WMLY/WICK BS30 81 D5
Woodwell Rd *AVONM* BS11 43 F5

Woodyleaze Dr KGWD/HNM BS15 .... 80 A3
Wookey Cl NAIL BS48 ... 87 E4
Woolcot St RDLND/MONT BS6 ... 63 F4
Wooler Rd WSM BS23 ... 141 D2
Woollard La HGRV/WHIT BS14 ... 104 B5
Woolley Cl BOAV BA15 ... 147 E2
Woolley Dr BOAV BA15 ... 147 E2
Woolley La CBATH/BATHN BA1 ... 113 E2
Woolley Rd HGRV/WHIT BS14 ... 104 C2 4
Woolley St BOAV BA15 ... 147 E3
Woolley Ter BOAV BA15 ... 147 E2
Woolpack Mdw TRWBR BA14 ... 157 E5
Woolvers Wy OMX/HUT/LCK BS24 .. 144 A4
Wootton Crs BRSG/KWL/STAPK BS4.. 78 C3
Wootton Pk HGRV/WHIT BS14 ... 93 F3
Wootton Rd BRSG/KWL/STAPK BS4 .. 78 C3
Worcester Buildings
CBATH/BATHN BA1 ... 113 F5 3
Worcester Cl MANG/FISH BS16 ... 67 F4
Worcester Crs CFTN/FAIL BS8 ... 75 E1 4
Worcester Gdns NAIL BS48 ... 86 A4
Worcester Pk CBATH/BATHN BA1 .... 123 F1
Worcester Rd CFTN/FAIL BS8 ... 75 E1
KGWD/HNM BS15 ... 68 B5 9
Worcester Ter CFTN/FAIL BS8 ... 75 E1
Wordsworth Rd CLVDN BS21 ... 84 C2 9
WSM BS23 ... 151 F2 2
World's End La KEYN BS31 ... 108 A2
Worlebury Cl MTN/WRL BS22 ... 128 A4 3
Worlebury Hill Rd MTN/WRL BS22 .. 128 B4
WSM BS23 ... 127 F5
Worlebury Park Rd
MTN/WRL BS22 ... 127 F4
Worle Ct MTN/WRL BS22 ... 129 E4
Worrall Rd CFTN/FAIL BS8 ... 63 E4
Worrel's La MANG/FISH BS16 ... 31 E5
Worsley St EVILLE/WHL BS5 ... 78 B2 13
Worsted Cl TRWBR BA14 ... 157 E5 4
Worth Cl KGWD/HNM BS15 ... 81 D3 4
Worthing Rd BRSTK/PCHW BS34 ... 12 A5
Worthy La WSM BS23 ... 141 D2 15
Worthy Rd AVONM BS11 ... 23 E1
The Worthys ALMDB BS32 ... 30 B2
Wotton Rd YATE/CS BS37 ... 17 F1
Wrangle Farm Gn CLVDN BS21 ... 85 E2 4
Wraxall Gv BMSTRD/HC/WWD BS13.. 91 D4
Wraxall Rd KGWD/HNM BS15 ... 81 E3
OLD/WMLY/WICK BS30 ... 81 E3
Wrenbert Rd MANG/FISH BS16 ... 68 B1
Wren Cl MTN/WRL BS22 ... 142 C2
Wren Ct TRWBR BA14 ... 156 B4
Wren Dr MANG/FISH BS16 ... 50 A5
Wrington Cl BRSTK/PCHW BS34 ... 29 D1
Wrington Crs
BMSTRD/HC/WWD BS13 ... 91 E5
Wrington La YTN/CONG BS49 ... 133 E1
Wrington Md YTN/CONG BS49 ... 133 E1
Wrington Rd YTN/CONG BS49 ... 133 F2
Wroughton Dr
BMSTRD/HC/WWD BS13 ... 102 B3
Wroughton Gdns
BMSTRD/HC/WWD BS13 ... 102 B3 3
Wroxham Dr BRSTK/PCHW BS34 .. 13 D5 3
Wyatt Av BMSTRD/HC/WWD BS13 .. 101 D2
Wyatt Cl BMSTRD/HC/WWD BS13.... 101 D2
Wyatt's Cl NAIL BS48 ... 86 C2
Wychwood KGWD/HNM BS15 ... 80 B3
Wyck Beck Rd HNBRY/STHM BS10.... 26 B4
Wycliffe Rd
HNLZ/SM/SNYPK/WT BS9 ... 46 C4
Wycombe Gv
BRSG/KWL/STAPK BS4 ... 94 B2 6
Wye Ct THNB/SVB BS35 ... 8 C4
Wye Croft Cl HNBRY/STHM BS10 ... 27 E5
Wyedale Av
HNLZ/SM/SNYPK/WT BS9 ... 44 C4
Wyke Rd TRWBR BA14 ... 149 E5
Wykis Ct KGWD/HNM BS15 ... 80 C4 5
Wyllie Ct MTN/WRL BS22 ... 129 F2 7
Wymbush Crs
BMSTRD/HC/WWD BS13 ... 102 A2
Wymbush Gdns
BMSTRD/HC/WWD BS13 ... 102 A2 4
Wyndham Crs
BRSG/KWL/STAPK BS4 ... 95 D1
PTSHD/EG BS20 ... 59 F2
Wyndham Wy PTSHD/EG BS20 ... 56 C1
The Wynstones KGWD/HNM BS15 .... 80 A2
Wynter Cl MTN/WRL BS22 ... 129 F4

Y

Yadley Cl WNSC BS25 ... 154 B5
Yanleigh Cl
BMSTRD/HC/WWD BS13 ... 100 A1
Yanley La LGASH BS41 ... 89 F4
Yarbury Wy OMX/HUT/LCK BS24 .... 144 A1
Yate Rd YATE/CS BS37 ... 17 E1
Yeo Cl WSM BS23 ... 7 G6
Yeolands Dr CLVDN BS21 ... 84 B3
Yeomans Cl
HNLZ/SM/SNYPK/WT BS9 ... 62 B1 5
Yeomanside Cl HGRV/WHIT BS14 .... 104 A2
Yeoman Wy TRWBR BA14 ... 156 C5
Yeomead NAIL BS48 ... 87 E1
Yeomeads LGASH BS41 ... 89 D3
Yeo Moor CLVDN BS21 ... 85 E2
Yeoward Rd CLVDN BS21 ... 85 E3
Yeo Wy CLVDN BS21 ... 84 B2
Yerbury St TRWBR BA14 ... 157 D3
Yewcroft Cl HGRV/WHIT BS14 ... 103 E3
Yew Tree Cl NAIL BS48 ... 86 B3 7
Yew Tree Dr KGWD/HNM BS15 ... 69 D3
Yew Tree Gdns NAIL BS48 ... 86 B3 8
PTSHD/EG BS20 ... 60 A2 10
Yew Tree Pk YTN/CONG BS49 ... 133 D3
Yomede Pk CBATH/BATHN BA1 .... 121 E3 2
York Av HORF/LLZ BS7 ... 65 D2
York Buildings TRWBR BA14 ... 157 D3
York Cl BRSTK/PCHW BS34 ... 29 E4
FRCTL/WBN BS36 ... 52 A2
MTN/WRL BS22 ... 129 F3 11
YATE/CS BS37 ... 19 F1
York Gdns CFTN/FAIL BS8 ... 75 D3
FRCTL/WBN BS36 ... 16 A5
York Pl CBRIS/FH BS1 ... 2 A4
CFTN/FAIL BS8 ... 75 F2
York Rd BMSTR BS3 ... 76 C5
EVILLE/WHL BS5 ... 66 A5
MANG/FISH BS16 ... 68 C2
RDLND/MONT BS6 ... 64 C5
York St CBATH/BATHN BA1 ... 4 C4 15
CBRISNE BS2 ... 65 D4 14
CBRISNE BS2 ... 65 E4 20
CFTN/FAIL BS8 ... 63 E4 13
EVILLE/WHL BS5 ... 78 A2 18
WSM BS23 ... 6 B1
Youngs Ct MANG/FISH BS16 ... 52 C3 1

Z

Zetland Rd RDLND/MONT BS6... 64 B4
Zig Zag CLVDN BS21 ... 71 D5

Index - featured places

Abbotswood Infant School
YATE/CS BS37 ... 35 E2
Abbotswood Surgery
YATE/CS BS37 ... 35 E1
ABC Cinema
CBATH/BATHN BA1 ... 4 B3
ABC Cinema
CFTN/FAIL BS8 ... 75 F1
Adam Gallery
CBATH/BATHN BA1 ... 4 B3
Adcroft Surgery
TRWBR BA14 ... 157 D2
Air Balloon Hill Junior & Infant School
EVILLE/WHL BS5 ... 79 E2
Allen School House
OLD/WMLY/WICK BS30 ... 81 E4
All Saints Exhibition Centre
CBRIS/FH BS1 ... 2 D2
Almondsbury Business Centre
ALMDB BS32 ... 13 E2
Almondsbury C of E VC Primary School
ALMDB BS32 ... 12 B1
Almondsbury Town Football Club
ALMDB BS32 ... 12 B1
Amberley House School
CFTN/FAIL BS8 ... 63 E5
Ambulance Station
BATHSE BA2 ... 123 E2
Amelia Nutt Clinic
BMSTRD/HC/WWD BS13 ... 101 D3
AMF Bowling
WSM BS23 ... 6 A2
Amphitheatre
CBRIS/FH BS1 ... 2 B5
Anchor Business Centre
RDLND/MONT BS6 ... 63 F5
Antrim Gallery
CBATH/BATHN BA1 ... 4 C2
Aretians RFC Clubhouse
BRSTK/PCHW BS34 ... 28 C1
Army Training Corps
CLVDN BS21 ... 70 C5
Arnolfini Gallery
CBRIS/FH BS1 ... 2 C5
Ashbrooke House School
WSM BS23 ... 6 B3
Ashcombe CP School
WSM BS23 ... 7 H1
Ashley Down Junior School
HORF/LLZ BS7 ... 64 C1
Ashley Down OB Rugby Club
HORF/LLZ BS7 ... 48 C3
Ashley Trading Estate
RDLND/MONT BS6 ... 65 D4
Ashmead Business Park
KEYN BS31 ... 107 F2
Ashton Gate Primary School
BMSTR BS3 ... 75 E5
Ashton Park School
BMSTR BS3 ... 90 C1
Ashton Vale Primary School
BMSTR BS3 ... 91 D2
Assembly Rooms Museum of Costume
CBATH/BATHN BA1 ... 4 B1
Avonbank Industrial Centre
AVONM BS11 ... 42 C4
Avonbridge Trading Estate
AVONM BS11 ... 43 D3
Avon Business Park
MANG/FISH BS16 ... 67 E3
Avon County Council
BMSTR BS3 ... 92 C2
Avondale Business Centre
MANG/FISH BS16 ... 68 A4
Avon Gorge Industrial Estate
AVONM BS11 ... 43 D4
Avonmouth C of E School
AVONM BS11 ... 43 D3
Avonmouth Group Practice Health Centre Doctors Surgery
AVONM BS11 ... 42 C3
Avonmouth Medical Centre
AVONM BS11 ... 42 C3
Avon Primary School
AVONM BS11 ... 43 E3
Avon Riverside Estate
AVONM BS11 ... 42 C4
Avon & Somerset Constabulary
CBRIS/FH BS1 ... 2 D1
Avon Trading Estate
CBRISNE BS2 ... 77 E4
Azure Gallery
HNLZ/SM/SNYPK/WT BS9 ... 46 A4
Badminton Road Trading Estate
YATE/CS BS37 ... 18 C4
Badminton School
HNLZ/SM/SNYPK/WT BS9 ... 63 E1
Badocks Wood Primary School
HNBRY/STHM BS10 ... 47 D3
Baileys Court Primary School
ALMDB BS32 ... 30 A2
Balaclava Industrial Estate
MANG/FISH BS16 ... 67 D3
Bandstand
CBATH/BATHN BA1 ... 122 C3
Bank Leaze Primary School
AVONM BS11 ... 44 C1
Bannerman Road Primary School
EVILLE/WHL BS5 ... 65 F5
Barley Close Primary School
MANG/FISH BS16 ... 52 B5
Barnack Trading Centre
BMSTR BS3 ... 92 A3
Barrs Court Primary School
OLD/WMLY/WICK BS30 ... 81 D4
Barton Hill Primary School
EVILLE/WHL BS5 ... 77 F3

Barton Hill Trading Estate
EVILLE/WHL BS5 .... **77** F3
Bath Abbey
CBATH/BATHN BA1 .... **4** C3
Bathampton Primary School
BATHSE BA2 .... **115** D5
Bath City Council
CBATH/BATHN BA1 .... **4** C2
Bath City Council
CBATH/BATHN BA1 .... **122** A3
Bath City Football Club
BATHSE BA2 .... **121** F4
The Bath Clinic
BATHSE BA2 .... **138** C3
Bath College of Higher Education
CBATH/BATHN BA1 .... **122** C1
Bath County Court
CBATH/BATHN BA1 .... **4** C4
Bath Cricket Club
BATHSE BA2 .... **4** D4
Batheaston Medical Centre
CBATH/BATHN BA1 .... **115** E4
Batheaston Primary School
CBATH/BATHN BA1 .... **115** D3
Bath Galleries
CBATH/BATHN BA1 .... **4** C2
Bath Golf Club
BATHSE BA2 .... **124** B4
Bath Media College
CBATH/BATHN BA1 .... **4** B2
Bath Natural Health Clinic
BATHSE BA2 .... **122** C4
Bath & North East Somerset Council
CBATH/BATHN BA1 .... **4** B3
Bath & North East Somerset Council
RDSTK/MIDN BA3 .... **161** D3
Bath Postal Museum
CBATH/BATHN BA1 .... **4** B2
Bath Rugby Club
BATHSE BA2 .... **4** D3
Bath Spa University College
BATHSE BA2 .... **119** F5
Bath & Sports Leisure Centre
BATHSE BA2 .... **4** D3
Bath University
BATHSE BA2 .... **124** C4
Bathwick St Marys C of E Primary School
BATHSE BA2 .... **124** A2
Baytree School
MTN/WRL BS22 .... **142** C1
Beacon Rise Junior School
KGWD/HNM BS15 .... **80** B3
Beazer Garden Maze
BATHSE BA2 .... **4** D3
Beckett Primary School
MTN/WRL BS22 .... **129** F5
Bedminster Down School
BMSTRD/HC/WWD BS13 .... **91** D5
Beechen Cliff Boys School
BATHSE BA2 .... **137** E1
Beeches Trading Estate
YATE/CS BS37 .... **18** B3
The Beehive Surgery
BATHSE BA2 .... **135** E1
Beehive Trading Estate
EVILLE/WHL BS5 .... **78** C2
Begbrook Primary School
MANG/FISH BS16 .... **50** A5
Birdwell Primary School
LGASH BS41 .... **89** E4
Bishop Road Primary School
HORF/LLZ BS7 .... **64** B2
Bishopston House Clinic
HORF/LLZ BS7 .... **64** C2
Bishopsworth C of E School
BMSTRD/HC/WWD BS13 .... **101** D1
Bishopsworth Swimming Pool
BMSTRD/HC/WWD BS13 .... **101** E1
Blackberry Hill Hospital
MANG/FISH BS16 .... **67** D1
Blackhorse CP School
MANG/FISH BS16 .... **52** B3
Blaise Hamlet (NT)
HNBRY/STHM BS10 .... **45** E1
Bonville Business Centre
BRSG/KWL/STAPK BS4 .... **95** D2
Book Museum
CBATH/BATHN BA1 .... **4** D5
Bournville County Junior & Infant School
WSM BS23 .... **7** F6
Bowling Hill Business Park
YATE/CS BS37 .... **20** B4
Bradford on Avon Hospital
BOAV BA15 .... **147** D1
Bradford on Avon Swimming Pool
BOAV BA15 .... **146** C3
Bradgate Surgery
HNBRY/STHM BS10 .... **26** B5
Brentry Hospital
HNBRY/STHM BS10 .... **46** C1
Brentry Primary School
HNBRY/STHM BS10 .... **26** C5
Briarwood School
MANG/FISH BS16 .... **67** F3
Bridge Farm Junior & Infant School
HGRV/WHIT BS14 .... **103** E3
Bridge Road Business Park
WSM BS23 .... **7** F3
Brimsham Green School
YATE/CS BS37 .... **19** E1
Brislington Retail Park
BRSG/KWL/STAPK BS4 .... **94** C3
Brislington School
BRSG/KWL/STAPK BS4 .... **95** D4
Brislington Trading Estate
BRSG/KWL/STAPK BS4 .... **95** D2
Bristol Baptist College
CFTN/FAIL BS8 .... **75** D1
Bristol Business Park
MANG/FISH BS16 .... **50** A2
Bristol Cathedral
CBRIS/FH BS1 .... **2** B4
Bristol Cathedral School
CBRIS/FH BS1 .... **2** A4
Bristol City Council
AVONM BS11 .... **42** B2
Bristol City Council
AVONM BS11 .... **43** E4
Bristol City Council
AVONM BS11 .... **44** B2
Bristol City Council
AVONM BS11 .... **44** B4
Bristol City Council
BMSTR BS3 .... **76** B5
Bristol City Council
BMSTRD/HC/WWD BS13 .... **101** F3
Bristol City Council
BMSTRD/HC/WWD BS13 .... **102** A4
Bristol City Council
BRSG/KWL/STAPK BS4 .... **78** A5
Bristol City Council
BRSG/KWL/STAPK BS4 .... **92** B5
Bristol City Council
BRSG/KWL/STAPK BS4 .... **93** E4
Bristol City Council
BRSG/KWL/STAPK BS4 .... **95** D1
Bristol City Council
CBRIS/FH BS1 .... **2** B2
Bristol City Council
CBRIS/FH BS1 .... **2** A3
Bristol City Council
CBRIS/FH BS1 .... **3** H5
Bristol City Council
CBRISNE BS2 .... **65** D5
Bristol City Council
CBRISNE BS2 .... **76** C1
Bristol City Council
CFTN/FAIL BS8 .... **2** A1
Bristol City Council
CFTN/FAIL BS8 .... **75** F2
Bristol City Council
CFTN/FAIL BS8 .... **75** E4
Bristol City Council
EVILLE/WHL BS5 .... **65** F4
Bristol City Council
EVILLE/WHL BS5 .... **77** F2
Bristol City Council
HGRV/WHIT BS14 .... **94** A4
Bristol City Council
HGRV/WHIT BS14 .... **103** D2
Bristol City Council
HNBRY/STHM BS10 .... **26** C5
Bristol City Council
HNBRY/STHM BS10 .... **46** C3
Bristol City Council
HNBRY/STHM BS10 .... **47** D1
Bristol City Council
HNBRY/STHM BS10 .... **47** F5
Bristol City Council
HNLZ/SM/SNYPK/WT BS9 .... **63** E4
Bristol City Council
HORF/LLZ BS7 .... **48** A2
Bristol City Football Club
BMSTR BS3 .... **91** D1
Bristol Civil Service Sports Club
HORF/LLZ BS7 .... **48** A5
Bristol Clifton & West of England Zoological Society
CFTN/FAIL BS8 .... **75** D1
Bristol County Court
CBRISNE BS2 .... **2** C1
Bristol County Sports Club
CBRIS/FH BS1 .... **2** B2
Bristol Crown Court
CBRIS/FH BS1 .... **2** C2
Bristol Dental Hospital
CBRIS/FH BS1 .... **2** C1
Bristol General Hospital
CBRIS/FH BS1 .... **2** D6
Bristol Grammar School
CFTN/FAIL BS8 .... **75** F2
Bristol Grammar School
CFTN/FAIL BS8 .... **88** C1
Bristol Harlequins RFC
BRSG/KWL/STAPK BS4 .... **95** E2
Bristol Ice Rink
CBRIS/FH BS1 .... **2** B2
Bristol Industrial Museum
CBRIS/FH BS1 .... **2** B6
Bristol North Baths
HORF/LLZ BS7 .... **64** B3
Bristol & North Somerset Sports Club
CFTN/FAIL BS8 .... **88** B1
Bristol Old Vic (New Vic Theatre & Theatre Royal)
CBRIS/FH BS1 .... **2** C3
Bristol Old Vic Theatre School
CFTN/FAIL BS8 .... **63** E5
Bristol Old Vic Theatre School
HNLZ/SM/SNYPK/WT BS9 .... **63** D5
Bristol Rovers Football Club
BRSG/KWL/STAPK BS4 .... **95** D3
Bristol Royal Hospital for Sick Children
CFTN/FAIL BS8 .... **2** B1
Bristol Royal Infirmary
CBRISNE BS2 .... **76** B1
Bristol Rugby Club
BATHSE BA2 .... **122** C4
Bristol South Swimming Pool
BMSTR BS3 .... **76** A5
Bristol Steiner Waldorf School
CFTN/FAIL BS8 .... **75** F2
Bristol University
CFTN/FAIL BS8 .... **2** B2
Bristol Vale Trading Estate
BMSTR BS3 .... **91** F3
British Empire & Commonwealth Museum
CBRIS/FH BS1 .... **3** G5
Broadlands School
KEYN BS31 .... **106** B1
Broadmead Lane Industrial Estate
KEYN BS31 .... **97** E5
Broadoak Community School
WSM BS23 .... **151** D2
Broadwalk Shopping Centre
BRSG/KWL/STAPK BS4 .... **93** F2
Broadway County Infant School
YATE/CS BS37 .... **20** A3
Brockeridge Infant School
FRCTL/WBN BS36 .... **33** D1
Brock Street Clinic
CBATH/BATHN BA1 .... **4** A1
Brockway Medical Centre
NAIL BS48 .... **87** E2
Bromley Heath Infant School
MANG/FISH BS16 .... **51** F3
Bromley Heath Junior School
MANG/FISH BS16 .... **51** F3
Brooklea Clinic
BRSG/KWL/STAPK BS4 .... **78** C4
Broomhill Infant School
BRSG/KWL/STAPK BS4 .... **95** D1
Broomhill JM School
BRSG/KWL/STAPK BS4 .... **95** D1
Bryer Ash Business Park
TRWBR BA14 .... **156** C3
The Building of Bath Museum
CBATH/BATHN BA1 .... **4** B1

Burnbush Primary School HGRV/WHIT BS14 .... 104 B2
Burnbush School HGRV/WHIT BS14 .... 104 B1
Bush Industrial Estate EVILLE/WHL BS5 .... 78 B1
The Business Park BMSTRD/HC/WWD BS13 .... 102 C4
BW Estates OMX/HUT/LCK BS24 .... 151 F2
CAB & Guildhall CBRIS/FH BS1 .... 2 D2
Cabot Primary School CBRISNE BS2 .... 77 D1
Cabot Tower CFTN/FAIL BS8 .... 75 F3
Cadbury Heath CP School OLD/WMLY/WICK BS30 .... 81 F3
Cadbury Heath Health Centre OLD/WMLY/WICK BS30 .... 81 E4
Callicroft Infant School BRSTK/PCHW BS34 .... 12 A5
Camden Works Museum CBATH/BATHN BA1 .... 4 B1
Canons House CBRIS/FH BS1 .... 2 B5
The Card Gallery YATE/CS BS37 .... 20 C4
Carla Trading Estate BMSTR BS3 .... 91 D1
Carlyle Business Centre CBRISNE BS2 .... 77 E3
Carrick Business Park BRSG/KWL/STAPK BS4 .... 95 D3
Castle Batch Primary School MTN/WRL BS22 .... 129 F2
Castle Business Centre THNB/SVB BS35 .... 8 B3
Castle CP School KEYN BS31 .... 106 B4
Castlemead Shopping Centre MTN/WRL BS22 .... 129 F2
Castle Place Leisure Centre TRWBR BA14 .... 157 D4
The Castle School THNB/SVB BS35 .... 8 B2
Catherine Cottage Surgery CBATH/BATHN BA1 .... 4 A1
Central Trading Estate BRSG/KWL/STAPK BS4 .... 77 F5
Chandag County & Infant School KEYN BS31 .... 107 E2
Charborough Road CP School BRSTK/PCHW BS34 .... 48 A1
Charlotte Keel Health Clinic EVILLE/WHL BS5 .... 65 E5
Chatterton House CBRIS/FH BS1 .... 3 E5
Cheddar Grove Primary School BMSTRD/HC/WWD BS13 .... 91 E4
Cherry Garden Primary School OLD/WMLY/WICK BS30 .... 97 F2
Chesterfield Hospital CFTN/FAIL BS8 .... 75 E3
Chester Park Primary School MANG/FISH BS16 .... 67 E3
Chinese Medical Centre CBATH/BATHN BA1 .... 4 C5
Chipping Edge Estate YATE/CS BS37 .... 20 C4
Chipping Sodbury Library YATE/CS BS37 .... 20 C4
Chipping Sodbury School YATE/CS BS37 .... 20 C5
Christchurch C of E Primary School CFTN/FAIL BS8 .... 75 E2
Christ Church C of E VC Infant School MANG/FISH BS16 .... 68 B1
Christchurch Junior School MANG/FISH BS16 .... 68 B1
Christchurch Primary School BOAV BA15 .... 147 D2
Christchurch VC Primary School WSM BS23 .... 141 D2
Christ the King RC School THNB/SVB BS35 .... 8 C3
Church Farm Business Park BATHSE BA2 .... 119 E3
The Church Street Practice BOAV BA15 .... 146 C2
Cinemas CBRISNE BS2 .... 76 B1
City Business Park CBRIS/FH BS1 .... 2 D2
City Business Park EVILLE/WHL BS5 .... 77 E2
City of Bath College CBATH/BATHN BA1 .... 4 B4
City of Bristol College BMSTR BS3 .... 92 C2
City of Bristol College CBRIS/FH BS1 .... 75 F3
City of Bristol College HORF/LLZ BS7 .... 65 D2
City & Port of Bristol Social & Sports Club AVONM BS11 .... 60 C1
Civic Centre KGWD/HNM BS15 .... 80 C1
Civil Service Sports Club BATHSE BA2 .... 138 C3
Claremont Special School RDLND/MONT BS6 .... 64 A1
The Clarendon School TRWBR BA14 .... 158 B1
Claverham Cricket Club YTN/CONG BS49 .... 117 D4
Claverton Manor American Museum In Britain BATHSE BA2 .... 125 E5
Clevedon Fruit Market CLVDN BS21 .... 85 D1
Clevedon Health Centre CLVDN BS21 .... 85 E1
Clevedon Hospital CLVDN BS21 .... 85 E1
Clevedon School CLVDN BS21 .... 71 F4
Clifton Cathedral Church CFTN/FAIL BS8 .... 75 E1
Clifton Clinic CFTN/FAIL BS8 .... 75 E2
Clifton College CFTN/FAIL BS8 .... 75 D1
Clifton College Preparatory School CFTN/FAIL BS8 .... 63 D5
Clifton College Sports Club CFTN/FAIL BS8 .... 73 F2
Clifton Down Shopping Centre CFTN/FAIL BS8 .... 63 F5
The Clifton Gallery CFTN/FAIL BS8 .... 75 D2
Clifton High Junior School CFTN/FAIL BS8 .... 75 E2
Clifton High School CFTN/FAIL BS8 .... 75 D1
Clifton Rugby Club HNBRY/STHM BS10 .... 26 A3
Close Farm Surgery OLD/WMLY/WICK BS30 .... 82 B4
Clyde House Surgery RDLND/MONT BS6 .... 63 F4
Coates Industrial Estate NAIL BS48 .... 87 E1
College House MANG/FISH BS16 .... 67 E1
College of St Mathias C of E (A) Infant School MANG/FISH BS16 .... 67 E1
Colston Hall CBRIS/FH BS1 .... 2 C2
Colstons Collegiate Lower School MANG/FISH BS16 .... 66 B1
Colstons Girls School RDLND/MONT BS6 .... 64 C4
Colstons Primary School RDLND/MONT BS6 .... 64 A5
Colstons School MANG/FISH BS16 .... 66 B2
Combe Down House Surgery BATHSE BA2 .... 138 A4
Combe Down Infant School BATHSE BA2 .... 137 F4
Combe Down Rugby Club BATHSE BA2 .... 137 F3
Community Health Authority KEYN BS31 .... 106 C1
Community Mental Health Centre CLVDN BS21 .... 70 C5
The Compton Clinic RDLND/MONT BS6 .... 63 E2
Coniston Primary School BRSTK/PCHW BS34 .... 12 A4
Connaught Infants & Primary School BRSG/KWL/STAPK BS4 .... 92 C4
Conygre Medical Centre BRSTK/PCHW BS34 .... 28 B5
Corbett House Clinic EVILLE/WHL BS5 .... 77 F2
Coroners Court CBRISNE BS2 .... 76 C1
Corpus Christi RC VA Primary School WSM BS23 .... 6 B4
Cossham Memorial Hospital KGWD/HNM BS15 .... 68 A4
Cotham Galleries RDLND/MONT BS6 .... 63 F5
Cotham Grammar School RDLND/MONT BS6 .... 64 A5
Cotham Park Rugby Club CFTN/FAIL BS8 .... 73 E3
Cotham Road Surgery RDLND/MONT BS6 .... 76 A1
Council Offices TRWBR BA14 .... 158 C2
Court De Wyck Primary School YTN/CONG BS49 .... 117 F2
Courtney Primary School KGWD/HNM BS15 .... 81 D2
Courtside Surgery YATE/CS BS37 .... 19 F4
The Craft Gallery HORF/LLZ BS7 .... 48 A2
Crescent Gallery CBATH/BATHN BA1 .... 4 A1
Cribbs Causeway Shopping Centre BRSTK/PCHW BS34 .... 27 D1
Crockerne Primary School PTSHD/EG BS20 .... 60 A3
Crofts End Industrial Estate EVILLE/WHL BS5 .... 66 C5
Crofts End Trading Estate EVILLE/WHL BS5 .... 66 C5
The Cross Bath CBATH/BATHN BA1 .... 4 B4
Crossways Junior & Infant School THNB/SVB BS35 .... 9 D3
Crown Court CBRIS/FH BS1 .... 2 D1
Culverhay Boys School BATHSE BA2 .... 135 F3
Culverhill School YATE/CS BS37 .... 35 E1
Custom House CBRIS/FH BS1 .... 2 D4
Cutlers Brook Junior School CBRISNE BS2 .... 65 E4
David Hamiltons Practice RDLND/MONT BS6 .... 63 F5
Dean Lane Family Practice BMSTR BS3 .... 76 A5
Deers Wood Primary School KGWD/HNM BS15 .... 69 E4
3-D Gallery CBRISNE BS2 .... 2 C1
Dixon Business Centre BRSG/KWL/STAPK BS4 .... 95 D2
Dodington Parish Council YATE/CS BS37 .... 20 B5
Dolphin Shopping Centre WSM BS23 .... 6 B2
Downend Cricket Club MANG/FISH BS16 .... 51 E5
Downend School MANG/FISH BS16 .... 68 C1
Downend Surgery MANG/FISH BS16 .... 68 B1
Downland Surgery MTN/WRL BS22 .... 129 F5
Downs Fitness & Health Centre RDLND/MONT BS6 .... 63 E4
Dral Health Centre CBATH/BATHN BA1 .... 4 B2
Dr Bells C of E School MANG/FISH BS16 .... 67 E2
Drove Road Hospital WSM BS23 .... 7 E4
Duckmoor Road Industrial Estate BMSTR BS3 .... 91 D1
Dundry Primary School LGASH BS41 .... 100 B5

Dunmail Primary School
HNBRY/STHM BS10 .... 47 D1
Eagles Wood Business Park
ALMDB BS32 .... 13 D2
East Clevedon VC Primary School
CLVDN BS21 .... 71 F5
Easton Business Centre
EVILLE/WHL BS5 .... 77 F1
Easton C E VA Primary School
EVILLE/WHL BS5 .... 77 E1
Easton Leisure Centre
EVILLE/WHL BS5 .... 77 E1
Eastpark Trading Estate
EVILLE/WHL BS5 .... 66 B5
East Twerton Infant School
BATHSE BA2 .... 122 B4
Eastville Health Centre
EVILLE/WHL BS5 .... 65 F4
Elmlea Infant School
HNLZ/SM/SNYPK/WT BS9 .... 63 D1
Elmlea Junior School
HNLZ/SM/SNYPK/WT BS9 .... 63 D1
Elm Park School
FRCTL/WBN BS36 .... 31 F2
The Elms Day Hospital
THNB/SVB BS35 .... 8 B3
Embleton Junior School
HNBRY/STHM BS10 .... 46 C2
Exhibition Centre
CBRIS/FH BS1 .... 2 B4
Explore @ Bristol
CBRIS/FH BS1 .... 2 B4
The Eye Clinic
CBRIS/FH BS1 .... 3 E1
Fairfield Grammar School
RDLND/MONT BS6 .... 65 D4
Fair Furlong Primary School
BMSTRD/HC/WWD BS13 .... 101 E3
Fairway Industrial Centre
BRSTK/PCHW BS34 .... 28 A5
Falconride Primary School
KGWD/HNM BS15 .... 68 C5
The Family Practice
RDLND/MONT BS6 .... 76 A1
Family & Youth Court
CBRIS/FH BS1 .... 2 D2
Ferry Steps Trading Estate
BRSG/KWL/STAPK BS4 .... 77 E5
Filton Avenue Junior School
HORF/LLZ BS7 .... 48 B4
Filton Clinic
HORF/LLZ BS7 .... 48 B1
Filton College
BRSTK/PCHW BS34 .... 28 B4
Filton High School
BRSTK/PCHW BS34 .... 29 E5
Filton Hill CP School
BRSTK/PCHW BS34 .... 28 C4
Filton Park School
BRSTK/PCHW BS34 .... 48 A1
Filton Recreation Centre
BRSTK/PCHW BS34 .... 48 B1
Filton Shield Road School
HORF/LLZ BS7 .... 48 B2
Filton Town Council
BRSTK/PCHW BS34 .... 48 B1
Filwood Swimming Baths
BRSG/KWL/STAPK BS4 .... 92 C4
Fire Station
CBRIS/FH BS1 .... 3 F3
Fishponds Health Centre
MANG/FISH BS16 .... 67 F2
Fitzmaurice Primary School
BOAV BA15 .... 147 D4
Five C Business Centre
CLVDN BS21 .... 84 B3
The Florence Brown School
BRSG/KWL/STAPK BS4 .... 92 B4
The Florence Brown School
CBRISNE BS2 .... 3 G1
Flower Gallery
FRCTL/WBN BS36 .... 31 E2
Folk House
CBRIS/FH BS1 .... 2 B2
Fonthill Junior School
HNBRY/STHM BS10 .... 47 F1
Fosseway Junior & Infant School
BATHSE BA2 .... 136 B4
Foster Almshouses
CBRIS/FH BS1 .... 2 C2
Fouracres Primary School
BMSTRD/HC/WWD BS13 .... 100 C3
Four Oaks County Infant School
NAIL BS48 .... 87 D2
Framing Workshop & Gallery & Archival Fine Art Print
CBATH/BATHN BA1 .... 4 C1
Frampton Cotterell C of E School
FRCTL/WBN BS36 .... 16 B5
Frenchay C of E School
MANG/FISH BS16 .... 50 C4
Frenchay Health Authority
MANG/FISH BS16 .... 68 A1
Frenchay Hospital
MANG/FISH BS16 .... 50 C3
Frenchay Village Museum
MANG/FISH BS16 .... 50 A4
Frome Bank Junior School
YATE/CS BS37 .... 19 E2
Fromeside Clinic
MANG/FISH BS16 .... 67 D1
Fulford Special School
BMSTRD/HC/WWD BS13 .... 102 A3
The Galleries Shopping Centre
CBRIS/FH BS1 .... 3 E1
Gay Elms Junior & Infant School
BMSTRD/HC/WWD BS13 .... 101 E3
Georgian House
CBRIS/FH BS1 .... 2 A3
Georgian House
CBATH/BATHN BA1 .... 122 C3
Gillies & Partners
CBATH/BATHN BA1 .... 123 F1
Glebe County School
YTN/CONG BS49 .... 133 D2
Glencoe Business Park
WSM BS23 .... 7 H2
Glenfrome Primary School
EVILLE/WHL BS5 .... 66 A2
Gloucestershire County Council
KGWD/HNM BS15 .... 80 C1
Gloucestershire County Cricket Club
HORF/LLZ BS7 .... 64 C2
Glynne Wickham Studio Theatre
CFTN/FAIL BS8 .... 2 A2
Golden Valley Primary School
NAIL BS48 .... 87 E2
Gordano Rugby Football Club
PTSHD/EG BS20 .... 58 A3
Gordano School
PTSHD/EG BS20 .... 56 A3
Gordon Fraser Gallery
CBATH/BATHN BA1 .... 4 A2
Graham Road Surgery
WSM BS23 .... 6 C2
Granby House Clinic
BMSTR BS3 .... 92 A1
Grand Pier
WSM BS23 .... 6 A1
Grange Road Surgery
BMSTRD/HC/WWD BS13 .... 101 D2
Great Western Business Park
YATE/CS BS37 .... 18 C2
Green Park Station
CBATH/BATHN BA1 .... 4 A3
Greystoke Business Centre
PTSHD/EG BS20 .... 56 B2
Grimsbury Park School
OLD/WMLY/WICK BS30 .... 81 F2
Grosvenor Surgery
CBATH/BATHN BA1 .... 124 A1
Grove County Junior School
NAIL BS48 .... 86 C4
Grove Industrial Estate
BRSTK/PCHW BS34 .... 28 C1
The Grove Primary School
TRWBR BA14 .... 158 B2
Grove Road Day Hospital
RDLND/MONT BS6 .... 63 E4
Grove Sports Centre
NAIL BS48 .... 86 C4
Hambrook CP School
MANG/FISH BS16 .... 31 E5
Hambrook Sports Club
MANG/FISH BS16 .... 31 E5
Hampset Cricket Club
BATHSE BA2 .... 136 B3
Hanham Abbots Junior School
KGWD/HNM BS15 .... 80 A5
Hanham Business Park
KGWD/HNM BS15 .... 79 F4
Hanham C of E Primary School
KGWD/HNM BS15 .... 79 F5
Hanham High School
KGWD/HNM BS15 .... 80 A5
Hanham Surgery
KGWD/HNM BS15 .... 80 B5
Hannah More County Infant School
NAIL BS48 .... 86 C4
Hannah More Primary School
CBRISNE BS2 .... 3 H3
The Happening Art Gallery
RDLND/MONT BS6 .... 63 F5
Hareclive Primary School
BMSTRD/HC/WWD BS13 .... 102 A3
Hartcliffe Health Centre
BMSTRD/HC/WWD BS13 .... 102 A3
Hartcliffe School
BMSTRD/HC/WWD BS13 .... 102 C3
Harveys Wine Museum
CBRIS/FH BS1 .... 2 B3
Haslemere Industrial Estate
AVONM BS11 .... 43 D1
Hawkins Clinic
CBATH/BATHN BA1 .... 4 B3
Hawthorne Industrial Estate
RDSTK/MIDN BA3 .... 161 F4
Hayesfield School
BATHSE BA2 .... 122 C4
Hayward Road Industrial Estate
MANG/FISH BS16 .... 68 B3
Headley Park Primary School
BMSTRD/HC/WWD BS13 .... 91 F5
Health & Fitness Club
WSM BS23 .... 6 D3
Heath House Priory Hospital
HORF/LLZ BS7 .... 65 F2
Henbury Court Junior & Primary School
HNBRY/STHM BS10 .... 26 A5
Henbury Manor School
HNBRY/STHM BS10 .... 45 F1
Henbury Old Boys AFC
HNBRY/STHM BS10 .... 46 A1
Henbury School
HNBRY/STHM BS10 .... 25 F5
The Henbury Surgery
HNBRY/STHM BS10 .... 26 A5
Henbury Swimming Pool
HNBRY/STHM BS10 .... 46 A1
Henfield Business Park
FRCTL/WBN BS36 .... 53 E1
Hengrove School
HGRV/WHIT BS14 .... 93 F5
Henleaze Infant School
RDLND/MONT BS6 .... 64 A1
Herschel House Museum
CBATH/BATHN BA1 .... 4 A3
Heywood Health Centre
PTSHD/EG BS20 .... 60 A2
Highbridge Infant School
BMSTRD/HC/WWD BS13 .... 101 D1
Highcroft Junior School
FRCTL/WBN BS36 .... 17 D5
High Down Infants and Junior School
PTSHD/EG BS20 .... 55 E2
Hillfields Park Primary School
MANG/FISH BS16 .... 68 A3
Hillside Infant School
MTN/WRL BS22 .... 129 D5
The Hindu Temple
EVILLE/WHL BS5 .... 78 A1
Hippodrome Theatre
CBRIS/FH BS1 .... 2 C3
Holbrook School
TRWBR BA14 .... 159 D1
Holburne Museum & Crafts Study Centre
BATHSE BA2 .... 5 E1
Holloway Dental Health Centre
HGRV/WHIT BS14 .... 104 C2
Hollywood Bowl
CBRISNE BS2 .... 78 A4
Holy Family RC Primary School
BRSTK/PCHW BS34 .... 12 C5
Holymead Infant School
BRSG/KWL/STAPK BS4 .... 94 B2
Holymead School
BRSG/KWL/STAPK BS4 .... 94 B1
Holy Trinity Primary School
ALMDB BS32 .... 13 D3
Homefield Industrial Estate
OMX/HUT/LCK BS24 .... 143 F5
Homeopathic Hospital
CFTN/FAIL BS8 .... 76 A1
Hope House Surgery
RDSTK/MIDN BA3 .... 162 C2

Horfield C of E School
HNBRY/STHM BS10 .... 47 E4
Horfield Health Centre
HORF/LLZ BS7 .... 48 B5
Horfield Sports Centre
HORF/LLZ BS7 .... 48 A4
Hornets Rugby Football Club
WSM BS23 .... 142 B3
Hospital
PTSHD/EG BS20 .... 60 C2
Hot Bath Gallery and
College of Art
CBATH/BATHN BA1 .... 4 B4
Hotspots Indoor Sports Centre
BRSG/KWL/STAPK BS4 .... 95 D2
Hotwells Primary School
CFTN/FAIL BS8 .... 75 D3
Hutton Moor Leisure Centre
WSM BS23 .... 142 A3
Hutton Primary School
OMX/HUT/LCK BS24 .... 153 D3
Hydro Estate
AVONM BS11 .... 22 C5
Ilminster Avenue Junior School
BRSG/KWL/STAPK BS4 .... 93 E4
Industrial Estate
BRSG/KWL/STAPK BS4 .... 95 D3
Industrial Heritage Centre
CBATH/BATHN BA1 .... 123 D2
The Institute of Cosmetic Surgery
CFTN/FAIL BS8 .... 63 E5
Iron Acton C of E School
YATE/CS BS37 .... 17 F1
John Cabot City
Technology College
KGWD/HNM BS15 .... 80 A2
John Govett Gallery
BOAV BA15 .... 146 C3
The John Milton Health Clinic
HNBRY/STHM BS10 .... 26 B5
The John of Gaunt School
TRWBR BA14 .... 156 B4
Jorrocks Estate
YATE/CS BS37 .... 35 D4
Jubilee Public Baths
BRSG/KWL/STAPK BS4 .... 93 F2
Kenn Business Park
CLVDN BS21 .... 85 E4
Kennedy Way Surgery
YATE/CS BS37 .... 19 F4
Kewstoke Primary School
MTN/WRL BS22 .... 128 A4
Keynsham County
Primary School
KEYN BS31 .... 106 B2
Keynsham Hospital
KEYN BS31 .... 107 D3
Keynsham Leisure Centre
KEYN BS31 .... 107 D2
Keynsham Rugby Club
KEYN BS31 .... 96 B5
Keynsham Town Football Club
KEYN BS31 .... 96 B5
Kilmersdon Magistrates Court
RDSTK/MIDN BA3 .... 162 B2
King Edmund Community School
YATE/CS BS37 .... 19 F4
King Edwards School
BATHSE BA2 .... 5 G1
Kings Business Park
CBRISNE BS2 .... 78 A3
Kings Chase Shopping Centre
KGWD/HNM BS15 .... 80 B1
Kings Court Primary School
YATE/CS BS37 .... 19 F5
Kingsdown Sports Centre
RDLND/MONT BS6 .... 76 A1
Kingsfield School
KGWD/HNM BS15 .... 81 E1
Kingshill Primary School
NAIL BS48 .... 86 C1
Kingsweston School
AVONM BS11 .... 44 B3
Kingswood Borough Council
MANG/FISH BS16 .... 68 B2
Kingswood District Council
KGWD/HNM BS15 .... 80 B2
Kingswood Health Centre
KGWD/HNM BS15 .... 80 C1
Kingswood Leisure Centre
MANG/FISH BS16 .... 68 B3
Kingswood Preparatory School
CBATH/BATHN BA1 .... 122 C1
Kingswood School
CBATH/BATHN BA1 .... 112 C5
Knowle Junior Mixed School
BRSG/KWL/STAPK BS4 .... 93 E1
Knowle Park Junior School
BRSG/KWL/STAPK BS4 .... 93 E3
The Lake Surgery
HNBRY/STHM BS10 .... 46 C4
Lancaster House School
WSM BS23 .... 141 E2
Lansdown Cricket Club
CBATH/BATHN BA1 .... 121 F2
Larkhall Football Club
CBATH/BATHN BA1 .... 113 F4
Larkrise School
TRWBR BA14 .... 157 F3
Lawnwood Road
Industrial Estate
EVILLE/WHL BS5 .... 77 F1
Lawrence Hill Health Centre
CBRISNE BS2 .... 77 E2
Lawrence Hill Industrial Estate
EVILLE/WHL BS5 .... 78 A1
Lawrence Hill Industrial Park
EVILLE/WHL BS5 .... 77 F1
Lawrence Weston School
AVONM BS11 .... 44 C2
Le Coree Gallery
BOAV BA15 .... 146 C3
Leigh Court Business Centre
CFTN/FAIL BS8 .... 61 E4
Leisure Pavillion
WSM BS23 .... 140 B3
Lewis Road Surgery
BMSTRD/HC/WWD BS13 .... 91 E4
Liberty Industrial Park
BMSTR BS3 .... 91 E3
Lime Grove School
BATHSE BA2 .... 5 E4
Little Stoke Junior School
BRSTK/PCHW BS34 .... 29 E2
Little Theatre
CBATH/BATHN BA1 .... 4 B4
Locking Road Business Park
WSM BS23 .... 7 G2
Lockleaze School
HORF/LLZ BS7 .... 49 D3
Lodge Causeway Trading Estate
MANG/FISH BS16 .... 67 D3
The Lodge Park School
CBATH/BATHN BA1 .... 122 A2
Long Ashton Surgery
LGASH BS41 .... 89 D3
Longbrook Trading Estate
BMSTR BS3 .... 90 C1
Longvernal Primary School
RDSTK/MIDN BA3 .... 160 C3
Longwell Green CP School
OLD/WMLY/WICK BS30 .... 97 D1
Lonsdale Business Centre
KGWD/HNM BS15 .... 68 A4
Lord Chancellors Department
CBRIS/FH BS1 .... 2 D2
Lord Chancellors Department
CFTN/FAIL BS8 .... 75 D2
Lovemead Group Practice
TRWBR BA14 .... 157 D4
Luckwell Road School
BMSTR BS3 .... 91 E1
Lyntony House Reading School
HORF/LLZ BS7 .... 64 B3
Malago Surgery
BMSTR BS3 .... 92 A1
Malago Vale Trading Estate
BMSTR BS3 .... 92 B1
The Mall Gallery
CFTN/FAIL BS8 .... 75 D2
The Mall
BRSTK/PCHW BS34 .... 27 E2
The Maltings Industrial Estate
CBATH/BATHN BA1 .... 121 F3
Mangotsfield School
MANG/FISH BS16 .... 69 F2
Mangotsfield United
Football Club
MANG/FISH BS16 .... 69 F1
Manilla Crescent
WSM BS23 .... 140 B1
Manor Brook School
THNB/SVB BS35 .... 8 C1
Manor C of E School
FRCTL/WBN BS36 .... 33 D2
Manor Farm Associated
Football Club
HNLZ/SM/SNYPK/WT BS9 .... 61 F1
Margaret Coates Special School
BATHSE BA2 .... 136 C5
Margaret Stancomb
Infant School
TRWBR BA14 .... 156 C3
Maritime Heritage Centre
CBRIS/FH BS1 .... 75 F4
Marlow Vetinary Surgery
CBATH/BATHN BA1 .... 122 A4
Mary Elton Primary School
CLVDN BS21 .... 84 B3
May Park Primary School
EVILLE/WHL BS5 .... 66 A4
The Meadows Primary School
OLD/WMLY/WICK BS30 .... 98 B4
Mead Vale Primary School
MTN/WRL BS22 .... 143 D1
Meltone Gallery
BATHSE BA2 .... 123 F2
Mendip Green First School
MTN/WRL BS22 .... 143 D1
Mendip Leisure Centre
PTSHD/EG BS20 .... 56 B2
Merrywood School
BRSG/KWL/STAPK BS4 .... 93 D3
Midland Way Business Park
THNB/SVB BS35 .... 8 B4
Midsomer Norton
County Primary School
RDSTK/MIDN BA3 .... 161 E3
Millpond Primary School
EVILLE/WHL BS5 .... 65 E5
Milson Street Clinic
CBATH/BATHN BA1 .... 4 B2
Milton CP Infant School
MTN/WRL BS22 .... 142 A1
Milton Junior School
MTN/WRL BS22 .... 142 B1
The Milton Surgery
MTN/WRL BS22 .... 142 A2
Minto Road Industrial Centre
RDLND/MONT BS6 .... 65 D4
Mizzymean Recreation Centre
NAIL BS48 .... 86 C3
Model Yacht Pond
WSM BS23 .... 6 A5
Model Yacht Pond
WSM BS23 .... 140 C2
Monks Park School
HORF/LLZ BS7 .... 48 A2
Monks Park Surgery
HORF/LLZ BS7 .... 48 A3
Monkton Combe Junior School
BATHSE BA2 .... 138 A4
Monkton Combe School
BATHSE BA2 .... 138 C4
Montpelier Health Centre
RDLND/MONT BS6 .... 64 C5
Moorlands Infant School
BATHSE BA2 .... 136 B1
Moorlands Junior School
BATHSE BA2 .... 136 B2
Mount Zion School
RDLND/MONT BS6 .... 64 B5
Museum
CBATH/BATHN BA1 .... 112 B3
Museum
RDSTK/MIDN BA3 .... 162 B5
Museum of Asian Art
CBATH/BATHN BA1 .... 4 B1
Museum of Costume &
Fashion Research Centre
CBATH/BATHN BA1 .... 4 A2
Nailsea Health Centre
NAIL BS48 .... 87 D2
Nailsea School
NAIL BS48 .... 87 E3
Natural Health Clinic
RDLND/MONT BS6 .... 75 F1
Newbridge Industrial Estate
BRSG/KWL/STAPK BS4 .... 78 B3
Newbridge Junior School
CBATH/BATHN BA1 .... 121 F3
Newbridge St Johns C of E
Infant School
CBATH/BATHN BA1 .... 121 F3
Newbridge Surgery
CBATH/BATHN BA1 .... 121 F3
New Court Surgery
WSM BS23 .... 141 D2

New Fosseway School
HGRV/WHIT BS14 .... 93 F5
New Siblands School
THNB/SVB BS35 .... 9 D3
New Theatre Royal
CBATH/BATHN BA1 .... 4 A3
Newton Park College
BATHSE BA2 .... 119 F5
Newtown County Primary School
TRWBR BA14 .... 156 C4
Northavon Business Centre
YATE/CS BS37 .... 19 D2
North Avon Magistrates Court
YATE/CS BS37 .... 19 F4
North Bradley C of E School
TRWBR BA14 .... 158 C5
North Bristol Rugby Football Club
ALMDB BS32 .... 12 B2
Northleaze Primary School
LGASH BS41 .... 89 F2
Northridge Business Centre
YATE/CS BS37 .... 19 D3
North Road CP School
YATE/CS BS37 .... 18 C1
North Somerset Council
CLVDN BS21 .... 85 D1
North Somerset Council
NAIL BS48 .... 87 D2
North Somerset Council
WSM BS23 .... 7 H2
North Somerset Council
WSM BS23 .... 140 C2
North Somerset Council
WSM BS23 .... 141 E2
North Somerset Council
WSM BS23 .... 150 B3
Northville Family Practice
HORF/LLZ BS7 .... 48 C2
North Worle Shopping Centre
MTN/WRL BS22 .... 130 A4
Norton Hill School
RDSTK/MIDN BA3 .... 161 E4
Norton Radstock College
RDSTK/MIDN BA3 .... 161 D3
Norton Radstock Town Council
RDSTK/MIDN BA3 .... 162 C2
Novers Hill Trading Estate
BMSTR BS3 .... 92 A3
Novers Lane Jmi School
BRSG/KWL/STAPK BS4 .... 92 A5
Oakfield Business Park
KGWD/HNM BS15 .... 80 B2
Oatley Trading Estate
KGWD/HNM BS15 .... 68 B5
Odd Down Football Club
BATHSE BA2 .... 136 A5
Odeon Cinema
CBRIS/FH BS1 .... 2 D2
Odeon Cinema
WSM BS23 .... 6 C1
Odeon Theatre
WSM BS23 .... 6 C1
Off Centre Gallery
BMSTR BS3 .... 92 B1
Old Bristolians Sports Club
CFTN/FAIL BS8 .... 73 D5
Oldbury Court Infant School
MANG/FISH BS16 .... 51 D4
Oldbury Court Jm School
MANG/FISH BS16 .... 51 D4
Old Culverhaysians RFC
BATHSE BA2 .... 136 A4
Oldfield Old Boys Rugby Club
BATHSE BA2 .... 122 C4
The Oldfield Park Surgery
BATHSE BA2 .... 122 C5
Oldfield School
CBATH/BATHN BA1 .... 121 D1
Old Knightstone Theatre
WSM BS23 .... 140 B2
Oldland Surgery
OLD/WMLY/WICK BS30 .... 98 A1
Old Mills Trading Estate
RDSTK/MIDN BA3 .... 160 B2
Oldmixon County Infant School
OMX/HUT/LCK BS24 .... 151 F3
Old Sucians RFC
CBATH/BATHN BA1 .... 112 B3
The Old Surgery
WSM BS23 .... 141 D2
The Open University
CBRIS/FH BS1 .... 3 E4
Optimax Laser Eye Clinic
CBRIS/FH BS1 .... 2 C3
The Orchard Medical Centre
KGWD/HNM BS15 .... 80 B1
The Other Surgery
CFTN/FAIL BS8 .... 63 F5
Our Lady of Lourdes RC School
KGWD/HNM BS15 .... 80 C2
Our Lady of the Rosary RC Primary School
AVONM BS11 .... 44 B3
Paddingham House
WNSC BS25 .... 155 D4
Paragon School
BATHSE BA2 .... 137 E2
Parish Wharf Leisure Centre
PTSHD/EG BS20 .... 39 F5
Park House Clinic
RDSTK/MIDN BA3 .... 161 D4
Park Preparatory School for Boys
CBATH/BATHN BA1 .... 122 A2
The Park School
KGWD/HNM BS15 .... 80 C1
Parkside Infant School
CBATH/BATHN BA1 .... 4 A2
Parkwall CP School
OLD/WMLY/WICK BS30 .... 81 E5
Parkway Trading Estate
CBRISNE BS2 .... 65 D4
Parnall Road Industrial Estate
MANG/FISH BS16 .... 67 E3
Parochial Junior School
TRWBR BA14 .... 157 D2
Parson Street Primary School
BMSTR BS3 .... 92 A2
Patchway C of E Primary School
BRSTK/PCHW BS34 .... 13 D4
Patchway Health Clinic
BRSTK/PCHW BS34 .... 12 B5
Patchway High School
ALMDB BS32 .... 12 C4
Patchway Town Council
BRSTK/PCHW BS34 .... 12 A5
Pavilion
BATHSE BA2 .... 4 D3
Pavilion
CBATH/BATHN BA1 .... 4 A2
Pavillion
BATHSE BA2 .... 4 D4
Paxcroft Primary School
TRWBR BA14 .... 157 F3
Pembroke Road Surgery
CFTN/FAIL BS8 .... 63 E5
Pen Park School
HNBRY/STHM BS10 .... 47 E1
Perry Court Junior & Infant School
HGRV/WHIT BS14 .... 103 E1
Petherton Road Infant School
HGRV/WHIT BS14 .... 93 F5
Phoenix Business Park
BMSTR BS3 .... 91 E2
Phoenix NHS Trust
KGWD/HNM BS15 .... 80 A5
Pilning CP School
THNB/SVB BS35 .... 11 F4
Pines Way Industrial Estate
BATHSE BA2 .... 122 C4
Pixash Business Centre
KEYN BS31 .... 107 F2
Playhouse Theatre
WSM BS23 .... 140 C2
Post Office
BATHSE BA2 .... 122 B4
The Podium Shopping Cente and Library
CBATH/BATHN BA1 .... 4 C3
Portbury Sawmills Industrial Estate
PTSHD/EG BS20 .... 42 A4
Portbury VA Primary School
PTSHD/EG BS20 .... 58 C3
Portishead CP School
PTSHD/EG BS20 .... 56 A1
Portishead Health Centre
PTSHD/EG BS20 .... 56 B1
Portishead & North Weston Town Council
PTSHD/EG BS20 .... 56 B1
Portrait Gallery
HORF/LLZ BS7 .... 48 A2
Portview Trading Estate
AVONM BS11 .... 42 C3
Portway School
AVONM BS11 .... 43 F4
Portway Trading Estate
AVONM BS11 .... 43 D4
The Practice
CFTN/FAIL BS8 .... 75 F2
Prim School
THNB/SVB BS35 .... 8 B4
Prior Park College
BATHSE BA2 .... 138 A3
Priory Doctors Surgery
BRSG/KWL/STAPK BS4 .... 93 F2
Priory Farm Trading Estate
PTSHD/EG BS20 .... 58 B3
Priory School
MTN/WRL BS22 .... 130 A4
The Priory Surgery
BRSG/KWL/STAPK BS4 .... 93 F2
QEH Sports Club
CFTN/FAIL BS8 .... 88 B1
QEH Theatre
CFTN/FAIL BS8 .... 75 F2
Quakers Friars
CBRIS/FH BS1 .... 3 F1
Queen Elizabeth Hospital
CFTN/FAIL BS8 .... 75 F3
Radstock County Infant School
RDSTK/MIDN BA3 .... 162 C1
Radstock St Nicholas Infant School
RDSTK/MIDN BA3 .... 162 C2
Radstock St Nicholas Junior School
RDSTK/MIDN BA3 .... 162 C2
Radstock Town Football Club
RDSTK/MIDN BA3 .... 163 D2
Ralph Allen School
BATHSE BA2 .... 138 C3
Ravenswood School
NAIL BS48 .... 86 C1
Raysfield Infant School
YATE/CS BS37 .... 20 A5
Raysfield Junior School
YATE/CS BS37 .... 20 A5
Redfield Edge Primary School
OLD/WMLY/WICK BS30 .... 82 B5
Redfield Leisure Centre
EVILLE/WHL BS5 .... 78 A2
Redgrave Theatre
CFTN/FAIL BS8 .... 75 D1
Redhouse Primary School
BMSTRD/HC/WWD BS13 .... 101 E2
Redland High Junior School
RDLND/MONT BS6 .... 64 A4
Redland High School
RDLND/MONT BS6 .... 64 A4
Red Maids Junior School
HNLZ/SM/SNYPK/WT BS9 .... 46 B5
Red Maids School
HNLZ/SM/SNYPK/WT BS9 .... 46 B5
Register Office
CBRIS/FH BS1 .... 3 E1
Registry Office
CBATH/BATHN BA1 .... 4 A2
The Ridge Junior School
YATE/CS BS37 .... 20 A3
Ridgeway Industrial Centre
EVILLE/WHL BS5 .... 66 C4
Ridings High School
FRCTL/WBN BS36 .... 31 E2
Riverbank Medical Centre
MTN/WRL BS22 .... 130 A4
Riverside Business Park
EVILLE/WHL BS5 .... 78 B3
Riverside Leisure Centre
CBRISNE BS2 .... 77 D1
Riverside Surgery
BRSG/KWL/STAPK BS4 .... 95 D1
Robin Cousins Sports Centre
AVONM BS11 .... 43 D3
Rockingham Works
AVONM BS11 .... 23 E3
Rodford CP School
YATE/CS BS37 .... 35 E1
Rodford Infant School
YATE/CS BS37 .... 35 D1
Roman Baths and Pump Rooms
CBATH/BATHN BA1 .... 4 C4
Romney Avenue Junior Mixed School
HORF/LLZ BS7 .... 48 C5
Rooksmoor Gallery
CBATH/BATHN BA1 .... 4 A1

Rose Green Sports & Leisure Centre EVILLE/WHL BS5 ..... 66 B5
The Rostra Gallery CBATH/BATHN BA1 ..... 4 B2
The Royal High School CBATH/BATHN BA1 ..... 113 D5
Royal National Hospital for Rheumatic Diseases CBATH/BATHN BA1 ..... 4 B3
Royal Navy & Royal Marines CBRIS/FH BS1 ..... 2 C2
Royal United Hospital CBATH/BATHN BA1 ..... 121 F2
Royal West of England Academy CFTN/FAIL BS8 ..... 75 F2
Royce Clinic TRWBR BA14 ..... 157 E2
Rps Octagon Galleries CBATH/BATHN BA1 ..... 4 B2
Rspca & Dogs Home CBRISNE BS2 ..... 77 E5
Russell Town Avenue Industrial Centre EVILLE/WHL BS5 ..... 78 A2
Rydal School CLVDN BS21 ..... 71 D5
St Andrews C of E VA Primary School CBATH/BATHN BA1 ..... 123 D2
St Andrews Trading Estate AVONM BS11 ..... 43 D1
St Andrews VC Junior School YTN/CONG BS49 ..... 132 C2
St Annes C of E Primary School OLD/WMLY/WICK BS30 ..... 98 A1
St Annes Junior Mixed School BRSG/KWL/STAPK BS4 ..... 78 B4
St Annes Park JMI School BRSG/KWL/STAPK BS4 ..... 78 C4
St Apollonias Surgery KEYN BS31 ..... 106 C1
St Augustine of Canterbury RC Primary School MANG/FISH BS16 ..... 51 F4
St Augustines RC School TRWBR BA14 ..... 156 B4
St Barnabas C of E VC Junior Mixed Infant School RDLND/MONT BS6 ..... 65 D5
St Barnabas C of E VC Primary School PTSHD/EG BS20 ..... 55 F1
St Bedes RC School AVONM BS11 ..... 44 B1
St Benedicts RC Primary School RDSTK/MIDN BA3 ..... 161 F5
St Bernadette RC School HGRV/WHIT BS14 ..... 104 A1
St Bernadettes RC Primary School HGRV/WHIT BS14 ..... 103 F1
St Bernards RC Primary School AVONM BS11 ..... 43 F5
St Bonaventures RC School RDLND/MONT BS6 ..... 64 A2
St Brandons School CLVDN BS21 ..... 84 C1
St Brendans Sixth Form College BRSG/KWL/STAPK BS4 ..... 95 D3
St Brendans Trading Estate AVONM BS11 ..... 42 C1
St Catherines Industrial Estate BMSTR BS3 ..... 76 B5
St Chads Surgery RDSTK/MIDN BA3 ..... 161 E3
St Francis RC School NAIL BS48 ..... 87 E3
St Gabriels Business Park EVILLE/WHL BS5 ..... 77 F1
St George Health Centre KGWD/HNM BS15 ..... 79 E1
St George School EVILLE/WHL BS5 ..... 77 F1
St Georges Industrial Estate AVONM BS11 ..... 22 C5
St Georges Primary School CFTN/FAIL BS8 ..... 75 F3
St Gloucester Co THNB/SVB BS35 ..... 8 A3
St Gregorys RC School BATHSE BA2 ..... 136 B5
St James's Gallery CBATH/BATHN BA1 ..... 4 A1
St James Surgery CBATH/BATHN BA1 ..... 123 D2
St Johns Church & Old City Gate CBRIS/FH BS1 ..... 2 D2
St Johns C of E Primary School KEYN BS31 ..... 106 C2
St Johns C of E VC Primary School CFTN/FAIL BS8 ..... 63 E4
St Johns Hospital TRWBR BA14 ..... 158 C1
St Johns Junior School RDSTK/MIDN BA3 ..... 160 C3
St Johns Lane Health Centre BMSTR BS3 ..... 92 C2
St Johns Mead C of E VC Primary School YATE/CS BS37 ..... 20 C4
St Johns RC Primary School BATHSE BA2 ..... 5 E3
St Johns RC School TRWBR BA14 ..... 156 B4
St John the Evangelist Primary School CLVDN BS21 ..... 84 C3
St Josephs RC School MANG/FISH BS16 ..... 67 F3
St Josephs RC School PTSHD/EG BS20 ..... 38 C5
St Katherines School PTSHD/EG BS20 ..... 60 C3
St Laurence School BOAV BA15 ..... 146 C2
St Margarets Surgery BOAV BA15 ..... 147 D3
St Marks C of E School CBATH/BATHN BA1 ..... 113 F5
St Mark's Community Centre BATHSE BA2 ..... 4 C6
St Marks VA Primary School MTN/WRL BS22 ..... 129 E3
St Martins Hospital BATHSE BA2 ..... 136 C4
St Martins Junior School MTN/WRL BS22 ..... 128 C5
St Martins Surgery BRSG/KWL/STAPK BS4 ..... 93 F3
St Mary Redcliffe Primary School BMSTR BS3 ..... 76 C5
St Mary Redcliffe & Temple C of E VA School CBRIS/FH BS1 ..... 3 F6
St Marys C of E Primary School YATE/CS BS37 ..... 19 F3
St Marys C of E School THNB/SVB BS35 ..... 8 A2
St Marys Hospital CFTN/FAIL BS8 ..... 75 F2
St Marys RC Infant School CBATH/BATHN BA1 ..... 121 F1
St Marys RC Primary School RDSTK/MIDN BA3 ..... 163 F2
St Mary's Redcliff CBRIS/FH BS1 ..... 3 E5
St Marys Rugby Club ALMDB BS32 ..... 14 A3
St Michael on the Mount C of E Primary School CFTN/FAIL BS8 ..... 2 B2
St Michaels C of E VC Primary School FRCTL/WBN BS36 ..... 31 F2
St Michaels Hill Clinic CBRISNE BS2 ..... 2 B1
St Michaels Hospital CBRISNE BS2 ..... 76 A1
St Michaels Primary School BRSTK/PCHW BS34 ..... 29 F3
St Nicholas Chantry Primary School CLVDN BS21 ..... 71 E5
St Nicholas Market CBRIS/FH BS1 ..... 2 D3
St Patricks RC School EVILLE/WHL BS5 ..... 78 B2
St Pauls RC Primary School YATE/CS BS37 ..... 19 F5
St Peter & St. Paul School RDLND/MONT BS6 ..... 76 A1
St Peters C of E VC Primary School PTSHD/EG BS20 ..... 56 B2
St Philips Junior & Infant School BATHSE BA2 ..... 136 B3
St Pius X RC Primary School BMSTRD/HC/WWD BS13 ..... 101 E2
St Saviours Infant School CBATH/BATHN BA1 ..... 113 F5
St Saviours Junior School CBATH/BATHN BA1 ..... 113 F5
St Stephens Business Centre OLD/WMLY/WICK BS30 ..... 82 A4
St Stephens C of E School CBATH/BATHN BA1 ..... 123 D1
St Stephens C of E VC Junior School KGWD/HNM BS15 ..... 68 B4
St Teresas Private Hospital BATHSE BA2 ..... 119 F2
St Teresas RC School HORF/LLZ BS7 ..... 47 F2
St Thomas More RC School HORF/LLZ BS7 ..... 65 E3
St Ursulas High School HNLZ/SM/SNYPK/WT BS9 ..... 46 B5
St Vincents Trading Estate CBRISNE BS2 ..... 78 A3
Sally Lunn's House CBATH/BATHN BA1 ..... 4 C4
Saltford Primary School KEYN BS31 ..... 108 C5
Salvation Army BMSTR BS3 ..... 76 A5
Salvation Army CBATH/BATHN BA1 ..... 4 A4
Salvation Army WSM BS23 ..... 6 B2
Sampson House Business Park HNBRY/STHM BS10 ..... 25 E1
Samuel Whites Infant School KGWD/HNM BS15 ..... 80 A4
Saracens Rugby Club HNBRY/STHM BS10 ..... 26 A3
Satellite Business Park EVILLE/WHL BS5 ..... 78 B2
Saville Court Business Centre CFTN/FAIL BS8 ..... 75 E2
Sawclose Health Clinic CBATH/BATHN BA1 ..... 4 B3
Scotch Horn Community & Sports Centre NAIL BS48 ..... 87 E2
Sea Life Centre WSM BS23 ..... 6 A3
Sea Mills Infant School HNLZ/SM/SNYPK/WT BS9 ..... 45 D4
Sea Mills Junior School HNLZ/SM/SNYPK/WT BS9 ..... 61 F1
Sea Mills Surgery HNLZ/SM/SNYPK/WT BS9 ..... 61 F1
Sefton Park School HORF/LLZ BS7 ..... 65 D3
Severn Beach CP School THNB/SVB BS35 ..... 10 B4
Severnside Trading Estate AVONM BS11 ..... 23 D3
Severnside Trading Estate AVONM BS11 ..... 43 D2
Sheene Court Industrial Estate BMSTR BS3 ..... 92 A1
Sheilding Schools THNB/SVB BS35 ..... 8 A3
Shirehampton Baths AVONM BS11 ..... 43 F5
Shirehampton Cricket Club AVONM BS11 ..... 44 A4
Shirehampton Health Centre AVONM BS11 ..... 43 F5
Shirehampton Infant School AVONM BS11 ..... 43 E5
Shirehampton Junior School AVONM BS11 ..... 43 E5
Showcase Cinema Bristol CBRISNE BS2 ..... 78 A4
Sidcot School WNSC BS25 ..... 155 D5
Sikh Temple EVILLE/WHL BS5 ..... 65 F5
Sikh Temple EVILLE/WHL BS5 ..... 66 A4
Silverhill School FRCTL/WBN BS36 ..... 31 F1

Simplex Trading Estate
OLD/WMLY/WICK BS30 .... **82** B5
Sir Bernard Lovell School
OLD/WMLY/WICK BS30 .... **82** A5
The Sisters of the Temple
CFTN/FAIL BS8................................ **75** D2
Sneyd Park Surgery
HNLZ/SM/SNYPK/WT BS9 .... **62** C3
Soaphouse Industrial Estate
EVILLE/WHL BS5 .... **78** C1
The Soga Gallery
CFTN/FAIL BS8................................ **75** E3
Somerton House Surgery
RDSTK/MIDN BA3........................ **161** D3
Somervale School
RDSTK/MIDN BA3........................ **161** D4
Soundwell College
KGWD/HNM BS15.......................... **68** C4
South Bristol College
BMSTRD/HC/WWD BS13 .... **102** B3
Southdown Junior School
BATHSE BA2 .... **135** F2
Southfield Road Trading Estate
NAIL BS48 .... **87** E1
Southgate Shopping Centre
CBATH/BATHN BA1.......................... **4** C4
South Gloucestershire Council
BRSTK/PCHW BS34......................... **12** A4
South Gloucestershire Council
BRSTK/PCHW BS34......................... **28** C5
South Gloucestershire Council
MANG/FISH BS16 .... **52** C5
South Gloucestershire Council
THNB/SVB BS35 .... **11** E5
South Gloucestershire Council
YATE/CS BS37 .... **19** D1
South Gloucestershire Council
YATE/CS BS37 .... **20** A4
Southmead Health Centre
HNBRY/STHM BS10 .... **47** D1
Southmead Health Services NHS Trust
HNBRY/STHM BS10 .... **47** E3
South Street Primary School
BMSTR BS3 .... **91** F1
South View Business Centre
MANG/FISH BS16 .... **68** C1
South View Business Park
MANG/FISH BS16 .... **68** C1
Southville Primary School
BMSTR BS3 .... **76** A5
Southville Surgery
BMSTR BS3 .... **2** B6
South Wansdyke Sports Centre
RDSTK/MIDN BA3........................ **161** E3
Speedwell Industrial Estate
CLVDN BS21................................... **84** C2
Speedwell School
EVILLE/WHL BS5 .... **67** E5
Speedwell Swimming Baths
EVILLE/WHL BS5 .... **67** D5
Springfield School
RDLND/MONT BS6 .... **64** C4
Springwater Park Trading Estate
EVILLE/WHL BS5 .... **78** C2
SS Great Britain
CBRIS/FH BS1 .... **75** F4
Stafford Business Centre
WSM BS23 .... **7** E1
The Stafford Clinic
WSM BS23 .... **150** C1
Stanbridge CP School
MANG/FISH BS16 .... **52** A5
Stanley Court Surgery
RDSTK/MIDN BA3........................ **161** E2
Staple Hill Primary School
MANG/FISH BS16 .... **68** B2
Staverton C of E School
TRWBR BA14................................ **149** D4
Steps Gallery
CBRIS/FH BS1 .... **2** C2
Sterling College International
CBATH/BATHN BA1.......................... **4** C1
Stockwood Green Primary School
HGRV/WHIT BS14 .... **104** C3
Stoke Bishop C of E Primary School
HNLZ/SM/SNYPK/WT BS9 .... **62** B1
Stoke Gifford Medical Centre
BRSTK/PCHW BS34......................... **29** F4
Stoke Lodge Infant School
BRSTK/PCHW BS34......................... **13** D5
Stokes Medical Centre
BRSTK/PCHW BS34......................... **29** D1
Stoke View Business Park
MANG/FISH BS16 .... **67** D2
Stonehill Business Centre
OLD/WMLY/WICK BS30 .... **80** C5
Stover Trading Estate
YATE/CS BS37 .... **18** C4
Stroud College
YATE/CS BS37 .... **19** F4
Stuckeys Furniture Gallery
HNLZ/SM/SNYPK/WT BS9 .... **63** E4
Stuckleys Pine Gallery
HORF/LLZ BS7 .... **64** C1
Studley Green Primary School
TRWBR BA14................................ **158** A1
Summerfield School
CBATH/BATHN BA1...................... **122** B1
Summerhill Infant School
EVILLE/WHL BS5 .... **78** C1
Sun Life Sports Club
HNBRY/STHM BS10 .... **26** A4
Sunnyside Farm Trading Estate
PTSHD/EG BS20 .... **60** A4
Sussex Place Surgery
RDLND/MONT BS6 .... **65** D4
Swainswick School
CBATH/BATHN BA1...................... **113** F2
Swimming Pool
PTSHD/EG BS20 .... **39** D3
Temple County Primary School
KEYN BS31.................................... **107** D1
Temple House Doctors Surgery
KEYN BS31.................................... **106** C2
Temple Trading Estate
CBRISNE BS2 .... **77** F4
Teyfant Primary School
BMSTRD/HC/WWD BS13 .... **102** C3
Thornbury Health Centre
THNB/SVB BS35 .... **8** C3
Thornbury Hospital
THNB/SVB BS35 .... **8** C3
Thornbury Leisure Centre
THNB/SVB BS35 .... **8** B5
Time Machine Museum
WSM BS23 .... **141** D2
Toll House Clinic
YATE/CS BS37 .... **21** D4
Totterdown Bridge Estate
CBRISNE BS2 .... **77** E5
Trimbridge Galleries
CBATH/BATHN BA1.......................... **4** B3
Trinity College
HNLZ/SM/SNYPK/WT BS9 .... **62** C2
Tropicana Leisure Complex
WSM BS23 .... **6** A4
Trowbridge College
TRWBR BA14................................ **158** A1
Trowbridge & District Hospital
TRWBR BA14................................ **156** C2
Trowbridge Mosque
TRWBR BA14................................ **157** D5
T T Trading Estate
YATE/CS BS37 .... **21** D4
Tudor Lodge Health Centre
WSM BS23 .... **151** D1
Twerton C of E Junior School
BATHSE BA2 .... **121** E4
Twerton Infant School
BATHSE BA2 .... **121** D5
Two Mile Hill Junior & Infant School
KGWD/HNM BS15.......................... **79** F1
Twyford House Cricket Club
AVONM BS11 .... **44** A4
Tyning Junior & Mixed School
HGRV/WHIT BS14 .... **93** E5
The Tynings CP School
MANG/FISH BS16 .... **68** C2
United Bristol Healthcare NHS Trust
CBRIS/FH BS1 .... **2** D1
University of Bristol
CBRIS/FH BS1 .... **2** B2
University of Bristol
CFTN/FAIL BS8.................................. **2** A1
University of Bristol
CFTN/FAIL BS8................................ **75** E3
University of Bristol
CFTN/FAIL BS8................................ **76** A1
University of Bristol
HNLZ/SM/SNYPK/WT BS9 .... **62** C2
University of the West of England
CBRIS/FH BS1 .... **2** D3
University of the West of England
MANG/FISH BS16 .... **66** C1
University of the West of England Bristol
BMSTR BS3 .... **74** C4
University of the West of England Bristol
MANG/FISH BS16 .... **49** E2
University of the West of England Bristol
MANG/FISH BS16 .... **67** E1
University of the West of England Bristol
RDLND/MONT BS6 .... **63** E3
Uphill CP School
WSM BS23 .... **150** C3
Upper Horfield Primary School
HORF/LLZ BS7 .... **48** B3
Victoria Art Gallery
CBATH/BATHN BA1.......................... **4** C3
Victoria Park County Infant School
BMSTR BS3 .... **92** C1
Victoria Rooms
CFTN/FAIL BS8................................ **75** F2
The Village Surgery
MTN/WRL BS22............................ **129** D5
Vines Industrial Estate
NAIL BS48 .... **87** F1
Wadehurst Industrial Park
CBRISNE BS2 .... **77** E2
Walcot Infant School
CBATH/BATHN BA1...................... **123** E2
Walcot Rugby Club
CBATH/BATHN BA1...................... **112** A2
Walliscote Primary School
WSM BS23 .... **6** C2
Wallis Estate
CBRISNE BS2 .... **65** D3
Wansdyke Business Centre
BATHSE BA2 .... **136** B1
Wansdyke District Council
RDSTK/MIDN BA3........................ **162** A2
Wansdyke School
BATHSE BA2 .... **136** C5
Wansdyke School
HGRV/WHIT BS14 .... **103** D3
Warmley C of E School
OLD/WMLY/WICK BS30 .... **82** A3
Waterloo Galleries
WSM BS23 .... **140** C2
Watershed Arts Complex
CBRIS/FH BS1 .... **2** C4
Waycroft Primary School
HGRV/WHIT BS14 .... **104** C2
Wellesley CP School
YATE/CS BS37 .... **35** E2
Wellsway School
KEYN BS31.................................... **107** E2
Welton CP School
RDSTK/MIDN BA3........................ **161** F2
Welton Rovers Football Club
RDSTK/MIDN BA3........................ **161** E2
Westbury Bazaar & Gallery
HNLZ/SM/SNYPK/WT BS9 .... **46** B4
Westbury on Trym C of E Primary School
HNLZ/SM/SNYPK/WT BS9 .... **46** B4
Westbury on Trym Practice
HNLZ/SM/SNYPK/WT BS9 .... **46** A5
Westbury Park School
RDLND/MONT BS6 .... **63** E3
Westcliff College of Further Education
WSM BS23 .... **140** A1
Westfield CP School
RDSTK/MIDN BA3........................ **161** F4
Westfield Surgery
RDSTK/MIDN BA3........................ **162** B3
Westhaven School
WSM BS23 .... **150** B3
Westlands Sports Club
OMX/HUT/LCK BS24.................... **151** F1
Weston All Saints C of E Junior & Infant School
CBATH/BATHN BA1...................... **111** E5
Weston Area Health Trust
WSM BS23 .... **151** D3
Weston College
WSM BS23 .... **140** C2

Weston County Infant School
CBATH/BATHN BA1 ...... **111** E5
Weston Park Primary School
AVONM BS11 ...... **44** A3
Weston St Johns Associated Football Club
WSM BS23 ...... **151** E2
Weston Sixth Form College
WSM BS23 ...... **151** D3
Weston-Super-Mare AFC
WSM BS23 ...... **7** H5
Weston-Super-Mare Borough Employees Sports Club
WSM BS23 ...... **7** E2
Weston-Super-Mare County Court
WSM BS23 ...... **6** B1
Weston-Super-Mare Cricket Club
WSM BS23 ...... **151** D2
Weston-Super-Mare General Hospital
WSM BS23 ...... **151** D3
Weston-Super-Mare Rugby Football Club
WSM BS23 ...... **6** D3
Westpoint Trading Estate
KGWD/HNM BS15 ...... **80** B2
West Town Lane Infant School
BRSG/KWL/STAPK BS4 ...... **94** A3
West Town Lane Junior School
BRSG/KWL/STAPK BS4 ...... **94** A3
West Walk Surgery
YATE/CS BS37 ...... **19** F4
Whitchuch Health Centre
HGRV/WHIT BS14 ...... **103** E2
Whitchurch Parish Council
HGRV/WHIT BS14 ...... **104** A3
Whitchurch Primary School
HGRV/WHIT BS14 ...... **104** A3
Whitefield Fishponds School
MANG/FISH BS16 ...... **67** D2
Whitehall Primary & Infant School
EVILLE/WHL BS5 ...... **66** B5
Whitehall Trading Estate
EVILLE/WHL BS5 ...... **78** A1
Whiteladies Medical Group
CFTN/FAIL BS8 ...... **63** E5
Wick School
OLD/WMLY/WICK BS30 ...... **83** F3
Widbrook Medical Practice
TRWBR BA14 ...... **156** A4
Widcombe C of E Junior & Infant School
BATHSE BA2 ...... **5** E5
Widcombe Surgery
BATHSE BA2 ...... **4** D6
Wildscreen @ Bristol
CBRIS/FH BS1 ...... **2** B4
William Budd Health Centre
BRSG/KWL/STAPK BS4 ...... **92** B4
Willow Green Infant School
CBRISNE BS2 ...... **65** E4
Wilverley Trading Estate
BRSG/KWL/STAPK BS4 ...... **94** C3
Wincombe Trading Estate
CBRISNE BS2 ...... **77** E5
Windmill Farm Business Centre
BMSTR BS3 ...... **76** B5
Windmill Hill City Farm
BMSTR BS3 ...... **76** B5
Window Arts Centre
CBATH/BATHN BA1 ...... **4** B4
Windwhistle CP School
WSM BS23 ...... **151** E2
Winscombe Cricket Club
WNSC BS25 ...... **154** C5
Winscombe & Sandford Parish Council
WNSC BS25 ...... **154** B4
Winscombe Woodborough Primary School
WNSC BS25 ...... **154** C3
Withywood School
BMSTRD/HC/WWD BS13 ...... **101** E2
Wood Road Industrial Centre
KGWD/HNM BS15 ...... **80** B1
Woodspring District Council
MTN/WRL BS22 ...... **129** D5
Woodstock Special School
KGWD/HNM BS15 ...... **80** C2
Worleburygolf Course
MTN/WRL BS22 ...... **128** A4
Worlebury School
MTN/WRL BS22 ...... **128** A5
Worle Health Centre
MTN/WRL BS22 ...... **129** D5
Worle School
MTN/WRL BS22 ...... **143** D1
Writhlington School
RDSTK/MIDN BA3 ...... **163** E3
Wyncroft School
WSM BS23 ...... **150** C1
Wyvern School
WSM BS23 ...... **7** F5
Yate Leisure Centre
YATE/CS BS37 ...... **19** F3
Yate Town Council
YATE/CS BS37 ...... **19** F3
Yate Town Football Club
YATE/CS BS37 ...... **18** C2
Yatton Family Practice
YTN/CONG BS49 ...... **116** B4
Yatton Infant School
YTN/CONG BS49 ...... **116** C3
Yatton Junior School
YTN/CONG BS49 ...... **116** C3
Yatton Parish Council
YTN/CONG BS49 ...... **117** D4
Yeo Moor Junior & Infant School
CLVDN BS21 ...... **85** E2
YHA
CBRIS/FH BS1 ...... **2** C5
YMCA
BRSG/KWL/STAPK BS4 ...... **77** D5
YMCA
CBATH/BATHN BA1 ...... **4** C2
Zhong Yi Clinic
CFTN/FAIL BS8 ...... **63** F5

Page 4

B3
1 Barton St
2 Beauford Sq
3 Bridewell La
4 Harington Pl
5 Kingsmead Sq
6 Kingsmead St
7 Old Bond St
8 Parsonage La
9 Princes St
10 Queen St
11 Quiet St
12 St John's Pl
13 Saw Cl
14 Trim Br
15 Trim St
16 Westgate Buildings
17 Westgate St

C2
1 Beehive Yd
2 Henrietta Pl
3 Saracen St

C4
1 Abbeygate St
2 Abbey Gn
3 Amery La
4 Church St
5 Henry St
6 Kingston Rd
7 Manvers St
8 New Orchard St
9 Pierrepont Pl
10 Pierrepont St
11 Southgate
12 Stall St
13 Swallow St
14 Terrace Wk
15 York St

Page 52

C4
1 Bromfield Wk
2 Cyrus Ct
3 Denton Patch
4 Howells Mead
5 Langley Mow
6 Pendock Ct

Page 63

F5
1 Chantry Rd
2 Collingwood Rd
3 Cotham Gdns
4 Cotham Hl
5 Hampton Pk
6 Imperial Rd
7 King's Parade Av
8 Oakland Rd
9 Warwick Rd

Page 64

B4
1 Brookfield La
2 Brookfield Rd
3 Cotham Brow
4 Edgecumbe Rd
5 Purton Rd

C1
1 Tennyson Rd
2 Willoughby Rd

C3
1 Denmark Pl
2 Princes' Pl
3 Rutland Rd
4 Surrey Rd

C5
1 Armidale Av
2 Barnabas St
3 Bath Buildings
4 Dalrymple Rd
5 Drummond Rd
6 Norrisville Rd
7 Woodmancote Rd

Page 65

E4
1 Boucher Pl
2 Boyce Dr
3 Cleave St
4 Dorset Gv
5 Durham Rd
6 Hereford Rd
7 John St
8 Lancaster Rd
9 Lynmouth Rd
10 Merstham Rd
11 Norman Rd
12 Ryland Pl
13 Seddon Rd
14 Stafford Rd
15 Tewkesbury Rd
16 Treefield Pl
17 Trentham Cl
18 Warminster Rd
19 Weedon Cl
20 York St

E5
1 Ashley Grove Rd
2 Baptist St
3 Barker Wk
4 Bean St
5 Blenheim St
6 Byron St
7 Conduit Pl
8 Dermot St
9 Gable Rd
10 Highett Dr
11 Kensington Pk
12 Lower Ashley Rd
13 Newfoundland Rd
14 Oxford Pl
15 Pennywell Rd
16 Rosebery Av
17 Summers Rd
18 Waverley St

F5
1 Chapel Rd
2 Church Av
3 Graham Rd
4 Greenbank Av West
5 Henrietta St
6 Lawrence Av
7 Moorhill St
8 Normanby Rd
9 Northcote St
10 St Mark's Ter
11 St Nicholas Pk
12 Warwick Av
13 Warwick Rd
14 Woodborough St

Page 66

A5
1 Cartledge Rd
2 Colwyn Rd
3 Leonards Av
4 Prudham St
5 Seaton Rd

C1
1 Blackberry Av
2 Cromwells Hide
3 Frome Pl
4 Glenside Pk
5 Kite Hay Cl
6 Lark's Fld
7 Pennyroyal Gv
8 Spires Vw

C3
1 Huyton Rd
2 Knowsley Rd
3 Marlborough Av
4 Marlborough St
5 Ridgeway Pde

Page 67

D3
1 Balaclava Rd
2 Drummond Rd
3 Halstock Av
4 Lodore Rd
5 Midland Ter
6 Stoke View Rd

Page 68

A3
1 Acacia Cl
2 The Chase
3 Glendale
4 Glenwood
5 The Greenway
6 Market Sq
7 Quadrant East
8 The Rosery

B4
1 Norman Gv
2 Wellington Rd
3 Whitfield Cl
4 The Wickets
5 Woodland Av

C1
1 Clarence Gdns
2 Heathcote Rd

C3
1 Gladstone Dr
2 Gloucester Rd
3 St Stephens Cl
4 Wiltshire Pl
5 Woodchester

C5
1 Collingwood Av
2 Frys Hl
3 Holly Crs
4 Runnymede

Page 75

D3
1 Albermarle Rw
2 Cornwallis Av
3 Cumberland Pl
4 Dowry Sq
5 Freeland Pl
6 Glendale
7 Hopechapel Hl
8 Hope Sq
9 Hotwell Rd
10 Joy Hl
11 North Green St
12 Oxford Pl
13 The Paragon
14 Royal York Crs
15 South Green St
16 Victoria Ter
17 Windsor Ter

E3
1 Ambra V
2 Ambra V South
3 Ambra V West
4 Camden Ter
5 Clifton Hl
6 Clifton Vale Cl
7 Cliftonwood Ter
8 Dowry Rd
9 Polygon Rd
10 Royal York Vls
11 St Vincent's Rd
12 Saville Pl

E5
1 Ashton Gate Ter
2 Baynton Rd
3 Leigh St
4 North Rd
5 St Francis Rd
6 Wells St
1 Berkley Av
2 Byron Pl
3 Queen's Av
4 Queen's Rd
5 Richmond Hill Av
6 Triangle South
7 Triangle West
8 Upper Byron Pl
9 Wetherell Pl

Page 76

A3
1 Bigwood La
2 Brandon Steep
3 Charlotte St South
4 College Sq
5 Culver St
6 Denmark Av
7 Frogmore St
8 Gaunt's La
9 Hobb's La
10 Lower College St
11 Lower Lamb St
12 Orchard Av
13 Orchard La
14 Orchard St
15 Partition St
16 Unity St
17 Upper Wells St
18 York Pl

A4
1 West End

B1
1 Barton St
2 Cherry La
3 Clevedon Ter
4 Cottage Pl
5 Earl St
6 Henrietta St
7 Hillgrove St North
8 King Sq
9 King Square Av
10 Lower Gay St
11 Marlborough Hill Pl
12 Montague Hl
13 Montague Hl South
14 Montague St
15 Princess Rw
16 Spring Hl
17 Terrell St
18 Whitson St

B2
1 All Saints' St
2 Bell La
3 Blackfriars
4 Bridewell St
5 Cannon St
6 Christmas St
7 Fiennes Ct
8 High St
9 Host St
10 Lewins Mead
11 Nelson St
12 Newmarket Av
13 Pithay
14 Pithay Ct
15 Quay St
16 St Stephen's St
17 Silver St
18 Union St

B3
1 All Saints' La
2 Assembly Rooms La
3 Bridge St
4 Broad Quay
5 Clare St
6 Coronation Pl
7 Crow La
8 High St
9 King William Av
10 Marsh St
11 Middle Av
12 Queen Square Av
13 Rackhay
14 St Stephen's Av
15 Telephone Av

B4
1 Barossa Pl
2 Challoner Ct
3 Draycot Pl
4 Farr's La
5 Grove Av
6 Jubilee Pl
7 Lower Guinea St
8 Redcliffe Pde East
9 Redcliffe Pde West

C1
1 Backfields
2 Backfields La
3 Brunswick Sq
4 Chapter St
5 Cumberland St
6 Dalton Sq
7 Gloucester St
8 Hillgrove St
9 Little Bishop St
10 Norfolk Av
11 Pembroke St
12 Portland Sq
13 Thomas St
14 Wilder St

C3
1 Church St
2 Ferry St
3 Long Rw
4 Narrow Pln
5 St Thomas St East
6 Three Queens' La
7 Tower St

C5
1 Nicholas St
2 Sargent St

Page 77

D1
1 Beggarswell Cl
2 Charlotte St
3 Cheapside
4 East St
5 Elton St
6 Eugene St
7 Frome St
8 Wilson Pl

D2
1 Asher La
2 David St
3 Eyer's La
4 Gloucester La
5 Hawkins St
6 Redcross St
7 St Matthias Pk
8 Tucker St
9 Waterloo St
10 Willway St

D3
1 Broad Pln
2 Louisa St
3 Midland St
4 New Kingsley Rd
5 New Thomas St
6 Providence Pl
7 Straight St

E3
1 Barton V
2 Dings Wk
3 Freestone Rd
4 Queen Victoria St
5 William St

E5
1 Angers Rd
2 Firfield St
3 Fitzroy St
4 Fredrick St
5 Highgrove St
6 Hillside St
7 Kingstree St

F1
1 Abraham Cl
2 Adelaide Pl
3 All Hallows Rd
4 Brighton Pk
5 Cattybrook St
6 Clayton St
7 Combfactory La
8 Eastbourne Rd
9 Elmgrove Av
10 Luxton St
11 Owen St
12 Pountney Dr
13 Thomson Rd
14 Tyndall Rd
15 Vining Wk
16 Westbourne Rd
17 Windsor Gv

Page 78

A1
1 Albion St
2 Alfred St
3 Arthur St
4 Clare St
5 Edward St
6 George St
7 Ida Rd
8 Lillian St
9 Samuel St
10 William St

A2
1 Beam St
2 Brook St
3 Brunswick St
4 Byron St
5 Cambridge St
6 Cowper St
7 Hanover St
8 Howett Rd
9 Lancaster St
10 Matthew's Rd
11 Milton Pk
12 Morse Rd
13 Osprey Rd
14 Oxford St
15 Verrier Rd
16 Weight Rd
17 Witchell Rd
18 York St

B1
1 Altringham Rd
2 Bourneville Rd
3 Charterhouse Rd
4 Congleton Rd
5 Hammersmith Rd
6 Mary St
7 Neath Rd
8 Oakleigh Av
9 Poets' Cl
10 Stretford Av
11 Tintern Av
12 Trelawney Av
13 Westminster Rd
14 Whitehall Gdns
15 Woodbine Rd

B2
1 Barnes St
2 Beaufort Cl
3 Ebenezer St
4 Gladstone St
5 Handel Av
6 Lewin St
7 Orchard Sq
8 Parkfield Av
9 Seneca Pl
10 Speedwell Av
11 Terrell Gdns
12 Weston Av
13 Worsley St

C4
1 The Beeches

Page 79

F4
1 Bence Ct
2 Churchward Cl
3 Collett Cl
4 Gillingham Hl
5 Hawthorn Av
6 Henbury Rd
7 Lovell's Hl
8 Polly Barnes Cl
9 Vicarage Ct

Page 80

C3
1 Elmfield Cl
2 Granny's La
3 High Elm
4 Kemble Cl

Page 81

D2
1 Brake Cl
2 Bredon Cl
3 Gee Moors
4 Kingsleigh Ct
5 Kingsleigh Gdns
6 Ladd Cl
7 Norton Cl
8 Penard Wy
9 Shilton Cl
10 Woodstock Rd

D4
1 Davis Cl
2 Downside Close
3 Forde Cl
4 Glastonbury Cl
5 Malmesbury Cl
6 Sassoon Ct
7 Scott Ct
8 Woburn Cl

D5
1 Alwins Ct
2 Bramley Ct
3 Britten Ct
4 Drummond Ct
5 Dudley Ct
6 Frampton Ct
7 Godfrey Ct
8 Greve Ct
9 Harris Ct
10 Hicks Ct
11 Laphams Ct
12 Logus Ct
13 Lynch Ct
14 Miles Ct
15 Park Farm Ct
16 Pippin Ct
17 Press Moor Dr
18 Stibbs Ct
19 Tindell Ct
20 Turners Ct
21 Woodington Ct

E4
1 Betjeman Ct
2 Churchill Cl
3 Coronation Cl
4 Dylan Thomas Ct
5 Earlstone Crs
6 Henry Williamson Ct
7 Laurie Lee Ct

F1
1 Crane Cl

Page 84

C3
1 Bradford Cl
2 Braikenridge Cl
3 Britannia Wy
4 Bryant Gdns
5 Stickland
6 Wickfield
7 Woodington Rd

Page 87

D4
1 Axbridge Cl
2 Broom Farm Cl
3 Bruton Cl
4 Church Hayes Cl
5 Langport Gdns
6 Wedmore Rd

F3
1 Cairn Cl
2 Cleeve Pl
3 Cricklade Ct
4 Falmouth Cl
5 Gleneagles Cl
6 Kemble Cl
7 St Agnes Cl
8 St Andrews Cl
9 St Ives Cl
10 Sherston Cl
11 Sunningdale Cl
12 Truro Rd
13 Vynes Cl
14 Woodford Cl

Page 92

A1
1 Clifton St
2 Diamond St
3 Eaton St
4 Graham Rd
5 Hebron Rd
6 Kent St
7 New John St
8 Rowley St
9 St John's Rd
10 St John's St
11 Sion Rd
12 South Rd
13 Stanley St
14 Victoria Pl
15 Victor Rd
16 Wesley St

C1
1 Almorah Rd
2 Newport St
3 Orwell St
4 Paultow Av

Page 93

E3
1 Green Wk
2 Greenwood Rd
3 Preston Wk
4 The Square
5 Teignmouth Rd

F5
1 Elderwood Rd

Page 104

C1
1 Beale Cl
2 Cornish Gv
3 Harrington Gv
4 Harrington Wk
5 Meardon Rd
6 Puxley Cl
7 Thompson Rd

Page 123

D3
1 Alfred St
2 Bartlett St
3 Bennett St
4 Brock St
5 Catharine Pl
6 Circus Ms
7 Circus Pl
8 Gloucester St
9 Guinea La
10 Hay Hl
11 John St
12 Milsom St
13 Old King St
14 Queen's Pde
15 Queen's Parade Pl
16 Rivers Street Ms
17 Russell St
18 Saville Rw
19 Upper Church St

D4
1 Amery La
2 Barton St
3 Bath St
4 Beauford Sq
5 Beau St
6 Bilbury La
7 Bridewell La
8 Burton St
9 Chapel Rw
10 Cumberland Rw
11 Harington Pl
12 Helting Ct
13 Hot Bath St
14 Kingsmead Sq
15 Kingsmead St
16 Kingsmead West
17 Monmouth St
18 Old Bond St
19 Palace Yard Ms
20 Parsonage La
21 St John's Pl
22 St Michael's Pl
23 Saw Cl
24 Trim Br
25 Trim St
26 Trinity Cl
27 Trinity St
28 Union St
29 Upper Borough Walls
30 Westgate Buildings
31 Wood St

D5
1 Magdalen Av
2 Magdalen Rd
3 Somerset St
4 The Square
5 Wood St

E2
1 Alpine Gdns
2 Bedford St
3 Clarence St
4 Cay's Hl
5 Lower Hedgemead Rd
6 Margaret's Hl
7 Nelson Pl
8 Nelson Ter
9 Pera Pl

E4
1 Abbeygate St
2 Abbey Gn
3 Abbey St
4 Boat Stall La
5 Church St
6 Green St
7 Johnstone St
8 New Bond St
9 New Orchard St
10 North Parade Pas
11 Northumberland Pl
12 Old Orchard St
13 Parade South
14 Pierrepont Pl
15 Southgate
16 Spring Gardens Rd
17 Stall St
18 Swallow St
19 Terrace Wk
20 Wine St
21 York St

F1
1 Frankley Buildings
2 Gillingham Ter
3 Hanover St
4 Southbourne Gdns
5 Tyning La

F5
1 Abbey Vw
2 Excelsior St
3 Gordon Rd
4 Hatfield Buildings
5 Pulteney Av
6 Widcombe Crs

Page 129

D3
1 Blake End
2 Collingwood Cl
3 The Dell
4 Frobisher Cl
5 Harwood Gdns
6 Jellicoe Ct
7 The Lindens
8 Mountbatten Cl
9 Nelson Ct
10 Ramsay Cl
11 Tovey Cl
12 Willowdown

E4
1 Atholl Cl
2 Constable Dr
3 Gainsborough Dr
4 Gleneagles Cl
5 Kielder Dr
6 Landseer Cl
7 Lynch Cl
8 Meadowbank
9 Reubens Ct
10 St Andrews Cl
11 Turnbury Cl
12 Turner Ct

F4
1 Becket Dr
2 Bishop Av
3 Blythe Gdns
4 Gilberyn Dr
5 Hogarth Ms
6 The Larches
7 Lester Dr
8 Parsons Gn
9 St Michael's Av
10 Torrington Crs
11 Vicarage Cl
12 Wentworth Cl

F5
1 Blenheim Cl
2 Cresswell Cl
3 Lynmouth Cl
4 Ricketts La
5 Salcombe Gdns
6 Simons Cl
7 Tavistock Rd
8 Totnes Cl
9 Trenleigh Dr

Page 130

A3
1 Austen Dr
2 Denning Ct
3 Fenners
4 The Fielders
5 Gill Ms
6 Goddard Dr
7 Kent Wy
8 Longdown Dr
9 Marindrin Dr
10 Portishead Rd
11 Sadbury Cl
12 The Saffrons
13 Saxby Cl
14 Spinners End
15 Taylor Ct
16 Tremlett Ms
17 Wainwright Cl
18 Wellard Cl

Page 140

C2

1 Cambridge Pl
2 Connaught Pl
3 Grove Rd
4 High St
5 Knightstone Rd
6 Market La
7 Old Post Office La
8 St Margaret's Ter
9 Victoria Pl
10 Wadham St
11 West St

Page 141

D2

1 Albert Quadrant
2 Burlington St
3 Edinburgh Pl
4 Gerard Rd
5 Glebe Rd
6 Hans Price Cl
7 Hopkins St
8 King's La
9 Longton Grove Rd
10 Orchard Pl
11 Poplar Pl
12 Prospect Pl
13 Tivoli La
14 Victoria Quadrant
15 Worthy La

D3

1 Back St
2 Beaconsfield Rd
3 Cross St
4 Meadow St
5 Orchard St
6 Station Ap
7 Station Rd
8 Walliscote Rd

F5

1 Axe Cl
2 Brue Cl
3 Buttermere Rd
4 Ennerdale Cl

Notes

Notes

Notes

Notes

Notes

Notes